THE STORY OF
GN

The Story of GN

150 Years in Technology, Big Business and Global Politics

© The author, GN Group and Forlaget Historika/Gads Forlag A/S

Editor: Anne Mette Palm
Translated from Danish by: Peter Sean Woltemade
Cover design and graphic design: Lene Nørgaard, Le Bureau
Layout: Lene Nørgaard, Le Bureau
Repro: Narayana Press

Printed by: GPS Group, Bosnien-Hercegovina

ISBN 978-87-93229-93-8
1. edition

KURT JACOBSEN

THE STORY OF
GN

150 Years in Technology,
Big Business and Global Politics

Historika

Contents

REBUILDING AND RENEWAL

FROM INDUSTRIAL CONGLOMERATE TO THE NEW GN

Preface

The story of the Great Northern Telegraph Society, which was founded by C. F. Tietgen in 1869 and laid the first telegraph cables to China and Japan, is a part of the Danish national story of the resurrection of the fatherland following the defeat in the war of 1864. Less well known—not to say unknown—is the story of what followed in the next 150 years.

Few private companies become as old as the Great Northern Telegraph Company, which was originally one of the world's leading international telegraph companies. With its network of undersea cables, the company contributed to creating the basis for globalization in the late nineteenth century by making possible intercontinental telegraphic communication.

Today, the company calls itself GN and is among the world's leading manufacturers of hearing aids and headsets, and the company's current activities are not obviously strongly connected with those of the telegraph company of the past. The products provided to the customers of the company of today differ greatly in nature from the services provided by the telegraph company during its early days. Nevertheless, there is an unbroken thread going back through the company's history to the days of telegraphy, in that the company has consistently used the newest technologies to create ways for individuals to communicate.

The transition from an international telegraph company to the global industrial company of today has been a lengthy and difficult—sometimes painful—process including failed investments and collapsed projects. But at the core, the company has pursued activities that have contributed to establishing the foundation for the cellular telephony and the Internet of our age before, not very many years ago, the company stabilized in its current form and with its current business areas. That is the story that is told in this book.

The structure of the book

No company gets to be 150 years old without having experienced decline, crises, and ultimately the threat of being dissolved. This is certainly true of Great Northern, which, with its original strong global involvement became entangled in many economic and political crises, regional wars, and two world wars, constantly seeking a balance among the interests of great powers. Technological developments constantly threatened to tear the foundation from under the company but also opened up new opportunities that were exploited with varying degrees of success until GN became the company it is today.

The history of Great Northern and GN to the present day cannot be told without simultaneously bringing in the global, geopolitical, and economic developments as well as technological innovation, particularly in the areas of telecommunications and electronics, in the last 150 years. Basically, developments from 1869 to today can be divided into four epochs, each of which presented its own characteristics, challenges, and opportunities. For this reason, the book is divided into four parts that reflect these epochs and the central and decisive moments in the company's development in interaction with influences from the surrounding environment.

PART ONE, "Establishment, expansion, and greatness," covers the years from the foundation of the Great Northern Telegraph Company in 1869 until the outbreak of the First World War in 1914. During the years 1869–1871, the company established two cable systems, in Northern Europe and East Asia, respectively, that were connected via a ten-thousand-kilometer-long telegraph line through Russia and Siberia, so that Japan and China were telegraphically connected with Europe. Great Northern thus became the first company to challenge the global dominance of the British telegraph companies, and there would be years of competition and outright clashes before a peace agreement was concluded.

During the years 1902–1905, Great Northern expanded, participating in the establishment of the United States' first and only cable connection across the Pacific Ocean to the Philippines and China, and in the European area, the company laid a cable to Iceland, which thus acquired a telegraphic connection with Denmark and the rest of the world. This is the time of the company's greatness as an international telegraph company, but the Russo-Japanese War (1904–1905) and the first Russian revolution (1905–1906) mark the dawn of a new age, as does the advent of new wireless radio telegraphy that made telegraph cables superfluous.

PART TWO, "With their backs to the wall," covers the years from the outbreak of the First World War in 1914 to the end of the Second World War in 1945, years in which Great Northern was put under increasing pressure and had to fight to retain its position and its business. Geopolitically, the company was affected on the one hand by the October Revolution in Russia in 1917, which led to the establishment of the Soviet Union and the Stalinist dictatorship, and on the other hand by Japan's increasingly aggressive expansionism and militarism, which was also directed against Great Northern, as the company stood in the way of Japan's own telegraphy ambitions.

At the same time, wireless telegraphy was continually gaining ground, offering more connections and lower prices, and when the global economic crisis of the 1930s led to a significant decline in international telegram traffic, Great Northern lost revenues to such an extent that telegraphy became unprofitable for the company. Great Northern had its back to the wall, and following the outbreak of the Second World War in 1939 and the German occupation of Denmark the following year, the decline culminated in the cutting of all of the company's cables and the interruption of the connection between the company's headquarters in Copenhagen and its stations abroad.

PART THREE, "Rebuilding and renewal," covers the years from the end of the Second World War until 1986, when the company's name was formally changed to GN Store Nord. The first postwar years were dedicated to the reestablishment of the company's international cable network. Following the communist revolution there in 1949, the company lost its connection with China. In the early 1960s, on the other hand, the company established the first cable connection between North America and Europe via Iceland and Greenland, and the trans-Siberian connection to Japan was modernized.

At the same time, Great Northern began a process of renewal via the establishment of a new industrial sector, with the important components of which were Great Northern's purchase of a bloc of shares in the battery manufacturer Hellesens A/S and not least the founding in 1947 of the company Storno, which became one of the world's largest manufacturers of car telephones and equipment for mobile telephony. In 1968, Great Northern acquired a stake in GNT Automatic A/S, which manufactured telephones and other equipment for land line telephony, and by the time of Great Northern's hundredth anniversary, most of its revenues were coming from the three industrial companies.

In the middle of the 1970s, Storno was sold, and in 1977, Great Northern acquired the hearing aid and headset manufacturer Danavox. Great Northern also became involved in the burgeoning computer industry and in the wholesaling of electronics articles. With the change of its name to GN Store Nord in 1986 the company emphasized its position as one of Denmark's large electronics groups with seven subsidiaries; the telegraphy business was ailing.

PART FOUR, "From industrial conglomerate to the new GN," covers a period in which globalization and rapid technological development changed the whole set of basic conditions under which several of GN Store Nord's subsidiaries operated; these subsidiaries were, therefore, sold. At the same time, the collapse of the Soviet Union and the Eastern bloc created new opportunities for the otherwise ailing telegraph company, which established new fiber optic cable systems. A new business area was cellular telephony; with Sonofon I/S, GN Store Nord became the first company to challenge the government monopoly on telephony.

However, it was three of the industrial companies that were responsible for key positive developments as the group headed into the new millennium, and after Sonofon was sold in 2000, GN Store Nord consisted of the hearing aid manufacturer GN ReSound and the headset manufacturer GN Netcom, as well as GN Nettest, a manufacturer of measurement, testing, and control equipment for various technological areas including fiber optic cables and the operation of the new Internet.

In 2001 and 2002, GN Store Nord was hit hard by the dot-com crisis, and a planned stock exchange listing of NetTest, the former GN Nettest, failed. The consequence was record deficits, and NetTest was subsequently sold, after which the group continued as "the new GN," with hearing aids and headsets as its only business areas.

In 2006, GN Store Nord concluded an agreement to sell GN ReSound, having been pressured to do so by shareholders, and GN Netcom subsequently represented GN's only activity. However, the planned sale of GN ReSound was prohibited by the German competition authority, and in the fall of 2007, GN began a turnaround that led the company to its current status as a global leader in the area of development of technologies for electronic processing of sound that are used in the creation of hearing aids and headsets by the two companies, GN Hearing and GN Audio.

The genesis of the book

This book has come into existence as the result of a research agreement between Copenhagen Business School and GN, which has wished to mark the group's 150th anniversary on June 1, 2019, with a research-based account of the company's development since 1869. GN has financed the project and thus given me time and good working conditions that have made it possible for me to produce the book. I have had free access to all of GN's archives, both those kept at the Danish National Archives and those kept at GN's headquarters in Ballerup, and I have had the freedom to produce a manuscript as I saw fit.

My work with the book has been followed by a group of readers and commentators consisting of project leaders and Brand Managers Anne Marie Preisler and Mette Rusholt, Vice President of Group Communication Steen Frentz Laursen, Senior Director of Audio Research Leo Larsen, and Vice President of External Relations Nikolai Bisgaard of GN, as well as Associate Professor and Center Leader Mads Mordhorst of CBS. This has led to a fruitful dialogue with many inputs, clarifications, and comments, but ultimately, I have determined the book's content and structure, and I, therefore, bear sole responsibility for any errors or misunderstandings.

In addition to the reading group, a number of individuals contributed to the work on the book by helping with archival studies at GN's headquarters: Eva Nielsen, Niels Strømmen, and not least Tina Gjørup Hansen, to all of whom I owe thanks. I have also had conversations with the former chief executive officer of GN Store Nord Jørgen Lindegaard, the former member of the board of directors Finn Junge-Jensen, and the former chairman of the board of directors Mogens Hugo, as well as the former head of the telegraph company, Vice President Frits Larsen; the former head engineer and member of the board of directors Erik Boye Jensen; and the former telegraphy administrator Karlo Andersen. I have also had a conversation with the current chairman of GN's board of directors, Per Wold-Olsen, and Vice Chairman Bill Hoover. I thank all of these individuals for having taken the time to help me with my work on the book.

KURT JACOBSEN, February, 2019

Prologue

On the morning of November 25, 1870, a Danish-chartered cable steamer, the *Great Northern*, anchored at the Wusong trading center on the Huangpu River, near the mouth of the Chang River. The crew immediately began unloading telegraph equipment and other materials intended to be used in the construction of a Danish telegraph station farther up the river, in Shanghai. Five days later, the passengers—Danish telegraphists and other technicians and office personnel—were picked up by Senior Lt. Edouard Suenson and transported to Shanghai. They had spent nearly four months getting here from London, and their longing to sleep in real beds was intense.

Immediately afterward, the *Great Northern* weighed anchor and steamed toward the mouth of the Chang River, where the ship anchored for the night. The following day, the ship steamed ninety nautical miles southeast, where the ship's crew began to lay a cable leading back toward Wusong. When the steamer had gotten halfway, things went wrong; it ran aground and damaged its engine. Af-

ter a provisional repair, the laying of the cable continued the following morning, and on the afternoon of December 4, the cable was cut at a point of land across from Wusong.

Four days later, the Danes laid another cable from two iron barges that were towed by two small steamships. During a night of bright moonlight, the ships sailed slowly up the river while the cable was laid and finally reached land on a lot in northern Shanghai, where the end of the cable was buried and all traces of it were eradicated. The telegraph had come to China.

The landing site for Great Northern's undersea cable at the Wusong trading center on the Huangpu River, north of Shanghai, where the company established a little station and built a cable depot. The picture conveys a sense of peacefulness, but in fact, the section of the river adjacent to the landing site was heavily trafficked by both Chinese junks and European steamships and sailing ships that anchored there and awaited high tide before proceeding to Shanghai.

The Great Northern Telegraph Company

CHAPTER 1

The landing of the telegraph cable in Shanghai was the central move in a grand operation that included a further two cable steamers and a Danish warship. The plan was to lay undersea cables between Hong Kong and Shanghai and connect these cables to Vladivostok in the Russian Far East via Japan. From Vladivostok, a telegraph connection to Denmark and Western Europe was to be established by laying cable through Siberia and European Russia so that China and Japan would be telegraphically connected to Europe and the rest of the world.

The man behind this operation was the forty-one-year-old Danish entrepreneur and chief executive officer of Privatbanken, C. F. Tietgen. If the project succeeded, Denmark would have a telegraph company that would stand comparison with major international players in the industry and a size that greatly exceeded what had thus far been seen in Danish business. For the Danish government, the project would result in significant transit income from the many telegrams that would pass through Danish territory on their way from the cables in East Asia.

The prospects of making money then were great, but the financial investments were corresponding-ly significant. Much was at risk, and much could go wrong; if the project were successfully completed, it would be a technical and commercial and also a national triumph.

The telegraph in Denmark – and to England

The electric telegraph came late to Denmark. After Samuel Morse had laid the world's first telegraph line for public traffic between Washington, DC, and Baltimore in the United States in 1844, this communication system using dots and dashes quickly spread to Europe. By 1850, the United Kingdom had approximately 3,500 kilometers of telegraph lines, Prussia approximately 3,900 kilometers, and France approximately 1,000 kilometers, and a number of countries were beginning to connect their national networks, thus creating an international telegraph system.

The establishment of a telegraph system in Denmark took place relatively late because of the Danish straits. When the first usable undersea telegraph cable had been laid under the English Channel between Dover and Calais, work on laying cable was begun in Denmark as well, but it took considerable time. It was not until February 2, 1854, that a telegraph line was established from Elsinore to Copenhagen and Korsør and on to Fredericia, from where a line led to Hamburg, thus establishing a connection to the rest of the European telegraph network.1

In 1857, a government telegraph line was established from Fredericia up through Jutland to Aalborg and Frederikshavn, and around this time, market towns and private individuals began establishing connections to the government lines, and Denmark thus acquired a national telegraph network. Norway and Sweden had been connected to the European network via a Dano-Swedish cable under the Øresund on January 1, 1855, and at the same time, Denmark became a transit country for international telegram traffic between the rest of Scandinavia and Europe.

It was not long before the business community in Denmark—particularly in Copenhagen—expressed interest in a direct cable connection with the United Kingdom, and there were also national security advantages that were inherent in being able to communicate directly with London without passing through Germany. The cable under the Øresund had been financed and was operated by the Swedish and Danish governments, but a cable under the North Sea would be far more expensive, and the British government had left telegraphy to private companies. Because of this, private financing and operating funds were required, as in the case of most undersea telegraph cables. In July 1857, the Danish government therefore issued a concession that gave the British company J. W. Brett & Co. permission to establish and operate a cable in Great Britain.

J. W. Brett was one of the main partners in the Submarine Telegraph Company, which had laid the first cable under the English Channel and then a number of others. There was then no lack of know-

At the age of just twenty-eight, the founder of the Great Northern Telegraph Company, C. F. Tietgen, was appointed chief executive officer of the newly founded bank Privatbanken, which was Denmark's first large commercial bank. During the years that followed, Tietgen and the bank participated in the creation of a large number of Danish businesses organized as limited companies, culminating in the creation of Great Northern in 1869. Tietgen was originally a wholesaler – he had been apprenticed in Manchester – and as the director of Privatbanken, he became the most important Danish businessman of his time. Probably, he was the most enterprising Danish businessman who had ever lived.

how and relevant experience, but owing to financial difficulties, the cable was not laid until July of 1859. The connection was made available for use starting on January 18, 1860, after the Danish government telegraph authority had laid the land-based connecting lines, and with this, Denmark had acquired a direct telegraph connection with Great Britain.

The cable had consequences not only for trade but also, owing to transit revenues from Swedish and Norwegian telegram traffic to Great Britain, for the finances of the Danish government. In 1861, Statstelegrafen, the Danish government telegraph authority, had transit income amounting to just under 47,000 rigsdaler, and the corresponding figure for 1863 was 59,000 rigsdaler. The director of Statstelegrafen, Peter Faber, developed a sense of the economic advantages that would be gained if Denmark became a nexus of international telegraphy, and he therefore got the country involved in two major cable projects.[2]

Denmark and telegraph connections with the United States

After a number of further cables had been laid under the English Channel and other European bodies of water, the great challenge was to establish a telegraph connection that crossed the Atlantic Ocean between Europe and North America. While it typically took two weeks to get a letter from London to New York, depending upon the weather, a telegram could be transmitted in a few minutes. A transatlantic telegraph connection would therefore revolutionize trade and relations between the Old and the New World in general—and would be quite profitable. Several consortia were working on the project both in the United States and in the United Kingdom, but the technical difficulties due to the distance and the depth of the ocean were considerable, and the costs were correspondingly great.

Most proposals involved laying cable between the west coast of Ireland and Newfoundland. An

Peter Faber was the director of the Danish telegraph authority from 1853 until his death in 1877. He shared C. F. Tietgen's vision of the exploitation of Denmark's geographical position in connection with the establishment of the global telegraph network and was also a constant driving force in the construction of a Danish national telegraph system. However, he is remembered in Denmark today most of all because of his songwriting, which included popular Christmas songs such as *Højt fra træets grønne top* and *Sikken voldsom trængsel og alarm* as well as his song from the beginning of the First Schleswig War (1848–1850), *Dengang jeg drog afsted*.

alternative proposal was to lay cable from New-foundland via Greenland, Iceland, and the Faroe Islands so the cable could be divided into relatively short segments. In the summer of 1854, the American Taliaferro Preston Shaffner was awarded a Danish concession for the laying of cable in the Danish territories in the North Atlantic with a connection to Copenhagen, which would result in further transit revenues for the Danish government.

In 1858, before this project could be completed, the American businessman Cyrus Field laid an undersea cable between Ireland and Newfoundland, but after having been used for a good two months, it no longer provided a working connection. However, the vision of a telegraphic connection between the United States and Europe was not dead, and while preparations for new attempts to lay a transatlantic cable were being carried out, Peter Faber got Denmark involved in a project with a completely different goal.

Faber wanted to lay a Dano-Russian cable so the transit traffic between Russia and the United Kingdom/France would pass through Denmark and circumvent Germany. In May 1863, the American Perry McDonough Collins had been awarded a Russian concession to lay cable from Alaska, then a Russian territory, under the Bering Strait to the harbor town of Nikolayevsk-on-Amur in the Russian Far East so that Europe could be telegraphically connected with North America via the Russian and Siberian landlines.

According to Peter Faber, Denmark could take advantage of the Russo-American project because a Dano-Russian cable would be preferred to the German landlines by the United Kingdom and France, and Denmark would become a nexus of international telegram traffic and therefore be able to count on receiving significant transit revenues.[3]

National catastrophe

In September 1863, Peter Faber got the United Kingdom's Submarine Telegraph Company to send an application to the Russian government for a conces-sion for the laying of a Dano-Russian cable, but this grand plan fell through a short time later. Early in 1864, Denmark went to war to retain the duchies of Schleswig, Holstein, and Lauenburg, but the Danish troops soon suffered a humiliating defeat.

When a peace agreement was concluded, Denmark had to give up the three duchies, and the country had suddenly become 33 percent smaller and lost almost 40 percent of its population. The new southern border was marked by the river Kongeåen and created a strong feeling that the fatherland had been "amputated at the hips," as the Danish author Herman Bang later put it.

With the relinquishment of the duchies, Denmark lost the Dano-British telegraph cable that had been brought ashore at Westerhever, one hundred kilometers south of the new Dano-German border. In the context of the general consequences of Denmark's defeat, the loss of the telegraph connection might seem minor, but both for foreign policy and diplomacy reasons and for business and economic reasons, it was unacceptable that Denmark's telegraphic communications with London would pass through German territory from that point on. Things took a further turn for the worse a short time later, when the cable connection stopped working and all telegram traffic to and from Great Britain had to be sent via Hamburg, which was both slower and more expensive.

Also, Danish government revenues were negatively affected when Sweden exploited the Danish "telegraph amputation" and got an undersea cable laid from Scania to the German Baltic island of Rügen. The cable was opened to traffic on July 1, 1865, and subsequently, almost all telegram traffic between Norway/Sweden and the rest of Europe bypassed Denmark, which suffered significant financial losses. Transit revenues, which had amounted to almost 59,000 rigsdaler in 1863, plummeted to 4,971 rigsdaler in 1866, and there was no prospect of improvement—on the contrary.[4]

The Danish government asked the Submarine Telegraph Company to lay a new cable to Great Britain but got nowhere with this request. The company was already operating several cables under the

English Channel and knew the Danish business community and government had no alternative to using these connections, so the company had no incentive to lay a competing cable. Neither the British company nor any other company was tempted by the prospect of attracting part of the Russian telegram traffic with Great Britain and the rest of Western Europe by laying a cable from Denmark to Russia. Getting a new cable to Great Britain laid therefore became one of the main tasks of the Danish government telegraph authority and its director, Peter Faber. The question was, who would do it?

C. F. Tietgen and the telegraph

One of Peter Faber's first initiatives after the loss of the telegraph connection to Great Britain was to resume negotiations regarding a Dano-Russian cable. In April 1865, he reached agreement with the Russian telegraph director to the effect that a cable connection between the two countries should be established via Bornholm. To generate interest in a connection with Great Britain, Faber had it made a condition that the company that got a concession for a cable between Denmark and Russia would receive the right of first refusal for a concession for a cable between Denmark and Great Britain and would therefore have access to the telegram traffic between Russia and Great Britain.

Neither the Submarine Telegraphy Company nor other companies that played dominant roles in undersea telegraphy were interested in this option. The thirty-five-year-old Danish bank director C. F. Tietgen did show an interest, however. In 1856, he had applied for the concession for the Dano-British cable but been rejected in favor of J. W. Brett, and from late 1857 onward, he had represented Taliaferro Shaffner's interests in Denmark with regard to the establishment of the North Atlantic cable connection to the United States.

In September 1865, Tietgen sent an application to the Danish Ministry of Finance regarding a concession for the North Atlantic project, which was thus revived. The application came from the consortium around the English member of parliament James

Wyld, who was represented in Denmark by Tietgen. The consortium planned to lay cable to Denmark via Scotland, thus establishing a new cable connection between Great Britain and Denmark.

Wyld was soon awarded the desired concession, which also included a cable between Denmark and Norway. Wyld declared that he would also be willing to lay a Dano-Russian cable if Russia were willing to provide sufficient financial support to make the cable connection profitable.

The director of the Russian telegraph authority was amenable, and the Russian foreign minister Count Tolstoy let it be known that Russia was quite interested in establishing a cable connection with Denmark in the west, "as Russia would thus acquire a direct connection with England that was independent of Germany." He also emphasized the possibilities that would arise when the Russo-American telegraph project was finished two years later and a telegraphic connection between Europe and the United States via Siberia and the Bering Strait became a reality.[5]

There were then two projects in competition for the establishment of telegraph connections between the United States and Europe, and in both cases, Denmark was a nexus. In the Russian Far East, the American Western Union Telegraph Company had already invested three million dollars in the Bering Strait project, and on March 1, 1866, when the North Atlantic Telegraph Company, which was to exploit Wyld's concessions, was established, the North Atlantic project too began to materialize.

The board of directors of the North Atlantic Telegraph Company included C. F. Tietgen, who was still an official representative of the English consortium, and his close friend and business partner, the wholesaler O. B. Suhr. With this, Danish businesspeople, with Tietgen as their driving force, had really assumed a central role in Denmark's efforts to become a major actor in international telegraphy.

Tietgen's fight for concessions

A short time later, however, the foundation of the entire project began to crumble. During the sum-

mer of 1865, a new attempt to lay a cable between Ireland and Newfoundland had failed, but the following summer saw the project successfully realized, and a further cable was laid, and in August 1866, it was therefore possible to establish two functioning direct connections between Europe and the United States. This achievement was much celebrated on both sides of the Atlantic— but not at the North Atlantic Telegraph Company

The Stock Exchange Building in Copenhagen in about 1865. This was where C. F. Tietgen had his office, and the Great Northern Telegraph Company was also housed here in the beginning. Behind the building on the left, one can glimpse masts from a sailing ship, in the background on the left a steamship. The building on the right is the Danish National Bank, which is connected to the Stock Exchange Building by an intervening building, and in the background on the right, one can see the spire of the Church of Our Savior.

It took the world's largest steamship, the *Great Eastern*, to lay the transatlantic cables in 1865 and 1866. The ship was originally a passenger ship that could accommodate four hundred passengers. With a length of over 211 meters, it was by far the biggest steamship of its day, and it was able to transport sufficient supplies to steam from Great Britain to Australia without stopping on the way. The ship was refitted for use in laying cables and fitted with three cable tanks that could store a combined total of 4,600 kilometers of submarine cable. Until 1868, Great Eastern laid more than 48,000 kilometers of undersea cable.

in London, which saw its North Atlantic project evaporate.

However, Tietgen did not lose interest in international telegraphy, and a new opportunity arose when the English cable producer R. S. Newall, who had begun work on production of the Dano-Norwegian cable without having received payment,

wished to acquire Wyld's concessions. He asked Tietgen to investigate whether this would be possible, and the Danish Ministry of Finance accepted the transfer on condition that Tietgen would personally guarantee the laying of the cable. If Newall got the Norway cable shipped by April 30, 1867, at the latest, he would also be awarded the concessions for the England cable and the North Atlantic project. If not, Tietgen was to ensure the laying of the Norway cable before the end of July or pay 15,000 pounds sterling to the Danish government, which Tietgen accepted.

However, the Danish Ministry of Finance hedged its bets in March 1867 by concluding a further agreement, an agreement with the United Kingdom's Telegraph Construction & Maintenance Company. If Newall did not get the Norway cable finished in time, all concessions would be transferred to the

British. Newall did not make the deadline, and immediately, on May 1, the Telegraph Construction & Maintenance Company demanded the concessions, while Tietgen asked the Ministry of Finance for a few extra days. The cable was shipped on May 4, but the British company insisted that the agreement it had concluded be honored. However, Tietgen insisted that he had a responsibility to lay the Norway cable before the end of July.

It all ended with the Ministry of Finance giving Tietgen and Newall permission to lay the Norway cable but giving the concessions for the much more important England cable and the North Atlantic project to the Telegraph Construction & Maintenance Company. Newall laid the cable between Arendal, Norway, and Hirtshals, Denmark, so it could be opened to traffic on July 1, 1867, while Tietgen got Newall's concession transferred to a company he had founded to operate the cable.

The Telegraph Construction & Maintenance Company was not able to raise the funds that would have been required to operate a Dano-English cable, and the Danish Ministry of Finance therefore transferred the concessions back to Newall, who had Tietgen waiting in the wings. With the Dano-Norwegian cable and the coming Dano-English cable, the outlines of a Nordic telegraph company began to become discernible.

The Danish-Norwegian-English Telegraph Company

On January 10, 1868, in Copenhagen and Newcastle, an invitation was issued to buy shares in the Danish-Norwegian-English Telegraph Company with the purpose of taking over the cable to Norway and laying and operating the cable to England. Shares were to be issued with a total value of 100,000 pounds or 900,000 rigsdaler, which was a significant amount of money for the small Danish capital market. In addition to C. F. Tietgen, the individuals behind this initiative included the wholesalers C. A. Broberg and O. B. Suhr, who respectively were the chairman and vice chairman of Privatbanken's banking committee; Imperial Count Wilhelm Carl

Eppingen Sponneck, a former Minister of Finance and Director General of Customs; and the wholesaler H. G. Erichsen, Tietgen's close ally in Newcastle.

The invitation was discussed in detail in the capital city press, and after having given an account of the previous unsuccessful efforts to reestablish a direct telegraph connection with England, *Dagbladet* welcomed the most recent turn of events, namely, "that here in Copenhagen some men who are respected in the financial markets have come together and taken matters in their own hands."[6]

The public offering was more successful than anyone had expected—its performance was greatly enhanced by the fact that the Danish government had agreed to provide just under 20 percent of the total capital and Tietgen and Erichsen had informed potential shareholders of this "in strictest confidence." Already on January 20, shares in the amount of more than 50,000 pounds sterling had been purchased, and on April 3, 1868, King Christian IX signed the concessions that gave the Danish-Norwegian-English Telegraph Company sole use rights both for the Dano-Norwegian and for the Dano-English connection for a period of thirty years.[7]

In all countries, a government permit was required if one was to land a telegraph cable, and by acquiring a monopoly, the company could protect itself against competition and thus guarantee that its costs would be covered and it would receive a return on its investment. A corresponding concession was granted by the Swedish-Norwegian government, while the British government—like the American government—did not issue monopoly concessions. Because of the Danish monopoly concession, however, no competing cables could be laid between Great Britain and Denmark.

The following day, April 4, 1868, the Danish-Norwegian-English Telegraph Society held a founding meeting at the stock exchange in Copenhagen. The first board of directors consisted of the five individuals who had called the meeting, to whom, at the first board meeting on May 7, the head of the secretariat of the Ministry of Finance Martin Levy, who represented the government's shares, was added.[8]

C. F. Tietgen's closest ally in the creation of the Great Northern Telegraph Company was Herman Gustav Erichsen, a Danish wholesaler in Newcastle.

neer and telegraph inspector for the sea forts and was given the task of following the production of the cables and assisting with the laying and landing of the England cable to begin with.

In early September 1868, R. S. Newall laid the Dano-English cable between Søndervig, on the west coast of Jutland, and Newbiggin-by-the-Sea, north of Newcastle in Northern England. The connection was opened on September 21 when Christian IX sent a telegram to his daughter Alexandra, who was married to the future King Edward VII of the United Kingdom, in London.

The opening of the connection quickly led to a dramatic increase in the transit traffic through Denmark and thus to the revenues of the Danish government. The Danish-Norwegian-English Telegraph Company also saw positive effects from this development; the company's net revenues from both cable connections during the last three months of the year amounted to approximately 40,000 rigsdaler.

Tietgen was a bank director, and neither he nor the other board members were familiar with the technical aspects of producing and laying cable or even of telegraphy more generally. It was necessary to attach a technical expert to the project, so Statstelegrafen, the Danish government telegraph authority, loaned out Commissioner of War C. L. Madsen to help with the project. He was an engi-

The Danish-Russian Telegraph Company

On March 2, 1868, already before the Danish-Norwegian-English Telegraph Company held its founding meeting, C. F. Tietgen applied for a concession for the operation of a cable to Russia on the basis of the telegraph convention concluded by Russia and Denmark on June 10, 1865. The concession was granted the following day under the

Great Northern's cable house at Hvide Odde Strand (beach) north of Rønne, where the cable from Møn was landed in December 1868. A landline led across Bornholm to Snogebæk, south of Nexø, from where the cable to Liepaja in Latvia, then a Russian territory, was laid in May 1869.

condition that Russia would also grant a concession.[9]

Tietgen immediately sent H. G. Erichsen to Saint Petersburg to negotiate with the director of the Russian telegraph authority, Gen. Karl Karlovich von Lüders. The main topic to be discussed was financing, for if a cable was to compete with the continental landlines to the English Channel via Germany, then Russian subsidies of telegrams sent via the Danish cable would be needed.

H. G. Erichsen was able easily to reach an agreement regarding the desired reduction in rates. To be sure, this would mean reduced revenues for the Russian government telegraph authority, but in his report to the Russian government, Von Lüders emphasized that on the other hand, Russia would acquire a telegraph connection with Great Britain that avoided Germany.[10]

At an international telegraph conference in Vienna in July 1868, Karl von Lüders and Peter Faber reached agreement on the last details so a Danish concession could be signed by Christian IX the following month. To ensure a quick Russian ratification, Tietgen got the king to raise the issue during the king's visit to Saint Petersburg in late August. Tietgen also got the Danish consul general in Saint Petersburg, the wholesaler Hans Pallisen, to work toward the same end by offering Pallisen the post as the Danish-Russian Telegraph Company's representative in Russia.[11]

In early September, Hans Pallisen was able to inform Tietgen that the heir to the Russian throne, Christian IX's son-in-law, Prince Alexander, had taken an interest in the matter following the Danish king's intervention. The Russian concession was, in fact, issued on September 18, 1868; like the Danish one, it granted a thirty-year monopoly on a cable connection between Russia and Denmark.[12]

The concession was granted to C. F. Tietgen and H. G. Erichsen, who transferred it to the newly founded Danish-Russian Telegraph Company with a share capital of 100,000 pounds sterling, which corresponded to 900,000 rigsdaler, most of which was provided by the most important shareholders in the Danish-Norwegian-English Telegraph Company—indeed, the two companies' boards of directors were identical. The shareholders included the Danish government; in the wake of the great interest in shares in the Dano-English company, Tietgen had convinced the Minister of Finance to replicate the government's investment in shares in the case of the Dano-Russian company.[13]

First, a cable was laid between the Danish islands of Møn and Bornholm with an extra strand intended for Danish traffic between Bornholm and the rest of Denmark, after which, in early May 1869, the cable between Bornholm and Liepaja, Latvia, was laid. A month later, the Denmark-Russia connection was opened to public traffic.

A total of 25 percent of the new company's share capital was earmarked for the possible laying of a new cable between Sweden and Finland, then a Russian grand duchy. A Swedish-Russian cable project had fallen through, and C. F. Tietgen and H. G. Erichsen had exploited the situation and secured the right to negotiate regarding the granting of a thirty-year monopoly concession both in Sweden and in Russia to keep it from falling into other hands.

The Norwegian-British Telegraph Company

The cable between Liepaja and Bornholm had been ordered earlier by the Norwegian-British Telegraph Company, a Norwegian company, to be laid between Norway and Scotland so Norway would have a direct telegraph connection with Great Britain that avoided Denmark and the Danish cables. However, the British parliament voted to nationalize all private telegraph lines so the liberal United Kingdom would follow the pattern from the other European states in which land-based telegraph lines were operated by the government. As the Norwegians had not previously secured an agreement with a British company regarding onward transmission of Norwegian telegrams, the Norwegians risked ending up with a cable that lacked a connection with the British telegraph network.[14]

C. F. Tietgen offered the Norwegian company an opportunity to become a party to an agreement the Danish-Norwegian-British Telegraph Company had with a British company that would be taken over by the British General Post Office, the administrator of the British postal and telegraphy systems, which would also take over the agreement regarding onward transmission of telegrams, in connection with the nationalization. If this occurred, the competition between the two cable companies would not be desirable, Tietgen argued, and on August 12, 1868, an agreement between the Norwe-

Draft head for the first stock certificates for the Great Northern Telegraph Company. The portrait in the middle is of the Danish physicist H. C. Ørsted, who created the foundation for the development of the telegraph with his discovery of electromagnetism.

gian-British and the Danish-Norwegian-British companies was reached. The total profits of the two companies were to be divided in accordance with their respective contributions of share capital, so the Danish company would receive two-thirds, the Norwegian, one-third.[15]

The Danes claimed that there were technical barriers to using the Norwegian cable with the Danish cable. However, the Danes indicated that the Norwegian cable could be used for the Danish-Russian connection, and at a general meeting in September 1868, the Norwegian company voted to sell their cable to the Danish-Russian Telegraph Company and order a new one for their own use.[16]

This all looked like a friendly favor done for the Norwegians by the Danes, but all the evidence suggests that it was, in fact, an element in a conscious long-term strategy designed to force the Norwegian company into cooperation with the goal of taking it over. The British company that was to be responsible for the onward transmission of the telegrams had been established by C. F. Tietgen and H. G. Erichsen when they had heard that the Norwegians had ordered a cable. The Norwegians thus ended up in the two Danes' pockets, and Tietgen could proceed with his plans.[17]

The Great Northern Telegraph Company

During the fall of 1868, C. F. Tietgen's notion of bringing about a merger of the Danish and Norwegian companies began to ripen, and it had probably been an element of his plans from the beginning. The reason for this would have been that he continued to believe in the North Atlantic project, which would be easier to realize with one large telegraph company than with three smaller ones.

That he nevertheless hesitated was because of his fear of the consequences of the introduction of a large proportion of the British capital into the project, which would require the investment of up to 1.2 million pounds sterling or almost 11 million rigsdaler that could not be raised by Tietgen himself, by Privatbanken, or by the Danish capital market. A large infusion of the British capital could disrupt Tietgen's control over the Scandinavian telegraph imperium, which had now otherwise really begun to cement itself. For the time being, however, he proceeded with the plans, and in February 1869, in cooperation with H. G. Erichsen and a Canadian attorney, he secured a Canadian concession for the landing of a cable from Greenland.[18]

In the course of the spring of 1869, however, it became clear that it would not be possible to secure the necessary financing, and Tietgen put the North Atlantic project on standby. Nevertheless, he proceeded with a merger of the three Scandinavian telegraph companies into the Great Northern Telegraph Company, which was founded on June 1, 1869, with a share capital of 40,000 pounds sterling or 3.5 million rigsdaler. The majority of the capital was acquired by offering the shareholders in the three existing companies the opportunity to transform their shares into shares in the new company with a value corresponding to 84.5 percent of the capital. Shares amounting to the rest of the company's capital were offered for sale on the stock exchange,

with the result that, as Tietgen put it, there was "an utter frenzy to buy Great Northern shares" that had soon all been sold.[19]

The members of the board of directors of the new Scandinavian company were previous board members: C. F. Tietgen was the chairman, and the other board members were the wholesaler C. A. Broberg; O. B. Suhr; Count W. C. E. Sponneck, who, in the meantime, had become the director of the National Bank; and M. Levy as the representative of the Ministry of Finance, which retained its proportion of shares. H. G. Erichsen was appointed the company's representative in the United Kingdom, while Consul Gen. Hans Pallisen was appointed the company's representative in Russia.

From the beginning, the new company had a de facto monopoly on international telegram traffic among Russia, Scandinavia, and Great Britain as the Swedish-Norwegian government had granted a thirty-year monopoly concession for the cable from Norway to Scotland. The cable between Bornholm and Russia was opened to traffic just five days after the company's founding meeting, and on August 21, 1869, the Norwegian-Scottish cable was opened. Finally, the Swedo-Russian cable was laid between Grisslehamn, Sweden, and Uusikaupunki (Nystad), Finland, and opened to traffic on November 1, 1869.

At the center of this network was Denmark, whose geographic position and neutral small-state status made it possible to establish the country as a telegraphic nexus between the great powers Russia and the United Kingdom as a basis for a Danish telegraph company's challenge to the otherwise all-dominating British companies.

The British telegraph companies' unwillingness to lay cables to Denmark and not least their underestimating of the Danish bank director in particular and of Danish perseverance in general were factors in Tietgen's success. After the opening of the Dano-English cable, C. L. Madsen was able to report to Tietgen that in English telegraph circles, people were saying that "these Danes [should not be allowed] to go on any further."[20]

However, the English had not heard the last of "these Danes." On the contrary, it would soon prove

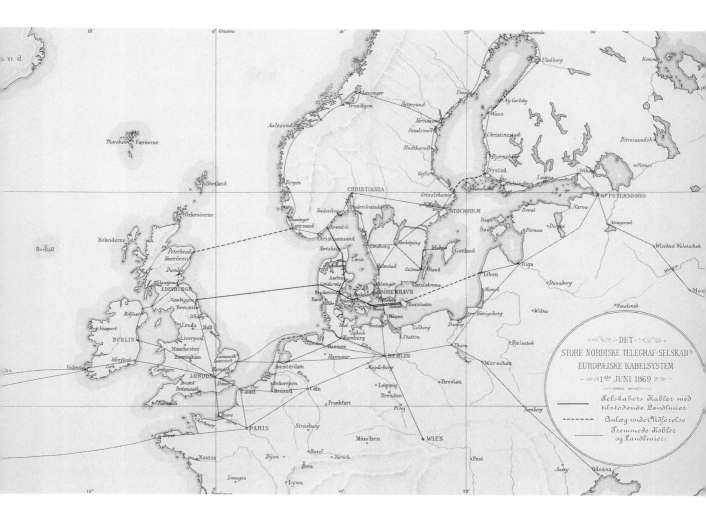

to be the case that Great Northern's Danish basis opened up possibilities in entirely different parts of the world where the British companies would hardly have expected it, and once again, it was Denmark's geographic location and neutral small-state status that provided the supporting foundation.

Map of the Great Northern Telegraph Company's cable system at the time of the company's founding on June 1, 1869. The dotted lines are cables laid in the months that followed. The significance of Denmark's geographical location—which constituted the basis on which the company was founded and achieved a de facto monopoly in Northern Europe—is clear.

Danish Telegraph Cables for China

CHAPTER 2

Trans-Siberian telegraph connection to China

His failed attempts to raise capital for the North Atlantic project did not cause C. F. Tietgen to abandon his international visions. He instead turned his gaze to the east, where the opening of the transatlantic cables had led to the shutting down of the Russo-American project of laying a cable via the Bering Strait. Russia's government had therefore stopped the completion of the trans-Siberian telegraph line, which had reached the town of Sretensk, six hundred kilometers east of Irkutsk. Much remained to be done if the line was to be completed, but the Russian government lacked the necessary financial resources.

However, Russia's political and strategic military interest in a telegraph connection with the Russian Far East was intact. In early April 1867, the governor of East Siberia and a previous governor of the Amur region asked the Danish consul general in Saint Petersburg Hans Pallisen to investigate the possibilities with regard to British financing of the completion of the trans-Siberian line as well as the installation of a landline from the town of Kyakhta south of Lake Baikal to Beijing. Pallisen subsequently had to report that no one in Great Britain was willing to finance such a project.[1]

There were good reasons for British investors' rejection of the proposed project. The completion of the trans-Siberian connection and the establishment and operation of a telegraph line extending almost 1,400 kilometers from Kyakhta in the south and through the Gobi Desert to Beijing would be a major technical challenge in itself. But in particular, it was the political challenges that were decisive as the emperor of China was strongly opposed to the introduction of a telegraph to China. In China, the telegraph—like the railroad—was seen as a tool

In November 1866, Denmark's Princess Dagmar married the heir to the Russian throne, Grand Duke Alexander. At the same time, she became a member of the Russian Orthodox Church and was given the name and title Maria Feodorovna, Grand Duchess of Finland. She used her position to support Great Northern's applications for concessions in 1868 and 1869, and as Czarina after her husband's accession to the throne in 1881, she sought to advance the business interests of Great Northern and other Danish companies in Russia.

Hans J. Pallisen was a Danish wholesaler, shipbuilder, and manufacturer who lived in Saint Petersburg all of his adult life. At the age of fifteen, he was hired there by the trading company Asmus Simonsen and Company. In 1855, he established his own business in the Russian capital. He became the Danish consul in 1860 and the general consul in 1866.

forced to open Shanghai, Guangzhou, Xiamen, and two other Chinese harbor towns to British tradespeople and hand over Hong Kong to the United Kingdom. In addition, China was to pay 21 million dollars in compensation for costs incurred by the British, including compensation for confiscated opium and the United Kingdom's expenses in connection with prosecuting the war.

The Treaty of Nanking was the first of a number of treaties that were referred to by the Chinese as unequal treaties and reflected the Western colonial powers' exploitation of their advantages with regard to military strength and weapons technology to force China to make concessions. The Tianjin treaties with the United States, the United Kingdom, France, and Russia followed in 1858, and further concessions were made in connection with the Beijing Convention of 1860, which obligated China to open fifteen harbor towns to Western tradespeople. The country was also to be open to Westerners, who were to enjoy freedom of movement and action and included tradespeople and missionaries.

In several of the harbor towns identified in the treaties, special so-called settlements that were not subject to Chinese jurisdiction were established for foreigners. Finally, a so-called most favored nation clause was introduced so that any Chinese concession or preferential treatment would be enjoyed by all nations that had concluded a treaty with China.

In 1861, after the ratification of the Beijing Convention, China established a ministry of foreign affairs, the Zongli Yamen, to manage relations with foreign powers. The head of this ministry and de facto foreign minister was Prince Gong, who had negotiated and signed the Beijing Convention. Now he and the new ministry were to determine the Chinese positions on the stream of applications

to be used by the Western colonial powers to force their way into the country and exploit its resources and population.

Chinese opposition to the telegraph had its roots in the previous decades' developments after China's defeat by Britain in the First Opium War (1839–1842), which ended with the conclusion of the Treaty of Nanking. Against its will, China had been

from Western private entities and governments that pressed China to accept the installation of telegraph and rail systems during the years that followed.

Russia, which wanted a telegraph line from Kyakhta to Beijing and on to the treaty harbor of Tianjin, was particularly insistent. The Chinese consistently rejected this application, but in 1862, the Russian government did manage to secure an assurance that "when foreigners [were] granted permission to establish telegraph lines, the Russians [would] be the first."[2]

Prince Gong and the Chinese Ministry of Foreign Affairs still had an attitude of utter rejection of any telegraph project. There was also massive cultural and religious resistance in the populace, which felt that the telegraph poles rising vertically from the earth would threaten human beings' harmony with nature and with their surroundings—the so-called feng shui, which is closely linked with Taoism.

On a number of occasions, it became evident that the threat to feng shui was taken literally when the local population tore down telegraph lines that

In 1867, the former American ambassador to China, Anson Burlingame, was appointed the leader of China's first diplomatic mission to the United States and Western Europe with a view to achieving the recognition of China as a country on an equal footing with the Western powers. The picture shows the entire delegation with Burlingame standing in the middle. He is flanked by two Chinese ministers and the delegation's two European secretaries—to Burlingame's right is the Frenchman Émile Deschamps, to his left the Irishman John Mc-Leavy Brown, who was the delegation's first secretary.

had been installed by Western entrepreneurs who had taken their chances. In 1864, a telegraph line between Fuzhou and Luoxingta was destroyed, in 1865, one between Shanghai and Wusong.[3]

For reasons of principle and political reasons and to avoid provoking the populace, all applications for the establishment of telegraph lines were consistently rejected by the Chinese authorities, and in 1865, all local authorities were instructed to send all telegraph matters directly to the foreign ministry in Beijing to ensure that no one gave in to Western desires or pressure.

Eventually, however, the Western powers' attitude toward China became less confrontational and more focused on cooperation. This was diplomatically recognized by the conclusion of the so-called Burlingame Treaty between China and the United States in Washington on July 28, 1868. The treaty established that the United States would abstain from pressuring China to establish railroad and telegraph lines because the United States recognized the Chinese emperor's "right to determine the time, manner and circumstances in which such changes would be introduced in his territories."[4]

The treaty is named after Anson Burlingame, who, despite his American origin, was the leader of China's first diplomatic mission to the United States and Europe. In 1861, Burlingame had become the United States' first ambassador to China, where he had won trust and respect from the Chinese, thanks to his understanding and recognition of Chinese points of view, including those responsible for Chinese reluctance to accept the introduction of telegraphy and railroads. In the fall of 1867, when China decided to send its first diplomatic mission ever to the West, the Chinese government therefore appointed Anson Burlingame the leader of the mission with extraordinary powers conferred by the emperor of China.

With the signing of the Burlingame Treaty, the United States became the first country to recognize China as an equal nation, and after the signing, Burlingame traveled to England, where, with the signing of the Clarendon declaration of December 28, 1868, he got the United Kingdom to abstain from pressuring Chinese authorities and citizens.

Chinese permission to land a cable?

At the same time, as he was seeking to obligate the Western powers not to force the telegraph and other Western technologies on China, Burlingame, paradoxically enough, became the cause of significant activity among Western telegraph companies and interested parties who suddenly saw an opportunity to introduce the telegraph to China.

As ambassador, he himself, despite his recognition of Chinese points of view, attempted to convince the Chinese government to introduce the telegraph but in vain. An application submitted in January 1865 by an American company, the East Indian Telegraph Company, regarding the installation of an undersea cable connection from Guangzhou up the Chinese coast to Tianjin with stations in the treaty harbor towns—which would have avoided the controversial installation of a cross-country telegraph line—was rejected.

However, in May 1865, when Burlingame was about to return to the United States for a lengthy leave of absence, the Chinese softened their position and approved the American company's application. The reason for this was that Prince Gong wished to have Burlingame's help in a matter that represented a great strain with regard to China's relationship with the United Kingdom. The application then was approved to acquire help in a matter regarded as of great importance to the Chinese government—not as the result of any change in the Chinese negative attitude toward the telegraph.

Nevertheless, permission had been granted, and Burlingame informed the East Indian Telegraph Company that he would confirm this to the United States Department of State in a dispatch. This did not occur, however, and finally, the company contacted the Department of State in Washington and asked what the status of the matter was. The department sent the question on to Burlingame, who, in a dispatch of May 1867, detailed the connection between the Chinese wish to receive diplomatic assistance and the application submitted by the American company:

"Wishing to please me, they assented to this, but not in writing. This is the only thing resembling a grant ever made to anyone. It should be understood, that a grant to me, under the favored nation clause is a grant to all. The first to occupy the ground will have the advantage but more than this I cannot say."[5]

There was then no written document from the Chinese, and the reason why Burlingame had never confirmed approval to the US Department of State was probably that given the circumstances, he had viewed the Chinese approval as a flimsy basis for a project such as this, which would require the securing of a large amount of capital and involved considerable risk. Indeed, he concluded his dispatch by remarking that he had "persistently refused to advice the Company or anyone else to risk money; and however much I should be pleased as a patriot to have Americans build the first line, I must still respectfully hold that position."[6]

This letter was published by the US Department of State in the spring of 1868, and in early July, the East India Telegraph Company reported in *Journal of the Telegraph* that "the Chinese government—via the honorable Anson Burlingame, the former American ambassador to the court of Beijing—has given the company permission to connect the large harbor towns from Guangzhou to Tianjin with undersea cables."[7]

With this, the Chinese approval was publicly known, at least in telegraphy circles, and when Burlingame's diplomatic mission arrived in London in September 1868, he was swarmed by representatives of individuals and companies from the telegraphy sector who wanted to land cables in the treaty harbor towns. Among these representatives was Commissioner of War C. L. Madsen, who met with Burlingame late in the month and passed on to him a letter from C. F. Tietgen. The exact contents of this letter are not known, but without a doubt, it had to do with a trans-Siberian telegraph connection between Europe and China that had been discussed in Moscow during the negotiations regarding the recently granted concession for a Dano-Russian cable.[8]

In early November 1868, C. L. Madsen was able to inform Tietgen that the former chairman of the board of directors of the East India Telegraph Company was also in London. "It must be the Chinese cable that is under discussion," Madsen reasoned. Then he asked, "Shall I consult with Mr. Burlingame on the subject?"[9]

He was instructed to do so, and on November 7, 1868, C. L. Madsen again met in London with Anson Burlingame, who told him that he had previ-

ously been sought out by a certain Mr. John Dunn and others for the purpose of discussing the same matter. In the meantime, Burlingame had read Tietgen's letter, and according to C. L. Madsen's report to Tietgen, he "spoke with great interest of the clear manner in which [Tietgen] had presented his plans to him."[10]

In late January 1869, Tietgen had an opportunity to present his plans to Burlingame himself when the two men met in Paris. A short time previously, Tietgen, having been asked to do so by the director of the Russian telegraph authority, Karl von Lüders, had prepared a memorandum regarding the extension of the trans-Siberian connection the last 1,500 kilometers from Sretensk to the little ice-free harbor town of Posyet on the coast of the Sea of Japan and the laying of cables from there to Shanghai via Japan. It was doubtless this project he now presented to Anson Burlingame, but Tietgen soon lost interest in this project and concentrated on the North Atlantic project, which had once again come to appear realizable in the near future.[11]

Close to a Russian concession

Russian interest in connecting Europe and China telegraphically by means of a landline through Siberia and a cable connection from Posyet to China was not new. The idea had originally been conceived by the English merchant in Shanghai John George Dunn, who, in 1864, had investigated the possibilities with regard to laying undersea cables from Shanghai to Nikolayevsk-on-Amur, Russia, where they would be connected with the planned telegraph connection between the United States and Russia.[12]

This plan was abandoned as a result of the laying of the Atlantic cables in 1866, but in the fall of 1867, Dunn instead presented to the governor of East Siberia a plan to extend the trans-Siberian telegraph connection to Posyet and to lay cables from there to Japan and Shanghai. The governor supported the project, and in February 1868, when Dunn had allied himself with the English banking company Chadwicks, Adamson, Colliers & Co., he began negotiations in Saint Petersburg, but disagreements arose with regard to financing, and the negotiations therefore took a relatively long time.

It was doubtless as an element of these negotiations that John Dunn sought out Anson Burlingame in London in November 1868, after which Burlingame confirmed the dispatch regarding Chinese landing permission with his own personal seal and his signature. Dunn took the confirmation with him to Saint Petersburg, but it did not change the situation, and at the beginning of 1869, negotiations appeared to have collapsed.[13]

However, the governor did not abandon his support for the project, and early in 1869, he again applied to the Russian government for approval for the completion of the trans-Siberian landline. David Chadwick and John Dunn were summoned to Saint Petersburg, but the negotiations proceeded only slowly, and in early May 1869, the Russian government decided to begin negotiating with another party. The party they had in mind appeared to have been the Danish investors who were interested in telegraphy—in any event, the telegraphy director, General Lüders, requested via Hans Pallisen that C. F. Tietgen's partner in Newcastle, H. G. Erichsen, who had negotiated with regard to the Dano-Russian cable, come to Saint Petersburg as soon as possible.[14]

The explanation for this decision was no doubt in part that the Russians had become impatient but also in part that a grand British cable project involving the laying of cables from England via Suez to India, Singapore, Hong Kong, and Shanghai had been presented a short time previously. The project was backed by the Telegraph Construction & Maintenance Company and several English telegraph companies that constituted an increasingly dominant cable and telegraph imperium controlled by the English financier John Pender. The first phases of the project were already being carried out, and to those contemplating the situation from Saint Petersburg, it appeared that there was a real risk that the English would get to Shanghai first, which would render the Russian project superfluous.

On May 24, 1869, after a stop in Copenhagen to discuss the matter with Tietgen, H. G. Erichsen arrived in Saint Petersburg to begin negotiations with telegraphy director Lüders. After four weeks, an agreement was reached, and on June 22, 1869, H. G. Erichsen and Hans Pallisen could sign a draft proposal for a Russian concession for the laying of cables among Russia, Japan, and China. The Russian government had yet finally to approve the draft and issue the concession, but the Danes were close to the finish line—just three weeks after the founding of the Great Northern Telegraph Company and two weeks after the opening of the Dano-Russian cable.[15]

However, John Dunn and his partners in Chadwicks, Adamson, Colliers & Co. did not give up. They had not been informed of the Russian government's decision to negotiate with the Danes and were still pushing to get their project approved. In early July, they were again summoned to Saint Petersburg, where, for the first time, they learned that the Russians were negotiating with others.[16]

In the meantime, a Russian consortium had also gotten involved. It was led by the Russian Sergey Abaza, who had worked for the Western Union Telegraph Company on the Bering Strait project and had highly placed, powerful supporters, thanks to his family network, which included the president of Russia's council of ministers and interior ministry.

It was probably precisely Abaza's connections that caused the telegraphy department to abandon the agreement with Erichsen and Pallisen. The department now proposed an open competition to be awarded the concession, and while everyone was awaiting the decision of the council of ministers, C. F. Tietgen acted. The experienced now retired diplomat, Chamberlain Julius Frederik Sick, took it upon himself to travel to Saint Petersburg and work to get the concession awarded to the Danes. Tietgen also wrote to Christian IX and requested his "most exalted protection" and a recommendation from the king in the form of a letter to the king's son-in-law, the successor to the Russian throne, Prince Alexander.[17]

Sick left with the intention of being admitted into the presence of the czar, but he was not successful in this. Instead, he was given an audience with the

Danish princess Dagmar, who had previously received a letter regarding the matter from her father, Christian IX. In 1866, Dagmar was married to the Russian successor and arranged to have him meet with Sick at an unofficial audience. Sick was well accustomed to walking the polished floors and the corridors of power; nevertheless, he was unable to prevent the approval by the council of ministers on July 27 of a competition to determine who would secure the concession. In a letter to Tietgen, he deplored that he had managed to achieve so little but also emphasized "the gain achieved" that the czar had learned of the matter from his son "and expressed his sympathy for the Danish position."[18]

Diplomatic fight over the concession

The decision of the council of ministers was sent to the Department of Telegraphy on August 3, 1869, and that same day, a further applicant was heard from. This was the French financier Baron Frédéric Émile d'Erlanger, who was a shareholder in a company that had laid a French transatlantic cable to the United States during the summer of 1869. In addition to financial strength, he had close connections to the circle around the Telegraph Construction & Maintenance Company.[19]

Chadwicks, Adamson, Collier & Co. were also associated with the circle around the Telegraph Construction & Maintenance Company, as was Sergey Abaza, who needed financing from the Telegraph Construction & Maintenance Company to be able to realize the project.[20]

Of the total of four applicants then, C. F. Tietgen, who was applying for the concession together with H. G. Erichsen and Hans Pallisen, was alone in not being connected to John Pender and the Telegraph Construction & Maintenance Company. The opposition appeared insurmountable, and the Abaza consortium in particular represented a threat, thanks to its Russian basis and its political connections.

Chamberlain Julius Frederik Sick, whom C. F. Tietgen sent on several diplomatic missions to Russia, China, and Japan, was a Danish career diplomat who left government diplomatic service as a forty-two-year-old in 1857 after a short but influential career. In 1869, he worked in Russia to advance Tietgen's efforts to secure Russian concessions, and in 1870, he was in Japan, where, as the official envoy of King Christian IX of Denmark, he concluded an agreement with the Japanese government with regard to Great Northern's landing of telegraph cables. In both Japan and China, he succeeded in obtaining audiences with the respective emperors.

However, Tietgen turned his underdog position into an advantage by addressing concerns raised by the international political situation in his application. While in connection with the Dano-Russian cable the Danes had exploited Russia's interest in a telegraph connection with England that would avoid Germany, Tietgen now exploited the strong anti-British feelings in Russia as a result of the crushing defeat Russia had suffered in the Crimean War (1853–1856) and as a result of the rivalry between the two empires in Central and East Asia.

Tietgen referred to the British project of establishing a telegraph line from India to Hong Kong, Shanghai, and Japan and mentioned that the companies involved could be behind the competing applicants for the Russian concession. If the Russian project ended up in British hands, Tietgen argued, all telegraph connections between East Asia and Europe would be controlled by the British, and this would ensure "England's commercial and political superiority in China and Japan." Russia's interests in the area of international politics would be threatened, and the trans-Siberian telegraph connection would be economically undermined as the British would certainly prefer that the cables be laid via India.[21]

Tietgen's conclusion was that the concession "cannot be awarded to any party but [the Danes], as [the Danes] are neither agents of British companies nor inclined to sell the concession to British businesses." The laying of the cable from Russia to Denmark and Sweden had already demonstrated that the Danish consortium was both independent and capable.

On September 1, 1869, the four applications were submitted, after which the fight to win the concession really began. All the parties had representatives in Saint Petersburg as well as contacts in the Department of Telegraphy and the government offices, and C. F. Tietgen once again sent out Chamberlain Julius Frederik Sick.

Sick immediately began attending a series of audiences with members of the council of ministers and other influential people, and he sent a French *exposé* to several key individuals. He focused in particular on the dangers inherent in handing over the concession to British interests, and the underlined passages in Tietgen's application suggested that the Russians took note of this argument.[22]

The French baron d'Erlanger appeared not to have been seen as a serious candidate by the Russian telegraph administration, and Chadwicks, Adamson, Collier & Co. hardly advanced their cause by expressing anger over the fact that others were now competing to be awarded a project that their company and John Dunn had conceived. Given the contents of Tietgen's application, it was hardly wise to emphasize the connection between the company and particularly David Chadwick on the one hand and the Telegraph & Maintenance Company on the other hand either.

The most dangerous competitor was Sergey Abaza, but his application too was negatively affected by the anti-British arguments. Because of this, he broke off his connection with the Telegraph Construction & Maintenance Company and declared that he wished to form a purely Russian company and finance the project with Russian money. However, this was a move that weakened his position vis-à-vis several ministers who lacked confidence in the Russian capital market. The battle raged back and forth, and various alliances were formed, and in the meantime, Tietgen and Sick prepared their decisive trump. In the middle of September, Sick sent a memorandum to Princess Dagmar, who was vacationing in Crimea, and asked her to exert her influence to get her husband, Prince Alexander, to delay the decision by the council of ministers until he was back in Saint Petersburg.

Around the same time, Tietgen had an audience with Christian IX at which he asked the king to address the czar to ensure that the concession ended up in Danish hands. On September 25, the king therefore wrote a letter to Dagmar, whom he asked to help ensure that the concession was given to Tietgen "as this would be in Denmark's best interests." The letter was brought to Saint Petersburg and handed over to Sick, who delivered it to Dagmar together with an account of the matter in French intended to be given to her husband.[23]

Before the decisive meeting of the council of ministers on October 12, the successor to the Russian throne spoke with the chairman of the council, Prince Gagarin, and assured himself of Gagarin's

When the Burlingame delegation came to Copen-hagen in October 1868, the Chinese participants attracted so much attention in the streets of the city that their visit was described in the newspaper *Illustreret Tidende.*

support; Prince Alexander also spoke with Grand Duke and Admiral Konstantin, who, as Sick put it, "made himself an organ for the prince and suc-cessor's strong interest in the matter, which the successor himself did not dare to make public-ly known." After two and a half hours of delibera-tions, the council of ministers voted unanimously to award the concession to the Danish consortium.

Final and formal confirmation followed the fol-lowing week, after which, on October 23, 1869, the czar signed the concession, which conferred a thir-ty-year monopoly.[24]

The Burlingame mission to Copenhagen

In connection with the concession, C. F. Tietgen, Hans Pallisen, and H. G. Erichsen had accepted re-sponsibility for laying undersea telegraph cables from Vladivostok to Japan and on to Shanghai, while the Russian government telegraph authori-

The British telegraph king John Pender was C. F. Tietgen's main opponent during the persistent rivalries between Great Northern and the British Eastern companies during the 1870s and 1880s until a peace agreement could finally be concluded. Over the course of his life, he created by far the largest group of telegraph companies in the world, a group that controlled more than 50 percent of the world's submarine telegraph cables.

and China, which it was the Danish concession holders' responsibility to obtain.

Tietgen was therefore more interested than was usual when the Burlingame mission arrived in Copenhagen the day after the Russian government had awarded the concession to the Danish consortium. There is no extant documentation indicating that Tietgen and Burlingame met in Copenhagen, but given the importance of the matter, it is difficult to imagine that this did not occur. In any event, Tietgen desired a written declaration from Burlingame regarding the landing possibilities in China for which he asked in a letter of October 21. An answer came already the following day:

"In response to your enquiry in relation to telegraphs in China I have to say that in 1865 as United States Minister, the Chinese Government, refusing to grant a right of way over the land, consented that if a line should be laid in the sea, it might be landed at the ports.

This assent is attested by two interpreters, Dr. W.A.P. Martin and Dr. Williams, eminent Sinologues.

By the favored nation clause in the treaties, what is granted to one is granted to all, so that the connection you propose by the way of Possiette [Posyet] with Shanghai may be securely made."[25]

Anson Burlingame then did not provide a permit to land the cable in China, and indeed, he had

ty would extend the trans-Siberian landline the last 1,500 kilometers through East Siberia, from Sretensk to Vladivostok. The concession was awarded without assurance of landing permission in Japan no authority to provide such a permit. He simply declared in vague terms that in his view, it ought to be possible to obtain permission. However, Tietgen did receive a transcript of Burlingame's original dispatch to the United States Department of State a few days later. This came from Chadwicks, Adamson, Collier & Co. in London, who offered to cooperate with Tietgen, who first responded positively but rejected the offer a short time later.[26]

It is hardly likely that Tietgen had previously been familiar with the exact wording of the dispatch; otherwise, there would have been no reason for him to receive a transcript at this time. He thus discovered on the one hand that the Chinese permission had only been granted orally and as compensation for diplomatic assistance and on the other hand that Burlingame had explicitly stated that he would not recommend basing a cable project on the Chinese indication of permission. Nevertheless, Tietgen had acquired a written, signed declaration from Burlingame on behalf of the Chinese mission that he, Tietgen, planned to use later to ensure that Burlingame supported him vis-à-vis the Chinese authorities if this should prove to be necessary.

When, on October 25, the Burlingame delegation left Copenhagen for Leipzig, it was aboard the steamship *Vesta* from Det Forenede Dampskibs-Rederi ("the United Steam Shipping Company"), which Tietgen had founded in 1866. A week later, the newspaper *Dagens Nyheder* reported that "the head of the recently departed Chinese delegation" had assured the Danish telegraph consortium that special permission to land cables in China was unnecessary as a result of the permission provided to the American company and the favored nation clause.[27]

Telegraph race and financial sabotage

The report in *Dagens Nyheder* regarding Burlingame's assurance that telegraph cables could be landed in China had surely come from C. F. Tietgen, who needed to raise money to lay the cables in East Asia. Not only in a Danish perspective but also in a European and global perspective, this was a grand and risky project Tietgen and his partners were embarking on. Undersea cables would need to be laid in faraway waters that had not been sounded, and cables were to be brought ashore on coasts where the prevailing conditions were not known and it was uncertain whether the respective governments would grant permission. Everything—cables, stations, wires, and apparatus—was to be brought from Europe and gotten to function as a coherent system. And then the project needed to be financed with 600,000 pounds sterling or almost 5.5 million rigsdaler that it would be difficult to acquire given the modest size of the Danish capital market.

To these problems was added the special challenge created by the fact that the project was being sabotaged by the circle around the Telegraph Construction & Maintenance Company. There was a real race to get to China first because on October 20, 1869—already before the Russian czar had signed the concession—John Pender established the British Indian Extension Telegraph Company to lay cables from India to Singapore. On December 11, he established the China Submarine Cable Telegraph Company to lay cables extending to Hong Kong, and on January 4, 1870, the company's share capital was increased to finance an extension to Shanghai. If the British got there first, the foundation of the Danish project could be threatened, and even the report regarding the British plans could make it difficult to raise the required capital.[28]

In Denmark at the same time, Tietgen established a new company to execute the project so as not to saddle the Great Northern Telegraph Company with an economic risk that could ruin it. On January 9, 1870, the Great Northern China & Japan Extension Telegraph Company was established by C. F. Tietgen, C. A. Broberg, O. B. Suhr, and Martin Levy as well as two new members of the circle, the manufacturer L. P. Holmblad and Julius Frederik Sick. The company's share capital amounted to 600,000 pounds sterling, 150,000 pounds of which was to be acquired from Privatbanken and 450,000 pounds from C. I. Hambro & Son in London.[29]

The *Tordenskjold*'s departure for Asia to participate in Great Northern's laying of cable was discussed in detail in the capital city press and mentioned even in small provincial newspapers all around the country. The picture shows *Illustreret Tidende*, which presented the moment at which the warship steamed out of the Port of Copenhagen on its front page.

Apparently, Tietgen was no longer entirely sure of the trustworthiness of Burlingame's declaration. It was not mentioned in the brochure issued in connection with the establishment of the company despite the fact that it would have constituted a trump card. All the evidence suggests that Tietgen was instead leaning toward landing the cables in Shanghai secretly, which would make it possible to confront the Chinese government with a fait accompli and expect the Danish project to be defended by the Western powers if there were Chinese protests.

The initial public offering took place in London on January 14, 1869, but that same day, the China Submarine Telegraph Company placed a notice in *The Times* regarding its own cable project and warned the public against confusing the British project with the Danish one. On the same page, the newspaper also published a letter by an anonymous reader who expressed wonderment over the notion that British investors should purchase shares in a Danish company that included no British partners and possessed a Russian concession. Furthermore, it was argued the landline went through Siberia, where maintenance would be practically impossible and profits would be modest.[30]

The Pender group doubtlessly also used other more hidden methods to sabotage the Danish public offering, methods whose nature and precise extent are not now known. In his memoirs, Tietgen later wrote, without going into detail, that "thanks to the opposition from Construction Company it [the public offering] completely failed in London."[31]

Officially, however, it was reported at the end of the share subscription that it had been complete. A valuation based on Tietgen's own records indicates that shares amounting to a maximum of 567,390 pounds sterling were purchased and that a significant proportion of the shares sold in London was purchased by Tietgen and Privatbanken and that the English cable manufacturer Hooper's Telegraph Works Ltd., which was to manufacture the cables, received shares in the amount of 100,000 pounds as a part of its payment.[32]

Preparations for laying the cables in East Asia

Because of the race with the Pender group, the production of cables was begun before the contract was signed. Hooper's Telegraph Works were located in South London and were not a part of the Pender group. According to the agreement, the company was to deliver 2,400 nautical miles of cable to be laid in the waters among Hong Kong, Shanghai, Nagasaki, and Vladivostok.

The cables, along with other equipment that were also purchased in England, were to be shipped from London and brought to East Asia and the Russian Far East via the newly opened Suez Canal. Traveling by the same route were a large number of Danish telegraphists, electricians, office personnel, and other personnel to carry out the laying of the cables and subsequently operate the systems and man the stations. For this purpose, two English steamships, the *Cella* and the *Great Northern*, were chartered and refitted for the laying of the cables. It would not be possible to ship all the cables in one cargo, and the plan was for the ships to steam back to London and pick up a new load of cables to be laid between Shanghai and Vladivostok after the cables to be laid between Hong Kong and Shanghai had been off-loaded.

In addition, thanks to action taken on the company's behalf by Minister of War and Maritime Affairs Gen. Waldemar Raasløff, the Danish government placed at the company's disposal the propeller-driven frigate *Tordenskjold*; expenses occurred in connection with operating the frigate were to be borne by the company. The warship was to sound the waters near Nagasaki and Vladivostok and also deliver personnel and a relatively small amount of cable. As a warship flying a burgee, it had the status of an official Danish vessel, and with its cannons, it could keep away pirates and other uninvited guests.

The company chose Senior Lt. Edouard Suenson, who was only twenty-seven years old, to lead the laying of cable and the operation in its entirety. As a young naval officer, Suenson had served in the French navy, first in the Mediterranean and then in East Asia, where his postings had included a year in Japan. During a battle in which he had been involved while in the service of the French, Suenson had been wounded in both legs, and when he had returned to Denmark, he had become the adjutant of William Raasløff, who now placed him at the disposal of the cable project. Despite his youth then, Edouard Suenson was familiar with the conditions in East Asia in general and in Japan in particular, and he was therefore an obvious choice to become the leader of the mission.

In the area of diplomacy too, preparations were made to secure permission to land cables in China and Japan. Tietgen had already secured the support of Russia and gotten the Danish Ministry of Foreign Affairs to seek the backing of the United Kingdom and France. In addition, Tietgen got the Danish government to send Julius Frederik Sick to China and Japan as an extraordinary diplomatic envoy.

Denmark had preexisting diplomatic relations with both countries. In 1863, Denmark and China had concluded a friendship, trade, and shipping treaty that had been negotiated and was signed in Tianjin by Waldemar Raasløff, and four years later, in 1867, Denmark and Japan had concluded a peace and trade treaty.

Sick's visit to Beijing had the status of a reciprocal visit following the visit of the Burlingame delegation to Denmark, while the visit to Tokyo had the official purpose of delivering a letter from the Danish king to the emperor. The real purpose of Sick's mission, however, was to secure the necessary landing permits, and because of this, Tietgen paid Sick's travel expenses, while Sick resigned from the board of directors of the Extension Company to take on the status of an independent diplomat.[33]

On April 3, 1870, *Tordenskjold* lay in Copenhagen Harbor, ready to depart for London, where the warship was to load cables and other equipment. There was a great gathering of people on the quay already early in the morning, and later in the morning, Christian IX arrived with several of his ministers and shook the hands of all the crew members and wished them a good journey. At noon, the company's board of directors and a number of honored individuals led by Tietgen arrived, and *Tordenskjold* sailed out of the harbor to the sounds of a cannon salute.

Two days later, Edouard Suenson left Copenhagen more discreetly for Marseille, from where he was to proceed through the Suez Canal to East Asia aboard fast French packet boats. He was accompanied by C. F. Tietgen to Hamburg, where the two men met with the first secretary of the Burlingame delegation, the Irishman McLeavy Brown.

Anson Burlingame had died of pneumonia in Saint Petersburg on February 23, 1870, and the question was what his declaration regarding landing permission in China was worth at this point. There is no extant record of Brown's response, but it was doubtless that the Chinese would not grant permission if they were asked. Certainly, this was the clear answer Julius Sick received when he met with this same McLeavy Brown late in the month in Brussels, where Brown indicated that Burlingame had made unjustified declarations not only in Copenhagen but elsewhere as well. Brown recommended that the Danish company act in accordance with Tietgen's plan to lay the cables secretly without having asked the Chinese government for permission.[34]

Having received this advice—and without any pre-existing sense of how he would be received in China or Japan—Sick traveled onward to Marseille, where he boarded a French packet bound for Japan and China.

Peace agreement between Tietgen and Pender

Others were on their way to China as well. John Pender was not going to stand passively by and watch while the Danish consortium prepared to lay their cables in East Asia. In early February 1870, he sent a trusted agent abroad to acquire a landing permit as he too had been assured by Burlingame that the Chinese government would not oppose the issuance of such a permit. This trusted agent was John Dunn, who had previously offered his services to Tietgen but been rebuffed.[35]

There was much at stake for Tietgen, not least financially, as he and Privatbanken risked great, indeed ruinous, losses. If Pender got to China first, the economic basis of the entire project would be threatened, and then there was the uncertainty regarding the landing permits, which could cause everything to collapse. Already in the middle of February 1870, Tietgen therefore took action to reduce the risk when he and H. G. Erichsen produced a draft for an agreement with John Pender that would eliminate the race between the two parties. Pender, who was unaware that the Danish public offering had, in fact, been a failure, saw an advantage in concluding an agreement, and one was therefore arrived at and signed by Tietgen and Pender in London on May 13, 1870.[36]

According to the agreement, which would remain valid for thirty years, the Danish company would lay a cable between Shanghai and Hong Kong and not expand south of the British crown colony. For its part, the Pender group agreed not to expand its activity north of Hong Kong. The Danish cable would therefore be the only one between Hong Kong and Shanghai, but it would be used jointly by the two companies such that it would be operated by Great Northern, and the gross rev-

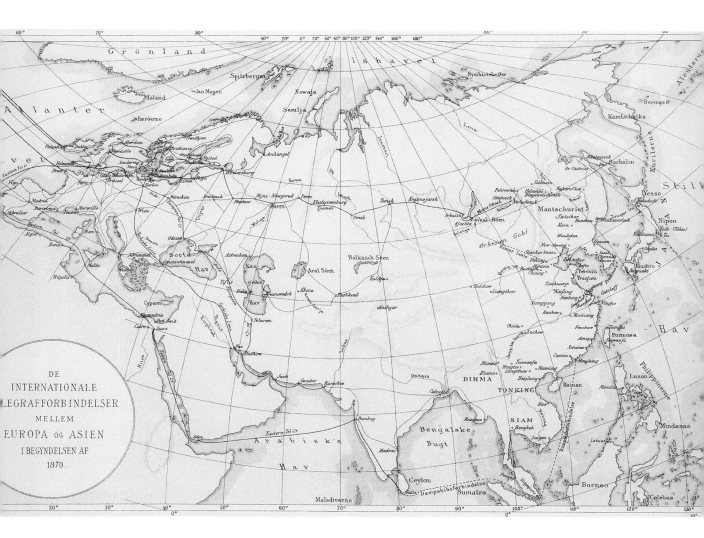

Map of the telegraph connections between Europe and East Asia early in 1870. One can see how the Russian landline had reached Sretensk, east of Lake Baikal, and was complemented by a courier connection between the end of the line and Beijing and how the British telegraph connections had reached Sri Lanka, from where one could communicate with the British crown colony of Hong Kong via steamship. There was a race between Great Northern and the British Eastern companies to be the first to lay cables in East Asia and connect China and Japan to the global telegraph system—a race the Danes won.

enues minus 15,000 pounds sterling for expenses and interest on invested capital were to be shared equally. The Pender group thus acquired a source of revenue, as well as a feeder line from the north to its cables, without having invested any money, while the Danish company got a feeder line from the south to its cables and an assurance that the English would not expand north of Hong Kong.

Danish Cable Action in East Asia

CHAPTER 3

Arrival in Hong Kong and Shanghai

When Edouard Suenson arrived in the British crown colony of Hong Kong in the middle of May 1870, he was unaware of the agreement between C. F. Tietgen and John Pender. John Dunn, who was in Beijing at this time, also knew nothing of the agreement. With the support of the British ambassador in China Thomas Wade, Dunn was to seek to acquire permission to land British telegraph cables in the harbor towns on John Pender's behalf. The Chinese Ministry of Foreign Affairs finally gave its permission but on the condition that the cables were not landed but instead ended on floating telegraph stations anchored outside the harbors. Land and sea were to be kept separate so the telegraph did not come in contact with Chinese soil—the declaration once made to Anson Burlingame notwithstanding.[1]

Prior to Edouard Suenson's arrival in Hong Kong, the Danish consul general George J. Helland had applied to the governor for permission to land a telegraph cable and establish a land connection between the landing site and the capital city of Victoria, where the company's station was to be established. The governor's attitude was positive, but the landing permit needed to be formally issued by the British government. This was a mere formality, however, as there was support in London for the establishment of a telegraph connection with China regardless of whether the company responsible was Danish or British.

After having rented the necessary buildings and gotten everything ready for the arrival of the Danish cable ships and their cargoes, Suenson traveled onward to Shanghai, where he arrived in early June 1870. At that time, about 200,000 people lived in the Chinese part of the town within the old town walls and surrounding areas. The Western settlements stretched along the Huangpu River; the British-American settlement had a common government, while the French settlement had a French government. At the time of Suenson's arrival, about 75,000 Chinese and only about 3,200 foreigners lived in the international settlements. About half of these foreigners were British, the rest a mixture of Frenchmen, Americans, Germans, Belgians, and others, including 16 Danes.

Despite the Chinese majority in their population, the foreign settlements were not subject to Chinese jurisdiction. The French settlement was governed by the French consul and the British-American area by a municipal council elected by foreign permanent residents who paid taxes. The powers enjoyed by the settlements' independent governments were evident in the fact that the settlements had two telegraph lines onsite, one that connected the American trading house Russell and Co.'s main office with its riverside warehouses and one that connected the two police stations in the American and British settlement, respectively. However, the landing of an undersea cable was an entirely different matter and one that was the business of the Chinese government.

Plan for a secret cable landing

Shortly after his arrival, Suenson, as he himself put it, was "pretty much destroyed by a serious case of cholera that exhausted [him] greatly." In general, his lengthy mission in East Asia was characterized by recurring attacks of cholera and other illnesses resulting in high and lasting fevers that sometimes kept him in bed and rendered him unable to work. He did begin work on his tasks, however, and in the middle of June 1870, after a week of investigations in Shanghai, he wrote to Tietgen that he had been strengthened in his conviction that they "would not encounter serious interference by the Chinese if [the Danes did] not provoke such interference by seeking permission or drawing attention to the preparations for and execution of [the Danish project] through the creation of unnecessary publicity."[2]

Suenson therefore kept a low profile, and there were only a few people who were aware of his activities, which, in part, consisted of purchasing a lot on which to land the cable and concluding

The leader of the cable-laying work in East Asia 1870-1871 was the young Senior Lieutenant Edouard Suenson. After he had returned to Copenhagen, Suenson became the secretary of Great Northern's board of directors, then head of business operations, and finally, in 1877, the company's first chief executive officer. He quickly became the driving force of the company and was its undisputed leader after he had also become the chairman of the board of directors in 1898. He held a number of other leading positions in Danish companies; he was a member of the board of directors of the salvage company Svitzer Bjærgnings-Entreprise and of the marine insurance company De Private Assurandører, where he became the chairman, as well as of the telephone company KTAS. He also became a member of Privatbanken's banking committee.

an agreement regarding the renting of a suitable building for the company station and dwellings for its personnel. Among those who knew what was going on was the French harbormaster S. A. Viguier, who came to play an important role in Edouard Suenson's mission.

The letter reached Tietgen in Copenhagen two months later, and in general, the mission was characterized by slow communications—telegrams took more than a month to arrive as they first had to be sent by packet boat to Point de Galle on Sri Lanka, where there was a telegraph connection with Europe. From the time when one sent a letter to the time one received an answer then, about four months or more would pass, while telegrams took two months and were very expensive. Suenson therefore had to make all decisions without previously having consulted with Tietgen and the rest of the board, and for this reason, he had brought with him a general power of attorney, giving him full freedom to act on behalf of the company.

However, there was a preexisting plan to land the cable from Hong Kong on a small island, North Saddle Island, off the mouth of the Chang River, and lay a cable from there up to the mouth of the Huangpu, a tributary of the Chang, and then, after an intermediate landing, lay the last length of cable up to Shanghai. All this was to be done in great secrecy to not attract the attention of the authorities or the public.

When Edouard Suenson arrived in Shanghai, the number of Westerners was not large in relation to the number of Chinese inhabitants. However, the city was undergoing a period of rapid change, and the number of foreigners was growing, and as the picture shows, the European immigrants made their mark on the city through the construction of the Bund, the harbor promenade that ran along the Huangpu River.

The navigable waters off the coast of Hong Kong in 1870. This is a picture brought home by Captain William Lund of the Tordenskjold.

Suenson succeeded in concluding an agreement regarding the landing of the cable at the trading center in Wusong below Shanghai on a lot on which there stood an uninhabited bungalow owned by the Danish consul Mr. Johnson and in acquiring a lot on which to land a cable in Shanghai's American settlement. To house the station and dwellings for the personnel, he rented a three-story building on Nanjing Road in the British settlement close to the Bund—the harbor promenade—so a telegraph line could be brought overland from the landing site that was within the Western settlements and therewith outside Chinese jurisdiction.

However, Suenson decided not to use North Saddle Island for the intermediate landing of the cables but instead to use the small island of Gut-zlaff, which was closer to the mouth of the Chang River. This island had a lighthouse and a house for the lighthouse keeper as its only buildings and was administered by the imperial customs authority, which was led by Europeans. In case of cable breaks in the Huangpu River, it would be possible to use a planned little telegraph station on the island and bring telegrams to and from Shanghai by ship—a system that could also be used on a more permanent basis if there were difficulties with the Chinese authorities or the local population.

The British head of the customs authority in Shanghai assured Suenson that there would not be problems in connection with the landing on Gutzlaff. He became concerned when he heard of the result of John Dunn's and Thomas Wade's negotiations in Beijing, however. He therefore left the final decision to the top administrator of the customs authority, the Irish-born Robert Hart.[3]

For his part, however, Suenson was not concerned by the Chinese rejection of the proposal that English cables be landed; on the contrary, it increased his confidence in his plan. He was irritated by John Dunn's activities in Beijing, though, as they could draw attention to his own project in Shanghai. For the same reason, he was dissatisfied with the Russian ambassador in Beijing, who was pushing for the introduction of the telegraph. "Every step taken in Beijing will only harm our enterprise," he wrote to Tietgen in late June. Then he added, "I still recommend following our plan, which is bold but right and good."[4]

Japanese landing permit

After having concluded the agreements regarding renting and purchasing lots and buildings in Shanghai, Suenson left in late June for Yokohama, where he arrived on July 8, 1870. He was received by the Danish general consul, the Swiss silk merchant Edouard de Bavier, at whose residence he met Julius Sick, who had been in Yokohama for some weeks and begun negotiations for a landing permit. Suenson presented his evaluation of the conditions in China to Sick, who supported the plans for a secret landing.

The two men discussed the situation in China in the wake of the massacre some weeks earlier in Tianjin, where a mob had attacked and burned Catholic churches and cloisters and killed the French consul and his assistant as well as ten French nuns and a number of additional foreigners and converts. Suenson found these events "horrible" but soberly concluded that the strong reaction by the Western powers must be expected to "attract the undivided attention of the Chinese government" and thus weaken interest in what was going on in Shanghai. Also, it seemed likely that there would be more active support from the United Kingdom and France if there were difficulties when it became known that the cable had been landed. Apparently, he had no concerns regarding his own safety or that of the future Danish staff—he never referred to such concerns, in any event.[5]

The situation in Japan was very different from the situation in China. For centuries, the country had maintained strict isolation from the West, but in 1868, a new ruling elite had come to power with the intention of exploiting Western technology and knowledge to strengthen Japan economically and militarily, in part, to be able to resist pressure from the Western powers. Because of this, the government had a positive attitude toward the telegraph; a landline between Tokyo and Yokohama had already been laid, and another was being laid between Kobe and Osaka. The landing of cables that could connect Japan with the global telegraph network was therefore welcome, but the Japanese were ambivalent about the prospect of having a foreign company operating the cables.

To begin with, Julius Sick had only brought up the question of whether a landing permit could be acquired for cables to Vladivostok and Shanghai, but Suenson expressed the wish that permission be acquired to lay and operate landlines from Nagasaki in the south to Hakodate on the northern island of Hokkaido. This wish was not granted, however; instead, the emperor issued a decree regarding the establishment of a government landline from Nagasaki to Tokyo, while the extension to Hakodate was approved a little over two years later.

Sick and Suenson did not get much support from Western diplomats in connection with the negotiations regarding the laying of cables near Nagasaki. The British ambassador was outright opposed—presumably under the influence of John Dunn, who was in Yokohama on the same errand as Sick and Suenson. On August 7, when Edouard Suenson left Japan to steam to Hong Kong and prepare for the arrival of the *Tordenskjold* and the two chartered steamers, no agreement had yet been reached. It was only on September 20 that Sick could sign an agreement that, in contrast to the company's other agreements, was not a landing permit issued to the company but

an agreement between national governments, concluded between the Japanese government and Julius Sick as the envoy of the Danish king.[6]

According to this agreement, the Great Northern China & Japan Extension Telegraph Company was to be granted a permit valid for thirty years to land and operate cables from Nagasaki to Vladivostok and Shanghai. In addition, the company was granted the right to purchase a lot in Nagasaki and rent or construct the buildings and other facilities that would be required for the establishment of a telegraph station and the operation of the cables. The landing permit did not in itself guarantee a monopoly, but the company was protected against competing projects by the Russian monopoly concession and the agreement with Pender.

In early October, after having had an audience with the emperor of Japan, Sick left Japan for Beijing. Here too he had an audience with the em-

Naval officers photographed between two cannons on the naval vessel *Tordenskjold*, which was on its way to Hong Kong in 1870. The identity of the woman in the background is unknown.

peror, but in accordance with his agreement with Suenson, Sick avoided bringing up the question of landing cables in Shanghai. Instead, he warmly recommended the Danish cable project to the foreign ambassadors.[7]

Uncertainty and illness

In the meantime, Suenson had arrived in Hong Kong. Shortly before his departure from Yokohama, he had received word from H. G. Erichsen that the *Great Northern* and the *Cella* and their cargoes of cables, equipment, and personnel had not left England as planned and would therefore not arrive by late August. As late as the middle of September,

Great Northern's telegraph station in Nagasaki seen from the beach.

Suenson had still heard nothing further about the ships except that the *Tordenskjold* had left Singapore ten days earlier. Suenson was unnerved by the uncertainty; he was worried that the Danish ship of the line had been stopped as a result of the Franco-Prussian War, which had broken out in the middle of July 1870. "In any event, it is certainly very unpleasant not to have any news," he wrote to Tietgen.[8]

Two days later, after a voyage of three months, the *Tordenskjold* slowly steamed into Hong Kong's harbor and dropped anchor. Suenson immediately had the ten telegraphists brought ashore and quartered at the Hotel l'Europe. As Suenson put it, they were in "such a neglected, not to say demoralized state" that in a letter to Tietgen, he complained of "the indefensible manner in which they

have been sent off without anyone at all who could take responsibility for their technical and general training." He therefore had telegraph equipment brought ashore and installed in the station building so the telegraphists would be able to practice their skills. He also moved from the house of the Danish consul George Helland, where he had been living up to this point, to the Hotel l'Europe "in order to have them under [his] oversight . . . and get them back into good shape, which [he thought could be accomplished] eventually."[9]

For the time being, Suenson was awaiting the arrival of C. L. Madsen before beginning the landing of the cable currently aboard the *Tordenskjold*. C. L. Madsen had joined the company as technical director of the cable-laying operation and should have arrived long ago. He had fallen ill in London, however, and it was uncertain when he would arrive. In the meantime, on October 2, the *Great Northern* arrived with its cargo of cables, equipment, and personnel who were traveling onward to Shanghai. The following day, C. L. Madsen and the company's station chief finally arrived in Hong Kong, and preparations for landing the cable began immediately.

Once again, Suenson was suffering greatly from illness and fever, which did more than just slow his activities. On October 9, 1870, he wrote to C. F. Tietgen and the board of directors of the Extension Company and requested permission to return to Denmark in the spring of 1871 despite the fact that his contract ran until September of that year. He also had to abandon his plan to travel to Vladivostok to prepare for the landing of the cable and to oversee the construction of a building comprising residences and a station and instead attempt to follow this work as best he could by mail. He was "so broken down and without health and strength that [he] did not believe [he] could get through another summer out here."[10]

Suenson obviously found the situation uncomfortable and emphasized that it was only "after careful consideration and only very reluctantly" that he raised the issue. His physician had forbid-

At the mouth of the Chang River lies the little island of Gutzlaff, on which Great Northern established a station and collected the cables from Nagasaki, Shanghai, and Hong Kong in a nexus. The station was operated by a single Danish telegraphist whose only company was the island's other inhabitant, a Chinese lighthouse keeper. The dwelling shown in the picture was built for the telegraphist in a style that was not particularly Chinese.

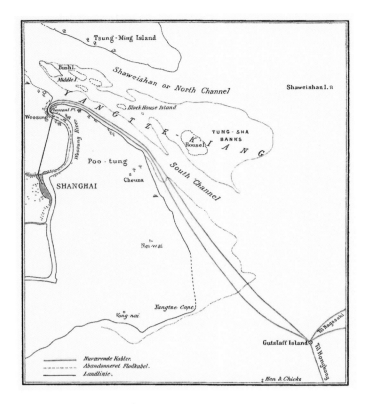

Map of Great Northern's cables from Shanghai to the Wusong River and leading out to the little island of Gutzlaff at the mouth of the Chang River, where the cables to Hong Kong and Nagasaki were also landed. This map was drawn after the river cable between Shanghai and Wusong (dotted red line) had been replaced with a landline connection and the cables connecting Shanghai, Gutzlaff, and Nagasaki had been supplemented with parallel extra cables.

been laid and things had progressed to a point at which it was possible for him to return home. He proposed Senior Lt. Georg Hannibal Napoleon Dreyer, whom he warmly recommended and who would immediately be able to acquaint himself with relevant conditions by working together with Suenson. "It has been unpleasant for me to have to take this step, but I believe that if the board could see me, then this would suffice to cause them to approve my request in their own interest," he wrote, concluding with the assurance that "if [his] request were denied [he] would of course continue in [his] position until the month of September."[12]

Despite his condition, Suenson toured the island with C. L. Madsen and Captain Lund of the *Tordenskjold*, after which they unanimously chose Deep Water Bay south of the capital city of Victoria, as a landing site. There was also support for Suenson's plan to land cables in Shanghai via Gutzlaff and Wusong.[13]

Around the same time, the Burlingame delegation stopped by Hong Kong on its way back to Beijing. The delegation's secretary, McLeavy Brown, was with the delegation, and despite his illness, Suenson had himself "dragged along to see him," as he put it. When Suenson met the delegation, Brown was not present, and Brown therefore later visited Suenson, who presented to him the plans to lay the cable secretly without having requested permission, of which Brown "completely approved."[14]

Cable landing in Hong Kong and defective cables

When Suenson requested permission to return home before his contract expired, he knew approximately four months would pass before he got the board's reply. At that point, the mission should have proceeded so far that the end was in sight, but before then, the most important and difficult task

den him to work, but he was nevertheless "forced to attend to business from morning to night," and because of his staff's lack of knowledge of local conditions, he had to become involved with the smallest details himself. He was unable to identify anyone who could replace him immediately and expected, as he wrote, that "even more difficult tasks [awaited him] in Shanghai." He expressed hope that the cold winter weather and better climate would make it possible for him to complete these tasks in a satisfactory manner.[11]

However, Suenson did have a suggestion with regard to who might replace him when the cables had

would need to be completed: the laying of the cable at Shanghai. However, the plan had been made, and after this, there would only be the laying of cable from Gutzlaff to Nagasaki and Vladivostok to take care of, and no one expected problems with that. He should be able to get done in time.

On October 20, 1870—already before the arrival of the *Cella*—the laying of the cable was begun with the landing of the cable from the *Tordenskjold* in Deep Water Bay. This occurred in the presence of the governor and other local authorities, after which lunch was served aboard the *Great Northern*. The landing had not been officially announced as Suenson wished to avoid attracting the attention of the Chinese to the project. Because of this, the local newspapers had not been informed, which led to sharply worded comments in these newspapers during the following days.[15]

As it turned out, there were entirely different reasons why it was fortunate that the landing was not a public event. Two days later, the *Tordenskjold* began laying its cable en route to a destination forty nautical miles from Deep Water Bay, where the end was to be spliced together with the cable on board the *Cella*, which would then lay its cable as it moved north on course for the mouth of the Chang River.

The *Great Northern* was one of the two chartered steamships the Great Northern Telegraph Company sent to East Asia with cables. On board was a Danish supercargo, Rasmus Petersen, and it was thanks to him that Great Northern did not have to see the entire project collapse. The cargo of cables was defective because the warship's cable tank was made of wood, and water had seeped out of it with the result that the isolating rubber had dried out and was full of cracks. The tank in the other steamship, the *Cella*, was of iron, but because the water had not been changed frequently enough during the voyage, the rubber had begun to rot, which had resulted in some flaws. However, Rasmus Petersen had eventually noticed this problem and changed the water, so the cables from the *Cella* were relatively intact, and the *Great Northern* could begin laying cable near Shanghai soon after it arrived in the area.

During the laying of the cable, however, it quickly proved to be the case that there were defects in the *Tordenskjold*'s cable; indeed, it was soon clear that the cable was so seriously flawed that it would have to be taken out of the water and sent home. "Unfortunately, our luck appears to have abandoned us for the time being," Suenson wrote to Tietgen.[16]

Things would get even worse, however. On October 28, when the *Cella* arrived with 754 nautical miles of cables, it was discovered that these cables were defective as well and that it would be neces-

The *Tordenskjold* and the *Cella* side by side on November 29, 1870, during the repair of a cable in Deep Water Bay. The repair was carried out such that the cable from the *Cella*'s cable tanks was pulled over to the deck of the *Tordenskjold* and carefully checked, after which the cable was fed back to the *Cella* once flaws had been addressed and damaged pieces of cable cut out.

sary to carry out a thorough inspection and repair or cut out all defective sections.

As Edouard Suenson later put it, the discovery "had an almost paralyzing effect on the project's leaders," who were Suenson himself, C. L. Madsen, and the captain of the *Tordenskjold*, William Lund. While the cables on board the *Great Northern* proved not to be defective, the plan had, in fact, fallen through. The laying of the cables could not be carried out as planned as on the one hand, it was unclear whether it would be possible to repair the *Cella*'s cables on site and, on the other hand, the *Great Northern*'s cables were sized to be laid near Shanghai, but the plan had been to begin in Hong Kong.[17]

In consultation with C. L. Madsen and Captain Lund, Edouard Suenson decided to put an emergency plan into effect. While the *Cella* and the *Tordenskjold* would remain in Hong Kong to inspect and repair the defective cables, the *Great Northern* would proceed to Shanghai to lay its cables. That ship would subsequently be able to return to England in time to participate in the expedition's second phase, which would not be possible for the *Cella* because of the repair work. To replace the *Cella*, it would be necessary to charter a further ship that, together with the *Great Northern*, would bring a new shipment of cables in the spring of 1871. A consequence would be the delaying of the entire project and thus the opening of the telegraph line through Siberia to Europe, and costs would also be significantly increased. A message to this effect was sent by telegraph to Tietgen, who would receive the message approximately four weeks later, when the emergency plan would already have been implemented.

On November 16, 1870, the *Tordenskjold* and the *Cella* pulled up next to each other in Deep Water Bay and began work on the inspection and repair of the cables, while the *Great Northern* steamed away, setting a northbound course for Wusong and Shanghai. "My work in Shanghai is done," Suenson wrote to Tietgen. The station and the landline had been completed, and the personnel were well settled at the Hotel l'Europe. "The situation here is characterized by discipline, order, and a very positive attitude." Five days later, Edouard Suenson and C. L. Madsen boarded a packet steamer bound for Shanghai, where they arrived the day after the *Great Northern* had dropped anchor at Wusong. The first stage of the mission could be embarked on.[18]

Secret cable landing at Shanghai

On the evening of November 30, 1870, after having quartered his staff, Suenson traveled down to Wusong together with C. L. Madsen and Lieutenant Dreyer, who, after having received instructions, boarded the *Great Northern*, which immediately weighed anchor to play its part in laying the cable. In the meantime, Edouard Suenson had to deal with unexpected problems as the Danish consul Mr. Johnson, on whose property in Wusong the cable was to be landed, had traveled back to England. The property had been taken over by his replacement, Mr. Keswick, who, as Suenson put it, wished to "secure personal profit" by exploiting the situation through an advantageous rental agreement or even the sale of the property. Suenson did not wish to be a party to this, and he therefore obtained permission temporarily to land the cable on a nearby property that was owned by the French government and housed a small naval unit.[19]

On Sunday, December 4, the *Great Northern* was back, having successfully laid cable from a position ninety nautical miles southeast of the mouth of the Chang River to a point close to Gutzlaff and up to Wusong, where the end of the cable was attached to a buoy on the other side of the river. A few days later, it was time for the nocturnal laying of the cable up the Huangpu River to Shanghai, where the cable was landed on the company's property in all secrecy. The following night, another cable was similarly laid from Wusong and spliced together with the end of the cable the *Great Northern* had laid.

The last part of the operation was the landing of the cable on Gutzlaff and was carried out on December 10 by a small steamship and three Chinese junks loaded with cement, bricks, telegraph poles, machinery, and artisans who were to build a small station with a dwelling for a single telegraphist who would monitor the connection after it had been established.[20]

To protect the cables in the river and at the landing site in Shanghai, the telegraphists were dressed in uniforms from the academic protection corps so they resembled a kind of river police, after which they sailed up and down the river from time to time to keep Chinese boats away from the cable.[21]

While the *Great Northern* off-loaded the last of its cargo, including a set of telegraph poles camouflaged as water pipes, and prepared to return to England to take on a new load of cables, Suenson confidentially informed the most important consuls in Shanghai of the landing of the cable. All these consuls were surprised by this report, for while they had been aware of the Danish plans, they had known nothing of their implementation in practice. The Danes had succeeded in keeping the project a secret.

All the consuls promised to support the Danish project if there should be difficulties with the Chinese, as did the Russian ambassador in Beijing, who was brought up to date by mail. "I think I can now calmly await the protest of the Chinese authorities," Suenson wrote to Tietgen.[22]

Opening of the telegraph connection between Shanghai and Hong Kong

Suenson's hopes that the winter climate in Shanghai would be good for his health were in vain. His illness was still "a great obstacle to [his] activity," as he wrote, but he nevertheless continued his work. On January 5, 1871, in his role as "general agent" of the Danish company, he applied to the chairman of the municipal council for permission to establish

Great Northern's first building in Shanghai, which was located on Nanking Road. It contained both a station and residences for the company's employees. The station was opened to traffic to Hong Kong on April 18, 1871, and three years later, it employed a total of forty-five Danes and eighty Chinese as a result of the rapid growth of the telegraph system.

a telegraph line between the American and British settlements to connect the landed cable with the company's station on Nanjing Road, where the company had established its East Asian headquarters. At the same time, it was officially reported that the Great Northern China & Japan Extension Telegraph Company had established itself in Shanghai.[23]

Permission was issued two weeks later, and when the line had been completed, a telegraphic connection to Wusong was established via the river cable so that the telegraphists could practice their skills. In the meantime, Mr. Keswick, the new Danish consul, had reduced his expectations with regard to extracting financial profits from his property in Wusong and had concluded a rental agreement with Suenson on the basis of which the end of the cable could be moved away from the French property.[24]

Around this time, the inspection and repair of the Cella's cables in Deep Water Bay was completed, after

which the Tordenskjold lifted anchor and set course for Wusong, where Suenson was impatiently waiting. On February 9, the Cella landed a new cable in Deep Water Bay, but because of the monsoon, the northward extension had to be interrupted. The Cella steamed back to Hong Kong, and it was not until March 12 that the laying of cable could be resumed.

A new storm forced the Cella to seek shelter behind a small island, but after fourteen days of waiting, the laying of cable could once again be resumed, and the ship reached the place where the Great Northern had laid the end of the cable and marked it with a buoy. The Tordenskjold had steamed out from Wusong and had waited near the buoy for seventeen days to meet the Cella. After the two cable ends had been spliced together, the two shops steamed up through the mouth of the Chang River and up the Huangpu River together to Wusong, where it proved to be the case that there was no signal coming through the cable. Electrical measurements showed that the cable had broken two hundred nautical miles from Hong Kong, and once again, the Cella had to steam out to repair the cable before, on April 16, 1871, there was finally a connection all the way from Shanghai to Hong Kong.

On Tuesday, April 18, 1871, the Great Northern China & Japan Extension Telegraph Company opened up public telegram traffic between the company's stations in Shanghai and Hong Kong. The Cella had completed its mission and set course for London, while the Tordenskjold headed north to sound the waters near Vladivostok and Nagasaki and prepare for the laying of the next shipment of cables when they had arrived from Europe.

Edouard Suenson was not present at the opening. Despite his illness, he had traveled to Japan in late February, and upon his arrival, he had been struck down by an attack of fever "stronger than [his] usual ones" that had forced him to stay in bed for the first week. He nevertheless completed his program with regard to preparing for the landing of the cable and the establishment of the station in Nagasaki as well as a diplomatic visit to Yokohama and Yedo (Tokyo), where he handed out presents to the ministers and officials who had been involved in the negotiations for the concession.

Two days after the arrival of the *Tordenskjold*, Suenson was back in Nagasaki, where he and Captain Lund agreed upon a landing site for the cables and upon how the process of measurements and soundings should continue. On April 15, he signed a contract for the renting of a station building, after which he left Nagasaki for Shanghai and was not back in time for the official opening of the Shanghai-Hong Kong cable.[25]

On April 24, after his arrival in Shanghai, Suenson informed all Danish consuls in China and Japan of the opening of the Shanghai-Hong Kong connection and, having made reference to the Danish government's interest, asked them to become agents of the Great Northern China & Japan Extension Telegraph Company and accept telegrams in return for payment and send these telegrams onward via the company's lines.[26]

Edouard Suenson was subsequently able to set a homeward course for Denmark. In late January, he had received the permission of the board of directors to return home, and Lieutenant Dreyer was appointed the new general agent in East Asia. "I would like to express my heartfelt thanks to the board of directors for my replacement," wrote Suenson, adding "that my replacement is even more important to me now than when I wrote my request."[27]

Chinese telegraph code

Before Edouard Suenson left Shanghai, he managed to complete a project that represented a watershed event in the development of the telegraph in China. In April 1870, when Suenson and C. F. Tietgen had met with the secretary of the Burlingame delegation, McLeavy Brown, in Hamburg, Brown had suggested that the Danes create a code that would make it possible to send telegrams in Chinese without translating them into English.[28]

This was a major challenge because Chinese had approximately 80,000 different written characters—and more were constantly being added—while Morse code had been designed to accommodate about fifty letters and numerals. It was estimated that around 7,000 written characters were necessary—and sufficient—for trade and everyday purposes, and if the company succeeded in creating a code system for converting Chinese characters into Morse signs and back again, then this could stimulate Chinese businesspeople's interest in the telegraph and weaken or even prevent a negative reaction from the authorities.[29]

When he returned to Copenhagen, Tietgen contacted the Danish astronomer and Sinologist Hans Schjellerup and asked him to design a system. Already on April 19, 1870, Tietgen received the two pages containing a preliminary proposal for a code system that would accommodate 5,454 Chinese characters based on the 214 root signs, each of which had been assigned a four-digit numerical code that could be converted into Morse code—and back to a Chinese root sign again. Tietgen immediately sent these two pages to McLeavy Brown, who had traveled to Berlin, and asked him for his opinion. It was positive, and Tietgen sent Schjellerup's proposal on to Edouard Suenson in East Asia.[30]

This was not the first time an attempt had been made to create a Chinese telegraph code—the first known proposals were presented as early as 1851—but all early proposals lacked practical applicability. However, the French harbormaster in Shanghai, S. A. Viguier, had succeeded in developing a system that was published in Shanghai in 1870—already before the Danish cables had been landed. Suenson had learned of the system when he had arrived in China and had found it "highly suitable." Like Schjellerup's system, Viguier's was based on the 214 Chinese root signs, but Viguier had placed them in a system of schematic coordinates so that each sign, like a chess piece, was assigned its own field.[31]

In October 1870, when Suenson had returned to Hong Kong from Japan, he got some Chinese tradespeople to compare and evaluate the two systems. There was agreement that both were good and us-

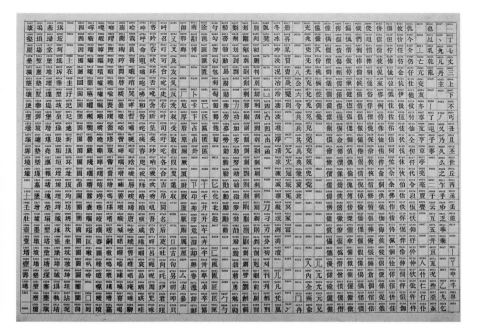

One way to overcome Chinese resistance to the telegraph was to make it possible for them to send telegrams using Chinese characters. Already before Great Northern had landed its cables at Shanghai, several attempts had been made to develop a Chinese telegraph code, but none of the resulting codes had been usable in practice. The first usable code was created when Edouard Suenson combined two systems respectively developed by the Danish astronomer and Orientalist Hans Schjellerup and the French harbormaster in Shanghai, Auguste Viguier. The result was a system in which the Chinese characters were entered into a chart based on the Chinese root signs and assigned four-digit numbers that were used in connection with sending telegrams and could be translated to and from the full Chinese characters. The first code book was published in 1871 and was soon widely used. The system continued to be used for many years, in fact until the advent of personal computers.

able, but Viguier's was seen as preferable because its graphic design provided a better overview. Suenson himself believed that "a combination of the two would be best."[32]

When he was back in Shanghai, Suenson convinced Viguier to incorporate Schjellerup's system into his own, and the Frenchman also came up with an idea for a stamp system such that the Chinese signs would be engraved onto one end and

Schjellerup's numerical code onto the other. In connection with delivering a Chinese telegram, the customer would take the stamps with the relevant Chinese signs and stamp the number codes on the telegram form. The numbers would be transmitted telegraphically, and at the receiving station, the process would be reversed so the telegram form was delivered with the Chinese signs.[33]

The stamps were to be stored in two frames such that the Chinese signs at the sending station were grouped in accordance with Viguier's coordinate system, while at the receiving station, they would be arranged in numerical order. Suenson found the system "really practical," and to begin with, he asked Viguier to produce two sets, each of which comprised approximately 10,000 Chinese characters, for the company's stations in Shanghai and Hong Kong.[34]

Suenson had hoped that the stamps would be ready in time for the opening of the Shanghai-Hong Kong cable, but Viguier was not able to get done in time. The sets were finished on April 27, 1871, and it was possible to begin using them a few days later, after one of the sets had been brought to Hong Kong. Despite the fact that only a short time remained before Suenson would return to Denmark, he found time to arrange demonstrations of the system for selected Chinese tradesmen to win over skeptics and open their eyes to the possibilities afforded by telegrams. In the middle of May, Suenson's successor in Shanghai, Lieutenant Dreyer, presented the system to a group of Chinese officials from the Kiangnan Arsenal whom he had invited to visit the company's station.[35]

Viguier also produced a printed telegraph code book so the Chinese themselves could fill out the telegram forms with numbers and send them to the station by messenger. The first eighty copies were delivered on June 1, and a short time later, an edition with instructions in English and French was published, ten copies of which were sent to Copenhagen. Already during the afternoon of the day of publication, the code book was distributed to other cities by organizations, including the American Presbyterian mission, which had received two hundred copies. A smaller number were sent to the head of the Chinese customs authority, the Irish-born Robert Hart, so that he could pass them on to the "highest authorities," and other Europeans in central roles received copies they could distribute.[36]

It was no longer a secret that the telegram had been introduced to China or that Great Northern had opened a telegraph station in Shanghai. However, this news provoked no reactions, let alone protests, from the Chinese authorities, neither locally nor in Beijing. During the first five months after the opening of the Shanghai-Hong Kong cable, 162 Chinese telegrams were transmitted from Shanghai to Hong Kong and 209 the other way, which certainly indicates that the publication of the Chinese code book had the desired effect.[37]

In 1872, an improved and expanded edition of the code book was published, and several new and updated editions were published during the following years. In January 1874, *The Chinese Recorder and Missionary Journal* wrote that the telegraph code had been widely distributed and was "much used by the Chinese."[38]

Trans-Siberian connection between East Asia and Europe

When the Pender companies opened their cables from Hong Kong to Europe via Singapore and India on June 3, 1871, six weeks after the opening of the Shanghai-Hong Kong cable, it became possible to send telegrams between Shanghai and Europe. At that time, Edouard Suenson was on his way home to Denmark, while the two Danish-chartered steamships *Great Northern* and *Africa* were headed the opposite way, steaming from London to East Asia with their cargoes of cables and equipment. Both

ships were delayed, the *Great Northern* by an accident with its propeller in the Suez Canal, the *Africa* by a collision on the Red Sea. With this, the ships had their worst accidents behind them, however, and on July 17, 1871, the *Great Northern* could land its cable on Gutzlaff and begin laying cable toward Nagasaki, where the cable was landed on August 4. Eight days later, public telegram traffic between Japan and China with an onward connection to Europe was opened.

In early August, the *Africa* arrived at Nagasaki, and in the middle of the month, the laying of cable toward Vladivostok was begun, the *Tordenskjold* steaming in front and sounding the waters. The *Great Northern* had previously laid a cable from Vladivostok to a position one hundred nautical miles from Nagasaki. After the two cables had been spliced together, the three ships sailed back to Nagasaki's harbor together.

With this, the Danish cable project had been completed, and the *Cella* and the *Tordenskjold* set course for home, that is, for London and Copenhagen, respectively. For the time being, the *Great Northern* remained in East Asian waters, having been chartered by the Great Northern China & Japan Extension Telegraph Company to carry out cable repairs.

A remaining task was the completion of the landline through Siberia, which had been greatly delayed because of the Siberian landscape and climate. On November 17, 1871, this connection was made available for a limited number of telegrams per day to test the connection, and on January 1, 1872, it could finally be opened to public traffic at full capacity. The trans-Siberian connection between Europe and East Asia was a reality.

Fusion of the two Danish telegraph companies

Just as the landing of the cable in Shanghai had been kept secret both from the Chinese and from the wider world, the information regarding the defective cables was restricted to a small circle of trusted individuals. C. F. Tietgen and the Danish company had no interest in giving the Pender companies or oth-

Port Said at the mouth of the Suez Canal in 1870. This picture was brought to Denmark by the captain of the *Tordenskjold*, William Lund, when he returned from the frigate's cable voyage to East Asia for Great Northern. The *Tordenskjold* was the first Danish ship to pass through the canal and the largest ship to have done so up to that point. Edouard Suenson had been assured by the company that operated the canal that the *Tordenskjold* would be able to get through without difficulties. Nevertheless, the Danish frigate scraped the bottom several times despite the fact that parts of the cargo had been transferred to barges and were pulled through the canal separately.

ers insight into the difficulties that had been experienced as this could create doubts regarding the project and have a negative effect on the value of shares in both Great Northern and the Extension Company and thus hinder Tietgen's plans.

Tietgen had always been planning to merge Great Northern with the Extension Company when the cable project in East Asia had been completed. With the opening of the trans-Siberian connection, the time had come, and on January 2, 1872—the following day—the newspaper *Berlingske Tidende* published an official announcement of the imminent merger, and an extraordinary general meeting was called for February 22–23, 1872.[39]

It seemed obvious that a merger would make sense as the two companies' cables in East Asia and Europe were to a great extent to be operated as a single system brought together by the trans-Siberian connection. Furthermore, the inner circle in the two companies was identical in all important ways. C. F. Tietgen, O. B. Suhr, C. A. Broberg, and M. Levy sat on both boards, while W. C. E. Sponneck and L. P. Holmblad sat on one each.

Also, both companies were in need of an infusion of fresh capital. The defective cables had saddled the Extension Company with an estimated deficit of 100,000 pounds sterling, and the company wished to continue the Hong Kong–Shanghai cable to Xiamen and establish a station with landline connections to towns in the Chinese interior. The company also wanted to build its own cable ship as a replacement for the *Great Northern*, which was both too large for repair work and too expensive to charter. In Europe, another cable to France and a cable between Sweden and Russia via the Estonian island of Saaremaa (Ösel) were planned.[40]

As well as the merger of the two companies, the new projects were approved at a common meeting of the boards of directors on January 9, 1872, at which the increasing of the share capital in the new company to 1.5 million pounds sterling, or 13.5 million rigsdaler, was also approved. The board of directors of the new company was to consist of all seven individuals who had sat on at least one of the two companies' previous boards of directors plus Julius Sick and Consul Helland from Hong Kong, who had recently established a residence in Copenhagen. The new company's statutes would be identical to Great Northern's existing statutes.[41]

When the extraordinary general meeting of the Great Northern China & Japan Extension Telegraph Company was held on February 22, 1872, approximately 40,000 shares valued at 10 pounds each were represented, which corresponded to two-thirds of the share capital. Of these shares, Tietgen alone represented just under 11,000 shares, while a power of attorney for the representation of 3,600 shares from England had been provided to Tietgen by H. G. Erichsen, who was not present. With support from the members of the company's board of directors and several other shareholders from his inner circle, Tietgen controlled about half of the shares represented at the meeting and was therewith in control of events.[42]

After Tietgen had defended the proposals of the board of directors in a report to the assembled shareholders, only a single shareholder expressed dissent. This was a certain James Higgins, a spokesman for an English shareholder group that was in no way able to threaten the board's majority. Also, Tietgen had reached agreement with Higgins the previous evening regarding the way in which the general meeting would proceed, and the exchange of words between the two men therefore took place in a very undramatic fashion, after which votes were cast, 34,289 votes being cast for

the board's proposals and 5,022 votes being cast against.[43]

The following evening, the Great Northern Telegraph Company held an extraordinary general meeting with voting immediately after Tietgen's report. With 26,424 votes in favor and only 539 votes against, the merger of the two companies was approved by a huge majority. The two companies were herewith unified under the name the Great Northern Telegraph Company, which, with a share capital of 13.5 million rigsdaler, was the largest limited company in the Nordic region.

C. F. Tietgen became the chairman of the new company's board of directors. Edouard Suenson was hired as the chief executive officer with re-

When Great Northern received its concession to lay cables from Vladivostok, the city had just been founded with a view to making it the home of Russia's Pacific Fleet. The company was, therefore, to be responsible for the construction of its own station and residential building, and all construction materials were to be purchased in Shanghai and brought to Vladivostok by ship. However, the local Russian authorities did provide the necessary lumber, so contrary to its original expectations, the company did not need to fell trees and saw boards itself. The photograph shows the residential building shortly after its construction in 1871.

sponsibility for day-to-day operations, bookkeeping, and accounting, while C. L. Madsen became the head of technical operations.[44]

Political balancing act

At the merged company's first general meeting on May 1, 1872, C. F. Tietgen could present a report and a balance sheet for 1,871 who showed success on all fronts. In all, the company had access to more than 3,343 nautical miles of cables, including over 2,200 nautical miles of cables in East Asia, where the company had stations in Shanghai, Nagasaki, and Vladivostok. In European Russia, the company had stations in Liepaja, Latvia, and Nystad, Finland, to handle the transfer from cables to landlines. In the United Kingdom, the company had stations in Newcastle and Aberdeen as well as in London, where a station and public office had been established in Great Winchester street buildings, in the central business district of the British capital. In Sweden, the company had a station in Gothenburg, while the company's cables in Norway and Denmark were operated by the government telegraph authorities.[45]

In Europe, the number of telegrams delivered had risen from approximately 403,000 to just under 421,000. The operating surplus for Europe amounted to about 355,000 rigsdaler; after 10 percent of this amount had been deposited in the company's reserve fund, 320,000 rigsdaler would be distributed among the shareholders.

Operations in East Asia were also turning a profit, though—not surprisingly—to a lesser extent. After the deduction of the Pender companies' share of the profits from the Shanghai-Hong Kong cable, the operating surplus amounted to 60,000 rigsdaler, of which 54,000 rigsdaler were distributed to the shareholders after a deduction for the company's reserve fund.[46]

Tietgen characterized the prospects for the future as good in both Europe and East Asia. The growth for the European cables had continued unabated during the first months of the new year, and things were going well in East Asia too as there was the prospect of a further increase in traffic

when the Japanese government telegraph authority opened up civilian international traffic via the company's cables. To be sure, the British companies had begun a price war with regard to traffic to and from Europe, but using the line though Siberia was both faster and cheaper than using the British cables. There was therefore "no reason to fear the English competition or show any weakness whatsoever in relation to it," Tietgen claimed, according to the Danish newspaper *Fædrelandet*. However, he declared that he was willing to conclude an agreement "under reasonable conditions."[47]

This statement indicated great self-confidence. In British telegraph circles, it had been said three and a half years earlier that "these Danes [should not be allowed] to go on any further." Since then, the company had won the Russian concession, acquired permission to land a cable in Japan, introduced the telegraph to China, and opened a trans-Siberian connection that was competing with the Pender companies.

The spine of the Danish system—or the life nerve as it was later called—was the trans-Siberian connection, which was operated by the Russian state telegraph authority. Without the 10,000-kilometer-long landline through European Russia and Siberia, Great Northern's system would be reduced to two regional cable networks in Northern Europe and East Asia. Because of this, Great Northern's position was dependent upon having a good relationship with Russia, and here, the company's position was for the time being protected by monopolistic concessions for almost the next 30 years. On the other hand, Russia had an interest in maintaining a good relationship with Great Northern because of the transit revenues and the political significance of the company's cable systems. This was a relationship of mutual dependence that would characterize the company's development for more than 125 years.

However, Great Northern was also dependent on having a good relationship with the United Kingdom and the Pender companies. The company needed to avoid getting into serious conflicts with British strategic interests, and the Pender companies were

many times larger than Great Northern and consti-tuted a global power in the area of international te-legraphy. With its constant expansion, the Pender companies' cable network contributed to connect-ing the entire British Empire and to ensuring that the government maintained control over its colonies and other possessions, and for this reason, it was supported by the British Foreign Office.

Like C. F. Tietgen, John Pender had merged his companies, or rather some of them, in November 1872, when he merged four companies into the Eastern Telegraph Company, which had cables leading from England through the Mediterranean region to India. The following year, he merged three companies with cables to India, Java, China, and Australasia into the Eastern Extension Australa-sia and China Telegraph Company. The two Eastern companies had a respective share capital of 3 mil-lion pounds sterling—twice what Great Northern had—and 3.8 million pounds sterling.

However, the English companies were depend-ent on the Danish cables in connection with traffic to and from China and Japan, and already in May 1870, the agreement between Pender and Tietgen had shown that despite its relatively small size, the Danish company was in a strong position. After the opening of the trans-Siberian connection, however, there was a price war with regard to the connection between East Asia and Europe that harmed both companies.

In February 1873, Great Northern and the Eastern companies therefore concluded a new agreement that expanded the agreement of 1870 by introducing a standardized rate of 150 francs per twenty-word telegram. In addition, a so-called joint purse was cre-ated into which the companies deposited their reve-nues to be distributed in accordance with a detailed agreement. This distribution agreement would re-main in force in cases of connections that were inter-rupted for up to 120 days, so the companies insured each other against loss of revenue in cases, for exam-ple, of cable breaks. This created economic security but also mutual dependence.[48]

European and Siberian Consolidation

CHAPTER 4

The Victorian Internet

In 1872, the length of Great Northern's undersea cables made up about 10 percent of the total global network of undersea telegraph cables, which amounted to over 60,000 kilometers of cables. The national landlines had a total length of over a million kilometers, and by far, the longest of these connections was the trans-Siberian one, which stretched 10,000 kilometers from the Baltic Sea to the Russian Far East.

Undersea cables connected Europe, North America, the Caribbean, Central America, the Mediterranean region, India, Australia, Indochina, East Asia, and the Russian Far East, and during the years that followed, the expansion continued so as to include South America and Africa. Already in 1880, the total length of undersea cables had more than doubled to just under 140,000 kilometers, and at the same time, the national landlines were being expanded so that the whole world was woven into an increasingly fine-meshed network of telegraph connections that constituted a cohesive, global communications system. The only exception was the Pacific Ocean, where the great distances and depths and the difficult conditions on the seafloor, where there were mountain ranges and deep valleys, created major obstacles to the laying and maintaining of cables.

This network has been called the Victorian Internet because it was built during the years in which Queen Victoria sat on the British throne and because it was dominated by the United Kingdom, from where telegraph cables were laid to all the parts of the world-spanning colonial empire. British telegraph companies were all-dominating, and John Pender's companies alone controlled more than half of the world's undersea telegraph cables.

Several times, Great Northern sent expeditionary teams to Russia that were to travel all the way through Siberia along the telegraph line to check its condition and make suggestions with regard to improvements. The first expeditionary team was the so-called Siberian Commission, which set forth in January 1876 and spent eight months on its journey. Pictured from the left are telegraph manager Adolf Severin Falck, telegraph engineer Julius Elias Nielsen, and Captain Wilhelm von Heinemann, who later became Great Northern's agent in Saint Petersburg.

In Japan, the company did not have its own telegram messengers to deliver telegrams to their addressees. The couriers of the Japanese telegraphy authority were responsible for this.

Pender's telegraph imperium constituted the spine of the Victorian Internet and was tellingly called the nerves of the Empire because of its importance to the British empire and British interests all over the globe.[1]

The Victorian Internet forever changed the world and people's conceptions of it because time and distance took on new meanings. At the Great Northern Telegraph Company's general meeting, C. F. Tietgen could brag that the company's trans-Siberian connection was "as fast as the Sun." Telegrams sent from Shanghai and Nagasaki in the morning normally arrived in Denmark at the same time of day as they were sent—and sometimes they even arrived more than three hours earlier in the day.[2]

The enormous speed with which news and other information was exchanged across national borders, oceans, and continents had revolutionary consequences for war and peace, politics and diplomacy, trade and investments, and the day-to-day-lives of human beings. While *The Times* of London, which took pride in being first with the latest news, had previously published eight-week-old reports from South Africa and news from New York and Berlin that was respectively four weeks old and one week old, the newspaper now published articles presenting day-to-day news from most of the world and posted a much larger number of such articles than before while the telegrams arrived in a steady and growing stream.

The consequences were great and often complex and unpredictable, as was dramatically demonstrated by the Crimean War (1853–1856). When the first British troops were sent to the front, the British government sent its usual wartime message to the public regarding the size, composition, and weaponry of its force. To generate enthusiasm for the war, *The Times* conscientiously reported the contents of this message, which were subsequently quickly passed on to the Russian general staff in Saint Petersburg via the cables under the English Channel.[3]

From then on, the British government had carefully considered what information it would make available, and to its irritation, it also found that *The Times*'s reporter in the Crimea reported on the poor British organization of the war effort, the great British losses, and the lack of medicine. The reporter sent his articles by steamship to Varna, Bulgaria, from where they were sent by telegraph to London, where they were read by the British population, which thus obtained insight into the prosecution of the war and its costs the British government would have preferred Britons not to have.

In fact, the English and French governments had laid a cable from the Crimea to Varna themselves, but not surprisingly, *The Times*'s reporter was not permitted to use that cable. However, the French government used it to interfere with the prosecution of the war, a state of affairs with which the French military leaders in the Crimea were not at all happy. It was not without reason that the English historian Alexander William Kinglake called the telegraph "the new and dangerous magic."[4]

The role played by the telegraph in the Crimean War demonstrated very clearly that governments, diplomats, and top military officers would need to learn that the increased volume and speed of the flow of information created new rules for their actions. Along with control over strategic telegraph connections, confidentiality and secrecy came to be seen as of central importance in the context of the use of the new communications technology. The establishment of the Great Northern Telegraph Company was inspired by precisely this perspective and the implications of the geographic locations of both Denmark and Germany.

International trade and the whole global economy down to the level of individual companies were also deeply affected by the expansion of telegraph technology. Information and time were money, and because of this, the great trading houses with offices in Shanghai were not initially in favor of the introduction of the telegraph to China as they would no longer have an advantage because of their fast private steamships, which brought messages to and from Sri Lanka, where there was a telegraph connection with England.

Thanks to the expansion of the Victorian Internet, anyone could have access to the fast transfer of information—anyone who was able to pay. Trading companies could therefore follow trends in the selling prices of coffee, tea, silk, rubber, spices, and other goods around the world, and they could conclude

agreements without using middlemen in distant harbor towns. As one historian of the telegraph has put it, telegrams were "like a narcotic for businessmen, who quickly developed a dependence."[5]

Telegrams were expensive, however, so for ordinary workers and functionaries, they were of limited significance as a form of communication. Via the newspapers, they did have a broad effect on the amount of information reaching the public and therefore on the development of public opinions and on political developments both at the national and at the international level. New newspapers such as *The Daily Telegraph*, *De Telegraaf*, and *Dags-Telegrafen* were named after the new technology, and news items became an independent ware with the established of the news bureau Reuters in 1849.

The International Telegraph Union

The growing number of international telegraph connections created a need for the regulation of telegram prices across national borders. The Victorian Internet was a hybrid of national, usually government-operated, telegraph systems and private telegraph companies that owned and operated undersea cables. A telegram sent from London "via Northern" to Shanghai was transmitted first through England and then via Great Northern's cables to Denmark or Sweden and through Scandinavia and onward via Great Northern's cables to Russia and the trans-Siberian landline to Vladivostok, from where it reached Shanghai or Nagasaki via Great Northern's cables. The questions were what it should cost to send such a telegram and how the revenues from it were to be distributed.

Already in 1849, Prussia and Austria concluded the first international treaty regarding charges for telegrams between the two countries. In the wake of the conclusion of several similar regional treaties, the International Telegraph Union, or ITU, was concluded in Paris in May 1865 by twenty European countries, including Denmark. The United Kingdom became a member in 1870, after its private telegraph lines had been nationalized, and eventually, most of the world's countries joined the ITU. The United States remained a notable exception as its private telegraph lines were never nationalized.[6]

Technically, the international telegraph companies were not subject to the ITU's convention, but the member countries were obligated to require companies to follow the convention and the rules established by the ITU. In 1868, a permanent office in Berne was established to oversee compliance with the convention, and that same year, companies were given the opportunity to join the convention. In 1871, they were given access to the ITU's conferences with speaking but not voting rights.

At the conference in Rome—and the following ones—Great Northern was represented by Edouard Suenson, who, following his return home from Shanghai, had, in addition to taking on the post of chief executive officer, assumed the position of secretary of the board of directors and thus C. F. Tietgen's right-hand man.[7]

The ITU's most important task was to create a harmonized and transparent pricing system, which, in 1865, was based on a fixed unit price for telegrams of up to twenty words. For each individual member, country rates were established for sending and receiving as well as for transit on the basis of countries' respective sizes. The rates were also to cover transmission via companies' cables, which created unequal conditions for the companies. Generally, landlines were cheaper both to establish and to operate, and in connection with the transmission of telegrams between the same two points, they were therefore able to outcompete undersea cables. This was why Great Northern received Russian subsidies for its Baltic Sea cables—to keep the rates from rising above rates for the continental landlines.

Consolidation in Northern Europe

While Eastern based its cable system on support points in the global British Empire, Great Northern based its system on cooperation with a number of countries, which was the reason why the Danish company—despite its relatively small size—was the first and for many years the only company to challenge the dominance of the British companies.

Instead of thinking of further expansion, the company, at first, concentrated on consolidating its position by increasing cable capacity in Northern Europe not only to cope with the growing amount of traffic and ensure fast and stable operations but also to guard against the effects of cable breaks by establishing several parallel lines. However, the company did expand its geographic coverage in one area.

Already in the fall of 1870, C. F. Tietgen had begun negotiations with regard to laying a cable between France and England with a land connection to the company's planned station in London. These plans were obstructed by the Franco-Prussian War (1870–1871), however, and the company instead hatched a new plan, and in accordance with this plan, the company succeeded in obtaining a French concession for the laying of a cable between Calais and the Danish island of Fanø.

It was of decisive importance in this connection that Russia became interested in a telegraph connection with France that avoided both Germany and the United Kingdom and therefore provided diplomatic support for the Danish project in Paris. For political reasons, Russia and France both provided financial subsidies to support the operation of the cable so it would be able to compete with the land lines, and on August 1, 1873, telegram traffic via a Danish cable station in Calais was opened up.[8]

Around the same time, the increasing traffic made it necessary to establish an additional connection between England and Scandinavia. Late in 1872, Great Northern obtained Swedish and Danish concessions for the laying of cables between Gothenburg and Skagen and between Hirtshals and Newcastle; the two Danish landing points were connected by a landline. This new connection was opened to traffic on September 11, 1873, on which day Great Northern also opened a cable station in Gothenburg.[9]

The connections to Russia too were doubled. When the Russian telegraph authority wanted to establish a cable connection between Finland and the Åland Islands in the Gulf of Bothnia, the company exploited the situation to propose the simul-

In Calais, Great Northern's station was established in a building belonging to the French postal and telegraphy authority. The station opened on August 1, 1873.

taneous doubling of the Sweden-Finland connection such that a new cable made an intermediate landing on the Åland Islands. In May 1876, an agreement was reached, and on July 1, 1877, Great Northern was able to open the connection.[10]

Another doubling became a reality in 1880 with the establishment of a connection between Gothenburg and Newcastle, the cable this time being brought ashore at Arendal, Norway, which meant that Norway got another direct connection with England. The reason for this was that at the ITU conference the previous year, a per-word pricing system for Europe had been introduced, so prices for international telegrams would subsequently be calculated per word and not, as had previously been the case, using a fixed price for the first twenty words. This change was expected to lead to a sharp increase in international telegram traffic and also have the effect of increasing intercontinental traffic, including traffic between Europe and East Asia.

The new cable was opened to traffic on October 1, 1880, and at the same time, Great Northern was able to secure the extension of its monopolistic concessions for Sweden until the end of 1910.

To cope with the growing traffic with Russia and East Asia and to prevent serious negative consequences due to cable breaks in the Gulf of Bothnia during the coldest half of the year, the company laid a new cable between Grisslehamn, Sweden, and Nystad, Finland, in September 1883.

Danish telegraphists in Siberia

In Russia too, there was a need for consolidation, though of a different kind. Along the landline east of the Ural Mountains, Russian telegraph stations had been established in Yekaterinburg, Omsk, Tomsk, Sretensk, Blagoveshchensk, and Khabarovsk—partly to connect these towns telegraphically with Saint Petersburg and their wider environment more generally, partly to be able to retransmit telegrams sent from Europe to East Asia and vice versa as the diminishing strength of the signal would otherwise have rendered the signs unreadable.

It was only at the stations in Nystad, Liepaja, and Vladivostok that Great Northern had Danish telegraphists who worked with the transfer of telegrams between the company's cables and the Russian landlines. The entire landline through Siberia was owned and operated by the Russian government telegraph authority and was to be operated by Russian telegraphists alone. However, the vital importance of this line to Great Northern had caused the company to pay very close attention to its operation from the beginning.

Tietgen therefore seized his chance when the Russian director of telegraphy Karl von Lüders asked him to help acquire twelve Danish telegraphists to be posted at the Siberian stations to assist with the transit traffic, in part because the Russian telegraphists did not know English. Tietgen assembled a band of adventurous young Danish men, only about half of whom had experience with telegraphy. The group included one veterinarian, one man with a cand.polit. degree, one man with a cand.phil. degree, and two lieutenants as well as a dancer and an actor from the Royal Danish Theater.[11]

The first group was sent to Saint Petersburg in the spring of 1871, and the second followed in June of the same year. They were all put to work in Russian service, and in August 1871, after having been trained in telephony, they took an official oath to serve the Russian directorate of telegraphy. The following month, the group traveled east, two of the men bringing along their wives and one a child as well. In Perm, they switched from train transport to the rather special tarantasses: four-person unsprung horse-drawn wagons that were later described by one of the company's employees as "torture instruments" as they thoroughly shook their passengers as they rolled down the always very uneven and sometimes almost bottomlessly muddy Russian roads.[12]

The first two Danes were stationed at Omsk in the middle of October 1871, the next at Irkutsk on Lake Baikal in November. The next two were placed at Sretensk, where the rest wintered, with the exception of a few who had fallen ill and been left behind. It was not until the spring of 1872 that the rest—with the exception of one who had died—could travel onward; by April, however, all the telegraphists had been placed, the last ones in Blagoveshchensk, Khabarovsk, and Vladivostok.

The Danish telegraphists were settled in remote, sparsely populated areas many thousands of kilometers from their former homes in Denmark and without other contact with the rest of the world than the telegraph and a horse-based postal system. None of them spoke Russian, and there were usually no other foreigners in the remote towns in which the Danes were posted. The climate was harsh. The winters brought severe cold, while the summers were characterized by great heat and violent, long-lasting thunderstorms. Most people—including most Russians—thought of eastern Siberia as a remote, inaccessible wilderness of tundra, steppes, vast forests, and wild animals, and of course, this was also where the authorities sent criminals as well as people who had been banished for political reasons.

The telegraphists had signed five-year employment contracts that expired at the end of 1876. A few returned to Denmark; one secured employment in the telegraph department in Saint Petersburg. Seven continued in their positions for a further five-year period, and two of these settled in their new places of residence permanently. In 1877, six new Danish telegraphists entered Russian service on five-year contracts, and more groups followed at five-year intervals; some of the new Danes became permanent residents, and a few acquired Russian citizenship. In addition to performing their contractual duties, these employees became an important source of information about operations and maintenance and about the operation of the vitally important landline for Great Northern.

Stabilization of the trans-Siberian connection

The telegraph line through Siberia was not just long; it was laid via sparsely populated areas, indeed through areas that were almost empty of human beings, and the terrain was sometimes inaccessible and rough, in many areas offering no roads, only horse and foot trails. On a stretch of more than

150 kilometers along the Shilka River east of Lake Baikal, the telegraph poles had been erected atop sheer cliff walls along a path known as the seven deadly sins because of the many travelers who had plunged to their deaths.

In a number of places, the line passed through dense primeval forests and was therefore susceptible to traffic interruptions because of fallen trees and branches. Other areas were extremely swampy, particularly during the spring thaws, so the poles loosened and fell over, while yet other areas consisted of granite-hard cliffs where the poles had to be supported with piles of rocks. The frequent violent electrical storms of the summers could also cause service interruptions. The most critical stretch was the one that followed the Amur River after Blagoveshchensk, where flooding during the spring could wash away the telegraph poles and interrupt the line, while the ice that came with the meltwater could damage the river cables where such cables had been used.

Already in July 1872, there was major flooding along the Amur River that washed away everything along long stretches of the line—telegraph poles, local telegraph stations, and river cables. The damage was so extensive that it was not possible to reopen the line until four months later. Traffic between East Asia and Europe was not interrupted, but Great Northern's traffic had to be sent via the British cables.

This interruption of service caused both the company and the Russian government telegraph authority to suffer great losses, and because there were constant interruptions due to fallen trees, lightning strikes, and other factors, Edouard Suenson raised the question of securing the connection when he was in Saint Petersburg in the fall of 1872. The Russian telegraph director Lüders was also interested in securing the line and was open to considering a Danish proposal that Great Northern be paid to take on responsibility for operating and maintaining the most problematic section of the line, the section along the Shilka River and the Amur River between Sretensk and Vladivostok—a section approximately 2,700 kilometers in length.[13] In the fall of 1873, the company began negotiations

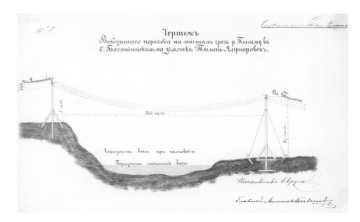

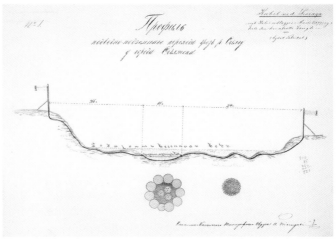

The trans-Siberian line passed over or under a large number of rivers, and in connection with plans to make a number of improvements to the line in 1877, Great Northern was provided with survey drawings of the individual rivers and indications of where the line crossed these rivers.

with the Russian telegraph directorate regarding a Danish takeover of the entire 6,000-kilometer-long section of line between Omsk and Vladivostok, but the Russians were unable to pay for the thorough renovation of the line that Great Northern demanded as a prerequisite for such a takeover, and no agreement was reached.[14]

The connection was nevertheless stabilized as a result of Russian repair and reinforcement work, but the line did not end up being entirely satisfactory, and Great Northern continued to see a takeover by the company of at least the eastern part of the trans-Siberian connection as the optimal solution. As there appeared to be little chance of this occurring, the company instead focused its attention on the stabilization of another part of the connection between Europe and East Asia.

It was not just the Russian landlines that were affected by constant breakdowns; it was also Great Northern's cables among Vladivostok, Nagasaki, and Shanghai. There were a number of places where the cables lay in exposed places where they risked being damaged or broken, either because of conditions on the seafloor or because of anchored ships or fishing boats. Usually, the cables were quickly repaired, but the situation was not satisfactory, and it appeared increasingly important that currently redundant cables be installed to ensure stable operations but also in reaction to the growing amount of traffic.

Around this time, however, Denmark was affected by an economic downturn, which made it difficult for the company to raise capital on the Danish financial markets. In addition, Great Northern's revenues fell from 3.2 million kroner in 1874 to 2.9 million kroner, and while the company's revenues did increase over the following two years to 4 million kroner in 1877, the reserve fund was far from sufficient to allow the company to raise the necessary funds itself.

At the same time, Great Northern's shares were under valuation pressure that would make the issuance of new shares difficult. The reason for this was that C. F. Tietgen and Privatbanken were still holding a large number of shares because of the English sabotage of the public offering in 1870. Simultaneously, a Copenhagen wholesaler, Svend Petersen, was wildly speculating in telegraph shares with significant financial help from Privatbanken and from Tietgen personally to keep prices high and avoid a stock market crash if Svend Petersen went bankrupt. There were many rumors in circulation about these transactions, but in 1878, Privatbanken managed to sell most of its shares to a French consortium, and the same year, the company's shares were listed on the stock exchange in Paris.[15] Unable to finance the doubling of the line itself, Great Northern had to trust in receiving help

from Russia. In the middle of March 1876, Edouard Suenson therefore traveled to Saint Petersburg to reach agreement with the Russian government regarding the financing of a doubling of the Vladivostok-Shanghai cables. After negotiations with the foreign ministry and interior ministry and with Minister of Finance Mikhail von Reutern personally, Suenson managed to secure approval of a loan from the Russian government in the amount of 500,000 pounds sterling under extremely advantageous conditions in the middle of May.[16]

Like Great Northern, the Russians saw a doubling of the line as being in their interest, but the Russian economy was not in a condition that would allow this loan to be paid out immediately. A war between Russia and the Ottoman Empire during the years 1877 and 1878 further worsened the finances of the Russian government, so the time at which the loan could actually be provided continued to remain uncertain.

The Siberian commission

On the other hand, another measure did get implemented, one the company had proposed to the Russians time and time again. Late in 1876, the company succeeded in getting the Russian government to approve sending a Siberian commission with Danish participants to inspect the trans-Siberian landline along its entire length from Saint Petersburg to Vladivostok and present suggestions for improvements with regard to possible route changes, the quality and condition of materials, service at the stations, and other aspects.[17]

On January 18, 1877, the Siberian telegraph commission left Saint Petersburg with Moscow as their first stop on the 10,000-kilometer journey along the Russian and trans-Siberian telegraph connection. The commission consisted of Chamberlain William von Hedemann, who had served in the Russian army after serving in wars on behalf of Austria and Mexico and spoke Russian; the station head A. Falck from Great Northern's station in Gothenburg; and the engineer Julius Nielsen, who had worked for the company in East Asia.

During the journey, there were always three Russian members of the commission from the various regions along to help with the Danish expedition, and in accordance with the wishes of the Russian department of telegraphy, it therefore had the status of a mixed Danish-Russian commission, which ensured an accommodating attitude on the part of local agencies and authorities.

In contrast to Edouard Suenson's mission in East Asia in 1870 and 1871, the telegraph line made it possible for Great Northern's leadership to be in constant contact with the commission on its long and time-consuming journey. The first stage of the journey, which was covered by rail, took the commission to Moscow and eastward from there. The telegraph line followed the railway to Nizhny Novgorod on the Volga River; this part of the journey was easy, and the line was in excellent condition.[18]

In Nizhny Novgorod, the railway ended, and the members of the commission were therefore transported onward through the Russian winter landscape wrapped in furs and sitting in sleighs respectively pulled by three horses—so-called troikas. Between the larger towns, the commission stopped to inspect selected sites as well as at postal stations to change horses or stay overnight. It was cold—in the Ural Mountains, the temperature dropped to thirty-five to forty degrees below zero Celsius—but in March 1877, when the commission approached Irkutsk, on Lake Baikal, spring had arrived, and the snow had begun to melt, which rendered transport more difficult despite the fact that teams of horses comprising up to sixteen animals each were used. Along this stretch too, the line was stable and operated dependably.

On April 11, after a stay in Irkutsk of a little less than three weeks, the commission traveled further eastward. The three Danes with their changing group of accompanying Russians had another 4,000 kilometers to cover before they would reach Vladivostok. Tarantasses were used instead of troikas until the commission reached Sretensk, after which the commission rode horses along the Shilka River, which unites with the Argun River to form the Amur River. With the Siberian spring came sudden great heat and consequent melting snow, lasting rains, and flooding.

The Danish and Russian members of the commission alternately rode along the river or floated down it in small boats and slept in small blockhouses along the line. On the stretch between Blagoveshchensk and Khabarovsk, the members of the commission spent half days and whole days on horseback in water that came up to the horses' knees. After Khabarovsk, the river was hit by huge amounts of water that flooded the line, the stations, and the houses and made it difficult to continue along the river, by which massive tree trunks were being carried along.

On September 19, 1877, the commission finally reached Vladivostok. The commission had been traveling for a total of eight months, and the five months after, Irkutsk had been spent traversing increasingly inaccessible terrain. After six weeks in Vladivostok, during which the team was debriefed, they enjoyed a well-earned recreational journey to Japan and China, after which they returned to Europe on the packet steamers via India and Egypt, where there was time for tourism.

On January 22, 1878, after a journey that had lasted a year, the three Danes were back in Copenhagen, where they presented a report to Edouard Suenson. Julius Nielsen and A. Falck returned to their former duties, while William von Hedemann was appointed the company's agent in Saint Petersburg, and after the death of Hans Pallisen in 1881, he replaced Pallisen as the company's representative.[19]

The commission's proposals led to a number of measures that had a remarkable effect on the stability of the connection. A very large number of telegraph poles were replaced with new and stronger poles, stations and lines along the rivers were moved away from a number of sites to higher elevations to avoid flooding, and in the forests, the corridors were broadened so the trees could not fall onto the line. These improvements were not carried out from one day to the next, but in 1880, a telegraphist who had traveled home to Denmark from his post in Shanghai along the line could deliver a positive report regarding its condition, and in Copenhagen, it was noted that the traffic was constantly getting faster and becoming more stable.[20]

Danish Telegraph Lines in China

CHAPTER 5

The first telegraph line in China

While Great Northern was consolidating its position in Northern Europe and also gradually improving and stabilizing its landline through Siberia, the company's challenges in East Asia, where Great Northern had plans to expand, were of a different and more complicated kind. To begin with, though, there was no friction when, in February 1873, the company opened a newly built telegraph station near the treaty harbor of Xiamen between Shanghai and Hong Kong.

This operation was carried out by the company's newly built cable ship, the *H. C. Ørsted*, which arrived at Xiamen in the middle of January 1873 after a voyage of two and a half months. The station and a residential building were erected on the little island of Gulangyu, on which the Western settlement was located, and the operation was carried out on February 21 and 22. On February 22, the station was opened to traffic, and the *H. C. Ørsted* departed for Shanghai, where it replaced the chartered *Great Northern*.

Cable repairs had kept the *Great Northern* very busy, and they would keep the *H. C. Ørsted* busy as well as there were constant interruptions of service due, in particular, to breaks in the river cables between Shanghai and Wusong. Anchored ships and junks tore apart or otherwise damaged the cables, and the Chinese fishermen's sharp fishhooks penetrated them and caused malfunctions. Also, local fishermen cut pieces out of the cable, which contained both iron and copper and could therefore be sold at a good price.

In the long run, basing operations on constant, endless cable repairs was unsustainable, and in the spring of 1873, Edouard Suenson's replacement, Lieutenant Dreyer, took the initiative to construct a landline from Shanghai to Wusong. This line was established along a new road that had been built by a private limited company with European owners,

Great Northern's *H. C. Ørsted* was the first ship in the world that had been specially built to repair undersea cables. The picture shows the ship in the spring of 1873 after its arrival in East Asian waters. Together with the cable machinery, the typical clipper bow was assembled in London before the ship sailed for East Asia and passed through the Suez Canal as the second Danish ship to do so, the *Tordenskjold*, as has been mentioned, having been the first.

including Great Northern, which was represented on the board of directors by Lieutenant Dreyer. The private limited company that owned the road intended to build a railroad along the road later.[1]

The telegraph line came to have three strands, two of which were connected to the cables to Shanghai and Nagasaki in Wusong, so the river cable became superfluous, while the third line was intended for local traffic between Shanghai and Wusong. With the exception of the short private lines used internally in the international settlements, this was the first telegraph line in China that was allowed to remain standing.

Despite the line's modest length—just under twenty kilometers—the symbolic significance of the line was great, and after it had opened on August 12, 1873, the local English-language newspaper *The North China Daily News* published an article on the event. The following day, another article appeared, one that praised not only Great Northern but also implicitly the local Chinese top official, who was called a taotai, because he had not obstructed the project.[2]

The taotai was unable to ignore this, and he immediately protested to the British consul in Shanghai, demanding that the landline be taken down and the cables that had been landed in Wusong be removed. The consul asked the taotai to address his protest to the entire group of thirteen Western consuls, and this group subsequently appointed a committee to consider the matter, after which, in late September, the American consul informed the taotai that he would have to negotiate with the Danish and Russian consuls. The Western powers obviously intended to delay the resolution of the matter as long as possible, but the taotai had already sent the matter upward in the system, and it reached the foreign ministry in Beijing on October 2, 1873.[3]

Eight days later, the foreign minister Prince Gong proclaimed in a note to all foreign ambassadors in Beijing and the Danish consul in Shanghai that the landline was to be taken down and the cables removed as the agreement concluded with the British ambassador Thomas Wade specified that telegraph cables were not to be landed. At the same time, orders were issued to the local Chinese authorities to the effect that they should see to it that the landline was taken down.[4]

Nothing happened, and the matter was further complicated for the local taotai when the Danish consul informed him that he could not take action against Great Northern without the approval of the Danish Ministry of Foreign Affairs. Around the same time, C. F. Tietgen succeeded in getting the Danish Ministry of Foreign Affairs to seek support from the Western ambassadors in Beijing. The controversy petered out, and Great Northern's board of directors rejoiced because the line had been allowed to remain in place but also because the matter had given the company's local leadership "an opportunity to have a detailed and friendly discussion with the Chinese authorities."[5]

In fact, the local taotai—despite his official protest—had displayed an accommodating attitude in his interactions with the company and put Lieutenant Dreyer in contact with the taotai in the adjacent Ningbo district. At Dreyer's request, this taotai issued a proclamation to the populace to the effect that the Danish cables in the mouth of the Chang River and around Gutzlaff should not be damaged, and all demands that the landline between Shanghai and Wusong should be taken down were soon forgotten.[6]

Danish plans for Chinese telegraph connections?

In Copenhagen, the board concluded that the taotai's initial reaction had been a formality and that there was "therefore no reason to interrupt efforts to introduce landlines to China." This remark referred to the fact that—as in Japan—the company had plans to supplement its cables with the establishment and operation of landlines. These plans had been discussed already in 1868, in connection with the negotiations with the Russian department of telegraphy in connection with the first Denmark-Russia cable.[7]

In Japan, the government had raised the matter itself and established telegraph lines on its own initiative, but nothing suggested that this would happen in China—on the contrary. This being the case, the construction of the Shanghai-Wusong line was only "the first step," as C. F. Tietgen put it when, in November 1873, he asked Russia's newly appointed ambassador in Beijing, Eugene de Bützow, to support the Danish plans. There were specific plans to establish four telegraph lines:[8]

- Between Shanghai and Nanjing with an extension to Hankou
- Between Xiamen and Fuzhou
- Between Hong Kong and Guangzhou
- Between Tianjin and Beijing with an extension to Kyakhta—the connection for which Russia had long wished

The sequence of events related to the Shanghai-Wusong connection confirmed the view of both Great Northern's board of directors and the company's leadership in Shanghai that it would be possible to press onward with the construction of landlines. This was expressed at the company's general meeting on April 25, 1874, when Tietgen characterized the taotai's proclamation "as [the company's] greatest achievement in China—that [the company

Great Northern was part-owner of the company that opened China's first railroad, which connected Shanghai and Wusong, on July 3, 1876. The news went around the world and was reported in publications including the *London Illustrated News,* which published an illustration based on an original photograph of the first train's departure from Shanghai for Wusong. The railroad was not in operation for long, however, as it was shut down by Chinese authorities on August 22, 1876. It opened again on December 1, remaining in operation until October 20, 1877, before being permanently shut down. During the railroad's second period of operation, a total of 176,000 tickets were sold.

has] gotten the Chinese authorities to proclaim that [the company's] cables must not be damaged."[9]

Tietgen painted with broad strokes and did not make reference to the Chinese demand that the landline and the station in Wusong be removed. In contrast, he dwelled on the company's plan to establish landlines and also referred to the company's involvement in the future railway between Shanghai and Wusong. A little scornfully, he spoke of how the major European powers had attempted to push into China "with the help of armies and armored warships and by making the Chinese receptive to the benefits of European civilization by selling them—opium."[10]

Things were different for Denmark, which was not a major power and therefore had to push into China along "a different path . . . along the path of conviction." The Chinese had to be convinced that the telegraph was a great force for good, and in this connection, the Danes had an advantage over the English and the French in that they were seen not as enemies but as friends—a designation that had been used by the taotai in the Ningbo district.

Thus far, the company had barely made a start, but the company was justified in hoping that it could "bring the whole Chinese population into [the company's] area," and if the company succeeded in this, it would have dramatic positive consequences. Three million people live in Hankou alone, and the city's volume of trade was comparable to that of London. If someone asked why Great Northern was working so hard in East Asia, Tietgen therefore answered as follows:

"This is because there is no place in the world where the telegraph has as bright a future as in China, and because there is no other nationality as suited as the Danish to establishing the telegraph there."[11]

Landline at Fuzhou and cable to Taiwan

While C. F. Tietgen was conjuring up a golden future in China from his podium at the stock exchange in Copenhagen, the company's hopes of establishing landlines in China suddenly appeared likely be fulfilled. The company had originally planned to connect the great trade and harbor city of Fuzhou with the Shanghai-Hong Kong cable in the same manner as in Xiamen, but the waters off the coast rendered landing a cable here difficult. Instead, the company began attempting to lay the groundwork in both Xiamen and Fuzhou for the construction of a landline between the two cities, which were about 215 kilometers apart as the crow flies.

In Xiamen, the company had received a sign that this would not be easy. A demonstration of the telegraph to the local taotai using a short landline set up for the occasion in March 1873 had to be canceled after all the invited Chinese suddenly indicated that they would not be attending. The taotai demanded both that the landline be shut down and that the cable be disconnected—apparently on the orders of the viceroy of Fujian Province, Li Henian. The Danes disconnected the landline but left the cable in place, and nothing further with regard to the matter happened subsequently.[12]

The construction of a telegraph line between Xiamen and Fuzhou did not then appear to be viable at this point. The station head in Xiamen, Jacob Henningsen, instead installed a courier line with regular messenger service between the two cities, but the plans for a landline had by no means been forgotten.[13]

An unexpected opportunity arose in a dramatic context in April 1874, when Japan sent a military expedition to Taiwan to carry out a punitive action following the mistreatment and killing of shipwrecked Japanese sailors by some local fishermen. In Beijing, preparations for war were begun immediately, at the same time as attempts were made to negotiate a peaceful resolution.

In May, Shen Baozhen was appointed imperial commissioner with full military and diplomatic powers for Taiwan and Fujian provinces. Originally, Shen Baozhen had been a strong opponent of the telegraph, but he now proposed to the emperor that a landline from Xiamen to Fuzhou be established and that cables be laid from there to Taiwan so that military activities could be coordinated as an ele-

ment of the defense of Taiwan. He was supported by the viceroy of Zhili Province and commissioner of the northern harbor towns, Li Hongzhang, who had long been a proponent of the introduction of the telegraph.[14]

Shen Baozhen's plans were approved in an imperial decree of June 14, 1874, which was the first positive reaction ever from China's top leadership with regard to the establishment of the telegraph in China. This was a radical break with the attitude of the Chinese up to this point, and it opened up possibilities for Great Northern, and indeed, the company started up the installation of landlines on its own initiative.

A short time later, Jacob Henningsen concluded an agreement regarding the establishment and operation of a fifteen-kilometer-long telegraph line between Fuzhou and the city's harbor, Luoxingta, which was known to the Europeans as Pagoda Anchorage and was the most important harbor for the exporting of Chinese tea. This line had no military value but was important in connection with the local Chinese and foreign trade, and for this reason, its construction was supported by the Western con-

In Xiamen, Great Northern built an entirely new station along with a residential building to go with the company's station, which opened early in 1873. The building at the top of the hill is the residence of the Danish employees, and at the bottom left, one can see the station itself near the beach where the cable was brought ashore. The station building still exists.

suls, while the local Chinese authorities could use the line as proof that they were in the process of realizing the imperial edict.

As soon as Lieutenant Dreyer in Shanghai received word from Xiamen by telegraph of the conclusion of the agreement, he steamed away from Shanghai aboard the *H. C. Ørsted* with the required materials, and on June 30, the first telegraph poles were set up. The line passed through local rice fields, and Lieutenant Dreyer therefore had to hold meetings with the inhabitants of several villages to get their permission to put up poles going through the areas in question. The line was finished on July 12 and opened the same day. This was the first officially approved telegraph line on Chinese soil, and shortly thereafter, it was visited by Viceroy Li Henian and the local taotai, and offi-

The *H. C. Ørsted* repaired and maintained cables in East Asia and the Russian Far East until the summer of 1881 when the ship made Denmark its new base so that it could undertake repairs to cables in Northern European waters. Over the years, the ship itself sometimes needed maintenance and repair, as here, where it was drydocked in Shanghai.

cial proclamations forbidding sabotage and theft were sent out.[15]

The agreement regarding the line from Fuzhou to Luoxingta confirmed the company in its belief that the Chinese were serious about establishing landlines, and further confirmation was forthcoming when, during his stay in Fuzhou, Lieutenant Dreyer was encouraged to travel to Taiwan to negotiate with regard to the laying of a cable from Fuzhou to Taiwan as an element of Shen Baozhen's plan.

On July 3, 1874, Great Northern decided to support developments in China by appointing Engi-

neer Capt. Col. Valdemar Hoskjær technical chief, reporting directly to the board of directors. In 1870, Hoskjær had left his position to participate in the laying of cable in East Asia during 1870 and 1871, and he was now again sent to East Asia so that he could participate in the establishment of the Chinese landlines, while C. L. Madsen was attached to the project as a technical consultant. On the same occasion, Edouard Suenson received the title of director of the entire company.[16]

Meanwhile, Lieutenant Dreyer traveled to Taiwan, where he arrived on July 11. His visit resulted in a contract for the construction of a telegraph system on Taiwan consisting of a landline from Tainan in the south to Tamsui in the north, from where a cable to Fuzhou on the Chinese mainland was to be laid. A cable was also to be laid from Taiwan to Penghu Lietao, a small group of islands in the Strait of Taiwan. A total price of 242,500 silver dollars was agreed upon.

Two weeks later, the board expressed its position on Lieutenant Dreyer's contract for the construction of a landline, and the board's attitude was negative as far as the cable between Taiwan and Fuzhou was concerned. The board saw the connection as lacking in commercial significance and irrelevant to the company's plans with regard to landlines, and the price that had been agreed upon would not cover the costs.[17]

Dreyer was therefore instructed to reach agreement on a higher price for the laying of the cable and not to use a new cable for the connection between Taiwan and Fuzhou but rather one the company already had in its cable depot in Wusong. On the other hand, the board of directors were strongly interested in the establishment of a landline between Xiamen and Fuzhou, and Dreyer was instructed to negotiate an agreement regarding the establishment of such a line so that the connection at Xiamen would be connected to the company's cable system.[18]

The Taiwan system then was not a high priority for the company's board, which was strongly focused on the connection between Fuzhou and Xiamen. For the Chinese, this was all one package, however, but when Dreyer received word in the second half of August that the Chinese had refused to pay a proposed higher price for the cable system, he reacted calmly. This was because in the meantime, he had succeeded in securing approval for the Fuzhou-Xiamen line via an alternative process, and negotiations regarding several other landlines were in progress.[19]

On the way to a breakthrough in China

While Lieutenant Dreyer was negotiating with regard to the Taiwan system, Jacob Henningsen was putting pressure on Viceroy Li Henian to conclude an agreement regarding the Fuzhou-Xiamen connection. The breakthrough came with a proposal that Great Northern establish the connection at its own expense, hanging up two telegraph wires, one of which was to be transferred to the Chinese, one to remain the company's. Great Northern was to maintain both wires until Chinese personnel could take over the Chinese wire.[20]

With the implementation of this proposal, the Chinese would get their own telegraph line between the two cities at no cost to them, and Li Henian interpreted the imperial decree of June 14 so that he had the authority to approve construction of this line. On August 1, 1874, he therefore gave Great Northern permission to proceed with construction work, and two weeks later, Henningsen signed an agreement, which would be finally approved by the local Board of Trade. In addition to a station in Fuzhou, Great Northern received permission to establish agencies in Xinghua and Quanzhou. The system in its entirety was to be owned and operated by the company until the Chinese authorities wished to purchase it.[21]

Lieutenant Dreyer had also begun negotiations regarding the establishment of a telegraph line between Ningbo and Hangzhou, from where a connection to Shanghai could be established, and at a meeting of Great Northern's board of directors on August 11, C. F. Tietgen announced that "China's currently most powerful man," the viceroy of Zhili Province and commissioner of the northern treaty harbor cities, Li Hongzhang, had plans to establish a landline between Tianjin and Shanghai. The company's Danish interpreter, Lt. C. A. Schultz, had therefore traveled to Tianjin to seek to initiate negotiations with Li Hongzhang.[22]

In general, Tietgen could report that local telegraph lines were desired in many parts of China as a result of the emperor's decree, which local authorities interpreted as a general approval of the establishment of telegraph lines. Because of this, a boom in the construction of telegraph lines was to be expected, and the leadership of the company had therefore—pending the approval of the board of directors, which was considered certain—ordered over 7,000 kilometers of telegraph wire and associated materials, which were to be shipped from London within the next few days. Tietgen recommended that the company immediately order a new shipment so as not to risk running out of materials, and this order was approved.[23]

After the opening of the station in Xiamen in 1873, Great Northern had a supply of telegraph stamps made for use in China. These stamps, which were decorated with a portrait of the Danish natural scientist H. C. Ørsted, were to be used for advance payment for telegram forms sent by courier to the company's stations in Xiamen and Shanghai, from where they were transmitted onward to their final destinations. The prices are given in Mexican silver dollars, which were used for telegram invoices in East Asia. There is no evidence to suggest that these stamps were ever actually used, but they are a reflection of Great Northern's ambitions with regard to the spread of the telegraph in China.

All the evidence suggested that this was the long-awaited breakthrough and that the company's great visions for its activities in China would not be realized. The company therefore immediately got to work: In August 1874, the engineer V. Hoffmeyer traveled by horse from Fuzhou to Xiamen, where, accompanied by two mandarins and an escorting group of soldiers, he undertook a survey of the stretch and strove to obtain a sense of the mood of the local populace. He noted that in several districts, there was "a restless and aggressive populace," but the company relied on the fact that the local authorities had accepted their obligation to provide protection. The preparations therefore continued, so it would be possible to begin work on the project as soon as the materials arrived from Europe.[24]

But then things began to go wrong. In a report to the board of directors in early September, Lieu-tenant Dreyer informed the board that the concession had not yet been signed by the local Board of Trade despite the fact that it had been approved by Viceroy Li Henian, the taotai of Fuzhou, and by other local authorities. Lieutenant Dreyer stated that he was optimistic with regard to the prospect of getting the concession finally approved soon and of subsequently receiving confirmation of permission to establish the line from Li Henian, but Lieutenant Dreyer's optimism proved not to have been justified.[25]

The reason for the missing signature was that Shen Baozhen had protested against the agreement and had informed Li Henian that a telegraph line established in accordance with the emperor's decree was to be owned and operated by the Chinese authorities and not by a Danish company. Li Henian replied that the Chinese would be able to purchase the line when they wished to, but Shen Baozhen was not mollified.[26]

The situation was made worse by the fact that the ministry of foreign affairs in Beijing found out what was going on without previously having been informed of the negotiations. Their source was the Russian ambassador Eugene de Bützow, who had reminded the Chinese of the guarantee that had been provided to Russia in 1862 to the effect that Russia would be given the right to establish a Kyakhta-Beijing-Tianjin line if other countries were given permission to establish landlines. As this had now occurred, the ambassador wished to begin negotiations regarding the establishment of the Kyakhta connection.[27]

Bützow had referred to the Danish Xiamen-Fuzhou agreement and to the already established Fuzhou-Luoxingta line, but the authorities firmly denied that foreigners would be operating the new lines. Around the same time, instructions were sent to the local authorities in Fujian Province to the effect that they should immediately take over the Fuzhou-Luoxingta line and that there should be an investigation into what had happened.[28]

Given the common interests of the Danes and the Russians, the Russians' actions were quite unfortunate, and indeed, they had not been coordinated with Great Northern. For the time being, the company attempted to delay a resolution of the matter and begin the construction of the Xiamen-Fuzhou line in the meantime. When the local Board of Trade asked the company to postpone the construction work, stating that the line could provoke the populace and be difficult to protect, the company ignored the board's request.[29]

The construction of the line from Fuzhou to Xiamen began on October 10, 1874, with Chinese workers under the leadership of Danish engineers and telegraphists. A little less than twenty kilometers of line was allegedly built without provoking protests or sabotage, but after a cable had been laid across the Min River, the work was delayed for a month during which it was necessary to negotiate with local mandarins regarding protection against possible reactions by the populace. At the beginning of December, the line had therefore only been extended by a further twenty kilometers.[30]

The local Board of Trade warned Great Northern that the authorities would be unable to protect the workers if there was violence and declared that Great Northern was establishing the line at its own risk as the concession had not yet received final approval. In late November, Jacob Henningsen reported to the Danish consul in Shanghai that telegraph material had been stolen and that he attributed this to the fact that Chinese officials had spread rumors to the effect that the construction of the telegraph line was taking place without per-

mission having been granted. And this was only the beginning.[31]

There were outright attacks by the local populace with which the Chinese authorities did not find it necessary to interfere. All the evidence suggested that it was a contributing factor that the crisis between China and Japan had been solved through diplomacy and that the risk of war had thus passed. There was no longer a military need for the line, and in 1874, the authorities ordered the construction work to be stopped and simultaneously announced that Chinese soldiers would be taking control of the line.[32]

Lieutenant Dreyer had repeatedly received instructions from Copenhagen not to interrupt construction of the line unless it was actually obstructed by force or the company was threatened with the use of force. Things had now gotten to that point, and construction was therefore stopped with that justification after less than fifty kilometers of the total stretch of more than two hundred kilometers had been set up. At this time, the Chinese offered to purchase the part of the line that had been built together with all the materials associated with the project, and Dreyer rejected this offer, claiming that the company had the right to build the line.

Extraordinary Danish delegation in China

The situation was now locked up, but Great Northern trusted in a Danish diplomatic delegation that arrived in Beijing early in December 1874. For some time now, C. F. Tietgen had been working to bring about the establishment of a Danish legation in China, but the Danish Ministry of Foreign Affairs had not shown much interest in this proposal. However, an extraordinary envoy was sent from Denmark to China, and in accordance with Tietgen's wishes, this was Waldemar Raasløff.[33]

The official purpose of the mission was to deliver Christian IX's congratulations to the new Chinese emperor, Tongshi, but Raasløff's real task was to bring about the official recognition and protection of Great Northern's cables. In its recommendation of the mission to the Council of State, the Ministry of the Interior had emphasized Great Northern's contributions to the revenues of the Danish government. The year before the founding of the company, the Danish government telegraph authority had had a deficit of just under 32,000 rigsdaler, but during the most recent financial year, there had been a surplus of 24,600 rigsdaler. During the years 1868–1873, Great Northern's activity had brought the Danish telegraph authority total revenues of 150,000 rigsdaler.[34]

In the area of foreign policy too, Great Northern was of great importance as the company contributed to supporting Denmark's ability to maintain its neutrality during any crises and wars given the fact that it would be necessary for all nations to maintain the telegraphic connections for which Den-

Former Minister of War Waldemar Raasløff, who had concluded the first friendship, trade, and maritime treaty with China in 1863, was sent to China in 1875 on an extraordinary diplomatic mission to support Great Northern's efforts to acquire official protection of their cables. He was accompanied by—standing, from the left—Denmark's general consul in China, the Swiss silk merchant Edouard de Bauvier; Captain Valdemar Hoskjær of Great Northern; Lieutenant Antonio Leigh-Smith; and Lieutenant C. A. Schultz from Great Northern in China, who functioned as an interpreter for Waldemar Raasløff.

mark was an important nexus. Finally, the ministry mentioned the very large amounts of capital that had been invested in Great Northern's systems and were predominantly in Danish hands.

The proposal had been signed by Minister of the Interior Fritz Tobiesen, who, as the director of the Postal and Telegraph Authority and as a representative of the Danish government's shares, had previously taken a seat on Great Northern's board of directors, a seat he still occupied. Two days later, the proposal received the support of Minister of Finance and Council Pres. Christian Fonnesbech, and the following week, the Ministry of Foreign Affairs added its support. The Council of State approved the proposal on September 2, 1874.

Waldemar Raasløff did not meet the newly crowned Chinese emperor, who was just eighteen years old and contracted smallpox and died in early January 1875. However, Raasløff did manage to secure the desired proclamation regarding protection of the Danish cables, probably due to the uncertain power relationships during the emperor's illness and after his death.

On December 20, 1874, Raasløff got the ambassadors of the United Kingdom, Russia, France, Germany, and the United States to participate in a joint action in which they sent almost identically worded notes to the Chinese foreign ministry demanding that the Danish cables be protected. On January 11, 1875, the Chinese government responded in a lengthy note that presented an account of all the events that had led up to the current situation and went on to state that the Chinese government would not be able to protect the cables. Nevertheless, in view of the notes that had been received and "considering what is due friendship and appropriate for maintaining mutual good will," the Chinese government would instruct the local authorities to take appropriate measures to protect the cables.[35]

It was difficult to interpret this note as anything but official approval of the landing of the Danish cables in China despite the fact that no actual landing permit had been issued. The Chinese had not found occasion to mention the circumstances under which the cables had been landed four years previously,

and in his report to the Foreign Ministry, Raasløff emphasized that the Western ambassadors were in unanimous agreement that the Chinese note constituted "the greatest concession it would be possible to obtain under any circumstances."[36]

The Battle of Kvankow

While Waldemar Raasløff was waiting for a reply to the ambassadors' notes, Great Northern resumed work on the Fuzhou-Xiamen line but not for long. On January 22, 1875, a work brigade was attacked by local residents who destroyed telegraph poles and other material and kidnapped a Chinese laborer—though he was released a week later—while two Danish engineers had to barricade themselves in a guardhouse. Several further attacks followed, and the Danes felt convinced that the local authorities and mandarins had encouraged the local populace to attack.[37]

A solution could only be reached in Beijing, and Raasløff therefore extended his stay and raised the matter with the Chinese foreign ministry. In contrast to the question of protecting the company's cables, he did not receive much support from the ambassadors, particularly not from Thomas Wade of the United Kingdom, who feared that the recognition of the Fuzhou-Xiamen line could lead to Russia's receiving permission to establish the Kyakhta-Beijing-Tianjin connection. In Copenhagen, a request for diplomatic support addressed to the Ministry of Foreign Affairs by C. F. Tietgen received a lukewarm reception, and Raasløff was, in fact, instructed not to entangle himself in matters whose ultimate resolution could not be foreseen or in controversial questions.[38]

While Waldemar Raasløff was negotiating in Beijing, events at Fuzhou culminated in the middle of February with the throwing of stones, the sawing through of telegraph poles, attacks on workers, and attempted arson. Two Danes were injured, and the company interrupted its work and concentrated on getting its workers and materials to safety in Fuzhou.

Unaware of what was going on near Fuzhou, Waldemar Raasløff negotiated in Beijing in the

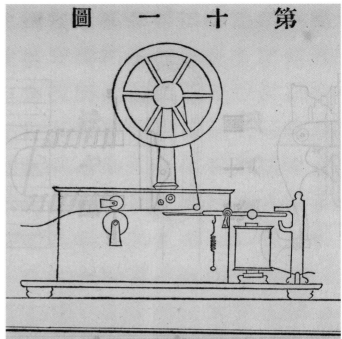

In the middle of the 1870s, Great Northern published a little book in Chinese that explained how a telegraph worked and why it was significant. The various apparatuses were explained in detail, and the company and its development were described. The book had been written by Lt. C. A. Schultz, who had taught himself Chinese.

meantime until, in the middle of February 1875, the Chinese Ministry of Foreign Affairs offered to pay Great Northern compensation for the damage and destruction the company had suffered and also offered to purchase the completed part of the line—without accepting any responsibility for building the rest of the planned line. Raasløff recommended that the company accept the offer as a prerequisite for "positive developments in China in the future." In contrast, Lieutenant Dreyer rejected the offer as a great defeat with regard to Great Northern's "legitimacy."[39]

In the meantime, work on the Fuzhou-Xiamen connection went nowhere, and at the same time, the unrest spread to the already built Fuzhou-Luoxingta line, which was sabotaged. When Raasløff heard about these events around this time,

he sent his interpreter, Lieutenant Schultz, to Fuzhou to find out what was going on and attempt to deal with the situation there while Raasløff himself traveled to Shanghai. After having investigated the matter, Raasløff sent a telegram to Great Northern's board of directors indicating that he "was not entirely convinced" that the company was legally in the right in the matter. He therefore recommended that the company concentrate on securing compensation for the damage and leave the question of its right to establish the line for later.

When C. F. Tietgen took the podium at Great Northern's general meeting in the Exchange Hall in Copenhagen on April 28, 1875, to report on the past year then, the situation in China was fluid. He spent most of his speaking time on Waldemar Raasløff's mission, which had led to the recognition of the company's cables, and on the work to build the Fuzhou-Xiamen system and the many attacks by the local populace that had taken place while that work had been going on.

It became evident that Tietgen had listened to Raasløff's recommendation when he reported that in view of what had occurred, the board of directors had created a new plan for telegraphy in China. It would no longer be the company that would own and operate the telegraph lines. Instead, Great Northern would build the lines for the Chinese government and ideally operate these lines as well. This appeared to be the government's wish, Tietgen declared, and on this basis, it was still the company's goal to encourage the construction of landlines in the Chinese interior, which—as in the case of landlines built in the Japanese interior—would increase the traffic on the company's cables significantly:

"Without any increase in or expansion of our capital, a wide field in the East is open to us in which we may increase our business activity, and I hope that this will become a field of honor on which, with God's help, we will be able to advance our great project and gain honor and benefit for all of you and for ourselves—gain honor and benefit for the peoples of the world and not least for our people and our country."[40]

Tietgen's account of the Chinese government's wishes did not accord with what China's ministry of foreign affairs had communicated to Waldemar Raasløff, but in the meantime, the negotiations with regard to the Fuzhou-Xiamen line had apparently taken a new turn. In any event, Tietgen told the assembled shareholders that Lieutenant Dreyer had gone to Fuzhou to negotiate with regard to the resumption of the construction of the telegraph line, which was to be owned and operated by the Chinese.[41]

On May 21, 1875, Dreyer, in fact, concluded a new agreement with the local Board of Trade according to which the Chinese would purchase the already built part of the Fuzhou-Xiamen line and all associated materials and also pay the company compensation for the damages of the last few months. On behalf of the Chinese and under the protection of the Chinese military, Great Northern was to complete the line and operate it until the Chinese themselves were ready to do so. Great Northern would contribute to this by training Chinese telegraphists so Russia could not demand the right to establish the Kyakhta-Beijing-Tianjin connection. The company was also to sell the Luoxingta line at a price to be determined.[42]

In Beijing, however, the agreement was seen as unsatisfactory as it was not in accordance with the offer presented to Raasløff. Also, Viceroy Li Henian wished to stop the construction of the remainder of the new line and tear down both the already built portion of the new line and the line to Luoxingta. The Chinese then were not in agreement internally, and perhaps it was for this reason that Lieutenant Dreyer pressed forward with new demands, including a demand for a higher price for the Luoxingta line. It was only on August 26, after the emperor had appointed a new Chinese negotiator, that the parties could conclude a new agreement that was based on the one Dreyer had previously concluded.[43]

In the meantime, on August 15, 1875, the construction of the Fuzhou-Xiamen line had been resumed on Dreyer's orders, but despite the fact that the local populace had been informed that permission for the work had been given by the Board of Trade, the work column was bombarded with stones and refuse, and there were instances of sabotage and theft of materials. In early September, there were outright riots during which workers were beaten while the Chinese guards fled. Jacob Henningsen, Great Northern's station head in Xiamen, who was one of the leaders of the work, later described what he called the Battle of Kvankow:

"The construction column had proceeded about a third of the way to Amoy and was about to cross the border between two districts. It had been known previously that posters had been put up in Kvankow [Guankou], a large village on the border of the next district, calling on the peasants to take up arms against the foreign barbarians who had come to destroy the fields' and houses' "feng shui" with their "lightning wires." But at that time there was a desire to provoke a crisis, and it arrived on a pretty morning in November. The camp was attacked by a mob of armed peasants, taken control of, and looted. We saved the tents and an insignificant amount of material; the engineers' private possessions, leather, and food fell into the hands of the enemy; one of the Danes suffered slight physical injuries, but otherwise no one was injured. The peasants were mostly interested in looting, and that they did."[44]

The catastrophe, as Jacob Henningsen called the episode, led to the stoppage of all continuation of the construction work while the arrival of the Chinese authorities with a force of soldiers was awaited. The company demanded that the stolen good be returned, but all that remained was empty boxes, cans, and bottles and other packaging—the contents were gone. The engineers and laborers were subsequently pulled back to Fuzhou, where new orders from Great Northern's leadership in Shanghai were awaited.[45]

Danish withdrawal

Three months after the Battle of Kvankow, the construction of the line was resumed, but new attacks from the local populace followed immediately, and on December 15, 1875, it was over. The Chinese authorities recognized that they could not restrain the resistance of the populace to the telegraph line, whose poles and wires disrupted the feng shui, and proposed to Great Northern that work on the line be permanently stopped and that the company receive suitable compensation.

In both camps, the leaders had already begun to assign blame for the failed project. Great Northern's board of directors focused on Lieutenant Dreyer, and so that the board would be prepared to make a decision with regard to his future role when his contract expired in the summer of 1876, the board asked Raasløff to express his opinion, which he did before he returned home.

When, on September 8, 1875, Great Northern's board of directors discussed Dreyer's future in the company, it was on the basis of "a number of very firm statements made by Waldemar Raasløff," as the minutes of the meeting have it. According to Raasløff, Dreyer lacked "the ability to perceive and characterize conditions accurately," and there was "a certain arrogance" in his behavior and statements that had caused a number of influential individuals to refrain from supporting the company in its undertakings.[46]

The board of directors shared the general's view, "evidence of the correctness of which the board of directors themselves had seen." In particular, Dreyer's "perception and presentation of the conditions around the Foochow-Amoy [Fuzhou-Xiamen] system had been wholly incorrect and had caused the board of directors to believe that a concession had in fact been granted to the company." A concession had not been granted, however, and it was for this reason that the complications and unrest had arisen.

Raasløff advised the board of directors to end Dreyer's employment at the company immediately, but the board of directors was not prepared to take this step. Instead, the board voted to give the former consul in Hong Kong, G. J. Helland, who was to travel to Hong Kong on his own business, a mandate to become acquainted with the company's situation and "present suggestions with regard to a change of representative" in Shanghai; it was, in fact, the board's wish that Helland replace Dreyer.[47]

Dreyer anticipated Helland's mission and, in October 1875, asked by telegraph about the attitude of the board of directors with regard to his future role. When Tietgen replied that this would be dependent on the outcome of a discussion but that he would not be offered permanent employment, Dreyer indicated that he intended to leave the company on June 1, 1876, when his contract expired.[48]

Dreyer's days as the company's executive officer in Shanghai were numbered. Formally, G. J. Helland took over the position on April 1, 1876, but it was he who signed the agreement regarding Great Northern's relinquishment of the Fuzhou-Xiamen connection and the sale of the Luoxingta line, both of which were transferred to the Chinese on March 20. As payment, Great Northern received the entire agreed-upon contract price for the former line and a previously agreed amount for the latter.[49]

The report to the company's general meeting in late April 1876 shows that Great Northern's management had not lost their belief in a bright future in China. Having reported on the setbacks and the sale of the two lines, Tietgen expressed the hope that the Fuzhou-Xiamen line would be completed. He noted that it was still Great Northern's goal

The first and only graduating class from the telegraph school Great Northern established in Fuzhou in 1876. The students subsequently contributed to establishing China's telegraph system, and several of them became employees of the Danish company. The European-looking gentlemen in the front row are, from the left, the Danes C. B. Christiansen, Julius Meincke Holst, and Jacob Henningsen; after them come two unnamed Chinese officials and then the Danes Carl Christian Bojesen and Carl Westring.

"to establish and organize landlines in the Chinese interior and thus create business for our cables without risking capital ourselves."[50]

Nevertheless, the Danish telegraph adventure in the interior of China was over, at least for the time being. The built part of the Fuzhou-Xiamen line was torn down, while the Fuzhou-Luoxingta line was allowed to remain standing and elevated to the status of a military installation, damage to which would be punished severely, after which attacks on it immediately ceased.[51]

The company's landlines between Shanghai and Wusong were also allowed to remain standing, and in 1877, two short landlines were built on Taiwan using the material from the Fuzhou-Xiamen line the Chinese had purchased. In all then, Great Northern's efforts led to the establishment of three short landlines in addition to the company's own Shanghai-Wusong line.

The lines on Taiwan were established with the participation of Chinese telegraphists who had been trained at a telegraphy school that had been established by Great Northern in Fuzhou with Danish instructors and Jacob Henningsen as the head at the request of the Chinese. On April 1, 1876, the school opened in the building intended to serve as a station building in Fuzhou with thirty students, whose one-year training course was paid for by the authorities. There would only be a single graduating class, however, as the next governor did not wish to keep the school open and had it closed.

From Danish Telegraph Monopoly to Dano-British Peace Agreement

CHAPTER 6

Chief executive officer in new domicile

The collapse of the landline project in China coincided with the conclusion of the favorable agreement with Russia regarding the doubling of the Vladivostok cables and the sending out of the Siberian commission. It was precisely the agreement with the Russians that was responsible for the appointment of Edouard Suenson to the position of chief executive officer, giving him the sole responsibility for the leadership of the company in both the economic and the technical areas on January 1, 1877. The board of directors noted that in reality, Suenson had already been functioning in this role for some time, and after this appointment, he increasingly became the company's leading person in interactions with the public and the driving force in its development. At the same time, Tietgen stepped more and more into the background, probably in part because the Svend Petersen matter was becoming increasingly serious and threatening Tietgen's position as the chief executive officer of Privatbanken and even had the potential to ultimately threaten the survival of the bank.[1]

At this time, Captain Hoskjær resigned from his position as the company's chief technical officer and returned to the army. He was voted onto the board of directors at the following general meeting in April 1877 and kept his seat on the board after he was appointed the king's adjutant two years later.[2]

The appointment of Suenson to the position of chief executive officer was followed by the moving of Great Northern's management and administration, which had been previously located in the Exchange Building since the founding of the company—first in two small rooms on the upper floor and, from 1872 onward, in a larger room on the ground floor where Edouard Suenson and a small personal staff had had their domain.

In 1875, the company's facilities were expanded to include a little mechanical workshop in Tuborg

Kongens Nytorv in the middle of the 1870s with the recently remodeled Hotel d'Angleterre on the left. It was in the white building on the right that Great Northern acquired offices on the third floor and Edouard Suenson moved in on the fourth floor in 1879. The shop on the left, on the corner of Ny Adelgade, is Brødrene Andersens Udsalg, and behind the windows to the right of the gate lay Privatbanken's first branch.

Harbor, where a mechanic was employed to repair and maintain the company's telegraph apparatuses and other telegraph equipment. In the summer of 1876, a further two mechanics were employed at the workshop, which quickly became too small.

The administrative room at the Exchange also became too small, and in December 1877, Edouard Suenson applied to the board of directors for the approval of a new space for the company "that had become an absolute necessity as a consequence of the rapid development of the company's business activity." Suenson also indicated that it was "of the greatest importance" that the chief executive officer live in the immediate vicinity of the company's administration as much administrative work was done and many decisions were made in the evenings, "and it was therefore necessary that he always be surrounded by the materials that were required for such activities."[3]

The board of directors approved Suenson's application, and in the spring of 1879, Great Northern moved its management and administration to a new space at the corner of Kongens Nytorv and Ny Adelgade. The building was owned by Privatbanken, which had established its first and thus far only customer service department on the ground floor, while Great Northern rented the upper floors. Edouard Suenson was herewith in direct contact with the company's bank, and the bank had installed a telegraph he could use for communications with London. The company's mechanical workshop moved to the second floor, where there were lathes, workbenches, vises, and other equipment, and the workshop's activity was expanded via the addition of three instrument makers.

In accordance with his wishes, Edouard Suenson got an apartment for himself and his family on the third floor, over the company's offices, so he could follow the progress of business around the clock and take appropriate action if necessary.

"[...] like a man without hearing"

In the wake of the collapse of the Chinese landline project, however, there was to begin with a quiet period that interrupted the expansive development that had characterized Great Northern up to this point. At the general meeting on April 16, 1879, C. F. Tietgen noted in his report that "the company's program has in a way been completed, and there are no new projects or plans." His report was therefore restricted to an account of the year's activities and results. Great Northern appeared to have reached its final dimensions, as far as expansion in East Asia was concerned in any event, and the North Atlantic plan was no longer on the agenda.[4]

Only two years would pass, however, before Tietgen could once again present grandiose plans at the general meeting, and once again, Tietgen's plans had something to do with China. The Chinese leadership had reversed their position on the telegraph question, and again, the triggering factor was the fear of war. During the summer of 1871, Russian forces had pushed into the Muslim Ili region of northeastern China, allegedly to protect Russian trade interests against local uprisings. The Russian government declared that its forces would leave the area when the Chinese government had put down the uprisings, and the Chinese government succeeded in doing so six years later. The Russian troops nevertheless remained in the area, and a Chinese diplomatic delegation was sent to Saint Petersburg to bring about the withdrawal of the Russian troops. It was only in October 1879 that an agreement that formally returned the region to China was concluded, and this agreement allowed Russia to retain control over a number of areas and to receive 5 million rubles and a number of trade advantages.

The agreement provoked shock in Beijing, and a Chinese diplomat was immediately sent to Saint Petersburg to annul the agreement and negotiate a new one. In the meantime, the Chinese army was mobilized, and the Russians had already assembled large forces along the border. The crisis was resolved without military conflict in February 1881 when a new agreement was concluded, specifying that Russia would give up the entire area and also its trade advantages but would have its monetary compensation increased to 7 million rubles.

For the Chinese government, the crisis had underscored the need both for fast communication between the country's regions and the capital and for a connection to the global telegraph network. The Chinese negotiators in Saint Petersburg had been in telegraphic contact with Beijing, but the lack of Chinese landlines had delayed the arrival of telegrams from both Shanghai and Kyakhta, from where they had been transported by couriers riding horses. Because of this, the top Chinese leadership had come to desire the construction of a network of landlines.

The driving force in this connection was Viceroy Li Hongzhang, who had been in contact with Great Northern several times and in 1878 had himself build a landline between the Taku Forts, located at the mouth of the Han River, and his headquarters in Tianjin. The Sino-Russian crisis had now laid the foundation for him to advocate more openly his points of view, and he got further ammunition from the English general Charles George Gordon, who arrived in Tianjin in July 1880 to function as his advisor.[5]

As a Briton, Charles Gordon created controversy with his presence and position with Li Hongzhang, and he soon left Tianjin, but before he did so, he prepared a memorandum that presented a number of suggestions with regard to the modernization of China's defenses, including the introduction of the telegraph. "A country without telegraph service is like a man without hearing," he wrote in the memorandum, which, in addition to the construction of landlines, recommended the creation of Chinese telegraph schools so that China would be able to operate its own telegraph service.[6]

"[. . .] hole in the Chinese wall"

Gordon's memorandum was water on Li Hongzhang's mill—and also on Great Northern's, as it would turn out. The memorandum was addressed to the leading circle in Beijing, but even before the memorandum was delivered, Li Hongzhang had already begun negotiation with Great Northern regarding the construction of telegraph lines. In May 1880, the company's staff in Shanghai had learned that the Chinese government "was showing an interest in having some telegraph systems established," and Lieutenant Schultz had immediately traveled to Tianjin to represent the Danish interests.[7]

After having made relevant inquiries, Lieutenant Schultz succeeded in arranging a discussion with Li Hongzhang, who confirmed that he intended to have a telegraph line built between Tianjin and Shanghai and that he would like to have Great Northern as the contractor. He requested an estimate of the costs of such a project and at the same time asked the company to perform the required preliminary analysis of the terrain between the two cities.[8]

In September 1880, before the preliminary analysis of the terrain had been completed, Li Hongzhang had already submitted a memorandum to the imperial administration proposing the construction of a telegraph line between Tianjin and Shanghai. He also proposed the establishment of a telegraph school with Danish instructors so it would be possible for China to operate the line itself. Only two days later, Li Hongzhang's proposal was approved by imperial decree, and the local authorities were ordered to protect the construction of the line. The establishment of the telegraph school was also begun with a view to begin instruction on January 1, 1881, with two of Great Northern's telegraphists as instructors.[9]

Li Hongzhang appointed a telegraph commission to complete the negotiations with Lieutenant Schultz, and on December 22, 1880, the parties signed an agreement that obligated Great Northern to supply all the materials required for the construction of a telegraph line between Tianjin and Shanghai, as well as leading the construction work, which was to be carried out by Danish engineers and telegraphists and Chinese laborers. At the same time, with the permission of the company, Lieutenant Schultz was temporarily employed by the Chinese to organize the creation of a Chinese telegraph administration on the basis of the commission that had been appointed.[10]

Despite the company's bitter experiences with the failed Fuzhou-Xiamen project, Great Northern's management were optimistic because there was a clear imperial decree this time. Furthermore, the final signature was on the agreement concluded after the peaceful resolution of the Sino-Russian crisis, and the current agreement with Great Northern was therefore not the result of the acute fear of war. In fact, C. F. Tietgen was almost euphoric when he characterized the perspectives opened up by the new agreement at Great Northern's general meeting on April 12, 1881.

The expansion of Japan's national telegraph network and their opening to international traffic had increased the traffic on the company's cables to many times what it had been before these changes had taken place, and a similar development was to be expected in China—but many times larger because of China's population, which was ten times that of Japan. The Tianjin-Shanghai connection would doubtless be followed up by a line between Tianjin and Beijing, and "then a hole will have been opened in the Chinese wall that it will be difficult to close in the future." Economically, the consequences for Great Northern would be positive, but the greatest satisfaction would come from the fact that "no one will have contributed more than we have to the ability of forty million Japanese and over four hundred million Chinese to benefit from the expansion of the telegraph system and not only reap the great material advantages, the democratization or spread of general well-being that will necessarily follow but also thus be affected by the whole European civilization and culture and moved in both a Christian and a humanistic direction to a much greater extent than could previously have been the case."[11]

The telegraph line between Tianjin and Shanghai opened on December 24, 1881, with seven stations along the approximately 1,500 kilometers of line. An engineer from Great Northern monitored the operation of the line, while seven Danish telegraphists monitored service at the stations, which were staffed with Chinese telegraphists who had been trained at the newly established school in Tianjin. In Shanghai, the Chinese telegraph station was established in Great Northern's building.

In order to make the telegraph popular among the Chinese, they were offered free telegrams during the first month, and in Tietgen's words, the company finally seemed to have made a "[h]ole in the Chinese Wall." In September 1881 the viceroy of Jiangxi Province addressed to the company a request that a landline be built from Nanjing to Zhenjiang, where it could link up with the Tianjin-Shanghai line. The connection opened in February 1882, but before that, the company was already receiving a stream of inquiries regarding the potential establishment of telegraph lines in various parts of China.[12]

Chinese monopoly with complications

Within a short time, the development of the telegraph in China had gained a great deal of momentum, with Great Northern playing a key role that unexpectedly opened up entirely new possibilities. Prior to the opening of the Tianjin-Shanghai line, Jacob Henningsen met with Li Hongzhang, who, according to a report from Great Northern's board of directors, "spoke of the company very positively." He indicated that he "would do everything in his power to provide advantages to the company in China both with regard to the construction of future systems and with regard to protecting the company's systems against competing lines on land and at sea."[13]

Li Hongzhang's announcement was quite far-reaching in its implications, as it had to do not only with official recognition of the Danish cables but also with the provision of a general preferred status to Great Northern in China. Great Northern's leadership in Copenhagen reacted quickly, immediately authorizing Jacob Henningsen to begin negotiations with regard to a Chinese monopoly on the landing of cables for a period not less than ten years as well as protection against competing cables and landlines, including Chinese ones. As compensation, the company would transmit all Chinese government telegrams via its cables free of charge.[14]

It is not clear what made Li Hongzhang take this surprising step, but it was hardly a sudden notion. It

In September 1880, Great Northern took delivery of a new cable ship from the Burmeister & Wain shipyard to replace the *H. C. Ørsted*, which was worn out, in East Asia. It was proposed to the board of directors that the new ship be called the *C. F. Tietgen*, after the founder of the company, but he himself rejected this idea. Instead, the ship was named for the company, receiving the name *Store Nordiske* (Great Northern). The *Store Nordiske* was both longer and broader than the *H. C. Ørsted*, but all the important equipment related to work with cables was the same as what had been used by the older ship. The ship arrived at Wusong in the summer of 1881, and the *H. C. Ørsted* set course for Denmark to undergo thorough repairs and refitting and then carry out work on cables in Northern European waters.

was probably the result of his intention of building a Chinese telegraph network, for which he would require foreign assistance—assistance that could not come from Eastern because of the United Kingdom's imperial interests and past events going back to the Opium Wars. In any event, the negotiations went very quickly, and an agreement had been concluded after only two days. The agreement was concluded after Jacob Henningsen had submitted a request for the fulfillment of six wishes on Great Northern's behalf on June 7, 1881, and Li Hongzhang had approved the granting of this request the following day in a short decree bearing his stamp and signature.[15]

According to this decree, which Great Northern consistently referred to as a concession, the company would be granted a monopoly on the landing of telegraph cables in China for the following twenty years, and China would undertake not to establish or allow others to establish landlines that could constitute competitors with the Danish cables—for example, a Shanghai-Hong Kong connection or a Beijing-Kyakhta connection via Mongolia.

Regarding the construction of a national Chinese telegraph network, Great Northern would be given the preferred right to erect the telegraph lines if the company was cheaper than or at the same price level as its competitors. Furthermore, all future Chinese telegrams to Europe were to be sent "via Northern," that is, via the Danish cables and the trans-Siberian connection, unless the sender explicitly requested a different routing.

In compensation, Great Northern would transmit Chinese government and diplomatic telegrams via its cables free of charge, while the Chinese themselves would pay for transmission via other cables and landlines. Great Northern succeeded in getting Russia to reduce its transit fee for such telegrams to a third of the regular fee because of the positive effect of the agreement on the trans-Siberian connection.[16]

In his report to Great Northern's board of directors, Edouard Suenson emphasized that "there can hardly be any disagreement with regard to this concession's extraordinary importance" and that with the agreement, the company had acquired "a position in China that it could not have expected to acquire at such an early stage and in which its influence on and benefits from the development of the telegraph in China will be largely dependent upon the company's own wisdom and capabilities."[17]

Suenson went on to state that it would not be possible to make an immediate public announcement regarding this concession, however; he wrote that it was because the monopoly could "cause complications of various kinds, the matter [was being] kept strictly confidential."

Suenson would turn out to be right—probably more obviously than he himself had expected. Only four days after Li Hongzhang's issuing of the decree, the British ambassador in Beijing appeared at China's foreign ministry together with his American colleague and criticized Great Northern's monopoly. The news spread quickly in diplomatic circles and throughout the business world, and on June 22, Tietgen's old opponent from the fight over the Russian concession, John George Dunn, again appeared in China to act on behalf of the Eastern, whose leaders had promptly found out what was going on.[18]

When Suenson informed the board of directors, the company's representative in London, H. G. Erichsen, had already begun negotiations in London with John Pender regarding the matter, and in early July, Great Northern was close to reaching an agreement regarding the participation of British companies in the monopoly. However, Pender demanded that the period of validity of any agreement should be the same as the period for which the Danes' monopoly lasted, while H. G. Erichsen desired an agreement with a period of validity of twenty years, the period of validity of the Chinese concession. Pender refused to accept such an agreement because he feared that the Danish monopoly could be extended by means of an agreement that was external to the concession itself, and the negotiations therefore collapsed.[19]

It was therefore something of an understatement when Suenson warned the board of directors in August that the Eastern had "gotten wind of the conditions established in the concession" and demanded to be included in the concession in accordance with the agreement made on May 13, 1870, but that this demand "would be rejected to the extent this proved to be possible." This formulation more than suggests that he, and doubtless also C. F. Tietgen, realized that they were on uncertain ground and would have difficulty maintaining the company's position.[20]

Between confrontation and strategic alliance

In the course of the fall, the relationship between Great Northern and Eastern deteriorated, and the Danish company had to recognize that its newly won monopoly had a weak point, as Li Hongzhang's signature and seal were not sufficient to render the decree legally valid in the absence of the ratification of the Chinese foreign ministry.

In 1881, John Pender therefore addressed the British foreign ministry and requested that it take action against Chinese ratification of the decree, re-

The interior of the station in Hong Kong, which was on Bundt's Lane, in the same building as the Eastern companies' station.

ferring to the fact that the concession would establish a monopoly and noting that the Danish company was cooperating closely with Russia. This request received a positive reception, and the British ambassador in Beijing, Thomas Wade, was telegraphically instructed to take appropriate steps.[21]

Thomas Wade was supported in his efforts by John Dunn, whose weapon of choice was portraying Great Northern as a Russo-Danish company that, in addition to seeking a monopoly, was advancing Russian interests at the expense of British interests—a message that contributed to strengthening the negative attitude of the British Foreign Office toward the Danish company.[22]

However, Great Northern's relationship with Russia was more complicated than Dunn suggested. In January 1882, Edouard Suenson learned that Li Hongzhang was negotiating in Beijing with representatives from Russia regarding the construction of a land connection between Kyakhta and Beijing. Not only would Li Hongzhang violate his own concession to Great Northern by concluding an agreement in this regard, but neither the Chinese nor the Russians had found it necessary or desirable to inform the company of the negotiations.

A short time previously, Great Northern had contacted the Russian government and proposed the doubling of the company's cables regarding the agreement to which Edouard Suenson had concluded in Saint Petersburg in 1876, but the establishment of a Sino-Russian landline would make this agreement meaningless. As Suenson understandably found this development extremely worrying, he sent the Russians a query regarding it, but he received no response.[23]

To use Edouard Suenson's earlier words, Great Northern's agreement with Li Hongzhang had indeed been followed by "complications of various kinds." Great Northern's alliance with Russia was threatened, and at the same time, the foundation under the Chinese concession had begun to crumble. Suenson trusted in the prospect that the opposing Chinese and Russian strategic interests in Mongolia, Manchuria, and the rest of the Far East would prevent the Chinese and the Russians from reaching agreement regarding the Beijing-Kyakhta line, but the big problem was what Suenson characterized as Li Hongzhang's "inclination to violate the company's concessional rights."[24]

The situation was made worse by the fact that at the same time, Eastern, via Thomas Wade, was seeking Chinese permission to lay a cable from Hong Kong to Guangzhou. This initiative had been triggered by news of Chinese plans to establish landlines between Guangzhou and Shanghai, as well as an onward connection to Beijing via Tianjin. With a Hong Kong-Guangzhou cable, Eastern would be able to use these lines to establish a connection with Shanghai, Tianjin, and Beijing—without using the Danish cable between Hong Kong and Shanghai.

The two telegraph companies were on course for a head-on collision, and at the same time, Great Northern was under pressure from the threat of a Sino-Russian alliance. In late February 1882, Edouard Suenson therefore traveled to London, after a discussion with C. F. Tietgen but without the knowledge of the other members of the board of directors to execute what he characterized as "a total reversal of the company's policies."[25]

In London, Edouard Suenson and H. G. Erichsen negotiated with John Pender and the rest of Eastern's top leaders, who, as Suenson put it, were "very agitated" about the company's monopoly, which they believed Russia was behind. After two days of negotiations, however, the parties reached an agreement regarding the basis of a new treaty that would mean the two companies would share Great Northern's monopoly and that Eastern would work to bring about the ratification of the Danish concession. As an element of this treaty, the joint purse agreement regarding the distribution of telegram revenues would be renegotiated, and a strategic alliance with broad implications thus seemed to have become a reality, though the treaty, which was concluded by Edouard Suenson on March 1, needed to be approved by Great Northern's board of directors.[26]

In his report to the board of directors, Edouard Suenson declared that given Li Hongzhang's behavior, the company "probably had no dependable support in China whatsoever" and that contrary to what had previously been assumed, the concession did not constitute a solid foundation for the company's business activities in China. The company was under massive pressure from Eastern and the British Foreign Office to give up the monopoly, and there was little hope that Russia would support the company.

Furthermore, the situation was critical because Great Northern's landing permit in Hong Kong had been granted under the condition that the company did not have exclusive rights in China. Therefore, the British government had a perfect right to demand that the cable in Deep Water Bay be removed so the company would lose its connection between

Shanghai and Hong Kong. The British were apparently not aware of this condition themselves, but nevertheless, it constituted a potential bomb under the Danish position.

Suenson's purpose in undertaking the negotiations in London was therefore to execute a total reversal of the company's strategy and seek to enter into an intimate and long-lasting alliance with Eastern, an approach Suenson found "doubly natural" because if such an alliance could be formed, Great Northern would be able to rely on the British diplomatic assistance in upholding the monopoly, assuming the monopoly was shared with Eastern. The members of the board of directors appear to have shared Suenson's point of view—in any event, the agreement with Eastern was unanimously approved at the board meeting on January 22, 1883.[27]

New complications arose, however, because Eastern's plan for a Hong Kong-Guangzhou cable was challenged shortly thereafter by a group of Chinese businesspeople in the middle of March 1882 when they sought permission to land a cable in Hong Kong that was to be laid in the narrow strait leading to Jiulong on the Chinese mainland, from where a landline to Guangzhou was to be built. Great Northern was to lead the construction of the landline and lay the cable, and Danish telegraphists were subsequently to function as inspectors at the stations along the connection.

A short time later, the Chinese created the telegraph company Wa-Hop, but in London, the Chinese plans were seen as an element of a new Danish attempt to exclude Eastern from China. At John Pender's request, the Foreign Office therefore instructed Hong Kong's governor to reject the application, and he did.[28]

The British reaction was an expression of the fact that at Eastern—despite the recent agreement on the formation of an alliance—Great Northern was not looked upon with a great deal of trust. The mood in London was not improved when, at Great Northern's general meeting on April 15, 1882, C. F. Tietgen referred to the Hong Kong-Guangzhou connection and declared that with it, the company "also would have pushed into Southern China."[29]

He subsequently spoke of the Chinese concession in bombastic tones, claiming that it had given the company "a monopoly for [the company's] cables forever" and guaranteed that no competing telegraph connections would be established. The company had taken another step toward the fulfillment of its historic mission, but the downside was that the concession "[had] provoked such intense enmity and such jealousy in the other foreign nationalities in China that they did could not say enough bad things about [the] company. They had even honored little Denmark by accusing the country of harboring ambitious plans for conquest in China as though Denmark were a major power."[30]

John Pender did not care for this characterization, and a protest from London arrived immediately. Edouard Suenson and H. G. Erichsen denied that Tietgen had said anything that ought to have offended Pender and accused Eastern of sabotaging Great Northern's contract with Wa-Hop. On May 18, 1882, Eastern provided written notice that all negotiations with Great Northern were viewed as having been terminated. The "total reversal" of Great Northern's policies had failed, and the company was instead again on a collision course with Eastern—and thus with the British government.[31]

Threat of an independent Shanghai-Hong Kong cable

The collapse of the approach to Eastern caused Great Northern to turn toward Russia again, which was made possible by the fact that the Sino-Russian landline project fell through as a result of the conflict of Chinese and Russian strategic interests. Therefore, on May 22, 1882, Edouard Suenson wrote a long letter in French to the Russian director of telegraphy in which he described the tension between the Great Northern and the Eastern and requested diplomatic assistance with the defense of the concession. At the same time, he emphasized that it was now "urgently necessary" to double the Vladivostok-Shanghai cables as had been agreed upon earlier.[32]

Edouard Suenson also sought help from the Danish Ministry of Foreign Affairs by means of a letter of June 2, 1882, and the conflict was thus elevated to the diplomatic level. Great Northern requested that the Danish envoy in London be instructed to cooperate with H. G. Erichsen to produce a memorandum to the Foreign Office regarding the Danish view of the situation in China and ask for a quick and positive response to Wa-Hop's planned landing of a cable in Hong Kong. The Danish Ministry of Foreign Affairs did as Suenson had requested, and on June 16, a Danish memorandum was delivered to the Foreign Office.

The results of Suenson's two initiatives were very different. In Russia, the government had assumed that the establishment of the Kyakhta-Beijing connection could not be realized, and Edouard Suenson was therefore invited to negotiations in Saint Petersburg, where he arrived on June 29. Suenson was received by Director of Telegraphy General Karl von Lüders, as well as Minister of Finance Nicolai Bunge and Minister of the Interior Count Dmitriy Tolstoy. An agreement was quickly concluded and could be sanctioned by the Czar already on July 15—doubtless because Great Northern was now in a position to finance the doubling of the cables itself. For its part, Russia was willing to provide an annual subsidy of 13,000 pounds sterling for a period of thirty years and also to extend the company's monopolistic concessions through the end of 1912.[33]

The reaction in London was less accommodating. The Foreign Office forwarded the Danish memorandum to Sir John Pender, who responded to it in a sharply formulated seventeen-page document. As a result, the British governor in Hong Kong was instructed to deny landing permission for the Chinese cable.[34]

At the same time, both Great Northern and Eastern were challenged by a new cable project: several companies in the treaty harbor towns planned to lay a new cable, one that would be independent of Great Northern and Eastern, not only between Shanghai and Hong Kong but also continuing further south to Singapore. By this time, Great Northern's Shanghai-Hong Kong cable was so worn and defective that the need for the laying of an extra cable was obvious, but the new project also threatened Eastern's position in the south of Hong Kong. This caused Eastern to propose that the two companies cooperate with regard to the doubling of the Shanghai-Hong Kong cable to prevent the establishment of a competing connection.[35]

There was skepticism about this proposal in Copenhagen, as it would give Eastern partial control over the Shanghai-Hong Kong connection. The company therefore secured verbal permission from Li Hongzhang for the landing of a new cable in Wusong, and on November 6, 1882, Great Northern's board of directors decided that the company would lay an extra cable between Shanghai and Hong Kong on its own.[36]

Summit in Boulogne-sur-Mer

The Danish decision caused John Pender, as Edouard Suenson put it, "to throw off his mask" and threaten Great Northern with the establishment of a new Eastern cable side by side with the Danish one. However, he declared that he would be willing to meet with C. F. Tietgen anywhere and at any time to reach a solution to the tense situation.

It was on neutral ground—in Boulogne-sur-Mer, on the French Channel coast—that the two main combatants, seconded by their chief executive officers, held their summit on November 16, 1882. Suenson described this meeting as "an outwardly friendly gathering" held in a formal and polite but not a friendly tone. Tietgen and Pender agreed that the threat of an independent cable should be met with an improved connection between Shanghai and Hong Kong, but this was the extent of their agreement, as both men defended their perceived right to lay a new cable.[37]

According to the detailed English minutes of the meeting, Tietgen and Pender reached agreement to the effect that Eastern would lay and operate the Shanghai-Hong Kong cable, which would be extended to Fuzhou. The British would also participate in the Danish monopoly, while Great Northern would be financially compensated via a change in the joint purse agreement.

It eventually became common practice to bury telegraph cables instead of establishing aboveground
lines. Here a cable is being laid in Hong Kong from the
landing site for Great Northern's sea cables in Deep
Water Bay to the crown colony's capital city of Victoria.

The agreement needed to be approved by the boards
of directors of the two companies, which might
well have appeared to be a mere formality. On November 24, however, Tietgen informed Pender that
Great Northern would immediately order and lay a
cable to block the independent cable initiative and
that there could be subsequent discussions of who
would own and operate that cable. Four days later,
Edouard Suenson reached an agreement with the
Telegraph Construction & Maintenance Company
regarding the manufacture and laying of a cable,
and on December 9, 1882, a contract that included
extra cables between Vladivostok, Nagasaki, and
Shanghai was signed.[38]

John Pender reacted immediately, announcing
that Eastern would begin work at once on the laying of a cable between Shanghai and Hong Kong

and recommending to the British government to
reject the renewed application from the Chinese
company Wa-Hop for the landing of a cable in Hong
Kong, which successfully occurred.

The submission of the Danish cable order was
approved at the meeting of the board of directors of
Great Northern on December 4, 1882, wherein Tietgen had presented a description of the meeting in
Boulogne-sur-Mer that differed from the characterization in the English minutes. He denied that an actual agreement had been reached and declared that
a draft proposal from John Pender regarding the
principles that would apply to the laying of the cable by Eastern had been "set forth on paper" so that
these principles could subsequently be presented to
the companies' respective boards of directors. According to Tietgen, those present at the Boulogne-
sur-Mer summit had not been in agreement on the
principles, and Tietgen could not recommend their
acceptance and had already informed John Pender
of this. The board of directors unanimously backed
Tietgen's point of view, and this was communi-

cated to Eastern in the middle of December, when Great Northern also threatened to pursue a lawsuit against Eastern if they laid a cable, as doing so would violate the agreement of May 13, 1870.[39]

Great Northern was under pressure. In 1870, this was all about which of the two companies reached Shanghai first, and this time, Eastern had an advantage because it could use a cable that had already been manufactured for use in the Red Sea. Great Northern, on the other hand, had to wait, as the Telegraph Construction & Maintenance Company had until April 1, 1883, to deliver the cables Great Northern had ordered.

Great Northern gave Eastern until December 26 to announce that they would refrain from laying a Hong Kong-Shanghai cable. The company heard nothing from Eastern, however, and on the Christmas Eve of 1882, Edouard Suenson left Copenhagen for London to work out an agreement with John Pender—or file a lawsuit.[40]

Dano-British peace agreement

Edouard Suenson arrived in London on December 26, the day of the Danish deadline. The Danish threat did not cause John Pender to cave in, however, and the following day, the *CS Sherard Osborn* left Singapore for Shanghai with a short cable on board to begin laying cable. Around the same time, the loading of the main cable into the *CS Scotia* in London had begun, and while all of this was going on, Suenson and Pender began negotiations.

Edouard Suenson was under considerable pressure, and the English were unwilling to budge. They held on to the principles from the meeting in Boulogne-sur-Mer but offered Great Northern increased economic compensation. Edouard Suenson felt he would be unable to reach a more advantageous agreement and telegraphically requested approval from Great Northern's board of directors of the negotiation of an agreement on this basis.[41]

When Great Northern's board of directors met on January 2, 1883, C. F. Tietgen recommended issuing the requested power of attorney, in part because he did not feel certain that the Chinese government would in fact provide the agreed-upon monopolistic concession to Great Northern. He was supported by a majority, while two members of the board of directors opposed approval of the negotiation of an agreement with Eastern on the grounds that such an agreement could damage the company's relationship with Russia. When the board of directors voted, the power of attorney for Suenson was approved by a vote of four to two.[42]

The day after he received telegraphic word of the decision of the board of directors, Edouard Suenson presented himself at the Foreign Office to ask the government to mediate in the conflict between the two companies, but not much help was to be had here. The British government unconditionally supported Eastern's resistance to the Danish monopoly and defended the English company's right to land a cable. The following day, the Danish envoy received the same message, and as a consequence, Great Northern was unable to count on receiving permission to land an extra cable in Hong Kong, and there was also a risk that the company would be asked to remove the existing cable from Deep Water Bay.[43]

Edouard Suenson subsequently caved in, and only two days later, on January 12, 1883, an agreement was concluded on the basis of the principles from the meeting in Boulogne-sur-Mer. Eastern would lay and operate the extra cable between Shanghai and Hong Kong, and the British company would share Great Northern's monopoly, while the joint purse agreement was changed to benefit Great Northern. The threat of competition between the two companies had been averted, and Great Northern had secured a strategic gain in that the company could now count on the support of the British government in its dealings with China.

Tietgen presented the agreement to Great Northern's board of directors at a meeting on January 22, 1883, wherein he began by declaring that he was in agreement with Suenson regarding "the necessity of making peace with the Eastern Extension Company." There was general approval of the result that had been achieved; even the two members of the board of directors who had opposed the negotiation of an agreement because of concerns about a possible Russian reaction approved of it.[44]

In fact, there were no protests from the Russian government when it was informed of the agreement. The Chinese government was also informed, and Li Hongzhang was personally informed that Great Northern had concluded this agreement because the company was unable to obtain permission to land a cable of its own in Hong Kong. Great Northern indicated that for this reason, the company had approved Eastern's laying of a cable between Shanghai and Hong Kong but that of course it was up to the Chinese government whether it wished to grant the British permission to land a cable or deny them such permission and thus "uphold [Great Northern's] concession with regard to this point."[45]

It was clear which of these options would be preferred by Great Northern itself, and indeed, Eastern would have to fight to be allowed to land its cable. When the CS *Sherard Osborn* arrived in Shanghai on January 15, 1883, with the first cable, a short one that Eastern wanted to land at Wusong, the Chinese did not want to permit an English cable landing and referred to the Danish monopolistic concession despite the fact that that concession had not been ratified.

Li Hongzhang was not well-disposed toward Eastern, either. He issued orders to the local authorities indicating that they should obstruct the landing of the cable in various ways, and on January 21, 1883, he issued a directive mandating the construction of a landline from Shanghai along the coast to Fuzhou and Guangzhou that would constitute direct competition with Eastern's cables south of Hong Kong.

On February 22, 1883, despite the difficulties in Shanghai, Eastern instructed the CS *Scotia* to begin laying the long cable from Hong Kong up to Shanghai, indicating that the steamship should drop anchor in the Saddle Islands until the situation had been resolved. The complications in Shanghai appeared never-ending, however, partly because the Chinese authorities were not in agreement internally and issued conflicting directives.

It was not until March 31 that Eastern and the Chinese reached agreement regarding the landing of the cable at Wusong, and a further supplementary section had to be added before a final agreement could be signed on May 7, 1883. The British cable was subsequently landed next to the Danish one, and on May 19, the Chinese purchased Great Northern's landline between Wusong and Shanghai after having threatened to remove it if it were not sold to them. Two extra wires were established for Eastern's traffic, and the British connection opened on May 23, 1883.

Eastern's cable was also brought to Fuzhou, but Eastern did not succeed in obtaining permission to land the cable there. Instead, Eastern established a floating telegraph station in the mouth of the Min River with a connecting courier service. The connection opened on June 19, 1883, and in April 1885, Eastern finally succeeded in acquiring permission to land its cable and have it connected to a landline to Fuzhou.

Japanese monopoly and cable to Korea

The relationship between Great Northern and Eastern had finally become calm, but the price had been Danish abandonment of the Chinese monopoly and a British cable between Shanghai and Hong Kong. Therefore, in contrast to his triumphant attitude the previous year, C. F. Tietgen now appeared conciliatory at the Great Northern's general meeting in late April 1883, when he explained the new situation by saying that Eastern had longed viewed the Danish successes in China "with a certain jealousy and wished to share a part of the whole development of the telegraph in China."[46]

As the Britons and British trade represented Great Northern's most important customers, "we found it right to accommodate them," Tietgen explained. Great Northern had been assured full economic compensation, and the company would avoid having to finance the manufacture and laying of a new cable and its subsequent maintenance. Tietgen claimed that the company had solely "sacrificed prestige" and noted that it still had its own cable, making no reference to the frail condition of that cable.

Tietgen was able to report that the planned doubling of the company's cables between Vladivostok, Nagasaki, and Shanghai would be carried out that same summer. By financing the doubling of the cables itself, the company had secured the extension of the Russian concessions until 1912, and the company had exploited the situation to ask Japan for monopolistic rights as compensation for the financial burdens the company was taking on in connection with the doubling.

The company's head engineer in East Asia Lieutenant Henrik Bohr had therefore been sent to Japan to acquire a monopolistic concession as compensation for the agreement Chamberlain Julius Sick had concluded in 1870. Bohr had fully succeeded, as the company had been awarded a concession that gave the company a twenty-year monopoly, lasting until 1902, on Japan's telegraph connections with the Asian mainland and nearby islands.

However, Japan's condition had been that Great Northern would lay a cable between Japan and Korea, which had been a closed country up to this point and was under the control of the Chinese but attracting increasing attention from the Japanese. The 120 nautical miles of cable were to be laid from a Japanese settlement at Fusan (today Busan) in Korea and via the Japanese islands of Tsushima and Iki to the north coast of Kyushu, from where a landline would lead to Nagasaki. The Japanese were not laying the cable themselves because they lacked necessary technical expertise and were unable to finance such a project. Great Northern would therefore own the cable and take responsibility for operating and maintaining it, while the station would be operated by the Japanese government telegraph authority.

In addition to the monopolistic concession, Great Northern received payment for the cable and its maintenance in the form of a fee for each telegram sent via the cable. It was not immediately clear that there was the prospect of large revenues, and the revenue stream would be dependent upon the development of trade with the previously closed country. The cable was opened on February 15, 1884, and when Tietgen again stood at the podium at Great Northern's general meeting, he declared that "we have earned great honor by becoming the first company to open a connection with a country that up to this point has not had a telegraphic or any other kind of connection with the surrounding world."[47]

"[. . .] a shameless conspiracy"

Great Northern was no longer alone in having a cable connection with China, but the company still had a strong position in East Asia as a result of the Japanese and Russian monopolies and the doubling of the Vladivostok cables. The common Dano-British concession remained to be ratified, and in June 1883, the two companies decided to take action, making a few changes to the text in order to accommodate their agreement of January 12 of that year. In accordance with the instructions he had received by telegraph, Great Northern's representative in Shanghai, Jacob Henningsen, traveled to Tianjin, where he met with Li Hongzhang, who refused to make changes to the concession.[48]

In December 1883, the matter was brought up again, but in the interim, the two companies had again been in conflict, as John Pender had become dissatisfied with several of the concession's conditions that he had accepted in the agreement of January 12, 1883, but that he now considered to favor Great Northern. In Copenhagen, Great Northern's leaders saw no reason to make further changes to the concession and referred to the agreement that had previously been concluded.

Once again, the controversies ended at the diplomatic level. They were brought up in late January 1884 by the Danish envoy in London, C. F. Falbe, in an unofficial letter to the permanent secretary of the Foreign Office, Sir Philip Currie. Currie tiredly replied that "it [was] a great shame that the two companies [could] not work together harmoniously in a spirit of mutual trust." He indicated that there must have been behavior on both sides that could be criticized, though he was unable to ascertain who should be accused of what. However, the Foreign Office ended up taking Eastern's side.[49]

The two companies were again on a collision course, and the situation became even more tense in early June 1884, when Pender learned from an unnamed agent in China—probably John Dunn—that Great Northern had attempted to get the concession ratified for Great Northern alone. Trembling with anger, John Pender asked the Foreign Office to instruct the British ambassador in Beijing to put a stop to the Danish project.[50]

In Copenhagen, Edouard Suenson was no less angry after he learned from one of Li Hongzhang's closest advisors, a European, that the British ambassador, acting on orders from London, had asked Li Hongzhang not to ratify the company's concession. In his report to the board of directors, Suenson declared that "this order [was] doubtless inspired by Mr. Pender" and that it was an indication of the existence of "a shameless conspiracy," as the company had made no efforts to get the concession ratified. However, Suenson stated that he would investigate the matter before he accused Eastern of anything.[51]

The result of Suenson's own investigation is not known, but in a report to the Danish Ministry of Foreign Affairs submitted around this time, the Danish envoy in Saint Petersburg indicated that it had been the Russian ambassador who had worked to bring about the ratification of the concession on his own initiative in order to prevent the British from gaining control over China's international telegraph connections.[52]

Great Northern's management, then, had not attempted to get the concession ratified and had also been unaware of the Russian initiative, and John Pender could have learned this by contacting the Danish company and asking about it. His reaction and Suenson's immediate suspicion were both symptomatic of the mutual mistrust between the two companies and their leaders.

"The final peace"

The matter was an example of how again and again great-power political tensions between Russia and

the United Kingdom affected the relationship between Great Northern and Eastern and how the Danish company constantly had to perform a balancing act between Chinese, Russian, and British interests. In this case, the Russian ambassador's actions had been due to an increasing tense relationship between Russia and the United Kingdom, which is a result of both countries' desire for influence in Afghanistan following the Russian annexation of an area in Turkmenistan that bordered on Afghanistan in the spring of 1884.

The danger of a conflict passed, but an outlier of this conflict caused the relationship between Great Northern and Eastern to take on, as Suenson put it, "a very tense character" once again. The reason for this was that in the middle of April 1885, the Royal Navy occupied a small group of Korean islands, Geomundo, which possessed a suitable natural harbor—called Port Hamilton by the British—in order to be able to counter a potential advance by Russian warships down through the strait between Korea and Japan.[53]

In order to be able to communicate with the British forces on the islands, the British government had a telegraph cable laid between Port Hamilton and the Saddle Islands at the mouth of the Chang River. The laying of the cable was carried out by Eastern's cable ships, which caused Great Northern to protest, as Great Northern felt this violated the agreement of January 12, 1883, according to which neither of the companies might carry out such tasks without the consent and possible participation of the other company.

According to the Danes, the laying of the cable could create a precedent, and therefore, Great Northern wished to appeal the matter to an independent arbitration panel, an option provided for by the 1883 agreement. The stage was thus set for a new confrontation between the two companies when the mood suddenly shifted.

On August 7, Edouard Suenson traveled to Berlin to participate in an international telegraphy conference. When he arrived, he met John Pender, who was unexpectedly "very friendly" and "unconcerned about all of the events of the past and felt

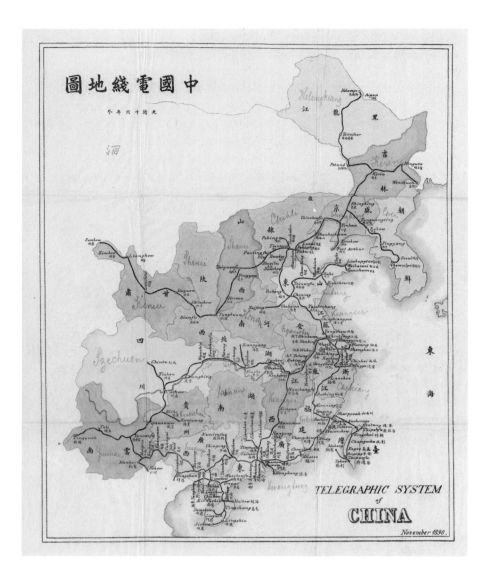

圖地綫電國中

光緒十六年冬

TELEGRAPHIC SYSTEM
of
CHINA

November 1890.

Map of China's national telegraph system in 1890. The vast majority of the land lines were established under the leadership of Danish telegraphists and engineers who also participated in the training of Chinese telegraphists and assisted in the operation of the telegraph.

This is hardly a sufficient explanation in itself, though, and the increasing price competition from the Chinese land-lines probably contributed. That competition had become such a serious threat that shortly before this, the two companies had agreed to reduce their prices to an agreed-upon standardized level, and on its own initiative, Great Northern had ended its free transmission of Chinese government telegrams. Finally, there were rumors that China and Russia were again negotiating regarding a Beijing-Kyakhta connection.

Whatever the reason for it, Pender's unexpectedly accommodating attitude caused Tietgen to travel to Berlin as well, where he and Suenson negotiated with Pender, who, according to Suenson's subsequent report to the board of directors, "appeared willing to make such great concessions that [Suenson] still [had] a hard time believing he [would] stand by them."[55]

Pender intended to, however, and on October 7, 1885, Suenson could present to Great Northern's board of directors with the basis for further negotiations with the goal of concluding an agreement that would replace the agreement of 1883. Eastern's board of directors had already approved the basic principles, and the Danish board of directors now did so as well.[56]

The principles now needed to be expanded into a contract with appropriate appendices and a new

that we should be able to arrange relations between the companies in a satisfactory manner." Suenson was both surprised and uncertain as to what the cause of the change in mood was. However, he suspected it was Great Northern's appeal of Port Hamilton to a neutral panel, which Suenson believed Eastern would lose.[54]

joint purse arrangement as well as instructions for the two companies' representatives in Shanghai. This was a demanding task in itself, and the negotiations were further delayed when Pender unexpectedly traveled south for a six-week vacation and subsequently spent time campaigning to be reelected to the British parliament.[57]

It was not until the middle of August 1886 that sufficient progress had been made for Pender, in the company of F. C. Hesse, secretary to the board of directors of Eastern, and the company's agent in Shanghai, William Judd, to come to Copenhagen to negotiate regarding the last remaining points with C. F. Tietgen, Edouard Suenson, and Jacob Henningsen, who had been summoned home from Shanghai for this purpose. It took just under a week for the men to reach agreement on a treaty that meant the introduction of cooperative operation of the cables between Shanghai and Hong Kong and the establishment of single common stations in the two cities that were run by equal numbers of employees from the two companies.[58]

All future orders and construction work for the Chinese telegraph administration would be shared equally by the two companies, and in general, they would act in common and present themselves as a single unit in their dealings not only with the Chinese but also with the Japanese. In general, the purpose of the agreement, which reflected the spirit in which it had been concluded, was "to eliminate all friction between the two companies by placing them on completely equal footing in all of their relations with the Chinese and Japanese governments and the public so that neither of the companies [could] assume a position that in any way could give them a preferred status in China."[59]

It was very difficult to reach an agreement because of Eastern's demand that neither of the companies might attempt to attract traffic to one of the routes at the expense of the other route. It was problematic for Great Northern to sign off on such a condition because if it became known to the Russians, it could be perceived as an agreement not to prioritize the trans-Siberian connection. Great Northern managed to persuade Pender to be satisfied with verbal assurance from the entire Danish board of directors that Great Northern would act in accordance with the condition. The British board of directors made a similar pledge to Great Northern.

Agreement with regard to the Port Hamilton cable was also reached: Eastern agreed to pay half of its net profit from the project, so Great Northern received 7,372 pounds, 10 shillings, and 2 pence.

On this basis, Great Northern's board of directors voted to approve the agreement, after which John Pender, F. Hesse, and William Judd, who had been waiting outside the meeting room, came in. The mutual verbal assurances that the companies would not seek to acquire advantages for their own lines were given, after which the agreement was signed by Pender and Tietgen. It was ratified by Eastern's board of directors on December 1 and was originally in force for three years as a trial arrangement, but it was otherwise intended, assuming there were no unexpected problems, to remain in force for twenty-five years, until 1912, with the possibility of being terminated with a year's notice.[60]

Suenson and Tietgen would later call this agreement "the final peace," and they would turn out apparently to have been right. In any event, there were no further open conflicts between the two companies.[61]

Power Shifts in East Asia

CHAPTER 7

"[...] go to war rather than give in on this point"

As an element of the peace agreement, Great Northern and Eastern decided to take "immediate common steps to retain the Chinese concession of 1881 or protect their interests in China in other ways." In March 1887, before they had had a chance to address the Chinese in this connection, Edouard Suenson received word that the Russian telegraphy department was working toward the establishment of a telegraph connection between Russia and China via Blagoveshchensk and that there was already a station on the trans-Siberian line.[1]

This was not the first time there had been rumors of Sino-Russian negotiations about a land connection between the two countries—indeed, there had been talk of such negotiations as recently as the summer of the previous year. Since then, an extension of the Russian telegraph lines in the Russian Far East to Posyet on the Sea of Japan had been completed, and in China, the landlines were nearing Heihe across from Blagveshchensk on the Amur River. It would only take the laying of a river cable to establish a connection, and both the governor of the Amur District and local interests in both China and Russia were pushing to get such a cable laid.

Via the company's representative in Saint Petersburg and the Danish Ministry of Foreign Affairs, Suenson tried to get the Russian government to instruct its envoy in Beijing to display a positive attitude toward a Sino-Russian land connection but at the same time declare that telegrams to and from cities in East Asia, where Great Northern had landed its cables, were not to be transmitted via the land connection. The company's own contacts in the Russian department of telegraphy were also asked to work to bring this about, and all in all, Suenson was confident.[2]

In 1892, the Store Nordiske laid thirty-three nautical miles of cable for the British authorities in Hong Kong from the crown colony to the steeply rising little island of Gap Rock, on which a lighthouse had just been erected. Even in calm weather, access to the island could only be gained using a jib crane at the foot of the rock. Landing the cable using this crane was a process that, as is indicated by the picture, was not completed without great difficulty.

As a visible expression of the cooperation between Great Northern and Eastern, the two companies built a new common building in Hong Kong that was inaugurated in 1898. Regardless of which of the two companies the customer chose, the telegram price was the same.

Great Northern and Eastern also took action in China. The two companies' representatives in Shanghai, Jacob Henningsen and Walter Judd, arrived in Tianjin on April 15, 1887, to negotiate with Li Hongzhang, who had not only issued the concession but was also the de facto leader of China and therefore the key to getting the concession ratified.

By way of an introduction to the meeting, the two envoys presented a memorandum in which they accused the Chinese government of having committed "a very serious violation" of the concession by exposing the companies to competition from the Chinese coastal lines. Great Northern claimed that

the government had also committed further violations of the concession including using other suppliers of telegraph equipment than Great Northern without having offered the company an opportunity to bid on the orders in question. Great Northern and Eastern therefore believed they "had a right to full compensation for the losses they had sustained because of such violations of the concession and a right to expect strict adherence in the future to all of the conditions established by the concession."[3]

This memorandum was hardly the best way to open negotiations, and according to Henningsen and Judd's minutes, Li Hongzhang in fact read the two documents "with obviously increasing dissatisfaction." He responded to this attack in what the company's representatives described as "strong and coarse language," declaring the concession annulled and invalid and that it had never been an actual concession. Rather, he had accommodated an application and could unilaterally withdraw his approval, and the so-called concession had been issued without the Chinese knowledge of its true purpose and therefore constituted a violation of Chinese sovereignty.

During the discussion that followed, Li Hongzhang became increasingly enraged until, in "strong and insulting language," he pointed out that Eastern had previously attempted to sabotage precisely the same concession on which it was now relying. He warned the companies against seeking help from their governments, as he would "go to war rather than give in on this point."

The meeting ended when Li Hongzhang threw the documents on the table and refused to receive them, in fact refusing to discuss the concession at all, calling it a matter for the head of the telegraphy administration, Sheng Xuanhuai, who was in Yantai (Chefoo). The two representatives therefore had to report to their companies that the conversation "provided no hope of reaching any friendly understanding with the viceroy, who obviously [had] strong personal feelings regarding this matter."[4]

Russian commission and Chinese freeze

When Edouard Suenson in Copenhagen received the minutes of the two representatives' conversation with Li Hongzhang, he also learned that contrary to his expectations, the Russian ambassador in Beijing had not been asked to support the company. Suenson had a bad feeling about this, a feeling that proved to be justified when it turned out that the action requested by Great Northern had been obstructed by the head of the Russian foreign ministry's Asian section, Privy Councilor Zinovyev, who did not have a friendly attitude toward Great Northern and wished to establish a commission to further the goal of establishing Sino-Russian telegraph connections. Suenson would be officially asked to meet with the commission, which predominantly consisted of "hostile elements," as the company's representative in Saint Petersburg put it.[5]

As the viceroy of Zhili Province during the years 1871–1896, the Chinese politician and diplomat Li Hongzhang was one of China's most powerful men. He sought to bring about the technological and economic modernization of China, and in 1881, he granted Great Northern a monopoly on the country's international cable connections and asked the company to help with the establishment of a national telegraph system. However, he ended up in conflict with the Danish company again and again, and it was not until 1899 that the monopoly concession was ratified. Nevertheless, a friendly relationship developed between Li Hongzhang and several of Great Northern's leading employees in China. This photograph of him at a quiet moment in his private residence in the late 1890s was taken by one of the company's employees.

In late April 1887, Suenson therefore traveled to Saint Petersburg, where the first meeting of the commission was held on May 3. After having given

After a fire at Great Northern's station in Liepaja, Estonia, in the middle of the 1890s, an emergency station was created and manned by Russian telegraphists in uniform and Danish telegraphists in civilian clothing. The Danes were responsible for the receipt of telegrams from the company's cables in the Baltic Sea, and the Russians were responsible for transmitting telegrams onward via the trans-Siberian landline connection. Great Northern had a strong desire to make Danish telegraphists responsible for all telegrams sent via the trans-Siberian connection.

a long account of the historic cooperation between Russia and Great Northern, Suenson declared that the matter of the landline was problematic for the company because Russian agreement to the creation of the land connections would be equivalent to the de facto annulment of the company's Chinese concession and would therefore deprive the company of "the only legal basis" for its activities in China.[6]

Suenson subsequently played the geopolitical card, declaring that if the company's position in China were undermined, then this would "deprive Russia of its independent telegraph connections" and make it dependent on the United Kingdom and China. This would have negative consequences in the event of diplomatic conflicts, and Russia would lose transit revenues. Suenson did not express opposition to the establishment of landlines between Russia and China but wished to secure the company's position in China and protect it against "completely ruinous losses" because of price competition from the land connections.

Suenson succeeded in getting a positive response to his arguments, and the result was that the Russians stopped their negotiations with the Chinese for the time being and telegraphically asked the Russian ambassador in Beijing whether he could support the Danish position. He could, and as the German and British envoys in Beijing also declared that they were willing to support the Danes, the assembled Russian commission approved instructing the ambassador in Beijing to support Great Northern in the negotiations with the Chinese.

On May 18, Suenson was back in his office in Copenhagen, where he learned that everything had gone as agreed and that Jacob Henningsen had left Beijing and was on his way to Yantai together with Walter Judd. After only six days of negotiations with Sheng Xuanhuai, agreement was reached regarding a joint purse treaty according to which both the companies and the Chinese would pay their telegram revenues into a common fund that would subsequently be distributed in accordance with a specified arrangement.[7]

A summary of the agreement was immediately sent by telegraph to the two companies' management, and in Copenhagen, Suenson felt that the agreement looked "fairly advantageous." A short time later, however, a telegram from Yantai arrived, indicating that Sheng Xuanhuai insisted upon renegotiating the entire agreement—probably because he had been ordered to do so.[8]

The companies had no choice but to resume negotiations, and in late July, they could finally sign a new joint purse agreement. Suenson found that it was "far from as advantageous as the agreement reached in May" but was the best that could be reached under the circumstances. The decisive point was constituted by conditions regulating standardized fees for international telegrams via cables and land connections that protected the cables against price competition and the fact that the agreement would remain in force for fifteen years.[9]

The agreement was signed by the companies' representatives on August 10, 1887, and was subsequently sent to Beijing for ratification. In accordance with the wishes of the Chinese, it was also to be approved by the British ambassador and the Russian ambassador in Beijing, with the latter ambassador functioning as the diplomatic representative of Denmark.[10]

Great Northern's entire European staff in Shanghai with station chief Jacob Henningsen sitting on a chair in the middle.

there had been a change of mood in Saint Petersburg, with the result that the Russian ambassador had been instructed to delay ratification until a Sino-Russian agreement had been concluded with regard to a Kyakhta-Beijing connection.[11]

The entire ratification process now got completely stuck while the resolution of the Sino-Russian negotiations was awaited, and those negotiations dragged on and finally ended up grinding to a halt without having produced a result. In his report to the board of directors in early December 1887, Suenson noted that the negotiations "[had] not undergone any change in the course of the month." A year later, the situation "still had the same status," and in July 1889 the situation "remained stagnant," and things continued like this in the years that followed.[12]

Sino-Russian agreement

The companies had to wait a long time for news from China. However, in November 1891, Russia got a new ambassador in Beijing, Count Arthuro Cassini, and in May 1892, he began negotiating with the head of the Chinese telegraphy administration Sheng Xuanhuai. Cassini wished to incorporate Great Northern's—and thus also Eastern's—circumstances into a Sino-Russian convention on telegraph connections between Russia and China. His intention was to avoid complications that might result from separate negotiations between Great Northern and Eastern on the one hand and the Chinese on the other hand.

Cassini succeeded in quickly reaching agreement with his Chinese negotiating partner, Sheng Xuanhuai, regarding a telegraph convention that included the circumstances of the companies. In Copenhagen, Edouard Suenson received word of the convention in late August 1892, and he found that "under the circumstances [the company] had reason to be satisfied, as all of [the company's] primary concerns [had] been taken into account."[13]

According to the convention, three landline connections were to be established between China and Russia. A connection via Hunchun and Kraskino close to the coast along the Sea of Japan was to be

In 1896, Li Hongzhang, the commissioner of the northern treaty harbors in China, attended the coronation of Czar Nicholas II of Russia, after which he traveled onward to several Western European countries and to the United States. In his journey, he met Germany's Chancellor Bismarck and—shown here—the United Kingdom's Queen Victoria. At a large banquet in London in honor of Li Hongzhang, Great Northern's chief executive officer, Edouard Suenson, gave a speech on behalf of the international telegraph companies.

The companies appeared to be on the verge of securing the long-desired Chinese recognition of the position, but the whole process suddenly froze. On the one hand, the Chinese were delaying ratification in an attempt to obtain greater concessions from the companies, and on the other hand, established immediately after the convention was ratified, a connection via Heihe and Blagoveshchensk was to be established as soon as a cable had been laid across the Amur River, and, finally, a connection from Beijing through Mongolia to Kyakhta was to be finished within five years. The postponement of the establishment of the Kyakhta connection was in response to a request from Great Northern, which most feared the competition from this route, as it was the shortest and therefore the fastest route with an onward connection to Europe.[14]

The fees for telegrams between China and Europe were basically to correspond to the fees charged by the companies. This was a condition Great Northern had wished to have in order to avoid price competition and was applicable to the cities where the companies had landed cables: Hong Kong, Fuzhou, Xiamen, and Shanghai. These cities accounted for 80 percent of all of China's traffic with Europe.

The contents of the convention soon became widely known, and, like the agreement that had been reached six years earlier, the convention provoked immediate protests from businesspeople in the harbor treaty towns and in London, who complained that it was monopolistic. There were demands that the Chinese and Russian governments refrain from ratifying it, but the protests were in vain, and on March 1, 1893, the first telegraph line between China and Russia, the line via Heihe and Blagoveshchensk on the Amur River, opened.

The Hunchun-Kraskino connection, which had been intended to be the first, opened to traffic on August 15, 1893, and came to have mostly local importance, while the Heihe-Blagoveshchensk line acquired a significant amount of international traffic. It was not until the beginning of 1900 that the connection via Kyakhta—which would be the most important of the three connections for transit traffic—opened.

Nationalization of European cables

During the 1880s, while Great Northern had been focused on the turbulent developments in the com-

Official portrait photograph of the leader of China's national telegraphy administration, Sheng Xuanhuai, with whom Jacob Henningsen negotiated regarding China's telegraph connections. The photograph is in Great Northern's archives because, like Western businessmen, Sheng Xuanhuai exchanged portrait photographs with others.

pany's relationship with Eastern, there had also been significant changes in the conditions applying to telegraph companies in Europe, though these changes were of an entirely different character.

A significant reduction of telegram fees at the international telegraph conference in Berlin in 1885 did not affect Great Northern much, as the capacity of the company's cables and a number of technical modernizations sufficed to cope with the increase in traffic that resulted from the reduced charges, and it was possible for Great Northern to

maintain profitability. One such modernization was the introduction of duplex technology, which made it possible to send telegrams both ways in a single copper wire, in contrast to simplex technology, which only allowed the sending of telegrams one way at a time. Duplex had established itself in the course of the 1870s, including on Great Northern's cables.

The consequences were greater when all of the cables between England and the continent except Great Northern's were nationalized by the governments of the United Kingdom, Germany, the Netherlands, Belgium, and France on April 1, 1889. For Great Northern, the consequence of the nationalization of the company's England cables would be that the company would be reduced to a regional East Asian telegraph company. There were already government-operated cables between Denmark and Sweden and between Sweden and Germany,

but nothing suggested that there were plans to nationalize Great Northern's cables between England and Scandinavia.

It was certainly the case that the company's cables had more far-reaching significance than the other cables between England and the continent, by far the greatest share of the traffic on which was European. Great Northern's England cables were an integrated part of the trans-Siberian connection between Europe and East Asia, and nationalization of those cables would necessarily affect the connection both economically and politically. For the Scandinavian countries, as well as for Russia, the consequence would be a predictable and significant reduction in transit revenues, as the connection would lose its politically neutral status.

The geopolitical consequences for Russia would be significant, as the trans-Siberian connection would be influenced by British interests, and the United Kingdom had an interest in preserving Great Northern's position, which was a prerequisite for Eastern's position in China and constituted a doubling of the English cables. There was, then, no one who was interested in nationalizing the company's England cables.

Great Northern's cables therefore remained the only private system in Northern Europe, and in the fall of 1890, the company reinforced its position by laying the first direct cable—a cable that avoided making an intermediate landing in Norway or Denmark—between England and Sweden. This connection was established to increase capacity, as the company expected a marked increase in traffic as a result of a new reduction of fees at the international telegraph conference in Paris the same year.

Map of Great Northern's telegraph system at the time of the company's twenty-fifth anniversary on June 1, 1894. The company owned only the undersea cables, but the red landlines in countries including Russia and China were a part of the Danish telegraph system, and international telegrams could be sent abroad "via Northern."

Another long-desired cable, one between Fanø and Calais, was laid in the summer of 1891. The existing cable between Denmark and France was extremely vulnerable to service interruptions as a result of the increasing use of trawlers for fishing, and the growing amount of traffic between France and Russia and on to China and Japan also made it necessary to provide an extra cable that was stronger and therefore more expensive. This required an increased subsidy from the French government, and by making reference to its major investment, the company succeeded in securing an extension of its French concession through the end of 1915.[15]

Twenty-fifth anniversary and change of board chairman

Despite the company's various worries and the turbulent developments in China, things were going

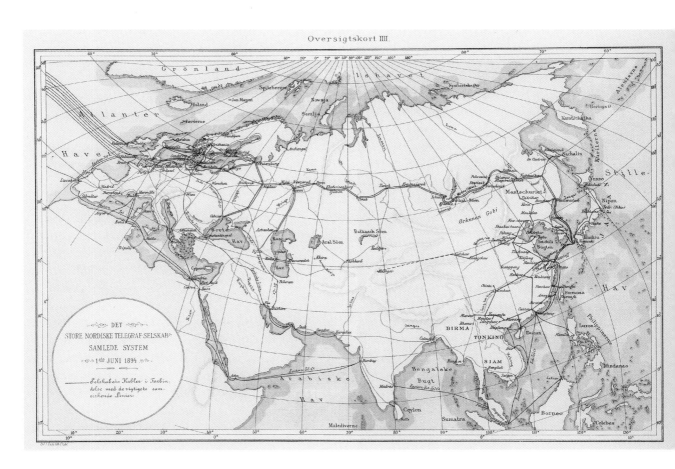

KØBENHAVN.   Store nordiske Telegrafselskab.

well for Great Northern—or fairly well, for the International Telegraph Union's repeated reductions of telegram fees restricted the company's revenues. Looking back at the company's history at the general meeting on 21 April 21, 1894, C. F. Tietgen thus dwelled on the developments regarding traffic and revenues since 1881, noting that there had been an increase in the number of telegrams transmitted from just under 800,000 in 1881 to more than 1.5 million in 1893, which represented an increase of approximately 92 percent.[16]

The development of telegram revenues looked different. These revenues had increased from 4.1 million kroner in 1881 to just under 5 million kroner in 1893, a modest increase of just 22 percent despite the marked increase in traffic on all of the company's cables. The stagnating revenues could be attributed to the ITU's regular price reductions, and despite the increase in the company's activity, the developments of the last ten years had not been "exclusively cause for rejoicing," as Tietgen put it.

Nevertheless, he felt that the shareholders had every reason to be satisfied because since its founda-

The headquarters of the Great Northern Telegraph Company in 1894 after remodeling and expansion. On the corner on the left is the shop Brødrene Andersen, which had also been there in 1879 when the company had moved in. From the main entrance in the middle of the building, the stairs led up to the offices of the telegraph company and to Edouard Suenson's apartment. To the left of the main entrance is Privatbanken's eastern branch, while the life insurance provider Graham Livsforsikring has offices on the right, on the corner of Gothersgade. On the top of the building one can see a sculpture of Electra executed by the Danish architect Emil Blichfeldt; Electra is a woman from Greek mythology who was used by the telegraph industry as a symbol of communication through the use of electricity. In her uplifted hand, she holds a torch that was later replaced with an electric lamp.

tion the company had had total revenues of just under 99 million kroner, of which 45 million kroner had been paid out as dividends despite the fact that the company had also financed a number of expensive cable projects and built up a considerable reserve fund. The average annual dividend had amounted to almost 7.5 percent, while the shares had increased in value to more than double their face value.

Tietgen used this opportunity to criticize the French shareholders who had repeatedly demanded increased dividends at the expense of increases in the size of the reserve fund. He declared that on the one hand, the stagnating revenues, in combination with necessary investments in the company's aging cable systems, meant that deviation from the company's dividend policy up to this point could be "fateful" and that on the other hand, it was precisely the interest revenues from the reserve fund that would make it possible to survive the expected future reductions in telegram fees.

After his triumph on Great Northern's twenty-fifth anniversary, on June 1, 1894, when he received great honors from all sides, C. F. Tietgen suffered a stroke in December of the same year during a trip to Paris and soon had to resign from all of his positions on the boards of directors of the limited companies he had helped establish—including Great Northern. He lived his last years quietly and out of the public eye.

The balance sheet presented with the annual account for 1893, which showed assets amounting to approximately 52 million kroner, indicated that the company had a healthy financial cushion to fall back on. Of the company's assets, the value of the company's systems and other property made up a little more than 40 million kroner and the company's portfolio of stocks and bonds just under 11 million kroner. Liquid assets amounted to about 375,000 kroner, and the company owned a little less than 900,000 kroner in outstanding debt. The share capital amounted to 27 million kroner and the reserve fund to a little more than 16 million kroner, and there was a debt repayment account containing 3.6 million kroner. Debts included only the remaining part of a bond debt—3.6 million kroner—plus debts to creditors amounting to approximately 670,000 kroner.[17]

The operating account for the year showed a surplus amounting to just under 5.8 million kroner, with interest revenues and other revenues having been taken into account. Given the transfer of the surplus from the previous year, which amounted to a good 800,000 kroner, there was a little under 6.4 million kroner to be distributed. Of this amount, 1.5 million kroner remained in the reserve fund, while 365,000 was used for the payment of interest and the partial repayment of the principal of a bond loan. About 50,000 kroner was transferred to the personnel pension and support fund, while the board of directors received 27,000 kroner in compensation.

After a transfer of just under 690,000 to the following year's budget, a little over 2.3 million kroner could be paid out to the shareholders, who, according to Tietgen, "had all reason to be satisfied with the first twenty-four and a half years of the company's activity and could meet the future with confidence if they trusted and backed the policies of the board of directors."

Tietgen was dwelling on history because about six weeks later, on June 1, 1894, Great Northern would be able to celebrate its twenty-fifth anniversary. In honor of this occasion, the company published a larger and more in-depth historical look back in the form of a 265-page large-format anniversary book. The author was Edouard Suenson, and the manuscript had been read by C. F. Tietgen—though this was not specified anywhere.[18]

Before the anniversary arrived, the book was sent to various individuals in Denmark and abroad, as well as the major Danish newspapers, which responded by publishing long front-page articles on the history of Great Northern. A visible sign of the company's greatness was the completion of an extensive renovation and expansion of the company's headquarters on Kongens Nytorv, which were enlarged via the purchase of the neighboring building. The whole grand project was finished by the erection of a bronze sculpture of the goddess Electra executed by the Norwegian sculptor Stephan Sinding.

On the actual day of the anniversary, the new headquarters was decorated with flowers and Dannebrog flags, and flags were also flown from other buildings in the capital city and by ships in the harbor. In the evening, there was a gala dinner at the Hotel d'Angleterre with two hundred guests including government ministers and notables from political and economic life, as well as envoys from Sweden, Austria, the United Kingdom, Russia, France, and the United States. In the evening, the company's building was illuminated, and the next day, the citizens of Copenhagen could read about the dinner and the many speeches in the newspapers.

The twenty-fifth anniversary of Great Northern was a high point in Tietgen's life, but shortly thereafter, in December 1894, he suffered a stroke during a journey to Paris, and because of this, the report of the board of directors was presented by Edouard Suenson, who had been elected to the board in 1890, at Great Northern's general meeting in April 1895. The following year, Tietgen participated in the general meeting but again left it to Suenson to present the report. In the years that followed, Tietgen no longer participated in general meetings or meetings of the board of directors but continued in his position as chairman of the board, as no temporary replacement was approved.

During the time when Tietgen could still attend the board meetings, Edouard Suenson had presented the various matters at the meetings of the board of directors wherein his proposals were always approved, and after Tietgen had stopped attending, it was Suenson who led the board meetings and presented the reports at the general meetings. This being the case, he was already functioning as the chairman of the board of directors in practice when Tietgen announced his resignation in January 1898, and at a meeting on February 8, the board of directors unanimously requested that Suenson take over, which he agreed to do.[19]

As both the chief executive officer and the chairman of the board of directors, Edouard Suenson now acted as the company's undisputed top leader formally and officially as well as in practice. There was no change in day-to-day leadership or daily routines, as this was very much a case of formalizing existing realities. However, it was not without significance that Edouard Suenson was now able to act with greater authority than in the past, and

he would need to do so, as the company was now facing one of the most turbulent and dramatic periods in its history.

"[…] peace and reconciliation […]"

The articles presented by the newspapers on the occasion of Great Northern's twenty-fifth anniversary emphasized in particular the laying of the cables in China in 1870 and 1871. However, it was precisely in China that the company had still not managed to secure recognized legal status, neither on its own

For the celebration of Great Northern's twenty-fifth anniversary in 1894, the company's leadership had a photograph collage made with portraits of all the company's Danish employees and photographs of the company's stations. In the middle are Edouard Suenson and C. F. Tietgen.

nor in cooperation with Eastern. To be sure, the Sino-Russian telegraph convention theoretically provided the companies with a stable framework, as the convention theoretically protected the companies against Chinese price competition, but this theoretical protection soon proved to provide insufficient security. In violation of the convention, the Chinese had halved the telegram fees for the landlines between Shanghai, Fuzhou, Xiamen, and Hong Kong, and Great Northern and Eastern asked the Russian ambassador, Arthuro Cassini, to complain to the Chinese about this.

On August 1, 1894, before this could happen, the situation changed dramatically when war broke out between China and Japan regarding control over Korea. The Japanese advanced quickly, conquering large areas in Manchuria and elsewhere. The war ended in April 1895 with a peace treaty with which China gave up its sovereignty over Korea, which became a sovereign state but was informally ruled by Japan. China also had to relinquish Taiwan to Japan.

Only the intercession of Russia, France, and Germany prevented Japan from also acquiring the strategically important Liaodong Peninsula in southern Manchuria. Russia in particular felt this would have conflicted with its interests, as Russia had its own territorial ambitions in Manchuria, but the other major European powers were also unenthusiastic about the prospect of a Japanese presence on the Asian mainland so close to Beijing. As compensation for not annexing Liadong, war reparations paid by China to Japan were increased to 230,000 taels, which corresponded to a little over 6.5 tons of silver.

For China, the defeat and the peace treaty were a humiliation that exposed the country's weakness. This situation was not exploited by Great Northern and Eastern, which accepted an agreement regarding the fees for the use of their cables and the Chinese coastal lines that Arthuro Cassini had negotiated with Sheng Xuanhuai. As had previously been the case, there would be equal and standard fees both for cables and for the Sino-Russian connection, and the companies and China would establish a joint purse into which all of the parties' revenues would be paid, after which these revenues would be distributed such that one-third went to China and two-thirds were divided between the companies. The agreement was to have a period of validity of twenty years.[20]

The agreement was to be ratified by the governments of Denmark, Russia, the United Kingdom, and China, but the British government was unwilling, as it viewed the agreement as a de facto monopoly and the payments in gold francs would cause price increases. Around the same time, the Chinese reopened price competition, and the companies subsequently accepted the lowering of the per-word rate from 8.5 to 7 francs for Western trade and businesses in China and the shortening of the period of validity such that it would expire at the end of 1910. The agreement could subsequently be ratified by all parties and go into force on August 1.[21]

In the report he presented at Great Northern's general meeting in April 1897, Edouard Suenson expressed his great happiness because "the company had finally succeeded in bringing about peace and reconciliation with the Chinese telegraph administration," and he expressed hope that the agreement would lead to "long-lasting friendly relations with the Chinese administration." His hopes proved justified to the extent that the following year, Great Northern concluded a separate agreement with Russia and China regarding a joint purse agreement for the Sino-Russian traffic according to which all revenues were shared equally among the three parties.[22]

This paved the way for Great Northern and Eastern once again to bring up the question of Chinese ratification of the 1881 concession or some other form of agreement that would secure the company's monopoly on the landing of cables in China, and they did so in 1898. The Chinese telegraph administration was now more open to such discussions, as American plans for a cable via the Pacific Ocean to China appeared more and more likely to be realized—if the Americans pressed forward with such plans, a Danish monopoly could protect China against the landing of American cables.[23]

Weather conditions in the Sea of Japan off the coast of Vladivostok in the Russian Far East could be extreme and could make work with cables difficult. The picture shows the deck of the *Store Nordiske* after a snowstorm in February 1892.

The new negotiations ended on March 6, 1899, with Jacob Henningsen and Sheng Xuanhuai signing a new concession establishing that the Danes had the sole right to land cables in China until the end of 1930. Before the concession was signed, its contents had been approved by the foreign ministers of Denmark, Russia, and China, all of whom subsequently ratified the concession. Eastern was not a signatory but was covered by the concession via Eastern's agreements with Great Northern.

In his report to the board of directors, Edouard Suenson viewed the matter from a historical perspective and declared that the company had "won back the cable monopoly in China that [the company] had in reality lost through the Chinese government's refusal to recognize Li Hung Chang's concession of 1881."[24]

Danish prince and extension of the Japanese concession

While China had been greatly weakened by its defeat, Japan now stepped into the role of a major power in the region, one that, with Taiwan, had annexed its first foreign territory. Given the new state of affairs, there was a need for a cable between Japan and Taiwan, and the government now began to free itself from its dependence upon Great Northern.

In August 1895, it became possible, thanks to the Chinese war reparations, for Japan to order a cable in the United Kingdom to be laid between Nagasa-

Kay Suenson in 1898, when he was hired as a secretary to the board of directors of Great Northern and his father, Chief Executive Officer Edouard Suenson. In 1908, he joined the company's top management team, and while he did consistently have to share power over the company with one or more co-directors, he was undisputedly the company's leading director until he resigned in 1933.

The first part of the cable was laid by the Japanese cable ship during July and August of 1896, the last part during May and June of 1897. The laying of the cable was carried out without the use of foreign engineers or other cable specialists, and in general, it marked a turning point in the development of the telegraph in East Asia, as it was the first cable that was not laid by Great Northern or Eastern. After this, the Japanese also used the *Okinawa Maru* for repairs made to cables between the Japanese islands, which had previously been a source of income for Great Northern.

Great Northern and Eastern were no longer alone in having cables in East Asia. In the area of telegraphy the Sino-Japanese war also brought changes that had consequences for the Danish company in particular. Suenson indicated that he was generally worried about Japan's new position at the company's general meeting in April 1895, when he declared that there was doubt as to whether the consequences of the peace agreement between China and Japan "[would] prove to be advantageous to the foreigners in the long run, particularly to the European nations in East Asia."[26]

Despite Suenson's pessimistic view, the company did not give up hopes of having its concession extended, and the company soon made a new attempt. The context was that there were plans for the Danish cruiser-corvette *Valkyrien* to steam to Siam under the command of Prince Valdemar. The Folketing was willing to approve but not to finance the voyage, but with the support of the East India

ki and Taiwan via the Okinawa group of islands. This order was placed through Great Northern and Eastern, which would also be responsible for transporting the first part of the cable to Japan. The Japanese also ordered a cable ship, the *Okinawa Maru*, that left Great Britain in May 1896, bound for Japan with the last part of the cable.[25]

Company and H. N. Andersen as well as the Wholesalers' Society, the necessary funds were raised.

In the spring of 1899, Great Northern was asked whether they would be willing to contribute to the financing of the voyage as well, and Suenson's attitude was positive, as he saw a possibility that a visit to Japan by Prince Valdemar could be beneficial to the company. Therefore, in late June, when it had been definitely decided that the voyage would take place, he contacted the Ministry of the Navy and offered to contribute 150,000 kroner if the voyage were extended to include China and Japan "and if the company had a right to influence decisions with regard to which harbors would be visited and with regard to the length of the respective stays."[27]

The ministry reacted positively, and when *Valkyrien* steamed away from Copenhagen on October 15, 1899, the plan for the voyage had been arranged such that Prince Valdemar would spend a month in Yokohama, followed by shorter stays in Kobe and Nagasaki. Prior to the ship's departure, Suenson had conferred several times with the prince, whose official mission in Japan was to present the Order of the Elephant to the Japanese crown prince.[28]

On its way to Japan, *Valkyrien* would make a stop at Shanghai, where Edouard Suenson's son, Kay Suenson, would board the ship so that he could accompany and assist the prince in Japan. The previous year, Kay Suenson had been hired by Great Northern as a secretary to the board of directors and his father. Shortly thereafter, he had been stationed in England so that he could become personally acquainted with the management of Eastern and the General Post Office and gain insight into Great Northern's relationship with England. He had subsequently been sent to Shanghai, where he was to continue his training in operational leadership after having accompanied Prince Valdemar to Tokyo.

During the voyage, Prince Valdemar was given a large confidential memorandum from Great Northern including several appendices related to the relationship between Great Northern and Japan.

Edouard Suenson had also asked the Danish envoy in Saint Petersburg to get Russia's foreign ministry to instruct the Russian ambassador in Tokyo to support Prince Valdemar in his undertaking, and Minister of Foreign Affairs Mikhail Muravyov had been accommodating in this regard.[29]

Suenson did not expect Prince Valdemar to succeed in bringing about actual negotiations but that he might succeed in creating an advantageous atmosphere. However, the prince succeeded beyond Suenson's expectations, and at a meeting of the board of directors on March 27, 1900, Suenson could report that the prince had secured approval of an extension of the company's concession in unchanged form by ten years. The extension was confirmed two days later in a declaration from the Japanese minister of communications and the general director of the Japanese postal and telegraph authority.[30]

As a gift memorializing the prince's voyage and his actions on behalf of Great Northern, the board of directors approved spending 10,000 kroner to have Otto Bache, who held a professor's chair at the Royal Danish Academy of Fine Arts, paint Prince Valdemar and his wife, Princess Marie of Orléans. The painting of the princess had been finished by the time *Valkyrien* returned home on July 21, 1900, and the prince agreed to pose for a painting of himself.[31]

The ship's return was celebrated in a gala dinner at the great hall of the Schimmelmann Mansion (now the Odd Fellows Mansion) attended by five hundred guests including the crew of the ship, the royal family, the prime minister, and other notables, after which there was a great folk celebration at Tivoli Gardens. At the gala dinner, Edouard Suenson addressed the commander and crew of *Valkyrien*, expressing the two companies' "unanimous recognition and deeply felt thankfulness for the excellent support they had received through Prince Valdemar's wise, strong, and effective intervention, thanks to which they had secured advantages whose effects would be felt for many years."[32]

American Transpacific Cable with Danish Participation

CHAPTER 8

Expansion into the Pacific Ocean?

It was not only the Chinese telegraph administration that felt threatened by a possible American transpacific cable—Great Northern did, too. The plans for such a cable had come about as a result of the United States' increasing economic, political, and military engagement in East Asia and the entire Pacific region, and on Kongens Nytorv developments in this regard were being followed closely.

At the same time, the British government was working on plans for a Pacific cable between Australia and Canada with an intermediate landing on the atoll Tabuaeran in the Pacific Ocean. This cable would be government-owned and would make it possible to telegraph all the way around the world with British cables landing on British territory. The project had been named the All British Line.

Both technically and economically, the laying of a Pacific cable was a task that differed greatly from the laying of an Atlantic cable. The first transatlantic cable had had a length of 3,500 kilometers, which was also the distance from San Francisco to Hawaii. However, the distance from Hawaii to Japan was approximately 6,500 kilometers, and the

great ocean depths, strong ocean currents, and undersea mountain ranges created great technical difficulties.

The costs would therefore be very great, but Edouard Suenson believed both cable connections would be established sooner or later, partly because of the United States' increasing interest in East Asia and partly because of the United Kingdom's strategic interest in a Pacific connection. The two cables would not compete with each other, which made it likely that both would be laid.

On January 20, 1896, Edouard Suenson sent a memorandum to the board of directors proposing that the company participate in the laying of a Pacific cable. He noted that the British cable between Australia and Canada would not affect Great Northern but would greatly affect Eastern, as the traffic between Australia and North America went via the English company's cables to Europe and on from there via the transatlantic cables. The American cable, on the other hand, would threaten Great

The American Pacific cable is landed on a beach near Honolulu in December 1902. The cable ship on the horizon is a British vessel, the *Silvertown*.

James Scrymser was a pioneer and dominant personality in American telegraphy. He founded the Pacific Cable Company, with which Great Northern and Eastern cooperated with regard to the American Pacific project until the cooperation collapsed in 1901.

Northern's and Eastern's traffic between North America and East Asia, which also went via Europe and the transatlantic cables. Finally, the cable connected to the American landlines could negatively affect both companies due to problematic competition between East Asia and Europe as a result of what Suenson called "absurdly low fees" for the use of the Atlantic cables.1

There were no longer insurmountable technical difficulties associated with the laying of a Pacific cable, and Suenson was convinced that sooner or later, the American and British governments would be willing to contribute to financing such a cable. It was therefore of decisive importance for the company to get involved with the American project,

"and the only appropriate way of doing this would be to participate in the project in order to be able to regulate the new route's fees so that the connection [did] not deprive [Great Northern] of [its] most important sources of revenue." At the same time, the United States' increasing interest in East Asia created the prospect of increased traffic, which could greatly benefit the company.

The question was what role could be played by the company. Suenson believed the company could create a role for itself if the British government could be persuaded to change the route of the Canada-Australia cable so that instead of using Tabuaeran as a landing site, the cable would be routed via the little uninhabited Necker Island near Hawaii. This would give the United Kingdom the desired All British Line, and if Great Northern and Eastern together laid a cable from Japan to Necker Island and a short cable from there to Hawaii, the two companies would have acquired a link both to the All British Line and to a future American cable to Hawaii.

Suenson therefore proposed to the board of directors that, having previously discussed this course of action with Eastern, the company initiate negotiations with Japan with regard to the matter and that the company seek contact with the proponents of an American transpacific cable in the United States in order to bring about a fusion of the interested parties rather than competition.

On January 24, 1896, before Great Northern's board of directors met to take a position on the matter, the company's director of operations in London, F. C. Nielsen, had already informed Eastern's management in strict confidence of the Danish plans, which "made a very great impression." Eastern rushed to summon its board of directors to an extraordinary meeting on January 29, where Eastern's board of directors voted fully to support the Danish proposal.2

However, the English themselves had not been inactive. It was revealed to F. C. Nielsen that Eastern was in contact with the Hawaiian businessman Colonel Zephaniah Swift Spalding, whom the president of Hawaii had granted a twenty-year monopolistic concession for the landing and operation of a

Among the powerful economic moguls with whom Great Northern's chief executive officer, Edouard Suenson, negotiated with regard to the American Pacific cable was the financier John Pierpont Morgan, who founded the American investment bank that today bears the name JPMorgan Chase & Co.

cable between Hawaii and the United States, as well as an annual economic subsidy of 8,000 pounds sterling for twenty years. This concession had been granted under the condition that Colonel Spalding would obtain an American concession including an economic subsidy by May 1, 1898.

For this purpose, Colonel Spalding had established the Pacific Cable Company, which was headquartered in New Jersey, and had presented to the American Congress a proposal that an annual economic subsidy amounting to a minimum of 22,000 pounds for twenty years would be provided. When the approval had been secured, Eastern would be responsible for the financing and laying of the cable and also for its subsequent operation, though not officially, as the system would formally be operated by a company registered in the United States. The project did not include an extension to Japan, but this was a perspective Eastern now wished to incorporate along with the possibility of a connection with the British government cable via Necker Island.[3]

Just before Great Northern's board meeting February 3, 1896, took place, however, another project became known, one that, in return for an annual American subsidy of 36,000 pounds, would establish a cable connection between the United States and Hawaii and lay a connecting cable continuing to Japan. This company too was called the Pacific Cable Company, but this one was registered in New York and associated with the Western Union Telegraph Company, which had a nationwide telegraph network in the United States in addition to two transatlantic cables. The men behind the new company were James A. Scrymser, who was the president of the Mexican Telegraph Company and the Central and South American Telegraph Companies, and John Pierpont Morgan, who was one of the United States' richest and most influential financiers and the founder of the investment bank J. P. Morgan & Co.[4]

Great Northern was now confronting some of the largest American businesses but that did not scare off the company's board of directors, which unanimously approved Edouard Suenson's proposal. The Danish company was on its way into a struggle over the laying of and the control over the first transpacific undersea cable.

American approaches and Dano-British alliance

In early February 1896, Edouard Suenson informed the Japanese general director of the department of telegraphy, Den Kenjiro, of the company's plans. The Japanese response was "not encouraging," as Den Kenjiro did not believe the government would grant a concession to the company that already had a monopoly on Japan's existing international cable connections. Because of this, Suenson chose for the time being to await developments in "the center of events," Washington, where the two competing cable projects were on their way through the Congress.[5]

In late February, however, the matter took an unexpected turn when, to his great surprise, Suenson received a telegram from James Scrymser, who proposed a meeting in the near future for the purpose

of initiating "friendly cooperation" between himself and Great Northern. Suenson immediately informed Eastern and recommended that he accept the invitation. At the same time, he proposed attempting to unite the various interested parties in a coalition in order to avoid destructive competition. Eastern shared Suenson's point of view, and Suenson telegraphed to Scrymser that he was prepared to travel to London on short notice.[6]

Suenson received no reply, but on March 6, he received another surprising message—this time from Eastern—to the effect that Colonel Spalding was on his way to London. Both of the American consortia, then, were seeking contact with the European companies, and Eastern "urgently" requested that Suenson come to London to meet with Colonel Spalding.[7]

For four days in the middle of March, Suenson negotiated with Eastern and Colonel Spalding, whom he attempted to persuade to join in cooperating with James Scrymser in order to form a large coalition that also included Great Northern and Eastern. He succeeded in his mission to the extent that when he departed for Copenhagen on March 25, he had secured Colonel Spalding's agreement to participate in the large coalition. He had also collaborated with Eastern to produce a separate heads of agreement document to the effect that Great Northern and Eastern would participate in the project on an equal footing, contributing the same amount of capital, enjoying the same rights, taking on the same responsibilities, and sharing all costs equally.[8]

Brito-American separate agreement

The following month, the whole project fell through after Colonel Spalding had decided to remain in competition with James Scrymser and both projects were rejected by the American Congress. There was no prospect of forming a large coalition, but Suenson confronted the situation calmly. The American Pacific project had certainly been delayed, but the company could continue its business activities undisturbed for the time being.

In contrast, both Colonel Spalding and Eastern's management were deeply disappointed and determined to press ahead as quickly as possible. Eastern was under pressure because the British government wanted to appoint an Imperial Pacific Cable Committee that would prepare a report on a British cable connection between Australia and Canada and present a recommendation.

In early May 1896, Colonel Spalding and Eastern's de facto chief executive officer, the secretary of the board of directors, F. C. Hesse, therefore arrived in Copenhagen to persuade Great Northern to participate in laying the cable between Hawaii and San Francisco. Spalding and Eastern wanted the coalition partners to pay for the project themselves, as in the absence of an American subsidy, they would not need a concession and could therefore begin immediately.[9]

Edouard Suenson rejected this proposal out of hand, as he saw no point in participating in creating a cable connection that only extended from Hawaii to the United States; in contrast, Eastern was fixated on the possibility of extending such a connection to Australia. However, Suenson did agree to have Great Northern pay half of a deposit in the amount of 10,000 pounds sterling to Hawaii's government and up to 5,000 pounds in preliminary costs. By concluding this agreement, Great Northern acquired the right to enter the consortium as a joint owner later if the company paid half of all of Eastern's expenses.[10]

There was no guarantee that the project would be completed, but if it went ahead, Great Northern would have the option of joining the coalition and thus influencing developments. On this basis, Suenson recommended to the board of directors that he be authorized to conclude an agreement, and the board approved this on October 23, 1896.[11]

However, Colonel Spalding did not sign the agreement, instead, he presented a new and more extensive project that involved laying cables to Japan and Australia in return for offering a significantly increased deposit amount to the Hawaiian government.[12]

Eastern immediately accepted the new proposal, but Suenson had had enough. However, he raised no objection when Eastern offered to pay the whole increased deposit amount and to let Great Northern participate in the project on the conditions previously established.[13]

"[…] a true Globe Company"

In late November, the Hawaiian government announced that it had utterly rejected Colonel Spalding's new proposal and was retaining the existing concession. Edouard Suenson reacted quickly, sending a strictly confidential letter to the secretary of Eastern's board of directors, F. C. Hesse, in which he warned Eastern against continuing its cooperation with Colonel Spalding. "In my view, the battle has practically been lost," Suenson concluded.[14]

According to Suenson, Colonel Spalding had not the slightest chance to win his struggle with James Scrymser, and when the latter had won the American concession, Hawaii's government would immediately transfer Spalding's concession to him. Great Northern and Eastern, Suenson wrote, could choose between opposing Scrymser and seeking to cooperate with him, and Suenson recommended the latter course of action.

Suenson proposed the unification of the interested parties in a coalition that would establish a Pacific system comprising cables between San Francisco, Hawaii, Australia, and Japan operated by a commonly owned company that was registered in the United States and under American jurisdiction and leadership. He indicated that the parties should try to involve one or two of the transatlantic companies in the coalition so the new company "would circle the whole Earth with [its] own lines and constitute a true Globe Company that extended its influence to all areas of the Earth."[15]

These were—perhaps particularly for an Englishman—provocative visions, as the nexus of the global combination would be the American Pacific company, in which the interests would be bound together. In London, the Victorian Internet was viewed from the perspective of the United Kingdom's globally leading position in the economic, political, and military spheres, and the notion that a Pacific coalition would be the point of departure for a Globe Company suggested a shift in this position.

In any event, F. C. Hesse was not receptive to this message but continued to prefer a coalition with Colonel Spalding alone. A verbal request from Great Northern's top representative in London, F. C. Nielsen, for Eastern's board of directors be allowed to discuss the Danish proposal—and ideally vote to break with Spalding before Spalding came to London on his way to Paris—also failed to secure approval.[16]

On Christmas Eve, Spalding arrived in London, where he had a brief meeting with F. C. Hesse and F. C. Nielsen before immediately traveling on to Paris, where his wife was ill. The London meeting brought no change in the situation, nor did several messages subsequently sent to Eastern by Spalding contribute to moving the project forward from its becalmed state.

Eastern's board of directors did not know what to do, and the company's new board chairman, Lord William Hay Tweeddale, asked Edouard Suenson to come to London together with Colonel Spalding. Suenson did not wish to meet with Spalding, however, and he replied that at the present time it was difficult for him to leave Copenhagen because of the company's business. He recommended that he come to London after Spalding's visit so that Eastern would have had an opportunity to clarify its attitude toward the American before Suenson arrived, and the two companies would be able to discuss their future policy on this basis.[17]

Lord Tweeddale followed this Danish advice with the result that at a meeting in early January 1897, Colonel Spalding succeeded in convincing F. C. Hesse to continue the fight against James Scrymser in the American Congress. Lord Tweeddale was more doubtful and "urgently" requested that Suenson come to London, as Eastern's board of directors was unable to reach a decision.[18]

Therefore, on January 14, Suenson arrived in London where, during a three-hour meeting with Lord Tweeddale and F. C. Hesse, he succeeded in winning over the chairman of the board to his point of view despite the fact that Hesse argued against him. When Eastern's board of directors met shortly thereafter, Suenson was called in to present his views after just ten minutes.

It was very unusual for Edouard Suenson to be invited to join a meeting of the board of directors of one of the world's largest companies because that board was unable to make a decision. The wavering attitude of Eastern's board of directors could probably be attributed to the fact that John Pender had died the previous year, and therefore, the board lacked a leading figure with the authority and forcefulness to drive a decision. In any event, Suenson succeeded in securing the British board's unanimous backing for his proposal that the two companies should seek an approach to Scrymser and that it would be left to Suenson to make contact "privately and solely on behalf of Great Northern."[19]

With this, Spalding had been parked on a side track, and immediately after the meeting of Eastern's board of directors, Suenson sought out Baron Everard Hambro, the son of the founder of Hambros Bank, which had been Great Northern's British bank ever since the company had been found-

At an early stage, Great Northern began production of telegraphy apparatuses in a mechanical workshop that was located on the top floor of the company's building on Kongens Nytorv from June 1878 onward. The apparatuses were manufactured both for the company's own use and for sale to other companies. The photograph shows Great Northern's stand at an exhibition in Stockholm in 1897. In the background, one can see the company's telegraph connections drawn on a map that covers two walls.

ed. The baron did not know James Scrymser, but he knew his business partner, the American financier J. P. Morgan, to whom he sent a warm recommendation of Edouard Suenson with a request that Scrymser be confidentially informed that he should expect to be contacted by the Dane regarding possible cooperation.[20]

James Scrymser sent a quick and accommodating reply by telegram, and immediately following his return to Copenhagen, Suenson sent Scrymser a letter in which he referred to Scrymser's earlier telegram and declared that he was ready to meet with

Scrymser at any time in Copenhagen or London but was not able to come to New York.[21]

Scrymser replied that he was not able to travel to Europe because of the debate in the Congress regarding the American concession. He stated that he had sent his telegram of February 1896 because he had been interested in possible cooperation in the context of a Pacific coalition but had been surprised by Spalding's mobilization in the Congress. He believed Eastern was behind Spalding, and he enclosed a number of documents as proof of this and did nothing to conceal his strong antipathy toward the English company.[22]

The reason for Scrymser's hostile attitude to Eastern was that starting in the 1870s, Scrymser and John Pender had fought a veritable telegraph war over the laying of telegraph cables along the coasts of Central and South American and in the Caribbean with connections to the United States and Europe via the Atlantic. This was not the best starting point for Suenson, as the purpose of his approach to Scrymser was precisely to create an alliance of all three companies. Nevertheless, he had established the desired contact, and there was no other way to go but forward.

Dano-American-English alliance

On February 18, 1897, Edouard Suenson sent a lengthy letter to James Scrymser containing "a rough sketch" of his thoughts about a global coalition. This sketch closely followed the scheme he had presented to Eastern's board of directors but was laid out as a cooperation only between Great Northern and Pacific Cable Company.[23]

However, Suenson succeeded in involving Eastern after having noted that Great Northern, like Scrymser, had had hard and long struggles against Eastern and that he therefore thought he could understand "the bitter feelings" that James Scrymser felt toward the English telegraph imperium. In the end, though, Great Northern and Eastern had succeeded in reaching agreement regarding cooperation, and Suenson was "very reluctant" to begin new competition with such a powerful company.

On the other hand—and here came Suenson's implicit suggestion that Eastern should be brought into the coalition—Great Northern's agreements with Eastern gave the Danish company "significant influence on the final arrangement under which the Eastern companies would participate in a Pacific coalition."[24]

James Scrymser did not reject Suenson's basic premises and found it particularly attractive that the planned Pacific company was to work under the American flag and jurisdiction. However, he was not accommodating when it came to his relationship with Eastern, with whom he firmly refused to cooperate.

There was an opening, however, when Scrymser recommended that Suenson meet with J. P. Morgan, who would come to London in May. J. P. Morgan had a close personal relationship with Lord Tweeddale and was to speak with Tweeddale informally regarding the plans for a Pacific cable. Scrymser had already brought J. P. Morgan up-to-date and in strictest confidence shown him the letter from Suenson, who declared that he was prepared to meet with the American financier.

In the middle of May, Edouard Suenson was again in London, where he met with J. P. Morgan, whose role in the Pacific project was purely financial. Probably for that reason, the American had a positive attitude toward involving Eastern in the coalition, partly because, as Suenson believed, it would make it easier to raise funds in Europe. The question was whether Scrymser was in agreement, but after he returned to the United States, Morgan succeeded in persuading Scrymser to participate.[25]

In the middle of June, Edouard Suenson therefore received a letter from Edmund Baylies, vice president of the Pacific Cable Company and the Mexican Telegraph Company, who was to begin negotiations with Eastern in London after having been authorized to do so by a telegram from Scrymser. Baylies requested that Suenson come to London in early July to participate.[26]

Suenson arrived on July 6, 1897, met with Lord Tweeddale and F. C. Hesse on the same day, and presented a basis for negotiations for which he se-

Electricians required particular knowledge to be able to work with telegraphy. Great Northern, therefore, created its own eight-week courses for electricians. The picture shows participants in the course that was offered in November and December 1896.

cured support. The following day, he met with Edmund Baylies, who, after eight hours of negotiations, agreed to accept the basis for negotiations Suenson had presented. Afterward, Baylies and Suenson drafted a telegram to James Scrymser recommending that he proceed with the project.[27]

Both Lord Tweeddale and F. C. Hesse were satisfied, and a meeting of representatives of all involved companies was scheduled for July 9, but the evening before that day F. C. Hesse came running over to Great Northern's offices and asked Suenson to postpone the common meeting, as it was "impossible" for Eastern's board of directors to accept the proposal. Eastern's main complaint was that in accordance with the wishes of the Americans, the proposal included a plan for a cable from Hawaii to Australia that Eastern insisted on establishing and operating itself.

This caused Suenson to threaten to abandon the whole project before, "after a heated discussion," he succeeded in obtaining support for a compromise proposal according to which the laying of the Australian cable would be postponed for five years. This would mean that in the meantime, Eastern could profit from its cables between Australia and Europe while a solution to the problem was found.

The postponed common meeting would be held on July 10, 1897, with Suenson previously having gotten Edmund Baylies to accept Eastern's point of view and new modification of the agreement. After a few days of negotiations, the parties prepared a heads of agreement document that Scrymser and Baylies intended to use as a basis for the drafting of a final agreement among the three companies.

A long series of further meetings followed before the three parties finalized four agreements late in the year, which are as follows: Each of the participating companies was to provide one-third of share capital totaling 8.5 million US dollars to establish a company that would lay and operate the cables. The new company would lay cables between San Francisco and Hawaii and from there to Japan and after five years to Australia. A specific agreement was to be reached regarding the regulation of all telegram fees, and this agreement was to take into consideration the interests of Great Northern and Eastern. Each of the participating companies was to appoint three members of the new company's board of directors, and the new company's establishment and activity were dependent upon the receipt of American and Hawaiian economic subsidies.[28]

The agreements were signed by James Scrymser on January 3, 1898, and then sent to Europe to be signed by the representatives of Eastern and Great Northern. Four days later, the proposed legislation was presented in both chambers of the American Congress with regard to granting the Pacific Cable Company a concession for the establishment and operation of a cable connection between San Francisco, Hawaii, and Japan, but before the proposal could be discussed, the political situation in the Pacific region changed dramatically when the United States went to war.

American colonies and interests in the Pacific Ocean

Of the once so mighty Spanish colonial empire in North, Central, and South America, only Cuba and Puerto Rico in the Caribbean remained. A growing independence movement was supported by the United States, and after a revolt broke out in 1895, many Americans were in favor of military intervention. The American government did offer to mediate in the conflict, but this offer was rejected by the Spanish government.

In January 1898, to protect American citizens and interests, the American warship *USS Maine* sailed to Cuba, dropping anchor in Havana Harbor. On February 15, the ship exploded here for unknown reasons, killing 250 American crew members and soldiers. Not many in the United States

doubted that Spain had been behind the explosion. The relationship between the two countries deteriorated, and on April 21, 1898, the American navy blockaded Cuba, making war a reality.

The Pacific Ocean too became a theater of war. The Philippines were still a Spanish colony, and on May 1, 1898, an American naval force sailed into the harbor of Manila, the capital city, and defeated the Spanish fleet there. In July, the last Spanish resistance was overcome, and on December 10, 1898, a peace treaty was signed according to which Cuba became an independent nation, while Puerto Rico was annexed by the United States. In the Pacific, the Philippines too became an American colony, as did the little island of Guam, which had a deepwater harbor and abundant supplies of freshwater, while the United States had annexed Hawaii already in August.

The war and its consequences caused Edouard Suenson to propose that the coalition change the whole Pacific project so that it was oriented toward the United States' new territories. The main line would be a cable connection from San Francisco to the Philippines via Hawaii and Guam, while the connections to Japan and Australia would be sidelines. Scrymser and Eastern backed this proposal, and when a new proposal for an American concession was presented to the two houses of Congress in January 1899, the proposal had been changed so that it followed Edouard Suenson's plan, for which there appeared to be political support.[29]

In a speech to the American Congress on February 10, 1899, the American president, William McKinley, declared that a cable between the United States and its newly won territories was an "urgent necessity." The current situation in which the telegraphic connection between the United States and the Philippines went via the Atlantic and several other nations and the connection between the United States on the one hand and Hawaii and Guam on the other hand was only provided by ship traffic "[could] not be permitted to continue a moment longer than absolutely necessary," the president told the members of Congress who were to discuss and decide upon the proposals for a Pacific cable that had been presented.[30]

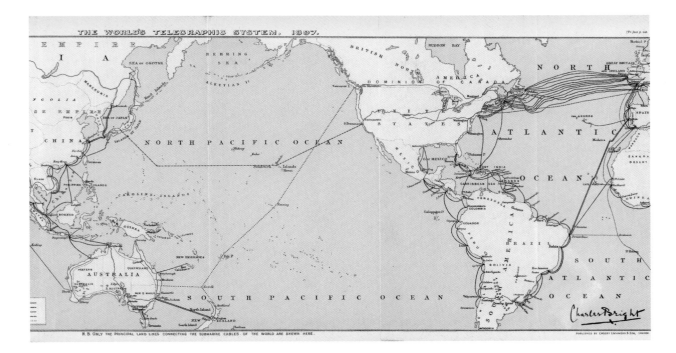

THE WORLD'S TELEGRAPHIC SYSTEM, 1897.

N. B. ONLY THE PRINCIPAL LAND LINES CONNECTING THE SUBMARINE CABLES OF THE WORLD ARE SHEWN HERE.

Map from 1898 of the international telegraph connections in East Asia and in the Atlantic and Pacific regions. While there is a dense group of transatlantic cables connecting North America and Europe, no cables have yet been laid across the Pacific Ocean. The two dotted lines respectively represent the planned American Pacific cable from California to Japan via Hawaii and the planned British government cable from Australia to Canada. Both cable projects were realized in the early twentieth century; the route of the American Pacific cable was altered, and Great Northern participated in laying it.

This speech did not have much effect, however. When the Congress finished its work in March 1899 and took a break until December, no decision concerning the cable matter had been made. The Congress did not reach a decision in 1900 or 1901, either, despite the fact that President McKinley repeated his message both in December 1899 and in December 1900 in his respective state of the nation addresses.

The reason for the lack of progress was that the American Congress was deeply divided on the issue of whether the Pacific cable should be private or—as an innovation—government-owned. The proponents of a government-owned cable argued on the basis of the fact that given the American annexa-

tions of Hawaii, Guam, and the Philippines, the Pacific cable would no longer be an international cable but rather a domestic cable, the operation of which, for strategic and security reasons, could not be left to a private company.

Reactions in Copenhagen to the repeated delays were calm. "Great Northern has no reason to be disappointed by the fact that the realization of the Pacific cable has again been delayed a year," Edouard Suenson wrote in his report to the board of directors after the Congress, in the spring of 1900, had again ended its session without having made a decision. As long as the Congress was unable to decide, the company could continue its activities in East Asia as it had up to this point, and Great Northern would avoid making the major investments a Pacific cable would demand.[31]

At Eastern, however, there was growing frustration over the dead calm in which the Pacific project had ended up, and finally the Britons lost patience. When James Scrymser's right-hand man, Edmund Baylies, announced that he would be coming to London during the last half of July 1901, Edouard Suenson and Eastern's top management therefore agreed that the time had come for "a friendly dissolution of the agreements that would give all of the parties free hands to conclude new agreements." However, the American declared that a dissolution of the coalition would require the unanimous consent of all parties. Eastern wanted to get out as soon as possible, while Suenson—according to his own report—maintained a low profile.[32]

When, after he had returned to the United States, Baylies sent a notice in writing that his view of the matter remained unchanged. Eastern sent a telegram indicating that the company considered all agreements terminated. Eight days later, on August 28, a message arrived from New York to the effect that the board of directors of the Pacific Cable Company declared that it was in agreement with Eastern and that all agreements had been annulled. There was no explanation.

Shortly thereafter, Great Northern received a transfer from Edmund Baylies of 323 pounds sterling, 19 shillings, and 3 pence, which constituted the remainder of the 8,500 pounds the company had paid as a deposit for the Hawaii concession and to cover expenses incurred. Suenson summed up the situation with the words "with this, our cooperation with Scrymser has been formally terminated as well." Suenson continued:

"That cooperation started in January 1897, and while it has cost us a not inconsiderable amount of money and an extraordinary amount of work, this money and work cannot be said to have been wasted, for the companies have thus succeeded in delaying the establishment of the Pacific cable for a further five or six years."[33]

The Commercial Pacific Cable Company

It was only now that Edouard Suenson learned that Eastern's eagerness to get out of its cooperation with Scrymser was because Eastern had a conflicting engagement as the British parliament had approved the laying of a government-owned cable between Australia and Canada. The Britons were in a hurry, and their new partner was the American Commercial Cable Company, which operated three Atlantic cables, and whose leader, John William Mackay, was also operating a nationwide American telegraph network via the Postal Telegraph Company.

In the middle of August 1901, already before he had received notice of Scrymser's acceptance of the termination of the agreements, Suenson received from Eastern the draft of an agreement regarding the immediate laying of a cable from San Francisco to the Philippines via Hawaii and Guam—without any economic subsidy from any government. This agreement had been worked out in detail between Eastern and the Commercial Cable Company, leaving room for the insertion of Great Northern's name.[34]

Around this time, Suenson received a telegram from the chairman of Eastern's board of directors, Lord Tweeddale, who, as Suenson put it, quite cold-bloodedly declared that Eastern had now decided to lay the cable in question. The company hoped that Great Northern would cooperate and accept the agreement without having an opportunity to negotiate in this regard.[35]

According to the agreement, the four companies—Eastern and Eastern Extension being treated as two independent companies—would each contribute one-fourth of the share capital of a maximum of 10 million US dollars to a new company named the Commercial Pacific Cable Company, which would lay the cable. The agreement would be signed by the other three companies on October 16, 1901, but this would not be required of Great Northern, for whom the door would be kept open for a year.

The previously so-wavering British board of directors had acted with decisiveness. Eastern's message was "take it or leave it," and Suenson clearly did not care for this approach, though he did find the agreement "quite advantageous for Great Northern," and he recognized the offer as an expression of Eastern's desire to involve Great Northern. Nevertheless, he made a formal protest to Eastern against the Britons' way of proceeding, which he found to be at odds with the two companies' agreements and with the spirit of cooperation that otherwise characterized their relationship.[36]

However, developments regarding the Pacific cable were unstoppable. On August 22, 1901, John Mackay presented the American Congress with an offer to lay the cable without receiving government subsidies and also promised to lower rates for telegrams between San Francisco and Honolulu by 60 percent. Just eleven days later, he established the Commercial Pacific Cable Company to build and operate the system—without informing the Congress of his ownership.[37]

John Mackay based his actions on the American telegraph law of 1866, according to which any American company had the right to "establish and operate telegraph lines throughout the whole territory of the United States as well as under and over the United States' navigable waterways." According to Mackay, with the annexation of Hawaii, Guam, and the Philippines, the Pacific Ocean had become an American navigable waterway, and he was supported by the American attorney general who issued a response indicating that every American company had the right to land cables in the United States and its territories. Armed with the attorney general's memorandum, Mackay went into action, immediately ordering a cable from England to be laid between San Francisco and Hawaii within the following ten months.[38]

The battle in the Congress was not yet over, however; the choice was now between Mackay's project and a government cable that was finally rejected by a large majority in June 1902. As Suenson put it, the question of Great Northern's participation was "now burning and *must* be resolved before long," as the company had been given until the middle of October to decide.[39]

Great Northern did not succeed in reaching a decision before the deadline expired. It was only after Eastern's entire top management team had been in Denmark in late September and after sometimes hectic telegraphic communication between the two companies' leaders that, on November 1, 1902, Edouard Suenson concluded the negotiations and led the company into the Pacific coalition.[40]

Around this time, the American Congress passed a law allowing the Commercial Pacific Cable Compa-

John W. Mackay was one of the great figures in American telegraphy both at sea and on land. Among other roles, he was the leader of Commercial Pacific, which became the American telegraph company with which Great Northern and the British Eastern companies cooperated in connection with the laying of the American Pacific cable.

ny to establish the cable connection from San Francisco to the Philippines via Hawaii and Guam. According to the conditions established by the permit, the American company was forbidden to cooperate

Preparation for the landing of the American Pacific cable on Midway Atoll in the spring of 1903. The cable was fed over onto the pontoon from the cable ship, which was subsequently towed toward the coast while the cable was laid out and finally pulled ashore. The atoll was uninhabited when the cable was landed, and the Commercial Pacific Cable Company's team, therefore, became the first permanent residents; they constituted the foundation for the establishment of a new community called Cable City.

with companies that blocked the landing of American cables in China and to enter into agreements with any other company or companies regarding the regulation of prices. Also, the company was not permitted to cooperate with other companies to extend the connection to China but should do this alone if it wished to do so.

These were the conditions which were more than difficult to comply, given that Great Northern and Eastern were to be not only business partners but shareholders in the Commercial Pacific. Also, the American antitrust legislation forbade the participation of companies with monopolistic concessions, which constituted the entire foundation of Great

Northern's existence both in East Asia and in Northern Europe.

Therefore, the ownership of Commercial Pacific was carefully concealed from the American authorities, in part by means of the insertion of—as Edouard Suenson put it—American "straw men" into the boards of directors of the European companies. In late 1904 a final board of directors was constituted in which Great Northern was represented by the Danish-born David Dessau, who was part-owner of the trading company Melchior, Armstrong, and Dessau in New York, and, on David Dessau's recommendation, by the attorney Stephen Williams.[41]

The share capital of 10 million US dollars was distributed such that one-fourth went to each of the four companies, which gave the two European companies a solid majority. It was not until 1905 that the last internal agreements for the American-English-Danish consortium were concluded, and these agreements were worded so as to prevent the two European companies from abusing their share majority.

Eastern's and Great Northern's shareholders were not given insight into the distribution of the share capital or of the two companies' involvement with the American Pacific cable, which would be both the first and the only telegraph cable from the United States under the Pacific Ocean. Already in 1898, and precisely so that they would be able to keep secret the company's possible future involvement in such a project, Great Northern's board of directors had secured approval of a change to the company's articles so they would not need to in-

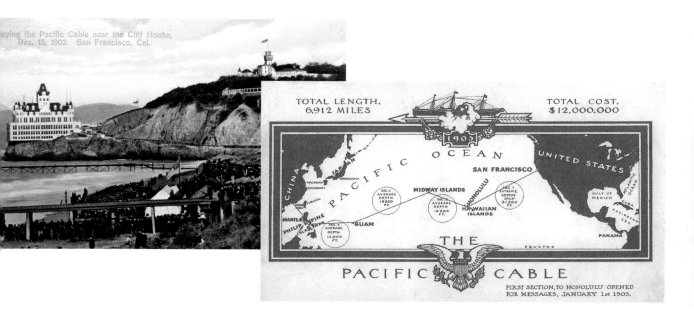

aying the Pacific Cable near the Cliff House, Dec. 13, 1902. San Francisco, Cal.

TOTAL LENGTH, 6,912 MILES

TOTAL COST, $12,000,000

THE PACIFIC CABLE

FIRST SECTION, TO HONOLULU OPENED FOR MESSAGES, JANUARY 1st 1903.

form the shareholders if they chose to participate in a Pacific project. This had been done by adding supplemental wording to the effect that in addition to engaging in telegraph or telephone business, the company's purpose was "participation in other projects with the same goal." According to what Edouard Suenson claimed at an extraordinary general meeting, the purpose of this addition was to give the board of directors "free hands to continue the development of the company."[42]

The Pacific cable between San Francisco and Hawaii was laid in December 1902 and could be opened to public traffic on January 1, 1903. This was not the first transpacific cable, as the British government cable between Australia and Canada via Fiji and Tabuaeran had opened on December 8, 1902.

After the laying of the cable between Hawaii and the Philippines via Guam and Midway, the connection between San Francisco and Manila could open to traffic on the United States' Independence Day, July 4, 1903. The first individual to send a telegram using this connection was the American president, Theodore Roosevelt, who wished "a happy Independence Day to the US, its territories and properties." The telegram took nine minutes to travel around the world.

Left: Postcard commemorating the landing of the American Pacific cable. On the cliff in the background, one can see the luxurious and legendary hotel Cliff House.

Right: American postcard showing the route of the Pacific cable from California to Manila in the Philippines. The average sea depth for the various sections of the cable is given in feet; for the section between California and Hawaii, it is specified that the cable was laid at depths all the way down to 31,500 feet, or nearly 10 kilometers. The opening of the cable made it possible to communicate with China and Japan by telegraph from the United States without having to send telegrams via Europe.

At Great Northern's general meeting in April 1903, Edouard Suenson called the American Pacific cable "very serious competition." Without referring to the company's involvement in the Commercial Pacific Cable Company, however, he indicated that Great Northern's leaders had reached "a preliminary understanding" with the American company, which "[had] required significant sacrifices from [Great Northern] but would protect [Great Northern] against ruthless competition that would be ruinous for both sides." He could not tell the truth about Great Northern's involvement with the American cable, so he rewrote history a little. The American cable would indeed cost Great Northern revenues, but to a modest extent.[43]

The Russo-Japanese War and Revolutions in Russia and China

CHAPTER 9

The Boxer Rebellion in China

The Japanese cable to Taiwan and the American Pacific cable were visible indications that the power relationships in East Asia and the entire Pacific region were shifting and that Japan and the United States were stepping into the roles of new major powers in the region. These two major powers were not alone in having territorial and geopolitical ambitions, however, and Great Northern had to confront the fact that more and more nations were planning to lay cables in the region.

The defeat by Japan had exposed China's weakness, which several major European powers did not hesitate to exploit. In his report to the board of directors for December 1897, Edouard Suenson noted that Germany had just annexed the Qingdao area and the adjacent bay, while Russia had annexed Port Arthur and the Liadong peninsula, which Russia had prevented Japan from annexing just two years earlier. In both cases, the purpose had been to acquire bases for the two major powers' respective navies.[1]

The Chinese government had no choice but to conclude long-term leasing agreements, and it was unable to prevent the United Kingdom from occupying the Weihai Peninsula near the mouth of the bay adjacent to Tianjin as well as another area on the Chinese mainland, at Jiulong across from the crown colony of Hong Kong. France also did not hold back in the spring of 1898, forcing China to conclude an agreement to lease the Guangzhou region, in southern China, to France for ninety-nine years. The governments of Belgium and Italy declared that they too, as Edouard Suenson put it, wanted to "share in the Chinese booty." China's territory had become a buffet at which the Western powers helped themselves, and in an internal note to the board of directors, Suenson referred to China as "this plucked and mighty country that only continues to exist thanks to the rivalries among the looters."[2]

The Siberian town of Kyakhta, south of Lake Baikal, became an important telegraph nexus when a telegraph line connecting the town with Beijing via the Gobi Desert and northern China opened at the beginning of 1900. The trans-Siberian connection from Europe to Vladivostok also passed through the city, in which a Great Northern station was established.

Among the 40,000 allied soldiers who were deployed during the Boxer Rebellion to put down the uprising and rescue the besieged foreigners and Christians in Beijing were a large force of Japanese soldiers. The picture shows a Japanese barricade in the international settlement in Tianjin.

While the Chinese government gave in again and again, the resistance of the Chinese populace to foreign incursions increased, and in May 1900, the so-called Boxer Rebellion broke out. Christians—both foreigners and Chinese—were attacked and murdered, railways were destroyed, churches were burned down, and there was extensive looting. The Boxers forced their way into Beijing and, together with imperial Chinese troops, laid siege to the embassy district, where 473 foreigners and around 3,000 Chinese Christians were protected by just over four hundred soldiers. The quarter lay in the Tatar city, which was protected by high walls,

but its defenders would not be able to hold out in the long run, and telegraphic appeals for help were sent to the Western powers.

The rebellion caused the major European powers as well as the United States and Japan to intervene militarily, and large naval forces were quickly assembled in the bay adjacent to Tianjin. The Taku Forts, at the mouth of the Hai River, were occupied on June 18, and a week later, Western military forces entered Tianjin, after which they moved north to come to the assistance of the besieged foreigners and Christians in Beijing. This caused the Chinese empress dowager to back the demand that all foreigners be expelled from China, and on June 20, the German envoy was murdered while he was on his way to the Chinese foreign ministry in Beijing.

A total of approximately 45,000 soldiers participated in the so-called eight-nation alliance consisting of the United Kingdom, Germany, France, Italy,

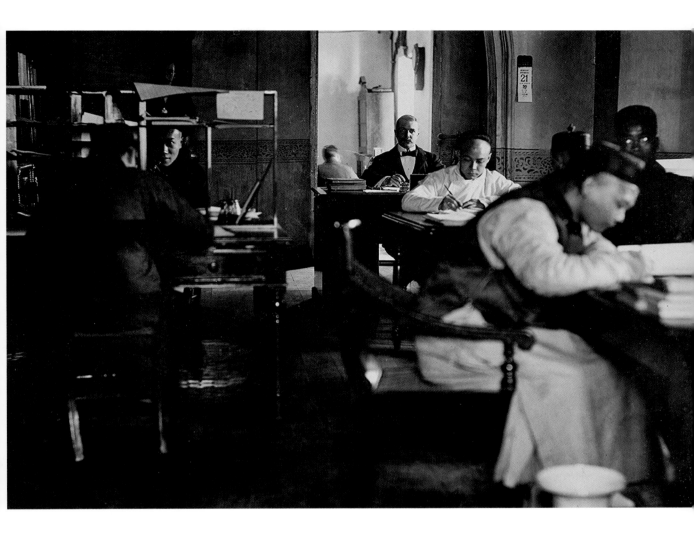

Austria-Hungary, Belgium, Japan, and the United States that took military action to put down the rebellion. Nevertheless, almost two months passed before, in the middle of August 1900, allied forces succeeded in rescuing the Western diplomats and other foreigners and Christians who had been trapped in Beijing, which was now occupied by the allied Western powers.

Great Northern and Eastern quickly became involved in the Western mission because the Chinese rebels responded to the Western powers' occupation of the Taku Forts by cutting telegraph connections throughout the region so the Western forces would be without the ability to communicate with their governments telegraphically. Great Northern and Eastern arranged for a small steamship to sail

The interior of Great Northern's first station in Yantai, which was opened in the offices of the French diplomatic mission. The station operated the cable connecting Shanghai, Yantai, and Taku that had been put in place as a result of the Boxer Rebellion in 1900.

daily between Taku and Yantai, from where there was a landline to Shanghai. However, service at the Yantai station was slow and undependable, and despite the fact that Great Northern sent one Danish and one Chinese telegraphist up from Shanghai to lead the work, the capacity and the stability of the connection were both completely inadequate.[3]

Great Northern did have large supplies of reserve cable in Wusong, though, and Eastern had an even greater amount of cable in Singapore. The two companies offered the allied powers the establish-

The cable house at Taku where the cable from Shanghai and Yantai was landed during the Boxer Rebellion in 1900. In the building, the cable was connected to the Chinese landline and brought up to the telegraph pole to connect it with Tianjin and Beijing.

ment of a cable connection between Taku, Yantai, and Shanghai that could also be used by the public, and the companies also offered strategic lines for the major powers from Yantai to their territories of Port Arthur, Weihai, and Qingdao.

This offer was accepted, and Great Northern's cable ship, *Store Nordiske*, subsequently laid a cable between Taku and Yantai that opened on August 22, 1900. After this, the cables were laid from Taku to Port Arthur and Weihai respectively, and when Eastern's cable ship arrived a short time later with a cargo of cables, new cables were laid between Yantai and Shanghai and between Yantai and the German territory of Qingdao. The allied forces also established a landline from Taku to Beijing.

Peace negotiations were initiated in late September 1900, but they dragged on, and it was only on September 7, 1901, that a peace treaty was signed. It was both expensive and humiliating for

China, which was forced to pay 333 million US dollars in war reparations. The Taku Forts, which had been built to protect Tianjin and Beijing, were to be closed, and the victorious powers were given permission to station troops in the embassy quarter and at selected sites in Beijing permanently.

New cables and landlines in China

Long before the peace treaty was signed, Great Northern was in the process of adapting to the new power relationships not only in China but also in the rest of the region. At Great Northern's general meeting in April 1901, Edouard Suenson referred to the company's and Eastern's laying of cable and efforts during the Boxer Rebellion as common efforts for "this matter of the public good," helping the allied forces rescue the people trapped in Beijing. What he did not tell the assembled shareholders—and what the allied forces were never told either—was that a part of these efforts had been initiated at the request of the head of the Chinese telegraph administration, Sheng Xuanhuai, who had heard in the summer of 1900 that the British government had plans to lay a cable between Taku and Yantai.

The prospect of a British government cable did not appeal to Sheng Xuanhuai, who turned to Great Northern's leadership in Shanghai with a proposal for the laying of a cable between Taku, Yantai, and Shanghai at Chinese expense so the cable would become Chinese property and be open to public traffic after the war had ended. Together with Eastern, Great Northern would finance the construction costs as a loan to the Chinese that would be paid back over the next twenty-five to thirty years, during which the cable would be operated by the companies. The companies had long wished to lay a cable between Shanghai and Yantai and up to Taku, and, like Sheng Xuanhuai, they were not eager to see a British government cable laid. Their attitude toward Sheng Xuanhuai's proposal was therefore positive, and already on August 16, 1900, an agreement could be signed that paved the way for the laying of the cable. In contrast, the major powers' strategic cables were financed by the major powers themselves and reserved for military use.[4]

During the negotiations in Shanghai, it proved to be possible to pressure Sheng Xuanhuai into agreeing, as compensation for Great Northern's laying of the cable, to let the company service international traffic on the landline between Taku, Tianjin, and Beijing, which had just been opened.

Around this time, the company also initiated negotiations with Russia with regard to operating the land connection between Kyakhta in Russia and Nystad in Finland, where the company's cables to Sweden had been landed. This would give Great Northern a new, land-based telegraph connection between East Asia and Europe that would add an alternative line to, and thus take pressure off, the cables between Vladivostok and Shanghai. In late August 1900, when Russia's minister of finance and future prime minister Count Sergei Witte was in Copenhagen for twenty-four hours, Edouard Suenson succeeded in arranging a meeting with Count Witte at which he brought the matter up. Count Witte "declared that he was in agreement with everything" and promised to use his influence in the Russian government.[5]

In late October 1900, the Chinese signed a contract that in addition to containing the agreement regarding the Shanghai-Yantai-Taku cable accommodated Great Northern's desire to operate the connection between Taku and Kyakhta, what remained was now to conclude a corresponding agreement with Russia.[6]

The contract also established the conditions under which Great Northern and Eastern would reestablish the destroyed Chinese landlines and operate them with European personnel until a peace treaty between China and the allies had been signed. In addition to the establishment of manned stations in Yantai, Taku, and Tianjin, the agreement led to the establishment of a Danish manned telegraph station in Beijing that opened on January 26, 1901.[7]

The Chinese themselves had opened the first telegraph station within Beijing's city walls in late March of the previous year, and this station was now taken over by Great Northern. Later in the spring, the station was moved to a complex of ten buildings of various sizes in the embassy quarter, where the establishment of a European business area was planned. The complex of buildings and the station were paid for and owned by the Chinese telegraph administration, which was kept secret so this station appeared to be a purely Danish station, the reason for this being concerns regarding the attitudes of embassy personnel and foreign residents who did not trust the Chinese. The same precaution was taken in connection with the newly opened telegraph line between Taku, Tianjin, and Beijing; the companies agreed to turn the operation of the line over to the Chinese administration when conditions had returned to normal.[8]

World politics and world telegraphy

Following the Spanish-American War, the Boxer Rebellion too had demonstrated the importance of telegraph connections in modern warfare, as did the Boer War, a conflict in South Africa between the British empire and two Boer republics, Transvaal and the Orange Free State, that took place at the same time as the Boxer Rebellion. At Great Northern's gen-

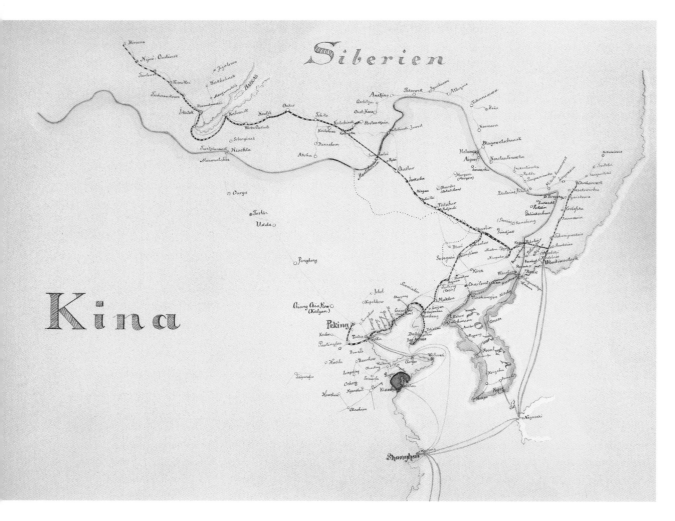

Map from 1901 of the area around Beijing, Korea, and the Yellow Sea. The thick red lines indicate Great Northern's cables connecting Vladivostok, Nagasaki, and Shanghai, while the thin red lines in the bay between Korea and China represent cables the company helped lay during the Boxer Rebellion to support the Western forces' military action.

eral meeting in April 1900, Edouard Suenson spoke of how the colonial powers' division of Africa, the ongoing dismemberment of China, the United States' annexation of Hawaii and the Philippines, and Japan's rise as a major regional power would affect the position and development of telegraphy:

"All of these rapid transformations, developments, and shifts of spheres of interest and of the center of gravity of the world society have necessar-ily opened the eyes of the great nations to the huge importance of the possession and exploitation of global means of communication in the struggle for political and commercial dominance."[9]

As a consequence, major powers such as France and Germany had built up a cable industry and established cable companies to break the British monopoly, which had previously only been seriously challenged by Great Northern and some American companies. The result would be increased competition based on both political and commercial factors, which would require Great Northern to make appropriate major changes to its operations and would require appropriately energetic responses from its leaders if the company was to survive future developments.

The company was already feeling the effects of the new trend, though Suenson did not specify in what way. Having annexed the Qingdao region of China, Germany wished to lay a cable from Qingdao to Shanghai, while France wished to lay a cable from Huê in French Indochina to Xiamen. Given its Chinese monopoly, Great Northern could deny both major powers permission to land their cables, but Suenson soberly reasoned that the company's position was not so strong "that [Great Northern] should dare to subject [itself] to a test of strength by opposing the planned *French and German telegraph invasion of China*."[10]

Germany had become a colonial power in Asia with the establishment of German New Guinea in 1885, which had been followed by the annexation of two groups of islands, the Carolines and the Marianas in the Philippines, as well as several small groups of islands in the Pacific after the Spanish-American War. The first German cable in the region was laid during the Boxer Rebellion between Qingdao and Shanghai, with the participation of the Danish cable ship *Store Nordiske*, which was also to carry out maintenance work on the cable in the future. It was to be anticipated that the German government would wish to lay further cables between its Asian colonies and create its own regional network connected to Germany, which already had its own Atlantic cable via the Azores.[11]

In contrast to Germany, France was an established colonial power in Indochina that wished to free itself from the British cables. There was already a French cable connection to the motherland, and a cable from Vietnam to Xiamen could therefore become a problematic competitor to both the Danish and the British cables. It therefore took many long negotiations regarding traffic and prices to reach agreement on the landing of a French cable at Xiamen in April 1901.[12]

Pacific telegraph cartel

Another established colonial power in the region was the Netherlands, which, like Germany, did not have an independent cable connection from the mother country to its colony, which in the case of the Netherlands was Dutch East India. In January 1901, the Dutch ambassador to Denmark therefore visited Edouard Suenson on Kongens Nytorv to ask about the possibility of establishing a connection between Dutch East India and the Dano-Russian system in order for the Dutch to be able to send telegrams that circumvented the British cables.[13]

The ambassador did not get a clear answer, as Suenson did not want to go behind Eastern's back, but around this time, German newspapers published reports of beginning cable cooperation between the Netherlands and Germany. By the summer of 1902, the plans had proceeded to the point where the two countries concluded a treaty regarding the establishment of a common cable connection between their Asian colonies and the American Pacific cable, in which the attachment point was intended to be the island of Guam. They also wanted to lay a cable from the Carolines to Shanghai, where they planned to connect to the Danish line through Russia. The purpose was to avoid the British cables, and in the fall of 1902, unaware of Great Northern's and Eastern's part-ownership of the American company, the two governments initiated negotiations not only with Commercial Pacific but also with Great Northern. The Danish company thus sat on two different chairs during the negotiations while also representing Eastern's interests without the knowledge of the Dutch and the Germans.

After negotiations that went on throughout all of 1903 and the spring of 1904 and took place at meetings in Paris, Hamburg, Cologne, Copenhagen, London, and Berlin, agreement was reached after Great Northern had secured the permission of the Chinese to land a German-Dutch cable at Shanghai. The reason for the very lengthy negotiations had been that the German-Dutch project would affect the Danish-British-American Pacific coalition and thus the traffic and price structure for the entire region and for the connections to the United States and to Europe. The main problem had been finding a way to avoid destructive competition, but this problem had ultimately been solved.

On July 26, 1904, no fewer than seventeen contracts had been signed by parties including Eastern, Great Northern, Commercial Pacific, the German-Dutch consortium, the Chinese and Russian telegraphy administrations—Great Northern signing on behalf of the Chinese—as well as the Commercial Cable Company, which operated a connection through the United States to Europe via the Atlantic, and The Indo-European Telegraph Company, which operated a connection between India and Great Britain via Persia, Russia, and Turkey. To lay the German-Dutch cables, the two governments established the government-owned Deutsche-Nederländische Telegraphengesellschaft, via participation of the two states, like Russia and China, in the complex of contracts. The two Dutch-German cables respectively to Guam and Shanghai were opened in the fall of 1905.[14]

The contract created a telegraphy cartel including both private and government interests that, via a complex of contracts regarding the distribution of traffic and the setting of prices and a joint purse, regulated the telegram traffic of the entire East Asian and Pacific region with the exception of the British government cable between Australia and Canada. In 1905, Commercial Pacific's shareholders—Great Northern, Eastern, and Commercial Cable Company—entered into a set of contracts regulating their internal relationships and actions as members of the Pacific cartel.

In May, Commercial Pacific opened a new cable between Manila and Shanghai, and in 1906 the cartel adjusted the complex of contracts to the new situation. Everything was kept strictly secret from the customers and the governments that were not participating—not least the American government, as American law forbade American companies to participate in such agreements. The Danish government was not informed of the arrangement, either.

Mission to Saint Petersburg

In the spring of 1901, Great Northern and Eastern began working to secure permanent status for their stations in Taku, Tianjin, and Beijing, and in this connection the companies sought diplomatic support in the United Kingdom and Russia. At the same time, Great Northern was pursuing its own agenda of bringing about a Danish takeover of the entire connection between Taku, Tianjin, Beijing, Kyakhta, and Nystad, and Great Northern was also trying to get its Russian concessions extended until 1930 as its Chinese concessions had been.

The situation was made more difficult by the fact that, according to messages from the Russian ambassador in Copenhagen to Edouard Suenson personally and from a leading official in the Russian foreign ministry to the company's representative in Saint Petersburg, "a certain antipathy" toward the company had developed in Russian government circles. The reason for this antipathy was Eastern's participation in Great Northern's monopoly in China and the two companies' cooperation with regard to the cable project during the Boxer Rebellion and the reestablishment of the Chinese landline network, which had caused some people in the Russian capital to speak of "a merging" of the two companies.[15]

Suenson immediately sent a memorandum regarding the matter to Russia's minister of foreign affairs, Count Vladimir Lamsdorf, and in July 1901, he traveled to Saint Petersburg to straighten things out personally. He had with him his son, Kay Suenson, who was going along in his role of secretary of the board of directors. On July 4, they arrived in the Russian capital, where they were met by the company's representative, the junior chamberlain Frederik Kjær. During their stay they were also assisted by the Danish ambassador, Chamberlain Poul de Løvenørn, who got them access to ministers and other high-ranking authorities.[16]

The day after his arrival, Suenson sought out the general director of the Russian postal and telegraph service, General Petrov, who reassured Suenson by saying that there had not been antipathy toward Great Northern in the department and that Suenson's memorandum had had a positive effect, causing everyone to view the company "in the correct perspective."

Edouard Suenson subsequently visited the ministry of foreign affairs, where he had an audience

The cable ship *Pacific*, which was built for Great Northern and the Eastern companies. The ship was delivered in 1903 and sailed under the Dannebrog with Great Northern's company flag flying from its mast.

with the foreign minister, who assured him "that all antipathy had disappeared." After having gotten a better feel for the lie of the land and learned that the foreign minister's opinion would have a decisive effect, Suenson, through Poul de Løvenørn, secured an audience with Count Sergei Witte, whom he had met in Copenhagen. Nevertheless, Suenson was given a "somewhat brusque" reception, as the minister of finance believed the matter was not his responsibility but that of the minister of the interior. If that minister supported the Danish project, however, Witte would not oppose it.

The following day, there was a larger conference in the department of telegraphy, and this was followed by several days of discussions with a member of the department's staff who was to prepare a report on the matter. As usual, Suenson played the geopolitical card, this time in a raw and direct fash-

ion, detailing how Russia risked becoming dependent on the Chinese landlines and British cables "when the evidently approaching war with Japan finally broke out" if Great Northern was not granted an extension of its concession and permission to operate the Kyakhta-Nystad line.

While Suenson was waiting for the report of the postal and telegraph service to be finished, he was granted an audience on July 13 with Empress Dowager Maria Feodorovna, to whom he described the purpose of his visit to Russia, a purpose he claimed was "in the interests of Russia as well as those of the company."

The empress dowager promised to have a word with General Director Petrov, and suddenly, the processing of the matter went quickly. A top staff member in the telegraph department was summoned home from Warsaw, and shortly thereafter, at a final meeting on July 18, agreement was reached, though the approval of the general director was still required before the project could move forward—as was the approval of the government.

What the parties had been able to reach general agreement on was letting Great Northern take responsibility for the transit traffic via the Kyakhta connection; in contrast, the Russians resisted extending Great Northern's concession, but Suenson made this a precondition for the company's investment in the Kyakhta connection.

On his last day in Saint Petersburg, Edouard Suenson was admitted to an audience with Czar Nicholas II, "who proved to be so gracious and showed such great interest that [Suenson] did not hesitate warmly to argue for the company's cause," as Suenson reported to Great Northern's board of directors. According to Suenson, the Czar was "well aware" of the importance of a stable telegraph connection with East Asia and expressed concern over the possibility that Russia could become dependent upon British or Chinese lines.

This caused Suenson to argue for the importance of an extension of the concession, and he did not fail to mention that several of the Czar's ministers did not look favorably on Great Northern's desire for such an extension. The Czar responded by noting that only two of the ministers were in fact opposed, and the audience ended with "his Majesty [giving Suenson] an explicit promise that the project would be carried out, though he could not promise [Suenson] that things would be arranged as [Suenson] wished in every respect."

On the evening of the same day, July 19, 1901, Edouard Suenson left Saint Petersburg by ship, his departure having been hastened by illness. He had begun suffering from strong "nerve pains," and after he had returned to Copenhagen, he was bedridden for a month and subsequently took a twenty-month leave of absence due to illness, participating neither in board meetings nor in the general meeting in April 1902.[17]

Supported by his son, Board Secretary Kay Suenson, Edouard Suenson continued to lead the company's business activity, including the continuing negotiations with regard to the Kyakhta connection. However, he was permanently finished with the long and exhausting trips abroad, which he now left to Kay Suenson and eventually

also to the head of the company's secretariat, Per Michelsen.

Danish telegraph line through China and Mongolia to Russia

After the conclusion of the peace treaty that ended the Boxer Rebellion, it was possible to begin normalizing telegraphy operations, and in late November 1901, the Beijing-Kyakhta line, which had been interrupted during the rebellion, was reestablished. Great Northern immediately carried out its first experiments with a direct telegraph connection between Beijing and the little Mongolian border station of Altanbulag, near Kyakhta, so the company could avoid establishing a manned transfer station in the Gobi Desert. The tests went well, and, thus encouraged, the company initiated the decisive negotiations with the Russians and the Chinese with regard to taking over the international traffic for the entire line connecting Taku, Tianjin, Beijing, Irkutsk, and Nystad. This would involve the hanging of a dedicated wire intended only for transit traffic as well as Danish servicing of the transit traffic along the entire stretch through both countries.

The negotiations took a long time, and it was not until September 1902 that two groups of Danish telegraphists traveled from Copenhagen to establish a transfer station in Kyakhta and prepare for direct telegraphy between Irkutsk and Beijing.[18]

On December 1, 1902, Great Northern's and Eastern's telegraph stations in Beijing, Tianjin, and Taku were transferred to the Chinese, while the Danish company continued to service the transit traffic with Danish telegraphists, and on January 1, 1903, Great Northern opened the connection between Beijing and Irkutsk with a Danish transfer station in Kyakhta and Danish operation in Irkutsk of the connection with China, while operation of the connection from Irkutsk onward to Nystad remained Russian. The company had originally feared that the connection, operated by China and Russia, could become a competitor to the company's cables, but now, it had instead become a doubling of the cable connection and therewith a welcome strengthening of the company's network of lines.

However, the company's efforts to secure a simultaneous extension of its concessions ended without success, and no agreement with regard to Great Northern's taking over operation of the connection between Irkutsk and Nystad was immediately forthcoming. On the other hand, Great Northern did achieve another gain in the spring of 1904 when, after having worked for many years to bring this about, the company received permission to open a station within the central Russian telegraph station in Saint Petersburg. On June 1, 1904, despite resistance from the Russian telegraph administration, the station opened to service not only transit traffic but all international traffic out of and into the Russian capital. A total of thirty to forty Danish telegraphists were hired and soon had more than enough work to keep them busy.[19]

The Siberian city of Irkutsk in about 1907. The telegraph station can be glimpsed behind the horse's neck.

The Russo-Japanese War

In the summer of 1901, when Edouard Suenson warned of a war between Japan and Russia during the negotiations in Saint Petersburg, he probably showed greater foresight than he realized himself. In connection with putting down the Boxer Rebellion, Russia had occupied large parts of Manchuria from which Russian forces were not withdrawn after the peace treaty had been signed, and in Japan, the Russian troops' presence in Manchuria was viewed with concern. The two countries had long been on course for a confrontation, and finally war broke out.

During the night of February 8–9, after a failed French attempt at mediation, the Japanese navy carried out a surprise attack on Port Arthur, destroying several Russian warships and blockading the rest. A Japanese declaration of war followed two days later, and large Japanese land-based forces moved north from Korea and besieged Port Arthur while some units moved on up through Manchuria.

Immediately after the Japanese attack on Port Arthur, Russia interrupted traffic on the Danish cables between Vladivostok and Shanghai; and Nagasaki, Japan, was declared to be in a state of emergency, and Great Northern's station was occupied by soldiers, after which Japanese telegraphists controlled all traffic.[20]

Great Northern declared that it was neutral with regard to the conflict, but the cables to Vladivostok remained closed. Even without the Vladivostok cables, though, the company was able to maintain its connection from Japan and China to Europe, via

Kyakhta, and transmit Russian traffic to and from Shanghai.[21]

The outbreak of war attracted attention all over the world, including in Denmark, where, on February 12, the daily newspaper *Politiken* began publishing a supplement on the war called *Politikens Ekstra Blad*. The following year, the supplement became an independent newspaper with its own editorial staff. Everyone had expected Russia to win a quick victory over the then unknown East Asian country. In fact, the war went differently: Japanese troops gained ground quickly, and all of the Russian warships in the Far East were eventually knocked out. At the beginning of 1905, Port Arthur fell.

The Russians now trusted in their Baltic fleet, which comprised eleven battleships and a number of cruisers and other ships and had steamed away from Liepaja in October 1904 to defend Port Arthur. The fleet had to sail around the southern tip of Africa, and it did not reach the Tsushima Strait between Japan and Korea until late May 1905. On the morning of May 27, the Japanese discovered the Russian squadron and initiated history's first naval

Japanese naval forces on their way to meet the Russian squadron in the Tsushima Strait in a battle that would take place on November 27 and 28, 1904, and end with a crushing Japanese victory. A factor that contributed to the outcome was the use by the Japanese of wireless telegraphy, which made it possible for their warships to communicate with each other and with their military leadership on land.

battle between two fleets of battleships. By the next morning, practically all of the Russian ships had been sunk or captured, while the Japanese had lost only torpedo boats. In Vladivostok there was fear of a Japanese siege, and Great Northern's personnel and their families were evacuated together with other foreigners. Japanese naval and army forces captured the island of Sakhalin, and the Russian defeat was a reality.

In connection with the signing of a peace treaty in September 1905, Russia had to surrender Port Arthur and the Liaodong Peninsula as well as the southern part of Sakhalin to Japan, leave Manchuria, and recognize Korea as part of the Japanese sphere of interest. The Japanese imperium had thus won a foothold on the Asian mainland, and Japan had previously secured an important strategic possession off the coast of China with its conquest of Taiwan in 1895.

Strikes and revolts in Russia

Reports from the Far East of the retreat of the Russian army, the encirclement of Port Arthur, and the destruction of the Pacific fleet fed previously existing unrest within Russia. The spark that ignited what developed into a revolutionary movement was the firing of two workers at the Putilov metal and machine factory in Saint Petersburg in January 1905. The workers at the factory responded by going on strike, and sympathy strikes soon brought the number of strikers in the capital up to 80,000. When 200,000 of the capital's men, women, and children marched toward the Winter Palace on January 22, 1905, Czar Nicholas II was not in his residence. Waiting for the marchers instead were military units, who opened fire on the crowd with disastrous results. Bloody Sunday, as the day of the massacre was called, caused strikes, demonstrations, and local revolts to spread across Russia.

In his report to the board of directors, Edouard Suenson soberly recounted how the unrest within Russia had arisen "and blazed up in the form of serious worker uprisings of a strongly revolutionary character in Saint Petersburg, followed by similar revolts in most major cities." With the help of the military and "apparently not insignificant bloodletting," however, the unrest had been calmed, and the Czar and the government had announced reforms.[22]

News from the war against Japan fanned the flames, and after the eradication of the Russian Baltic fleet in the Tsushima Strait, Suenson, in his report to the board of directors, noted that there had been unrest among sailors in Liepaja and in the Russian Black Sea fleet. Great Northern felt the effects of the strikes when the Russian telegraph lines were repeatedly shut down and the company was therefore unable to maintain the transit traffic, which had to be sent along the British lines.[23]

The Czar promised the introduction of a parliamentary assembly, the Duma, but when its lim-

A Russian naval officer aboard the *Store Nordiske* during operations to repair cables near Vladivostok after the Russo-Japanese War (1904–1905). These operations were assisted by a Russian minesweeper.

ited powers became known an all-encompassing general strike broke out. At the same time, workers and peasants established so-called Soviets—directly elected councils—that challenged the power of the government and the Czar himself. This development culminated on October 13, 1905 with the formation of the Saint Petersburg Soviet, which presented itself as the leadership of the revolution. As Suenson put it, the general strike left the government "helpless," while the Saint Petersburg Soviet quickly grew to comprise four to five hundred members elected by around 200,000 workers from five trade unions and almost a hundred factories.

The Russian czar Nicholas II involved himself in Great Northern's affairs in Russia on several occasions, probably having been urged to do so by his mother, Dowager Empress Maria Feodorovna. A single time, in July 1901, he met with Great Northern's chief executive officer and board chairman, Edouard Suenson, and promised to take a positive view of Suenson's wish to secure an extension of the company's concessions.

The general strike also included the Russian government telegraph organization and thus the stations in Nystad, Liepaja, Saint Petersburg, Irkutsk, and Kyakhta, where the Danish telegraphists suddenly found themselves in the heart of a revolutionary movement that seemed unstoppable. During the following months, the telegraph connection through Russia was almost constantly nonfunctional, and at several stations, Danish telegraphists who attempted to service the transit traffic were threatened with negative consequences if they did not go on strike.[24]

The revolts gradually calmed, and on December 3, 1905 the Czar's police arrested all of the members of the Saint Petersburg Soviet. There were some aftershocks including serious unrest and an outright revolt in Vladivostok in January 1906, wherein it was feared in Copenhagen that Danish telegraphists and other personnel and their families, who had returned after the signing of the peace treaty between Japan and Russia, could be harmed. Ultimately, all of the Danes escaped without injury.[25]

New Dano-Russian cable and extension of the Russian concession

With the decline in revolutionary activity, it became possible to reestablish the telegraph connection all the way through Siberia as well as the Kyakhta connection to Beijing. It was also possible to resume use of the cables from Vladivostok to Nagasaki after one of the two cables had been repaired with the help of a Russian icebreaker in the middle of January 1906. The other cable could only be repaired later in the year with the assistance of Russian minesweepers.

The inspection and repair of the Vladivostok cables brought several surprises. It was revealed that both cables had been cut off the coast near Vladivostok and that the ends had been brought to two islands in the mouth of the city's harbor so the Russian forces that had been stationed on the islands would be able to communicate with military leaders in the city's fort.

It was also revealed that the Japanese had used one of the Danish cables for a similar purpose in the waters off Nagasaki. Ten nautical miles of cable had been spliced into the Danish cable, and the Danish cable had been cut and subsequently repaired. The other Danish cable, too, had been used by an unauthorized party which, in Suenson's view, is "the Japanese government, of course."[26]

Both sides in the war, then, had followed the pattern from the Spanish-American War and made the cutting of cables and the securing of their own cable connections a part of their prosecution of the war. To be sure, the Kyakhta connection had

The entrance to Great Northern's station in Saint Petersburg being guarded by Russian soldiers during the revolutionary uprising of 1905 and 1906.

demonstrated that its construction had been justifiable, as it had remained functional throughout the war, but the revolutionary unrest and general strike had exposed another weakness in Russia's international telegraph connections.

As a result of the conditional strikes in the Russian telegraph service and during the total general strike, Saint Petersburg and therefore the government had been without a telegraphic connection to the surrounding world. This caused Great Northern to propose the laying of an undersea cable between the Danish island of Møn and Saint Petersburg, which would mean that Russia's telegraph connections with the West would not be dependent upon the vulnerable landlines. This cable would pass by Liepaja but be operated solely from the company's station in Saint Petersburg and transmit directly to

the Danish government telegraph authority's station in Fredericia. Both at Liepaja and in Saint Petersburg, the wires between the respective landing sites and the telegraph stations would be buried to prevent cutting or other sabotage in the event of new unrest.

The cable was laid in July 1907, and in compensation for financing the cable and its installation, operation, and maintenance, Great Northern was granted an extension of all of its concessions through the end of 1926. The company's longstanding wish to open an independent Danish station in Irkutsk, where up to this point the company had had Danish telegraphists stationed in the Russian telegraph station, was also granted.

Japanese wish to be liberated from Great Northern

With the reopening of the Vladivostok cables, Great Northern's situation in East Asia and the Russian

After the Russian revolt in 1905 and 1906, Great Northern laid a cable between Bornholm and Saint Petersburg that was landed in Liepaja, Latvia, on the way. The picture shows the cable being pulled ashore, where it was buried so that in the future, it would not be possible to interrupt the telegraph connection between Saint Petersburg and the rest of the world simply by cutting some telegraph wires.

Far East had been normalized to the extent that the company had reestablished its connections, and the company had also acquired new positions through the establishment of the Kyakhta-Beijing connection and the laying of the cable between Taku, Yantai, and Shanghai, though formally, this was Chinese territory. Geopolitically, however, the situation in the region was much changed given the internal dissolution of China, Russia's humiliating defeat, and not least Japan's new position of power, some of the implications of which were soon made clear to Great Northern.

At the time of the Japanese attack on Port Arthur, Japan's telegraph administration contacted Great Northern, Eastern, and Commercial Pacific regarding desired assistance with purchasing up to 1,000 nautical miles of deep-sea cable. The Japanese provided no information about the intended purpose of such a purchase, but it was soon obvious that the Japanese wished to lay a government cable to Guam in order to establish a connection with Commercial Pacific's cable to San Francisco, which would allow the Japanese to circumvent Great Northern's cables.[27]

The Japanese were evidently unaware of Commercial Pacific's ownership structure, and the three companies all declined to help the Japanese, though the companies gave respectively different reasons. The American government hesitated to grant permission for the landing of a Japanese government cable, so instead, a Japanese company sought permission to land the cable on Guam. Neither the three companies nor the American government had any doubt that the Japanese company was a front for the Japanese government, but it was difficult for the Americans to deny the Japanese company permission to land its cable. As a solution, Commercial Pacific offered to lay a cable from Guam to the Bonin Islands, a part of Japan, from where the Japanese government could lay a cable to one of the main Japanese islands.[28]

The American authorities gave the project a green light, but because of disagreements with regard to prices, which the Commercial Pacific owner companies wanted to prevent from undermining the new cartel agreement for the Pacific Ocean, about which the Japanese did not know at this point and were never told, a contract was not signed until September 1905. After this, another year passed before the Japanese could finally open the cable connection to Guam via the Bonin Islands.

After the victory over Russia, the prevailing mood in Japanese leading circles was increasingly characterized by the desire for a new structure for the country's international telegraph connections. In particular, a greater degree of independence was desired, and the military formulated a clear wish to be liberated from Great Northern.

"All of the countries of the world view independence in communication as a basic principle of national defense. Possessing their own communication systems is a goal for all of them. During the time of the Meiji rule, however, Japan surrendered itself to the Great Northern Telegraph Company, which represented Russian interests, and since then Japan has been unable to break free of the company's choking grip."[29]

The military found the situation dishonorable and demanded the termination of Great Northern's monopolistic concession, which would expire at the end of 1912, and in the fall of 1906, the company's management anoted that the company's relationship with Japan "was constantly becoming increasingly confrontational."

In response to a Japanese request for such negotiations, negotiations began with regard to the conclusion of a new agreement that could replace the concession. Japan wished to have the right to lay its own cables to China and Russia. This was obstructed by Great Northern's monopolistic concessions in the two countries, and Japan wanted the company to grant permission for the landing of Japanese cables if Japan previously was able to secure permission from the governments of the two countries. However, the company refused to agree to this.

The main concern of the Japanese was getting rid of Great Northern, while Great Northern wanted to secure its position in Japan after the expiration of the concession. Theoretically, the company was in a stronger position than the Japanese, as the right to land cables had no time limit and would therefore not be lost together with the monopoly. The mood was nevertheless pessimistic when the matter was discussed by Great Northern's board of directors in March 1907. There was an expectation that it would be possible to reach agreement regarding a new contract at the end of the year, but according to the minutes Edouard Suenson and other members of the board declared that without any diplomatic as-

In 1906, Great Northern built a new cable depot at Wusong. This picture was taken from the Huangpu River and shows the Dannebrog flying at the entrance to Shanghai.

sistance from Russia, the United Kingdom, and Denmark, the company would "be fairly helpless as a result of Japan's dominant position and have to accept whatever that country was willing to give it."[30]

New top management team at Great Northern

It would not be Edouard Suenson who would negotiate a new agreement with Japan. At a meeting of the board of directors in early April 1907, he announced that he wished to resign from his position as chief executive officer. Not least as a result of his long and difficult illness in 1901 and 1902, he lacked the strength to continue, and he had already chosen his son, Kay Suenson, and the head of the company's secretariat, Per Michelsen, as his replacements. They would constitute a two-man top management team, as the workload and amount of responsibility had increased to the point at which the daily leadership of the company was too much for a single individual.[31]

At the general meeting in April 1908, Edouard Suenson made an official announcement to the effect that he wished to step down as chief executive officer later in the year and that he would be replaced by a top management team "made up of several persons who will offer the greatest guarantees for the company's reliable administration in the future thanks to their personal qualities and knowledge and their excellent cooperation with the chief executive officer." At the same time, he indicated that he would continue in his position as chairman of the board of directors and that in that capacity, he would participate "in the leadership of the company's business in broad strokes as well as controlling daily business until the new top management team have become accustomed to working together and are sufficiently consolidated."[32]

When Edouard Suenson stepped down from his position as chief executive officer on October 1, 1908, he was replaced by a top management team of no fewer than four individuals. In addition to Kay Suenson and Per Michelsen, who were both given the title of director, Chief Engineer K. Gulstad and Operations Inspector Captain H. Rothe joined the top management team. The two directors were given the power to sign documents on behalf of the company either together or individually; if signing individually, they were to have their respective signatures accompanied by the signature of a further member of the top management team. At the same time, the chairman of the board of directors was appointed the board's representative in the top management team with responsibility for following its work.[33]

In 1907, Great Northern moved from Nanjing Road to the newly built East Asian headquarters on the Bund, the harbor promenade in Shanghai. The building was known as the Telegraph Building because in addition to Great Northern's station and offices, it housed the British Eastern companies and the American Commercial Pacific Cable Company.

This was a structure within which Edouard Suenson—in accordance with his announcement at the general meeting—could continue to play a leading role as the chairman of the board of directors with two directors with equal powers under him. While Kay Suenson's main task would be to take care of contacts and negotiations with other companies and authorities, Per Michelsen's main task would be the administration of the company. Kay Suenson continued in his role as secretary of the board of directors.

Chinese republic

The new top management team did not immediately engage in negotiations with Japan in the context of new realities, and neither of the parties showed any willingness to soften its position. The situation, then, was still locked up when the geopolitical map

of the Far East was once again radically changed. On October 10, 1911, a revolt broke out in the Chinese cities of Wuchang, Hankou, and Hanyang, after which it spread along the Chang River and quickly gained the support of Chinese military units. The revolt soon developed into an actual revolution, and demands were presented that the imperial state be abolished and a republic be established. There was fighting between revolutionary forces and troops that were loyal to the emperor, but it quickly became clear that the imperial state could not be saved.

The interior of Great Northern's new building on the Bund, which was inaugurated in 1907. The telegraph apparatuses and furniture could have been found in any of the company's stations—what makes the scene in this building distinctive are the male Chinese employees with their braids.

A truce was agreed upon, and on December 6, Prince Chun, who had ruled on behalf of the child emperor Puyi, abdicated. During the revolutionary events, Shanghai, Fuzhou, and Yantai had fallen into the hands of the rebels, but there had been no attacks on Great Northern's employees or their families, and in contrast to the Boxer Rebellion, foreigners had generally not come under attack.

However, panic broke out in Beijing in late February and early March 1912, when rebellious government troops burned parts of the city and engaged in looting and other uncontrolled behavior that caused the Chinese populace to suffer greatly, while all foreigners sought refuge in the walled embassy quarter, where Great Northern's personnel and other Danes were given protection in the Russian embassy.

Great Northern's personnel managed to keep the telegraph station just outside the embassy quarter operational, and there was continually a connection from there to both Kyakhta and Tianjin. British and Japanese troops secured the road between Beijing and Tianjin so that it could be used for an evacuation if necessary. In Tianjin, too, the company's personnel were close to the violent events but did not suffer because of them.[34]

On March 10, the change of regime form from imperium to republic was completed when a provisional president took an oath in Beijing, and a prime minister was appointed two days later. Already before this, Great Northern, partly via diplomatic contacts, had begun working to get the new government to recognize the company's concession and all of the other agreements into which the company had entered—one reason for these efforts being that the company feared Japan would exploit the situation. The new government quickly approved all international agreements into which the previous regime had entered, and Great Northern's monopolistic concession remained in force.

Japanese cable to Shanghai and Danish-Japanese joint purse

In early July 1912, with the company's position in China having been secured, Great Northern's head of operations in Shanghai, Captain Jesper Bahnson, could begin negotiations in Tokyo about the company's position, given the new realities in Japan. Back in 1891, Great Northern had sold the eastern section of the Korea cable to Japan, and Japan had bought the western section of the cable as well after having annexed Korea in the summer of 1910. Great Northern had attempted to use that situation as an occasion to reopen concession negotiations, but without any luck. Now, though, the company wanted to make it happen.[35]

Captain Bahnson was received by Count Preben Ahlefeldt-Laurvig, who had been appointed Denmark's first ambassador to China and Japan in April 1912 after having been the secretary of the delegation at Russia's embassy in Beijing since the spring of 1908.[36]

Count Ahlefeldt-Laurvig's promotion to ambassador occurred on the initiative of Great Northern and the East India Company, who wished to have a Danish representative in China and Japan with the status of an independent diplomat and greater authority to represent the interests of the companies directly. Count Ahlefeldt-Laurvig presented his credentials to the Japanese emperor on May 25, 1912, which left plenty of time to prepare for Bahnson's arrival in Tokyo.[37]

Count Ahlefeldt-Laurvig introduced Captain Bahnson to all of the relevant embassies and consulates, after which negotiations with the Japanese vice minister and general director of the telegraphy authority began. The Japanese press had previously presented a series of attacks on the company, which had been accused of setting prices much too high, and demanded that the government take over the Danish cables.

Precisely, prices became a main topic of the negotiations, which were engaged in by Captain Bahnson, while Count Ahlefeldt-Laurvig sought support from the embassies of the major powers. However, the Japanese had a wish that went further than laying their own cables to China. The Japanese negotiators presented their views in a memorandum that was not given to Bahnson until early August as a result of the death of the Emperor of Japan. He immediately returned to Shanghai to await the making of a decision in Copenhagen, while Count Ahlefeldt-Laurvig remained in Tokyo to advance the Danish company's cause at the embassies of the major powers.[38]

In the memorandum, the Japanese expressed the wish that rates be reduced by fifty percent for traffic between Japan and China and by twenty percent for all other traffic. The rate reductions would not affect the transit traffic between Vladivostok and Shanghai, and from the beginning, the company was prepared to accommodate this wish. In contrast, the company was not immediately prepared to accommodate Japan's wish to take over the station in Nagasaki, as such a takeover would represent "a very great loss of prestige" that could reduce both Russia's and China's interest in the company, since a change to Japanese operation of the Nagasaki station would interfere with the neutrality of the service. Therefore, the position of the company's management was that the company would oppose this wish "to the utmost possible extent."[39]

Finally, Japan wished the company to accept the landing of one or more cables in China and the establishment of Japanese stations staffed by Japanese personnel. Even if the cables were to transmit only government telegrams or telegrams bearing Japanese written characters (kana), Great Northern would oppose the fulfilment of this wish "by all means." The company did recognize that it might be necessary to give in a little and accept a single cable between Nagasaki and Shanghai, but the establishment of a Japanese telegraph station in China would "be absolutely rejected."

After a break, the negotiations were resumed in early November 1912. The Japanese were satisfied with the company's acceptance of the rate reductions but insisted upon the fulfilment of their demands with regard to laying their own cables and taking over the station in Nagasaki. The negotiations were interrupted, but late in the month, there was a turning point when the Japanese general director unexpectedly declared that "the only decisive point" was that, like the Americans, the British, and the Germans, the Japanese should have their own cable to China and their own station in Shanghai. If this were made possible, Great Northern could retain its station in Nagasaki and be given a new contract valid until the end of 1930.[40]

Great Northern and Eastern had already previously been willing to give in to the Japanese demand for a cable to China, and as the Russian ambassador in Tokyo also recommended accepting the Japanese offer, it was accepted. While Captain Bahnson continued to negotiate, Count Ahlefeldt-Laurvig traveled to Beijing to secure the agreement of the Chinese government, in which he succeeded.[41]

Captain Bahnson and the Japanese general director could therefore sign a heads of agreement document in December 1912, but it was not until eight months later, in August 1913, that a contract valid until the end of 1930 could be signed. Great Northern lost the monopoly it had held until this point but retained its landing permission for and station in Nagasaki. Japan secured the right to lay a cable to Shanghai for traffic with Japanese characters and telegrams sent between the governments of China and Japan, and the lowering of rates was also accommodated.

By way of compensation, Great Northern demanded the conclusion of a joint purse contract regulating the distribution of revenues for all traffic to and from Japan both on the Danish cable and on the Japanese cable. The major sticking point in the negotiations was establishing the respective percentages of revenues to be received by the parties. These ended up being 64.5 percent for Great North-

Some of Great Northern's Danish employees posted in foreign countries never returned to Denmark. In some cases, this was because they chose not to return but in others because they died while in the company's service. Oscar Christian Terkelsen joined the company as a trainee in 1890; he was trained as a telegraphist in London and subsequently sent to Shanghai. He died there on November 18, 1910, at the age of thirty-four.

ern and 35.5 percent for Japan. The Japanese were dissatisfied with the contract they finally signed, not because they found these particular percentages unfair but because they found it generally unacceptable that the Danes should receive part of the revenues from a Japanese cable.[42]

With this contract, Great Northern had secured its position in East Asia and thus in the Pacific cartel through the end of 1930, while Japan had brought about the fulfillment of a long-held wish to have a government cable to China. After this contract had been signed, a further three months passed before a Sino-Japanese contract regarding the landing of the Japanese cable could be concluded. The cable was opened to traffic on January 1, 1915.

Wireless Telegraphy

CHAPTER 10

With its victory over Russia, Japan had demonstrated not only its military strength but also that it was at the forefront of the development of a new communication technology. The crushing victory of the Japanese in the naval battle in the Tsushima Strait could be attributed not least to their use of wireless telegraphy, which in the long run would present the most serious threat to the position not only of Great Northern but of cable companies all over the world.

In 1896, the world's first patent on wireless technology was issued to the Italian Guglielmo Marconi, who had succeeded in sending signals over a distance of a little less than three kilometers. He demonstrated his invention in London and on the limestone plateau Salisbury Plain as well as over the Bristol Channel. In the spring of 1899, he succeeded in transmitting signals across the English Channel.

At that point, the technology had still not been sufficiently developed for it to be used for practical purposes, but the imperial Japanese navy had now become interested in it, and in 1900, that navy established a research and development unit that presented a prototype of a wireless telegraphy system for use on ships the following year. The range was 18.5 nautical miles, but already in 1903, the range was extended to eighty nautical miles, and the system immediately went into production and was installed on all large Japanese warships.[1]

When the Russian Baltic Sea fleet approached Japan, a number of Japanese merchant vessels had also been equipped with wireless telegraphy so they would be able to function as an early warning system. It was from one of these ships, the *Shimano Maru*, that the Russian squadron was spotted and the flagship of the Japanese fleet warned. The Russian ships had installed a German Telefunken wireless system, but this did not prevent the squadron from being discovered or the Japanese fleet commanders from being warned—without the knowledge of the Russians.[2]

The press also exploited the new technology to get news and transmit it to the rest of the world. In

A Marconi radio station at Inchkeith in the Firth of Forth off the coast of Scotland, equipped with the new beam technology using reflections of short waves in the ionosphere. This technology further strengthened wireless telegraphy in competition with classic wire and cable telegraphy and contributed to putting Great Northern's business under pressure.

the spring of 1904, the English newspaper *The Times* chartered a steamship that was equipped with a wireless system and sailed around the waters outside Port Arthur with journalists who telegraphed their stories to a wireless station in the British territory of Weihai, from where news telegrams were sent to Europe and the United States by cable.

The correspondents also intercepted wireless telegrams sent internally between both Japanese and Russian warships, which caused the Russians to issue a warning that if neutral ships with wireless equipment and newspaper correspondents on board were found within the Russian sphere of operations, the ships and their equipment would be confiscated and the correspondents regarded as spies.[3]

Wireless telegraphy had been used already during the period 1899–1902, in the Boer War, but the military possibilities of the new technology were made particularly apparent by the naval battle in the Tsushima Strait, which resulted in increased interest in the technology not least in the navies of the major powers, which had already previously been experimenting with wireless telegraphy.

"Telegraphy without wires"

Great Northern and the other cable companies too were following the development of the wireless telegraph. Edouard Suenson informed the board of directors of Great Northern after Guglielmo Marconi had established the Wireless Telegraph and Signal Company Ltd. in July 1897 to develop and commercialize the technology, though Suenson did not comment on this event.[4]

In October 1899, Edouard Suenson reported that signals had successfully been transmitted 150 kilometers, between Chelford northeast of London and Wimereux on the French Channel coast. Also, the British ministry of war had concluded an agreement with Marconi's company regarding the use of the wireless system in the war against the Boers in southern Africa. The system, then, had been not only improved but also put to practical use, and "Telegraphy without wires" was subsequently a regular rubric in Edouard Suenson's monthly reports.[5]

After a successful six-month trial in South Africa, the British Admiralty purchased thirty-two sets of Marconi's equipment for use on British warships. The technology appeared best suited to use on the open sea, where the range was longer than elsewhere, and the size of the sending and receiving equipment meant that it could be installed on ships and used during voyages. Great Northern, too, was interested in the possibilities—at least, the company asked for a price quote for the installation of Marconi equipment in the company's cable ships in 1901, though the company did not end up placing an order.[6]

A major breakthrough came in the middle of December 1901, when Marconi claimed to have transmitted a wireless signal across the Atlantic Ocean. As Edouard Suenson wrote in his report to the board of directors, this announcement "came as quite a surprise to the world, which had not expected his system to be developed so fast." In the United States, Marconi had received a signal from Ireland using a very sensitive microphone that was attached to a reception wire that had been sent up high above the ground using a kite, so it was not without reason that Suenson found it "rather unlikely" that Marconi would immediately be able to establish a commercial connection across the Atlantic. Nevertheless, there was now "no reason to doubt that the technology could become a serious competitor to cables, particularly over short distances, when his apparatus has been more nearly perfected."[7]

The report of the transmission across the Atlantic sent shockwaves through the telegraph sector, whose stocks declined in value sharply. The following month, however, Suenson was able to calm his board of directors, noting that "the panic that gripped the telegraphy market following the first report of Marconi's telegraphing across the Atlantic [had] become much less severe." Highly regarded engineers and technicians claimed that telegraphy without wires "[was] not at the present time dangerous for the cable companies in any way, as Marconi [had] not yet succeeded in achieving speed, secrecy, and dependability." Doing so would require very great improvements that could be classed as actual inventions in their own right, these individuals maintained, and the cable companies could therefore refrain from worrying about wireless competition.[8]

This was confirmed by a report around this time that the functioning of five stations Marconi had established on five of the Hawaiian Islands in late June 1900 had proved to be "completely unsatisfactory." This was Marconi's first commercial system, but the telegrams often did not reach their intended recipients. Marconi lost customers, and in early February 1902, it was over when the company in Hawaii went bankrupt.[9]

Not only at Great Northern but at all cable companies there was relief over Marconi's difficulties. However, Marconi was undeterred, continuing with his efforts to commercialize his system, and on April 1, 1902, he registered a company in the United States. Shortly before Christmas of that year, he announced that he had now solved the problems with telegraphing across the Atlantic wirelessly and that he would soon open a public connection with lower prices than those of the cable companies.[10]

Edouard Suenson and the rest of the cable sector were skeptical, as they had not been convinced that the connection would be so fast, secret, and secure that it could be used for commercial and political telegrams. Nevertheless, the cable companies' stocks fell steeply again, but they rose again when it became clear that Marconi had been too optimistic.

In the middle of January 1903, the American president was able to send a wireless telegram of congratulations to the British king, Edward VII, but there was still a long way to go to create a stable connection across the Atlantic. In general, the technology had not been sufficiently developed to be used for commercial purposes, and the cable companies were assuring themselves and their shareholders that cables would continue to be the superior and preferred medium for telegraphy in the future—when Great Northern was suddenly challenged by the wireless technology on its own home territory.

Cable or wireless connection with Iceland

Since the early 1870s, not much had happened with regard to the North Atlantic project involving cables between Scotland, the Faroe Islands, Iceland, Greenland, and Canada, but in late 1896, Edouard Suenson learned that three Britons had sought a Danish concession for the laying of a cable from Iceland via the Faroe Islands to the Shetland Islands, from where there was a cable connection to Scotland. Inquiries to members of Iceland's Alting, the Danish Ministry of the Interior, and the cable manufacturer Henley's in England confirmed what Edouard Suenson had been told.[11]

Back during the years 1880–1882, Great Northern had tried to lay the groundwork for the laying of a cable to Iceland via the Faroe Islands, the plan having been to secure the project's economic basis by means of subsidies both from Altinget and from various European countries other than Iceland because of the importance of weather reports from the North Atlantic. It had proved to be the case, however, that interest in the project outside Denmark and Iceland was modest at best, certainly as far as participating in the financing was concerned, so nothing had come of the company's efforts.[12]

Now, the plan was once again relevant, and Suenson immediately sought to obstruct the English project, which would invade Great Northern's sphere and furthermore was based on the financing model he himself had presented fifteen years earlier. He did not refrain from mentioning this in a letter to the Ministry of the Interior in which he warned against leaving the installation of an Iceland cable to a group of Englishmen with no experience in international telegraphy. The project should instead be given to Great Northern, Suenson argued, and the Ministry of the Interior declared that it was in agreement. Suenson also succeeded in persuading the Danish attorney representing the Englishmen to distance himself from them, and already in January 1897, Suenson could note with satisfaction that in government circles the English project was seen as "dead in the water."[13]

At this time Great Northern revived the possibility of completing the project itself, presenting a possible extension from Iceland to Canada via Greenland as part of the plans. Applications to the Ministry of the Interior and the Ministry for Iceland as well as to Altinget secured the approval of annual subsidies from Iceland in the amount of 35,000 kroner for twenty years and from Denmark in the amount of 54,000 kroner for twenty years. What remained was to obtain economic support from other European countries by justifying such support with reference to the project's meteorological importance and to seek support from fisheries organizations in Germany, England, and France that had an interest in weather prognoses for the waters off Iceland.[14]

Despite the support of the Danish Ministry of Foreign Affairs and the Danish Meteorological Institute, however, the results were not encouraging. There was a clear interest in getting regular and up-to-date weather reports from the North Atlantic, but there was no similar clear interest in helping to cover the costs. Only Sweden and Russia had a positive attitude in this respect—the latter country after Empress Dowager Maria Feodorovna had become involved in the matter.[15]

The company continued to work on the project, however, now turning to the acquisition of landing permission in England for an Iceland cable, and in February 1902, the company requested that it include a wireless connection, as it was possible that "even at a relatively undeveloped stage" Marconi's system could be used for a connection between Iceland, the Faroe Islands, and the Shetland Islands.[16]

A wireless connection would be much cheaper to establish than a cable connection, and Great Northern therefore did not reject the possibility of using wireless telegraphy itself for connections where it did not have preexisting cables and in areas in which it wanted to block competitors. Great Northern therefore asked the Marconi company to present a price quote with regard to the establishment of a wireless connection, but the Marconi company replied that it did not see the possibility of accommodating Great Northern's request, as the Marconi company was already negotiating with the Danish government regarding a corresponding project.[17]

This information came as a great surprise to Edouard Suenson, who felt that the Danish government telegraphy authority had gone behind his back. A few months later, when he learned through an agent for the Marconi company that its negotiations with the government had ground to a halt, he offered the Marconi company the opportunity to cooperate with Great Northern, and Suenson and the agent promised to notify each other if the status of the matter changed.[18]

Later in the year Danish newspapers reported that a group of interested parties in Copenhagen had created a syndicate for the purpose of establishing a wireless connection between Iceland and Scotland using Marconi equipment. This caused Great Northern to obtain its own price quote for the installation of a wireless connection for Denmark's North Atlantic possessions—but not from the Marconi company, which had not honored the agreement regarding the mutual provision of information. In June 1903, Great Northern instead asked the French company Société Française des Télégraphes et des Téléphones sans Fil to present an offer for the establishment of two stations on Iceland, one on the Faroe Islands, and one in Denmark.[19]

In late 1903, while Great Northern's management were considering the offer they had received, Denmark's Postal and Telegraphy Authority received a new offer for the establishment of a wireless connection to Iceland via the Faroe Islands. It was the German company Siemens & Halske that presented this offer, which the Danish director of telegraphy found attractive. Finally, in the summer of 1904, the Marconi company announced it was prepared to establish a corresponding connection for a group of Icelanders in return for an annual subsidy of only 2,000 pounds sterling.[20]

Danish government pressure for a cable to Iceland

Iceland and Denmark had suddenly and quite unexpectedly found itself at the center of a battle over the choice between telegraph cables and wireless telegraphy. For the company, the connection would not in itself have great economic significance, but on the other hand, the loss of prestige would be significant if the establishment of the connection

The landing of Great Northern's cable at Seyðisfjörður in the summer of 1906. In connection with cable landings, it was usual for the position of the cable to be marked with barrels or buoys until all the installations were in place.

were assigned to a foreign company, and there was also the possibility of a continuation to Canada via Greenland to consider.

The entire matter acquired a further dramatic perspective in November 1903, when Edouard Suenson was summoned on short notice to a meeting with Minister of Finance and Traffic Christopher F. Hage (Danish Liberal Party), who described the projects involving a wireless connection with Iceland—after which he referred to the possibility of extending Great Northern's Danish concessions, which were due to expire in 1910, if the company "were willing to make sacrifices in connection with the cable to Iceland."[21]

This was a thinly veiled threat to the effect that a prerequisite for an extension of the company's Danish concessions would be the company's willingness to contribute to the financing of an Ice-

landic cable. However, an extension of the Danish concession might pave the way for an extension of the other Scandinavian concessions, and at a new meeting that was also participated in by Council President and Minister of Foreign Affairs Johan Henrik Deuntzer, Suenson was promised that the government would work to bring about an extension of the concessions for Norway and Sweden and put pressure on the United Kingdom to extend the company's English landing permits—if the company manifested the right attitude toward the Iceland project.[22]

While at this point wireless telegraphy had hardly been sufficiently developed to be used to create a stable connection with Iceland, it could be assumed that it was only a matter of time before it could be used for that purpose. When it could, the Danish government would be able to establish a connection without involving Great Northern, and Suenson had now also learned that the three Scandinavian directors of telegraphy were in agreement that the company's concession should not be extended past 1910 and that the government telegra-

Great Northern participated in financing and establishing a landline from the station at Seyðisfjörður to the capital city of Iceland, Reykjavik. The line needed to withstand severe climatic conditions, including heavy winter snowfalls.

phy authorities should be able to take over the cables themselves.[23]

In a lengthy written document he subsequently sent to Christopher Hage, Suenson expressed doubt that a stable and secure wireless connection with Iceland could be established at all and indicated that "non-extension of the company's Scandinavian concessions would mean its ruin." The entire basis of Great Northern's international system would be gone, and this would also be damaging to Denmark, which would lose "the very significant amount of transit traffic handled by the government telegraphy authority."[24]

The company was therefore open to the proposal, requiring that as compensation for a "cheap" agreement regarding the laying of a cable between Ice-

land, the Faroe Islands, and the Shetland Islands the government would extend the Danish concessions until 1930. In addition, the government would be expected to recommend to the British government that it grant Great Northern a corresponding extension of the company's English landing permits, arguing that such an extension was justifiable because the laying of the cable would provide the United Kingdom with a "free" telegraph connection with Iceland. At this time, the British government was under renewed pressure from fisheries organizations to provide a cable connection that would make it possible to receive weather predictions for the waters around the Faroe Islands and Iceland, and this pressure could be relieved by an Iceland cable without cost to the British government.[25]

The minister reacted positively, but it was not until early in 1905 that an agreement was concluded. There were no major obstacles in London or Stockholm, but Norway was "on the warpath," as the government did not want to renew the Norwegian concessions and also demanded special conditions including rate reductions for Norwegian traffic on Great Northern's cable between Sweden and England, which made an intermediate landing in Arendal.[26]

With the support of the Danish Ministry of Foreign Affairs and the envoys in London and Stockholm and thanks to independent initiatives on the part of the British postal and telegraphy authority, the company succeeded in blocking the Norwegian directory of telegraphy's demand for rate reductions. Subsequently, on May 24, 1905, Denmark's King Christian IX could sign the concession for a cable to Iceland, and at the same time, the company's Danish concessions and English landing permits were extended so they would expire in 1925.[27]

The only economic support for the project came in the form of the previously approved subsidies from Denmark and Iceland amounting to a total of 90,000 kroner for twenty years. Great Northern also paid 300,000 kroner for the installation of a landline from the landing site in eastern Iceland to Reykjavik, to which the towns along the route could connect their telegram stations.[28]

On September 5, 1905, Great Northern, Denmark, and Sweden concluded a joint purse agreement covering all of the traffic on the company's cables, and at the same time the company's Swedish concession was extended until 1925. The cable between the Shetland Islands and the Faroe Islands opened on August 1, 1906, and a little over three weeks later, the connection with Iceland was opened, giving Iceland a telegraphic connection not only with Denmark, the mother country, but with the whole world. The openings were marked by two ceremonies respectively in Tórshavn and Reykjavik in which the King of Denmark and a large number of members of Denmark's Rigsdag participated.

Norway continued to refuse to extend its concessions, and Great Northern therefore had to sell its cables between Norway and Denmark and between Norway and England to the governments of Norway and the United Kingdom after long negotiations regarding the price and other conditions, though the cable between Sweden and England continued to make an intermediate landing in Arendal.

Valdemar Poulsen's arc transmitter

Great Northern's request for a price quote from the French company reflects the fact that Marconi was not the only serious player in the area of wireless telegraphy; rather, there were developments in this area in several countries on the basis of various patents and technologies. The obvious military and political implications of wireless systems caused

Christopher Friedenreich Hage was a wholesaler and earned a cand.polit. degree from the University of Copenhagen for a thesis on the economist John Stuart Mill. He went into politics for Venstre, the Danish Liberal Party, and was Minister of Finance during the years 1901–1905 as well as Minister of Traffic during the years 1902–1905. In the latter capacity, he pressured Great Northern to lay a cable to Iceland under conditions that were favorable for the Danish government. He later became a middleman between Valdemar Poulsen and Great Northern in the negotiations regarding the company's possible exploitation of the arc transmitter. He subsequently became a member of Great Northern's board of directors.

the great powers to devote a great deal of attention to the new technology from the beginning.

Denmark was among the countries that experimented with the new wireless technology. As early as in 1898 and 1899, both the Telegraph Authority and the Danish navy had carried out experiments with systems purchased in France and Germany, and in 1901, a permanent system was established at Blåvandshuk Lighthouse and aboard the *Vyl Fyrskib*. During the years that followed, systems of German manufacture were installed on some Danish warships, and in 1905 the Danish navy installed its first land station on the islet of Holmen in Copenhagen.[29]

Danish engineers also developed wireless systems themselves. In the fall of 1903, the engineer Alfred Grut contacted Great Northern and offered to sell the company a patent. This was while Great Northern was in the middle of the battle over the Iceland connection, and on Edouard Suenson's recommendation, the board of directors approved the use of up to 40,000 kroner for a series of experiments. The results were not convincing, and the offer of an opportunity to purchase the patent was therefore declined.[30]

In the summer of 1906, Great Northern received another offer when the two engineers Valdemar Poulsen and Peder Oluf Pedersen contacted the company via Christopher Hage, who had left the government. While Marconi's and most other systems were built using so-called spark transmitter technology, Valdemar Poulsen and Peder Oluf Pedersen had developed a competing arc transmitter system. In 1903, the two men had taken out a patent for this system in Denmark and thirteen other countries, and on the same year, they had founded a consortium to exploit the patent. In 1905, they built a permanent testing station near Lyngby.[31]

The two engineers offered Great Northern an opportunity to share the patent with a view to develop it into a practically usable and stable technology for wireless telegraphy. However, the company felt unqualified to evaluate the system and contacted Eastern, which sent two engineers to Denmark to carry out a series of tests. Their report was positive and praised the inventors, but the English company nevertheless declined to enter into a cooperative arrangement with regard to the technology, as Eastern was not convinced of wireless telegraphy's commercial potential.[32]

In fact, there were still a number of serious weaknesses such as low transmission speed and instability as a result of meteorological phenomena as well as the failure to ensure security and secrecy. The last problem in particular was decisive in connection with commercial and not least political, military, and diplomatic applications, as it was easy to intercept wireless telegrams. Also, Great Northern was in the process of preparing to lay the cable to Iceland, and the company had no plans to establish other new connections and therefore no immediate incentive to acquire the patent. Like Eastern, the company therefore declined the opportunity to cooperate with Poulsen and Pedersen.[33]

Valdemar Poulsen and Peder Oluf Pedersen did not give up, however. With the exception of the American rights, they sold their patent rights to a group of English investors who were behind England's De Forest Wireless Telegraph Syndicate Ltd. In the middle of July 1906, the Amalgamated Radio-Telegraph Company Ltd. was established in London, and later in the year, two of the investors purchased the American rights as well.[34]

Shortly after the establishment of Amalgamated, the German company Lorenz AG bought a license to exploit Valdemar Poulsen's patent in Germany. The company developed three transportable testing stations for the German military leadership, which concluded after a demonstration in late 1907 that Poulsen's system was superior to all other wireless systems. Systems based on Poulsen's technology went into production, and the following year, the first mobile and stationary stations were delivered to the German army and navy.[35]

The arc transmitter had a number of advantages over the spark transmitter. The station was considerably smaller, and the arc transmitter was almost soundless, while a spark transmitter created an ear-splitting racket. The arc transmitter had a longer range over land, and because the receiver could be more precisely set, problems due to atmospheric noise were reduced. Finally, a decisive difference was that the arc transmitter made possible a much faster rate of transmission for telegraphy.[36]

The expectations of Valdemar Poulsen and Peder Oluf Pedersen, as well as those of Amalgamated, were therefore great. After a series of successful tests including transmissions across the North Sea, the construction of a large Poulsen station on the west coast of Ireland was begun. This station was intended to be used to establish a transatlantic connection that would compete with that of Marconi, who was still working on establishing a stable connection.

An agreement was concluded with DFDS to the effect that four of that company's steamships that brought passengers from Denmark to the United States and vice versa would be equipped with Poulsen stations, and in July 1907,

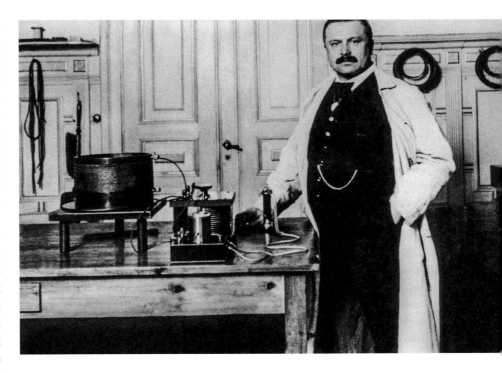

the steamship *Hellig Olav* succeeded in maintaining a connection with land over distances of up to 1,200–1,500 kilometers. It even proved possible to receive signals from one steamship over a distance of 3,300 kilometers, which was the greatest distance telegraph signals had ever been sent by a ship before being successfully received.[37]

Shortly thereafter, however, Amalgamated began to collapse owing to economic problems and difficulties in cooperating. All of this ended with a lawsuit, and after the American rights had returned to Valdemar Poulsen and Peder Oluf Pedersen, the two men went to Christopher Hage, who, in February 1908, collected a group of Danish investors and founded Det Kontinentale Syndikat A/S ("the Continental Syndicate Company") with himself as chairman of the board of directors.

The syndicate bought back all of Amalgamated's rights except for the transmaritime rights and the rights for the British Empire. The German rights were immediately sold to Lorenz AG, after which the syndicate sought funding for further development and commercialization of the system. Poulsen and Pedersen now again looked to Great Northern,

The Danish engineer and inventor Valdemar Poulsen was not educated at the College of Advanced Technology (today the Technical University of Denmark) but began his career as an apprentice at the machine manufacturing company Frich's Efterfølgere in Aarhus, after which he came to Københavns Telefon Aktieselskab (KTAS, "the Copenhagen Telephone Limited Company") as an engineering assistant. In addition to the arc transmitter, he invented the telegraphone—a forerunner of the gramophone—which he patented in 1899. He came to play an important role in the development of radio technology, and his cooperation with the engineer P. O. Pedersen—who was a professor at the Technical University of Denmark from 1912 onward—resulted in the adoption of weak-current electronics as an academic field at the Technical University before the field had been granted this status anywhere else in the world.

which both had an established position in international telegraphy and possessed significant wealth.

Since his first contact with Great Northern, Poulsen had demonstrated his system's strengths and potential, and in late 1907, Great Northern, on its own initiative, had asked Amalgamated to provide a price quote for a wireless station to be constructed on Iceland. The system was to be able to reach both Great Britain and Canada, so at the request of the Icelandic government, the company established a backup connection with Great Britain, and at the same time, Taliaferro Shaffner's and later C. F. Tietgen's 1860s plan to establish a North Atlantic telegraphic connection with the United States could be realized.[38]

The project had gotten no further as a result of Amalgamated's economic crisis, but Great Northern's interest in the arc transmitter had shown that the ongoing development of wireless telegraphy had changed Great Northern's previously extremely skeptical attitude.

Also, in October 1907, the Marconi company had finally opened a commercial wireless connection between England and the United States, and the prices for telegrams sent via that connection were only half what the cable companies charged for telegrams. While the connection was still unstable and of poor quality, the symbolic significance was enormous, and at Great Northern's general meeting in April 1908, Edouard Suenson recognized that the challenge could no longer be ignored.

"No matter how unconditional our trust in the absolute and lasting superiority of wired telegraphy in the context of the transmission of political, commercial, and private telegrams between the continents and between countries, the newly opened connection between two parts of the world does show that in the future we will have to view the new invention not only as a competitor but also as an ally and a supplement to wired telegraphy—it could be a competitor, however, if it should succeed in freeing itself from the serious flaws that are still associated with it."[39]

Purchase of Valdemar Poulsen's patent rights

In May 1908, when Christopher Hage again contacted Great Northern with a proposal regarding possible cooperation, Edouard Suenson responded positively, indicating that the company would "benefit more from using this technology than from awaiting future competition from the various wireless companies."[40]

To begin with, however, Great Northern desired a demonstration of the system's practical applicability, and after having seen positive results from a series of tests the company offered Eastern the opportunity to cooperate with Great Northern in this area, an offer the British company declined. Suenson's impression was that "the English cable companies would not mind seeing the wireless companies fail utterly." Suenson's own attitude was no different, but this was obviously not the direction in which developments were going. His view was therefore that it would be entirely defensible for Great Northern, situated as the company was, "to use a relatively small but not insignificant amount of money—even if this should be for naught—to acquire a wireless system for telegraphy between the countries that are connected by its cables and thus to some extent protect itself against competition."[41]

Suenson's primary motive was to prevent wireless competition from the Poulsen system from impacting Great Northern's established connections in Northern Europe and East Asia. The company was therefore interested in the transmaritime rights for these areas, which were still owned by Amalgamated. Thus, when a preliminary agreement was concluded in November 1908, it included a provision that the Continental Syndicate, with economic support in the amount of 10,000 pounds sterling from Great Northern, would attempt to buy back the transmaritime rights from Amalgamated, which was now in the process of being liquidated. The company's motive in doing this, as expressed by Suenson, was clear: to ensure that the patent "could not be used by others to compete with the company's cables without [the company's] permission and that [the company] might be able to establish and operate wireless connections parallel to the cables [itself] if circumstances should allow or necessitate this."[42]

Christopher Hage did succeed in buying back the transmaritime rights, but the agreed-upon 10,000 pounds were nowhere near enough money. The price ended up being 33,000 pounds, and it was only after several urgent requests that the compa-

In the summer of 1909, a nationwide industrial, craft, and art exhibition took place in Aarhus, and Great Northern participated. In a sixty-five-meter-high tower, the company had erected a pillar-like structure that reached almost all the way to the top. At the bottom was a display of telegraphy instruments and cables, and halfway to the top, there was a map of the company's cables and telegraph connections around the world. The structure was crowned by a marker buoy for use in laying undersea cables. Elsewhere in the exhibition, a little telegraph station based on Valdemar Poulsen's patent had been built as a sign of a new technological future. During the exhibition, 2,416 wireless telegrams were sent from this station.

ny finally provided Christopher Hage with the money as a personal loan because in his time as a minister he, as Suenson put it, "had shown the company not inconsiderable good will."[43]

It was subsequently possible for the company and the syndicate to conclude a new agreement on April 10 and 11, 1909, after which Great Northern received the transmaritime rights to Valdemar Poulsen's patent for Northern Europe and East Asia. A condition requiring the establishment of a company for the exploitation of the rights in these areas was subsequently removed, and subsequent requests from Christopher Hage that such a company be created were rejected. The agreement was not final, as a final agreement was to be concluded only after an English Poulsen company had been created for the purpose of establishing a transatlantic connection.

"The Death Bell of Ocean cable has rung"

While Great Northern was only interested in protecting its position with regard to its traditional

DET·STORE·NORDISKE TELEGRAF SELSKA

territory, the company could see how the wireless technology was gaining ground in other areas. In the fall of 1909, the British postal and telegraphy directorate took over all coastal radio stations in Great Britain with the exception of Marconi's transatlantic station. Near Gothenburg, the Swedish government established a powerful Marconi station for maritime use. A proposal presented by Guglielmo Marconi personally during a visit to Stockholm late in 1909 that a powerful wireless station be built near the Swedish capital was not realized, however. In Norway it was decided that a number of coastal stations would be built, also for maritime use.[44]

Plans for large and small wireless projects shot up everywhere like mushrooms from a wet forest floor. Most of these plans were never realized, but both Great Northern and Eastern became worried when, in the spring of 1909, a wireless transmitter was installed at the Palace Hotel on the Bund in Shanghai. The Chinese administration had no way of interfering, as the station was located within the British settlement, but in reaction to requests from Great Northern and Eastern, the British consul had the transmitter shut down.[45]

Nevertheless, such plans were constantly becoming more practical in nature, and the range of

Like other large Danish companies such as F. L. Smidth and the East Asiatic Company, Great Northern had a large mural displayed at the world exposition in San Francisco in 1915 that was intended to reflect the company's activities and importance. The inspiration for Great Northern's mural, which was in color, appears to have been provided by a photograph of the landing of the Pacific cable near Honolulu in 1902 (which is described in chapter 8) despite the fact that the company kept its participation in the Commercial Pacific Cable Company secret.

the transmitters involved was increasing. The most ambitious plan yet was presented in the fall of 1910. Swedish newspapers reported that the General Post Office was negotiating with the Marconi company regarding the establishment of a world-spanning system of wireless systems that would connect the British colonies as the All British Line had done. Great Northern's top management team responded to the news calmly, however, as it was regarded as "probably mostly an indication of the Marconi company's wild dreams."[46]

Nevertheless, an agreement regarding the project was concluded between the General Post Office and the Marconi company, and in the spring of 1912, the Marconi company announced a plan for a further wireless system, one connecting the United

States and East Asia. In Germany, plans to connect the country's colonies and territories in the Pacific Ocean and East Asia with wireless telegraphy were announced.[47]

The world now seemed to in the process of being spun into a network of wireless connections that spanned oceans and international borders just as undersea cables had previously spun the world into a communication network that in the year 1900 had a total length of 400,000 kilometers.

The great breakthrough came in the United States, and the technology was Valdemar Poulsen's arc transmitter. Shortly after the conclusion of the agreement between Great Northern and the Continental Syndicate, the young American engineer Cyril F. Elwell came to Copenhagen to visit Valdemar Poulsen and examine his system. In January 1911, after having purchased the American rights to the Poulsen patent, Elwell established the Poulsen Wireless Corporation, which came to be responsible for the development and commercialization of the Danish wireless technology in the United States, working with the Federal Telegraph Company, an operating company.[48]

In June 1911, the first commercial connection was opened in California, and in 1912, the Federal Telegraph Company was operating about ten wireless telegraphy stations in the United States and more were under construction. The network stretched along the west coast of the United States and offered a connection from Los Angeles via El Paso and Fort Worth, Texas, and Kansas City, Missouri, to Chicago, Illinois, on the Great Lakes near the Canadian border. Rates were at least thirty percent lower than those of the established telegraph companies, so traffic increased rapidly.

This process culminated in the summer of 1912, when the Federal Telegraph Company opened a wireless connection between California and Hawaii using Valdemar Poulsen's arc transmitter. At Great Northern, the top management team noted the opening of this connection without commenting on it in any detail. The achievement was in fact remarkable, however, as the distance of 3,800 kilometers was considerably greater than that of Marconi's transatlantic connection. "The Death Knell of Ocean cable has rung," wrote the San Francisco newspaper *The Call*.[49]

This prediction of death had been issued rather too early, as it would turn out, but the opening and operation of the wireless connection increasingly affected Commercial Pacific as the connection became more stable and, with rates considerably lower than those for the Pacific Cable, took over a growing part of the traffic. The cable company was forced to lower its rates, and later in the year, Great Northern's top management team did remark that Poulsen's system "finally [seemed] to have gotten wind in its sails."[50]

The Poulsen system's success and obvious advantages were convincing and indisputable, but this did not make Great Northern change its attitude. What was important to the company was to defend its own existing position rather than pursuing new initiatives of its own that might well expand the company's business area and activities but would also challenge the existing world order in international telegraphy and put the Danish company in the position of confronting other companies, including companies with which it had been cooperating, e.g. cooperation partners who also avoided using the wireless telegraph. When the English Poulsen company was established in 1913, Great Northern did not wish to cooperate with it because it would challenge the transatlantic cable companies, including the Commercial Cable Company, that were partners in the Pacific Ocean coalition.

In contrast, a final contract between Great Northern and the Syndicate and Christopher Hage could be signed in May 1913. Great Northern finally acquired the transmaritime rights for the Poulsen patent in Scandinavia and East Asia for 5,000 pounds sterling, and the company had no interest in or influence on what went on outside this area.[51]

European War and Two Russian Revolutions

CHAPTER 11

Special mission to Saint Petersburg

While Great Northern was following the development of wireless telegraphy from the sidelines, the company made considerable efforts to take over the entire trans-Siberian land connection with an independent wire for transit traffic alone and with Danish personnel at all transfer stations. The Russian government telegraph authority resisted these efforts, but that did not cause the Danish company to give up.

During the years after the Russo-Japanese War, the functioning of the service for transit traffic was degraded as a result of insufficient maintenance of the line, of great increases in Russian domestic traffic, and of the prioritization of the Russian telegraphists at the expense of transit telegrams. The reason for the increase in domestic traffic was the construction of a trans-Siberian railroad, which had resulted in a growing number of people moving to towns in Siberia and the construction of new residential and commercial areas and therefore increased telegram traffic.

When the railroad was built, the telegraph line was moved so that it followed the tracks, which made maintenance much easier and cheaper. However, the poor state of the Russian economy after the defeat by Japan resulted in insufficient funds being budgeted for maintenance and the installation of new equipment—and money for an extra wire was out of the question.

After the government's budget department had once again refused the approval of funding for an extra wire along the route from Omsk to Saint Petersburg, which was particularly overloaded, Great Northern finally succeeded in getting the support of the Russian director of telegraphy for an offer from the company for the financing of the hanging and operation of an extra wire.

The company offered to pay the cost of an extra wire for the transit traffic, which would thus be enhanced without negatively affecting the wires for the domestic traffic. Great Northern's expenses for establishing the extra wire would be reimbursed out of Russia's transit revenues, which were expected to increase as a result of the increased transit traffic.[1]

In January 1910, the director of telegraphy sent the offer to the government together with his recommendation that it be accepted, and shortly

Wilhelm Weimann held a law degree and became a supreme court attorney in 1897. The same year, he was sent to Chicago as a Danish vice consul, and for a time he was acting consul before he became general consul in Hamburg in 1901. In October 1909, he became Minister of Trade and later became Minister of Traffic in the first Social Liberal government. In 1911 he joined the East Asiatic Company as a manager, and in 1913, he became the director of the company's activities in Thailand, but he had to return to Denmark in 1914 because he had contracted climatic fever. As the chairman of the board of directors of Great Northern during the years 1916–1938, he led the company through great economic and political upheavals and increasing economic pressure due to the spread of wireless telegraphy.

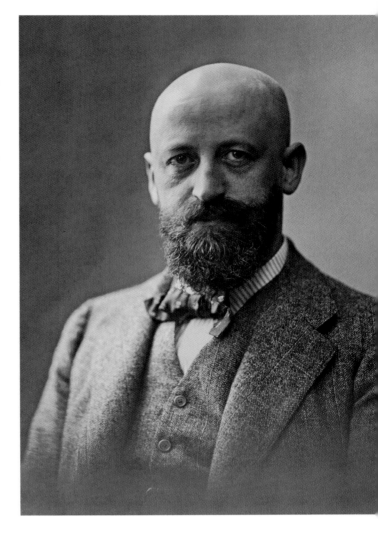

thereafter, Kay Suenson traveled to Saint Petersburg to present the company's arguments. However, the Russian Imperial Controller declared that the company's offer had to be regarded as an actual loan to the Russian government, which required the approval of both the imperial council and the Duma, and it was hardly realistic to expect such approval to be secured. As an internally circulated company description of events related to the matter put it, the Imperial Controller's decision had "again knocked all hopes of a satisfactory solution to this dragged-out matter to the ground."[2]

Things looked hopeless, and Great Northern's top management team and board of directors feared for the company's future cooperation with Eastern and, by extension, feared for the company's international position in general. In the long run, the English were hardly likely to accept the continually degraded performance of the trans-Siberian connection, which was causing increased traffic on the English cables, unless the distribution of revenues from their joint purse was changed to reflect the shift in traffic.

"Extraordinary envoy to Saint Petersburg"

In early September 1910, the chairman of the board of directors of Great Northern, Edouard Suenson, wrote a lengthy memorandum in which he pointed out the importance of reestablishing the compa-

ny's position in Russia, where the government and the department of telegraphy appeared "to have lost all interest in the Dano-Russian connection to the world we originally established as a result of their own initiative." Suenson believed it would be necessary to take what he called "extraordinary steps to reawaken the government's and the administration's interest in the common Dano-Russian project." This was to be accomplished by sending "to Saint Petersburg an extraordinary envoy with sufficient status, personality, abilities, and savoir faire to gain access to and be listened to by the authorities, particularly the ministers of the interior, foreign affairs, and finance, a few of their department heads—including, of course, the General Director of the Postal and

As one of his first actions on behalf of the company, Frederik Kjær, who was Great Northern's representative in 1891, undertook an expedition along the trans-Siberian connection.

Telegraph Authority—and possibly a few influential members of the Duma who are not too steeped in extremely chauvinistic views and prejudices."[3]

Because of his advanced age and poor health, Suenson felt he could not take on the proposed mission himself, and he found that it would be "most appropriate" if the mission was not carried out by one of the company's directors. Instead, a person should be chosen who would appear independent to the Russians and who would primarily emphasize not the interests of the company but "the origins and development of the *Dano-Russian* telegraph system in the context of cooperation between the imperial government and the company [...] and the eminent practical, political, and strategic significance of that cooperation for Russia."

As his envoy, Suenson had chosen the attorney and former minister of trade, Wilhelm Weimann (Danish Social Liberal Party), who had left the government a short time earlier and was not quite forty-two years old. According to Suenson, the ministerial post Wilhelm Weimann had recently held would give him "the necessary social position and access to the highest authorities in Russia." In addition, Suenson believed that Wilhelm Weimann, with his "sympathetic personality, lively spirit, clear vision and ability to acquire quick insights, energy, and savoir faire, would, it was to be hoped, be able to awaken the Russian authorities from their slumber and bring about the realization of the company's legitimate and reasonable wishes."[4]

Suenson's emphasis of Wilhelm Weimann's qualifications and personal qualities appears strikingly exaggerated and perhaps with good reason. According to Suenson's own memorandum, the mission to Saint Petersburg would have a decisive effect on the company's future, and Weimann had absolutely no preexisting knowledge of telegraphy, much less of undersea cables and concessions specifically.

Indeed, at the meeting of the board of directors on September 7, there was obvious skepticism with regard to whether Wilhelm Weimann was in fact the right person. There was general support for the chairman's proposal that a special envoy be sent to Saint Petersburg, but according to the minutes, "a few individuals asked whether an even more qualified person might not be found." There was a lengthy discussion of the matter that is not preserved in the minutes, but in addition to his lack of insight into international telegraphy, Weimann had had no experience with negotiations on the level in question.

Several names not recorded in the minutes were suggested without winning support, and the board, therefore, voted to approve authorizing the chairman to proceed with Wilhelm Weimann if none of the members of the board of directors put forward a new name in the following few days. Given Edouard Suenson's prestige and position, it is remarkable that there was even a discussion, but things went as he had wished as no new suggestions were made.[5]

On November 16, 1910, Wilhelm Weimann left for Saint Petersburg by ship with letters of introduction and recommendations from the Danish Ministry of Foreign Affairs and Suenson personally. He was received by the company's representative, Junior Chamberlain Frederik Kjær, and the Danish envoy, O. C. Scavenius, who supported his mission.

Weimann spent about two months in the Russian capital and appeared to achieve only modest results. When it came to ministers, he had "a satisfactory meeting" with Minister of Finance Vladimir Kokovtsov, but that was Weimann's only such meeting. On the basis of a Danish draft, the director of telegraphy had previously composed a letter to the Ministry of Finance containing strategic economic and traffic-related arguments for accepting Great Northern's proposal for financing a new transit wire. Minister of Finance Kokovtsov supposed-ly listened with "great interest" to Wilhelm Weimann's presentation of the matter and promised to view the company's proposal "positively" as did his department head.[6]

Great Northern appeared to have come no closer to its goal. After he returned to Copenhagen, Weimann's association with the company ended as Weimann became the manager of the operations of the East Asiatic Company (today the Santa Fe group) in Thailand and moved to Bangkok, where, in 1913, he became a director. However, he returned to Denmark the following year because he had contracted climatic fever, and on Edouard Suenson's recommendation, he was elected to Great Northern's board of directors.

"[...] close to the goal of their dreams"

While the results of Weimann's mission appeared limited, the accommodating attitude of the director of telegraphy nevertheless did lay the foundation for quick Danish action that itself led to significant results. Weimann had hardly left Saint Petersburg before the company's representative, Frederik Kjær, sought out the director of telegraphy to obtain written confirmation of the director's assurance that he would work to bring about the establishment of a dedicated transit wire and Danish staffing of the Russian transfer stations. As it turned out, Kjær was in fact able to obtain nothing more than verbal assurance, but at the same time, the need for an extra trans-Siberian wire was becoming more urgent as domestic traffic through Siberia was increasing rapidly and drastic reductions in prices that could be expected to increase traffic volume had been announced.

Frederik Kjær went to see Minister of the Interior Pyotr Stolypin, who was responsible for the telegraphy authority. In May 1911, Stolypin went to Minister of Finance Vladimir Kokovtsov and expressed a strong wish to secure financing for new telegraph connections through Siberia, and the following month, the Danish ambassador, O. C. Scavenius, also sought out Kokovtsov, who indicated that the budget for 1912 could already include funding for an extra wire.[7]

The pressure had an effect, and in August 1911, 210,000 rubles for the 1912 budget year were allocated for the hanging of an extra wire, to which an additional 260,000 were to be added for the following budget year if necessary. In the meantime, domestic traffic was increasing more or less explosively, partly as a result of the fact that Russia had introduced a single standard rate for all telegrams regardless of the distance. This caused the local section heads and operating leaders to demand that the new line be used for domestic traffic, while Great Northern referred to the pressure from Japan, which was threatening to lay its own cables to circumvent the Danish lines, and to the fact that Eastern was now servicing 80 percent of the traffic between East Asia and Europe, which was reducing Russia's—and Great Northern's—transit revenues.

The company did not get its own wire, but Great Northern did secure an agreement that the new wire would be used both for domestic and for transit traffic. At the same time, as it had wished, the company had transferred to it the servicing of the transit traffic all the way from Vladivostok via Irkutsk to Saint Petersburg—to begin with only for a one-month trial period as the director of telegraphy had made it a prerequisite for the establishment of a corresponding permanent arrangement that the company could produce an increase in the transit traffic of 10,000 words per twenty-four-hour period.

On March 15, 1913, Great Northern was, therefore, able to open its own telegraph service along the entire trans-Siberian landline with operators in Vladivostok, Irkutsk, and Saint Petersburg. The eight transfer stations in between were still manned by Russian telegraphists in the future, but at each station, the company was provided with two staff members using perforated telegram strips for the transit traffic alone, and the staff members in question were given an opportunity to earn bonuses for good service. The company had no difficulty meeting the volume target, which was exceeded by a large margin, and the arrangement was, therefore, extended indefinitely.

Like the domestic traffic, the transit traffic was now increasing rapidly—in the case of the transit traffic, the increase was due in part to the fact that Germany and the Netherlands, as well as the German-Dutch telegraphy company, were supporting Great Northern by diverting increasing amounts of the traffic away from Eastern's cables and over to the company's connection. If this development was to continue, it would be necessary to increase capacity and improve service for the connection.

During the spring of 1914, the company, therefore, presented to the Russian telegraphy administration a proposal for the hanging of a further wire that would be fully paid for by the company, which would also contribute to the financing of the operation of the transfer stations if Danish telegraphists were employed. Neither in the Russian telegraphy administration nor in the Ministry of the Interior was there resistance now to the wishes of the Danish company, and in the middle of July 1914, the Russians offered to hang a further wire that would be paid for by the Danes and intended solely for transit telegrams, and the Russians were also amenable to the employment of Danish telegraphists at all transfer stations if the company would pay two thirds of the operating costs for these stations. "The company was finally close to the goal of its dreams" as a document for Great Northern's internal use put it—and then everything fell through.[8]

The outbreak of war, censorship, and cut cables

On August 1, 1914, after a long period during which the political situation in Europe had become increasingly tense, Russia began a general mobilization of its army and navy, and a German declaration of war followed the same day. Three days later, German troops invaded Belgium, after which France and the United Kingdom declared war on Germany. A major European war was a reality, with the Central Powers, consisting of Germany and Austria-Hungary and their allies, on one side and the Entente Powers, consisting of France, Russia, the United Kingdom, and their allies, on the other side.

The outbreak of war had an immediate effect on Great Northern despite the fact that the company, like Denmark, had declared that it was neutral. On August 2, the British government already took over the company's stations in Newcastle and London and subjected them to military censorship. Russia and the other combatant countries followed suit, and the sending of encoded private telegrams was forbidden.[9]

Japan also declared war on Germany, blockading Qingdao and immediately subjecting Great Northern's station in Nagasaki to censorship. A few days later, Sweden introduced inspection of incoming and outgoing telegrams, while Denmark introduced a prohibition against using codes in private telegrams and in January 1916 introduced actual censorship. On the other hand, Great Northern—at least in the beginning—escaped the combatant powers' cutting of each other's cables. The first was a German Atlantic cable to the United States via the Azores, which was cut by the British shortly after the outbreak of war.

However, a representative of the company was summoned to a meeting in the French department of telegraphy on August 10 because the department feared that Germany would intercept traffic sent via the company's Dano-French or Dano-Russian cables, which were used to send telegrams between the two allied powers. The French had not noticed anything suspicious, but they could not understand why the company's cables had not been cut immediately after the outbreak of war. The expla-

An artist's rendering of the murder of Grand Duke Franz Ferdinand and his wife in Sarajevo, Bosnia, on June 28 1914. This assassination was the event that triggered the First World War following a long period in which political tensions had increased and military forces had been upgraded. Denmark remained neutral throughout the war, and Great Northern succeeded in maintaining traffic on its cable systems in Northern Europe and East Asia. The company's trans-Siberian connection continued to operate.

nation, they believed, could only be that the Germans were intercepting traffic on one or more of them, but both the company and the Danish government telegraphy authority carried out measurements that did not reveal anything unusual, let alone suspicious.[10]

In early November 1914, however, the company's Dano-Russian cables in the Baltic Sea were cut. Suspicion fell on the German Navy, and this suspicion was confirmed when Great Northern, via the Danish Ministry of Foreign Affairs, requested permission from Germany to repair the cables so that the cable ship *H. C. Ørsted* would not be exposed to danger. In its reply, the German Ministry of Foreign Affairs admitted that the cables had been cut by the German Navy, which would not hinder the *H. C. Ørsted* in repairing them. However, Germany would not promise not to cut the cables again, and the company viewed this as refusal to allow repairs. A Danish demand that damages be paid was rejected, but the German telegraphy authority promised to consider the matter after the war.[11]

The war had now been going on for seven months, and it was clear that it would not be brief. As the combatant powers adjusted to the prosecution of a long war, censorship became stricter. At the company's station in Petrograd, as Russia's capital had been called since the beginning of the war to not have a name that sounded too German, the number of censors was already increased to eighteen early in 1915. These eighteen were under the command of a functionary. At the same time, the company lost its right to service the direct connection between Petrograd and Irkutsk.[12]

The Dano-Russian cables were not repaired before the end of the war, and it would have made no difference if they had been as Liepaja was occupied by German troops advancing toward Petrograd in the summer of 1918. Neither the cables between Denmark and England nor the cables between Sweden and England were cut; the cables between Sweden and Finland also remained intact. On the other hand, it became more difficult to repair both the company's own and other cables because of the laying of mines and because the United Kingdom and, in particular, Germany increasingly refused to provide guarantees that the *H. C. Ørsted* would be able to work without risking being attacked or stopped.

The company did succeed in carrying out a fair number of repairs, however, and in October 1915, a royal resolution made it permissible for the company's cable ships to fly the Dannebrog burgee as special protection. To a great extent, it was therefore possible to maintain the traffic between the United Kingdom and Russia via Sweden, and special ac-

tion by the United Kingdom and Russia contributed to reducing pressure on the Danish cables.

Immediately after the cutting of Great Northern's Baltic Sea cables, the two countries carried out a spectacular secret laying of cable from Aberdeen, Scotland, around Norway to the north and to the harbor city of Aleksandrovsk on the Kola Peninsula. In December 1914, Great Northern was notified in strict confidence of the existence of the cable, which was already being used for British, Russian, and French government telegrams in late January 1915.[13]

In East Asia, the company's cables were not subjected to cutting or other form of sabotage. After having taken Qingdao in November 1914, however, Japan exploited the situation to expand its telegraphic network further. In addition to taking over the cables Great Northern had laid in connection with the Boxer Rebellion, the Japanese established a new cable connection between Qingdao and Japan, which was announced to the bureau of the International Telegraph Union in Berne as a "temporary" cable. In the eyes of Great Northern, this was, nevertheless, a "violation," and both China and Eastern saw it similarly, but because of the war, no protest was registered.[14]

Under suspicion of espionage

Much as Denmark managed to remain neutral during the whole war, balancing its trade relations and political actions between the combatant powers, Great Northern succeeded in remaining neutral. Nevertheless, both of the warring blocs feared espionage, and they continually tightened censorship at the company's stations. However, censorship and the relationships between censors on one hand and operating leaders and personnel on the other in the various countries differed greatly. When Colonel Hore, the head of military censorship at the company's station in London, left his position at the beginning of 1916, he thanked head of operations P. Westergaard for "their assistance and the friendly relations" there had been between him and them.[15]

Developments were very different in Russia, where the authorities' tone in dealing with the company became sharper as the Russian armies were increasingly put on the defensive and shortages of food and other supplies became acute. Both in the countryside and in the cities, dissatisfaction increased, so there were demonstrations for peace and bread, and among the soldiers, dissatisfaction also smoldered, partly as a result of the lack of weapons, ammunition, and other equipment, as well as insufficient supplies of food.

The military defeats and the increasing internal dissatisfaction and unrest led to growing fears of German espionage and suspicion of foreigners, including the representatives of Great Northern. In October 1915, the military in Petrograd forbade the company to hire more Danish personnel, and early in 1916, the censorship became so strict that the transit traffic on the Russian lines ceased completely.[16]

In late June, military censors occupied Great Northern's stations in Petrograd and Nystad and removed all Danish telegraphists from the apparatus and replaced them with Russian telegraphists. Frederik Kjær protested, but the company otherwise accepted the situation to avoid provoking even more drastic Russian action.[17]

In early July 1916, Kay Suenson traveled to Petrograd, where he remained for a little under four weeks. The purpose of his visit was to obtain a written declaration to the effect that the Russian action had not been the result of inappropriate behavior on the part of the company or suspicion of a lack of

During the Russian Revolution in 1917, Dowager Empress Maria Feodorovna was in Kiev, from where she traveled to the Crimea, thus avoiding arrest by the Bolsheviks. Here, in July 1919, she received the news that her son and his entire family had been murdered. In May 1919, she fled to the United Kingdom on a British warship, and the following year, she moved from there to Denmark, where she moved into the small mansion Hvidøre in Gentofte, north of Copenhagen. Her living expenses during her last years were covered by several large Danish companies, including Great Northern, which provided its support in deep secrecy to avoid challenging Lenin and the Soviet government. The picture shows her being helped out of her car by one of her Cossack Life Guards, who had come with her from Russia. Maria Feodorovna died in 1928; her funeral service was held at the Russian Orthodox Saint Alexander Nevsky Church on Bredgade in Copenhagen.

discretion on the part of the company's personnel.[18] The head of the military censorship unit, General Mikhail Adabash, and Director of Telegraphy Mikhail Poskvisnev assured Kay Suenson that "not the least shadow of mistrust had fallen over the company," and the general staff also declared that the company's behavior had been "beyond reproach." Nevertheless, Kay Suenson met resistance to his request for a written declaration, and in the end, he had to leave Petrograd without having received one. In fact, on the very day of his departure, July 31, he received notification that all Danish personnel would be removed from the company's stations as soon as Russian personnel could be acquired.[19]

Kay Suenson did not get a reason for this—or maybe he did. Though this was not explicitly linked to the Russian measures taken at the company's stations, he was informed during his stay that on June 29, the station in Petrograd had received ten German telegrams sent from Berlin to Stockholm. This glitch could have been caused by a technical problem in Sweden, but it had nevertheless caused the Russian military censors to react with horror and sparked rumors that Great Northern had a secret connection with Germany. The company immediately prepared a written report on the matter but was unable to localize the cause of the glitch.[20]

In fact, the removal of the Danish telegraphists was later officially justified by the Russians with reference to the famous telegrams, as well as by the allegation that a Danish telegraphist had been seen on the street tearing off a piece of an official Russian proclamation that had been pasted to a wall.[21]

The situation was worsened when it was announced from London that at the request of the Russians, it had been decided that the employment of Danish telegraphists at Great Northern's stations in the United Kingdom would not be allowed in cases in which the Danes in question had worked in Petrograd within the past year. The company's management knew from confidential sources that the English were not dissatisfied with the Danish telegraphists from Petrograd but that the British government did not wish to decline to fulfill a request from an ally.[22]

Kay Suenson's fellow director, Per Michelsen, traveled to London promptly in early October 1916, and at the same time, the matter reached the highest level in Russia after telegrams to Grand Duke George Mikhailovich from his wife, the Princess, who was in London, had arrived after such a delay that the Prince demanded an explanation. Great Northern's representative in Petrograd presented the company's view of the matter to him, after which the Grand Duke summoned the head of military censorship and announced that he planned to mention the matter to Czar Nicholas II, whom he was to accompany to the military headquarters at the front that same day.[23]

Word of the Grand Duke's plan was welcomed in Copenhagen, where there was also rejoicing over the fact that there was no sympathy for the Russian measures in London. The British postal and telegraphy directorate also indicated that it would contact the Russian department of telegraphy and try to influence Russia's Ministry of Foreign Affairs and military authorities.[24]

In order "not to leave any means of obtaining justice in Russia untried," the company's management also briefed Prince Valdemar on the matter and got him to transmit a French memorandum to the Russian Czar. "With his usual helpfulness," the prince promised to send the memorandum on to Empress Dowager Maria Feodorovna and ask her to present it to her son, the Czar.[25]

Per Michelsen subsequently traveled to Petrograd again but was again unable to achieve positive results. The British had not sent the promised letter, and the British representative attached to the military censors in Petrograd was unwilling even to receive Per Michelsen. An account of the matter sent by the Danish Ministry of Foreign Affairs to the corresponding ministry in Russia had no effect either—no response was ever received.[26]

This was a matter no one wanted to touch. Only Empress Dowager Maria Feodorovna appeared to take an interest in the company's problems—she sent Great Northern's memorandum on to her son, the Czar, who wrote a note to the effect that the matter should be investigated and the result reported to him. After this, the matter disappeared in the Russian bureaucracy, and Great

Northern heard nothing further regarding the fate of the memorandum before overall developments took a dramatic turn.

Russian revolution and dissolution

On the morning of March 15, 1917, Copenhagen and other European capital cities were reached by the first telegrams from Petrograd to the effect that the Russian Czar had abdicated in favor of his brother, Prince Mikhail, who had declined to take over the throne. The abdication represented the culmination of a long period of increasing strike activity, unrest, and demonstrations in Petrograd and other cities against the prosecution of the war and the worsening shortages of food and other vital necessities.

After the Czar's abdication, the Duma appointed a provisional government to lead the country and call a constitutional assembly that would approve a constitution. The power shift quickly led to changes in the Russian department of telegraphy, where the general director was replaced by one of his subordinates. General Mikhail Adabash disappeared from the military censorship unit and was replaced by a young lieutenant for whom Great Northern had high hopes as regarded the possibility that he might know something about telegraphy as he was the son of an official in the postal service.[27]

Despite the tenacious efforts of Frederik Kjær, however, the personnel changes did not lead to changes in Russian censorship or in the staffing of Great Northern's station in Petrograd. Instead, the service for both the domestic and the transit traffic was degraded to such a degree that in the course of the spring, the British postal and telegraphy directorate got the British Foreign Office to instruct the embassy in Petrograd to support the Danish company. The embassy refused to do so, however, declaring that under the existing circumstances, the Russian government could not be faulted for the poor state of the telegraph service.[28]

The attitude of the British embassy reflected the fact that revolutionary chaos in Russia was increasing and the power of the provisional government had begun to crumble. Already before the abdica-tion of the Czar, soviets had been founded at factories and in army units in the capital, and during the revolution in 1905, the Petrograd Soviet had been established, an organization that was increasingly playing the role of an organ of power that constituted an alternative to the provisional government, which was gradually losing its authority.

In the middle of April, the rivalry between the two organs of power became more acute when the revolutionary Bolshevik Vladimir Lenin arrived in Petrograd from his exile in Switzerland and urged the people to overthrow the provisional government and transfer all power to the Soviets. The Bolsheviks quickly gained ground by means of simple slogans about peace, bread, and freedom and with the growing number of soviets as their power base, and Great Northern saw the effects of this. "In the telegraphy sector, as in the army, it is the subordinates who rule, dictating their orders to their superiors via a committee, after which the superiors simply carry out these orders," the top management team reported to the board of directors in April 1917. The following month, the company's top management team described the situation as chaotic and characterized by a lack of top leadership.

"Every telegraph station appears to constitute a little republic whose members are too busy approving resolutions to carry out their work and appear not to recognize any authority; the postal and telegraphy authorities have determined that the department of telegraphy is entirely superfluous, and the superior officials are fired on the orders of their subordinates, as in the case of the acting general director."[29]

In the course of the summer, the situation deteriorated further. Russia was on the brink of collapse, and the Germans exploited the situation for a military advance toward Petrograd. The newly established Postal and Telegraphy Ministry was preparing to move to Kharkiv in southern Ukraine, and Frederik Kjær also found the increasing anarchy so threatening that he recommended evacuating the approximately fifty Danish employees who were still working at the station in Petrograd.[30]

Great Northern's top management team refused to approve such a measure as it would constitute failure to carry out the duties the company had taken on in connection with its concessions. If an evacuation was to be carried out, it should be at the initiative of the Russians so as not to damage the company's position in a future postwar Russia. With the permission of the Danish authorities, the company, therefore, arranged for weekly shipments of four hundred kilograms of food to Petrograd to help the Danes in the Russian capital, while the Danish personnel were warned not to go out after dark and to observe further safety rules.[31]

Bolshevik takeover

The Danish personnel, therefore, remained in Petrograd while Russia disintegrated more and more until November 7, 1917, when the Bolsheviks carried out an armed uprising that introduced a government via the Soviets and brought the Bolsheviks to power with Vladimir Lenin as leader of the government. No reports indicate that any of the company's employees or their families were in danger or were subjected to persecution during the Petrograd uprising, which took place without significant bloodshed.

In contrast, there was violence in Irkutsk, which the revolution reached after some delay. Shortly before Christmas 1917, the city was shelled by the Bolsheviks' artillery and severely damaged; the entire neighborhood was burned down. The telegraph station was damaged and looted, though the company's rooms and equipment escaped this fate, and despite intense street fighting, none of the Danish telegraphists or members of their families were among the thousands who lost their lives in the fighting around and in the city.

When the battles were over, the personnel managed to reestablish the connections with Petrograd, Vladivostok, and Beijing, and the transit route was, therefore, intact, though private telegrams were not being transmitted. The local Bolsheviks considered closing the Danish station, but the Soviet government vouched for the company and its personnel.[32]

In Kyakhta, the Bolsheviks did not seize power until April 1918, and they did not succeed in taking power in Vladivostok, where Japan landed troops to support the local opponents of the Bolsheviks while Great Northern's station was able to keep operating as it had been.

Much as the personnel at all Russian stations got through the revolutionary events unharmed, the Bolsheviks' takeover had no immediate consequences with regard to Great Northern's concession rights. The top management team's report to the board of directors simply notes that "in Lenin's/Trotsky's government, which came to power in Petrograd after the maximalists had toppled Kerenski, the postal and telegraphy sector has been taken over by Mr. Avilof."[33]

In connection with the takeover, the previously existing ministries were transformed into People's Commissariats. Nikolai Glebov-Avilov, who had been a Bolshevik and one of Vladimir Lenin's supporters since 1904, became Soviet Russia's first People's Commissar of Posts and Telegraphs and thus the individual with whom Great Northern would negotiate in the future.

The first time this happened was after the Soviet government had nationalized the banks and confiscated all deposited funds in December 1917. Frederik Kjær was unable to get access to the company's account at the government bank for foreign trade, and the company was owed more than 5 million gold francs for telegram invoices. This was a debt the Soviet government was not immediately willing to recognize, but in February 1918, Frederik Kjær succeeded in securing a transfer from the People's Commissariat of 2 million gold francs to the Russian government bank as partial repayment of the debt. The money was released in June 1918 on condition that it not be exported from Russia.[34]

In contrast, other Danish companies, several of which were owed significant sums, were unable to get their money paid out—even after an official protest by Ambassador Harald Scavenius.

Agreement with independent Finland

Among the first decisions made by the Soviet governments was the decision to issue a decree that

When Kay Suenson arrived in Helsinki in the middle of
January 1918, there was a civil war brewing between
the revolutionary Red forces and the counter-revo-
lutionary White forces. The picture shows the White
militia marching into the Finnish capital, where fighting
broke out on January 27, while Kay Suenson was still
negotiating with the Finnish government regarding a
telegraphy contract.

gave all nations within the Russian imperium the
right to detach themselves and become independent
nations. The first nation to exploit this right was Finland, which declared its independence on Decem-

ber 6, 1917, but already earlier, via the Danish Ministry of Foreign Affairs, the Finns had sought contact
with Great Northern and requested "quick negotiations." When two representatives of the Finnish government came to Copenhagen just a week after the
Finnish declaration of independence to negotiate
with regard to official Danish recognition of Finland
as an independent state, they, therefore, also met
with Kay Suenson and Per Michelsen at Great Northern's headquarters in Kongens Nytorv.[35]

The company had previously discussed its position with the Danish Ministry of Foreign Affairs,

and the two Finns' predictable wish to have an independent direct cable connection with foreign countries that circumvented the Russian lines was, therefore, "in principle" positively received. Given that there were four cables between Finland and Sweden, there would not be a technical problem in this connection, but the station in Nystad was still occupied by the Russian military. It was also of relevance that the company was still bound by duties related to its Russian concessions and that Finland's independence had still not been recognized by Russia or any other state and thus had to be regarded as Russian.

The first recognitions of an independent Finland came on January 4, 1918, from Soviet Russia, Sweden, Germany, and France, while Denmark and Norway followed on January 10. At that point, Great Northern had already received an official Finnish request for negotiations as well as notification that the Finnish government would begin negotiations with the Soviet government regarding taking over the country's telegraphy authority.[36]

Therefore, on Sunday, January 13, Kay Suenson departed for Helsinki, and as there was no sea connection to the Finnish capital, he had to undertake a three-day rail journey via Stockholm and Haparanda at the northern end of the Gulf of Bothnia. His willingness to undertake this difficult journey was no as much for the sake of helping independent Finland establish international telegraph connections as for the sake of securing the company's position and not least the maintenance of its connection with Russia and its access to the trans-Siberian connection in the future.

The day after his arrival, Kay Suenson met with Councilor of State Ahonen, who was the chairman of the government committee that was negotiating with the Soviet government regarding the taking over of the telegraph authority in Finland. The following day, Frederik Kjær arrived from Petrograd, and he and Suenson met with the head of the Russian telegraph administration in Finland, Mr. Kouzov, who assured the two men that the Soviet government had a positive attitude toward the Dano-Finnish negotiations.[37]

Kay Suenson subsequently produced a draft agreement that required Great Northern to establish a direct cable connection between Finland and Sweden, while Finland was to recognize the company's Russian concessions as the basis of the connection, including the economic subsidies, as well as their responsibility for maintaining a number of landlines between Nystad and the Russian border for the sake of the transit traffic.

Via Councilor of State Ahonen, the Finnish minister of traffic rejected acceptance of the Russian concessions and indicated that if necessary, Finland would lay a cable to Sweden itself, something Kay Suenson claimed Finland would be prevented from doing by the company's Swedish concessions.

For Great Northern, Finnish recognition of the Russian concessions was a key point because of the company's relationship with Russia, where conditions continued to be unstable. Kay Suenson recommended that the Finns "seize the current situation" as the Soviet government was not expected to retain power for very long and a new Russian government might take a very different position on Finland. If that happened, it might have consequences for Great Northern, and he, therefore, did not wish to sign an agreement that did not recognize the Russian concessions as the basis of Finland's telegraph connections before conditions in Russia had stabilized. If the Finns did not give in, he declared, he would return to Copenhagen and confer with his board of directors, which could result in "a very unfortunate delay in resolving the matter."

The Finns gave in, and a new agreement was drafted indicating that they accepted the Danish demands. Kay Suenson was ready to sign, but on January 27, 1918, before he could do so, an armed uprising broke out in Helsinki. The Finnish social democrats were opposed to the Finnish declaration of independence and now seized power in the capital. From their hotel, Kay Suenson and Frederik Kjær could watch armed Red Guards taking control over the city and occupying banks and public buildings. The bourgeois government was declared deposed and replaced by a revolutionary government on the Russian model.

Nevertheless, the following day, Kay Suenson and Frederik Kjær, met with Councilor of State Ahonen, who told them that troops loyal to the government were on their way to the capital under the command of the newly appointed commander-in-chief of the country's armed forces, Baron Carl Mannerheim. A civil war had broken out, and while Ahonen tried to find the minister, Kay Suenson and Frederik Kjær sought out Mr. Kouzov of the Russian telegraph administration to secure his approval of the agreement.

During Suenson and Kjær's meeting with Mr. Kouzov, shooting broke out in the vicinity, and the Swedish general consulate was fired upon. The same evening, there was what Kay Suenson called "lively shooting" on the square in front of the hotel, and at two o'clock in the morning, armed Red Guards and Russian sailors forced their way into the hotel and got all the guests, including the two Danes, out of bed and ransacked their rooms.

The following day, Kay Suenson again sought out Councilor of State Ahonen, while Frederik Kjær brought Mr. Kouzov up to date by telephone. Mr. Kouzov was satisfied with the loyalty of the Danes and approved the agreement. As Mr. Kouzov was going to travel to Petrograd himself, he offered Frederik Kjær an opportunity to accompany him on his journey, and Kjær gratefully accepted this offer. Councilor of State Ahonen was unable to reach the minister of traffic, but Kay Suenson persuaded Ahonen to sign under the condition that the agreement would subsequently have to be ratified by the government before it could go into effect.

Kay Suenson was now able to return home, something the civil war made difficult. On February 1, he left Helsinki on an extra train for Scandinavians that had been arranged for by the Swedish general consul. His journey subsequently featured transport by dogsled to the Finnish east coast, where he boarded the Danish steamer *Heimdal*, which was an element of a squadron of ships that were evacuating fleeing foreigners.

On February 9, Kay Suenson was back in Copenhagen with the agreement, which, as it bore not only Councilor of State Ahonen's signature but also his reservation regarding government approval, was not legally binding. However, the agreement was immediately recognized by the Soviet government, and the resolution of the matter subsequently depended on which way the Finnish civil war went. The war ended on May 5, 1918, with the surrender of the last Red Guards.

Kay Suenson subsequently returned to Helsinki. The Finnish government was initially unwilling to recognize the agreement Councilor of State Ahonen had signed but ended up giving in, and after two weeks of negotiations, Suenson was able to leave Helsinki with the signed agreement in his briefcase. The agreement was temporary and to be renegotiated when the world war was over and the question of who would hold power in Russia had been resolved.

The Russian Civil War and the Soviet Russian Concession

CHAPTER 12

Danish evacuation of Petrograd

In June 1918, both Great Northern and the Finnish government received an official request from the Soviet government that the transit line through Finland, which had been interrupted as a result of the civil war, be restored. At this time, the company was also given permission to operate the station in Petrograd again, but despite the fact that the Russian and the Finnish lines were reestablished all the way to the border, starting up operations again was not easy. The Finnish general staff forbade the connecting of the lines after pressure from representatives of the German military leadership in Finland who had reacted to the stationing of British troops in northern Russia.

In March 1918, the Soviet government had withdrawn from the war after having concluded a separate peace with Germany, which had caused the United Kingdom to send military units to Murmansk. In June, a further large contingent of British troops arrived, and shortly thereafter, the government of the United Kingdom announced that it would not recognize Finland's independence because of the German influence on Finland. At

the same time, Finland was blockaded, and Great Northern had to recognize that the company's hopes for the reopening of the telegraph connection with Petrograd had not been justified.

At this point, the telegraph connection between Petrograd and Irkutsk had also been interrupted. In connection with the conclusion of the Russo-German peace agreement, a Czech legion comprising 40,000 to 50,000 soldiers who had fought on the Russian side had been pulled out of the war. The Soviet government had concluded an agreement with the Western powers according to which the legion would be transferred to Vladivostok via the trans-Siberian railway and the soldiers would be transported by sea from Vladivostok to Western Europe to fight against Germany.

In May 1918, when the legion was spread out along the trans-Siberian railway, fighting broke out between the Bolsheviks and the Czechs, with the result that the heavily armed legion started a revolt and seized power in Vladivostok and large areas along the railway, causing the telegraph connection

The proclamation of Soviet power in connection with the Bolshevik takeover in Vladivostok in October 1922.

In May 1920, Harald Scavenius replaced O. C. Scavenius
as Minister of Foreign Affairs. During the Russian Civil
War, Harald Scavenius advocated for Western military
intervention against the Bolsheviks, and he supported
the British-led international blockade against Soviet
Russia. This conflicted with Great Northern's efforts to
reach agreement with the Soviet government regarding
the landing of the company's cables and the reopening
of the trans-Siberian connection, and Harald Scavenius's behavior therefore provoked great irritation at
Great Northern, whose board chairman, Wilhelm Weimann, declared that "the man [was] insane."

sian Central Asia, and an allied military delegation
was attached to a Siberian government that had established itself in Omsk.

In a report to the Danish Ministry of Foreign Affairs on August 10, 1918, Ambassador Harald Scavenius reported that the pressure on the Bolsheviks
had triggered "a kind of wildness" in the local authorities, who had carried out mass arrests of both
Russians and foreigners. Later in the month, he
wrote that the Bolsheviks had "become like wild
animals" fighting for survival.[1]

In a somewhat more subdued tone, Kay Suenson
and Per Michelsen reported to the board that "circumstances in Petrograd are becoming increasingly
intolerable." To be sure, Danish citizens were not being arrested, but this might be a temporary state of
affairs. At the same time, it was becoming more difficult to continue delivering food from Denmark, and
the company's top management team, therefore, decided to evacuate the Petrograd station. The company left behind a small number of telegraphists intended to carry out a quick reopening of the station
when the Soviet government was overthrown as the
company's leaders hoped it soon would be.[2]

However, the situation in Petrograd continued
to become increasingly tense, and in September
1918, Frederik Kjær returned to Denmark "as there
was no prospect of an improvement of conditions."
A number of telegraphists continued to remain at
the station, but in the middle of December 1918,
when Harald Scavenius evacuated the embassy in
Petrograd and the general consulate in Moscow
and returned to Denmark, Great Northern pulled
its remaining personnel out, though four telegraphists and their families remained behind of their
own free will to protect the station.[3]

Danish telegraph connections
and British geopolitics

Everywhere in the world, the Soviet government
was seen as a pariah, and in Denmark, as in most
other countries, the mood favored an allied military intervention now that the war in Europe had
been ended by the conclusion of a truce agreement

to be interrupted. Soviet power was neutralized in
large parts of Siberia, and the Soviet government,
which had moved to Moscow in March 1918, was
under pressure from anti-Bolshevik forces on all
sides.

Pressure from abroad increased as well in early August when the Entente Powers established a
general blockade of Soviet Russia that included
telegraph traffic. British, French, and American
troops went ashore in Arkhangelsk, and in Vladivostok, Japan increased the size of its force to 70,000
soldiers. From Iran, British units pushed into Rus-

At an early stage, Great Northern built a cable depot at Tuborg Harbor in which the company stored cables to be used in connection with repairs and the establishment of minor lines. In 1920, this depot was moved to the building whose interior is shown in the picture, which is located on the Redmolen pier. The depot had been designed by the Danish architect Osvald Rosendahl Langballe.

on November 11, 1918. On his return to Copenhagen, Harald Scavenius warned that if the allies did not chase the Bolsheviks out of Russia, they would see "the general European revolution" for which the Bolsheviks were agitating.[4]

Danish business leaders such as Harald Plum, Alexander Foss, and H. N. Andersen also desired the military overthrow of the Soviet government, and the mainstream press backed them. The Danish government expressed itself with caution, however, and there was silence from Great Northern as the company would be dependent on being able to work with the coming Russian government regardless of who emerged from the conflict victorious.

Within the company, though, sympathies were unconditionally on the side of the counterrevolutionaries, and the company materially supported the fight against the Soviet government. With the establishment of the Siberian government and the allied military mission in Omsk, the telegraph connections from there to foreign countries became of decisive importance for the further development of the civil war. In September 1918, Great Northern had reopened its lines from Irkutsk to Vladivostok as well as to Beijing via Kyakhta, and in October, the British government asked the company to increase capacity as a result of the increasing amount of traffic between Omsk and the capital cities of the allied countries, and the company accommodated this request.

In Europe, Great Northern was also asked to support the United Kingdom's foreign policy. Like Finland, the Baltic countries, Estonia, Latvia, and Lithuania, wished to separate from Russia, as did

In January 1919, the cable ship *H. C. Ørsted* carried out an unusual rescue mission when it entered the harbor at Liepaja to have its anchor system repaired during an operation in the Baltic Sea. Here the Latvian prime minister, Kārlis Ulmanis, unexpectedly boarded the ship with two other ministers who were fleeing the Russian Bolsheviks, who were seeking to reestablish control over the three Baltic countries, which had declared their independence after the October Revolution of 1917. The three ministers who had fled their own country were set ashore on Bornholm on January 20, and the *H. C. Ørsted* subsequently continued with its cable repairs.

Poland. In October 1918, Great Northern received a message from the British Foreign Office, which wished to connect the Baltic countries and Poland with the Western powers telegraphically "while avoiding Germany." This would be in the interests of the United Kingdom, and Great Northern too could, it was suggested, "have a future" that was represented by such connections.[5]

At a meeting in London in November and December of 1918, Kay Suenson presented a plan that would make Liepaja, Estonia, a telegraphic nexus in the region. The company would operate stations in the three Baltic countries and in Poland that would be connected via landlines to Liepaja, from where a new cable to Denmark would be laid.[6]

However, the plan required economic subsidies from the United Kingdom and not least the acceptance of the new states, and Kay Suenson, therefore, used the opportunity offered by his stay in London to meet with the ambassadors of Estonia and Poland. As it turned out, both countries had such a strong desire for independence that they categorically rejected a connection via Liepaja; they wanted instead to have their own cables to Denmark.[7]

The Baltic countries' push for independence did not cause Great Northern to waver in its resoluteness, and the company asked France and the United Kingdom to implement the plan at the coming peace conference in Paris. In a report on the matter submitted to the board of directors, Kay Suenson and Per Michelsen made no secret of how "it is to be desired that England and France raise the matter in the way described and if necessary dictate their will to the three named states and Poland."[8]

On January 18, 1919 the peace conference in Paris began; there was a Danish delegation whose primary interest was Southern Jutland. Kay Suenson arrived in the middle of March, but he was not attached to the official Danish delegation. He had traveled from Copenhagen to London before proceeding to Paris, and the Foreign Office had confirmed its support for the company's plan but added that France would have to contribute a part of the economic subsidies if the plan was to be realized. The French refused to do so, however.[9]

The company's grand plan for the telegraph connections in the Baltic Sea region had collapsed, and Kay Suenson was both bitter and disappointed: "In contrast to the [British] Post Office, they preferred to see correspondence sent via the German lines and to become dependent on those lines to paying higher prices to avoid them."[10]

Agreements with Latvia and Finland

In March 1919, while the Paris Peace Conference was going on, the anti-Bolshevik forces in Siberia launched a major offensive and pushed the Red Army back almost six hundred kilometers in just four weeks. During April and May, a new front aimed against the Soviet government was created when a force based in Estonia advanced toward Petrograd. In June, the fall of the city appeared imminent, and at the request of the British government, Great Northern began stockpiling materials and personnel in Stockholm, from where it would be possible to transfer everything to Petrograd quickly.[11]

But then the fortunes of war shifted. Petrograd held out, and in the course of the summer, the Red Army made major gains in Siberia. This caused the United Kingdom and other powers to withdraw their troops from Russia, and in the fall of 1919, the anti-Bolshevik forces were left to their own devices. By the middle of November, Western Siberia was in the hands of the Bolsheviks, and while the fighting still continued, it was clear that the civil war was nearing its end and the Bolsheviks would emerge as the victors.

Great Northern began to adjust to the idea that the Soviet government had come to stay and that there would be no getting around initiating negotiations with the revolutionary government. The matter was complicated by the fact that the company's cables in the Baltic Sea and the Gulf of Bothnia no longer landed in Russia but rather in Latvia and Finland. Resuming traffic would, therefore, require an agreement with Latvia, and a new agreement would have to be negotiated with Finland.

In December 1919, Kay Suenson was, therefore, again in Helsinki, this time to negotiate with the Finnish minister and the Latvian director of telegraphy, who had come to Helsinki for this purpose. It was easy to reach an agreement with the Latvian director of telegraphy, and in December 1920, the Latvian government ratified a concession that would expire on January 31, 1946.[12]

The Finns were more difficult as they refused to provide an economic subsidy to the company, which caused Kay Suenson to threaten to lay a cable directly from Denmark to Petrograd so Finland would miss out on significant transit revenues. The was also disagreement with regard to the running time of the concession: the Finns wished to borrow 10 million kroner from Great Northern in return for granting the company a concession that would run until 1939. From two Finnish bank directors, Kay Suenson knew Finland could not borrow money abroad, and he, therefore, offered to loan the Finns 4 million kroner in return for a period of validity until the end of 1946. The Finns had no choice but to accept, and an agreement was signed in January 1920.[13]

On their way into a geopolitical minefield

The company now still had to deal with the Soviet government, with which Great Northern had had no experience. But as late as in August 1919, the company had learned from a Red Cross staff member who had returned to Denmark that the four telegraphists who had remained behind with their families were well and that "their special position would protect them from being intentionally harmed in the future as well."[14]

The serious situation in which Great Northern found itself was due to the fact that since the interruption of the connection via Finland in April 1918, the company had profited from the agreements it had made with Eastern, which secured the company's revenues for up to two years in case of an interrupted connection between East Asia and Europe. The period during which Eastern would continue transferring support money to Great Northern was due to expire in April 1920, after which the company could lose annual revenues amounting to 8 to 9 million gold francs or a third of the company's total telegram revenues. Eastern and the Commercial Cable Company could also require Great Northern to give up its share in Commercial Pacific and pull out of the Pacific agreements. This was to say that the consequences for Great Northern could be fatal if the connection to Russia was not reopened.[16]

The main obstacle to reopening the connection, though, was not the Soviet government but the Western powers. As recently as in October 1919, the allies had asked the Danish government to prevent Danish citizens from being connected to the Soviet government by telegraph, and Denmark was explicitly asked to break off all postal and telegraphic contact with Soviet Russia.

The Danish government had assured the Western powers that measures taken to blockade and isolate Soviet Russia would be supported; if Great Northern initiated negotiations with the Soviet government, then this would constitute a violation

The celebration of Great Northern's fiftieth anniversary in 1919 was somewhat muted because of the interruption of the trans-Siberian connection, but there was a party for all the company's staff in Denmark, at which this picture was taken. The relationship between the staff and the leadership had been strained in recent years by dissatisfaction among the employees with salaries and other conditions of their employment that had been affected by the war and its aftermath. In 1912, an association of functionaries had been created that now wished to represent the personnel in connection with their dealings with management, and this was not agreeable to the company's board chairman and previous longtime chief executive officer, Edouard Suenson. He gave in, however, and the party could subsequently be held without conflicts.

There was reason to be confident, and indeed, the Bolsheviks had no choice but to treat Great Northern and its local staff well as they would be dependent on the Danish cables if they wanted to have a telegraphic connection with the surrounding world. However, Great Northern was also dependent on Soviet Russia. In September 1919, Kay Suenson and Per Michelsen warned the board that the consequences could be dire if the company did not secure a new agreement before April 1920.[15]

of both the allies' blockade policy and Danish foreign policy. Over the years, to be sure, Great Northern had always carried out a balancing act between often-conflicting British and Russian interests, but now the company was entering a political minefield that could cost it its life.

However, there was nothing to be done but begin negotiating with the Bolsheviks. In March 1920, before undertaking this, Kay Suenson traveled to London to negotiate with Eastern regarding an extension of the arrangement under which Great Northern's revenues were ensured during periods in which service was interrupted. The English company offered Great Northern a year's extension under the condition that the Danish share be halved, which Kay Suenson accepted after having protested appropriately. Speaking confidentially within the company, Kay Suenson characterized the Britons' attitude as "a pleasant surprise" as he had feared demands for a greater reduction in Great Northern's share. In the long run, however, Eastern's cables were unable to service the very significant amount of traffic that had been shunted over to them, which caused delays and complaints. The British company, therefore, had an interest in seeing Great Northern reestablish its connection, but if this had not been achieved within a year, the matter would be discussed again.[17]

Vice Foreign Commissar Litvinov on Kongens Nytorv

On March 18, 1920, before Kay Suenson had returned to Copenhagen, Per Michelsen already sent a request to the Danish Ministry of Foreign Affairs for support with regard to getting the trans-Siberian connection reopened. Great Northern was interested in arranging a meeting with the commissar of foreign affairs of the Soviet government's vice people, Maksim Litvinov, who had been staying in Copenhagen since November 1919. Officially, Litvinov had come as a representative of the Russian Red Cross to negotiate with representatives of the United Kingdom regarding an exchange of prisoners of war, and in January 1920, he was also appointed the chief foreign representative of the Russian cooperative movement, the allies having issued permission for trade with the Russian cooperative organizations.

In contrast to businesses engaging in industrial or trade activity, Great Northern could not justify addressing Litvinov with reference to his status as a representative of the Russian cooperative organizations. It was his status as vice foreign commissar and official representative of the Soviet government in which Great Northern was interested, and the allies' explicitly established blockade of postal and telegraph communications was still in force.

The Danish Ministry of Foreign Affairs was well aware of Great Northern's actual business with Litvinov. The head of the first department and therewith the top official at the ministry was the former ambassador to Petrograd and Stockholm, Chamberlain O. C. Scavenius, who had assumed this current post in October 1919. At the same time, he had been elected to Great Northern's board of directors, and he had, therefore, been fully informed of what was at stake. The company's message regarding the reestablishment of the trans-Siberian connection was in fact read already the same day by Minister of Foreign Affairs Erik Scavenius—the brother of O. C. and Harald—and a meeting was scheduled for two days later between Per Michelsen and Captain Frits Cramer, who, in his capacity as the head of the ministry's section for prisoners of war and civilian prisoners, was in contact with Maksim Litvinov.

Per Michelsen now said to Cramer straight out what he had not been able to write in his letter to the Ministry of Foreign Affairs, and he asked Cramer to tell Litvinov that if Soviet Russia wished to have its telegraph connections to foreign countries reopened, then there would be a good opportunity to discuss this. The Ministry of Foreign Affairs had every sympathy for the company's wishes, but because of concerns about the allies' priorities, the ministry was reluctant to bring up this matter with the Russian vice foreign commissar itself. It was, therefore, Danish businessman Hjalmar Lange who arranged the contact during a meeting with Litvinov.[18]

In April 1920, a Soviet Russian delegation arrived in Copenhagen to negotiate with regard to a trade agreement. In Copenhagen, the delegation met with the vice foreign commissar of the Soviet Union, Maksim Litvinov, who had been in Denmark since November 1919. In the middle is the leader of the delegation, the commissar of trade and industry Leonid Krasin; Maksim Litvinov is on his left.

The following day, March 25, 1920, the Soviet Russian vice foreign commissar already discreetly met with Per Michelsen for a preliminary discussion. The two men quickly concluded that they had something to talk about, and they agreed to initiate actual negotiations. Therefore, on Saturday, March 27, 1920, Soviet Russia's vice foreign commissar appeared at the Great Northern Telegraph Company's headquarters directly across from Harsdorff's Palace, the building that housed the Danish Ministry of Foreign Affairs at Kongens Nytorv 3–5.[19]

Maksim Litvinov was received by Per Michelsen and Kay Suenson, and the parties soon reached an agreement as Litvinov was strongly interested in getting Soviet Russia's international telegraph connections reopened. Great Northern was given not only the right to reopen its station in Petrograd but also the right to open a new station in Moscow, now the Russian capital. The vice foreign commissar also promised that the Soviet government would provide an uncensored telegraph wire to be used exclusively for transit traffic through Siberia—finally fulfilling a wish the company had waited many years to see come true—and that telegram invoices would be paid monthly in gold francs.

The only remaining matter to be settled was the matter of the company's credit from the time of the Czar in the amount of 5 million gold francs, 2 million of which had previously been transferred to an account at the Soviet foreign trade bank, but most of which had not been withdrawn. As a matter of basic principle, the Soviet government refused to recognize that kind of debt, but after Kay Suenson and Per Michelsen had explained that much of this money came from invoices sent to other countries and companies for services rendered on Russia's behalf, Litvinov promised to investigate what could be done.

With good reason, the top management team were satisfied when they said goodbye to the Soviet Russian vice foreign commissar after a few hours of discussions. Three days later, a draft of an agreement was sent to Maksim Litvinov by messenger with the request that he secure authorization from Moscow to sign the document as soon as possible. When this had been done, the agreement would be signed by Great Northern, and the company would subsequently contact the relevant governments to obtain permission to reopen the connection.[20]

Time-consuming Soviet processing

Great Northern could not act without the approval of the United Kingdom, however, and Litvinov had hardly left the company's headquarters before the company's representative in London, Captain Paul Westergaard, was instructed by telegraph to inform the British government that "Moscow had accepted all of [the company's] conditions" and that the Danish government had no objection to the reopening of the telegraph connection. The draft of the agreement was also sent to London with a request that it be approved quickly.[21]

From Denmark, the Ministry of Foreign Affairs involved itself in the matter when Section Head Count Eduard Reventlow sought out the British ambassador and asked him to recommend to the Foreign Office that Great Northern's request be approved. The ambassador promised to do so, but he did not keep his word, though in his report, he did loyally pass on the company's request and indicate that this request was supported by the Danish Ministry of Foreign Affairs.

In London, there was not a great deal of sympathy for the Danish wishes. On April 9, the ambassador in Copenhagen was instructed that an agreement between Great Northern and the Soviet government was to be obstructed, and Count Eduard Reventlow was informed of this a week later.

The company did not give up, however, as it had informed the British government two days previously that there was a telegraphic connection between Petrograd and the town of Rakvere in Estonia, from where there were landlines to the rest of Europe. In other words, as the British ambassador in Tallinn was able to confirm, the blockade had been broken. Shortly after this, Great Northern discovered that the cable between Aberdeen and Aleksandrovsk on the Kola Peninsula that had been laid during the war was being used for civilian telegrams. "This appears to prove that the General Post Office has—and permits others to have—contact with Russia via their cable," Great Northern concluded on Kongens Nytorv, instructing the company's representative in London to bring this state of affairs to the attention of the appropriate authority.[22]

Three days later, the matter was again examined by the Foreign Office, which concluded that it could no longer justify forbidding Great Northern to open its cables to Russia. This decision was approved on May 7, 1920, by British Secretary of State for Foreign Affairs Lord George Curzon, and at the Ministry of Foreign Affairs in Copenhagen, Reventlow was notified of it the same day.[23]

Now all that was missing was to receive word from Maksim Litvinov, who had promptly sent the Danish draft agreement to Moscow by telegraph and had already received a reply from the People's Commissar for Foreign Affairs, Georgy Chicherin, on April 22. However, Litvinov was busy working on the possible establishment of trade relations between Soviet Russia and the United Kingdom and did not react to the company's telegram.[24]

It was not until early June that Great Northern received word from Litvinov regarding the Soviet government's attitude. In Moscow, there was clearly eagerness to get the telegraph connections reopened, and the company was asked to inform the Soviet government of when the cable between Liepaja and Petrograd could be expected to be in use again. Nevertheless, the message was "rather disappointing" for Great Northern as it provided no specifics with regard to the promised establishment of a station in Moscow and indicated that the

Russians would not immediately be able to provide an independent transit wire. The desired guarantees regarding personnel and property were also not mentioned.[25]

At a meeting with Litvinov, Kay Suenson presented the company's objections and proposed that direct negotiations take place between the company and the Soviet government. Litvinov replied that the desired transit line would be established and that it would be "greatly appreciated" if the company's previous representative in Petrograd, Frederik Kjær, would come to Moscow and initiate direct negotiations.[26]

On July 29, 1920, Frederik Kjær left for Moscow accompanied by Alfred Schønebeck, who had been a telegraphist in Russia during the years 1904–1914. During their stay in Russia, they did not communicate with the top management team at Kongens Nytorv apart from a few wireless telegrams that contained no confidential information as they assumed such telegrams would be read by the Cheka, the Soviet Russian security service—which they were.[27]

At a meeting with representatives of the Soviet government and the secret police, Frederik Kjær and Alfred Schønebeck were presented with a draft agreement that accommodated the objections Kay Suenson had presented to Litvinov. When the two envoys returned home in late August, Kay Suenson and Per Michelsen characterized the draft as "quite satisfactory," though there were contentious points, including a Soviet requirement that transit telegrams be subject to military censorship.[28]

Kay Suenson and Per Michelsen wanted to try to get the condition removed from the draft via negotiations with Litvinov, who had been authorized to sign the agreement, but he had since gotten stuck in Kristiania, having been denied permission to reenter Denmark as a result of pressure from the French government. Therefore, in the middle of September, Alfred Schønebeck was sent to Kristiana to communicate the company's objections to Litvinov, after which Litvinov promptly sent these objections on to Moscow by wireless telegram. Great Northern then heard nothing further.[29]

The reason for this was that a disagreement had arisen within the Soviet government. The Commissariat of Foreign Affairs supported approving the Danish wishes as the government needed "regular business connections" that could only be supplied by Great Northern. In contrast, the head of the security service, Felix Dzerzhinsky, warned against concluding an agreement, and in late October 1920, the Commissariat of Foreign Affairs, therefore, presented the matter to the leader of the Soviet government, Vladimir Lenin, personally.[30]

The commissariat argued that the Aleksandrovsk cable was owned by the British directorate of telegraphy and thus under the control of the British government, while Great Northern's cables were "neutral." Wireless connections were useful in connection with agitation and propaganda, but they could not satisfy the need for stability and security. The only option was to cooperate with the Danish company, which could "assure stable and secure satisfaction of our needs in return for being provided with commercial earnings." The message was that the Danish company was not associated with a major power with imperialistic ambitions but was solely interested in money.[31]

On December 4, the Commissariat of Foreign Affairs sent the government a request for a response regarding the matter, noting that the commissariat considered the matter to be of "extraordinarily great importance." The Soviet government subsequently decided to appoint a three-person commission to carry out the final processing of the matter and present the result to the Soviet government within a week.[32]

Danish ultimatum and English pressure

Great Northern's leadership at Kongens Nytorv lacked knowledge of what was going on in Moscow, and in late November 1920, the company sent a telegram to Litvinov requesting a response. While the company was waiting, interest in reopening Great Northern's cables arose in England as it was expected that a trade agreement between Soviet Rus-

This Soviet Russian poster bears a didactic slogan formulated by Vladimir Lenin: "Communism is Soviet power and electrification." A radio transmitter spreads the message that a national electricity network will give the country and its people electricity while telegraph poles with a large number of lines emphasize the importance of the classic telegraph.

In effect, this was an ultimatum, and as such, it represented a high-stakes gamble with the fate of the company. However, the company needed to have the matter resolved by April 11 when Eastern's new extended deadline would expire. The top management team, therefore, informed the Russian trade delegation in Stockholm of the situation, and the company's representative in Helsinki was sent to Tallinn to speak with Litvinov. Litvinov declared that he had already sent the proposal to Moscow "with his strong recommendation that it be approved" and that he expected it to be signed and returned to him soon. It was not, for in Moscow, the matter was being dragged out despite the fact that in early February, the Commissariat of Foreign Affairs asked the government to resolve the matter soon, stating that it was "extremely important" that the matter be handled quickly.[34]

Things did not start moving until March 16, 1921, when the United Kingdom and Soviet Russia signed a trade agreement that included a section on reopening the telegraph connections between the two countries. This caused the British directorate of telegraphy to impress on the secretary of the Soviet Russian trade delegation in London that the British government wished an agreement between Great Northern and the Soviet government "to be concluded with all possible speed."[35]

Already the same day, the head of the Russian trade delegation sent a telegraph to the Commissar of Foreign Affairs, Georgy Chicherin, in Moscow to the effect that an agreement needed to be signed quickly, and he sent copies, respectively, to the Commissariat of Posts and Telegraphs, the Soviet government, and Lenin personally. In Moscow, Chicherin immediately wrote a memorandum to Lenin and declared that it was "necessary to get them [the commission] to hurry."[36]

The following day, Georgy Chicherin again wrote to Vladimir Lenin, warning that if the matter continued to get dragged out, the company would "simply break with [Soviet Russia] and refuse to cooperate with us in any way," which could lead to a damaged relationship with the United Kingdom.[37]

sia and the United Kingdom would soon be concluded.

This caused Great Northern to send two signed copies of a draft agreement to Litvinov by courier on February 1, 1921. At the beginning of the year, Litvinov had become Soviet Russia's first ambassador to Estonia. Enclosed with the drafts was a declaration to the effect that the Danish signatures would be invalid if the company had not received signed copies from the Soviet government by April 1.[33]

Lenin had not previously been involved in the matter; he had simply referred to the fact that it was being processed by the government. Now he did get involved, and he shifted the matter onto a new track, asking the People's Commissariat of Justice to examine the company's concessions from the time of the Czar and use them as the basis for preparing a completely new draft concession.[38]

On March 30, the question was handled by the Soviet government's so-called narrow cabinet with the participation of the appointed commission as well as officials representing the Commissariats of Foreign Affairs, Posts and Telegraphs, and Foreign Trade. By a vote of four to two, the conclusion of a concession agreement was approved. Among those who voted in favor was Vladimir Lenin, while the head of the security service, Felix Dzerzhinsky, voted against.[39]

Soviet Russia's first concession

On March 26, 1921, while the Soviet government apparatus was working, Great Northern received a telegram from Litvinov to the effect that the Soviet government was inviting representatives of the company to come to Moscow to negotiate a new agreement that would replace the "three old agreements." This telegram surprised staff at the company's headquarters on Kongens Nytorv, who asked for specification of which agreements were meant.[40]

The company received no reply, but the prospect of concluding an agreement meant that Great Northern could extend its agreement with Eastern regarding compensation for the missing revenues from the transit connection before. On April 30, Frederik Kjær and Alfred Schønebeck once again traveled to Moscow without knowing what awaited them. The only sign of life received from them in Denmark during their stay in Moscow was a radio telegram sent on May 10, with the message "New concession presented to us." Therefore, all anyone on Kongens Nytorv knew was that the drafts signed previously had been discarded and replaced by a new one.[41]

After having been away for nearly six weeks, Frederik Kjær and Alfred Schønebeck were back in Denmark on June 8, and in contrast to the reaction to their last return, Per Michelsen and Kay Suenson's reaction was unreservedly positive. "Extremely satisfactory results," they found. It was not often the two men used such effusive words in their reports to the board of directors, but this time, there was justification for enthusiasm as the draft of the new concession accommodated the company's wishes in all significant respects.[42]

The company was particularly glad to see its long-desired separate transit wire with Danish staff at all transfer stations poised to become a reality, and the company was also to be permitted to open a station in Moscow. A new and special aspect of the proposed agreement was that it addressed the Russian debt from the time of the Czar, which the Soviet government now agreed to repay via monthly payments amounting to 25 percent of Soviet Russia's transit revenues. This arrangement conflicted with the government's official policy of not accepting responsibility for debts incurred by the Czar's government, and in general, the concession violated the regime's principles for relationships with foreign companies.

These principles established that concessions could only be issued to companies from countries that had recognized Soviet Russia, which Denmark had not done. Nevertheless, Great Northern was now granted the first concession ever issued by the Soviet government. The Russians considered the concession a replacement for the company's previous concessions, which would all expire in 1926, but Frederik Kjær and Alfred Schønebeck succeeded in extending the period of validity until the end of 1946.

The only little flaw in the agreement was that the company had not managed to get the condition regarding military censorship of transit telegrams removed. Nevertheless, there was happiness at Great Northern. "The result is quite satisfactory," was the conclusion, and to not risk further delays, the company decided to sign.

Two copies of the agreement were signed on June 24, 1921, by Wilhelm Weimann, who had been

elected chairman of the board of directors in 1916, having been proposed by Edouard Suenson, who had resigned on the same occasion. These two copies were sent to Moscow. On July 21, the leader of the Soviet Russian government, Vladimir Lenin, and People's Commissar of Posts and Telegraphs Lyubovitsh signed the two copies, and in early August, a further copy was signed by People's Commissar of Foreign Affairs Georgy Chicherin and the People's Commissar of Posts and Telegraphs and sent to Denmark. On August 12, 1921, a copy was inserted into the Foreign Commissariat's record of concession agreements as the Soviet Union's concession number 1.[43]

Reopening of the trans-Siberian connection

In late July 1921, before Great Northern had received the signed concession, Frederik Kjær already traveled to Petrograd with two telegraphists to establish the company's station and to find a suitable residen-

Originally, Great Northern recruited its telegraphists from the Danish government telegraph authority or had them trained in the United Kingdom. Around the time of the First World War, however, the company established its own telegraph school. The picture shows the class of February–August 1919.

tial building for the Danish employees. Around this time, two telegraphists left Copenhagen by ship with materials and equipment for the station and for the reestablishment of the trans-Siberian connection.

In Petrograd, the Danish delegation was lodged at the Hotel Internationale, which had previously been the fashionable Hotel d'Angleterre and was one of the few buildings in the former capital in which the Soviet government could lodge foreigners. Despite the fact that the city had not been the site of battles during the civil war, it was characterized by the war's shortages, anarchy, and lawlessness. In 1917, the city had had two and a half million inhabitants—now there were about 700,000, and they lived a hard life characterized by the lack of food, fuel, and the most basic of necessities.

After the October Russian Revolution in 1917, the Soviet government moved to Moscow, and when Great Northern reopened its cables generally and the trans-Siberian connection in particular, the company also moved its business office to Moscow. The building shown in the picture, which is still there, on Tverskoy Boulevard, close to Pushkinskaya Square in central Moscow, housed the residence and administration of the company's representative.

it from the secret police in June 1919, everything had lain in ruins; furniture was smashed, the wallpaper had been ripped off, ceilings had fallen down, paneling and floors had sustained water damage, and toilets had been shattered. "An earthquake could not have caused worse damage," Frederik Kjær wrote in a letter he mailed home to Denmark.[45]

Finally, however, it proved possible to find "a suitable house," which was a small palace in a formerly wealthy quarter. The house had belonged to the respected attorney and liberal politician Vladimir Nabokov, who had fled the country. The building needed thorough renovation, however, as it had been used as barracks for a few hundred soldiers and, therefore, been rather severely damaged.

In early October, Frederik Kjær returned to Denmark, and forty Finnish artisans and laborers began renovating the residential building. They had not finished with this task by late November when Alfred Schønebeck traveled back to Petrograd as the company's new representative. He established his headquarters at the Hotel Internationale, where the Danish staff were also quartered while they awaited the completion of the renovation of the residential building. On January 18, 1922, after the station in Petrograd had been fully equipped and the necessary telegraph wires across the Finno-Russian border had been provided, Great Northern could open the connection between Petrograd and Western Europe.

However, there were a few positive aspects. In the middle of March 1921, Lenin had carried out a certain liberalization of the economy so that the peasants were allowed to sell their surplus grain, and small private businesses were now permitted. "In the few days in which we have been in the city, the right to own money and the right to engage in trade have led to the reopening of many cafés and shops," Frederik Kjær wrote in a letter sent home to Denmark in the middle of August.[44]

Despite the fact that the number of inhabitants had fallen dramatically, it was difficult for the local Soviet organs to find a suitable residential building for the company as most of the city was in a process of decay. Frederik Kjær was first assigned to the Danish embassy's previous rooms, but since a vis-

In August 1921, two Danish telegraphists had left Petrograd with three rail cars fully loaded with telegraphic equipment to assist the repair work to be carried out on the line through Siberia. By late October, they had reached Irkutsk, from where there was a telegraphic connection with Petrograd. However, the line to Beijing via Kyakhta could not be reestablished as a result of political instability in Mongolia, and in the Russian Far East, the existence of an independent Far Eastern Republic as well as the presence of Japanese troops prevented the continuation of the line to Vladivostok.

In March 1922, the company instead succeeded in establishing a temporary connection to Beijing via Blagoveshchensk, Heihe, and Harbin, and the trans-Siberian connection could finally be reopened after an interruption that had lasted nearly four years.

In Moscow, the company rented a residential building for its staff and a house for Alfred Schønebeck's residence and representative purposes. In Irkutsk, the company managed to rent two wooden buildings, but in Omsk and Blagoveshchensk, the Danish telegraphists had to accept rented accommodations in the homes of residents. In Vladivostok, the company waited for Japan to pull out its troops, which occurred in October 1922. Shortly thereafter, the Red Army marched into the city so the Bolsheviks could proclaim that Vladivostok was under Soviet rule. In late February 1923, Great Northern could reopen the connection to Nagasaki and Shanghai via the cables from Vladivostok after an interruption that had lasted nearly four years.

When the landline connecting Kyakhta with Beijing via the Gobi Desert was to be reestablished after the Russian Civil War, the entire connection was inspected by a team of Danish telegraphists assisted by natives and carried by a caravan of cars. As the area had previously been the site of a military conflict involving Russian, Mongolian, and Chinese troops, the group traveled under the American flag for protection. The picture shows the group taking a rest at a mountain pass near the Chinese city of Zhangjiakou in January 1921.

The following month, the company's service was back at full capacity, and already in April 1923, half of the total traffic between East Asia and Europe was transmitted via the Danish connection. The company, therefore, applied for an extra wire on the Petrograd-Irkutsk section for the peak time periods, and this extra wire was approved.[46]

During the summer of 1924, a total of thirty-five to forty Danish telegraphists were stationed in Siberia, thirty to thirty-five in Petrograd, ten to fifteen in Vladivostok, and fifteen to twenty in Moscow. The company's relationship with the Soviet Russian authorities both locally and in the capital was good, and the monthly installment payments on the debt to Great Northern were coming in punctually while the Soviet government began to receive significant transit revenues.

Pressure to conclude a Dano-Russian trade agreement

Following the conclusion of the Russo-British trade agreement, there was interest in both Russia and

The repair of a telegraph pole on the Kyakhta–Beijing line is undertaken.

Denmark in the conclusion of a similar Dano-Russian agreement, and in February 1923, the Soviet government presented proposals regarding the initiation of negotiations. In the middle of March, a Danish delegation traveled to Moscow, and on April 23, 1922, an agreement was signed, but this was not viewed positively by everyone in Denmark. The matter was sent for processing to the Folketing's newly created Committee on Foreign Policy, which postponed making a recommendation in the middle of May as the result of an escalating Russo-British crisis.

This caused Great Northern to get involved. The company saw the conclusion of a Dano-Russian trade agreement as the beginning of normalization of the relationship between the two countries that could finally cement the company's position in Soviet Russia. Therefore, on May 28, 1923, Per Michelsen and Kay Suenson signed a confidential letter to the Ministry of Foreign Affairs in which they warned of "the fateful consequences the rejection of the trade treaty negotiated in Moscow between Denmark and Russia could have for the company."[47]

In a firm, didactic tone, Kay Suenson and Per Michelsen established the significance of the company's relationship with Russia. If Denmark rejected the conclusion of a trade agreement with the Soviet government, the two men argued, it would result in "revenge and harassment wherever possible," and they feared this would negatively affect the company, which was the only Danish company with interests in Russia.[48]

Great Northern was not alone in putting pressure on the government. When asked directly for their input by Minister of Foreign Affairs Christian Cold, the Danish Industrial Council (Industrirådet), the Committee of the Wholesalers' Society, and the Danish Steamship Owners' Association recommended ratification, while the East Asiatic Company and other large businesses felt it would be best to await the stabilization of the relationship between Russia and the United Kingdom.

The matter was raised at a meeting of the Council of Ministers on May 29, 1923, at which the Minister of Foreign Affairs reported that the United Kingdom would hardly break off relations with Russia. The minister indicated that Denmark should, therefore, ratify the trade agreement as the country's prestige would otherwise suffer. He then read aloud Great Northern's letter regarding "the very damaging consequences that would result if the treaty were not approved." Prime Minister Niels Neergaard declared that he was in agreement with his minister of foreign affairs.[49]

After the Russian Revolution and Civil War, it took great and sustained efforts to find a residential building for Great Northern's Danish personnel in Petrograd. In 1922, however, Great Northern's staff were able to move into a palace close to Bolshaya Morskaya Ulitsa that had belonged to the prominent attorney, author, and liberal politician Vladimir Nabokov, who had fled after the revolution. His eponymous son is the author of the novel *Lolita*. Today the palace contains a museum dedicated to the Nabokov family.

The remaining ministers were in agreement, and on June 8, 1923, the Folketing voted to approve the agreement by 105 votes to twenty-one, and the Landsting followed suit, fifty-three votes being cast in favor and ten against there—which resulted in feelings of great relief on Kongens Nytorv. In June 1924, Denmark recognized Soviet Russia *de jure* and thus adjusted to international developments in the wake of the recognition of the Soviet regime by the United Kingdom the previous February and other countries' recognition of the regime shortly thereafter.

Telegraph Mergers and War in East Asia

CHAPTER 13

Threat of liquidation

With the acquisition of its concessions in Finland, Latvia, and Russia, Great Northern had secured its position in those countries through the end of 1946. In China, the company was protected by its monopoly until the end of 1930 when the agreement with Japan would expire as well, but the situation in Northern Europe was different as the concessions for Denmark, Sweden, and the United Kingdom would expire at the end of 1924. A preliminary feeler put out in London resulted in a positive announcement to the effect that the agreement with the British could be extended by five years, but Great Northern feared a situation like the one that had arisen in 1910 when Norway had refused to extend the company's concession and thought it possible that Denmark and Sweden would follow Norway's example this time. This was not an unrealistic scenario as the Swedish director of telegraphy had told Kay Suenson that the Swedish government was planning to take over the company's cables and the Danish director of telegraphy made no secret of the fact that he wished to do the same.

Great Northern's strategy was to secure first a Danish extension and then a British one so Sweden would be checkmated. In the middle of February 1921, Kay Suenson, therefore, had a sixteen-page letter delivered to the Danish Ministry for Public Works in which the company applied for an extension of its Danish concession by twenty years until the end of 1944. Suenson described the positive attitude of the United Kingdom, which was a result of the British interest in reopening the trans-Siberian connection and desire to preserve the company "as a bulwark against Japan's extensive and energetic efforts to pervade China and Eastern Siberia telegraphically." With regard to Sweden, he noted simply that, as was well known, the government had thus far been "most inclined to free itself from the company."[1]

So that the Danish government would not be tempted to take over the company's cables, Suenson claimed that this would be expensive in itself and that it was to be expected that a government takeover would result in reduced transit revenues, which in turn would result in reduced revenues for

After a fire in the company's East Asian headquarters on the Bund in Shanghai, Great Northern erected a new building that was inaugurated in 1922 and still housed the Eastern companies and Commercial Pacific. The building was not on the Bund but just around the corner.

Thorvald Stauning, Denmark's first Social Democratic prime minister, with his wife on Christiansborg Palace Square on April 7, 1924 after having been received by King Christian X. The creation of the first Social Democratic government meant that Denmark's Post & Telegrafvæsen (postal and telegraphy authority) was put in a stronger position vis-à-vis Great Northern, whose cables the authority wished to take over. The company first noted this in connection with negotiations regarding an extension of its concessions by twenty years the Danish government of 1920 had suggested could be possible. No actual contract granting Great Northern such an extension was concluded, as the company was simultaneously negotiating with Sweden and the United Kingdom, and when everything appeared to have been settled, Denmark got a new Social Democratic government, which P & T immediately exploited in order to force Great Northern to accept a concession with shorter validity and greater economic expenses for the company.

the Danish government. However, Suenson's main argument was that it would have an "utterly fatal effect on the company" if it lost its connection with Great Britain as the company's agreements were dependent on it having its own lines from Great Britain to East Asia.

He underscored the seriousness of the situation by "confidentially" revealing the company's participation in Commercial Pacific and the Pacific cartel. This was the first time the Danish government had learned of the company's involvement with the organizations in question, and Suenson declared that if the company's Danish concession were not extended, it would "sink to the level of a local East Asian company." If this occurred, the company's management "would be forced to propose the complete liquidation of the company" out of consideration for the shareholders.[2]

Kay Suenson sent a copy of this letter to the Ministry of Foreign Affairs, and Prime Minister Niels Neergaard, who had a seat on the company's board of directors, also received a copy. This was probably the reason why the general director of the postal and telegraphy authority was full of understanding when he appeared on Kongens Nytorv in March 1920 to propose an extension of the company's concession by twenty years and indicated that he found such an extension "natural and necessary." Subsequently, in the middle of May, the Ministry of Public Works informed Great Northern that the desired extension of the company's concession had been approved.[3]

"Fooled by the Danish government"

Immediately thereafter, Kay Suenson traveled to London to convince the British government to extend the company's concession beyond 1930 by way of compensation offering to lay a new cable from Great Britain to Sweden as the existing cables had nearly been worn out. As a matter of basic principle, the British government issued landing permits only for five years at a time, but Suenson succeeded in creating the possibility of achieving a longer extension, and the chances of this were improved when the Soviet Russian concession was signed later in the summer.[4]

The United Kingdom's good will became evident in late October 1921 when Great Northern was confidentially informed that the British government had informed the Swedish government that it planned to extend Great Northern's landing permits at least until the end of 1930 and that it recommended that the Swedish government to do the same.[5]

In the middle of November, with this knowledge, Great Northern asked the Danish Ministry of Foreign Affairs to instruct the Danish ambassador in Stockholm, Herluf Zahle, to raise the matter of the extension of the concession with the Swedish Ministry of Foreign Affairs. With the Danish Ministry of Foreign Affairs's director, O. C. Scavenius, as a go-between, there was lively correspondence during the following weeks among Great Northern, the Ministry of Foreign Affairs, and Herluf Zahle, who informed Great Northern in early December 1921 that an extension of the concession until the end of 1930 had now been secured and indicated later in the month that Sweden would be willing to agree to an extension until the end of 1934 if necessary.[6]

O. C. Scavenius was an envoy first in Saint Petersburg and then in Stockholm before he was summoned back to Denmark and appointed a department head in the Ministry of Foreign Affairs. On the same occasion, he was elected to Great Northern's board of directors, on which he remained after he had been appointed a director in the Ministry of Foreign Affairs. In 1924, he was appointed a director at Great Northern while remaining on the company's board of directors. He was chairman of the board of directors from 1938 until his death in 1945.

However, the Swedish government was under strong pressure from the public, which did not understand why it would not take control of the country's international telegraph connections. Great

In 1918, a Poulsen arc transmitter was built at Croix d'Hins near Bordeaux, which was the world's most powerful wireless telegraph transmitter at that time. The purpose of building this transmitter was to take over some of the telegrams that would otherwise have been sent via the transatlantic submarine cables, which had been overused following the United States's entry into the First World War and dispatching of troops to Europe. The tower masts were 250 meters tall, and the antenna covered an area of more than half a square kilometer. Normally, the signals could be received anywhere in the world.

Northern exerted corresponding pressure, threatening to move the transit traffic away from Sweden and over to the Danish cables to Russia, and after the United Kingdom had announced a short time later that it was willing to extend the company's landing permits until the end of 1934, the Swedes gave in.[7]

In July 1923, the British government approved an extension of the company's concessions until the end of 1934, and in late September, Sweden followed suit. The extension of the Danish concession had not been officially announced, but on Kongens Nytorv, there was confidence that such

approval could be regarded as a mere formality. However, over a year passed before, on November 8, 1924, the company received a letter from the Ministry for Public Works with a draft of a new concession and operating agreement that, as Kay Suenson put it, contained "quite surprising and in [the company's] opinion unjustified demands."[8]

In April 1924, there had been a change of government when Thorvald Stauning had become prime minister and the leader of Denmark's first social democratic government, and the general director of the postal and telegraphy authority had exploited this. A precondition for the desired extension of the company's concession was that in the future, Great Northern would pay Statstelegrafen, the Danish government telegraphy authority, for the operation of its cables as the company did not have stations of its own in Denmark. The feeling at Kongens Nytorv was that Statstelegrafen received more than adequate compensation in the form of the significant transit revenues, but the general director did not agree, nor did the social democratic minister. Furthermore, the general directorate wished to upgrade Denmark to the status of a so-called "large country" so that Statstelegrafen could raise transit fees—at the expense of the company.[9]

The worst change, however, was that in contrast to what had originally been promised, the extension of the concession would not be valid until 1944 but only until the end of 1934, after which an extension for the following ten years would be dependent on Great Northern's success in securing corresponding extensions in Sweden and the United Kingdom. Finally, the government was to appoint two representatives to the company's board of directors and not, as had previously been the case, only one.

There was room for negotiation, but it took the parties three months to agree on a new concession and operating agreement. The company managed to limit its economic losses to approximately 357,000 gold francs per year, which the top management team and board of directors found to be a modest sacrifice in return for an extension of the company's concession. In contrast, the company was not able to eliminate the requirement that in the future, the government would be able to appoint two members of the board of directors, and on February 16, 1925, when the board unanimously approved the concession and the operating agreement, Wilhelm Weimann gave expression to the feeling all the way around the board's table when he said he "felt very much fooled by the Danish government."[10]

The new member who joined the board was the general director of the Danish telegraphy authority, T. F. Krarup, who thus acquired the ability to follow Great Northern's decisions and business activities from very close at hand. He joined the board in the wake of a number of changes in the company's top leadership, Director Per Michelsen having resigned in the fall of 1923. Kay Suenson had continued as sole director, but he had difficulty handling all the tasks that presented themselves, and in the spring, the top management team was expanded to four members.

In the fall of 1922, O. C. Scavenius had been forced to leave his director post at the Ministry of Foreign Affairs because of his involvement in the collapse of Landmandsbanken. In the spring of 1924, he was elected to the board of directors of Great Northern and at the same time appointed as the board's full-time representative in the top management team. At the same time, cand.polit. Alf Ussing, who was stationed in Shanghai, and the head of accounting, Lieutenant Commander Harald Bonde, were appointed under-directors.

Also, at the same time, Kay Suenson was elected to the board, and he was subsequently referred to within the company as the leading director.[11]

"[...] after all, mighty forces were in motion"

Great Northern's new leadership soon encountered great challenges. While the company had once again secured its concessions and rights for a relatively long period, Great Northern was now put under pressure by a new threat.

During the world war, the wireless telegraph had made great advances, and in particular, Valdemar Poulsen's arc transmitter had developed into what has been called "the world's most important radio transmitter technology." One of the organizations that exploited it was the United States Navy, which needed wireless connections between its headquarters in Arlington, Virginia, on the east coast of the United States, and the American naval bases in the Pacific Ocean and in other regions, as well as for the Navy's ships everywhere on the seas of the world.[12]

In 1912, a wireless connection had successfully been created between Arlington and Honolulu—over a distance of 4,200 miles—and in 1913, the United States Navy had ordered the first of a number of Poulsen stations for American naval bases and subsequently ordered smaller stations for warships. Hundreds of arc transmitters were also installed on British, French, and Italian warships, while the system had already previously been used by the German Navy.[13]

Civilian use of Poulsen's system was also increasing. Not least in the Pacific region, but also in Europe, long-range radio stations were established, including one installed at the top of the Eiffel Tower in Paris. The culmination came in December 1920 with the opening of the world's most powerful wireless station near Bordeaux, France, which caused Great Northern's top management team laconically to remark that "the system [appeared] to be the one to which the company once bought the rights."[14]

Production of magnet tanks for thousand-kilowatt generators used by the Federal Telegraph Company of the United States for its Poulsen arc transmitters.

The wireless systems from other companies, including the Marconi company and the German company Telefunken, were also making great progress, and during the years after the war, Great Northern began really to feel the competition from wireless telegraphy in the form of declining telegram revenues, something that the company's shareholders inevitably noticed.

At Great Northern's general meeting in June 1922, Chairman of the Board of Directors Wilhelm Weimann was asked about his and the company's view of the development of wireless telegraphy and its consequences for the cable companies, and he responded by admitting that radio telegraphy "had made huge advances and caused the company to suffer significant losses." No one could know what further technological advances would bring, "but

after all, mighty forces were in motion, and large amounts of capital had already been invested, and the chairman was therefore not able to reassure the asker of the question other than by underscoring that in his view the investment of this capital would not return a profit and that he therefore did not expect that wireless stations would continue to be established, as their operation was not proving profitable."[15]

Fusion of cables and wireless

Wilhelm Weimann turned out to have been right to the extent that powerful forces had indeed been set in motion—so much so, in fact, that he would have to abandon his skepticism about the operational stability and profitability of the technology. The development and rapid spread of radiophony accelerated the spread of the wireless technology, and in the course of 1923 and 1924, Marconi introduced a new wireless beam technology, which was based on

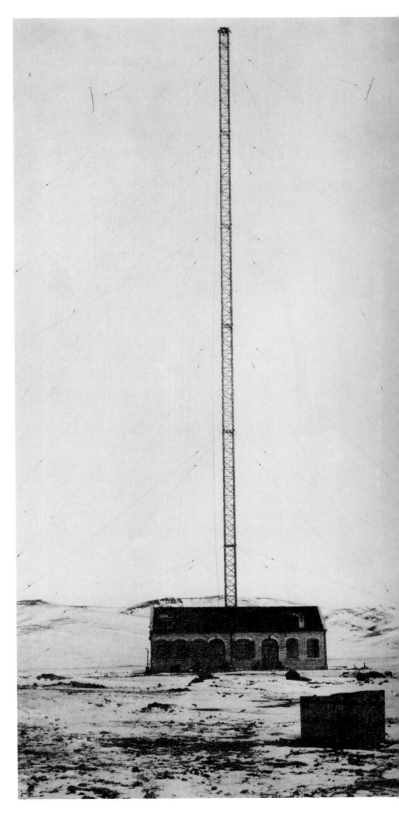

Around the time of the end of the First World War, China began work on the construction of a national network of wireless stations based on various systems as the Chinese, like the Japanese, saw the new technology as a means of freeing themselves from Great Northern and the other cable companies. The picture shows a station near Urga (today Ulaanbaatar) in Outer Mongolia early in 1921.

the so-called skip effect. He exploited the fact that in contrast to long waves, short waves did not follow the curvature of the Earth but were instead reflected in the ionosphere; he used a parabolic antenna so that the radio waves were aimed at the receiving station.

In the summer of 1924, Marconi concluded a contract with the British government for the supply of shortwave stations for an Imperial Wireless Chain that began operating in October 1926 with the opening of a connection from Great Britain to Canada, which was followed by radio stations in other British possessions. According to the agreement, the British General Post Office was to own and operate the stations within the British Empire, while Marconi would have the rights to the connections between the empire and the rest of the world.

The beam technology quickly pushed other technologies, including Valdemar Poulsen's arc transmitter, out of the market. The big losers, however, were the cable companies, which experienced marked reductions in traffic as a result of the lower prices for radio telegrams. When the British shortwave service to Australia opened, its prices for telegrams were a sixth of what the cable companies charged, and while Eastern lowered its rates, the company was unable to match the wireless rates without losing money.

In just six months, the General Post Office took over 65 percent of Eastern's traffic to India and Australia, and by the end of 1927, the company had lost about half of its total traffic. Eastern ended up in a deep economic crisis and facing the prospect of bankruptcy, which was a problem for the British government as well as for the company itself as this was a matter of the empire's telecommunications structure, and cables were still preferred for confidential and secret telegrams because of wireless telegraphy's exposure to surveillance.

Representatives from all parts of the empire were summoned to an Imperial Cable and Wireless Conference in the middle of January 1928, but before then, the chairman of Eastern's board of directors, Sir John Denison-Pender, contacted his counterpart in the Marconi company, Lord Inverforth, to initiate negotiations with regard to a merger. On March 16, 1928, the two chairmen appeared at the imperial conference and announced that their companies had decided to merge via the creation of a holding company that would own and operated the two companies' telegraphy systems.[16]

A little over a week later, there was news of another major merger when the International Telephone and Telegraph Company, or ITT, an American wireless company, took over the Mackay companies' cable interests, including their shares in Commercial Pacific. All in all, a dramatic restructuring of the whole international telegraphy sector was taking place, partly as a result of the fact that cable-borne and wireless telegraphy were now merging and working together within the same companies and partly because of the size and capital strength of the companies that had resulted from the mergers.

The new English company would have share capital amounting to 53.7 million pounds sterling or nearly a billion Danish kroner, while the American company would be marginally larger, with share capital of 55 million pounds. These amounts contrasted sharply with Great Northern's own share capital, which amounted to 1.5 million pounds, in addition to which the company possessed a reserve fund containing approximately 4 million pounds. "English-American battle for world domination in telegraphy?" asked the Danish newspaper *Nationaltidende* in a dramatic headline. Great Northern's top leadership team was calmer—and doubtless also more resigned—in its report to the board of directors: "In later times this month of March will be remembered for its major mergers of companies that were well suited to complement each other but had up to that point more or less competed with each other."[17]

The Great Northern Telegraph Company's Holding Company

Great Northern also felt the effects of the new beam technology, though not to the same extent as Eastern. The company saw its telegram revenues decline from 25.4 million kroner in 1924 to 21.9 million kroner in 1925. The decline continued in 1926 with a drop to 18.1 million kroner, after which it flattened out, with operating revenues gradually sinking and ending up at 17 million kroner by 1929.

The constant decline was due to a combination of reductions in traffic and lower prices. To some extent, the decline in revenues was offset by a simultaneous decrease in expenses. Nevertheless, in 1925, the company's primary operations—telegraphic operations—contributed only 2.1 million kroner to a total surplus of just under 5 million kroner, while in 1926, primary operations contributed 1.6 million kroner to a total surplus of 4.6 million kroner. The rest of the surplus for the respective two years came from interest revenues and "various revenues."[18]

The company, nevertheless, maintained a dividend of 20 percent of the share capital by taking money from its liquid assets for running expenses, and for 1928, the company also had to transfer interest revenues in the amount of 2.4 million kroner from the reserve fund to pay out the dividend. This occurred after, in the fall of 1927, the board of directors had received a request from Banque Nationale de Crédit, a shareholder, that a dividend of 30 percent be paid out in the future—though the board did not agree to raise the dividend to that level.

With a reserve fund of more than 80 million kroner, the future of the company was in no way threatened, but the board of directors did not consider this an appropriate time to be increasing the dividend. The French bank claimed that it was in possession of 16,000 shares and could assemble a considerable number of votes. Approximately, two thirds of the company's share capital was in French hands, and while the board of directors could count on support from English shareholders, the board was not certain that "it would be able to dominate a possible general meeting," as the chairman put it.[19]

This was a frightening perspective, and partly to seek to get the French shareholders to behave in an orderly fashion and partly to "create considerable security as protection against future actions," Wilhelm Weimann presented to the board of directors a proposal that free shares be issued in the amount of 9 million kroner (500,000 pounds sterling), which would be transferred to a holding company in which the company's shareholders would have a right to purchase a pro-rated proportion of shares.

The holding company's articles of association were written so that Great Northern's board of directors would appoint half of the holding company's board of directors, including the board's chairman, who would have the decisive vote in cases of split votes. With this, Great Northern secured voting rights for itself for shares in the holding company corresponding to 25 percent of Great Northern's increased share capital of 36 million kroner. This would give the company's board of directors a considerable basis on which to exercise power at the future general meetings.[20]

The bait for the French shareholders was that keeping the dividend at 20 percent with the increased capital basis would lead to a larger dividend in terms of the cash amount, and the board of directors would guarantee a dividend of 20 percent, which Banque Nationale de Crédit accepted.[21]

A space at the eastern entrance to Great Northern's new building in Shanghai contained a bust of Edouard Suenson with an accompanying inscription: "Edouard Suenson. The Dane that introduced the telegraph into China." In 1962, when Great Northern pulled out of China, the bust was only allowed to be brought to Denmark after the company's representative had signed a declaration to the effect that the bust had been cast in metal that had been mined in Europe and, therefore, did not constitute a Chinese strategic raw material. In 2011, the bust returned to its place in the building in Shanghai as a gift from GN Store Nord. Today the building houses the Shanghai Telecom Museum, which contains Great Northern's archives from the company's time in China.

Subsequently, on May 24, 1928, a formal articles of association document for Det Store Nordiske Telegraf-Selskabs Holding Selskab A/S (the Great Northern Telegraph Company's Holding Company A/S) could be drawn up by Wilhelm Weimann, Kay Suenson, and O. C. Scavenius. Two days later, the issuing of free shares, and therewith the entire maneuver, was approved at Great Northern's ordinary general meeting. The holding company's first board of directors consisted of Wilhelm Weimann (chairman), Kay Suenson, O. C. Scavenius, and Bank Director Roger J. Audap of the Banque Nationale de Crédit. With the holding company's share of votes at Great Northern's general meetings, control of the company had been secured, and in the words of the chairman, this was "a fortunate turn of events for the company, one that has offered [Great Northern] very strong protection against future assaults, something [the company] had lacked up to that point—one could say

that a barbed-wire fence was erected around the capital."[22]

American takeover attempts and a major English merger

The reports of the major mergers of telegraphy companies came just as the establishment of the Great Northern Telegraph Company's Holding Company was on its way into its last phase. The threat from the French shareholders had been averted, but the mergers constituted an entirely different threat that could have far-ranging consequences for Great Northern. Great Northern's top management team was particularly worried about the consequences of the British merger, which meant that the company no longer stood united with Eastern in the fight against the wireless telegraph and probably also meant that Great Northern's connection with the English company would be dissolved. It was also to be feared that the British government would no longer back the company's interests in China and that the company would, therefore, end up "very isolated."[23]

Joining one of the two new combinations was something the company could consider, but only the British one represented a real possibility, and if there were to be a merger with the British combination, then a form would have to be found in which "the company's outward

In September 1930, Denmark's Crown Prince Frederik visited China together with Prince Knud, Prince Axel, and Princess Margaretha. The official visits were to Beijing and Guangzhou, but there were also visits to the many Danes in Shanghai, and a dinner was arranged in the French club.

Great Northern's telegram messengers lined up with their bicycles in Shanghai about 1930.

independence" would be preserved because of the desirability of being able to retain the company's concessions, not least the Soviet Russian one.[24]

What the company's top management team was interested in was an expansion of the company's joint purse agreements with Eastern so that these would come to include the traffic of the whole British combination as well as that of Great Northern. At a meeting of the board of directors on November 27, 1928, Kay Suenson presented the plan and reported that he had spoken to Eastern and the Marconi company about the proposed arrangement and that "in principle," both companies had accepted such an arrangement. After a lengthy debate in which particularly the fear of the company's possible future isolation was a dominant theme, the board of directors unanimously approved the top management team's proceeding with the plan that had been sketched out.[25]

The American merger also had consequences for Great Northern. After a meeting with East-

ern and the Mackay companies in July 1928, it was Suenson's impression that ITT would attempt to liberate Commercial Pacific from the control of the European companies. This was an impression that was confirmed at a meeting in London in September 1928 at which ITT's leader, Colonel Sosthenes Behn, made it clear to Suenson that he wished the two European companies to sell their shares in Commercial Pacific to ITT.[26]

Already before Suenson had taken any further action with regard to this matter, there was a fundamental change in the entire situation. It had been agreed that representatives of Great Northern, Eastern, and ITT would meet in London in the middle of December 1928, but the meeting was cancelled because Colonel Behn had had to travel to the United States because of an "unexpected and very urgent business." Subsequently, Great Northern's stock price began rising sharply because of purchasing activity, and after a few quiet months, there was a new wave of share purchases in April.[27]

At Kongens Nytorv, Great Northern's management was in no doubt that ITT was behind the purchases. Colonel Behn had previously said that he needed a link between Europe and East Asia to complete his circuit of the whole Earth, and in September 1928, he had asked Kay Suenson directly whether the Danish company would have any objections to his purchasing a large minority bloc of shares in the company.[28]

Suenson had indicated that, in fact, the company would have such objections, and Colonel Behn had responded by declaring that in that case, he would not try to purchase such a post in the company. Now he had apparently, nevertheless, begun purchasing shares in the company, and at the meeting of Great Northern's board of directors in April 1929, Suenson expressed the judgment that the American was not interested only in acquiring a minority post, for in similar situations he had made it a point to acquire a majority, and it could be assumed that

In the early 1920s, Great Northern built new dwellings in Beijing for the company's Danish employees in an arrangement and an architectural style that was not particularly Chinese. The area looks like a neighborhood of Danish houses that was moved to China unaltered.

this was his intention in the case of Great Northern as well.[29]

Great Northern's leaders feared that the holding company structure would not be able to resist an American takeover attempt if Colonel Behn really wished to take over the company. However, the purchasing of shares ceased, and the colonel's intention to purchase the European companies' shares in Commercial Pacific also remained unrealized.

Instead, there was another American approach in November 1929 when Western Union contacted the company and informed it that Western Union had been offered "a large number of" shares in the company. The prospective seller was not identified, but Western Union wanted to know whether the company was aware of this offer, and the reply was that the company had not been aware of it and that the company would do "its utmost" to resist speculators' purchasing of shares.[30]

There was then significant American interest in Great Northern, and when the president of Western Union, Newcomb Carlton, came to Europe in late November 1928, Kay Suenson traveled to London to meet him. Kay Suenson's purpose in undertaking this journey was to "dissuade Western Union from considering purchasing shares in the company." Suenson achieved this by declaring that the holding company structure would prevent outsiders from taking control of the company via the purchasing of shares.[31]

Kay Suenson underscored the importance of maintaining Great Northern's independence, and Newcomb Carlton declared that he was in agreement with Kay Suenson on this point. This caused Suenson to turn the game around and attempt a cautious approach with regard to an alliance between the two companies with the goal of resisting ITT, but this proposal was rejected by Carlton, who found such an alliance unnecessary, and Suenson abandoned his attempt.[32]

The efforts to obtain an agreement associated with the merger of East-

The vast majority of Great Northern's employees were men, and in most of East Asia, women were at the stations only rarely. This was not the case in Nagasaki, however. The picture shows the Danish station chief Jessen with the station's female staff in 1919.

ern and the Marconi company also had to be abandoned as the British government approved an even more far-reaching plan to merge all British overseas telegraphy interests, both public and private, into a single company.

The idea was to create a holding company that would acquire all of the shares in Eastern, the Marconi company, and the other telegraphy companies. The holding company would own all the shares in an underlying company that would take over undersea cables and cable and wireless stations. The two companies would have identical boards of directors with two representatives appointed by the government, and an Imperial Communications Advisory Company with representatives of the British Empire would supervise the two companies.[33]

The merger was executed on April 9, 1929, with the establishment of the holding company, which was given the expressive name Cable & Wireless Ltd., while the communications company was named Imperial and International Communications Ltd. The result was a telecommunications giant that owned 253 cable and radio stations in locations around the world, as well as more than half of the total length of the world's undersea cables. The company could not act in accordance with normal business behavior as it was subject to the government's control and strategic interests, one of the consequences of which was that the now-unprofitable cables had to continue to be operated. The world saw what was called "a new form of business, formally private, but in reality government-regulated and monopolistic—a pillar of the empire."[34]

This construction, which was known colloquially simply as Cable & Wireless, became involved in and complicated all aspects of Great Northern's preexisting relationships with both Eastern and the British directorate of telegraphy. For the time being, all existing agreements continued to be applicable to their respective areas, including Great Northern's monopolistic concession in China, which would expire at the end of 1930—that is, already the following year—and in connection with which there would be discussions that could decide the company's future.

Sino-Japanese telegraphy alliance

Great Northern had long had its gaze fixed on the expiration of the Chinese concession, which the company wished to have extended at least through the end of 1940. However, the concession provided no protection against the invasion of China by wireless telegraphy. In February 1918, the Japanese company Mitsui Bussan Kaisha received an order from the Chinese government for the construction and operation of a radio station near Beijing that would be powerful enough to connect Beijing with Japan, the United States, and Europe. Great Northern and Eastern both protested, making reference to their concession, but their protest was rejected out of hand.[35]

The construction of the wireless station was a result of the fact that during the world war, Japan had experienced considerable industrial and economic growth, with growing interests not least in Manchuria. As a consequence, the country's international telecommunications had expanded explosively; the number of telegrams to and from the United States alone had quintupled during the period from 1914 to 1920. For the Japanese government, wireless telegraphy became a means of increasing capacity and a way of achieving independence from Great Northern.

However, Japan was not alone in wishing to establish wireless telegraphy stations in China. Leading wireless companies such as Germany's Telefunken, England's Marconi, and the United States' Federal Telegraph Company were swarming around China with offers to build radio stations, and the Chinese government, like the Japanese government, saw wireless telegraphy as a way of achieving telegraphic independence.

Around this time, there was a new wave of anti-Western movements in China in the wake of the refusal of the Versailles peace conference at the end of the world war to accommodate Chinese demands that the so-called unequal treaties be nullified. This was a factor that contributed to the development of a closer relationship between Japan and China that included the telegraphy sector, and Great Northern and Eastern noted this in the fall of 1922 when the companies negotiated with the two countries with regard to the operation of the cable Japan had laid to Qingdao after having taken the area from Germany. The companies exploited the opportunity to apply for an extension of their concession past 1930, but the Chinese presented "a new and quite worrying" demand that the companies' landing rights should expire at the same time as the agreements that had been concluded.[36]

At the same time, the Japanese refused to consider an extension of the company's concession beyond 1930. Therefore, the result of the negotiations was that in November 1922, Japan and China concluded an agreement with regard to the Qingdao cable that contained a Chinese declaration to the effect that China did not intend to create new monopolies. In the perspective of the Danes, Japan and China together appeared to be attempting "to liberate themselves from the companies and in particular from Great Northern, whose existence and business activity are particularly hindering Japan in acting freely with regard to telegraphy."[37]

Great Northern's fears proved justified when, early in 1923, the company received information to the effect that the Sino-Japanese contract contained a supplementary agreement regarding a major expansion of the cooperation between the two companies in the telegraphy sector. This agreement meant that China would not extend the companies' monopoly beyond 1930 and that the two countries together would take over and operate Great Northern's cables between Shanghai and Nagasaki.[38]

Great Northern believed that a possible Danish diplomatic action would be unlikely to have any effect. In contrast, it might be hoped that other governments than the Danish one, particularly the British government, could react to Japanese advances in the telegraphy sector, but otherwise, the company would have to hope "that the political situation in East Asia could change before 1930 in such a way that Japan's intentions [could] not be realized."[39]

Japanese attack on Shanghai

Great Northern got what it had hoped for, but the background was tragic. During the 1920s, internal conflicts in China developed into an actual civil war, and Japan backed the sitting government in Beijing. In 1927 and 1928, however, the situation finally stabilized with the nationalist Kuomintang party under the leadership of Chiang Kai-shek as the victor, and after the party had established its government at Nanjing, Japan's influence in China crumbled.

In late 1928, the nationalist Kuomintang government presented its basis for the upcoming concession negotiations with both the companies and Japan. The government intended to take over all foreign cables in Chinese waters but was evidently aware that nothing would be gained by owning one end of an undersea cable. However, the time of the monopolies had passed, and foreign companies doing business in the telegraphy sector in China would be required at least to have landing permits and would not be allowed to operate stations of their own that were in direct contact with customers.[40]

On December 9, 1928, the Chinese government gave notice of termination of the agreements with Great Northern, Cable & Wireless, and Commercial Pacific at the end of 1930 and gave notice of termination of the agreements with Japan. At the same time, the parties were invited to participate in negotiations; the government wished to negotiate with each government and with the Japanese individually.

As far as the companies were concerned, Great Northern's negotiations, which began on March 26, 1930, ended up showing the way things were going. The Danish company had feared that in the wake of the merger with Marconi, the English company would cut its ties to Great Northern, but on one hand, Cable & Wireless would doubtless be weaker if it faced the Chinese alone, and on the other hand,

Chiang Kai-shek was the leader of the Republic of China from 1928 until 1949, when he had to flee to Taiwan in the wake of the civil war with Mao Zedong's communist revolutionary forces. He governed Taiwan until his death in 1975. He had received a military education, and, with the title of Generalissimo, he had led China's army in the war against the Japanese and subsequently in the civil war against the communists after the Second World War. He took a positive view of Great Northern's wish to reopen the cables to Shanghai, but because of the course taken by the civil war, no agreement was finally concluded.

Great Northern's cables to Nagasaki were still the only technically and politically reliable connection with Japan.

For the companies, the decisive goals were to secure the validity of their landing permits as far into the future as possible and to keep their stations. The companies achieved both of these goals: A preliminary agreement signed on December 31, 1930,

During their service in Shanghai, Great Northern's Danish employees were part of an international community of Westerners that had its own sports clubs and restaurants. One tradition maintained by this community was the annual "cable match" among the three telegraph companies, Great Northern, Eastern, and Commercial Pacific. Here the teams had assembled in connection with the tournament in the early 1930s. In the front row on the right is Great Northern's East Asian director, Jesper J. Bahnson.

included a landing permit valid through the end of 1944 and provided for an arrangement under which the companies would keep their stations. However, the sending of telegrams itself would be carried out by Chinese personnel in Chinese telegraph stations inside the companies' building.[41]

The Japanese achieved a corresponding agreement, so despite the fact that a number of unresolved points remained, Kay Suenson was guard-edly optimistic as the long period of validity of the landing permits and the guarantee of the continued existence of the stations would provide the company with "firmer ground under its feet in the negotiations that remained."[42]

It initially appeared that he would turn out to have been right as the operating chief in Shanghai, Captain J. J. Bahnson, reported in late February that the negotiations were going well, and the following month, the Chinese government approved a draft with which Great Northern was satisfied. After this, however, the process ground to a halt.

Chiang Kai-shek's government had had its attention diverted as military revolts had broken out in northern China and a communist revolutionary government had been established in Guangzhou and now controlled several so-called liberated areas that were being run as Soviet communes. In July

1931, when the companies asked that the new agreements be signed, their request was rejected with the explanation that Chiang Kai-shek was at the front and the acting leader of the government council did not dare to sign the documents on his own initiative. However, the minister of telecommunications assured the companies that they had nothing to fear as Chiang Kai-shek had personally approved the agreements and found them "quite reasonable."[43]

This reassuring statement notwithstanding, the delay was probably partly attributable to the fact that the negotiations with Japan had broken down and the Chinese negotiators had been summoned home. In general, the relationship between the two countries had continually worsened, and in the middle of September 1931, Japanese army units in Manchuria initiated an attack on China's three northeastern provinces. This attack had not been sanctioned by the top military leadership or the government in Japan, but faced with a *fait accompli*, the government had no choice but to support its rebellious army units, which gained ground quickly, conquering most of Manchuria.

In reaction, a strong anti-Japanese mood quickly spread throughout China, and Japanese goods and companies were systematically boycotted. In Shanghai, where thirty thousand Japanese constituted by far the largest foreign population group, five Japanese Buddhist monks were attacked by a mob, and one of these monks was killed.

On January 26, 1932, a state of emergency was declared for the entire Shanghai area, except for the international settlements, and in the settlements, the Municipal Council announced its own state of emergency and mobilized the small foreign military units and a corps of volunteer soldiers to defend the borders of the settlement areas. On the evening of that same day, Japanese naval units landed four hundred marines to protect Japanese citizens, and when Chinese troops engaged these marines in battle, the Japanese began a bombardment of the Chinese positions.

During the weeks that followed, the Japanese sent additional 20,000 soldiers as well as heavy artillery and airplanes supplemented by bombard-

ments from the Japanese warships. The international settlements were not directly involved in combat actions, but they did notice the effects of the war as approximately 600,000 refugees arrived in the settlements. The telegraph companies were affected by the Japanese bombardments, which tore apart several underground cables. Great Northern laid a river cable between Shanghai and Wusong and established an emergency station at Wusong.[44]

When the Chinese forces pulled back after a little over a month of fighting, about 14,000 civilians had been killed. In early May 1932, a peace agreement was concluded according to which the Chinese would have to accept the establishment of a neutral zone around all of Shanghai and the stationing of 2,000 Japanese marines to protect the Japanese component of the populace.

Great Northern's telegraph station had found itself in the middle of the fighting, but despite significant technical difficulties and significant danger to the personnel, the company had succeeded in maintaining the city's only stable telegraph connection to the surrounding environment without any of the company's employees having come to harm.

The company's efforts to conclude a new agreement were resumed, but it was not until early April 1933 that the final agreements were signed. With regard to all significant points, these agreements were identical to what the Chinese government had approved a year previously. Great Northern's and Eastern's monopolies were gone, but the companies' landing permits and right to have their own stations had been secured through the end of 1944.

During the war, in March 1932, Japan had declared that occupied Manchuria had become an independent state called Manchukuo. Both the League of Nations and the United States condemned Japan's de facto annexation of Manchuria. While Japan was not subjected to any actual sanctions, the creation of Manchukuo contributed to worsening the tense relationship between China and Japan and made the laying of new Japanese cables to China impossible. On the other hand, the new Chinese landing permit for the Japanese cables allowed them to be used for international traf-

An emergency station in Great Northern's cable depot in Shanghai that the company established during the Japanese military action near Shanghai in 1932 to maintain the telegraph connection between the city and its local and wider environment.

fic and not as had previously been the case only for Japanese traffic between the two countries.

Shortly thereafter, the Japanese administration unilaterally gave notice of termination of the joint purse agreement with Great Northern of 1912, thus "liberating [Japan] from one of the fetters that had limited Japan's independence in the area of communications," as a leading member of the Japanese telegraphy administration later put it. Great Northern accepted this with resignation and chose not to take action in response.[45]

A national security problem for Japan

Despite the Japanese efforts to force Great Northern out, the company's cables from Nagasaki to China and Russia were still in use. The company was also maintaining its station in Nagasaki, which in the eyes of the Japanese was "a foreign enclave on Jap-

anese soil, which was of the greatest concern and also a serious and difficult problem for the Japanese telecommunications authorities."[46]

In general, Great Northern was seen as a foreign body in the region that with its cables and position was blocking Japan's own ambitions in the telegraphy sector, and Great Northern's relationship with Japan was gradually worsened after the signing of the Chinese landing permits, which had extended the Danish company's presence for a further number of years.

The problems began in Manchukuo, where the local telephone and telegraph company began systematically ignoring the customers' via-specifications in cases in which customers had specified "via Northern" or "via Eastern." The telegrams were instead sent from a powerful radio station capable of reaching not only Japan but also Europe and the United States, which provoked repeated protests from the companies to the Japanese telegraphy authorities, none of which had any effect.[47]

The Japanese telegraphy authority now initiated a campaign to get residents to use the country's own wireless stations rather than the Danish cables. Japanese companies that preferred to send their telegrams "via Northern" were visited by the local government telegraphy agency, which implied that the customers in question risked getting inferior service from the local telegraph stations if they did not use Japan's own wireless service. Once again, Great Northern protested but in vain.[48]

For the Japanese, the campaign against Great Northern was to a significant extent about money. In 1935, the Japanese telegraphy authority paid out over 10 million yen in gold francs that the Japanese government could have used for other important purposes. At the same time, Japan—in contrast to Russia—had no transit revenues as the telegrams between Europe and China did not pass through Japanese territory.

In August 1936, Great Northern's presence was made a matter of Japan's national security when the government approved a program that proclaimed that Japan would act as a stabilizing power in the region and in opposition to the United Kingdom and the United States. In the press and in the government's propaganda, concern was expressed about the Danish company's relationship with the United Kingdom, and the company was characterized as "British" or "British controlled." Early in 1937, the Japanese Ministry of Communications began considering possible ways of ending Great Northern's presence in Japan and in East Asia generally as the company was viewed as a national security problem in the context of preparations for new territorial expansion.[49]

Japanese control over all East Asian telegraphy

In early July 1937, Japan launched a major military attack on China. Both of Great Northern's cables to Nagasaki and the cable to Hong Kong had soon been cut, and while the cuts occurred near Gutzlaff, two Japanese destroyers prevented them from being repaired. On August 10, Japanese army units reached Shanghai, and during the following two months, there was a bloody battle for the city that has been called China's Stalingrad because of the intensity and brutality of the fighting, the many military and civilian deaths, and the pervasive destruction.[50]

As in 1932, Shanghai's international settlement was spared involvement in the actual fighting but was flooded with refugees. The Danish embassy, which had been moved to Shanghai, moved into Great Northern's building, which became a collection point for the whole city's Danish expatriate community. The personnel at Wusong were evacuated by a British destroyer and brought to Shanghai, while the cable depot's buildings were badly damaged. However, the cable tanks and the cables they contained, which had a value of 700,000 to 800,000 kroner, remained largely undamaged.

On September 23, 1937, after lengthy negotiations with the Japanese, the company succeeded in repairing and reopening the cable to Nagasaki, and after further difficulties, the company also managed to repair the cable to Hong Kong, which opened in the middle of January 1938 after a five-month interruption. Apart from regular inspections, Great Northern had no access to the cable depot at Wusong, however, as Japanese troops were using it as barracks.

When the battle for the city was over, the Japanese were "masters of the Shanghai area," as a report to Great Northern's board of directors put it. In general, the Japanese forces respected the international settlement's international status, but with regard to telegraphic connections with the surrounding world, they did not.[51]

On November 20, 1937, representatives of the three telegraph companies were summoned to a meeting with the Japanese general consul in Shanghai, who demanded the introduction of Japanese military censorship and that the companies ceased paying money to the Chinese telegraphy administration instead transferring the money to a Japanese bank. The companies and the three Western general consuls protested but achieved nothing by doing so. The general consuls recommended that the Japanese demands be accommodated so that telegram traffic could be maintained and argued that there was no alternative to this course of action. This resulted in protests from the Chinese government to the companies and their governments, which could only respond by referring to force majeure.[52]

This Japanese action did not affect the telegraph service itself, but in July 1938, the Japanese military announced that it intended to take over the Chinese telegraph stations inside Great Northern's building in Shanghai. Once again, the companies, supported by their general consuls, protested, and they had no choice but to accept the Japanese action and refer to force majeure. This meant that Japanese soldiers were now stationed inside Great Northern's building on the Bund and that these soldiers controlled all local, regional, and international telegram traffic coming into and leaving the city, including transit traffic to and from Europe.[53]

Great Northern and Stalin

CHAPTER 14

Soviet Russian campaign against foreigners

At the same time as Great Northern came under increasing Japanese pressure in East Asia, things began to be tightened up in the Soviet Union. During the 1920s, the company's representative, Alfred Schønebeck, had succeeded in developing good personal relationships with a number of employees at various levels in the telegraphy administration. In 1926, however, there was a controversy when the Soviet authorities declared that the debt from the time of the Czar had now been paid. Great Northern believed that the company was, in fact, still owed 2 million gold francs, and after the company had made a statement to this effect, a department head in the People's Commissariat had threatened to terminate the company's concession.[1]

Around the same time, Alfred Schønebeck reported to the company in Copenhagen that "in various ways [he had noted] a tendency toward suspicion and jealousy of the company," though there was not an actually hostile mood. In fact, things were much as they had been in the old department of telegraphy in the time of the Czar when the Russians had not liked to see foreigners in charge of Russian telegraph connections.[2]

However, Great Northern was aware that the Soviet Union's top concession committee, which administered the Soviet government's concessions for foreign companies, was considering the company's position. Not long before this, the committee had asked the foreign commissariat whether Great Northern's concession might not be in need of "interpretation, supplements, or changes," but Maksim Litvinov, who was still the vice foreign commissar, had replied that this was not the case: "SNTS [*Store Nordiske Telegraf-Selskabet*, the Great Northern Telegraph Company] was the first foreign company to which Soviet Russia issued a concession; this concession was signed by Lenin, and in the opinion of the Foreign Commissariat it is in not in need of interpretation, nor is it necessary that supplements be added or changes made to this concession." Litvinov confidentially sent a copy of his letter to the concession committee to Alfred Schønebeck, who informed Great Northern's headquarters in Copenhagen.[3]

In other words, Great Northern enjoyed a special status that had been conferred by the for-

In 1927, Moscow's new central telegraph building opened. It housed the Soviet government telegraphy authority and Great Northern's station in Moscow. The building is still there, on Tverskaya Ulitsa, close to Manezhnaya Square and Red Square.

As an eighteen-year-old, Alfred Schønebeck was hired by Great Northern as a telegraphist and stationed in Russia, from where he returned to Denmark in 1914. In 1920, he participated in the negotiations in Moscow regarding the reopening of Great Northern's cables and the trans-Siberian connection, and in 1921, he was appointed the company's first representative in the Soviet Union. He returned to Denmark again in 1930.

eign commissariat and had Lenin's signature, and the threat to terminate the concession came to naught. However, the matter of the remaining debt from the time of the Czar ended up being processed and ultimately presented to the top concession committee, which was to present a recommendation to the Soviet government. While the case was being processed, Alfred Schønebeck received legal advice from a Russian attorney, Mr. Glass, who was arrested following the decisive meeting of the concession committee in early January 1928. Schønebeck was given no explanation of this arrest, not even when Mr. Glass was sentenced to five years' banishment to the Solovetsky Islands in northern Russia. In Denmark, Kay Suenson judged that "there [would hardly be]

any attorney who would dare to replace him after what had happened," and this turned out to be correct. When Schønebeck asked some of Glass's colleagues whether they would be able to take over, their replies were "evasive or negative."[4]

Great Northern subsequently gave up its attempts to get involved in the matter and let it go its course without having an opportunity to appear before the various organs, and in late July 1928, the Soviet government, not unexpectedly, decided the matter in favor of the People's Commissariat.

A contributing factor with regard to the progress and resolution of the matter was a new tendency for foreigners to be viewed negatively, a tendency that was growing stronger. After the death of Vladimir Lenin in January 1924, the general secretary of the Communist Party of the Soviet Union, Joseph Stalin, had increasingly established himself as an absolute ruler, outmaneuvering or eliminating his opponents.

In the middle of the 1920s, when the Soviet government began preparing for the implementation of the Soviet Union's first five-year plan and the collectivization of agriculture, this was accompanied by increasing and hostile propaganda against foreign countries and foreigners. In April 1928, Stalin warned against economic sabotage carried out by foreign specialists and companies in the Soviet Union. The following month, the first of a series of show trials took place in Moscow. In this trial, more than fifty so-called bourgeois specialists, including several foreigners, were accused of sabotage and so-called parasitic activity in the coal mines in the Shakty area of the Donbass region. This trial led to an increase in propaganda against foreigners and a change in the official concession policies.

After the number of businesses holding concessions had peaked at sixty-eight in 1928, the Soviet government began systematically forcing the foreign companies out. The companies that did not voluntarily conclude agreements to terminate their concessions were subjected to harassment in the form of failures to deliver raw materials as well as restrictions on imports and exports, and

the companies' ability to export their surpluses was obstructed.

Soviet Russian special treatment of Great Northern

Great Northern was not affected by the aggressive attacks on foreign specialists and companies, but Alfred Schønebeck, who had written in confidential reports to Great Northern of the "oppressive, depressing, and foreboding mood" that pervaded the society, took precautions. Instead of waiting for the authorities to implement various measures, he took the bull by the horns by seeking permission to appear before the top government planning commission, Gosplan, which was responsible for forced collectivization and the execution of the first five-year plan.[5]

Schønebeck succeeded in obtaining such permission, and on January 30, 1930 the absolute cream of the political-economic elite of the Soviet Union listened to what the representative of a private capitalist telegraph company had to say. Schønebeck emphasized the planned-economy aspect of the company's system, which was operated rationally and "from a center" across national borders and geographic boundaries and freed the Soviet Union from the need to negotiate with foreign powers itself. And then Schønebeck emphasized Great Northern's greatest advantage, the advantage that constituted the very foundation of the company's existence:

"An international telegraph company such as ours, which works in ten different countries and has close relationships with an even greater number of governments and international organizations, must of course manifest the strictest neutrality in all political questions, complete loyalty to all governments with which it cooperates, and full compliance with all of the conditions of the concession."[6]

There is no record of how Schønebeck's speech was received by Gosplan, but all the evidence suggests that it had a positive effect. In any event, the

The People's Commissar of Communications of the Soviet Union, Alexei Rykov, was the host of Great Northern's Director Alf Ussing when Ussing visited Moscow in May 1933. Alexei Rykov shared the fate of most of the other Bolsheviks who had been closest to Vladimir Lenin during the Russian Revolution in October 1917: As Joseph Stalin's power increased, Rykov fell out of favor, and he was finally executed following a public show trial.

Soviet government's hysterical campaign against foreigners did not negatively affect Great Northern, which, in fact, received special treatment in a positive sense in February 1933 when, as the only foreign company to be so favored, Great Northern was excepted from new immigration restrictions. In the future, Russian-born women who had married foreigners and changed their citizenship would not be able to return to the Soviet Union once they had left, even if they had left only for a vacation. Great Northern was excepted from this

rule, which would otherwise have affected approximately thirty of the company's Danish telegraphists and their wives.[7]

The special treatment continued in May 1933 when Alf Ussing arrived in Moscow "to pay his respects" to the Soviet Commissariat of Communications. In 1932, he and Kay Suenson's nephew, cand. polyt. Bent Suenson, who had been an employee of the company since 1925, had been appointed to directorships in preparation for Kay Suenson's planned resignation the following year. Kay Suenson intended to retain his seat on the board of directors following his resignation from the top management team. At the same time, Lieutenant Commander Harald Bonde had been appointed director of accounting outside the top management team, so the company now had a three-man top management team including O. C. Scavenius.

Great Northern's leaders had planned to avoid having Alf Ussing engage in "business discussions" on this occasion; nevertheless, the company considered his visit an event of considerable importance. Hans Christiansen, who had replaced Alfred Schønebeck as the company's representative in Moscow in 1931, had indicated a number of times to the company's headquarters in Copenhagen that it "would be desirable and would be appreciated by the Soviets if a member of the company's top management team would come to Moscow at some point." An internal document from the People's Commissariat for Communications indicates that there was a Soviet wish for "maintenance of the good relationship with the Great Northern Telegraph Company in harmony with our own interests."[8]

When Director Ussing arrived in Moscow on May 24, 1933, he was, therefore, met by no lesser personage than the People's Commissar of Communications of the Soviet Union, Alexei Rykov, as well as a number of high-ranking functionaries to whom Hans Christiansen did not normally have access. Rykov belonged to the revolutionary guard that had surrounded Lenin at the time of the October 1917 revolution, but in the late 1920s, he had fallen out of favor with Stalin and been removed from his post as a government leader and member of the

After the Russian Revolution and Civil War, the living quarters for Danish staff were not as luxurious in Moscow as in Leningrad, as is indicated by this photograph of the residential building in Moscow.

party's powerful Politburo. He had instead become the People's Commissar of Communications of the Soviet Union, and it was in this capacity that he was now hosting the Danish director, Ussing, and his wife at an official dinner and a performance at the Bolshoi Theater.

One can only guess at the impression left on the Russians by this visit, but as the People's Commissariat's purpose had supposedly been to maintain the Soviet Union's good relationship with the company, Alexei Rykov had every reason to be satisfied. The evaluation of the encounter presented to Great Northern's board of directors by the top management team indicates that the team was left with a positive impression: "Director Ussing was received with great friendliness, and the statements made by the Russians during the social gatherings

that took place during the visit confirmed the good will with which our company's business is in fact viewed in Moscow."[9]

A year and a half later, the Russians would use a very different tone in their dealings with Great Northern.

Deportation of seven Danes in Leningrad

In November 1934, Alf Ussing again traveled to Moscow, and this time, it was not for a social visit. A short time previously, the Soviet government had taken over one of the company's wires through Siberia, and when the company's representative in Moscow had tried in vain to get it back, Alf Ussing traveled to Russia to negotiate with Alexei Rykov in person. To Alf Ussing's great surprise, Rykov offered to provide the company with all the wire facilities it desired—if it agreed to replace the Danish telegraphists with Russian ones.[10]

The commissariat had long desired a reduction of the Danish staff, a reduction Great Northern had resisted, arguing that Russian telegraphists were not as well trained as Danish ones. Alf Ussing repeated the company's arguments, but these arguments had no effect, and he had to return to Denmark without having made any progress.[11]

A short time later, the Soviet authorities ratcheted up their game. On January 9, 1935, Hans Christiansen received an official letter from the People's Commissariat of Communications of the Soviet Union. In this brief letter, Great Northern was asked to fire seven named Danish functionaries then employed at the company's telegraph station in Leningrad, formerly Saint Petersburg and Petrograd, in accordance with § 4, section 2 of the concession agreement. The individuals in question were the station chief and the duty chief as well as four leading employees and an assistant mechanic.[12]

Hans Christiansen was shocked. To be sure, the agreement did give the commissariat the right to demand, without providing a reason, that functionaries at the company's stations in Russia be fired immediately, but the Russians had not previously made use of this right, and he immediately telegraphed the top management team at Kongens Nytorv and asked for instructions. He reported that he had heard nothing about the reason but that it was probably a manifestation of the "nervosity" that characterized the Soviet Union in the wake of the "recent events" in precisely Leningrad.[13]

What he was referring to was the murder of Leningrad's party leader, Sergei Kirov, in December, which had been followed by a large number of arrests and a massive wave of propaganda that had triggered a witch hunt for all kinds of potential enemies of the Soviet state, including foreign spies. For Great Northern, the consequence was that the station in Leningrad was placed under increased surveillance by the NKVD, the Soviet interior ministry, a unit of which was the secret police, whose officers were not so secret that they could not be easily recognized thanks to their uniforms and high-shafted boots. According to Hans Christiansen, the demand had "hardly" been presented by the Commissariat for Communications; he believed there were other forces behind it.

Also, the Soviet telegraphy administration had asked to be provided with a number of copies of the code books Hans Christiansen and the Danish station chiefs used in their internal communications and in communicating with Great Northern's headquarters in Copenhagen. Hans Christiansen believed that this demand had also originated with the NKVD, and for this reason, he had telegraphed to Kongens Nytorv using the Danish foreign service to preserve his "freedom of expression in his correspondence with the top management team.[14]

The situation was serious, and Great Northern's board of directors was immediately summoned to a crisis meeting, while the Danish Ministry of Foreign Affairs notified the company that the ministry was prepared to support them. An operation to soften and, if possible, ward off the Soviet Russian demand was initiated, but everyone understood that this would be difficult, and it was indeed to be feared that this was only the beginning of a major wave of purges of the company's stations.

On Monday, January 14, 1935, at 4:30 PM, Great Northern's board of directors met to discuss the situation in Leningrad. The board consisted of the chairman, Wilhelm Weimann; the Venstre (Danish Liberal Party) representative, Niels Neergaard; O. C. Scavenius; Kay Suenson; the University of Copenhagen professor dr.jur. Poul Johannes Jørgensen; the manufacturer Thomas B. Thrige; Frederik Hoskjær, a department head in the Ministry of Public Works; and the social democrat Frederik Andersen, who was a member of the Folketing and a Copenhagen councilman. The last two of these men had been appointed to the board of directors by the government.[15]

O. C. Scavenius briefly detailed the People's Commissariat's demands, noting that "formally the commissariat had a perfect right to make these demands." Nevertheless, he said, the demand had the character of "intentional misuse of the condition in question" because of the extensiveness of the firings and because they affected "a number of the company's most trusted individuals, people who have served well and long in Russia." He was not in any doubt that this had to do with the murder of Kirov, nor was he in any doubt that the People's Commissariat "has had to carry out the orders of the all-powerful secret police, probably without knowing why." He was, therefore, pessimistic with regard to the chances of getting the decision changed but felt that an attempt should be made.

To be sure, it would not be difficult for the company to replace the seven functionaries, but "if the situation were repeated at other Russian stations the company's position could end up being entirely untenable," Scavenius declared. Also, the company had to fear the consequences that could arise if the Russian measure were to become public knowledge, and it would doubtless attract attention from and create insecurity among the Danes at the company's other Russian stations. Therefore, the matter would need to be treated with the strictest confidentiality.

No one asked questions, and after some other matters had been discussed, the meeting ended, having lasted just forty minutes.[16]

Appeal to Maksim Litvinov

A little over two hours after the meeting of the board of directors, O. C. Scavenius received a telephone call from the Ministry of Foreign Affairs, which notified him that the Danish ambassador to the Soviet Union, Ole Engell, had presented himself at the Foreign Commissariat the previous Sunday and been received by the head of the division for the Scandinavian countries, Mr. Berosov, who had declared that he knew nothing of the matter. Ole Engell had emphasized "that the matter was of great importance not only to the company but also to the country," and Mr. Berosov had promised to investigate it.[17]

Hans Christiansen had also been in action; on January 10, he had sought out the head of the international department of the Commissariat of Communications, Mrs. Dobruskina, but she had been unable—or unwilling—to provide any information about the reason for the deportation demand. However, she requested that the company send her written notice of when the seven functionaries could leave Leningrad.[18]

She did not receive such written notice. Instead, Hans Christiansen appeared at the commissariat on January 14 with an account in which he referred to "the many years of friendly cooperation" and appealed to the commissariat, asking that the matter be reexamined. Mrs. Dobruskina softened and promised to do what she could, letting herself be persuaded to try to arrange a meeting between Christiansen and People's Commissar Alexei Rykov in person.[19]

The matter was heading for the top of the People's Commissariat for Communications, and at Great Northern, O. C. Scavenius decided to try a similar strategy with the Commissariat of Foreign Affairs, where Maksim Litvinov had risen to the post of Commissar of Foreign Affairs. The day after the meeting of the board of directors, Weimann sent a memorandum to the Ministry of Foreign Affairs in which he noted that Great Northern's former representative in Moscow, Alfred Schønebeck, "had on several occasions spoken with Litvinov about the conditions under which the company was working and had always found a sympathetic listener." Scavenius, therefore, trusted that Litvinov would take an interest in the matter, and he asked Minister of Foreign Affairs P. Munch to present the matter to his Russian colleague "in a brief and unofficial form" at the upcoming meeting of the League of Nations in Geneva.[20]

In Moscow, Ambassador Ole Engell supported the initiative, though he was not optimistic, as the wave of purges in Russia was escalating at this time. On January 16, 1935, nineteen formerly leading members of the Communist Party were sentenced to five to ten years for conspiracy in connection with the murder of Kirov. According to Ole Engell, the trial had led to "a mood of such panic that it would be even more difficult for the Commissariat of Foreign Affairs to get its way in the face of resistance from the secret police, and to the Russian mentality it must seem a small thing that seven people are being ejected from the country when at the same time hundreds of people are being executed more or less because of unproven suspicions."[21]

Nevertheless, the appeal to Maksim Litvinov appeared to have paid off. Late in January of 1935, Minister of Foreign Affairs P. Munch reported that he had mentioned the matter to Litvinov and that Litvinov had promised it would be investigated. And on February 23, when Hans Christiansen was finally admitted to see People's Commissar Alexei Rykov, the Russian demands had, in fact, been softened, though not decisively.[22]

According to Rykov, the matter had been "thoroughly investigated," and on the basis of the investigation, the commissariat retained its demand that the seven Danes be fired; the station chief and three leading employees were to leave immediately, while the remaining three were to be gone "within a few months." Hans Christiansen tried to save the station chief, but Rykov, whose behavior was otherwise "characterized both by sympathy and friendliness," rejected Hans Christiansen's efforts, claiming that the individual in question was "very problematic."[23]

To prepare for the removal of the Danish personnel from all the stations in the Soviet Union in 1937, Great Northern was to train Russian telegraphists to take over servicing these stations. The picture shows a classroom in Omsk.

Hans Christiansen did not learn what the problematic aspect was, nor did he learn the fundamental reason why the seven individuals were to leave the Soviet Union. He did not ask about these things either, and he reported to Great Northern that he did not think the ambassador should try to investigate the matter as doing so would risk making a bad situation worse. There was nothing more to be done, but the company could take comfort in the fact that not all seven were expected to leave Leningrad immediately: "That has to be regarded as an achievement not many have managed."[24]

The ambassador shared Christiansen's view, and all in all, the matter had ended well under the circumstances. The company would avoid negative publicity, and the deportations could be publicly presented as ordinary staff replacements. On March 11, 1935, Great Northern's top management team, therefore, wrote to the Ministry of Foreign Affairs, thanking the ministry for its efforts on the company's behalf but declaring that it had to be viewed as "unproductive and inappropriate further to resist the Soviet Union's demands or seek to establish the reason for the presentation of these demands."[25]

"In greatest harmony"

The deportation of the seven Danes was only the beginning. In May 1935, Hans Christensen had to sign an agreement regarding the replacement of fourteen Danish telegraphists with Russian ones, and the company would have to train the replacements. As an element of the agreement, Great Northern got the transit wire that had been taken over by the Russians back, and at Kongens Nytorv, it was hoped that there would be no further Russian demands. "Fortunately, there seem to be certain signs that the suspiciousness that has characterized the Russian authorities' attitude toward the company's personnel for several months is now in the process of evaporating," the top management team noted hopefully. This statement was justified in part by the observation that the NKVD's oversight of the station in Leningrad had now "been relaxed somewhat."[26]

The replacement of the fourteen Danish telegraphists did take place in a planned and orderly fashion and "in greatest harmony," but in May 1936, new difficulties appeared on the horizon when the People's Commissariat, "first in the form of a gentle inquiry and later in a firmer tone," asked whether the company would be willing to give up its station in Moscow's central telegraphy building, which was located close to Red Square. The company indicated that it would not in fact be willing to give up this station, but to appear accommodating, it offered to give up one of its rooms in the station—though without real hope that this would be sufficient.[27]

However, the company received help from an unexpected quarter. During a show trial in the middle of August 1936, the public prosecutor, Andrei Rykov, announced that during the trial, evidence had been uncovered that incriminated People's Commissar Alexei Rykov, who was arrested shortly thereafter. His successor was named on September 26 and was no lesser personage than the former head of the NKVD, Genrikh Jagoda, who had not engaged in enough purging to suit Joseph Stalin and, therefore, had been replaced by Nikolai Yezhov, the new and current head of the NKVD. However, neither Hans Christiansen nor other representatives of Great Northern would have occasion to negotiate with Genrikh Jagoda as he would be arrested seven months later and convicted in a show trial together with Alexei Rykov in March 1938 and subsequently executed.

A new commissar was immediately appointed, but the People's Commissariat appeared to be more or less paralyzed, and after sporadic negotiations in January and February of 1937 with regard to the company's rooms in Moscow's telegraphy station, discussion of the matter quieted down. This was the calm before the storm, however.

"Socrates against a machine gun"

Hans Christiansen was unexpectedly summoned to a meeting at the People's Commissariat at 3:30 p.m. on July 21, 1937. He was received by the director of the international department, Mr. Anikeyev, who informed him that the Soviet government wished to no longer have foreigners at its telegraph stations. Therefore, the government wished to have the company's concession of 1921 replaced with an agreement that would guarantee Great Northern the same revenues as the company had had previously but would establish that the trans-Siberian connection would be operated by the telegraphy authority of the Soviet Union using Russian personnel. For this reason, all sixty-seven Danes were to be removed from the stations, and the Soviet government requested that the company appoint a representative with a mandate to negotiate with regard to the matter. Mr. Anikeyev emphasized that this was a "serious" request and that the Soviet government wished the matter to be taken care of as soon as possible. He himself believed that it would be possible for Great Northern to hand over the company's station within three months.[28]

Hans Christiansen attempted to protest but soon realized that there was no point in discussing the matter. He, therefore, proceeded directly to the Danish general consulate and informed the Danish chargé d'affaires, Count Ivar Moltke, who sent a telegram regarding the matter to Denmark the same evening. Hans Christiansen did so as well, so by the next morning, the Ministry of Foreign Affairs and Great Northern's top management team were both aware of what had happened.[29]

The telegrams caused shock on Kongens Nytorv. Hans Christiansen was immediately summoned home for consultations, but previously, he had already made it clear to the company's leaders that it would hardly be possible to get the Russian decision reversed. Following the appointment of Nikolai Yezhov as the new head of the NKVD, the Soviet Union had been hurled into a blood fury, and mass arrests, terror, and trials had taken on vast dimensions.

In Hans Christiansen's view then, the reason for the commissariat's demand was "obvious enough, namely the fear of spies and the general 'liquidation' of foreigners." It could not be expected that a foreign company's protest would have any effect under the circumstances, but if an attempt were to

be made, a diplomatic action would be required: "There might be a little hope that Litvinov could be moved to do something for us, but this is not certain, in part because no one knows how strong his position is at the moment."[30]

What Hans Christiansen did not know was that the decision to terminate the company's concession had been made by the Soviet government on July 19 and that it had been Litvinov himself and the new People's Commissar for Communications, Ivan Khalepsky, who had established the procedure for implementing the decision. Having recognized that there were no usable "formal reasons" for terminating the concession, the two men had decided not to send the company official written notification of the termination but instead simply to have Mr. Anikeyev inform Christiansen of the decision.[31]

It did not help that it was obvious that the Soviet government's decision was not only a symptom of the general fear of spies but also a result of the fact that Great Northern had ended up in the NKVD's spotlight. In June, the company had gotten a sign of what was to come when the newspaper *Leningrad Pravda* had published an article about "tricks used by some of the foreign espionage organizations and their Trotskyist-Bukharinist agents." The article, which was also published as a brochure, had been written by Leonid Zakovsky, who was presented as "a commissar first rank for government security and head of the NKVD's administration in the Leningrad district." As the right-hand man of the local party chief, Andrei Shdanov, Zakovsky was among the forces driving the bloody purges that had hit Leningrad like a tidal wave in the summer of 1937, and in his article, he now directed his gaze toward Great Northern's activities during the First World War and the matter of the German telegrams that had ended up in Petrograd:

"The Danish telegraph company's lines went through Saint Petersburg. This was a concession business, an international limited company, that connected the West with the Far East. In Saint Petersburg attention was not paid to the fact that spies could freely act in the Scandinavian countries for which the Danish telegraphy agency worked. In reality, messages were sent to the German general staff via Saint Petersburg over a long period during the imperialistic war with the help of the Danish telegraphy company."[32]

The article made no reference to Great Northern's current activities, but the message was clear enough. While Hans Christiansen was not aware of the circumstances surrounding the Soviet government's decision or of Maksim Litvinov's true role then, he was certainly justified in assuming that the chances of getting the Russians to change their decision were "not particularly great." The company had no power but that of its arguments, and in this connection, Hans Christiansen found inspiration in Russian literature, characterizing the company's situation by quoting the Russian author Leonid Andréyev: "Of what use are the arguments even of a Socrates against a machine gun?"[33]

"[...] the bottom and some side boards of the company's coffin"

On Tuesday, August 17, 1937, the Great Northern Telegraph Company's board of directors met to discuss "the company's position in the USSR." Since the meeting in January at which the deportations from Saint Petersburg had been discussed, Niels Neergaard and Frederik Andersen had passed away and had been replaced with His Majesty the King's cabinet secretary, Chamberlain C. P. M. Hansen, and the chairman of the Folketing, the social democrat Hans Rasmussen, respectively. The engineer Per Kampmann had been elected to the board in November 1936.[34]

O. C. Scavenius presented a brief report on Mr. Anikeyev's message to Hans Christiansen and emphasized the seriousness of the situation, noting that the company's whole position was threatened. The matter had been discussed with both Hans Christiansen and the ambassador in Moscow, and both men "[saw] it as completely pointless and extremely risky to offer resistance on grounds of principle." This being the case, Scavenius believed there was nothing to be done but to try to achieve "a gradual and gentle transition to a new arrange-

ment" and "if possible the *formal* retention of the current concession."

The top management team proposed to the board of directors that the company should offer the Russians a new arrangement under which the whole line through Siberia would be automated and the staff in Leningrad would be moved to Helsinki. To be sure, this would mean that a cable would have to be landed on the south coast of Finland, and there was no guarantee that the Russians would accept the proposed arrangement, but it did offer the advantage that all the Danes would be able to leave the stations in Russia. The top management team had already asked Hans Christiansen to try to get a feel for the Russian telegraph authority's position with regard to such an arrangement, and Scavenius had just received a telegram to the effect that owing to yet another change of commissar, there was as yet no news to report in this regard.

Scavenius's portrayal of the situation was businesslike and characterized by an experienced diplomat's cool and neutral approach. In contrast, the statements made by Wilhelm Weimann, who had been chairman of the board of directors for many years, reflected strong emotion. He declared that the proposed new arrangement "could become the bottom and some of the side boards of the company's coffin." He emphasized that a number of the company's fundamental agreements with other governments and companies were dependent on the company's operation of the trans-Siberian line and that fulfillment of the demands presented by the Soviet government could give the company's partners the right to terminate their agreements, which would mean the death of the company.

Even if things did not go that badly immediately, the result would be the same in the end, just at a later time and as a result of the degraded quality of the service and the consequent loss of traffic. Given this situation, it was natural to ask why the company did not offer resistance and demand that the concession be honored—and according to the minutes of the meeting, Weimann answered his own question, stating that "Great Northern was in fact powerless against the 'Russo-Asian Cheka treatment,' and if the company fought back the result would be arrests and the usual Soviet Russian acquisition of 'confessions.'"

The board chairman's words caused Kay Suenson to take the floor. Like Scavenius, he adopted a sober tone, responding to Weimann by remarking that he did not fear having the company's partners terminate their cooperation with the company. However, he did indicate that he was aware of the danger, saying that the company's partners would "in any case want to see how the new arrangement worked before they decided to take drastic measures."

Per Kampmann subsequently uttered a brief remark, but there were otherwise no further speakers. Therefore, discussion of this item on the agenda could be closed with the conclusion that "there was *no objection* to negotiation with Russia on the basis of the arguments detailed above." However, Weimann did get a final remark reflected in the minutes: "It appeared clear to the chairman that if this arrangement became a reality, it would at best mean a very serious, indeed fateful, weakening of Great Northern's system."[35]

To the Secretary of the Central Committee of the Communist Party of the Soviet Union, Comrade J. V. Stalin

A few days before the meeting of the board of directors, Hans Christiansen had arrived in Moscow, where he had sought out Mr. Anikeyev at the People's Commissariat and presented an official letter from Great Northern's top management team containing a proposed new arrangement, but as O. C. Scavenius had indicated at the meeting of the board of directors, no reply had been forthcoming because there had recently been a change of commissars.[36]

In June, three Soviet marshals and a number of high-ranking officers had been convicted in secret trials and subsequently shot on Stalin's orders, and the People's Commissar who, after having been the commander of the Soviet armored forc-

es, had replaced Genrikh Jagoda after Jagoda had been arrested in April had now met the same fate. The new commissar was Matvei Berman, who had been the top administrator of the GULag, the Soviet system of penal camps, and had received the Order of Lenin for his work in that connection before being promoted to vice commissar of the NKVD in September 1936. Now he had been transferred to the post of People's Commissar for the Soviet Union's communications, where, in light of the fate of his predecessors, he must have felt as if he were sitting in a waiting room until he would be arrested and subsequently executed. Nevertheless, Matvei Burman proceeded to carry out the order to liquidate Great Northern's concession, letting Mr. Anikeyev take care of the actual negotiations, and when the People's Commissariat realized that the company was willing to agree on a new arrangement that would accommodate the Soviet demands, things went fast.

The Russians were insistent only with regard to a single point, namely, that all Danes were to be out of Russia within three months. In a report to the Ministry of Foreign Affairs submitted around the same time, the Moscow legation described how "the pervasive and pathological fear of espionage" had now also affected neutral Denmark, and during the following months, the legation reported how Danish citizens were being expelled "on inconsiderately short notice." In general, the expulsion of foreigners had reached a level that had caused the commission shops in which private individuals could sell their private furnishings and possessions to be flooded with goods.[37]

Mr. Anikeyev had no choice but to insist on the expulsion of the Danish telegraphists, though he did agree to take into consideration that some stations might need extra time. It was also possible to convince him to allow Great Northern to retain a Danish representative in Moscow. With regard to the landing of a cable in Finland and the transfer of the service staff from Leningrad to Helsinki, he had no objections.

In contrast, there were difficulties because Great Northern wanted formally to retain the old concession and add to it a kind of supplemental written agreement regarding the new arrangement. Mr. Anikeyev would have liked to have accommodated the company's wish, but in accordance with a government decision, he had been explicitly instructed to terminate the concession and conclude a new contract. However, he did pass the Danish request upward in the system, and apparently, People's Commissar Matvei Berman was convinced that it would be reasonable to allow Great Northern formally to retain the old concession, and Maksim Litvinov also appeared to be sympathetic to this point of view.

In any event, the two people's commissars produced a joint letter "to the Secretary of the Central Committee of the Communist Party of the Soviet Union, *Comrade J. V. Stalin.*" This letter was dated September 8, 1937, stamped "strictly secret" and signed by Matvei Burman, while First Vice Minister of Foreign Affairs Vladimir Potemkin signed for Litvinov. The letter was not sent directly to Stalin but via the head of the government, Vyacheslav Molotov, who got the opinion of his vice head, Anastas Mikoyan, before he sent the letter to Stalin via the Secretariat of the Central Committee.[38]

In their letter to Stalin, the two people's commissars described the way the matter had gone and stated that Great Northern's wish to formally retain the concession would not collide with the Soviet government's demand that it take over the company's stations. Also, the commissars declared that formal nullification of the concession would "doubtless create a number of difficulties and cause the company to present questions regarding compensation for its losses." Finally, the commissars played their trump card: "Furthermore, elimination of the agreement could lead to the complete cessation of transit traffic through the USSR, and in addition to providing other advantages that traffic has provided considerable hard-currency revenues."

The two commissars no doubt expected that the danger of losing hard-currency revenues was what it would take to convince Stalin to accommodate the Danish company. Stalin's response arrived on September 23 in a letter from the Secretariat of the Central Committee to Molotov, the leader of the government. Stalin's decision was justified with the declaration that it would be inappropriately formal to retain the old agreement and that "operation of the undersea cables between the Soviet Union and Denmark, Japan, and China should be the exclusive domain of the People's Commissariat for Communications." The most important point was that all Danish personnel should be removed from the stations, and as Great Northern had agreed to this, there was, in Stalin's view, "no reason to allow the old agreement to remain in force." Nevertheless, Stalin declared that "all of the company's wishes with regard to the use of the undersea cables can be taken into consideration in the general agreement between the People's Commissariat and the Great Northern Telegraph Company."[39]

The response to their letter to the general secretary that Matvei Berman and Maksim Litvinov received was not very clear or very direct. While Stalin did not see any reason to maintain the old concession, he had not explicitly forbidden its continuation, though it had been characterized as "inappropriately formal." Despite this characterization, it was possible to interpret the general secretary's response as indicating that the old concession was insignificant as long as all the Danes left the stations, and thus, the People's Commissariat acquired control over incoming and outgoing telegram traffic.

Apparently, this was how the general secretary's response was interpreted by the two people's commissars, who doubtless checked to make sure they had not misread Stalin's letter. For this reason, a draft of a new government decision was produced according to which the People's Commissariat for Communications was instructed to carry out the liquidation of Great Northern's concession in such a way that "the old concession is not formally nullified, but it is established via an exchange of letters that the Great Northern Telegraph Company's stations are placed at the unrestricted disposal of the People's Commissariat for

Communications." In addition, all Danes were to have left the stations by March 1, 1938, at the latest.[40]

The last Soviet Russian concession

At Great Northern, there was no knowledge of what was going on in the corridors of power in Moscow, and a meeting of the company's board of directors on October 20, 1937, proceeded accordingly. The meeting began at 4:30 p.m. with a report from O. C. Scavenius on what had been achieved thus far, including the granting of additional time to leave the stations. The next board member to take the floor was Kay Suenson, who stated that it was his understanding that the People's Commissariat had offered the company a new agreement but that the top management team preferred an oral agreement. His own view was that the company should strive to secure some kind of written agreement.[41]

It was the absolute top political leadership of the Soviet Union that, in the fall of 1937, considered Great Northern's request that the company's concession not be nullified: the vice president of ministers of the Soviet Union, Anastas Mikoyan; the president of ministers and leader of the government, Vyacheslav Molotov; and not least, General Secretary Joseph Stalin. The picture shows them standing on the Lenin Mausoleum at the May Day demonstration on Red Square the previous year.

Scavenius confirmed that the information Suenson had received was correct but noted that both Hans Christiansen and the Danish ambassador had "most emphatically" advised against making any attempt to secure a written agreement as such an attempt would have to be viewed as very risky under the current circumstances. "The question of the concession and other important questions could end up being presented to the Soviet government directly and perhaps subsequently to the military authorities," he said, adding that this could lead to decisions "that could end up having a fatal effect on the transit route."

Kay Suenson replied that he had not envisioned a new concession but rather a "supplement to the existing concession that would cover the new state of affairs." In his view, this was "the most opportune [point in time] at which to ask for the establishment of an arrangement that had been set down in writing, as the Russians themselves had envisioned the company having something in writing."

There was not much sympathy for Suenson's arguments, however. On the contrary, the chairman of the board of directors, Wilhelm Weimann, stated that the company was standing there "with its hat in its hand" while the Soviet government demanded that its will be done. Under the current circumstances, he did not dare act contrary to the recommendations of Hans Christiansen and Ambassador Engell, and while he would like to see something in writing, "in this case the concession had, after all, not proven to be worth much more than any other piece of paper." Suenson remained alone with his point of view, and the meeting was adjourned after it had been established that the top management team would continue working to secure an oral agreement.

In the meantime, the processing of the matter in Moscow had ground to a halt. Like Hans Christiansen and Ole Engell, the employees of the People's Commissariat for Communications were evidently afraid to suggest anything, let alone put anything down on paper. In the words of Ambassador Ole Engell, they had been frozen by "the fear of responsibility" not because they feared the possible reaction of Great Northern but because they feared the possible reaction of "the higher powers."[42]

Also, the People's Commissariat for Communications had been affected by the purges. It was not only the commissars who were being replaced in a rapid tempo. The lower-ranking officials were also affected as indicated by a report submitted to Great Northern's board of directors in October 1937: "When the company's representative, Mr. H. H. I. Christiansen, visited the People's Commissariat in Moscow to inform the commissariat that the

change had been made, Mr. Anikeyev was gone, and a new man, Mr. Stolyarov, was sitting at his desk."[43]

The change regarding which Hans Christiansen had gone to notify the commissariat was the agreed-upon landing of a cable in Finland and the transfer of the service staff from Leningrad to Helsinki. Now he had to present the whole matter anew to Mr. Stolyarov, who "appeared to have nothing to say about what had been done."

It was then the case that in the fall of 1937, there was a willingness both on Kongens Nytorv and in Moscow to conclude an agreement according to which Great Northern's concession of 1921 would formally be allowed to remain in force, while the removal of all Danish functionaries from the company's stations and the commissariat's takeover of these stations would be confirmed by some less formal kind of agreement. As a result of the Stalinist terror and apparently because the Soviet government never made the decision to accommodate the company's wish that had in fact been prepared after the two commissars' letter to Stalin had received a response, however, such an informal agreement was never concluded.[44]

While, as Christiansen had noted, Great Northern's successful delaying of the expulsion of seven Danish functionaries from Leningrad had been an achievement, the company's retention of its concession and of the right to continue its operations must be regarded as nothing less than historic. A Soviet government decision formulated in December 1937 makes it clear that the government had intended to eliminate the concession arrangement entirely. What had remained at that point were a few Japanese fishing, forestry, and oil concessions on and off the Pacific coast and on Sakhalin that did not survive the military collision between Japan and the Soviet Union in the summer of 1938.[45]

Great Northern then was not only the first foreign company to be awarded a concession by the Soviet government but apparently also the only one that did not lose its concession, a concession that remained in force until it expired in 1946. There must have been compelling reasons for the

The station in Blagoveshchensk manned by predominantly Russian telegraphists in the middle of the 1930s.

"higher powers" in the Soviet Union not to nullify the concession, and the explanation can hardly be assumed to have much to do with anything but money, though the company's persistent efforts to maintain its position and the effect of the purges on the processing of the matter by the people's commissariat no doubt also played a role.

And then Maksim Litvinov may have been the company's guardian angel again. It was certainly on the initiative of the Commissariat of Foreign Affairs that the danger of losing transit revenues was mentioned in the letter to Stalin. The two commissars did not mention the specific transit revenue amounts, but Stalin surely had access to the figures. In 1935, the People's Commissariat for Communications calculated that they amounted to pre-

cisely 2,163,234 so-called currency rubles and, in 1936, that they amounted to 2,134,318 currency rubles. In September 1937, it was already clear that because of the outbreak of war in East Asia, a significant increase in transit revenues was to be expected, and in fact, the income for the whole year ended up amounting to 3,343,876 currency rubles. The Soviet government, therefore, had its own pecuniary interests in refraining from entirely eliminating Great Northern's presence in Russia.[46]

The last two telegraphists in the Soviet Union

The company managed to keep the public from finding out about the removal of the Danish personnel from the Soviet Union, which was an achievement in itself. Indeed, the company succeeded in this in part because it paid a former telegraphist who had gone to *Ekstra Bladet* with the story to remain silent. The newspaper was also provided with what the board of directors' negotiation records called "a contribution to one of its charity funds, one that could be considered neutral, and the origin of this contribution was kept secret from the public."[47]

However, it was not possible to refrain from referring to the new arrangement at all, and reference was in fact made to the matter at Great Northern's general meeting on June 24, 1938: "The automatic relaying of telegraph traffic that until now has taken place in Leningrad has been transferred to Helsinki, which therefore works with Nagasaki via direct lines, and in part because of this change a number of functionaries have been moved out of the USSR in the course of 1937."[48]

At that point, all Danish employees had, in fact, left the Soviet Union, except the representative in Moscow, who had been allowed to remain so that the company and the Soviet government would be able to remain in contact, and two Danish telegraphists who had been imprisoned by the secret police. One had been arrested in Irkutsk in December 1937 and accused of being a German spy; the other had been arrested in the common dining room in Leningrad in March 1938 because of alleged contacts with Russian Trotskyists and Zinovyevists—a designation for enemies of Stalin and the Soviet regime.

The Danish Ministry of Foreign Affairs immediately contacted the Soviet Commissariat of Foreign Affairs and, in cooperation with Great Northern, made energetic efforts to get the two Danes released, including numerous meetings with First Vice Commissar of Foreign Affairs Vladimir Potemkin and several meetings with Commissar of Foreign Affairs Maksim Litvinov. Both men showed great understanding of the Danish wish to see the two arrested men freed, but they had to refer to the fact that the matter was the responsibility of the Soviet Commissariat of the Interior. At a meeting with the new Danish ambassador, Laurits Bolt Bolt-Jørgensen, at the Commissariat of Foreign Affairs on April 9, 1938, Potemkin promised to send a letter to the Commissariat of the Interior in which, speaking for himself, he would "emphasize the Soviet Union's interest in having its cooperation with the Great Northern Telegraph Company proceed without disruptions" and recommend that the two men's cases be terminated with their deportation, an initiative Bolt-Jørgensen welcomed.[49]

Later in April 1938, when Bolt-Jørgensen emphasized that the Danish government found it remarkable that the matter could be dragged out for such a long time, "Mr. Potemkin referred with a sigh to the completely overwhelming amount of work" the Commissariat of the Interior had needed to perform recently.[50]

Bolt-Jørgensen's subsequent reports to the Danish Ministry of Foreign Affairs suggest that Potemkin and the Commissariat of Foreign Affairs made determined efforts to get the two imprisoned telegraphists deported despite the fact that the matter had been dragged out. On December 18, 1938, however, the telegraphist from Irkutsk was finally found guilty of engaging in espionage on behalf of Germany and, after "the reception of a telegraphic message from the Vice Commissar of the Soviet Union's Commissariat of Foreign Affairs, Comrade Frinovskogo," was sentenced to deportation. A similar sentence was doubtless handed down in the other matter.[51]

On January 20, 1939, the Danish legation in Moscow received a message from the Commissariat of Foreign Affairs to the effect that both of the imprisoned telegraphists had been sentenced to deportation. This was confirmed by verbal notification on February 2 when the legation received the additional information that the two telegraphists would be deported via Beloostrov on the Finnish-Russian border near Leningrad, and the deportations were subsequently carried out as planned.[52]

With this, all of Great Northern's Danish telegraphists in the Soviet Union had returned home to Denmark, and just as it is remarkable that Great Northern was not stripped of its concession, it is also remarkable that the two telegraphists were both convicted of serious crimes that normally resulted in execution or at least sentencing to many years in penal colonies but in this case led only to deportation.

World Crisis and World War

CHAPTER 15

Liquidation of Great Northern?

While Great Northern defended its position in Japan, China, and the Soviet Union in the 1930s, its business was gradually undermined by a new threat of a different but no less life-threatening kind. After the negotiations with Colonel Behn in London in October 1929 with regard to ITT's possible purchase of the European companies' shares in Commercial Pacific, the top management team considered whether, "given the financial crisis in the United States at the present time, [the American] would find it opportune or be able to proceed with his plan." The remark in question made reference to a dramatic devaluation of ITT's stock, which had been up to 149 points but had subsequently fallen to a third of that.[1]

What the top management team had observed had been the effect of "Black Thursday," October 24, 1929, when the bottom had dropped out of the American stock market. ITT had actually gotten off lightly as many other American companies had been thrown into bankruptcy, and the crisis had just begun. What no one had been able to foresee

was that the world was on the threshold to a global economic recession that would quickly spread and lead to a significant decline in global trade.

The effects of the American stock market crash soon had consequences for Great Northern as well as for the other telegraph companies. In July 1930, the top management team determined that the telegraph revenues from the first five months of the year had declined from 8.1 million gold francs the previous year to 7.5 million gold francs. Calculated in Danish kroner, the decline in revenues was even greater as a result of a decline in the price of silver, which was a common payment medium in China and Hong Kong.[2]

The crisis also affected the United Kingdom's Cable & Wireless, which had expected normal annual income of 1.9 million pounds sterling but had a total income of only 2 million pounds for the post-merger company's first twenty-one months. Western Union also experienced a significant decline in revenues.[3]

The decline continued, and "the bad times" became a recurring item in the top management team's reports to the board of directors. The situation was not improved by the fact that the expansion of wireless telegraphy across borders, oceans, and continents continued despite the crisis. In addition to taking traffic away from the cable lines in this crisis-impacted market, the increased capacity of the overall global telegraphy network contributed to pushing prices downward.

When the annual accounts for 1930 had been prepared, they showed a decline in telegram revenues from 17.5 million kroner to 15 million kroner. Expenses amounted to 13.5 million kroner, and while interest and other revenues did amount to 2.8 million kroner, it was necessary to supplement the annual result with 3 million kroner from the reserve fund's interest revenues to keep the promise to the French shareholders to the effect that a dividend of 20 percent would be paid out.[4]

Before the general meeting at which the annual accounts were to be presented, the question was raised at a meeting of the board of directors whether "the possibility of liquidation might not tempt the shareholders" if the operating result ended up at zero. Board Chairman Wilhelm Weimann declared that he, like the asker, considered this something that might happen if the company were unable to produce an acceptable operating result "during a period in which economic conditions were normal," and there did not appear to be "any way to bring about a decisive change in this situation."[5]

The problem was that there was no prospect of a return to the normal economic conditions that had

The British prime minister Neville Chamberlain proclaims "peace for our time" after having signed the Munich agreement that gave Nazi Germany the Sudeten region of Czechoslovakia and left the country without defensive lines. Great Northern did not have much faith in the British message, and the company began to prepare for a coming war, in part by transferring considerable sums of money to its offices in London and in other cities outside Denmark.

A crowd of people gathered on the steps of the Sub-Treasury across from the New York Stock Exchange on October 24, 1929, the day known as Black Thursday, when the bottom fell out of the American stock market, plunging the world into the biggest and most long-lasting economic crisis yet experienced. Because of the crisis, world trade was greatly reduced. So was international telegram traffic, and by the late 1930s, Great Northern was no longer able to turn a profit from telegraphy operations.

existed in earlier times. The decline continued in 1931 with the reduction of telegram revenues to 14 million kroner. Therefore, it was necessary to add 3.75 million kroner to the operating result to keep the dividend at 20 percent.[6]

The following year, there was a further decline, but this was more than offset by a Danish devaluation, so telegram revenues calculated in Danish kroner increased to 16 million kroner. As expenses amounted to 14 million kroner, it was, nevertheless, necessary to transfer 4.5 million kroner to the operating result from the interest revenues to pay out the dividend.[7]

When the annual accounts for 1933 were ready, the amount of traffic had declined again, and if Denmark had not devalued its currency the previous year, the accounts would have shown a deficit. As it was, there was a modest surplus of 1.5 million kroner, and to secure the dividend, 5.5 million kroner had to be transferred from the reserve fund's interest revenues, which amounted to 5.7 million kroner. Thus, the company was reaching the limit for this way of securing a 20 percent dividend, assuming the company would not begin to eat away at the reserve fund itself and thus at the company's equity.[8]

With stocks and bonds with a total value of 100 million kroner and cash assets of 12 million kroner in Danish and foreign banks, the company was unusually well cushioned—and then there was the value of cables and other materials. Nevertheless, continuing the company's operations would be unsustainable if the operating result were not improved, and the board of directors discussed a possible liquidation of the company. This topic was not mentioned at the general meeting on May 31, 1934, however.[9]

Preparations for a major European war

During the following years through 1938, revenues stagnated at around 15 million kroner, and every year, all the interest income from the reserve fund was transferred to the operating result to maintain the dividend. At the same time, the situation in both the Soviet Union and Japan became more problematic in the wake of the first deportations of telegraphists from Leningrad in 1935 and the Japanese attack on China in 1937.

Furthermore, the international political situation in Europe became more tense after Adolf Hitler and the Nazis had come to power in Germany in January 1933. In violation of the Versailles Treaty of 1919, Germany began massively rearming, and at the same time, Hitler generated aggressive anti-Semitic and anti-Bolshevik propaganda and demanded *Lebensraum*.

In March 1938, Germany violated a number of international agreements and annexed Austria, after which Hitler turned his gaze toward Czechoslovakia, where, in the Sudety region along the border with Germany, more than three million Germans lived. Hitler claimed that Germany had a right to annex this area, and in a speech, he accused the Czechs of oppressing 3.5 million Germans.

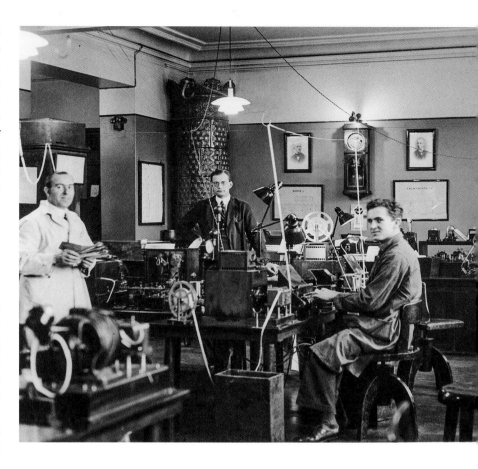

Great Northern's station in Helsinki, which was opened in 1937 to service the whole line through Russia and Siberia to Nagasaki after the Soviet government had deported all Danish employees from Russia. Note the two photographs of C. F. Tietgen and Edouard Suenson, respectively, on either side of the grandfather clock. These two photographs were displayed in the same way in all the company's stations, at least from the beginning of the twentieth century onward. This photograph is from 1939, and the station was evacuated the following year during the Soviet Union's attack on Finland, in the course of which Helsinki was bombed from the air.

A new major European war was on the way, and at Great Northern, the top management team undertook a number of "preparations for war" intended to enable the company to maintain telegraph service and protect the company's personnel. Steps were also taken to secure the foreign stations' and offices' monetary funds "in the event that contact with the company's headquarters should be interrupted," and the cable steamer *Edouard Suenson* was sent to Germany to pick up a supply of reserve cables that had been ordered for use in East Asia but were now stored in the company's cable depot in Copenhagen's free harbor.[10]

The crisis passed when the Western powers gave in to Hitler's demands, and in Munich on September 30, 1938, the leaders of the governments of the United Kingdom, France, Italy, and Germany concluded an agreement according to which Czechoslovakia—which was not represented at the meeting—was to withdraw from the Sudeten region within a day. Therefore, the following day, German troops advanced into the area and annexed it, and when he returned to London, the British prime minister, Neville Chamberlain, proclaimed "peace for our time."

However, there was skepticism about this at Great Northern, where the preparations to confront a coming war continued. On March 15, 1939, Nazi Germany annexed the remainder of Czechoslovakia, and after a nonaggression pact had been concluded between the Soviet Union and Germany in August 1939, German troops crossed the Polish border on September 1. France and the United Kingdom declared war on Germany, and a new major European war was a reality.

Great Northern was well prepared. The cable stocks in Copenhagen and Wusong were expected to last several years "if they were used very efficiently," but for safety's sake, the company had previously ordered two new cables from an English and a German factory, respectively. Both of these cables were almost finished, and the company tried to arrange for one to be shipped to East Asia and the other to Copenhagen. As an extra backup measure, the company concluded an agreement regarding the manufacture of a cable in Singapore to be delivered to Wusong.[11]

The stations' supplies of consumable goods, such as telegraph paper and other necessities, had been bolstered by means of increased deliveries over a lengthy period of time. Liquidity was increased by means of the sale of British war bonds with a nominal value of 75,000 pounds sterling, 50,000 pounds of which was transferred to New York so that it would be possible to supply the stations in East Asia with money from there.[12]

The personnel were also taken care of. Most of the employees at the station in Calais, which was in an exposed position on the French Channel coast, were evacuated. The wives and children of Danish employees at the stations in Finland and Latvia were evacuated to Denmark after the Red Army had advanced into Poland from the east on September 16, thus dividing Poland between Stalin's Soviet Union and Hitler's Germany.

Severed cables and Japanese termination

Immediate effects of the outbreak of war felt by Great Northern were an increase in correspondence as well as the prohibition of the sending of encoded telegrams and the introduction of censorship, which caused delays in transmission. On September 19, 1939, however, all telegram traffic connections between Latvia and Poland were discontinued, which led to a decline in traffic sent via the company's station in Liepaja. There were more serious consequences when Germany began the evacuation of Latvian citizens of German Baltic extraction, which affected eight of the company's employees, and in general, the situation constantly became more uncertain.[13]

For the time being, the company was able to maintain its traffic to and from Russia and East Asia at a relatively normal level as none of the cables in the North Sea had been cut—yet—and the cables in the Baltic Sea were protected against German or Soviet attacks by the German-Soviet nonaggression pact.

During the night of November 29/30, 1939, however, the situation was radically changed when the Red Army crossed the Finnish border, while Helsinki and other Finnish cities were bombed by the Soviet air force. The outbreak of war between the Soviet Union and Finland led to an immediate cessation of all traffic to and from the Soviet Union and therefore to a cessation of all traffic to and from East Asia as all telegrams had been sent via Helsinki after the landing of the cable in Finland in 1938. While the company's station was not damaged in the bombings, twenty-two of the forty Danish employees were evacuated to the little town of Grankulla (today Kauniainen) sixteen kilometers west of the Finnish capital.[14]

The interruption lasted a month until it became possible for the company to get the use of a landline between Riga and Moscow, and as direct service between Riga and Nagasaki was established at the same time, traffic once again "was fully satisfactory" until the line between Helsinki and Nagasaki could be reopened in May 1940 as the result of a Finno-Russian peace agreement.[15]

On the other hand, four of the company's seven North Sea cables were cut in December 1939. As Germany refused to allow the cables to be repaired and it was to be expected that the remaining cables would be cut sooner or later, Great Northern established a wireless connection between Denmark and the United Kingdom in the spring of 1940, having reached an agreement regarding this connection

with the British and Danish telegraph authorities. Between London and Stockholm too, the company established a wireless connection so the traffic to and from East Asia could continue normally in all important ways.[16]

However, there was alarming news from East Asia in March 1940 when Great Northern's director H. S. Poulsen, who had come to Tokyo to discuss the company's tax situation, was called to a meeting at the Japanese department of telegraphy. According to the general director, the Japanese government had decided to nullify the company's concession as

In connection with the Soviet Union's military attack on Finland in late November 1939, the Russians bombed Helsinki and other cities from the air, causing great destruction. While Great Northern's station and the residences of the company's employees were not damaged, an evacuation of most of the Danish employees was begun immediately after the bombing started. The picture shows Helsinki, where rescue and cleanup operations are in progress following a Russian bombing mission.

a result of direct contacts between Great Northern and Japanese customers over a period of years. Such contacts, according to the general director, had violated paragraph 1 of the concession agreement.[17]

The Japanese decision was "final and offered no possibility of compromise," and the company was warned that there could be "serious consequences" for both individuals and the company if the Japanese telegraph authority were asked to provide documentation to support the accusation of direct contact with the customers. Between the lines, it was implied that some of the company's employees had been involved in espionage.

The general director emphasized that Japan had a right to nullify the concession with immediate effect but said that as a result of the "many years of friendly relations," the Japanese would grant the company a three-year landing permit, though the cable in Nagasaki would have to be operated by Japanese personnel. The general director wanted to have a response to this offer within four weeks, and after he had informed the Danish ambassador in Tokyo of the situation, H. S. Poulsen hurried back to Shanghai to confer with Kongens Nytorv.

After consultations with the Danish Ministry of Foreign Affairs and the company's British attorney, the conclusion was that the situation was "very difficult," regardless of whether the accusations of contact with the customers were groundless. The concession was considered to be basically "very weak" because it did not have a specifically identified period of validity, something that had previously been regarded as a strength. According to the Ministry of Foreign Affairs and the attorney, the concession had been formulated in such a way that Japan could terminate it at any time if a reasonable justification were provided.

The battle was lost, and H. S. Poulsen was telegraphically instructed to accept the offer of a three-year landing permit under the conditions that had been specified. Therefore, on April 9, 1940, H. S. Poulsen was back in Japan, where the Japanese director of telegraphy was able to inform him that Denmark had been occupied by German troops during the morning of that same day.[18]

More than twenty additional meetings for negotiations were required before an agreement could finally be signed. The Japanese telegraphy administration would take over the operation of the company's cables at Great Northern's station in Nagasaki on June 1, 1940, and Great Northern's landing permit would expire on April 30, 1943.

On April 30, 1940, the Japanese director of telegraphy wrote to H. S. Poulsen to notify him officially of the consequences of the agreement that had just been concluded and took the opportunity to "thank [Poulsen] on his own behalf for [Poulsen's] friendly cooperation over so many years." On his own behalf and on behalf of Great Northern, H. S. Poulsen thanked the director "for the never-lacking friendship that has been offered to us and for the warm and harmonious atmosphere that has characterized all of our negotiations."[19]

Allied with the United Kingdom

In Denmark, Great Northern's top management team and board of directors were unaware of what was going on in Tokyo. As a result of the German occupation of Denmark on April 9, all of Denmark's international telegraph connections other than the connection with Germany were severed, and the company's cables connecting Sweden and Britain had also soon been severed. It was not until after a brief Japanese press release had been sent out on May 7, 1940, that Great Northern's headquarters at Kongens Nytorv learned—via a German wireless connection—of the agreement H. S. Poulsen had concluded. There was no news of the Danes in Nagasaki, and it was not until a few months later that Kongens Nytorv received word that all of them were well and some had been employed by the Japanese as consultants at the station.[20]

In general, Great Northern in Copenhagen lacked a connection with its stations and representatives abroad, and this situation had been foreseen by the company's leaders. In late August 1939, the company's director in London, O. E. Nielsen, had received a power of attorney that authorized him to act and make decisions with regard to any pressing matters

In February 1940, Great Northern purchased the steam-ship *Kabel* and had the ship refitted for cable work. It had time to carry out a number of minor cable repairs before it was sold to the Soviet Union in October of the same year after pressure had been put on Great Northern by the Danish Ministry of Foreign Affairs, which was strongly interested in encouraging the conclusion of a Dano-Russian trade agreement. The picture shows the ship in the winter of 1940 with a Dannebrog burgee and painted Dannebrog on the hull for protection.

if contact between Kongens Nytorv and the company's business representatives abroad were to be interrupted. He was also authorized to instruct the company's offices in Shanghai, Paris, and Calais that if they were unable to communicate with Copenhagen, they should contact him for guidance regarding any matters they were unable to resolve on their own.[21]

Therefore, on April 9, 1940, O. E. Nielsen was the de facto leader of Great Northern's entire telegraph system to the extent that he was able to get in contact with the stations. With the help of the Foreign Office and the General Post Office, he was able to present his authorization to the British Trading with the Enemy Branch, whose task it was to pre-vent companies from engaging in economic deal-ings with Germany or its allies. This step was nec-essary because the company's headquarters were located in a country that had been occupied by Ger-many. The authorization was recognized, and O. E. Nielsen received official permission to lead the company's overall activities on condition that no money would be transferred to Denmark.[22]

In accordance with an agreement with Cable & Wireless, O. E. Nielsen telegraphed to Shanghai on April 11 and ordered the company's two cable ships to steam to Hong Kong to avoid complying with a German demand that the ships be dry-docked. On arrival in Hong Kong, the ships' status was changed so that they would sail under the Union Jack, and O. E. Nielsen also considered transferring the com-pany's building and materials in Shanghai and the cable reserves in Wusong to Cable & Wireless. He abandoned this project after consultations with the British Foreign Office as it could have compromised both the company and the United Kingdom.[23]

The United Kingdom was displeased with the Danish government's cooperation with Denmark's German occupiers, but this did not have a negative

The United Kingdom's prime minister during the Second World War, Winston Churchill, in an iconic pose with a cigar and the index and middle finger of his right hand forming a *V* for "Victory." During the time of the Blitz, when nocturnal German bombing attacks on London and other English cities occurred frequently, he found time to become involved in Great Northern's affairs by approving the company's transfer of money to Denmark's ambassador in Japan. In general—as during the First World War—the company enjoyed the support of the British government, and Great Northern's two cable ships fought on the side of the Allies against Japan and Germany in the Indian Ocean and the Mediterranean Sea, respectively.

effect on the British government's view of Great Northern, which, under O. E. Nielsen's leadership, acted as a British ally. Because of this, Nielsen had no problem getting permission to rent a wireless station in London despite the fact that doing so conflicted with the terms of the company's landing permit and agreements with Cable & Wireless, which owned the station. Thus, O. E. Nielsen suc-

ceeded in establishing a wireless connection with Sweden, Finland, and Latvia, from where it was possible to reestablish the connection with East Asia, which the British government viewed as an achievement "of national importance."[24]

It became clear that the British had not expressed themselves merely for the sake of politeness after both Cable & Wireless and O. E. Nielsen, in the middle of May 1940, had received confirmation of the accuracy of the press release regarding the Japanese government's action against Great Northern. Cable & Wireless expressed the view that the foundation for the two companies' agreements, which had been collected in a so-called consolidation agreement in 1938, no longer existed, and Cable & Wireless informed O. E. Nielsen of this in a letter of August 30. The letter indicated that "since the German occupation of Denmark, your company has been considered an enemy," and in addition, there had been a decline in the traffic with East Asia and now the taking over of the station in Nagasaki by the Japanese. Cable & Wireless, therefore, indicated that the consolidation agreement had to be regarded as no longer in effect as of April 9, 1940, and that the company was not willing to continue loaning its radio station to Great Northern.[25]

The main reason for Cable & Wireless's action was of a financial nature as the agreements between the two companies that had been in effect during the Russian revolution and civil war had predominantly benefited the Danes. Given Japan's planned termination of Great Northern's concession in 1943, there was now no prospect of a resumption of the company's connection with East Asia, so the consolidation agreement could be terminated in Cable & Wireless's view.

The consequence for Great Northern would be a significant loss of revenues, and with the loss of the radio station, the company would lose its connections with neutral countries such as Sweden, Finland, Latvia, and the Soviet Union. This would mean that the company would be unlikely to survive the war regardless of who won it. Cable & Wireless probably did not care about that, but the British government did.

O. E. Nielsen countered Cable & Wireless's arguments and got the British government to consider the matter, after which the Foreign Office got the government to establish that a resolution of the matter and its economic consequences would have to wait until the war was over. This did not prevent Cable & Wireless from withdrawing the loan of its radio station, though. The postal and telegraphy directorate, therefore, made available facilities that enabled Great Northern to maintain its connection with Stockholm.[26]

The British government's position was based not on law but on politics and consideration for the postwar period that would come. Great Northern was, in fact, seen not as an enemy but as an ally whose activity could benefit the United Kingdom after the war. In March 1941, when the Danish ambassador in Tokyo, Lars Tillitse, ran out of money, there was further evidence that people in the highest circles in London were sensitive not only to Great Northern's but also to other Danish companies' and Danish individuals' perceptions of the United Kingdom. The Danish government was unable to supply him with currency, and he, therefore, wished to borrow 4,000 dollars from Great Northern's Shanghai office, which the Treasury—the British Ministry of Finance—was not immediately willing to allow. However, the matter ended with Winston Churchill personally instructing the Foreign Office to inform the Treasury that the loan should be allowed as both the company and Ambassador Tillitse were pro-Allies and "any assistance rendered to him [Tillitse] would be in the interests of His Majesty's Government."[27]

The British government provided further assistance to Great Northern in July 1943 when Cable & Wireless applied to open a wireless connection with Stockholm and compete with Great Northern's connection. The government said no, however, as the British Foreign Office was protecting the Danish company:

"Before the war Great Northern always maintained good relations with the countries in which they operated their connections as well as with the Post Office. It therefore appears to be in our interests to support Great Northern with a view to their reestablishment of the same effective services they were offering before the war."[28]

Orderly relations in "the home country"

In Denmark, Great Northern's top management team and board of directors were unaware of what O. E. Nielsen was doing in London—and vice versa. However, Great Northern's headquarters were able to establish sporadic communications with H. S. Poulsen in Shanghai via German wireless stations that could be used until the company's own connection with East Asia could be reopened. This occurred some time after a German officer had appeared at Kongens Nytorv to obtain information that would confirm the Danish nationality of the company and its leadership and provide insight into the ability of foreign shareholders to receive dividend payments.

He received the desired documentation, which showed that any dividend for foreign shareholders would be paid into an inaccessible Danish bank account but also that the board of directors would propose at the next general meeting that no dividend beyond the already-paid 5 percent be paid out. The German occupation authorities appeared to have been satisfied by this—in any event, the company was permitted to reopen its cables to Liepaja on May 10, though to begin with not for traffic with East Asia.[29]

German troops crossed the border into the Netherlands, Belgium, and Luxemburg the same day and subsequently advanced into France. On May 26, 1940, the Germans captured Calais after air bombardments and hard fighting that left much of the city, including the company's station and all its equipment, in ruins. The four Danes who had remained in Calais all survived and returned to Denmark, but without their possessions, which had been lost.[30]

After France surrendered in late June, the Germans allowed Great Northern to reopen traffic to and from East Asia. There was only limited rejoicing over this, however, as the company had learned via German radio of the Japanese takeover of the station in Nagasaki and the nullification of the company's concession. Also, the Baltic countries had been annexed by the Soviet Union, though this did not immediately affect the company as the Danish employees in Latvia were allowed to remain at their posts, in contrast to all other Danes who were expelled.

The Soviet Union's annexation of Latvia did create some uncertainty at Kongens Nytorv. There were calming words coming from Moscow, however, and the good relationship between the company and the Soviet Union was strengthened in the fall of 1940 when Great Northern sold the cable steamer *Kabel* to the Soviet government. The company had purchased this cable steamer the previous year so it would be able to assist the *Edouard Suenson* with repairing the many cable breaks it could be assumed the war would bring. Great Northern then had a great need for this cable steamer itself, but the Russians were quite insistent, and in accordance with a recommendation of the sale by the Danish Ministry of Foreign Affairs—partly because it could render the conclusion of a Dano-Russian trade agreement more likely—the company accommodated the wish of the Soviet government, which thus acquired its first cable ship.[31]

In the midst of the turbulent international conditions, Great Northern managed to secure its position in Denmark relatively painlessly when, shortly before Christmas 1940, the company reached agreement with the General Directorate and the Ministry of Public Works regarding a new concession under conditions that would be identical in all important ways to the conditions that had been applicable to the existing concessions. The company had argued that it would be important to have "[the company's] circumstances in the home country in order" in a few years when the agreements with Sweden, Finland, and the United Kingdom were to be renewed.[32]

The new concession would be valid through the end of 1950, and with it in his briefcase, Bent Suenson traveled to Stockholm to negotiate with the telegraphy directorate. In April 1941, it already proved possible to reach an agreement regarding a new Swedish contract that, like the new Danish concession, would remain valid through the end of 1950. Negotiations with the United Kingdom remained, and for the time being, engaging in such negotiations was impossible because of the war, and before Great Northern contacted the Finns, the war took a new and dramatic turn.[33]

Distance from the occupying power

Early on the morning of June 22, 1941, 4.5 million German and German-allied troops invaded the Soviet Union via a front almost three thousand kilometers in length, and three days later, Finland declared war on the Soviet Union, and the telegraph connections between the two countries were interrupted. The Danish government summoned its ambassador in Moscow, Laurits Bolt Bolt-Jørgensen, home, but on June 26, he informed the Danish government by telegram that after careful consideration, he felt that he "could best protect the interests of the [Danish] government and those of the Great Northern Telegraph Company by remaining at [his] post." Only a few days later, however, both the ambassador and Great Northern's representative, Henrik Christiansen, were evacuated by the Soviet authorities and helped to return to Denmark via Istanbul.[34]

The invading German army advanced quickly, partly through the Baltic countries, on its way toward Leningrad. On July 5, Great Northern already received a German message to the effect that the company's station and cable house in Liepaja were intact and that the Danish personnel, of whom there were only a few, had not been harmed.[35]

On the other hand, there was a cable break near Liepaja, and the Germans asked Great Northern to repair the cable so contact with Germany's ally Finland could be reestablished. After having conferred with the Danish Ministry of Foreign Affairs, the company informed the Germans that the company would not be able to carry out the repair because the break was located in an area that had been "closed to sailing," presumably because of mines. The Germans decided to repair the cable themselves and requested precise information about its location, which the company—after a new consultation with the Danish Ministry of Foreign Affairs—provided.[36]

In the fall of 1941, Great Northern received another German request, this time a request that the company provide a cable ship to be used to repair a cable near Norway. After having reached agreement with the Danish Ministry of Foreign Affairs regarding the response to this request, Great Northern responded by stating that because of the great risk and the great importance of such ships to the company and the countries whose cable connections the company maintained, the company "felt great reservations about providing ships" and risking their loss.

Given that the *Edouard Suenson* was at the quay in Copenhagen and that the company used smaller chartered ships to carry out repairs of the Danish cables in the Baltic Sea and other repairs, this was a daring response. Nevertheless, the Germans displayed an understanding attitude, and the *Edouard Suenson* remained at the quay until it was towed to Køge and dry-docked late in 1942. [37]

In contrast, Great Northern was unable to prevent the Germans from renting the company's cables between Møn and Bornholm and between Liepaja and Helsinki starting in the summer of 1942. This rental was arranged with the Danish General Directorate of Postal and Telegraph Systems as a middleman, so the company avoided direct contact with the occupying power.[38]

Great Northern wished to avoid assisting the Germans to the greatest extent possible, and to avoid having them take matters in their own hands, the company moved the *Edouard Suenson* to Kalmar, Sweden, in August 1944, officially in response to a Swedish request that the company repair cables but, in reality, to prevent the confiscation of the ship by the Germans. At the same time, some of the company's reserve cables were moved to Sweden and the rest laid between Anholt and Zealand, officially as a temporary replacement for a worn-out cable but, in reality, to prevent the confiscation of the cables by the Germans.[39]

A freight steamer the company had bought after selling the *Kabel* to the Russians, the *Karla*, was

After its military attack on China in 1937, Japan expanded its military operations to the Pacific region with the attack on the American naval base at Pearl Harbor, Hawaii, on December 7, 1941. The picture shows the damaged American battleship *USS Pennsylvania* behind the wrecks of the two destroyers *USS Cassin* and *USS Downes* after the attack, which destroyed large parts of the United States Pacific Fleet.

also secured against German confiscation. The company had abandoned the notion of refitting the *Karla* for cable work, and the steamer had instead brought supplies such as coal from Germany to Denmark. In January 1945, the steamer was dry-docked in Copenhagen's South Harbor, and after the company had received a tip from the Danish Steamship Owners' Association regarding the risk of confiscation by the Germans, vital parts were removed from the engine room. When German officers boarded the ship and saw the condition of the engine, "they shook their heads and left the ship."[40]

Japanese takeover of the East Asian cable system

In East Asia and on the Pacific, the war was also escalating. On the morning of December 7, 1941, Japanese airplanes had attacked the naval base at Pearl Harbor, Hawaii, and sunk the American Pacific Fleet. The next day, the United States and the United Kingdom had declared war on Japan, and two days later, Germany and Italy had declared war on the United States. The European war and the Sino-Japanese war had been merged into a coherent world war.

The attack on Pearl Harbor had been the beginning of a major Japanese offensive. The Japanese took Guam three days later, while Hong Kong fell on December 25. On February 15, Singapore was conquered. On March 2, Jakarta fell, and Burma's (Myanmar's) capital, Rangoon (Yangon), fell five days later. On May 6, 1942, the Philippines was under Japanese control.

Because of the general war, the Japanese did not leave the international settlement in Shanghai in peace as they had during the Japanese attack on Shanghai in 1932; rather, they sent troops in "to suppress enemy activity and maintain law and order," as an official proclamation put it. The company's East Asian cable system was still operating, but in the middle of January 1942, Great Northern's East Asian director, H. S. Poulsen, and the Danish general consul were called to a meeting with the Japanese general consul in Shanghai. Here they were told that because of "military necessity," the Japanese military authorities had decided to take over the company's building, station, and structures and replace all Danes with Japanese personnel.[41]

H. S. Poulsen and the general consul had difficulty seeing any military necessity, and they informed Great Northern's top management team and the Danish Ministry of Foreign Affairs of the situation via German wireless connections. As a result, the Danish ambassador in Tokyo, Lars Tillitse, was instructed to raise the matter with the Japanese Ministry of Foreign Affairs and argue that "appropriate supervision" should be sufficient.

At the Japanese Ministry of Foreign Affairs, the ambassador was received by the vice minister of foreign affairs, who asked about Great Northern's ownership structure and particularly about the extent to which Britons owned a share of the company. The ambassador responded by saying that "only a small part" of the shares in the company were in British hands and that the company's management was "completely Danish." The Japanese interest in the company's ownership structure had arisen because the Japanese intended to confiscate all American and British property in Shanghai, and the vice minister of foreign affairs implied that neutral property could also be confiscated in accordance with international law if there was a "military necessity."

That was, in fact, how things went. On February 25, 1942, H. S. Poulsen and the representatives of the other telegraph companies and a number of British and American businesses in Shanghai were summoned to a meeting with the Japanese military authorities, who informed them that from now on, they would be working under a Japanese "supervisor" and no longer be able to dispose of their property and revenues as they saw fit. A few days later, the Japanese decided to take over Great Northern's building and station in Shanghai and the operation of the cables, and H. S. Poulsen was informed of this in writing on March 19. In accordance with instructions from Copenhagen, the general consul in Shanghai and the ambassador in Tokyo both protested, but they achieved nothing by doing so, and the Japanese de facto takeover of the company's East Asian cables system was a reality.[42]

When Great Northern's Japanese concession expired on April 30, 1943, the top management team noted laconically in their report to the board of directors that "sixty-three years of business activity in Japan were over."[43]

Purchasing of properties and stocks

The only connections Great Northern had in operation after the Japanese takeover of the building in

Shanghai were the cable from the Shetland islands to Iceland and the wireless connection between London and Stockholm that O. E. Nielsen had succeeded in establishing, and that was protected by the British Foreign Office.

The future was more than uncertain, regardless of who won or lost the war, as the expiration of the Japanese concession deprived Great Northern of the possibility of resuming the company's activities in East Asia. Furthermore, the Chinese concession would expire at the end of 1944 and the Soviet and Finnish concessions two years later. Even if Great Northern managed to reestablish its operations in Sweden, Denmark, and the United Kingdom, the company would be reduced to a Northern European telegraph company in a region in which the government telegraphy authorities had previously shown an appetite for taking over the company's cables.

The question was what should happen. This was a question Great Northern's management had discussed already before the war had broken out as the crumbling profitability of telegraph operations had provoked consideration of a possible future without telegraphy or in any event with new business areas as supplements to telegraphy. Probably for this reason, the vice chairman of the board of directors of Den Danske Landmandsbank ("the Danish Agricultural Bank") and the business attorney and member of the boards of directors of many Danish companies, Kristian Steglich-Petersen, had been elected to the board of directors of Great Northern in December 1938 to open doors to investments in Danish businesses.

In July 1939, Kristian Steglich-Petersen had already been able to present Great Northern's board of directors with an opportunity to acquire a large number of shares in the Danish manufacturer of dry batteries A/S Hellesens Enke & Ludvigsen. The

Supreme Court attorney Kristian Steglich-Petersen became a member of Great Northern's board of directors in 1939 and was its chairman from 1945 to 1958. He supported the efforts of Chief Executive Officer Bent Suenson to transform Great Northern from a classic telegraph company into a modern industrial group.

company's share capital amounted to 3 million kroner fully owned by Landmandsbanken, which would sell 40 percent to Great Northern, while 20 percent would be divided between a family foundation and the board of directors of the company.[44]

Alf Ussing held a cand.polit. degree and worked at the Danish Ministry of Foreign Affairs for three years as a volunteer and secretary before he was hired by Great Northern in 1917. He became a vice president in 1924 and a director in 1932. After the Second World War, he lost influence at the company, and in 1950 he was pressured into resigning so his fellow director since 1932, Bent Suenson, could become sole director—chief executive officer.

Great Northern had originally intended to take over all of the share capital or at least a dominating majority and take over the leadership of the company to enter a new business area. However, a prior question put to the Limited Company Registry (today the Danish Business Authority) regarding the practicability of this had gotten the reply that dry battery production was not covered by the company's mission statement and that a takeover would violate the limited company law.

Great Northern, therefore, had to be satisfied with acquiring 40 percent of the share capital at 150 points as "a component of the company's efforts to achieve a somewhat broader spreading of the risk that is associated with the company's capital investments." Thanks to this investment, Great Northern acquired a seat on the board of directors that was occupied by Director Bent Suenson, while Kristian Steglich-Petersen acquired a seat as the representative of Landmandsbanken.

A subsequent discussion of Great Northern's investments generally and in particular "the possibility of participating in or controlling other business activity than what is covered by the mission statement" made it clear that the company's leaders were not thinking solely in terms of spreading risk. Among the possibilities discussed was investment in aviation connections—a topic that was probably introduced by the engineer Per Kampmann, who was the chairman of the board of directors of Det Danske Luftfartsselskab A/S (Danish Air Lines).[45]

Around the time of Great Northern's acquisition of the shares in Hellesens, Great Northern began spreading the company's capital investments, which had very predominantly been placed in bonds. In early September 1939, just after the beginning of the war, Great Northern converted 300,000 pounds sterling in British government bonds into telegraph stocks. The following month, the board of directors voted to invest a large part of the reserve fund's Danish cash in stocks and residential properties.[46]

In early February 1941, the board of directors approved the purchase of three large residential complexes in Copenhagen, and during the following two years, a number of further residential properties were purchased so that by the end of the year, the company had invested over 15 million kroner in Copenhagen, Aarhus, and Odense. The purchases continued, and in September 1943, the company established the new company Dansk Ejendomsadministration (Danish Property Administration) A/S with share capital of 10,000 kroner to take responsibility for the operation and renting out of the properties.[47]

Parallel to these purchases, Great Northern invested in shares and mostly relatively small blocs of shares in a broad spectrum of Danish companies such as Kjøbenhavns Telefon Aktieselskab (Copenhagen's Telephone Limited Company), De Forenede Papirfabrikker (the United Paper Factories), the East Asiatic Company, De Forenede Teglværker (the United Brick Factories), the steam shipping companies Orient and Norden, Glud & Marstrand, and Det Danske Petroleumsselskab (the Danish Petroleum Company). Great Northern also bought blocs of shares in banks and other financial institutions and, to an increasing extent, in insurance companies.[48]

Three investments stood out from the rest. One of these was Great Northern's participation in the initial public offering for the establishment of a Danish steel rolling plant in Frederiksværk following the receipt of a message regarding the possibility of such participation from the shipowner Arnold P. Møller. The purpose of the establishment of this plant was to secure deliveries of steel to Danish industry and shipyards, and "because this was seen as being in the interests of the Danish society," Great Northern's board of directors voted to buy shares with a value of 300,000 kroner, to which shares with a value of 50,000 kroner were added later that year.[49]

The second remarkable investment was the acquisition at 140 points in the fall of 1942 of a bloc of shares valued at 450,000 kroner in Ole Sørensen & Co. A/S in Kolding. That company, which sold agricultural machinery, had share capital of 1.2 million kroner, all of which had until recently been owned by Landmandsbanken. The bank wished to reduce its engagement, however, and after Hellesens and its board chairman had each acquired shares in the amount of 100,000 kroner and the Wessel Foundation had also acquired shares amounting to 100,000 kroner, Landmandsbanken presented an offer through Kristian Steglich-Petersen that Great Northern would purchase shares amounting to 450,000 kroner, while the remaining 450,000 kroner would remain in the bank's hands. Ole Sørensen & Co. A/S accepted the offer, and Director Alf Ussing received a seat on the board of directors.[50]

Finally, Great Northern received an invitation to participate in an expansion of the share capital in Det Danske Luftfartsselskab A/S (Danish Air Lines) by 7 million to 12 million kroner, which would bring the share capital up to between 10 and 15 million kroner—a significant increase then, one that was justified with the argument that international air traffic would doubtless experience a mighty surge when the war was over.[51]

When the board of directors was to discuss and vote on the matter on June 25, 1943, Director Alf Ussing had sent out a note in which he strongly recommended that the company purchase shares amounting to 3 million kroner. Not only was air traffic looking forward to rapid development, but Kastrup Airport was also well positioned, and cooperation with the Swedes after the war was assured. Economically, this would "currently [be] a wise disposition with fair prospects of success," and there was also a "special Great Northern aspect" that he conjured up in almost euphoric phrases.

"When Tietgen's magnificent work, bulging with money, must await its dissolution as a result of the unfavorable times and because of the course of developments, something no one could be too blind to see that it is in fact doing ... what would now be a more obvious thing to do or more in accordance with our duty than that we make a sensitive contribution to helping the new phoenix in the area of communications—aviation, which is partly walking in our footsteps—to develop under good conditions in Denmark and show Denmark's colors out in the great world."

There are no records of the actual statements made and questions asked during the discussions of the board of directors, but the minutes do show that there were "very detailed discussions of the matter, in particular of the size of the amount for which Great Northern should purchase shares." The discussions ended with a unanimous vote to purchase shares for 500,000 kroner, though Per Kampmann did not participate in the voting.[52]

This was not what Alf Ussing had wanted, and the modest scale of the purchase of shares apparently indicated that Great Northern's search for new business areas did not include aviation.

A mission statement that is in the way

Parallel to the purchases of property and the investments in the stock market, the top management team had begun to probe the possibilities with regard to circumventing or changing Great Northern's mission statement, which was preventing the company from playing an active role in or completely taking over companies with operations in business areas other than telegraphy. In March 1942, Bent Suenson prepared an internal memorandum in which he predicted that the company's shareholders, who up to this point had accepted the considerable size of the reserve fund as the basis of Great Northern's international and political strength, would hardly maintain this attitude in the event that activity in the area of telegraphy ceased—rather, the shareholders would likely demand that a part of the company's wealth be paid out and thus drain Great Northern of money that could otherwise be used for investments.

Therefore, it would be necessary to find ways in which the company could invest in industrial businesses, and in August of the same year, Bent Suenson discussed the possibilities with a head registrar in the Limited Company Registry, who believed it could be done. He referred to the possibility of acquiring an exemption from the requirements of the mission statement or making small changes in it and including industrial activity without coming into conflict with the law.

The question was subsequently discussed by the board of directors on August 28, 1942, without a detailed record of the discussion being entered into the minutes of the meeting, but in March 1943, Bent Suenson took the initiative to arrange a meeting with an office head at the Ministry of Trade to discuss the possibility of making "such a change in the company's business purposes paragraph that the company's investment activity could continue even if the company's telegraphy activity ceased."[53]

In a memorandum that had been sent to the section head before the meeting, Bent Suenson had described the company's situation, which "had looked bleak" already before the outbreak of the Second World War. Since then, the company's business activity had ceased entirely, and there was a risk that national governments would take responsibility for their own international telegraph connections in connection with the imminent expiration of Great Northern's concessions. In contrast, Great Northern's investment activity had increased, and in Denmark alone, the company and its retirement fund had invested 117 million kroner, not including salaries and taxes paid.[54]

In general, Bent Suenson put things in nationalistic terms, emphasizing how the company's leaders "both from a narrow company point of view and with a view to serving the interests of the Danish society" had considered how they might maintain the company's investment activity if the company's activities in telegraphy ceased entirely.

The problem was § 57 of the Limited Company Law, according to which substantial changes in the company's purposes required that shareholders representing nine tenths of the share capital vote in favor. Given the extent to which Great Northern's shares were distributed among many different owners in various countries, it would be impossible to accumulate such a majority. Bent Suenson, therefore, appealed to the section head to seek to bring about the passing of legislation that either modified § 57 or gave the minister the option of granting an exception from the requirements of the law.[55]

According to Director Bent Suenson, the office head was "very understanding," and he promised to report back on the matter when he had discussed it with others in the ministry. He did so in the middle of July 1943 when he reported in a letter that he had discussed the matter not only with the department head but also with the Conservative Minister of Trade Halfdan Hendriksen.

The minister had not believed that under existing law, it would be possible to grant a dispensation from § 57, which was "one of the very most important conditions" for the protection of shareholders in the Limited Company Law. As far as a possible change in the law was concerned, the minister did not believe there was a sufficiently strong argument as "it could hardly be said [...] that it was a precondition for the company's survival that its mission be altered." The ministry, therefore, took the view that the matter would have to rest until after the war when "after all, it would be a little easier to see 'where the company was.'"[56]

As a consequence of the general situation during the German occupation, Great Northern's seventy-fifth anniversary on June 1, 1944, was not publicly celebrated. A staff party was held, however.

This message was briefly summarized at the meeting of the board of directors, apparently without any detailed commentary—no such commentary is reflected in the minutes, in any event. There was nothing to be done but to await the end of the war. This was particularly clear after the revolt of August 1943 when extensive unrest in the populace as well as the government's refusal to pass legislation mandating the death penalty for sabotage caused the occupying power to declare a state of emergency. As a consequence, the Danish government resigned on August 29, 1943, eliminating any chance of the passage of new legislation.

With the current state of affairs in mind, the top management team had the most important components of the company's accounting documentation reproduced on microfilm that was deposited in one of Privatbanken's branches in the Greater Copenhagen area. All Danish bonds held by Great Northern were, to the extent this was possible, deposited with the issuers—the Ministry of Finance, the credit associations, and the municipalities respectively—while the company retained the proofs of registration, which, as a form of extra security, were photographed and deposited at a bank branch. All of the company's stock certificates were also deposited in a bank, and a receipt for this deposit was obtained and photographed so a copy could be stored in the company's box in Privatbanken's Eastern Branch. A deposit book detailing all the papers in the box was drawn up in two copies, one of which was kept outside the company's building.[57]

Copies and documents providing an overview were subsequently updated and the copies secured by means of photography, in connection with the company's ongoing investments in property and stocks, while the top management team, the board of directors, and the employees awaited the end of the war.

"The Darkest Time"

CHAPTER 16

Liberation and the beginnings of normalization

On Tuesday, April 17, 1945, Great Northern's board of directors met to prepare for the upcoming general meeting. The written report was approved, as was the annual account, the account of the company's status, and the agenda for the general meeting, which had been scheduled for May 31. Immediately after the meeting of the board of directors, the accounts statement was sent out to the public with a remark to the effect that an inability to acquire relevant information from abroad meant the account was incomplete.1

The year's gross revenues amounted to 4,272,571.13 kroner, which had been exclusively generated by capital investments, as all telegraphy activity had been suspended, while there were operating expenses in the amount of 4,245,444.59 kroner. As during the past five years, it was proposed that the modest surplus be transferred to the "account for later disposition."[2]

A little less than three weeks later, on the evening of May 4, it was announced from London that the German forces in the Netherlands, northwest Ger-

many, and Denmark had surrendered. The next morning, Denmark was once again a free country, and after Germany's complete and unconditional surrender on May 9, the war in Europe ended.

To carry out a normalization of the situation, a temporary government was formed including representatives of the political parties and the resistance movement; this government was to resign when the time was ripe for holding ordinary elections to the Danish Rigsdag. An election to the Folketing was scheduled for October 30, 1945, and government by the people was reestablished with the creation of a new government a week later. However, the years of the occupation had a significant effect on the years that followed because of the worn-out production apparatus and shortages of goods and currency, and there was no immediate return to the situation before the Second World War and the German occupation.

For Great Northern, too, a transition to normalized conditions began. On May 10, 1945, after a five-year interruption, the company could reopen Den-

The day of Denmark's liberation, May 5, 1945. Flags are flown in Bredgade in Copenhagen.

mark's telegraph connection with England via a rented radio station in London and a radio station in Denmark. On Great Northern's initiative, the first telegram was sent to the Post Office from the Danish General Directorate and had the purpose of ensuring that it would be Great Northern and not Cable & Wireless that would be responsible for the radio connection until Great Northern's cables could be reopened.[3]

The preparations for the many coming cable repairs were immediately begun, partly in Kalmar, where Great Northern began to get the *Edouard Suenson* ready, and partly in Copenhagen's South Harbor, where the machine parts that had been removed from the *Karla* were reinstalled. Great Northern received a message from London to the effect that the Post Office had reserved fifty nautical miles of cable for the company's repairs and that there would be no shortage of fuel oil for the *Edouard Suenson*. In cooperation with the Danish and British marine authorities, preparations were made for clearing mines and carrying out the cable repairs.[4]

In contrast, efforts to contact the Soviet authorities via the Danish Ministry of Foreign Affairs were to no avail. There was no getting an overview of the situation in East Asia, partly because the war against Japan was continuing with no reduction in ferocity and partly because the company had no information about the condition of the cables and the concessions for both China and Japan had expired.

Because of the conclusion of the peace agreement for Europe, the conditions under which the upcoming general meeting would take place were very different from the conditions that had applied when the general meeting had been scheduled. The board of directors therefore met again on May 29, 1945 to discuss the running of the general meeting that would take place two days later. A new oral report was prepared and subsequently presented at the general meeting by O. C. Scavenius, who described the current situation and noted the continuing uncertainty with regard to the situation in East Asia.

The ruins of Great Northern's station in the French city of Calais after the end of the Second World War.

With regard to the annual account, he declared that as it was now possible to contact the London station and the company's other stations in Europe and as it would therefore—despite the continuing lack of complete information—soon be possible to present "a more accurate annual account," the board of directors did not consider it appropriate to ask those present at the general meeting to approve the annual account that had been sent out. Instead the board of directors would present a new annual account as quickly as possible and schedule a new general meeting "at which the question of a dividend would also be addressed." Those present at the current general meeting unanimously approved this course of action.[5]

Cable repairs in Europe and contact with Moscow

Two days after the general meeting, the *Edouard Suenson* sailed from Kalmar toward Copenhagen, and after a thorough inspection at Orlogsværftet (the Danish naval shipyard) and refitting for the

Cable machinery on the deck of the *Edouard Suenson*. At the front right of the picture, one can see a marker buoy that was used in connection with cable repairs, of which there were many in the postwar years.

upcoming voyage, the steamer departed on June 20, 1945, to carry out cable repairs in the North Sea, and the *Karla* joined the *Edouard Suenson* half a year later after having been refitted for cable work. The *Edouard Suenson* had soon carried out a large number of repairs, and Great Northern was able to reestablish the cable connection between Denmark and England on October 9, 1945, after two cables between Sweden and England had been repaired. Because of mines, it was not possible to repair the cables connecting Denmark and France before the beginning of the new year, and the reestablishment of the station in Calais, which had been completely destroyed, also had to wait.

It was much more difficult to reestablish the connections with the Soviet Union than it had been to reestablish several of the European connections. Great Northern managed to arrange a meeting on Kongens Nytorv on June 13, 1945, with the newly appointed Danish ambassador to the Soviet Union, Thomas Døssing, who promised to help the company with matters including acquiring permission for Great Northern's previous representative, H. P. Andersen, to travel to Moscow to initiate negotiations with regard to an extension of the company's concession. The Danish Ministry of Foreign Affairs instructed Døssing to inform the Soviet authorities that the Danish government wished to have the cable connection between the two countries reestablished.[6]

It was not until the beginning of September that a response came from Moscow, but it was positive. According to Thomas Døssing, the People's Commissariat for Communications was "very interested" in the reopening of the Siberian connection, but to begin with the reopening of the cable connections with Western Europe was a higher priority for the commissariat. The following month, the Soviet Commissariat of Foreign Affairs declared in an official note that Great Northern could begin repairing cables in cooperation with the Soviet marine authorities and that H. P. Andersen would be welcome to come to Moscow "to negotiate with regard to the exploitation of the cables in the future."[7]

The cable repairs were begun in November 1945 by the *Edouard Suenson* and a rented Finnish cable ship, but the company did not succeed in repairing the Helsinki-Leningrad cable before the winter, partly because there were cable breaks in areas that had not been cleared of mines. On the other hand, H. P. Andersen was able to travel to Moscow in late November, and the negotiations there proceeded more quickly than the cable repairs. Already in the middle of December he was able to send a telegram to Denmark to the effect that the Soviet Union was willing to conclude a new long-term agreement with a period of validity of fifteen years.[8]

The Russians did not intend to issue a new concession; rather, they wished to conclude an agreement between "equal partners" such that Great Northern would maintain the cables in Soviet waters while the People's Commissariat would operate and service the connection through Russia and Siberia without Danish participation. The Russians wanted to proceed immediately with the reestablishment of the land lines, which were largely intact east of Moscow but damaged in the entire area to the west.[9]

Contact with East Asia

Great Northern still needed to get an overview over the situation in East Asia, where the war continued until two atomic bombs were dropped on the cities of Hiroshima and Nagasaki on August 6 and 9, 1945, respectively, and Japan had unconditionally surrendered. The declaration of surrender was signed on September 2, and with this, the war in East Asia—and the world war—was over.

Shortly after the Japanese surrender, Great Northern received word from Shanghai to the effect that all was well with the personnel, including employees in Japan, and after the company had received further telegrams and air mail the current situation could be described in late October: In Shanghai, the company's building and material were still in place, while the reserve cables and other equipment and inventory in Wusong had been removed by the Japanese, after which the depot had been looted by local gangs—even the reserve tanks were gone. In Xiamen, the company's buildings and inventory remained, and in Hong Kong there was enough material to reestablish the station.[10]

With regard to the cables, it was known that all of the ends near Gutzlaff had been removed, and the cables leading to Shanghai had been severed at Wusong. Large parts of the underground cables between Wusong and Shanghai had been dug up and stolen, and near Hong Kong local fisherfolk had stolen parts of the cable to Xiamen. Also, the Japanese had rerouted several of the company's cables, and there were breaks in both cables between Nagasaki and Vladivostok in the Tsushima Strait, which had been heavily mined.[11]

The first reports from Nagasaki indicated that the company's building could be repaired, but when a telegraphist who had previously been an employee of the company had an opportunity to inspect the building in November 1945, he concluded that 70 percent of it had been damaged and that 80 percent of the equipment, inventory, and instruments had been lost as a result of the destruction caused by the atomic bomb.[12]

In East Asia, too, then, extensive repair work needed to be done, but the main challenge was diplomatic, as the company's Chinese and Japanese concessions had both expired. Also, in 1944, Cable & Wireless had once again and with immediate effect terminated the two companies' consolidation agreement—this time with reference to the fact that Great Northern's trans-Siberian connection had long since been interrupted for more than two years. At the same time, Cable & Wireless insisted that the original termination of April 9, 1940, had been valid.[13]

In July, already before Japan had surrendered, Great Northern's director Bent Suenson had therefore traveled to London to negotiate with Cable & Wireless's board chairman Sir Edward Wilshaw, who "expressed good will and indicated a desire to continue [the companies'] cooperation." However, there was skepticism about the English company at Kongens Nytorv, as there was a clear feeling that Cable & Wireless wished to dissociate itself from the Danish company.[14]

On the other hand, Great Northern could be glad that both the Foreign Office and the General Post Office had received Bent Suenson with "a friendly attitude" in accordance with the position the British authorities had expressed during the war. The Britons were interested in maintaining the cables between Denmark and England rather than going over to wireless telegraphy, and there was support for the reestablishment of the company's position in East Asia—support the company would need.

Despite their internal disagreements, Great Northern and Cable & Wireless were forced to present a united front vis-à-vis the Chinese telegraph administration, which sent a letter to the two companies as well as to Commercial Pacific and reminded them that their concessions had expired. The companies therefore had no right to resume their activities before new agreements had been

concluded, and until then the companies' cable ends and stations in China would remain sealed.[15]

After having discussed the matter for some time, the two European companies agreed to take the first step via diplomacy. One factor that had contributed to this decision was the uncertain political situation in China, which now had two governments: Chiang Kai-shek's government in Chongqing and Mao Zedong's communist government in Ya'nan. These two governments had cooperated during the war against the Japanese and were now negotiating with regard to the formation of a common government. Denmark had no diplomatic representation of its own in China, as Denmark had broken off diplomatic relations with China in 1941 under pressure from Germany, and after having consulted with the Danish Ministry of Foreign Affairs, Great Northern therefore asked the United Kingdom's Foreign Office to represent the company's interests.

The company's point of departure was a desire to operate its cables using its own stations and establish a joint purse including the various companies and the Chinese administration. Commercial Pacific was asked to inform the American ambassador in China, and Great Northern sent a memorandum on the company's own behalf to the Danish ambassador in Washington, Henrik Kauffmann, and asked him to inform the United States Department of State with a view to transmitting the relevant information to the American ambassador.[16]

The first foreign businessman in Japan

The uncertain political situation caused Great Northern's director in Shanghai, H. S. Poulsen, to abandon a planned visit to the Chinese ministry of communications. He decided instead to visit Japan, where the situation was no less complicated, as the country was occupied by American troops and subject to a formally Allied but de facto American military government under the leadership of General Douglas MacArthur.

The reestablishment of the company's position in Japan and of the station in Nagasaki was of decisive importance in connection with reopening the trans-Siberian connection with an extension to Shanghai. If H. S. Poulsen were to travel to Japan, however, he would require the permission of the American military administration.

With the assistance of Cable & Wireless's board chairman, Sir Edward Wilshaw, Great Northern was able to get the commander of the Allied South East Asia Command, Lord Louis Mountbatten, to recommend the Danish project. H. S. Poulsen was therefore able to travel to Japan in November 1945 as the first civilian to visit Japan for business purposes after the war, having received permission from General MacArthur personally.[17]

After his arrival in Tokyo, H. S. Poulsen discovered that he would need to negotiate with the communications department of the American headquarters. The Americans made it clear that "for the time being," as a matter of basic principle, Japan would not be allowed to conclude agreements of a commercial nature or take on international obligations. It was also the position of the military administration that "for a long period of time" Japan would not be permitted to have access to commercial correspondence with foreign countries via telegraph, telephone, or mail. The only permissible telegraph correspondence was official telegrams, press telegrams, and telegrams to and from the American occupation forces.[18]

With regard to Great Northern's wish to reestablish the company's position prior to 1940, when the Japanese, in the view of the company, had forced new concession conditions on Great Northern and taken over the station in Nagasaki, the Americans responded that the reestablishment of that position was hardly a possibility. The Americans recommended that the company instead conclude a completely new agreement with the Japanese when the conclusion of such an agreement became relevant.

However, H. S. Poulsen did manage to secure permission for the company to reestablish its station in Nagasaki as a transfer station for the cables between Shanghai and Vladivostok to which traffic to and from Japan would not have access. There was rejoicing over the granting of this permission

on Kongens Nytorv, but before the Nagasaki station could be reestablished, the trans-Siberian connection needed to be reopened, and the company's East Asian cable systems needed to be repaired and in some cases completely replaced. It was not clear when these steps could be taken.[19]

Extraordinary general meeting

On December 13, 1945, when Great Northern was finally able to hold the planned extraordinary general meeting, it was the responsibility of a new board chairman to present the updated annual report and the adjusted account. O. C. Scavenius had died in early September, and attempts to find a suitable person outside the board of directors had been unsuccessful. As late as November 20, the individual who had held the post of vice chairman up to this point, law professor Poul J. Jørgensen, was persuaded to take over the post.[20]

The written report that had been sent out, which briefly indicated that the Soviet Union had shown an interest in a quick reopening of the trans-Siberian connection, made it quite clear that the company's prospects for the future were uncertain. In Japan and China the situation was "unclear" though the Chinese government had expressed a desire to begin negotiations with regard to the reestablishment of the cable connections.[21]

At the same time, the shareholders were warned that growing competition from wireless telegraphy had to be expected and that air mail would doubtless become "a more serious competitor than it was before the war." Nevertheless, the board of directors believed "that cables would continue to hold an important place in international communications in the future."[22]

The account covered all of the years in the period 1939–1944. Since the presentation of the annual account for 1940, the annual surplus had been transferred to a special "account for later disposition," in which there were now 20 million kroner. A good 15 million kroner had come from the transferred part of the surplus for 1939, while the rest represented the total accounting result for the years 1940–1944,

after the company had gotten access to its foreign accounts. The board of directors proposed to those present at the general meeting that 20 percent of the share capital be paid out as a dividend amounting to 7.2 million kroner while the remaining 13 million kroner were transferred to the following accounting year.[23]

Not all of the shareholders approved of this. After the account notification had been sent out on October 23, the board of directors received a message from a Danish shareholder, the wholesaler and general consul for Yugoslavia Th. Olesen, who, "on behalf of a number of shareholders," expressed the wish to receive a larger dividend, as the proposed dividend would not even come close to covering the wealth tax for their shares for the past five years, during which no dividend had been paid out. He also wished to receive a statement from the board of directors regarding the possibility of the liquidation of the company, and finally he wished to receive a response from the board of directors to

A selection of grapnels and other grappling hooks that were used to get a grip on the cables on the seafloor after the Second World War.

the question of whether the company would continue to pay out an annual dividend of 20 percent regardless of the operating results so that the money in the reserve fund would gradually be paid out to the shareholders. He stated that he wished the holding company to be dissolved and its shares and assets distributed to the shareholders.[24]

The last thing the board of directors wanted was to have these questions discussed at the general meeting. Before the general meeting, board member and supreme court attorney Kristian Steglich-Petersen managed to get the general consul to abstain from pressing his demand for an increased dividend by referring to the need for funds with which to rebuild the company's systems, while the remaining questions were fended off in writing—it was established that the board of directors had no plans for

liquidation of the company and that the dissolution of the holding company would have very significant negative tax consequences for the shareholders.[25]

The general meeting then took place without critical questions and sounds of discontent, but the fear of possible shareholder demands for the liquidation of the company that the board of directors had felt before the beginning of the Second World War had proven justified—and this was not the last the board of directors would hear about this topic.

Reestablishment of the connections with the Soviet Union

At the extraordinary general meeting it was announced that in the course of the summer the *Edouard Suenson* had repaired a total of fifty-five breaks and flaws in the company's cables, after which the work had been interrupted because of the winter and the danger from mines. In the spring of 1946, the cable steamer, assisted by the *Karla*, resumed repair work, and the cables between Møn and Bornholm could be opened in April 1946 and the last two cables between Denmark and England during the months that followed. Because of the danger from mines, it was not possible to repair the

In February 1941, Great Northern purchased the steamship *Karla* with a view to refitting it as a cable ship when the Second World War was over. The picture shows the ship after refitting; it has been fitted with the typical clipper bow with a cable wheel. During a cable repair operation in the Gulf of Finland in January 1947, the *Karla* struck a mine that exploded, and despite the fact that Russian minesweepers that had been assisting the *Karla* soon arrived to help, sixteen men died, and one more was injured. This is the only known loss of human life in connection with Great Northern's cable repairs.

first of the two Dano-French cables until October 1946, and as a result of the extreme destruction in Calais, it was not until December that a house could be purchased and the furnishing of a new station could be begun. The last cable was reopened as late as in the summer of 1952.

As after the First World War and the Russian Revolution, it was of decisive importance that a telegraphic connection with the Soviet Union be established. This would require cable repairs along with the conclusion of an agreement that could replace the concession that had expired in 1946.

In the middle of February 1946, Great Northern sent a draft of a new agreement to Moscow via the Danish Ministry of Foreign Affairs and the Soviet embassy in Copenhagen. The People's Commissariat quickly replied that a delegation from the company would be invited to Moscow when the commissariat had reviewed the draft—and after this, nothing happened.[26]

In late May, H. P. Andersen managed to get himself attached to a Danish trade delegation that traveled to Moscow, where he had an opportunity to negotiate with the People's Commissariat, which, with the exception of "a few relatively insignificant changes" found the company's draft to be in accordance with what the commissariat had wished to see. Having received an invitation from the People's Commissariat, Great Northern's director Alf Ussing and H. P. Andersen subsequently traveled to Moscow, where, on August 8, 1946, they signed a new fifteen-year contract according to which Great Northern would be responsible for the maintenance and operation of the cables in Europe and East Asia, while the Soviet telegraph administration would operate the land lines from Leningrad to Vladivostok. At the same time, the Soviet government took over all the Great Northern properties it had maintained after the expulsion of the Danish telegraphists before the war.[27]

The next link in the chain was Finland, which concluded a ten-year agreement with Great Northern in the middle of November. In the meantime, the last break in the Helsinki-Leningrad cable had been repaired, and on December 12, 1946, Great Northern reopened the telegraph connection between the Soviet Union and Western Europe via the Finno-Swedish cables.

A few days later, the repair of the Bornholm-Liepaja cable was completed, and what remained was the repairing of the last break in the Liepaja-Helsinki cable in the Gulf of Finland, on which the *Karla* was working on New Year's Day 1947 when the catastrophe occurred. The cable steamer struck a mine that exploded, and despite the fact that Soviet naval vessels in the vicinity immediately came to help, sixteen crew members perished in the icy water. These were dangerous waters, and it was not until October 1947 that Great Northern succeeded in completing the repair so

the connection via the Liepaja cables could be reopened.

New cable connections were also established. In April 1946, Great Northern received a message from the Polish telegraph administration, which wished to establish a direct telegraph connection between Poland and Denmark in order to have an onward connection to Western Europe. During the war, the Germans had laid two cables between Poland and Bornholm, and the laying of a new cable between Bornholm and Zealand made it possible to establish the desired connection.[28]

Repairing the German cables required the permission of the Allied Control Commission in Berlin. Such permission was soon issued, as the cable was a component of Allied plans to establish a European network of telegraph and telephone connections that avoided Germany. After an agreement had been concluded by Great Northern, P & T, and the Polish telegraphy administration, a cable was laid between Bornholm and Zealand early in 1948. Because of the danger from mines and the extensive destruction in the Polish city of Kołobrzeg, where the cable was to be landed and connected to the Polish land line network, the connection could not be opened until the middle of June 1948. This was the first new cable connection the company had opened since the Iceland cable in 1906.[29]

Lack of progress in China and reestablishment in Japan

Great Northern still needed to reestablish its connections in East Asia, which would be more difficult than reestablishing the connections in Europe. In the fall of 1945, the negotiations between Chiang Kai-shek's government and the communists broke down and a civil war broke out. The Americans backed Chiang Kai-shek, as did Great Northern. When H. S. Poulsen visited Chiang Kai-shek's telegraph director in January 1946, however, he did not hear any inspiring words. According to the telegraph director, the government had made "a final decision" to take over and operate all cables that were landed in China. Furthermore, radio telegra-

When Great Northern's employees gained access to the company's cable depot in Wusong after the end of the Second World War, they encountered Japanese fortifications.

phy had proved able to fulfill China's telegraphic needs, and cables would therefore be of "secondary significance."[30]

The following month, however, the Danish ambassador in London received a message from his Chinese counterpart to the effect that the Chinese government wished to have Great Northern resume its activity in East Asia. In March 1946, after this surprising positive development, the company therefore sent an application to the American military administration in Japan for permission to re-establish the station in Nagasaki for transit traffic between Shanghai and Vladivostok.[31]

The company received a depressing rejection in June, when the Americans informed Great Northern that at this time they would not be permitting any other business activity in Japan than what was necessary for the occupation but that the company could send a new application "when more stable conditions had been created."[32]

However, the Soviet government was also interested in the reopening of the cables to Shanghai, and during the negotiations in Moscow in the summer of 1946, Alf Ussing received word that the Allied Control Commission in Japan would support the approval of a new application from Great Northern. From London, too, there came a confirmation of support, and in October 1946, when H. S. Poulsen began negotiations in China regarding a new agreement, he brought the Chinese government, which was represented on the Allied Control Commission, up to date on the matter.[33]

In the meantime, the cable companies had negotiated with the Chinese, but the parties had not come any closer together. The situation was complicated by the fact that the companies were not in agreement, as Great Northern and Commercial Pacific were willing to allow the Chinese to take over and operate the cables, but the English resisted this. The Danish company gave in to Cable & Wireless, however, as the British parliament had voted to nationalize Cable & Wireless on January 1, 1947, and Great Northern feared that insisting on maintaining the company's earlier position with regard to operations in China could damage Great Northern's position in the United Kingdom. In December 1946, the three companies therefore sent a new proposal to the Chinese in which the companies maintained that they wished to keep the cables and operate them themselves.[34]

While the negotiations with the Chinese dragged on, there was a breakthrough in Japan. In January 1947, when Ambassador Tillitse arrived in Tokyo, he delivered a new application from Great Northern to General MacArthur personally together with a note in which, on behalf of the Danish government, he "recommended that the Allied Control Commission take a positive view of the application." He also contacted the Allies' civilian communications department, which promised that the matter would be viewed "in as positive a light as possible."[35]

To the great surprise of both the ambassador and Great Northern, there was a response from the military headquarters already on March 23, 1947, and it was more positive than anyone at Great Northern had expected, as the Japanese government would be directed to reopen the station at Nagasaki.[36] A negative aspect of the planned arrangement, however, was that the Japanese were to be responsible for the operation of the cables in accordance with the system the company felt had been "forced upon" Great Northern in 1940. During a stay in the United States in June 1947, Bent Suenson, thanks to the intervention of Ambassador Henrik Kauffmann, was able to convey the company's point of view to the future leader of the United States Army's communications authority, to which the American communications authorities in Japan were subordinate. According to Bent Suenson, the American was "friendly and objective," but he could not promise to support Great Northern.[37]

Negotiations between H. S. Poulsen, who was assisted by Ambassador Tillitse, and the military administration in Tokyo that lasted the whole month of August did not get the Americans to change their position. The promised Russian and British support had no effect, either, as the military administration was completely dominated by the United States.

On September 24, 1947, the Allied military headquarters in Japan issued a license to Great Northern for the reopening of the Nagasaki station, which was to be operated by the Japanese administration in accordance with the 1940 agreement. The Japanese made no secret of the fact that they preferred not to see the Danish cables reopened, as that would undermine the profitability of their own radio connections. However, the American military administration insisted that the cables were to be reopened, and it was left to the Japanese administration to negotiate a new operating agreement that regulated rates and invoicing.

As H. S. Poulsen was completely occupied by the negotiations in China, another representative of Great Northern, F. Lassalle, traveled to Tokyo in January 1948 to begin negotiations with the Japanese administration as an accredited Civil Communications Advisor attached to the Danish embassy. Great Northern was sensitive to the Japanese resistance to reopening the station in Nagasaki, but despite an accommodating attitude toward the Japanese, the negotiations dragged on until the middle of September before the parties reached agreement on a contract that could be approved by the occupation authorities.[38]

In the meantime, Great Northern had begun work on the Vladivostok cables, and they became usable again on October 12, 1948—the day the company and the Japanese administration signed the new contract. A little over three weeks later, the agreement was approved by the American military administration, and on November 15, 1948 the trans-Siberian connection reopened after having been interrupted for more than seven years.

In the beginning, the volume of traffic was extremely modest. Japan's international telegraphy amounted to only 15 percent of the level in 1938, and some of Japan's telegrams were sent via seven wireless connections with Europe. There was no transit traffic to China, as the connection with China had not yet been opened.

Chinese revolution and new geopolitical world order

One reason why the negotiations with the Chinese took a long time was that Cable & Wireless and Commercial Pacific were not in as great a hurry as Great Northern, and the Chinese also appeared to have plenty of time. Furthermore, the Chinese wished to negotiate with the three companies separately so as to be able to play them off against each other, and they confidentially let the other two companies know that China could easily do without the Danish company.

However, the Chinese tactic was not effective, and in fact Great Northern received official American support when the American military administration in Tokyo, having been asked to do so by the company and Ambassador Tillitse, presented the Chinese ambassador in Tokyo with a note in which it was requested that Great Northern receive permission to reopen the cable connection between Nagasaki and Shanghai as soon as possible. Two months later, the American embassy in China presented a corresponding request in a note to the Chinese ministry of foreign affairs.[39]

In the end, this support would prove not to have any effect, however. While the companies were negotiating, the situation in China deteriorated as the civil war escalated, and the communist forces advanced and forced Chiang Kai-shek to assume a defensive position. Late in 1948, the three companies agreed to stop the negotiations and "await further military and political developments for a time," and Great Northern began to prepare for a possible critical situation as a result of the civil war."[40]

It soon arrived. In late January 1949, H. S. Poulsen reported from Shanghai that there was an increasing lack of food and other vital supplies and that general anarchy reigned as a result of "the presence in the city and its environs of a large number of undisciplined soldiers." In March, the communists' troops crossed the Chang River and advanced toward Shanghai, where a large number of government troops had arrived to defend the city, and Great Northern's cable depot in Wusong was occupied and armed as a defensive position.[41]

As the only one of the three cable companies' representatives, H. S. Poulsen remained in Shanghai, and in the spring of 1949, when the British carried out an evacuation, he and Great Northern's other personnel remained in the city of their own free will. None of them suffered on May 25, 1949, when communist troops marched into the city. The civil war continued in southern China, but it was clear to everyone that it would only be a matter of time before the communists took over completely.

On October 1, 1949, Communist Party Chairman Mao Zedong proclaimed the creation of the People's Republic of China on Tiananmen Square in Beijing. Great Northern's leaders had no doubt that the Chinese communists planned to "align themselves with the Soviet bloc," and indeed the Soviet Union recognized communist China the same day, as the first nation to do so, while the great Western powers continued to recognize Chiang Kai-shek's government, which had fled to Taiwan.

"The company's darkest time"

The developments in China contributed to increasing the uncertainty with regard to Great Northern's prospects for the future that had been created by the slow reestablishment of the company's cable connections and not least the uncertainty regarding the situation in Japan. The annual accounts were not inspiring, and there did not seem to be a way out of the dead calm that had left the company a shadow of its former self. Later, Bent Suenson would refer to the years after the Second World War as "the company's darkest time."[42]

In December 1945, when the revised annual account and the proposal that a dividend of 20 percent be paid had been presented, Board Chairman Poul J. Jørgensen had stated that the board of directors expected to be able to maintain a corresponding level during the years that followed. When the notification of the annual result was sent out in May 1946, however, the board of directors proposed a dividend of 18 percent, and it was only the statement that had been made by Poul J. Jørgensen the previous year that kept the board of directors from proposing an even lower percentage.[43]

The board's proposal immediately provoked General Consul Th. Olesen to send the board a letter expressing the wish to receive a dividend of 20 percent, a wish the board of directors rejected with reference to the fact that the board's proposal was based on an evaluation of "all factors that needed to be taken into consideration, including the operating result for the year and the prospects for the immediate future."[44]

There was in fact not much money to go around. Telegram revenues amounted to only 4.7 million kroner, in addition to which there was incoming revenue from the war years in the amount of 2.2 million kroner. Given expenses amounting to just under 11 million kroner, the revenues from capital investments and interest from bank balances, which amounted to a total of 5 million kroner, were not sufficient to create a surplus, and it was only by tapping the transferred surplus of 12.5 million kroner from 1945 that Great Northern was able to pay out a dividend at all.[45]

The situation was similar the following year, when the revenues from telegrams had risen a little but 2 million kroner had to be transferred from the surplus for the previous year in order to pay out a dividend of 15 percent. Once again a letter arrived from General Consul Th. Olesen, who referred to the fact that Great Northern's former chairman of the board of directors Wilhelm Weimann had said that "if the day ever came when the company could not produce a reasonable operating surplus, he would support the liquidation of the company." This would have had significant tax disadvantages, however, and as an alternative Th. Olesen proposed the payment of an annual dividend of 20 to 25 percent so that the company's assets could be transformed into payments "without excessively burdensome effects on the shareholders." He presented this proposal together with a thinly disguised threat: He indicated that he represented a group of shareholders who wished "to negotiate in a peaceful manner" and that it would be unfortunate "if, because of a lack of sensitivity to the justifiable wishes of the shareholders, a mood of strong antagonism should develop."[46]

Some of the fighting of the Chinese Civil War took place near Great Northern's station in Xiamen. The photograph shows P. E. V. Jørgensen of Great Northern in a Nationalist trench in October 1949 after the Communists had won and Mao had proclaimed the establishment of the People's Republic of China.

As the great majority of the company's shares were held outside Denmark, and as there were no protests coming from abroad and the board of directors controlled the holding company and thus 25 percent of the shares, there was no way for the Danish group of shareholders to gain control over a general meeting. Nevertheless, an open revolt by Danish shareholders was the last thing the board of directors needed, and in his response, Board Chairman Poul J. Jørgensen therefore expressed his hope that "Danish shareholders would show at least as strong a tendency as foreign ones to have sympathy for the ongoing efforts to get Great Northern back on its feet."[47]

Great Northern succeeded in preventing the dissatisfaction of the shareholders from being openly aired—also after Th. Olesen had been replaced as the rebellious shareholders' spokesman by the stockbroker S. A. Jensen the following year and Jensen had proposed selling off the company's East Asian cable systems. This occurred already before the notification of the annual result had been sent out, in connection with which it was suggested that the dividend again be reduced—this time to 12 percent. The response was that the board of directors "could not take responsibility for giving up the efforts to re-establish the company's activity," which the selling of the East Asian cables would amount to.[48]

However, the annual account for 1947 did not provide much reason to believe in the revitalization of the company. Telegram revenues decreased to 6.3 million kroner, while there were revenues from previous years amounting to 4.2 million kroner. The revenues from capital investments amounted to 4.1 million kroner, and 1.5 million kroner of the surplus transferred from the previous year had to be used to make up part of the dividend.[49]

"The situation has not yet gotten to the point at which we should haul down the flag"

The downward trend continued in 1948, though there was a modest increase in telegram revenues. In combination with revenues from capital invest-

ments and miscellaneous revenues, the revenues from telegrams were not sufficient to keep Great Northern from posting an operating deficit of nearly 1 million kroner.

Denmark's newspapers took notice in March 1949, when the company published the notice of the annual result for 1948 and at the same time announced that the dividend would be reduced by almost half, from 12 percent to 7 percent. "A sad development," wrote *Ekstra Bladet* with regard to the constant reduction of the dividend since 1945.[50] An a conto dividend of 5 percent had already been paid out, so the shareholders could only look forward to a further dividend of 2 percent. Because of the operating deficit, the entire dividend had to be funded out of the so-called dividend equalization fund. This fund had been created in 1918 in order to even out annual deviations in the dividend amount and not to make possible the paying out of a higher dividend "than was ultimately supportable." The fund, then, was intended for funding dividends for individual, anomalous bad years, and tapping the fund was therefore not appropriate in the current situation, in which bad years had become the new normal situation. Nevertheless, the fund was now used for the first time—and this would not be the last time.[51]

When the annual report was sent out in April 1949, it was followed by a new series of newspaper articles about the company's difficulties, and the uncertain situation in China was in focus in these articles. During the preceding years, despite the company's difficulties, the newspapers' articles had included positive news about the repairing of cables, the agreement with Russia, the reopening of the connection with Japan, and the new cable to Poland. Attention to positive developments had now been replaced by headlines such as "Great Northern struggling with difficulties," "Serious discussions at Great Northern," and "Great Northern does not want to give up."[52]

The articles were inspired by the company's annual report, which contained a lengthy account of the situation in the telegraphy sector and in particular the situation in China. It was explained that the reason why the company had not scaled down, let alone sold off, its system in East Asia but rather kept the stations in Shanghai, Xiamen, and Hong Kong on standby was that Great Northern wished to be able to resume its work in China when this became possible.[53]

In general, the board of directors found it to be "in accordance with the interests of the company" to continue Great Northern's efforts to rebuild the company's telegraphy activity. At the same time, the board of directors recognized that "in the long run, of course, the company cannot continue an activity that does not produce a profit"—without elaborating on what the consequences of this recognition might be. Nevertheless, this was the first time Great Northern had ever suggested the possibility of liquidating the company in its annual report.[54]

The scene was therefore set at the general meeting on May 12, 1949, in the great hall of the Stock Exchange. The supreme court attorney, Kristian Steglich-Petersen, who had become chairman of the board of directors after Poul J. Jørgensen, who had died in 1947, presented his report and went over the annual account, after which the floor was given to a shareholder, the government-accredited auditor Einar Nissen, who was not satisfied. Nissen called the annual account "sad and depressing" and called the announced dividend of 7 percent "an unusually bitter pill to swallow."[55]

Einar Nissen immediately proposed to the board of directors that they "show some sense of social responsibility" and at least increase the remaining dividend to 5 percent so that the shareholders would receive a total of 10 percent, "which must be considered a very modest dividend." And then he expressed basic doubt with regard to whether the company, given the situation in China, the company's financial situation, and the prospects for the future in general, would continue to be able to generate an appropriate dividend from a share capital of 36 million kroner—and here he referred to the fixed dividend of 20 percent that had been paid out before the Second World War.

He believed it might be better for the shareholders to depreciate the share capital and begin to distribute the remaining very large reserves rather than let them be eaten up by annual operating deficits. This was a thinly disguised demand that the company be liquidated, and Einar Nissen concluded by expressing the opinion that at least the holding company should be liquidated immediately. He thanked those present for their attention.[56]

With its control over the holding company's votes and a large supply of powers of attorney, the board of directors could react calmly to such criticism, but the board chairman was nevertheless obviously irritated when he responded by saying that there "[was] no justification at all for criticizing the company's leaders." He described in detail the situation and the board's ongoing discussions and dispositions, and then he firmly rejected the proposal that the company be liquidated and, according to the account of the meeting in *Berlingske Tidende*, declared that in the view of the board of directors "the situation was not yet one in which [the company] should haul down the flag." He added that the purpose of having the large reserves was precisely that the company should be able to get through a difficult situation "in the hope that there would be light ahead," but on the other hand it was also the case that "if one "[saw] that there was darkness ahead," then the natural consequence would be that one liquidated the company. The board of directors did not believe that this point had been reached yet.[57]

The annual report and the account and the proposal that a dividend of 7 percent be paid out were subsequently unanimously approved, as neither Einar Nissen nor anyone else demanded a vote. Nevertheless, it was in particular the criticism of the board of directors and the modest dividend that were reflected in the newspaper articles during the following days, and the company's board of directors later remembered this general meeting for its "gloomy mood."[58]

Cold War, New England Cable, and Shutdown in China

CHAPTER 17

New world order

It is not surprising that some of Great Northern's shareholders had difficulty seeing "light ahead," as the chairman of the board of directors apparently could. The prospects for the future were not promising, and while the connection to Japan had been reopened, this did not provide a foundation for East Asian traffic at anywhere near the level Great Northern had experienced before the Second World War.

In addition, the proclamation of the People's Republic of China represented the culmination, thus far, of the emergence of a new economic and political world order. The spirit of cooperation among the Allied powers in the fight against Germany and Japan had quickly cooled, and already on March 5, 1946, the United Kingdom's wartime prime minister, Winston Churchill, held a watershed speech in Fulton, Missouri, in which he warned of an iron curtain that had come down, dividing Europe into an Eastern and a Western bloc.

The following year, the American president, Harry Truman, picked up this thread in an equal-

ly groundbreaking speech on March 12, 1947, in which he proclaimed a new American foreign policy of containing the Soviet Union and fighting against communism all over the world. Less than three months later, the United States Secretary of State, George Marshall, presented a grand plan for offering economic aid to support the reconstruction of war-ravaged Europe, the so-called Marshall Plan.

The Soviet Union declined the American offer, as did the countries in Eastern Europe that had been liberated by the Soviet Union, in which communists had come to power and units of the Red Army were still in place. In September 1947, the communist parties in Eastern Europe as well as France and Italy established the organization Cominform, which declared that there were now two geopolitical camps under the respective leadership of the United States and the Soviet Union.

In the spring of 1949, the Western bloc established the military alliance NATO, in which Denmark participated after having accepted Marshall aid. In the fall of that year, Germany was divided into two separate states belonging to different

American visit to Great Northern's station in Nagasaki after the reopening of the cable to Vladivostok in November 1948.

blocs, and the Soviet Union detonated its first atomic bomb. With the alignment of the People's Republic of China with the "Soviet bloc," not only Europe but also the entire northern hemisphere was divided into two opposing political and ideological camps. In February 1950, the Soviet Union and the People's Republic of China signed a 30-year mutual aid and friendship treaty.

The world war had been replaced by a new globe-spanning cold war, which placed Great Northern in a completely new position on the borderline between the two blocs. It was not new that the company was balancing between great powers' imperial and political interests—that had been a condition of the company's existence ever since the company was founded and had gained an extra dimension after the October Revolution in Russia in 1917 and the creation of the Soviet Union.

What was new was the global separation into two blocs that were sharply divided and faced each other with great hostility, a separation that caused Great Northern's original foundation in national politics, Danish neutrality, to crumble, as Denmark had unambiguously chosen the side of the American-led Western bloc.

The increasing tension between the Eastern and Western blocs did not immediately affect Great Northern's work on reestablishing the telegraph connections in Northern Europe and with the Soviet Union. Nevertheless, the development caused the shareholders to worry as the international political climate became increasingly tense, while the board of directors believed it could see a light in the darkness—a light that had been lit in London.

New coaxial cable to the United Kingdom

At a meeting of the board of directors in October 1947, Bent Suenson presented a proposal to lay a

The coaxial cable between Denmark and Great Britain was landed in Weybourne from the *Edouard Suenson* in the summer of 1950.

new type of undersea cable, a so-called coaxial cable, between Denmark and England. In contrast to traditional cables, a coaxial cable could exploit carrier frequencies to accommodate several channels, which made it suitable not only for telegraphy and telephony but also for a new form of telecommunications—the telex, which made it possible for major clients such as press bureaus and aviation companies to rent a channel to communicate with one another directly, avoiding the telegraph stations.[1]

Great Northern's existing cables did not allow for telex connections, nor were there existing telex connections between England and Scandinavia. However, a coaxial cable had just been laid between England and the Netherlands, and a projected gov-

ernment-owned coaxial cable from the Netherlands to Denmark would therefore open up the possibility of telex connections between England and Denmark.

The telex appeared to represent a threat to Great Northern's telegraphy business, but the company chose to confront the challenge by laying its own coaxial cables and offering telex connections. However, the cables required a very significant financial investment if their capacity was to be great enough to allow a sufficient number of channels to make them profitable. A newly developed undersea amplifier that sent electricity through the cables made it possible to accommodate a larger number of channels in cheap types of cables than had previously been achievable, but even with such an amplifier, a coaxial cable between Denmark and England would perhaps cost between 5 and 5.5 mil-

lion kroner. And as not only the technology but also the use of the telex was quite new, there was no guarantee that such an investment would let Great Northern break even, let alone produce a profit.

According to Bent Suenson, there was no getting around it, however. The connections with England were of decisive importance for the company, and according to the minutes he stated at the meeting of the board of directors that "refraining from laying the cable would mean that the company gave up trying to follow technological developments, which would hardly harmonize with the company's efforts to continue its business activities." The alternative would be to liquidate the company, and the board of directors did not hesitate to approve further work on the project by the top management team.[2]

The laying of a new cable and the establishment of telex connections required approval from both Denmark and the United Kingdom. Approval from the Danish General Directorate arrived in early May 1948, and in June, Bent Suenson secured permission from the British authorities not only for the desired landing but also for the Danish company to operate all telex traffic between England and Denmark and possibly also the other Scandinavian countries via the Danish coaxial cable. Despite the nationalization of Cable & Wireless and that company's attempts to sideline Great Northern during the Second World War, the British then stood by their statement that there would be room for the Danish company after the war.[3]

Complications with regard to production meant that the cable was not delivered until May 1950, but in June and July the cable could finally be laid. In August, the British approved making the cable the "main route" for all telex traffic between the United Kingdom and Scandinavia, and at the same time they reserved five of the eleven duplex channels the cable could accommodate. The cable had no amplifier, but the company had already ordered two, so the capacity could be increased when there was a need. In November 1950, when the cable opened, Great Northern shut down two of the old cables, which led to great savings in operating and maintenance costs, and a large number of telegraphists in Newcastle were dismissed.[4]

Great Northern characterized the opening as "a milestone in the company's history," and this was certainly justified. The multichannel capacity and the undersea amplifiers represented the company's first real technological leaps since Great Northern had been established in 1869. Worldwide, the Weybourne cable, as it was called, was the longest undersea coaxial cable that had been installed up to that point. At the same time, the cable had been specifically constructed for telex and telegraph traffic and not, as in the case of most other coaxial cables, primarily for telephony.[5]

The number of circuits rented out for telex traffic grew quickly, and already in 1954, the company increased the number available to 24 duplex circuits. In the spring of 1954, the two amplifiers that had been ordered were installed, so the capacity was increased to 74, and in the spring of 1956, five new amplifiers were ordered to replace the original two so the capacity could be increased to 144 duplex circuits plus a telephone line for service purposes.[6]

It was the England cable that had once laid the foundation for C. F. Tietgen's establishment and development of the Great Northern Telegraph Company, and now the Weybourne cable became the light in the darkness that the board of directors had hoped would appear. The company had regained its role as a major player on the international cable scene, and the revenues from the cable and the savings thanks to the shutting down of the old cables, together with general growth in international telegram traffic, helped to improve the company's operating economy. The company was therefore able gradually to increase dividends by half a percent annually so that the dividend for 1956 amounted to 12 percent, and this calmed the Danish group of shareholders and gave the board of directors some peace while they were working to get the company back on its feet.

New leadership

It was with new leadership that the work to get Great Northern back on its feet continued, as Board Chairman O. C. Scavenius had initiated a discussion by the board of directors of the composition of the top management team. It was not the identity of the company's leaders he placed on the agenda but rather the principle of having two equal directors. This system had been in operation since Edouard Suenson had resigned as chief executive officer in 1908, but O. C. Scavenius did not find that it functioned satisfactorily. He therefore felt that "the en-

Upon the Communist takeover and the proclamation of the People's Republic of China on October 1, 1949, Chou En-Lai was appointed the new government's first Premier of the Government Administration Council. This gave Great Northern hopes that the company's cables to Shanghai could be reopened, as the company had learned that Chou En-Lai viewed the Danish company's wish positively. The outbreak of the Korean War in 1950 got in the way, however, and Great Northern had to abandon the notion of resuming its activities in China.

tire management should be reorganized in the relatively near future," and the other members of the board of directors supported him in this, so a committee was formed to develop and present proposals for a new structure.[7]

Neither the documents of the top management team nor those of the board of directors suggest that there were major disagreements, let alone controversies, in the current situation or that such disagreements or controversies had existed earlier. The documents do indicate, however, that the driving force with regard to getting the company involved in manufacturing activity was Bent Suenson, while Alf Ussing was alone in recommending that the company become involved with Det Danske Luftfartsselskab (Danish Air Lines).

A short summary of the meeting of the board of directors that took place on June 13, 1945, when each of the two directors was asked to present his view of the company's leadership, does indicate that the two directors had different views with regard to O. C. Scavenius's comments. While Alf Ussing preferred the current arrangement, as he preferred "a treble tone" to a "double tone," Bent Suenson declared that he had always found the existing arrangement "heavy" though he did not explain what he meant by that—no such explanation is reflected in the summary of the meeting, in any event.[8]

While Alf Ussing's declaration can be read as the expression of a wish to have a mediator and arbitrator, Bent Suenson clearly was interested in having a faster and more effective decision-making and executive process—and doubtless would have liked to see such a process created by means of the establishment of a position for a chief executive officer to be occupied by Bent Suenson himself.

The board of directors was not prepared to take such a step immediately, however, so while the working group continued its discussions the two directors' tasks were divided so they shared the area of telegraphy and each had responsibility for a distinct group of countries. Within the company itself, Alf Ussing was responsible for the administration, the company's investments and financial dealings, and the top management team's relationship with the board of directors and the shareholders.[9]

While the two men were supposed to divide responsibility for the area of telegraphy, Bent Suenson, given his other areas of responsibility, was clearly the leader in the top management team, and his position was reinforced when, as the only director, he was elected to the board of directors at the extraordinary general meeting in Decem-

ber 1945. After the death of Board Chairman Poul J. Jørgensen in 1947, he rose higher under the new chairman, Kristian Steglich-Petersen, becoming Vice Chairman. His position within the top management team was subsequently uncontested.

In the fall of 1949, the board of directors was finally ready to implement the definitive restructuring of the company's leadership when Alf Ussing was persuaded to resign effective June 1, 1950, when Bent Suenson would become the sole director. As the chairman of the board of directors put it, the company had thus carried out the "reconfiguration of the top management team that appears appropriate given the company's position."[10]

Negotiations with China's communist government

While the emergence of the Cold War did not influence Great Northern's reestablishment of the telegraph connections between Western Europe and the Soviet Union, the increasing tension between the two blocs probably was a contributing factor with regard to the reopening of the connection with Japan, as the United States became interested in a quick rebuilding of the country's economy.

On the other hand, the Cold War influenced the attitude of the Chinese toward Great Northern, as Chinese nationalism now acquired both a communist ideological quality and a strongly anti-American quality, not least because during the civil war the United States had provided massive economic and military support to Chiang Kai-shek and his forces.

This became clear to Great Northern's director in East Asia, H. S. Poulsen, shortly after the communists had marched into Shanghai, when he received an invitation to a meeting in a newly established office for foreign affairs, where, on June 24, 1949, he met with the head of the department of telecommunications. The Chinese were interested in Great Northern's relationship with Cable & Wireless and in particular with Commercial Pacific and in whether Great Northern was controlled by one or both of these companies. H. S. Poulsen could honestly answer no to this last question, and he wisely avoided mentioning the European companies' involvement with Commercial Pacific.[11]

On Kongens Nytorv, there was no knowledge of what was going on in Shanghai—and vice versa—as sending coded messages via wireless telegraph connections was forbidden. With the exception of short messages and the transmission of neutral information, correspondence was carried out through letters, and such correspondence was restricted by a harbor blockade put in place by Chiang Kai-shek's naval forces. It was not until August 27 that Great Northern's management received H. S. Poulsen's report on the meeting.[12]

Prior to this, however, the company had received from the Danish Ministry of Foreign Affairs a copy of a report from the Danish ambassador in Shanghai, who described H. S. Poulsen's meeting with the Chinese. The board of directors decided to act immediately to "break the ice," and H. S. Poulsen was instructed to initiate negotiations in Beijing.[13]

It was not until the middle of October 1949 that H. S. Poulsen received this instruction, and in late November, he traveled to Beijing at the personal invitation of the Chinese minister of communications. The ministry in question had barely been established, and it made contact with Great Northern not via official channels but via the minister's younger brother, a retired former employee at the company's station in Shanghai.[14]

H. S. Poulsen said that he was probably the first foreigner to be invited to negotiations with China's communist government in Shanghai. The special treatment of Great Northern was remarkable, and according to H. S. Poulsen his reception at the ministry was "almost warm." The negotiations ended with the Chinese asking Great Northern to prepare a document as a basis for further negotiations, and when H. S. Poulsen learned from the minister's brother that both the minister and the vice minister had been "quite satisfied," the situation initially appeared promising. Furthermore, both H. S. Poulsen and Ambassador Mørch of Denmark had been told that Prime Minister and Minister of Foreign Affairs Chou En-Lai, who was among Chairman Mao Ze-

dong's closest comrades in arms, had supported Chinese cooperation with Great Northern.[15]

When he had returned to Shanghai, H. S. Poulsen applied for an exit visa, which was immediately approved, but because of a more rigorous blockade of the harbors, he had to give up his planned journey. A draft agreement was therefore produced in Copenhagen and sent to H. S. Poulsen around the beginning of 1950, and Poulsen was given a power of attorney to negotiate an agreement. It was around this time that, as the first Western countries to do so, Denmark, Finland, Sweden, the United Kingdom, and Switzerland recognized the People's Republic of China.

H. S. Poulsen received the material from Copenhagen in the middle of February 1950, but a request for negotiations sent to the ministry of communications received no response. It was not until late May, after H. S. Poulsen had gotten the minister's brother to send a follow-up message, that Poulsen received a message in response to the effect that he should send his interpreter to Beijing with the company's proposal. H. S. Poulsen would have preferred to make the journey himself, but he did as the Chinese wished.

The Korean War and the closing off of China

When they had returned to Shanghai, the interpreter and the minister's brother reported that the government was no longer interested in the reopening of the cables. On the one hand, the wireless connections were adequate for China's immediate needs, and on the other hand, the People's Republic of China had concluded an agreement with the Soviet Union the previous year regarding an expansion of the landline connections between the two countries. Finally, the vice minister had noted that the company's cables had been landed in Nagasaki and therefore must be under the control of the Americans.[16]

That the company's station in Nagasaki had now become a problem was doubtless because on June 25, 1950, North Korean tanks and troops had crossed the 38th parallel and advanced into South

Korea. Following the Second World War, Korea had been divided into a Soviet zone of occupation in the north and an American one in the south, and by 1948, these two zones had become two independent countries. The North Korean leader, Kim Il Sung, was now attempting to unite Korea through military force, but two days after the invasion, it had been condemned by the United Nations Security Council, which encouraged the member countries of the United Nations to intervene on South Korea's behalf. The Soviet Union did not veto the Security Council's resolution, as the Soviet Union was boycotting the United Nations in protest against the fact that Chiang Kai-shek's government was still representing China as a permanent member of the Security Council, while the United States was blocking the admission of the People's Republic of China.

On June 30, the first United Nations troops entered South Korea under American leadership, af-

The Korean War, which broke out in late June 1950 and lasted nearly three years, gave the coup de grace to Great Northern's business activities in China; the Chinese government did not wish to reopen the cables because they had been landed in Nagasaki. The picture shows a South Korean border post at the thirty-eighth parallel a few weeks before it was crossed by North Korean troops and the war broke out. In the picture, South Korea is on the left; North Korea, including the valley in the middle, is on the right.

ter which the Soviet Union and China moved to support North Korea and the Cold War suddenly became hot. The situation was viewed with concern on Kongens Nytorv, but for the time being, H. S. Poulsen remained in Shanghai, though other personnel in China were reduced so that, other than H. S. Poulsen, there were only two employees left in Shanghai and one in Xiamen.

On September 30, 1950, the situation in Korea became even more tense when American-led United Nations troops crossed the 38th parallel and advanced northward. In the middle of November, the forwardmost American forces reached the Chinese border. This caused Chinese army units to cross the border to Korea and begin a major military offensive that brought them into direct conflict with American forces.

The two other telegraph companies had long since evacuated their entire staffs, and in January 1951, H. S. Poulsen and the lone Dane in Xiamen were summoned back to Denmark. However, the ministry of communications indicated around this time that it was not impossible that negotiations could soon begin, and H. S. Poulsen subsequently extended his stay. In late May, both he and Great Northern's management in Copenhagen decided that there was no point in waiting any longer, and in July 1951, H. S. Poulsen embarked on his homeward journey.

By this point, the company had summoned home the oldest of the two remaining Danish employees in Shanghai, and after H. S. Poulsen's departure, there remained only a single Danish functionary in Shanghai, Poul Arnvig, whose task was to "keep his foot in the door" and keep an eye on Great Northern's building and equipment, which were still being maintained by 20 Chinese employees.[17]

Great Northern's management at Kongens Nytorv adopted the attitude of waiting for the Korean War to end before once again beginning to attempt to open negotiations with the Chinese government. In the spring of 1952, however, the company received intelligence to the effect that the Chinese communists had begun an anticorruption campaign that was directed in part against foreigners and foreign companies. Chinese employees were pressured to denounce their foreign superiors, while company leaders were held responsible for their own actions and those of their predecessors. Foreigners were subjected to humiliating and undignified treatment, and there were also some arrests. Applications for exit visas were denied, and according to the Danish Ministry of Foreign Affairs a number of foreigners ended up "in serious difficulties."[18]

Great Northern's Chinese employees, too, held anti-corruption meetings, which resulted in a de-

mand that Poul Arnvig admit to capital extraction and tax fraud, as the rental revenues from Commercial Pacific and Cable & Wireless for their offices in the company's building in Shanghai had been paid abroad and not reported to the Chinese authorities.[19]

While these accusations had no consequences for the company or its remaining representative in China, foreign companies were shutting down their businesses in China and often having to surrender all of their assets and transfer additional payments in order to obtain exit visas for their personnel, and Great Northern had to recognize that the prospects of reestablishing the company's activities in China were not good.

In October 1952, via the Danish envoy in Beijing, Great Northern made a new attempt to get a clear answer from the Chinese. The Chinese response constituted a rejection of Great Northern's project "in view of the current global situation." Further probes in the spring of 1953 led to no progress, and on July 1, 1953, when a ceasefire went into effect in Korea, Great Northern decided not to contact the Chinese again but instead to wait and see how the situation would develop.[20]

A contributing factor in this decision was the reception of a confidential report from the Danish Ministry of Foreign Affairs on attempts by other Western companies to pull out of China. The liquidation of a company could drag on for years, and in the meantime the respective company's leaders were held hostage as a way of ensuring that there would be sufficient funds to pay the Chinese personnel, who could not be dismissed. Companies were confiscated along with all of their liquid and other assets, so the foreign owners were forced to transfer money to cover the living expenses of the staff until exit visas had been issued, which could take months.[21]

There was, then, much to be said for not forcing developments in general and in particular for not forcing the Chinese to take a position. In reality, Great Northern was shutting down its operations in China despite the fact that the company retained its buildings in Shanghai and Xiamen and continued to pay the salaries of Chinese personnel and that of a representative of the company. Rental revenues from Chinese companies using space in the building in Shanghai and the deduction of pension payments to previous Chinese employees meant that the net cost of "keeping a foot in the door" amounted to only 75,000 kroner annually. However, there was hardly anyone among Great Northern's management who seriously believed that the Chinese door would be opened again.[22]

Liquidation of Commercial Pacific

While Great Northern was seeking to reach an understanding first with the nationalist and from 1949 onward with the communist authorities in China, the company's American partner in Asia, Commercial Pacific, was moving toward its dissolution. Like Great Northern, the American company had been hit hard by the Second World War, and only the Guam–Midway–Honolulu–San Francisco cable connection had been reestablished by the beginning of 1946. Then there was the uncertainty about the future in China and Japan, and as an American company Commercial Pacific was particularly vulnerable.

This situation was reflected in the American company's annual account for 1945, which Great Northern's top management team, in an example of extreme understatement, characterized as "not good," and things got worse in 1946, when the annual account showed a deficit of 90,000 dollars—after 75,000 dollars had been transferred to the revenues from the interest yield from the reserve fund.[23]

This poor result caused Great Northern to consider the future of its involvement with Commercial Pacific, while Cable & Wireless waited to see how things would develop. In the spring of 1948, however, Commercial Pacific again presented an annual account showing a deficit—this time amounting to 209,000 dollars.[24] A decisive blow came when the cable between Guam and Midway was broken in the middle of August; the cable could not be reopened until the middle of April 1949. The cable break had occurred at a depth of almost six kilometers, and

the repair costs amounted to 760,000 dollars. Then came the Chinese revolution and the outbreak of the Korean War, and in the fall of 1950, when Great Northern and Cable & Wireless received a document from Commercial Pacific showing an operating deficit of 339,000 dollars for the first six months of the year, the two companies pulled the plug.[25]

At a meeting in London in November 1950, Great Northern and Cable & Wireless decided to propose to ITT, which owned a fourth of the shares in Commercial Pacific, that the company be liquidated "as soon as possible." The Americans did not wait long to back this proposal, but it required the approval of the American Telecommunications Coordinating Committee, which represented the communications interests of the United States' government and armed forces. Commercial Pacific was finally able to end its operations at the end of October 1951.[26]

It took a further year and a half before everything had been sorted out with regard to pension commitments, creditors, and the American authorities, and then Commercial Pacific could finally be liquidated in October 1953. The three shareholders received 39.4 percent of the share capital, 350,000 dollars of which went to Great Northern. On January 1, 1954, Commercial Pacific's office in New York closed, and an epoch in Great Northern's history—and that of American and international telegraphy—came to an end.

Charm offensive in Japan

With the shutting down of the company's operations in China and the liquidation of Commercial Pacific, Great Northern's position in East Asia had shrunk to the cable connection with Japan, where the company's presence was based on the American military authorities' directive, with which the Japanese government was openly and obviously dissatisfied. Eventually, the occupation would end and the Japanese would again take control of the country's international telecommunications connections, and Great Northern therefore made great efforts to build up a good relationship with the Japanese authorities.

In June 1953, Japan's young Crown Prince Akihito—the current Emperor of Japan—visited Denmark. In addition to meeting the Danish royal family, he met with Bent Suenson and the world-famous Danish physicist Niels Bohr at a dinner at Tivoli Gardens.

international department was in Paris together with two other high-ranking officials. Great Northern invited the delegation to spend five days in Copenhagen in early August, when they were invited to a dinner with Bent Suenson at his private residence. He and the company's other leaders could subsequently rejoice over the fact that after their return to Tokyo the three Japanese "expressed their great satisfaction with their visit to Denmark." No doubt the friendly reception of H. S. Poulsen in Tokyo and the delegation's indications of their great satisfaction with their visit to Copenhagen were expressions of ordinary Japanese politeness and etiquette. Nevertheless, the Danish charm offensive appeared to be paying off.[28]

In February 1950, the American military administration nullified all of its directives concerning the conditions for Japan's telecommunications, and on July 1 of that year, all licenses that had been granted to foreign companies were nullified. In September 1951, Japan and the Allies concluded an actual peace treaty, and in the same month, the Japanese telegraphy administration announced that it wished to begin negotiations with regard to a new contract with Great Northern, a prospect the company's leaders at Kongens Nytorv viewed with some uncertainty. "It is to be expected that the coming negotiations could be rather difficult," declared Bent Suenson.[29]

In the spring of 1949, H. S. Poulsen visited Tokyo, and he and the company's permanent representative in Tokyo, Ferdinand Lassalle, met both officially and privately with leaders and employees of the ministry of communications. Everywhere the two men were received "with the greatest accommodation and friendliness," and on Kongens Nytorv the top management team concluded that Poulsen and Lassalle had succeeded in establishing "an extremely good relationship with the Japanese authorities, which should have a significant effect on the company's position."[27]

The charm offensive continued in the summer of 1949, when the head of the Japanese ministry's

Before the negotiations began, the outbreak of the Korean War led to an economic upswing in Japan and an increase in trade both with Europe and with the United States. This was soon reflected in the traffic to and from Japan carried by Great Northern's cables, which by the fall of 1951 already exceeded the volume the company had experienced before the Second World War. Contrary to all expectations, Japan was becoming an important market, and in order to strengthen Great Northern's position vis-à-vis the Japanese authorities, Bent Suenson took what he himself described as a purely diplomatic visit to Tokyo.[30]

After Suenson's arrival in Tokyo, the minister of communications, whom Suenson had not expected to meet, gave a welcome dinner, during which the minister gave a speech where he reassuringly declared that the Japanese did not "expect to make major changes in their cooperation with Great Northern." Nevertheless, it later emerged that Japan was planning a reorganization of its entire telephony and telegraphy sector so that the operation of the country's international connections would be handed over to a private company. Despite the minister's reassuring statements, such a reorganization would necessarily influence the conditions under which Great Northern operated, and Bent Suenson therefore asked for a meeting with the general director of the telegraphy administration to discuss the possible consequences for the company despite the fact that this conflicted both with his intention to make a purely diplomatic visit and with etiquette.[31]

A meeting was immediately set up under the leadership of the vice minister and with the participation of the general director. To begin with, the vice minister assured Bent Suenson the Great Northern "should not be fearful," though he was not particularly specific, and the general director was less accommodating and reminded Bent Suenson that Great Northern's cable connections with Japan existed solely because of the American military authorities' directive. However, he expressed gratitude for the company's accommodation of the ministry's wishes after the war and declared "that the ministry was not interested in changing its policies now, after having shook hands with Great Northern."[32]

At the farewell dinner a few days later, the vice minister declared that Bent Suenson "should not make too much of the episode," but it was nevertheless with some concern that Bent Suenson returned to Denmark. He could report that he had been received with "strikingly great friendliness and hospitality even given the Oriental context," but on the one hand, the reorganization of Japan's international telecommunications connections created uncertainty, and on the other hand, it was clear that in the Japanese administration there were differing opinions regarding the administration's relationship with Great Northern.

Agreement with Japan

The reorganization was carried out on April 1, 1953, with the creation of Kokusai Denshin Denwa Company Limited (KDD), which took over all of Japan's international telecommunications connections. Already before this, Great Northern had sent the Japanese a proposal with regard to an agreement that would put the company in a better position, and at the same time, the company had played a somewhat risky card.

The peace treaty that had been concluded between Japan and the allies included a paragraph regarding war reparations, and Great Northern judged that there were good chances of securing compensation for lost revenues as a result of the confiscation of the cables in 1940. The Danish demand was set at 7 million dollars, an amount the company had no hopes of receiving, but after discussions with the Danish Ministry of Foreign Affairs and the Danish ambassador in Japan, the company intended to use the demand for compensation as a means of exerting pressure on the Japanese during the negotiations with regard to a new agreement.[33]

Great Northern was playing a dangerous high-stakes game, as the demand for compensation formally had nothing to do with the negotiations regarding an agreement—and certainly had nothing to do with KDD—and there was also a risk that the company would offend the Japanese by digging up the past. The presentation of the demand for compensation was carried out via the Danish ambassador in Tokyo, Lars Tillitse, and the Japanese response was predictable—that on the one hand they, KDD, rejected the company's proposed agree-

Bent Suenson during his first visit to Japan in April 1952. On the right-hand side of the picture is Great Northern's director, H. S. Poulsen, who had concluded the 1940 agreement regarding the nullification of the company's landing permit, and on the left-hand side is Director Sasaki of KDD.

ment and on the other hand the demand for compensation had nothing to do with KDD. KDD recommended that the company present its demand for compensation to the Japanese government and did not neglect to refer to the fact that Great Northern's resumption of its activities in Japan had taken place solely as a result of the actions of the American military administration and "was not welcome" in Japan.[34]

With regard to a new agreement, KDD proposed a reorganization of the distribution of traffic and fees between wireless and cables that would cause Great Northern to lose 1.5 million kroner in annual income and also mean that Finland, Russia, and Sweden would experience a significant loss of transit revenues, which could threaten the company's position in those countries. As the maintenance of the connection with Japan was "a precondition for the maintenance of [the company's] relationship with the other countries," Bent Suenson therefore decided to travel to Tokyo together with the director H. P. Andersen in February 1954.[35]

The two men spent a good four weeks in Japan, but they succeeded in reaching agreement on the basic questions, and Suenson reported on this at a meeting of Great Northern's board of directors on April 8, 1954. H. P. Andersen had remained in Tokyo to negotiate the final agreement so it could be signed on May 17, 1954. The contract had a period of validity of five years, after which it could be terminated by either of the parties with two years notice.[36]

In the meantime the matter of Great Northern's demand for compensation proceeded until, in September 1954, Japan's ministry of foreign affairs indicated in an oral communication to the Danish ambassador that Great Northern's demand was legitimate. The Japanese determined that payment of compensation amounting to 220,000 dollars would be appropriate—not the 7 million dollars at which the company had arrived. In order to achieve "the best possible relationship with the Japanese authorities and the Japanese government," Great Northern indicated that the company would be willing to reduce its demand, and in May 1955, Bent Suenson was back in Tokyo to encourage the conclusion of an agreement.[37]

The result was that the Japanese ministry of foreign affairs offered the company 833,000 dollars, which Great Northern accepted in July 1955. It was of decisive importance to Great Northern that the company reach a solution "that all Japanese authorities would find reasonable and satisfactory." Apparently Great Northern succeeded in this—in any event, Suenson wrote in his report to the board of directors that the Japanese ministry of foreign affairs had "expressed its hearty thanks and in particular its gratitude for the company's gentlemanly attitude." The Japanese ministry of communications and KDD had followed the negotiations closely and made statements Suenson interpreted as an expression of how "Great Northern [had] succeeded . . . in creating the good will [the company had] made an effort to generate."[38]

With the conclusion of the matter of war compensation, Great Northern and Japan had put the past behind them, so the mutual mistrust of earlier days was replaced by a new friendly tone and way of interacting. A decisive role in this connection had doubtless been played by Bent Suenson's trips to Japan and his personal involvement with and participation in the negotiations, which, according to an official who had then held a high position in the Japanese communications hierarchy, "changed what up to that point had been pretended friendly relations into real friendly relations in the true sense of these words."[39]

Slow shutdown in China

Paradoxically enough, the agreement with KDD became the reason why Great Northern finally decided to end its presence in China. In August 1954, H. P. Andersen traveled to China to propose the doubling of the trans-Siberian connection in order to be able to handle the constantly increasing traffic to and from Japan. In addition to acquiring an additional trans-Siberian line, the company wished to strengthen its cables in the Vladivostok area, which often suffered breakdowns.[40]

This was not the first time Great Northern had presented these wishes, but in contrast to earlier occasions they were now accommodated. When H. P. Andersen raised the question of a renewal of the company's concession, which would expire two years later, the mood was again positive, and in the middle of April 1955, after further negotiations, a new contract could be signed.[41]

The following month, Bent Suenson traveled to Tokyo to give KDD a brief overview of the agreements with the Soviet Union, and in November

1955, H. P. Andersen arrived in Tokyo to provide the Japanese with more detailed information. During his stay in Tokyo, H. P. Andersen asked KDD what KDD's position could be expected to be if Great Northern contacted China to ask about a possible reopening of the company's cables between Nagasaki and Shanghai. The response was "very clear and negative," namely that KDD was not interested in using the Danish cables to China, as the existing radio connections were more than adequate.[42]

The response from KDD was the coup de grace for Great Northern's engagement in China, and at a meeting of the board of directors in March 1955, Bent Suenson declared that "there was no longer any reason to continue to adopt a wait-and-see attitude." Raising the question with the Chinese again would certainly "lead to a decision to pull the company out of China," but this was the path the company now wished to take.

The Danish Ministry of Foreign Affairs took a similar view of the matter, and a unanimous board of directors decided "to continue handling the matter along the lines that have been proposed," as the minutes laconically put it. Great Northern's withdrawal from China, a country to which the company had introduced the telegraph seventy-five years previously and one that had been an axis of the company's existence as an international telegraph company ever since, had begun.[43]

However, it was one thing to make the decision and another thing to put it into effect. The first message from Great Northern to the Chinese related to the company's withdrawal from China was delivered by the Danish ambassador in Beijing in the summer of 1956 and proposed negotiations regarding the future use of Great Northern's cables. A response arrived in September, and the message was that China had gotten along quite well for fifteen years without cooperating with Great Northern and therefore had no desire to resume cooperation.[44]

In March 1957, Great Northern had a proposal with regard to a withdrawal process ready, and in late May, H. P. Andersen and Poul Arnvig traveled to Beijing to participate in the ambassador's pres-

Great Northern's station at Saint Helen's Place in London in 1952. Teleprinters are being used, and in general, the interior is very different from the interiors of the telegraph stations that could be seen before the Second World War.

entation of the proposal to the Chinese Ministry of Foreign Affairs. After this, there was a long period of waiting before, in March 1958, the Danish Ministry of Foreign Affairs received a note from the Chinese ministry of foreign affairs to the effect that Great Northern should negotiate with the postal and telegraphy authorities in Shanghai. H. P. Andersen again traveled to China, where the postal and telegraphy authorities refused to comment on anything at all. However, they did bring up the old demand for compensation for the period 1937–1941, when Shanghai had been occupied by the Japanese, to which H. P. Andersen responded that the compa-

ny had acted under force majeure and done what it could to protect Chinese interests.[45]

The Chinese pressed their demand, however, and they put the ball in Great Northern's court by requesting documentation of the company's assets and liabilities in China and a more specific proposal for Great Northern's withdrawal. This material was ready early in 1959 and featured a reduction of the company's assets to 5 million kroner that the company further reduced to half "as a contribution to a harmonious resolution." With regard to the years 1937–1941, the company noted that Great Northern itself had suffered significant losses as a result of dramatic inflation and several Chinese devaluations in the absence of corresponding rate increases, and the company therefore proposed that both parties abstain from presenting demands for reparations for the period in question.[46]

However, the Chinese did not feel that the Danish account was conducive to a harmonious withdrawal process. When H. P. Andersen presented the account to the postal and telegraphy administration in Shanghai in June 1959, the response was that the account was unacceptable. The Chinese proposed a new step-by-step negotiation process during which the parties would come to agreement regarding all unresolved payment issues, finishing with the matter of the years 1937–1941.[47]

The negotiations subsequently bogged down in procedural discussions, during which the Danish representatives proposed that the company's permanent representative in Shanghai should be permitted to return to Denmark when agreement had been reached with regard to everything but the years 1937–1941. The Chinese rejected this proposal out of hand, saying that "in accordance with the usual rules" he would not be allowed to leave China until all currently unresolved issues had been resolved. As Bent Suenson put it, the Chinese had taken "a hostage," so there was no alternative to accepting their proposed procedure.[48]

Shortly before H. P. Andersen's arrival in China, Great Northern's new permanent representative, Henry Kruse, had arrived in Shanghai, and it was his fate to become responsible for reaching an agreement with the Chinese. His first meeting with the telegraphy administration took place on July 22, 1959, but it was not until three and a half years later that Great Northern's withdrawal from China could be completed, most of the intervening time having been used for getting the Chinese to the negotiating table.

There was an unexpected breakthrough in the middle of May 1961, when the Chinese demanded that Great Northern give up its demand for compensation and devaluations during the years 1937–1941. After having consulted with Kongens Nytorv, Henry Kruse responded that if Great Northern were to do as the Chinese wished, the company would want the Chinese to abandon their own demand for compensation for the same period, which they did at a meeting in late May.[49]

After this, things went fast, and on December 9, 1961, the documents regulating the termination of Great Northern's activities in China were signed. The company left behind its building in Shanghai but received approximately 278,000 kroner that were paid into the company's account in Zurich in Swiss francs on January 8, 1962. This was a modest amount in the context of Great Northern's original account, but as Bent Suenson explained to the board of directors, "[i]t [was] unusual that a Chinese payment in free currency [was] received in connection with the withdrawal of a foreign firm from China."[50]

On January 18, 1962, Henry Kruse received his exit visa, and a few days later, he left China. Great Northern's existence in China was history, and in a look back, Suenson characterized the historic perspective from his paternal grandfather's mission back in 1870 and 1871.

"With the shutting down of the company's division in China, an epoch in Great Northern's history comes to an end. It was in East Asia and not least in China that in its first years the company carried out pioneering deeds that appear in an adventurous light and created the foundation for seventy years of activities in that country.

The first cable between Shanghai and Hong Kong was commissioned on 18 April 1871, and the telegraph connection between Europe and East Asia via Russia was opened the same year. The company's activities in China were stopped by the Japanese military on 8 December 1941, the day after Pearl Harbor."[51]

The final closure of the company's Chinese division, then, occurred ninety years after the opening of telegraph business in China and twenty years after the cessation of telegraph activity there.

Storno Radio Factory

CHAPTER 18

The first manufacturing activity

The coaxial cable to the United Kingdom was not the only light in the darkness the company's board of directors could sense. But while the telegraph activity was the subject of a detailed description at the general meeting in May 1949, the board of directors avoided dwelling on a new activity, manufacturing. The board referred briefly to the fact that a newly created division for the manufacture of shortwave radio equipment had begun limited activity and expected to make its first deliveries soon. The board did not mention that already in 1946 the company had acquired a cash register factory that—except for the real estate company—became Great Northern's first subsidiary.

The purchases of the cash register factory and the radio equipment factory were both expressions of the company's efforts to create a new future for Great Northern via manufacturing activity. This had started in 1939 with the purchase of the bloc of shares in Hellesens A/S, when the company's mission statement had stood in the way of a complete takeover of the factory and the investment had therefore been placed in the capital investments section of the annual account without more specific information.

Late in 1945, a new opportunity arose when Great Northern was offered a bloc of shares in a new limited company that was to manufacture a Swedish accounting machine. Members of Great Northern's board of directors were strongly interested in having Great Northern take over production itself, and when, while investigating the possibilities in this regard, the company was offered an opportunity to purchase a Danish cash register factory, A/S KARV, instead, Great Northern jumped at the chance.[1]

KARV had been founded in 1938, was based in the Nørrebro district of Copenhagen, and employed thirty to forty people. Every year the company had shown a deficit due to technical flaws in the construction of the machines. However, technical and economic evaluations had shown that there was potential for a significant improvement of KARV's operating economy, as a new type of cash registers had "really good and robust construction that appealed to the customers," and two electric models were soon to go on the market.[2]

In its decision, the board of directors emphasized that "the board had long wished to expand the company's manufacturing activity [. . .] and that the manufacturing in question was so closely related to the company's other production that it might later profitably be combined with that production."[3]

The board of directors was referring to the fact that early in the war the company's mechanical workshop, GNT Works, had expanded its production of telegraph apparatus and telegraphy instruments with the manufacture of control clocks. Late in 1942, a business specializing in the construction of control and signal clocks, Viggo Arp, acquired the sole right to manufacture the product line under the name STONO. After the war, when it became possible to resume selling telegraphy instruments, the production of control clocks continued.[4]

KARV's relationship with the company's GNT Works manufacturing activity was purely mechanical, and indeed it was clear to Great Northern's board of directors that its production lay "outside the company's [Great Northern's] area of experience." On the other hand, Great Northern's board of directors saw potential efficiency gains in the fact that it would be possible to unite the production types in one factory building on the island of Amager south of the core of Copenhagen, a building Great Northern had acquired in order to be able to move the apparatus factory out of the complex on Kongens Nytorv, in which it had been housed since 1879.[5]

The takeover of KARV was effected by liquidating the existing company as of October 10, 1946, and having the business taken over the same day by a newly created limited company, A/S Union Mekaniske Værksteder ("Union Mechanical Workshops"), with a share capital of 400,000 kroner. Great Northern owned shares for 397,000 kroner, while a director, H. L. Smith, who had acted as a straw man for Great Northern, owned the shares for the remaining 3,000 kroner. H. L. Smith became the chairman of the new company's board of directors, while the other board seats were occupied by the company's director and attorney. Because Great Northern's leaders wanted to keep Great Northern's involvement with the new company a secret, Great Northern was not represented on the new company's board of directors, and for the same reason, the investment was shown under capital investments in the annual accounts.[6]

The reason for keeping Great Northern's ownership of Union a secret was in part that it conflicted with Great Northern's mission statement and in part that knowledge of Great Northern's involvement with Union doubtless would provoke those shareholders who desired the liquidation of Great Northern. Under relevant law, a legalization of Great Northern's involvement with Union via a change in Great Northern's mission statement would require the support of 90 percent of Great Northern's shareholders, support that would be impossible to secure because of the wide geographic distribution of Great Northern's shareholders and because the names of those shareholders had not been recorded. In March 1947, Bent Suenson therefore again contacted Head Registrar Lage at the Limited Company Registry, and proposed what he characterized as "a minor change" in the mission statement.

On paper, the change looked reasonable enough, as the mission statement was to be expanded so in addition to telegraphy and related activities the company would engage in "the production and repair of telegraph and telephone apparatus and other electrical and mechanical apparatus and articles, etc., possibly by means of participation in other companies with similar goals."[7]

The head registrar indicated that he viewed the matter positively, but a few days later he warned Great Northern by telephone that not all of his colleagues felt that the change could be viewed as minor. Nevertheless, Great Northern sent the proposed change to the Limited Company Registry in the middle of April, and two weeks later the registry sent the company notification of its approval of the change. It is not clear what had happened behind the scenes, but the way had been paved for the presentation of the proposal at Great Northern's general meeting on June 27, 1947, when the change was justified with reference to the desire to "make possible a certain expansion of the company's manufacturing activity." No one spoke in opposition, and the proposal was unanimously approved.[8]

Despite the understated presentation, this was a very significant change, as the production of "electrical and mechanical apparatus and articles" was given status as an independent purpose on the same level as the telegraphy business. Great Northern's existence was no longer dependent upon the continuation of telegraphy activity.

STORNO

The change in the articles of association was hardly made solely for the sake of Union, which never became a profitable business and whose ownership remained a secret until the company was quietly liquidated in 1954. Rather, the move would have been made in order to create opportunities to get into manufacturing activity more generally, and in fact the change came at the right time, as this was around the time Great Northern was contacted by two Danish engineers, Erik Petersen and Svend Falck Larsen, who presented Bent Suenson with a forty-page document titled *Memorandum Ang. Firma for FM Tovejsradio* ("Memorandum Regarding an FM Two-way Radio Company"). The memorandum presented an ambitious project involving the formation of a Danish industrial business "with radio equipment in particular as its manufacturing focus," and in addition to a description of the technical basis and usage possibilities it contained a sketch of the formation, organization, and operation of the business.[9]

The radio equipment, which was based on shortwave technology—*VHF* for "very high frequency"—was to be used for two-way communication using so-called frequency modulation, or FM. This was a technology that was still in its infancy but was being used for regular radiophony transmissions in the United States and—the only other country where this was the case—Denmark, where Erik Petersen had been involved in the development work in Statsradiofonien ("the Danish Government Radiophony Authority," today the Danish Broadcasting Corporation) from the beginning.

FM technology had a number of advantages that made it well suited to two-way radio communication between mobile units, including constant signal strength, low weight, and low electricity consumption. Erik Petersen and Svend Falck Larsen

had already built a system that was used for a remote connection between the Frederiksberg Fire Department and one of its emergency response vehicles. This had resulted in the gaining of "valuable experience," and the Frederiksberg Fire Department had already ordered a further mobile system for an emergency response vehicle.

The technology could be used to create a two-way connection between a stationary mother station and a number of mobile units or between the mobile units themselves. There were numerous contexts in which the technology could be useful: It could be used by police and fire departments; in medical emergency response vehicles and by ambulance services; by the Danish National Railways; by physicians in rural areas; in electric, gas, and water service repair vehicles; in taxis; by the military; and by transport companies as well as, of course, in motor vehicles for commercial or private use.

Also, the technology could be used for mobile transmissions from transmitters so small that they could be carried in backpacks, a possibility Statsradiofonien had already exploited. Other use possibilities included two-way communication within shipping and aviation, and in the United States portable so-called walkie-talkies or Handie-Talkies were manufactured for military use and also for many other types of use. According to the two engineers, it was only in the United States that the new technology had reached the production stage, though a few factories in Europe were already carrying out relevant testing. There were, then, significant opportunities with regard to sales and exports for a company that was among the first to deliver usable systems.

The current situation was reminiscent of the one in which Great Northern had been contacted by the consortium behind Valdemar Poulsen's arc transmitter forty years previously, but now Great Northern had a different attitude. This project was not a competitor of the failing telegraphy business but would mean an expansion of the company's area of activity, in fact an expansion into a related business area based on electronic telecommunications. Given the company's years of efforts to establish itself in manufacturing activity, then, the approach by Erik Petersen and Svend Falck Larsen was the best Great Northern could have wished for.

By way of references, Erik Petersen and Svend Falck Larsen named the technical chiefs of Statsradiofonien and the Postal and Telegraphy Authority as well as the professor of weak-current technology at the Technical University of Denmark, J. Oscar Nielsen. All of these individuals, according to Bent Suenson, spoke "extraordinarily highly" of the two engineers.[10]

The top management team therefore did not hesitate to conclude a contract with Erik Petersen and Svend Falck Larsen, and the new company was founded on July 15, 1947. The immediate investment costs amounted to 1 million kroner, which was to be used primarily for laboratory equipment and salaries for engineers and other technically specialized employees—and no one knew how much more money would need to be invested before production could be begun.[11]

While it appeared obvious that there were positive business perspectives, the market situation and the situation with regard to possible competition were nevertheless uncertain. A completely new market had to be created from the ground up, as did a usable radio system. A number of foreign companies, for example in England, were already working with the same technology, and it could be difficult to secure permission to import the necessary components, particularly radio tubes, because of Denmark's shortage of currency. However, Suenson had been in contact with the Directorate for the Supply of Goods, which had indicated that it would take a positive view of the matter, as Great Northern would be manufacturing goods for export as well as for use in "socially useful institutions" such

To spread knowledge of its radio technology and its car telephones, Storno acquired a large van and outfitted it with equipment to demonstrate the system. The photograph shows the van in Oslo in 1949.

as fire departments, police forces, and ambulance services.[12]

The company also needed a transmitting permit, and in the middle of September 1947, Great Northern wrote to the General Directorate for the Postal System and Telegraphy and requested that the company be granted two frequencies to be used in testing the equipment, and the company also proposed a meeting for preliminary discussions of the use of the system at the national level.[13]

The General Directorate was accommodating, and the following month, Great Northern's board of directors voted to expand the business to include radio equipment based on ultrashortwave technology—UHF for "ultra high frequency." The extra investment for the first year was estimated to amount to around 100,000 kroner, primarily for the employment of several technicians including the engineer Leif Christensen, who had just returned to Denmark from the United States, where he had worked with microwave equipment.[14]

Erik Petersen and Svend Falck Larsen had wished to establish a limited company with themselves as leading engineers and part-owners but were convinced to accept that the business would be operated as a division of Great Northern for the time being. The business was established in the company's newly purchased building on Amager, while the manufacture of telegraphy instruments and control clocks remained on Kongens Nytorv for the time being. Svend Falck Larsen became the administrative head of the division, while Erik Petersen became the technical chief.

The name of the business was to be STONORA, but this name could not be registered for all types of goods, as it was too similar to a trademark that had already been registered. Instead, Great Northern chose the name Storno, which Great Northern had registered as a replacement for the name GNT Works in 1946 but never used.

"[K]nocks out the United States' car telephones"

It was with the name Storno that the new division demonstrated its new products at the Industrial Exposition in Forum, which attracted attention. "At the Great Northern Telegraph Company's stand innovations of a completely different kind from those for which that global Danish company is known were seen," wrote the industry newspaper *Dansk Radioindustri*. Next to the telegraphy materials from GNT Works, Storno presented a portable FM radio transmitter unit that could be carried in a backpack and a walkie-talkie system in radiophony quality. At the exposition, according to *Dansk Radioindustri*, there was "only praise for the excellent results Great Northern's talented engineers have achieved."[15]

It is clear that potential customers also saw Great Northern's new products positively, as Statsradiofonien ordered a number of mobile FM systems for ra-

dio transmissions, while P & T ordered VHF radio telephone systems for the airports in Kastrup, Aalborg, Tirstrup, and Rønne, to be used in communications with pilots during takeoffs and landings. None of the orders was effected in 1948, for which reason Storno had no revenues that year, but in May 1949, there were orders for 239,000 kroner, and the company began delivering Storno products over the summer.[16]

Storno's intended main product, mobile radio telephone systems for automobiles, had not been completely developed by the time of the industrial exposition, partly as a result of import difficulties. Early in 1949, however, the company had reached the point at which it could carry out the first tests in Copenhagen. With the permission of P & T, a base station was established at the top of a forty-meter-tall corn silo that had just been built in Nørrebro by Arbejdernes Fællesbageri ("the Workers' Common Bakery"), and the same year the first demonstrations for P & T and potential customers—and for journalists—were carried out.

The press coverage of Storno's products contrasted dramatically with the understated presentation at Great Northern's general meeting in May 1949. "Telephone at the wheel!" was the headline in *Social-Demokraten*, which continued, "The Storno radio factory is ready to begin serial production of radio telephone systems that are unparalleled on the global market." The newspaper's journalist, who had placed a call from a car radio telephone via the base station in Nørrebro, noted how quickly and easily the call had been placed and how "the connection had been just as clear as an ordinary telephone connection while the car was still being driven."[17]

The daily newspaper *B. T.* also expressed itself enthusiastically, in an article on how Storno had begun the production of its first car radio telephone in August 1949. "Denmark's fleet of cars is calling the whole world" was the article's headline. In the article's main text, it was reported that Denmark would probably be the first country in the world to solve the problems with the establishment of a public car radio network.[18]

The newspaper was enthusiastic because Storno had developed a system that made it possible to use a telephone with duplex technology—both ways at the same time—while other systems used simplex and necessitated switching between the sender and the recipient. It was also possible to make selective calls to a specific radio telephone to which other parties could not listen. Calls were made by calling a main station, after which one's call was transferred by Rigstelefonen, the Danish national telephone agency. If one received a call, a green light on the dashboard lit up and there was a buzzing sound. It was expected that telephony would soon be fully automated and that when this happened car telephones would only have to be equipped with rotary dials for them to work like ordinary telephones.

In the United States, which was the only country in the world in which radio telephones were used in private automobiles, work on developing duplex and selective calls was still ongoing, and the Danish newspapers' articles were therefore characterized by nationalistic pride. "Danish invention knocks out the United States' car telephones" was the headline in *Berlingske Aftenavis*, and the tone was the same elsewhere.[19]

In Sweden, too, the Danish car telephone attracted attention. *Teknikens Värld* described "a revolutionary Danish radio telephony system" and "sensational advances in the area of radio telephony" that made it possible to sit in one's car and speak to anyone via a telephone. After a test drive, the magazine's radio expert wrote that as a result of the frequency modulation the sound came through without noise and fluctuations in strength so that "the illusion of making an ordinary wired telephone call was total."[20]

In the industry magazine *Brandskydd* ("Fire Protection"), Hälsingborg's fire chief presented a sober article in which he particularly emphasized the system's "simplicity" and the duplex technology as well as the possibility of making selective calls. He also placed an order with Storno—probably the first—for a complete radio telephone system for the fire department in the Swedish city.[21]

Things did not go as quickly in Denmark, but Storno was optimistic. In *B. T.*, the engineer Knud Diemar, who was behind the selective calls, declared that in the foreseeable future Denmark would get a public telephone network for car radio telephones. The construction of approximately twenty-five base stations at elevated locations would be required to cover the country and achieve a capacity of five thousand users. Further development was dependent upon P & T, which would build up the network of base stations, and Knud Diemar predicted that socially useful functions would be prioritized and that private use would be a secondary priority.[22]

P & T had an eye on the new technology. In November 1949, P & T's chief engineer Niels Erik Holmblad declared in the course of a telephone interview with the Danish newspaper *Politiken* in which he participated from his car that "for the time being [P & T was] experimenting" but that a public network in Copenhagen would probably be opened in about half a year. This telephone interview, which was presented as "Interview no. 1 via the car radio telephone," was conducted via a radio station Storno had built for P & T on Amager Fælledvej. It was planned that the station would ultimately play a role in servicing Copenhagen, which could be fully covered by the addition of a further base station. P & T would subsequently proceed slowly, building stations in central and densely populated areas and along heavily trafficked main roads.[23]

P & T had not yet determined whether a car radio was to be rented like equipment used by ordinary telephony customers, who rented their equipment from the telephone companies. Niels Erik Holmblad estimated that the price of a car radio telephone would be 4,000 to 5,000 kroner, while a base station would cost 8,000 to 30,000 kroner, depending on the capacity. He did not know whether the system would become nationwide. "But let us see what it all leads to. The first experiences have been good."[24]

The first customers

Under Danish law, only police, fire departments, and medical emergency response personnel had permission to use car radio telephones. In March 1949, a revision of Radiospredningsloven, the Danish radio proliferation law, was proposed, and in this connection Niels Erik Holmblad stated that not everyone would be able to acquire a car radio telephone. "The system is not intended for relatively unimportant private conversations," he told *Politiken*, but people with a valid justification such as rural physicians could be granted permits after having sent an appropriate application to P & T.[25]

In November 1949, after the law had been passed, P & T issued a proclamation according to which providers of electric power, veterinarians and rural physicians, taxi companies, telephone companies, and certain other professional individuals or organizations could establish their own closed networks. In contrast, use by private companies and individuals would have to wait until a public network, which was to be operated by P & T, had been established.

Storno began receiving its first orders already before the proclamation had been issued. The systems could be provided with either duplex or simplex technology, and most customers chose the latter option, partly for economic reasons. The first permit to operate a system was issued to the so-called Lillebiler ("Little Cars"), which competed with Københavns Taxa ("Copenhagen Taxi"). A total of one hundred little cars were fitted with radio telephones that were connected with a base station at a common central dispatching station for all such little cars. The idea was that by calling a central number, customers could request a car that would be sent to the desired address.[26]

Københavns Taxa also considered putting radio telephones in its cars, but that company hesitated because of the cost and did not begin to install the system until November 1952. Aarhus Taxa purchased car radio telephones from Storno the following year, and by the middle of the 1950s, the taxi companies in several major provincial cities had begun using radio telephones. A factor that contributed to the sales success was that Storno sold its systems on installment payment plans, so the companies and drivers did not need to pay the entire purchase price at once.

Another group of customers was made up by electricity and other energy plants across Denmark. Among the first of these was Aarhus, Randers og Kaløvigegnens Elektricitetsselskab, ARKE, which provided electric power to most of Djursland. The system was supplied in May 1950 and consisted of a telephony center in the company's central electricity plant in Mesballe, an antenna mast on the 102-meter-high hill Bavnehøj, and five car telephone systems for the assembly vehicles. The price was 50,000 kroner, but the electric company believed it would soon recover this amount, as the company saved both time and money because the drivers did not need to return to the dispatching center to be assigned new tasks.[27]

Companies that bought car radio systems from Storno the following year included Nordsjællands Elektricitets og Sporvejs Aktieselskab (NESA, "North Zealand's Electricity and Tramway Company"), which received a system with a radio connection from the central transformer station in Vangede to four subordinated transformer stations. A radio connection to Nordvestsjællands Elektricitetsværk ("Northwest Zealand's Electricity Works") in Svinninge was also established, as was a system comprising radio telephone connections to—initially—five work vehicles. The main station's antenna was placed on top of a gas holder.[28]

Odense Kommunale Elektricitetsværk ("Odense Municipal Electricity Works") was among the six electric companies that received a radio telephony system in 1952, and by the end of that year, a total of eleven electric companies had acquired mobile radio telephony systems from Storno. In addition, P & T, Jydsk Telefon-Aktieselskab ("the Jutland Telephone Limited Company"), DSB (Danske Statsbaner, "the Danish National Railways"), Københavns Politi ("the Copenhagen police"), Esbjerg Dampvaskeri ("Esbjerg Steam Laundry"), Frederiksberg Fire Department, and Civilforsvaret ("the Civil Defense") were among the customers.[29]

In addition to car telephones, P & T acquired a radio chain system for the transmission of radiophony and telephony. In 1952, Civilforsvaret acquired the first stations that would become components of a nationwide radio chain system, and the same year, Storno delivered three radio chain systems to the Faroese telephone authority.[30]

Left: Storno's first car telephone installed under the dashboard in a Ford personal car. The radio transmitter itself was placed in the car's trunk together with the power supply.

Right: The car telephone's radio transmitter and receiver were housed together with the power supply in a cabinet that could easily fit in a normal personal car's trunk.

Portable radio telephone systems that could communicate directly with other portable radio telephones or with base stations also became part of Storno's assortment of products. This telephone—which was called a walkie-talkie—could be carried in one's hand or in a backpack. Among the first customers were Jydsk Telefon-Aktieselskab and P & T, and in 1952, the system was installed at the B & W shipyard to connect crane operators with the workers on the ground.[31]

The company's success in the taxicab sector in particular caused Storno to develop a new model called CAB with greater receiver selectivity so that the channels could be closer together and the capacity of the system could thus be increased. In 1953, fifteen taxi and little car companies bought more than three hundred radio car telephones of the new type, which was also used by nine electric companies, the Danish military, and Fyrdirektoratet (the Danish lighthouse authority) as well as the DFDS shipyard.

The same year, however, Storno began to notice that the company was not alone on the market for car radio telephones. An early competitor was the engineering company M. P. Pedersen, another Nordisk Svagstrøms Industri A/S ("Nordic Weak Cur-

rent Industry"). It was when the Danish subsidiary of the American electronics giant Standard Electric created a division for mobile radio telephony that Storno began really to feel the competition, though. In 1953, when Københavns Taxa wanted to acquire one hundred car systems, it was only after what Bent Suenson described as "very hard" competition that Storno won the order. According to its own claims, Standard Electric supplied an unspecified number of base stations and "several hundred" car telephone systems to taxis and other cars for hire all over Denmark.[32]

Denmark as a "first mover country"

While the number of private car radio telephone systems grew steadily, the construction of the pub-

Taxi telephone at a taxi stop in Copenhagen in the 1950s. Before Storno introduced its car radio telephones, the taxis in Copenhagen stopped at such taxi stops. This telephone was connected to the dispatch center, which could call the taxis at the stop if there were orders. Also, customers could use the telephone to call the dispatch center if there were no free taxis at the stop. In that case, the dispatch center would call other stops to find out whether there were any free taxis. This was a complicated and time-consuming process and caused the taxis to waste a great deal of time. Storno's car radio system made it possible for the dispatch center to call every individual car directly or all cars at once to find out whether there were any free cars and, if so, to send a car to a specified address.

lic car radio network went slowly. On August 11, 1950, P & T opened this network for a limited number of subscribers in Copenhagen. The base station was placed on top of Fællesbageriet's silo in Nørrebro, where Storno had had its testing transmitter. The system had only two channels, so its capacity was limited, but on the other hand, it was equipped with duplex technology. Among the first customers was the brewery Tuborg, which installed a Storno car telephone in a repair vehicle so the brewery's beer keg repair service could be sent out to customers who had problems with their beer keg systems.[33]

Supposedly, this was the world's first public car radio telephone network, and in fact the Swedish magazine *Populär Radio* identified Denmark as a "first mover nation" in May 1951, when it published a report on a test drive including a telephone conversation in one of Storno's cars. Regarding the car radio telephone itself, the article's author wrote that it was superior to the American models in that it offered both duplex and selective calls.[34]

It was expensive to become a car radio telephone subscriber. In addition to purchasing or renting the system, subscribers had to pay 40 øre per minute of talk time plus a further fee to Rigstelefonen and the local telephone company for calls going outside the local area. Thus far, there were only a few subscribers—according to the Swedish journalist, ten employees of Post & Generaldirektoratet (the Danish postal and general directorate) and a small number of private customers. However, Storno's intention was to build up a national network with the capacity for ten thousand subscribers—and in the long run to create a Scandinavian car radio telephone network with a common standard based on the company's own radio telephone.[35]

This is not how things ended up going. The Copenhagen car radio network remained in operation, but in its existing form, it never acquired more than twenty private subscribers. On the one hand, it experienced technical difficulties and was—despite the Swedish praise—not at all particularly user-friendly, and on the other hand, there was a limited market in a time of import restrictions on automobiles and given a very high price.

Export and military orders

While sales in Denmark were increasing sharply, Storno was working on getting a foothold on the export market for its three main products: mobile radio telephones, radio chains, and radiophony transmitting equipment. The company's first target was Sweden, where, in 1950, Storno got its first foreign representative, the radio electronics company Elektron AB. The order from the fire department in Hälsingborg for a complete radio telephony system was followed by corresponding orders from the Swedish national railroads, while the Royal Swedish Army Materiel Administration and the Royal Swedish Air Force Materiel Administration both acquired a number of walkie-talkie systems. Storno subsequently received orders for walkie-talkies for the Stockholm police and the Swedish telegraphy authority.[36]

In Norway, there was also an interest in Storno's products. In 1950, the police and fire department in Oslo wished to acquire car radio systems, but the negotiations had to be abandoned due to Norway's currency situation. In June 1951, Storno carried out a successful demonstration in Helsinki, and a short time later the company concluded an agreement with Finland's largest radio electronics company, A/S Helvar, regarding Helvar's becoming Storno's sole representative in Helsinki, which soon led to orders for portable radio telephones for the Finnish national railroads, among other orders.[37]

There was also foreign interest in Storno's mobile radiophony transmitting equipment, and systems were sold to the national radiophony authorities in Norway, Italy, Poland, Egypt, and Ireland. As Bent Suenson put it, the material passed "its test of fire" during the 1952 Winter Olympics in Oslo, and this led to further orders from the Norwegian Broadcasting Corporation.[38]

In 1953, Storno concluded a sole representation contract with a radio electronics company in Portugal, and negotiations were begun with a company in Johannesburg regarding a similar agreement for South Africa. A sales engineer traveled to Pakistan, Egypt, and Syria, and in Karachi, the capital of Pakistan, Storno negotiated regarding the delivery of a radio system to the Pakistani air force as well as an order for walkie-talkies for 750,000 kroner and other military car radio systems for about 600,000 kroner. Pakistan's economic situation was poor, however, so these orders were never in fact placed.[39]

Nevertheless, military customers both in and outside Denmark became a quickly growing market that offered a great deal of potential. Together with other Danish electronics companies, Storno participated in putting together a bid with regard to supplying a large network of microwave connections for NATO of a total of 8 million kroner. In communications with Bent Suenson, Minister of Finance Thorkil Kristensen (of Venstre, the Danish Liberal Party) confirmed the Danish government's interest and that the government would be willing to support the Danish companies via credit and foreign exchange guarantees, and there was also strong support from the Danish Industrial Council and the Danish army's signals service during the decisive negotiations during the first months of 1953.[40]

Nevertheless, Storno failed to secure the order. On the other hand, the Danish Ministry of Defense confirmed that a delivery of UHF radio equipment to the Danish air force that had previously been discussed with Storno could be viewed as definite. Also, Storno's work on the bid for the order for the American forces in Germany resulted in an order from the Danish army's signals service for one thousand walkie-talkies for a total value of 4 million kroner. This order was not for Storno's own portable radio telephones but for a sixteen-channel American Motorola AN/PRC 10 that was to be manufactured under license.[41]

Not giving up at the halfway point

Storno's increasing sales both in and outside Denmark did not result in an economic surplus. There are no separate accounts for the company for the 1950s, and in Great Northern's overall annual account the firm's revenues, together with those of GNT Works, are shown under the heading "various revenues," a category that also contained revenues from other sources including revenues from the renting out of cable steamers and buildings. A factor that had contributed to this state of affairs was that Storno feared that the poor results could be exploited by the company's competitors to damage Storno's reputation.

At the meeting of Great Northern's board of directors on March 20, 1951, however, Bent Suenson calculated that the accumulated deficit since Storno had been established amounted to 868,000 kroner, of which 372,000 had been accounted for by the most recent year. Revenues from sales for that same year amounted to only 264,000 kroner, but on the other hand, the company had current orders for 2.8 million kroner, of which 1.7 million kroner were accounted for by a recently placed order from Civilforsvaret.[42]

The factory then had plenty of work to keep it busy, and the numbers show how because of the relatively long periods that elapsed between the placement of some of the larger orders and the respective deliveries invoicing and payment would not always occur already during the year in which the order in question had been placed and how the results could consequently vary greatly from year to year. In 1951, for example, Storno received orders for 2.75 million kroner, but revenues amounted to 1.3 million kroner. In 1952, the value of orders received fell dramatically, to 724,000 kroner, while revenues increased sharply, to 2.3 million kroner, because of earlier orders.[43]

The modest volume of orders received in 1952 and the poor operating results caused concern among Great Northern's board of directors, which discussed the situation at a meeting late in the year. Bent Suenson felt there was a need for a new leader with "practical and industrial and commercial experience," and other members of the board agreed with him.[44]

The minutes of the meeting indicate that the engineer Per Kampmann found it necessary to underscore that "it was by no means surprising that a new business such as Storno would have difficulties during its first years," and this suggests that some board members felt deep pessimism with regard to Storno's future. One should not give up when Storno was halfway to its goal, Per Kampmann felt, "but of course it was of decisive importance that the right leader be found."[45]

On April 1, 1953, Storno got its first director, Tage Nielsen, who came from Hede-Nielsens Fabrikker ("Hede-Nielsen's Factories") in Horsens, which had more than six hundred employees and manufactured television sets and radios. The employment of Tage Nielsen by Storno might have been the reason why Svend Falck Larsen, who had had the title of administrative head, left the company to take a job with NATO's Production and Logistics Division. The other of Storno's two founders, Erik Petersen, remained with Storno, as did Leif Christensen, who led the company's development work.[46]

The employment of a director did not lead to the desired improvement. Despite the fact that "1953 saw increased activity in the home market and in the export markets," the annual result was poorer than the one for the previous year. Revenues declined by 400,000 kroner to 1.9 million kroner, and the operating result was a deficit, the size of which is not specified in the annual account.[47]

However, the year was saved by the fact that the expected orders from the Danish army's signals service for one thousand walkie-talkies valued at 4 million kroner were finally signed late in the year, which tripled the value of orders received that year, bringing the total up to 6 million kroner. A problematic aspect of this situation, though, was that the orders would not be reflected in the operating result before 1955, when deliveries were supposed to begin. The orders were subsequently delayed so that deliveries did not in fact begin until 1957. The reason was the relevant ongoing technical development, which caused the army to postpone fulfillment of the order twice in order to get the latest model.[48]

Global product without a surplus

There was no major change in the trend in 1954, though there was a steady stream of orders for car stereo systems from both previous and new clients, including an order from Falcks Rednings-korps ("Falck's Emergency Response Corps"), and one from DSB (Danske Statsbaner, the Danish National Railways) for the train ferries. Not much happened on the export markets, however, and this caused the company to replace its agents in Norway and Sweden.

The situation did improve the following year, though, when the volume of orders received increased by 55 percent and the revenues by 37.5 percent. Among the new customers was Rigshospitalet (the Danish national hospital) and the daily newspapers *Politiken* and *Berlingske Tidende*. The security company Danske Securitas A/S and Københavns Frihavn (the Free Port of Copenhagen) were also among the new customers, as were a number of physicians and veterinarians across Denmark. Among the biggest customers was Rigspolitiet (the Danish national police force), which bought radio equipment, including mobile radio telephones for use on motorcycles. Following a round of bidding, Storno received an order for more than 200,000 kroner, and an earlier oral agreement for an order valued at 500,000 kroner was finally realized. The company also received an order from Nordisk Mineselskab ("Nordic Mine Company") for devices to be used in Thule on Greenland and an order from the Ministry for Greenland.[49]

There was progress on the export markets as well, after Storno had begun making systematic efforts to represent the company via stands at expositions and trade fairs as well as participation in rounds of bidding for orders around the world and the establishment of a network of agencies. Storno received orders from Norway, particularly from Civilforsvaret (the Norwegian Civil Defense) and taxi companies as well as the telegraphy authority, while orders from Finland included ones from organizations including the Finnish police and air force. In Sweden, it was difficult to compete because there were several domestic suppliers, including L. M. Ericsson AB, but Storno nevertheless sold products there for approximately two

hundred thousand kroner. Equipment was supplied to an engineering firm in Iceland.

Storno received orders from Ireland for more than 600,000 kroner, a third of which was for radio systems for the airports in Dublin and Shannon. The company sold products for 110,000 kroner in the Netherlands, including a car telephone system sold to Royal Dutch Shell for use on New Guinea. Only modest results had been achieved in Germany, but the company had achieved some sales via an agent, including the sale of systems to a whaling company owned by the Greek shipowner Onassis. In Egypt, the company participated in several major rounds of bidding for orders but secured only small orders for the fire departments in Cairo and Alexandria. In South Africa, too, the company participated in rounds of bidding and secured small orders while the police in India appeared to want to place an initial order to sample Storno's products.[50]

The company's turnover for 1955 was its highest ever, and this was the year in which the company received its most valuable group of orders to date, orders that provided Storno with work and secured the company's revenues for the following year. The company's successes continued in 1956 with an increase in the value of orders received to 4.7 million kroner and an increase in revenues by more than a third, to 4.5 million kroner. Among Storno's spectacular deliveries was a specially developed VHF system for use by Shell in tropical areas in New Guinea, Borneo, and Sumatra and fixed and mobile telephone systems for Artic Contractors, to be used on the American base at Thule in North Greenland and by Norwegian whalers in Antarctica.[51]

Storno's success was noticed by the public. "Danish radio equipment has become a global article" was a headline in *Danmarks Handels- og Søfart-Tidende*, which reported that private companies and public institutions in seventeen countries "[were using] these Danish quality products." Most recently, the company had developed a radio telephone system for use at sea that quickly gained widespread use.[52]

Great Northern was not satisfied, however, for despite the successes, Storno's operating result was still unsatisfactory, and at Great Northern's general meetings, only brief mention was made of Storno's development. Bent Suenson's private diagnosis was that the causes of the problems were rising costs and that "getting the production through the factory [was] not going well." He was dissatisfied with Storno's leadership, and in the fall of 1955, he asked a streamlining consultancy company to examine Storno's processes from one end to the other and seek to increase efficiency.[53]

The streamlining report was presented to Great Northern's board of directors in September 1956 and confirmed Bent Suenson's belief that a number of situations particularly with regard to cost control and pricing calculations were "extremely unsatisfactory" and that a change in Storno's leadership was needed. The board of directors approved of the fact that efforts had already been begun to find a replacement for Tage Nielsen, who was given notice that he would be dismissed at the end of the year.[54]

The increasing volume of orders meant that an expansion of the factory would be necessary if Storno was not only to maintain acceptable delivery periods but also have adequate space and offer reasonable working conditions. Such an expansion was expected to cost approximately 800,000 kroner, and despite the company's poor economic state the top management team was authorized to proceed with the project, which in fact ended up costing 2 million kroner.[55]

New leadership and transformation into a branch

It took time to find a new director, and in the meantime, the Great Northern board member and director of Hellesens A/S Poul Norsman agreed to work on improving the leadership situation. This led to discussions regarding the possibility of transforming Storno into a limited company "in order to make it easier for the new leader and create a clearer situation with regard to the placement of authority and responsibility," as Bent Suenson put it.[56]

In June 1957, Great Northern placed an advertisement in the national daily newspapers and in *Ingeniøren* for the position of a director who would lead the transformation of Storno into a limited company as well as the expansion of the company. The job advertisement noted that the technical side of Storno was "highly developed" and that in connection with the choice of a candidate there would be a particular focus on "development of the commercial and administrative part of the business, a very great deal of the revenues from which comes from exports."[57]

Børge Bentsen became Storno's new director on December 1, 1957, and at the same time, Poul Norsman was appointed representative of Great Northern's board of directors at Storno. At the same time, it was decided that the transformation of Great Northern into a limited company would be put off until the following year—perhaps even until the end of that year—so that Børge Bentsen would be able to participate in establishing the new company's initial status. For the time being, Storno was registered with the Limited Company Registry as a branch of Great Northern with Børge Bentsen as its branch director and sharing the right to sign on behalf of the company with Erik Petersen. Also, for the time being, "an informal board of directors" of Storno was created consisting of Bent Suenson and Niels Erik Holmblad as well as the member of Great Northern's board of directors and director of Superfos H. Stevenius-Nielsen and Poul Norsman. However, the transformation of Storno into a limited company was not in fact carried out—the records of Great Northern's board of directors give no reason for this, though there is a suggestion that tax considerations may have played a role.[58]

Storno therefore continued its existence as a branch of Great Northern and was required to maintain a separate account for the business that was to be presented independently, but there was no legal requirement that an annual report be presented as there was in the case of limited companies. Great Northern remained fully responsible for Storno's liabilities, but the intention behind the transformation of Storno into a branch was never-

Storno's development was characterized by constant growth and progress; the company's development and production facilities were continually enlarged. The picture shows the celebration of the completion of a new factory hall in October 1957.

theless to get the business to act like an independent company to a greater extent.

While Storno did not become a limited company, then, the business nevertheless ended up having a kind of opening balance after depreciation of inventories and other assets of 1.3 million kroner. In connection with the discussion by the board of di-

rectors of the branch's first annual account, the one for 1958, Bent Suenson declared that "the currently greatly depreciated status values must be viewed as the values for which Storno's leadership would be responsible in the future"—and then he added that "at the same time it should be remembered that the amounts invested were in fact significantly larger." The previous year he had presented to the board of directors a document that indicated that over the years Storno had cost Great Northern 13.7 million kroner in investments. Now the time had come for the business to stand on its own feet.[59]

New Cables in the North Atlantic and Modernization in the Far East

CHAPTER 19

Deep Freeze and the North Atlantic connection

While Storno was expanding and increasing its sales both in Denmark and on the export markets, Great Northern's telecommunications business was spinning its wheels. To be sure, the traffic and thus the revenues were increasing, and the capacity of the Weybourne cable was increased several times, but there were no new cable projects, as the establishment of undersea cables in Europe became a matter for national governments.

As long as Storno was not generating a surplus, however, it was the revenues from the telecommunications operations that, together with the revenues generated by capital investments, kept Great Northern alive and ensured an annual surplus. Because of this situation, the company's leaders paid more attention than usual when, early in 1954, they learned of plans that could constitute a threat to the company in its European core area.

On February 18, 1954, Bent Suenson informed Great Northern's board of directors that "there are signs that a secret American cable project involving

the establishment of a new transatlantic telecommunications connection via Greenland, Iceland, the Faroe Islands, and England is at a fairly advanced stage." If completed, the project would realize the North Atlantic cable project that had been a part of C. F. Tietgen's original visions, but what was worse was that a coaxial cable between Iceland and Great Britain would be the coup de grace for Great Northern's outdated 1906 Iceland cable and mean a loss of both prestige and revenues for Great Northern.[1]

In June 1954, before Suenson had investigated the matter further, Great Northern's director in London was informed "orally and in strictest confidence" by an official in the British telegraphy administration that there were plans to lay a coaxial cable between the Shetland Islands and Iceland. The official could not tell Great Northern's director who was behind the plan, but he said that the cable would be owned by the British, though they would not pay for it. The plan was so secret that it was not to be mentioned even to the Icelandic telegraphy administration.[2]

Bent Suenson assumed this was a NATO project, and in fact NATO was behind the laying of a coaxial cable between Great Britain and Norway around this time, a cable for which the British telegraphy administration was officially responsible. During a visit to Kongens Nytorv in August 1954, the Icelandic general director confidentially confirmed that something was up by reporting that the Americans had told him about the plans for a cable between Iceland and the Shetland Islands. Apparently the Icelanders did not take the plans seriously, but Suenson did, and he wanted to contact the British "in order to find out more about the matter and protect the company's interests."[3]

Suenson managed to find out that the project in question was called Deep Freeze and had been presented by the Commercial Cable Company, an American company that was a part of ITT—and a former partner of Great Northern in connection with the Pacific cable. The project had originally been presented to the British as purely military in nature, but it had soon proved to be the case that the project in fact had a primarily commercial purpose and that the military aspect was reflected in the fact that the United States Armed Forces were to lease a number of channels corresponding to 11 percent of the cable's capacity.[4]

It was not until the middle of August 1954 that the Danish government was confidentially informed of the cable project by the American embassy in Copenhagen. Corresponding information was provided simultaneously in the United Kingdom, Iceland, and Canada, and the Americans indicated that in addition to meeting the communication needs of the United States Air Force and NATO, the cable also had a commercial purpose. To begin with, the Americans were asking for permission to carry out surveys of stretches of coastline in Greenland to find suitable places to land cables and establish a station.[5]

The permission of the Danish government was given on September 1 after a meeting at the Danish Ministry of Foreign Affairs in which representatives of the Prime Minister's Office and the Department for Greenland, the Ministry of Defense, the Ministry for Public Works, and the General Directorate for Postal and Telegraphy Systems participated. In the response sent to the Americans,

The Icecan cable, which Great Northern participated in laying in the early 1960s, was brought ashore at Frederiksdal at the southern tip of Greenland. As is indicated by the picture, conditions on the coast were problematic, which made the landing of the cables difficult.

which was approved by Acting Prime Minister Viggo Kampmann, it was emphasized that the granting of permission to carry out the desired surveys did not mean the project itself would necessarily be approved by the Danish government. The Danish response also drew the Americans' attention to the fact that the cable could conflict with the interests and concessions of the Great Northern Telegraph Company. Despite the Americans' desire for confidentiality, the Danish government therefore intended to inform the company.[6]

The American embassy's reaction came in a note to the Danish Ministry of Foreign Affairs of September 8, 1954, that strongly emphasized the project's "high priority" and its military necessity both for the United States and for NATO. Because of this military necessity, the project was fully supported by the United States government.[7]

Nevertheless, the Danish authorities were skeptical as a result of the project's commercial content, the extent of which was unknown. That skepticism was proved justified when the president of the Commercial Cable Company, Admiral Ellery W. Stone, came to Denmark late in September 1954. At a meeting at the General Directorate for Postal and Telegraphy Systems, the admiral emphasized that the project would not be carried out if the commercial circuits were eliminated from it, which caused the Danes to conclude that "with regard to all important aspects the cable project must be viewed as a civilian matter."[8]

The project involved the establishment of a station in Greenland, which the United States Air Force insisted was to be manned by employees of the Commercial Cable Company. However, Denmark was not willing to permit foreign companies to carry out commercial activities in Greenland, and Admiral Stone was notified of this at a meeting at the Danish Ministry of Foreign Affairs on November 9, 1954. At a meeting at the General Directorate the following day, he was informed that the Commercial Cable Company would have to conclude an agreement with Great Northern that ensured that Great Northern's interests would be protected.[9]

With regard to Great Northern, Admiral Stone declared "that he had an excellent relationship with the company and was in no way interested in competing with it," and he also assured Bent Suenson of this at a meeting at Great Northern's headquarters. However, Bent Suenson doubted that the project would leave room for the continued operation of Great Northern's Iceland cable, and at the meeting at the General Directorate Admiral Stone indeed indicated that he saw no reason for Great Northern to continue operating that cable.[10]

Denmark's prime minister was continually provided with up-to-date information regarding the matter, which was sensitive as a result of the American government's emphasis on the project's military significance, an aspect the United States' embassy and Admiral Stone underscored again and again. The Danes avoided rejecting the project outright, but this was not true of all of the governments involved. Canada and the United Kingdom rejected the project out of hand because of its commercial character. The previous year, the two countries had concluded an agreement with regard to the laying of the first transatlantic telephone cable, TAT 1, and they saw no need for a further such cable—and particularly not for an American one that would more than double the capacity of the transatlantic connections.[11]

The governments of both countries were subjected to strong American pressure, and finally, in the spring of 1955, they gave in and announced that they were willing to issue landing permits—but only for a purely military cable. This killed the Deep Freeze project and caused the plans to be shelved—but only for a time.[12]

Military and civilian communication needs in the North Atlantic

The American armed forces' wish to lease channels in the now shelved cable was a reflection of the fact that Greenland, Iceland, and the North Atlantic had generally taken on an important role in the military strategy of the Cold War. After the detonation of the Soviet Union's first atomic bomb in 1949, the Americans had become aware of the danger of Soviet air attacks via the Arctic region—and of the potential for American attacks on the Soviet Union via this same region. The North Pole lies exactly halfway between New York and Moscow, and because of this having a military presence in Greenland in particular but also in Canada and Iceland became a central component of American defense strategy.

In April 1951, the United States and Denmark concluded an agreement regarding the establishment of American military bases in Greenland, and the same year the United States began construction of Thule Air Base, which was to be used by American strategic bombers and surveillance planes. The United States concluded an agreement according to which the American military would defend Iceland, and in 1951 the United States also returned to Keflavik Airport near Reykjavik, which the United States had left in 1947 after a World War II–era agreement according to which the United States would have defended Iceland against Germany had expired. Now there was a new enemy.

Given their development of a strategic defense system and a strategic offensive capability vis-à-vis the Soviet Union, the American armed forces and NATO came to need stable and secure communications connections between North America on the one hand and Greenland and Iceland on the other hand, and onward connections from Greenland and Iceland to Great Britain were also needed.

At the same time a corresponding interest in such connections developed in the area of civilian aviation. When the Commercial Cable Company was trying to get Deep Freeze realized, the International Civil Aviation Organization (ICAO) identified a number of requirements for air safety with regard to telecommunications in the North Atlantic as a result of the now considerable and constantly increasing air traffic in the area between Europe and North America. A milestone event in this connection was SAS's flight over the North Pole en route from Copenhagen to Los Angeles late in 1952; no airline had previously flown this route.

A central wish was the wish for the development of reliable telephone, telex, and telegraph connections via both Iceland and Greenland. Such connections could not be established using the existing radio technology, which was sensitive to the aurora borealis and other weather phenomena, for which reason service disruptions—so-called polar blackouts—lasting up to several days could occur, a problem that was also of concern to the American armed forces and NATO.

The optimal solution would be a cable connection using the route that would have been used by Deep Freeze, but on the one hand the costs for such a connection would be so great that they could not be borne by the ICAO and on the other hand there were major technical difficulties associated with landing cables in Greenland. Americans were therefore working on the develop of a new wireless ionospheric forward scatter technology that would not be vulnerable to polar blackouts.[13]

Regardless of which technological solution would be implemented, it was clear to Great Northern's leaders on Kongens Nytorv that in the foreseeable future the increasing both military and civilian needs would lead to the establishment of communications connections in the North Atlantic that accommodated telegraphy, telex, and telephony. It was to be expected that unless Great Northern succeeded in involving itself in a North Atlantic project, this would lead to the closing of the company's Iceland cable.

At the same time, Great Northern had to confront the fact that with the exception of the Weybourne cable the company's entire existing cable system was out of date. Cable and in particular amplifier technology was being developed at a rapid pace, and the use of telex connections was increasing rapidly. If Great Northern's telecommunications business was to have a future, it would therefore require a general modernization of the company's cables, a prerequisite for which would be the addition of individuals possessing technical expertise to the company's management.

In the fall of 1954, Bent Suenson therefore recommended to Great Northern's board of directors that the company again have a technical director, and he recommended P & T's chief engineer, Niels Erik Holmblad, for this position. In a conversation with Suenson and Great Northern's board chairman, Holmblad had indicated that he would be interested in taking on such a role.

The board of directors approved the establishment of the position without much discussion, and on September 1, 1954, when Niels Erik Holmblad assumed the position, Great Northern again had a top

SAS's DC-6B *Arild Viking*, the first passenger airplane to fly over the North Pole. The plane took off from Los Angeles on November 19, 1952, with twenty-two VIP passengers and set course for Copenhagen, where it landed twenty-eight hours later. This opened up a new era in international aviation and created a need for international telecommunications connections in the North Atlantic, which Great Northern exploited when the company laid cables between Great Britain and the United States via Iceland and Greenland.

management team with more than one director. However, the two directors were not equal as they had been in the past. This was emphasized by the fact that "to establish his leading position in day-to-work" Bent Suenson was given the title of chief executive officer—thus becoming the first the company had had since Edouard Suenson had resigned back in 1908.[14]

Swedo-English coaxial cable in the shadow of the Americans

While Great Northern was following the American attempts to force Deep Freeze upon other countries, the company took the initiative in connection with a new cable project of its own in June 1954, when the board of directors voted to propose to Sweden and the United Kingdom that a coaxial cable in-

tended for telex and telegraph traffic and possibly also telephony be laid between the two countries.[15]

The company's cable plans were first officially presented to the Swedish telecommunications authority at a meeting in Stockholm in October 1954, a way of proceeding that was not without risk. The Swedish telecommunications authority had repeated indicated that it wished to take over the company's cables, but the United Kingdom had opposed such a takeover. The Swedish traffic gave Great Northern annual fee revenues amounting to approximately four million kroner, which represented a third of the company's total fee revenues, and if the Swedes and Britons agreed to lay a coaxial cable themselves, these revenues would be lost. On the other hand, Great Northern's only possible means of retaining the Swedo-English traffic in the long run was the laying of a coaxial cable, so there was no alternative to presenting the proposal and risking inspiring the Swedes and Britons to lay such a cable themselves.[16]

The Danish delegation was greatly gladdened by the fact that the Swedish reaction was extremely positive, and it was agreed that Great Northern would contact the British administration and that the Swedish Telecommunications Authority would follow up with a visit to London. According to Bent Suenson's report, the Swedish general director had assured the Danes that the Swedes "had a significant interest in the new cable and that Great Northern could rest assured that this would be expressed."[17]

In contrast to the Swedes' accommodating attitude, the proposal's reception in London was a disappointment. Already in response to an initial inquiry early in November 1954, the British vice general director expressed himself "very cautiously." He indicated that the question of the foreign telecommunications companies' position in the United Kingdom was sensitive as a result of the controversy surrounding the Deep Freeze project, which had provoked strong resistance by the Post Office and discussion of the position of particularly the American but also other foreign countries' telecommunications companies.[18]

During more detailed discussions late in the month, the British were "very cool," and Bent Suenson was informed that the proposal was "inconvenient" because of the ongoing negotiations with regard to Deep Freeze. However, he was assured that London continued to have "friendly feelings toward the company" and that there were no British plans to terminate cooperation with Great Northern. The problem was the Americans, as granting a landing permit to Great Northern would set a precedent in relation to a possible American cable, and in general the British wished to keep American telecommunications companies out.[19]

It was only late in November 1955, after a year of negotiations in London, Copenhagen, and Stockholm, that Great Northern received notification from Sweden that the Swedes and the Britons had agreed upon "a negative attitude" so that the British would be able to say no to the Americans. At the same time, Bent Suenson was invited to Stockholm for a meeting on December 6—the day after Sweden and the United Kingdom were to make their final decision. In a letter, the British telecommunications minister had previously assured the Danish ambassador to the United Kingdom that[20] the company can be quite sure that in considering its proposals we shall not forget the excellent service that they give and our long cordial relationship with them.

Indeed the British did not forget these things; at the meeting in Stockholm, Bent Suenson was assured that after the coming Swedo-British government cable had been opened in 1960 Great Northern would be ensured a certain portion of the resulting traffic. The Swedes and Britons would determine later how this would be accomplished.[21]

This all ended with a leasing agreement concluded in the fall of 1959. In return for paying 25,000 pounds sterling annually, Great Northern was able to lease twelve channels in the Swedo-British cable. The capacity made it possible for the company to shut down its two remaining cables and its station in Newcastle, which gave Great Northern savings corresponding to the lease fee. It remained possible to send telegrams between Sweden and Great Britain "via Northern," and Great Northern found the leasing conditions "reasonable." However, it was with a certain melancholia that the company accepted no longer having its own cables.[22]

Coaxial cable between Iceland and Scotland

There was further confirmation that the British were sincere about recognizing the positive aspects of their many years of collaboration with Great Northern and that the Americans were the problem when the matter of the North Atlantic connection came up again. In the summer of 1956, sufficient progress had been made in the United States with the new ionospheric scatter technology that an official plan was presented to the ICAO for a wireless North Atlantic telephony, telex, and telephony system, which caused the Icelandic directory of telegraphy to contact Great Northern.

Iceland wished to exploit an ICAO connection in order to carry out a modernization of the country's international telecommunications connections, which were connected to Europe via Great Northern's cable to the Shetland Islands as well as a radio telephone connection via the Faroe Islands and to the United States via radio connections. If the desired modernization were carried out, the new connections were to be given adequate dimensions to cover the needs of both Iceland and the ICAO as well as being able to respond to possible wishes from NATO and other defense organizations.[23]

Iceland's problem was that the country did not have sufficient currency to finance the fulfilment of its wishes, and the Icelandic government therefore wanted to continue its cooperation with Great

Northern in the expectation that the company would carry the economic burden in return for being assured of the Icelandic government's support in connection with protecting Great Northern's interests in the region.

A scatter connection between Scotland and Iceland was estimated to cost 10 to 11 million kroner, and it was uncertain whether the traffic generated by such a connection would cover the costs of establishing and operating it. Great Northern itself preferred a connection that would be a few million kroner more expensive to establish but cheaper to operate and more reliable. In any event, however, it was of decisive importance that Great Northern become involved in the project, as the company would otherwise be left with only its old cable, which would "be the beginning of the end of all of the company's activity in the region."[24]

In October 1956, Niels Erik Holmblad therefore traveled to the United States to take a closer look at the scatter technology, and at the same time Great Northern asked an American engineering consulting company to investigate the technical and economic possibilities with regard to a potential alternative project. One such possibility would involve the use of UHF-based tropospheric forward scatter technology, which did not have the range of the ionospheric forward scatter technology but offered a significantly greater capacity.

Both the investigation carried out by the American consulting company and that carried out by Niels Erik Holmblad himself, however, raised doubts with regard to the quality of both systems, and the respective operating costs for both systems would be greater than the costs for a cable solution. On December 4, 1956, Great Northern's board of directors therefore voted to propose to the ICAO the establishment of a new cable connection between Iceland and the Shetland Islands and an option for the ICAO of leasing the desired number of channels for use in connection with civilian aviation.[25]

The British telegraphy administration had reached the same conclusion, and at a meeting with Great Northern in London on December 11 in which the Icelandic general director and representatives of P & T also participated, there was general agreement on presenting a proposal for a cable solution before the ICAO would take a position on the American scatter proposal at a meeting in Montreal the following month.[26]

With support from the United Kingdom, Iceland, and Denmark, Great Northern had secured the best imaginable position. What with Deep Freeze had started as a project that could threaten the company's business activity in the North Atlantic was now developing into a cable project between Scotland and Iceland with Great Northern in a key role.

On January 3, 1957, when the ICAO conference in Montreal began, the European alliance had previously secured American support for the Scotice project, which was presented by the Icelandic delegation. The recommendation to the ICAO's governing council was therefore that a cable solution be used for a connection between Scotland and Iceland via the Faroe Islands and that a scatter solution be used for a connection between Iceland and Canada via Greenland.[27]

The ICAO's governing council followed this recommendation, and on May 28, 1957, after a series of negotiations to clarify fine points with regard to the collaboration, Great Northern's board of directors voted to participate in Scotice. The British were to pay half the costs of and become half-owners of the cable between Scotland and the Faroe Islands, while Great Northern would finance and own the remaining portion of that cable. However, the time when the cable would be laid was dependent upon when a scatter connection linking Iceland, Greenland, and Canada could be established. The lease revenues from the ICAO would be of decisive importance with regard to making Scotice profitable, and the ICAO did not wish to conclude an agreement before the construction of the whole line to Canada was ensured.[28]

Coaxial cable between Iceland and Canada

On September 25, 1956, while Great Northern was working on establishing its position with regard to

the ICAO connection with Iceland, the first transatlantic telephone connection via cable, TAT 1, which connected Scotland with Canada, was commissioned. The connection consisted of two coaxial cables—one for traffic in each direction—and was equipped with a total of 102 amplifiers. It had a capacity of thirty-five circuits for telephony as well as a circuit with a capacity of twenty-two telegraph connections.

The opening was marked by ceremonies and enthusiasm in both Canada and the United States that was hardly less impressive than the reactions to the opening of the first transatlantic telegraph cable. Because of the ICAO's needs and the strategic military significance of the region, however, there was still a need for the North Atlantic connection.

For this reason, Great Northern got an unexpected opportunity to become involved in the Iceland-Canada project when an examination of the bids for establishing a scatter connection showed that the costs for such a connection would be significantly greater than had been expected and that the

technology was not as good as the ICAO had expected. Great Northern confidentially contacted the Canadian telecommunications administration, which had a positive attitude toward more detailed discussions of a possible cable solution, and early in December 1957 Bent Suenson and Niels Erik Holmblad traveled to Montreal.[29]

Suenson and Holmblad quickly reached agreement with the United States Department of Transportation and the Canadian Overseas Telecommunications Corporation with regard to proposing to the ICAO that instead of a scatter connection a cable be laid from Iceland to Canada via Greenland and that the ICAO would be able to lease the same number of channels as in the Scotice cable. The Canadian partner in the project work would be the government-owned telecommunications company, which would own the western half of the cable between Canada and Greenland, while Great Northern would own the other half. In addition, the company would own the cable between Greenland and Iceland and establish a station at Frederiksdal on the southern tip of Greenland, where the cables from Canada and Iceland were to be landed and connected.[30]

The process was delayed by a Canadian parliamentary election, but on April 23, 1958, the Cana-

Niels Erik Holmblad had a long career. In 1930, when he had just received his cand.polyt. degree and finished his training as an electrical engineer, he was hired by Post- og Telegrafdirektoratet (Denmark's postal and telegraphy directorate), where he had soon been promoted to head of the Technical Division. In 1954, he was brought to Great Northern and appointed Technical Director, as the company needed technical expertise in its top management because of the technological developments in the area of mobile telephone communications as well as wireless and cable-borne telecommunications. He retired in 1971.

dian government sent the proposal for a cable connection between Canada and Iceland to the ICAO. The following month, representatives of the Danish, British, Icelandic, and Canadian aviation authorities met in London for a weeklong conference on the Icecan project. Niels Erik Holmblad and Poul Laursen of Great Northern and a representative of the United Kingdom's Post Office participated in some of the meetings.[31]

The conference resulted in unanimous support for the cable solution, and the final report was presented and discussed at an informal meeting at the ICAO in late May 1958. A final decision could be expected in the course of the fall, but in the meantime, the Americans were heard from again.[32]

American obstruction

While the conference in London was going on, there were reports of a new American cable project involving the laying of a cable between Canada and England via Greenland and Iceland. This project was called Quick Freeze and presented as a purely military project, but according to "confidential information" received by Great Northern, the organization behind the project was again the Commercial Cable Company, and the project again was commercial in purpose. Great Northern therefore saw Quick Freeze as American obstruction of the Icecan project, obstruction that in the worst case could derail the Scotice project as well as the Icecan project.[33]

In early June 1958, however, the company learned that neither the Canadian nor the Icelandic, British, or Danish government had received official notice of the project's existence, though everyone knew about it. This led to an unofficial Canadian request for information from the United States Air Force, and in England the Foreign Office asked the American embassy about the matter.[34]

At the same time, via the Canadian Overseas Telecommunication Corporation, Great Northern attempted to encourage a common Dano-Canadian diplomatic inquiry in the United States with regard to whether the Americans would be interested in leasing a number of channels in a Dano-Canadian cable. The purpose of such an inquiry would have been to force the Americans to admit to their own cable plans, but the Canadian government was hesitant, and in late July, when Great Northern received word that an official American presentation of Quick Freeze was imminent, the Danish Ministry of Foreign Affairs was mobilized in order to ensure that Icecan would be presented first.[35]

On August 1, 1958, the Danish ambassador in Washington presented an official note to the United States Department of State in which Denmark gave notice of the existence of the Icecan project and of the expectation that the ICAO would support that project. The note requested information regarding any American interest there might be in having channels made available to the American armed forces.[36]

The American reaction came three days later in the form of notes to the Danish, Canadian, and British governments in which Quick Freeze was presented as a United States Air Force project "of urgent strategic importance to national defense." The note to the Danish government contained no reference to possible commercial use of the cable, but the note to the British government did indicate that such use was possible and that if there were to be such use, then there would be appropriate negotiations among the parties involved. Detailed information about the ownership structure for the cable was not provided, though the Americans did indicate that non-American interests might own up to 49 percent of the cable.[37]

The American note caused the Danish Ministry of Foreign Affairs to call a meeting that would be participated in by the Ministry of Public Works, the General Directorate of Postal and Telegraphy Systems, the Aviation Directorate, the Ministry of Defense, the Ministry for Greenland, and Great Northern. The parties agreed to support Great Northern in the company's efforts to realize Icecan and to discuss the matter with the other interested parties before responding to the American note. In Canada and the United Kingdom, too, there was an interest in discussing the situation and arriving at a common position with regard to the American plans.[38]

At a meeting in London on August 28, 1958, led by the general director of the British postal and telegraphy directorate and participated in by P & T, the president of the Canadian Overseas Telecommunication Corporation, and Cable & Wireless as well as Bent Suenson and Niels Erik Holmblad of Great Northern, it was found that there was "complete agreement" among the parties that the American project should be rejected. It was also agreed that

the Americans should be offered the opportunity to lease Icecan channels under favorable conditions for use by the United States Air Force (USAF).[39]

Iceland was not represented in London, but after the meeting, Suenson and an official from the United Kingdom's General Post Office traveled to Reykjavik to meet with the Icelandic postal and telegraphy director, who fully supported the conclusions that had been reached at the meeting in London. The Euro-Canadian position was subsequently indicated to the Americans via the usual diplomatic channels.[40]

By way of response, the Americans indicated that they would like to hold a meeting in early October at which the United States, Denmark, Canada, and the United Kingdom would participate and at which the communications needs of the USAF and the ICAO in the North Atlantic and ways of accommodating these needs could be discussed. All of the countries involved responded positively to this proposal, and the Danish Ministry of Foreign Affairs indicated that Denmark would be represented by Great Northern.[41]

Euro-American summit in London

The decisive negotiations took place at a conference held in London from October 9 to 14, 1958. The United States were represented by a delegation of at least ten men under the leadership of the head of the Department of State's division for civilian aviation and including representatives of both the civilian American aviation authorities and the United States Air Force. The even larger British delegation consisted of representatives of the Post Office, the ministry of transportation and civilian aviation, the Foreign Office, Cable & Wireless, and the ministry of aviation. Canada was represented by the president of the Canadian Overseas Telecommunication Corporation and representatives of the ministry of transportation and the Canadian air force.

Given the importance of this meeting and the size and composition of the American and British delegations, the group of individuals sent to represent Denmark was remarkable. The Danish delegation was made up mostly of representatives of Great Northern led by Bent Suenson; the official

The Soviet general secretary Nikita Khrushchev was famous and notorious for his impulsive and sometimes unpredictable behavior. Great Northern experienced such behavior early on the morning of July 1, 1960, when the general secretary sent a rush telegram to the French president, General de Gaulle, appealing to him to pardon an Algerian who was to be executed for terrorism. This telegram was severely delayed and did not arrive until after the execution had already been carried out, which caused the national government in Moscow to send a sharply worded complaint to Great Northern and interrupt all telegram traffic from the Soviet Union via the company's cables. As the company was able to prove that the delay had been the fault of the French government telegraph authority, however, Great Northern's cables were reopened to traffic two days later.

Denmark was represented only by an embassy secretary. It was also remarkable that Iceland—which had not been officially informed of the existence of the American project—was not represented by a delegation but did have a voice at the meeting, as the general director of the Icelandic postal and telegraphy authority had indicated that Bent Suenson could speak on Iceland's behalf.[42]

Immediately before the meeting, the United States had officially requested that Sweden support the American plans in the ICAO, and Bent Suenson had therefore expected that "the Americans would display an extremely stubborn attitude." This was not the case, however, as the Americans declared at the beginning of the conference that their position had changed and that they now intended to lay a purely military cable that directly connected Canada and Great Britain without making an intermediate landing in Greenland or Iceland. The reason for this was that there was political uncertainty with regard to the future of the Keflavik base and that the Americans therefore planned to provide for the USAF's need for circuits to Iceland by means of the leasing of channels in commercial cables.[43]

With this the greatest obstacle to the reaching of an agreement had been eliminated, and the parties soon in fact reached agreement that the ICAO's needs could best be met via the leasing of circuits in Scotice and Icecan. The Americans also indicated that the USAF would conclude a leasing agreement for one telephone and four telegraph circuits in the whole cable system. On this basis, it was agreed that Canada should present an official proposal to the ICAO as soon as possible, and such a proposal was presented to the ICAO on November 6, 1958.[44]

In the meantime, Great Northern secured a twenty-five-year monopolistic concession in Iceland, which for its part received access to telephone, telegraph, and telex connections with other countries without having to invest in the relevant systems. The Danish government had also agreed to change Danish law so that Great Northern could be granted a twenty-five-year concession for the landing of cables in Greenland. Everything seemed to have turned out to Great Northern's advantage when another opportunity in Greenland and the North Atlantic arose.[45]

Distant Early Warning Line in Greenland

At an early stage, the United States became aware of the importance of an early warning in the case of a Soviet air attack via the Arctic. In 1952, a report from the Massachusetts Institute of Technology proposed that the United States establish a radio chain at the Arctic Circle from Alaska along the northern coast of Canada to Greenland in order to give the American defenses extra advance notice of three to six hours. The need for such an early warning system became clear in 1953, when the Soviet Union detonated its first hydrogen bomb—a year after the United States had detonated its own. The establishment of the Distant Early Warning Line, or DEW Line, as the radar chain was called, was foreseen by an agreement between the United States and Canada concluded on May 5, 1955.

The plans for the DEW Line came to involve Great Northern on November 21, 1955, when, during a conversation at the Ministry of Greenland with Department Head Eske Brun, Bent Suenson was informed of a message received from the Americans regarding their desire to extend the DEW Line to Iceland via Greenland. In a secret memorandum, a copy of which Eske Brun provided to Suenson, it was claimed that Greenland constituted a problematic hole in this line [the DEW Line], a hole that, given today's possibilities as regards aviation, must in fact be said to compromise the entire line."[46]

To begin with, the Americans wished to carry out some preliminary surveys with a view to establishing a number of radar warning stations on Greenland. Assuming these stations were in fact established, the responsibility for operating them was to be borne by Danes, and Eske Brun indicated that he would like to see Great Northern take on the task in question. Suenson declared that the company would like to become involved in the matter and requested additional information regarding the staffing of the stations. He agreed to maintain

"strict confidentiality" with regard to the matter— the necessity of which Eske Brun strongly emphasized—but drew attention to the fact that it would be impossible for him to work on the matter without discussing it with others at the company. However, he indicated that such individuals would be limited to "a very small circle," and in fact, no members of the board of directors other than the chairman were provided with any information about the matter.[47]

Bent Suenson was kept appraised of progress with regard to the matter by Eske Brun until a meeting was held on July 8, 1957, with the participation of representatives of the Department for Greenland, the Ministry of Foreign Affairs, the Danish company Artic Contractors, who were intended to build the American radar stations, and Niels Erik Holmblad of Great Northern. Eske Brun reported that the Americans had carried out a preliminary survey and now wished to carry out a final survey.[48]

Eske Brun wanted to know whether Arctic Contractors and Great Northern could select representatives who would participate, and both companies replied affirmatively, though Niels Erik Holmblad added that Great Northern had "various serious reservations" with regard to the possibility that Great Northern would be responsible for operating the warning stations itself. In part, these reservations had to do with the company's relationship with the Soviet Union, though he did not say so directly. Holmblad indicated that it was of decisive importance to the company that the radar stations should not become areas belonging to the American armed forces, as that could be "a major obstacle" to the company's participation. To begin with, however, he found it "extremely important" for the company to send a representative along on at least one of the two expeditions that were to carry out the final American survey.[49]

Participation in the American expedition had no influence on Great Northern's attitude toward participation in the operation of the American warning system. Already before that operation had begun, Bent Suenson informed Permanent Secretary Finn Nielsen of the Ministry for Greenland that "the reservations as a matter of basic principle had been more strongly expressed" by the company's leaders.[50]

Vice Director Poul Laursen expanded upon this on October 21, 1957, when, in a conversation with Finn Nielsen, he stated clearly and directly that the company had "special political reservations, as [the company's] relationship with Russia meant that [the company] had to step lightly and take care not to provoke the Russians."[51]

On November 29, 1957, Suenson confidentially informed Great Northern's board of directors of the inquiry from the Ministry of Greenland regarding the possible operation by Great Northern of the warning stations on Greenland. According to the minutes of the meeting in question, "the board of directors was in agreement that Great Northern should not pursue the matter," and the ministry was informed of this. Great Northern had thus—for the sake of its relationship with the Soviet Union—rejected a request from the Danish government that the company take on a task that was of importance in connection with cooperation with the Americans in establishing defenses of Greenland and the NATO members against precisely the Soviet Union. The ministry subsequently made a number of attempts to get the company to reconsider its position—the last in April 1959—but Great Northern stuck to its decision not to participate, and this had no negative effect on the Danish government's continued support for the company.[52]

This was evident when an outlier of the DEW Line project came in contact with Great Northern's cable projects. In the middle of November 1958, Ole Buhl of the Ministry for Greenland, who was the Danish member of a project commission that was responsible for the establishment of the DEW Line in Greenland, received a letter from his American colleague Colonel Richard Critchfield, who informed Buhl that the Americans intended to lay a cable between Kulusuk on the east coast of Greenland and Iceland and that the Americans wished to secure the approval of the Danish government without going through the usual diplomatic channels.[53]

The matter, which was given the name Green Eyes—presumably an adaptation of *GreenIce*—end-ed up in the NATO office of the Danish Ministry of Foreign Affairs, which, after having exchanged a number of messages with Great Northern's leadership, scheduled a meeting at the ministry for December 15, 1958. The perceived importance of the matter is attested to by the fact that the participants in the meeting were practically the same group of individuals who had participated in the meeting regarding Quick Freeze earlier in the year.[54]

After the background of the meeting had been described by Section Head Axel Serup of the Ministry of Foreign Affairs, Bent Suenson presented Great Northern's view of the American cable, which he saw as another attempt to "obstruct" Icecan. It was to be feared, according to Bent Suenson, that, contrary to what had been agreed, the United States would not lease a number of channels in Icecan, which was of great importance in connection with the profitability of the connection, but instead use the American cable in combination with the scatter connections over Greenland. Also, the Canadians had reported that in other cases the Americans had used military cables for civilian traffic.[55]

There was agreement among the participants in the meeting that Icecan should be protected against American competition, and Section Head Serup also declared that the American request would necessarily have to go through the usual diplomatic channels. Permanent Secretary Eske Brun of the Ministry for Greenland declared that he agreed, and the meeting ended with the decision that in cooperation with the Ministry of Foreign Affairs and Great Northern the Ministry for Greenland would prepare a response to be sent to the Americans.[56]

The realization of Scotice-Icecan

Great Northern was happy to have gotten this support but also worried about the possibility that a request sent via the diplomatic channels could drag the matter out and thus delay the conclusion of a contract with the United States Air Force regarding the leasing of circuits in Icecan. The number of American military circuits would have an influence on the dimensions of the cable and its profitability and therefore on the price and other conditions for the ICAO's lease. The ICAO had originally scheduled a conference for late September 1958 to reach a final position on the Canadian Icecan proposal, but the presentation of the American Quick Freeze project had caused this conference to be moved back to January 12, 1959. Great Northern now feared a further delay.

Things did not end up going that badly. At the meeting of the ICAO in Paris on January 12, 1959, delegations from the fourteen governments that were involved unanimously recommended the use of Icecan in association with Scotice so that the communication needs of civilian aviation in the North Atlantic would be met by the coherent cable system. The final decision was subsequently made by the ICAO's governing council late in the month, and the construction of both Scotice and Icecan had thus been assured.[57]

It was not until three months later that the Danes heard of the resolution of the matter of the American Kulusuk cable. At a meeting in the Ministry of Greenland in the middle of April 1959, an American delegation reported that the United States had abandoned the plans and instead planned to establish a tropospheric scatter connection. The decision in question had supposedly been made by the United States Department of Defense after a Russian trawler had cut TAT 1 and several other cables off Newfoundland.

It remained for Great Northern to agree with the United States Air Force on a contract regarding the leasing of the four telegraph circuits and the one telephone circuit that Great Northern had been promised. However, it only proved possible to reach a resolution of this matter at the very last minute. In August 1960, the last contracts regarding the construction and operation of the Scotice-Icecan system were signed by the two companies, the governments involved, and the ICAO.

Scotice was opened to traffic in January 1962, and it was not before December of that year that a contract with the United States Air Force could be signed. On January 1, 1963, Icecan was opened to traffic, and C. F. Tietgen's original vision for the Great Northern Telegraph Company's cable system,

a vision of that system stretching both to North America and to East Asia and thus embracing the entire northern hemisphere, had been realized.

Modernization of the trans-Siberian connection

The Scotice-Icecan connection with North America brought with it a shift in Great Northern's cable interests, as China was no longer a part of the system in East Asia, but there was also a technological imbalance. While all the cables leading west were now coaxial cables, all of the cables in both the Baltic Sea and the Far East were traditional telegraph cables, and Great Northern had long been discussing a modernization of the trans-Siberian connection that would make it possible to use it for telex and telephony. Similar thinking was going on in Moscow, and at Kongens Nytorv "confidential secret notification" had been received that a director from Great Northern's Japanese cooperation partner Kokusai Denshin Denwa (KDD) had visited Moscow in December 1959 to discuss the modernization of the trans-Siberian connection.[58]

The relationship between Japan and the Soviet Union was somewhat tense, however, and according to Great Northern's sources the Japanese probe had not led to "encouraging results." On the other hand, KDD became interested in a Dano-Japanese alliance on the basis of Great Northern's good relationship with Moscow, and on Kongens Nytorv it was therefore expected that KDD would bring the matter up in the near future.[59]

The contact came in October 1959, when a KDD director, Mr. Hachifuji, "in strict confidence," informed Great Northern of KDD's plans in Copenhagen. It was agreed that the parties would continue their discussions of the matter and exclude the Soviet ministry until agreement had been reached on a basis on which to bring the matter up in Moscow, but at the same time, the Russians began making approaches to the company.[60]

During the second half of the 1950s, Great Northern and the Soviet Ministry of Communications had begun new forms of cooperation involving mutual visits by delegations that both had a business agenda and engaged in more relaxing activities. This resulted in a closer and more familiar relationship, and when a Russian delegation was in Denmark in December 1959, the first vice minister raised the question of a possible modernization of the trans-Siberian connection.[61]

This Soviet probe was more than welcome, and according to Bent Suenson it created "fertile soil" for the project at the same time as Great Northern was in a key position and had good opportunities to maneuver because the Russians and the Japanese found it difficult to speak to each other. In the spring of 1960, Great Northern produced a memorandum that was discussed with KDD during a series of meetings in Tokyo. According to H. P. Andersen, the Japanese had shown a "positive interest," but the summer and fall passed without Great Northern hearing anything new. Danish requests for an update were responded to with indications that KDD was still interested but busy with other cable projects.[62]

Finally, in March 1961, Great Northern found it necessary to provide information to the Soviet Ministry of Communications about the company's discussions with the Japanese. The Russians were still interested, and in May 1961, Bent Suenson therefore traveled to Tokyo to orient KDD's chairman, Mr. Shibusawa, with regard to the position of the Soviet government and to put some pressure on KDD to participate in the development of a common foundation on which to proceed, but he had to return home without having achieved what he had wished to.[63]

It was not until early June 1962 that KDD clearly indicated that KDD supported the project. A delegation from the Soviet Union's Ministry of Communication traveled to Copenhagen immediately. There Great Northern had prepared a foundation for the project for which the Russians expressed their support. They also proposed that three-way negotiations be initiated, but the Danes rejected this proposal because they feared a Russo-Japanese alliance. The Russians subsequently accepted that Great Northern would initiate parallel negotiations with them and the Japanese.[64]

In the fall of 1962, when H. P. Andersen was again in Tokyo, the Japanese indicated that there were discrepancies between his portrayal of the Russians' position and the impressions the Japanese themselves had received during their diplomatic probes in Moscow. Uncertainty with regard to the Russians' attitude led to a number of meetings in Tokyo, Copenhagen, and Moscow before H. P. Andersen and the Soviet ministry signed a document indicating that the Soviet government fully support the Danish foundation proposal.[65]

In early October 1963, H. P. Andersen sent a copy and a translation of the Dano-Soviet protocol document to Director Hachifuji, who declared that there was now "clarity with regard to all points" and that it would therefore be appropriate to study the Danish foundation document more closely. Having been pressed by H. P. Andersen, he even indicated that the Japanese would begin "immediately," but the Japanese did not in fact proceed that quickly.[66]

Threats of collapse from the beginning

In the spring of 1964, Bent Suenson and others traveled to Tokyo, where the first practical negotiations with KDD took place on April 24 and 25—four years after Great Northern had presented their first related memorandum to the Japanese. In addition to Director Hachifuji, participants from KDD included the company's president, Mr. Hamaguchi, and vice president, Mr. Ohno. The Japanese presented a number of proposals that in the view of the Danes deviated "with regard to very important points" from Great Northern's proposed basis for the project.[67]

The most important point of contention was economic. Great Northern assumed that the Soviet Union would continue to receive transit revenues and the companies would receive revenues calculated on the basis of the amount of traffic being carried by the cable. The Japanese wanted this system to be replaced with one in which foreign telecommunications companies and telecommunications authorities would be able to lease circuits in the modernized connection at a fixed price per one hundred kilometers of cable both on land and in the seas—a new principle for international billing. Leasing revenues, the Japanese foresaw, would be divided among the Soviet Union, KDD, and Great Northern according to an arrangement that would be developed by means of future negotiations among the parties.

The Japanese point of view did not come as a surprise to Great Northern, and the Danes had prepared a document that showed that such a system would hardly provide a viable economic basis for the new cable, as it would not enable Great Northern to recover its investment. This document surprised the Japanese and caused Hachifuji, as Bent Suenson put it, "to present a tough view of the problem" and declare that if the Danes were right, then there would be no adequate economic basis for laying the cable in question and that in this case KDD would manage by using satellite and radio connections.

This was the first-time satellites had been mentioned. On July 10, 1963, the first experimental satellite for television transmissions and telephony, Telstar I, had been launched by the United States, and while Great Northern and KDD were negotiating, the preparations for launching the first geostationary satellite, Syncon 2, were ongoing. It was only a question of time before satellites would be used for telecommunications.

Hachifuji, then, was not making an empty threat, and in fact, he was threatening to take the project off the table before the negotiations had even begun. Bent Suenson responded by declaring that if it were not possible to develop an arrangement that would be acceptable to both parties "then it would be necessary to recognize that the JASC [Japan Sea Cable] could not be realized," and with this, the negotiations ended.[68]

The following day, however, Vice President Ohno told H. P. Andersen that on the morning of that day KDD's management had held "a meeting for a small circle" and that the Japanese felt that it was only now that the actual negotiations were beginning.

Bent Suenson—second from the right ion the back—leading a Danish delegation visiting KDD during the negotiations with regard to the JASC connection in the middle of the 1960s.

The leasing principle could not be changed, but KDD was willing to establish a leasing fee and a system for distributing revenues that would ensure that Great Northern would be able to recover its investment.

To some extent, this calmed the Danes, but the question was what the reaction in Moscow would be. On May 6, 1964, Great Northern provided the Soviet Ministry of Communications with information regarding the meeting in Tokyo, and a few days later, the Soviet vice minister Ivan Klokov arrived in Copenhagen. While the leasing principle would result in a significant reduction of the Soviet Union's revenues, the Russians appeared not to be concerned about this. "Modernization is so important that economic considerations should not be decisive," Klokov felt, and he gave Great Northern a green light to continue on the basis the company had described.

Negotiations with a blind partner

The negotiations with KDD continued in two rounds in Copenhagen and Tokyo in August and October 1964 respectively. The negotiations involved a blind partner in the sense that the Soviet ministry did not participate. The negotiations involved three main points, the most important of which was the size and distribution of the leasing revenues per circuit. KDD and Great Northern had a common interest in seeing the Soviet Union receive as little of the leasing revenues as possible, but Great Northern was forced to take Soviet interests into account. Preliminarily, Great Northern and KDD agreed that the Russians should have leasing revenues per circuit in the amount of 1,200 gold francs per one hundred kilometers of cable on Russian territory, which was only a fifth of the applicable price for cables in Europe.[69]

Great Northern considered it to be of decisive importance that the company should receive a binding guarantee that KDD would ensure that the cable carried a certain minimum amount of Japanese traffic so that Great Northern could be certain that the company would recover its investment, but the Japanese were only willing to provide a declaration of intent, so this question remained unresolved for the time being.

Finally, KDD wished to own that part of the cable that would lie in Japanese territorial waters and receive the corresponding part of the revenues. Great Northern accepted this, but because the company feared that the Russians would present a corresponding demand, Great Northern insisted that the Japanese part-ownership be kept secret so "to the public the whole JASC cable system [appeared] to be fully owned by Great Northern," and KDD accepted this condition.

The next step was to get the Soviet Ministry of Communications to accept the leasing revenues, but Bent Suenson had the sense that the ministry would "not let itself be guided by narrow economic considerations alone but to a great extent consider general issues." He appeared to have been right when the Soviet Minister of Communications Nikolai Psurtsev "gave his general blessing to moving forward with the matter" at a meeting in Moscow.[70]

It did not end up being quite this easy, however. A Soviet delegation that came to Copenhagen to con-clude an official contract in April 1965 claimed—"presumably correctly"—that the 1,200 gold francs were less than what it had cost to establish the land connection. Great Northern insisted upon this amount, however, and it was only after a week of negotiations during which the leader of the Soviet delegation had to go to the telephone a number of times and consult with Moscow that a document establishing that the Russians would receive 1,200 gold francs per one hundred kilometers of cable could be signed. The reason for the Russians' acceptance of the conditions was probably that the Soviet Union needed modern international communications connections and that the lease revenues would be paid out in hard currency.[71]

The project had thus received an official green light from Moscow, and in Tokyo KDD was satisfied with the results of the Dano-Russian negotiations. However, KDD continued to reject Great Northern's wish to be guaranteed a certain amount of traffic and also presented a demand that KDD become part-owner of the entire cable. Shared ownership was not new to Great Northern, but the company nevertheless resisted accommodating the Japanese demand, as doing so could necessitate reopening the negotiations with the Russians. The Danes promised to study the Japanese proposal, however, and a new meeting was scheduled for October in connection with a telecommunications conference in Montreux. At the same time, Great Northern asked KDD to reconsider the Danish wish for a guarantee, but this request was "quite categorically" rejected.[72]

The Japanese wish for part-ownership was expressed in the context of an ultimatum, and there appeared to be no possibility that KDD would modify its consistent rejection of a guarantee system. On September 27, 1965, Great Northern's board of directors therefore met to reach what was described as "a kind of decision in principle with regard to the further handling of the matter."[73]

The chairman of the board of directors, H. Stevenius-Nielsen, emphasized the significant economic risk associated with the project and that future competition from satellites constituted an unpredictable factor. On the other hand, rejection of participation

The laying of the JASC was carried out such that the *Store Nordiske* laid the cable from Nakhodka, in Primorsky Krai in the Russian Far East, while the Japanese cable ship *KDD Maru* laid the deep-sea cable and executed the landing of the cable on the Japanese coast. The photograph shows the ceremony aboard the *KDD Maru* on April 12, 1969, in which a hawser is cut so the cable can sink to the seafloor. The two men carrying out this operation are, from the left, Engineer V. S. Christoffersen of Great Northern and Technical Director Dr. S. Shimura of KDD.

in the project could mean that the company lost its connection with Japan and was reduced to a Northern European and North Atlantic telegraphy company. His position was that Great Northern should attempt to avoid the proposed shared ownership and that the company should certainly acquire the desired guarantee before proceeding with the project.

The other members of the board of directors expressed their agreement, after which Bent Suenson expressed the seriousness of the situation with a statement to the effect that the negotiations had reached a "showdown" stage at which, as in poker, the parties would lay their cards on the table and reveal their hands. There was the risk of a breakdown, but Bent Suenson indicated that he nevertheless intended to present KDD's representative with a document containing a demand—not for guarantees but for "certain assurances," the implication being that a formulation would be used that could be perceived as softening up the discussion somewhat.[74]

In the words of Bent Suenson, however, Director Itano of KDD was "categorically negative" when the two men met in Montreux in early October. Itano promised to make his board of directors familiar

with the contents of the document immediately, but according to Bent Suenson Itano "despondently expressed his expectation that this would not lead to anything good."[75]

He proved to be right. The following day, Bent Suenson received a message to the effect that Itano had gone to bed with a bad cold that no one in Tokyo had any comments on the Danish document and that Itano did not believe there would be any point in continuing the discussions. Later in the day, Director Itano had suddenly regained his health—or at least he indicated an interest in having "a final meeting." The parties came no closer together, however, and Bent Suenson ended the meeting by declaring that he would write to KDD's president, Katsuzo Ohno, and propose a meeting in Tokyo.

"[…] [A] bright future"

On October 25, 1965, Bent Suenson wrote to Katsuzo Ohno, and the response came on November 16 in the form of a telegram from Director Itano, who was in Switzerland and requested a meeting with Suenson on his way home to Tokyo. According to Itano, Katsuzo Ohno did not see the point of a new meeting, as such a meeting would simply be a repetition of the earlier ones. All the arguments were subsequently repeated until Suenson asked Itano to "make it completely clear" in Tokyo that Great Northern required assurances that there would be a certain amount of traffic.[76]

A few days later, a letter arrived from Katsuzo Ohno that got straight down to business and in a sharp tone declared that the relationship between the companies had come to "a parting of the ways" and that KDD insisted on its demand for part-ownership and that issuing guarantees or assurances with regard to the volume of traffic was out of the question.

At Kongens Nytorv, the letter was read as "a pretty clear threat regarding the possible end of [the two companies'] cooperation," and Great Northern subsequently gave in. In a letter to Katsuzo Ohno on December 6, 1965, Bent Suenson declared that Great Northern was now ready to contact Moscow. He made no reference to the Danish wish for a guarantee or assurances, and Great Northern thus implicitly accepted abstaining from receiving such a guarantee or assurances.[77]

Katsuzo Ohno adopted a very different tone in his response, in which he expressed his deepest appreciation of Great Northern's decision. He foresaw "a bright future" and praised Great Northern as "the best business partner for the future as well as in the last hundred years."[78]

When a Danish delegation traveled to Moscow in April 1966, it was with the knowledge that "this would not be an easy task." Not only would the Soviet government have to accept Dano-Japanese

ownership of the cable, but KDD had also proposed reducing the previously agreed-upon leasing revenue in order to be able to compete with a global chain of satellites, the first of which was called Early Bird and had been launched in April 1965.

The Russians were "not enthusiastic" about the first condition but ended up accepting it. They refused to accept the second condition but indicated that the ministry would consider the matter. At the same time, Vice Minister Ivan Klokov proposed that a three-way meeting be held in Copenhagen in the near future so that the three parties would meet at the same time for the first time.[79]

The three-way meeting was held on Kongens Nytorv from September 5 to 10, 1966. There were no difficulties in reaching agreement with regard to the ownership of the cable, and in accordance with a proposal from Great Northern the originally agreed-upon leasing amount of 1,200 gold francs was also retained. However, the company wished to obtain a statement from the European telecommunications authorities regarding the leasing amount before making a final decision.[80]

This was an attitude that caused pressure to be put on Great Northern both by the Japanese and by the Russians. KDD in particular displayed "great impatience," and Hachifuji pushed hard to get the situation resolved before the end of 1966, declaring that "if necessary" KDD would finance the JASC in its entirety. At the same time, Hachifuji declared that if Great Northern pulled out of the JASC project, the company's cooperation with Japan would end completely.[81]

The Soviet ministry was also impatient, and Great Northern was told that the company would need to reach a decision soon. Confidentially, Vice Minister Ivan Klokov told Bent Suenson that KDD had proposed completing the project without the participation of Great Northern, a proposal the Russians had rejected. Nevertheless, this information indicated what could happen if there were not a Danish decision in the near future.[82]

After the three-way meeting, Great Northern contacted the various European telecommunications authorities to obtain their reactions to the leasing price, and when the board of directors met on January 16, 1967, to make a final decision, all of the organizations in question with the exception of that of West Germany had accepted the 1,200 gold francs. Bent Suenson and Niels Erik Holmblad both recommended that Great Northern participate in the JASC project, and the board of directors voted to approve such participation. On the same occasion, the board approved two identically worded telegrams to KDD and the Soviet ministry respectively in which the company's positive decision was announced with the reservation that West Germany, too, would need to approve the leasing amount before the project could proceed.[83]

It was only in March 1967, after having received several follow-up messages, that West Germany announced that it did not wish to lease circuits in the JASC and would use only satellite connections with Japan. As a way of reducing Danish risk, KDD now offered to let Great Northern reduce its ownership to 25 percent in return for reducing its revenues proportionally. If the company subsequently wished to increase its ownership share, it would have the right to do so.

This required approval in Moscow, and in late May 1967, Vice Minister Ivan Klokov declared that "under the circumstances" the Russians would be willing to accept a further reduction of the Danish ownership share if the company ended up owning the part of the cable that landed in the Soviet Union. The matter needed to be presented to the Ministry of Finance of the Soviet Union, but on June 20, 1967, Klokov no-

The signing of the JASC agreement took place on August 24, 1956, at Great Northern's headquarters on Kongens Nytorv. Pictured from the left are Director Toki Hachifuji of KDD, the Soviet Union's Vice Minister of Communications Ivan Klokov, and Chief Executive Officer Bent Suenson.

tified Great Northern that everything was all right.[84]

On August 24, 1967, Great Northern and KDD signed a contract with regard to the establishment and operation of a coaxial cable between Japan and Russia. This contract established that Great Northern would own one-fourth of that cable. The following year, Great Northern and the Soviet Union concluded a new twenty-five-year contract regarding the trans-Siberian connection, and in April 1969, the JASC was laid between Nakhodka in the Soviet Union and Naoetsu in Japan. In the meantime, the Soviet Union had modernized the connection between Siberia and European Russia, and on July 25, 1969, the opening of the entire connection was marked by a series of ceremonies in Tokyo, Moscow, Prague, Bern, and Copenhagen.

"We Want to be World Leaders"

CHAPTER 20

Military deliveries and civilian products

While in the area of telecommunications Great Northern was balancing between east and west and succeeding first in establishing the North Atlantic connection and then in realizing the modernization of the trans-Siberian connection to Japan, the radio factory Storno was experiencing almost explosive growth.

During the period 1957–1960, revenues almost tripled, and at the same time operations began producing a surplus. The reason for this was not least that deliveries of the Motorola PRC 10 Walkie Talkies to the Danish army's signals service, which had been ordered a long time previously, began in 1958. At the same time, Storno was receiving further orders for the PRC 10, and in combination with the first orders, which were valued at 4 million kroner, these orders made a significant contribution to the increase in revenues. However, the military deliveries also meant that Storno was forced to make a strategic choice with regard to the future of the business.

In 1958, the military deliveries contributed just under 2 million kroner to revenues, which were in-creased from 4.9 million kroner to 6.7 million kroner. In 1959, such deliveries accounted for approximately 3.5 million kroner, which lifted the total revenues to 9.8 million kroner, and in 1960, they contributed 7.5 million kroner, which brought the revenues up to 16.2 million kroner. And then it was over.

In 1961, military deliveries declined to just 1 million kroner, and as a consequence, Storno's revenues declined by just under 25 percent, to 12.2 million kroner. This reduction did not come as a surprise to the company's leaders, as there were no new military orders as far as the eye could see. At the same time, however, the numbers also showed that revenues from civilian orders had more than doubled in just three years and that it was sales of car radio telephones in particular that had been responsible for this growth. The operating surpluses, though, had very predominantly been accounted for by deliveries to the army, while the civilian part of the business was weighted down by high costs and a competitive market that pushed prices downward.

Bent Suenson had previously identified high and constantly increasing development costs and not least the salaries of engineers as the perhaps largest problem in connection with creating profitable operations. The reason for this situation was the technical developments within the radio sector, which, in contrast to the undersea telegraphy sector, was highly competitive and characterized by constant and rapid technological development. It was not enough to develop and launch a new product—new and improved model and variants had to be developed constantly.

This was precisely what Storno had done, spreading out across five business areas: mobile radio telephony, airport equipment, radiophony equipment, radio chains, and most recently, in the late 1950s, maritime telephony, an area in which the company had launched a series of radio telephones under the name Marinephone. At the same time, the business constantly became more export-oriented so that by the late 1950s over 60 percent of revenues came from exports, and here Storno was in fierce competition with foreign companies in all of its business areas. The individual countries had differing technical standards in various areas including radio telephony, so Storno had to adapt its products to each individual market.

Storno's technical excellence is attested to by the fact that in the fall of 1959, the American radio electronics giant Motorola contacted Storno to propose cooperation. Motorola was among the absolute leaders in the radio electronics sector; the company's achievements included developing the walkie-talkie for the United States Army after the outbreak of the Second World War. However, the company did not have a presence on the European car radio telephone market, and it now wished to use Storno as a wedge.[1]

The Americans proposed that Storno become an agent for Motorola in Europe and be given access to Motorola's designs and knowhow in that connection. Storno would be given an opportunity to manufacture what were called "special systems" for Motorola that would be sold on the American market; in return, Motorola wished to acquire a minority bloc of shares in Storno.[2]

The offer does not seem to have resulted in great enthusiasm in Storno or Great Northern, and in fact there were never any actual negotiations in this regard. One reason for this was probably that at the same time the leaders of Storno were engaged in fundamental discussions regarding a possible future for the business on the basis of production for the civilian market.

"A turning point in Storno's history"

Storno's products were characterized by their very high quality and use of the latest technology, but they had difficulty competing with regard to prices. The situation was particularly difficult because of the company's many business areas, in connection with which the company was too small to be a global player, and there was also the problem of adjusting to international standards within each individual product area. Early in 1960, Storno's leaders therefore decided to shut down the company's divisions for airport systems, radio chains, and radiophony and focus on what had been intended to be Storno's central business area from the beginning: mobile radio telephone systems. In 1960, the value of mobile radio telephone systems had increased to 54 percent of the overall production in 1960—and the tendency was for growth to continue.

The market for mobile radio telephony was growing, and a strategy report based on the systematic collection and analysis of a large number of international statistics showed that in the United States there had been constant growth in the car telephone market amounting to 23 percent a year for the last fourteen years, while Europe was seven to ten years behind. The conclusion was that the material "removes all doubt with regard to whether a business of Storno's type would be able to live on developing and selling mobile VHF systems, assuming the product in question is competitive technically and with regard to pricing."[3]

The concept for the future was for Storno to become "specialists in mobile communications" who developed and manufactured a series of basic elements that in combination could represent all popular products. Further specialization would not be possible if the company was to compete in the international markets, and a decline in quality would not be acceptable. The goal was for the company's product assortment to be "very nearly complete,"

though Storno would leave very complicated systems to the company's foreign competitors.

A reduction in development costs, which made up about 10 percent of total costs, was not viewed as a possibility, but it was expected that the simplified product range would result in savings in the area of salaries and other production costs. At the same time, there was to be a strengthening of Storno's performance in the export markets, which had become increasingly important. Since 1952, exports had grown from 22 percent of the total revenues for the civilian market to 68 percent in 1960, and because of the modest size of the Danish market, continued growth would be dependent upon growth in the export markets.

Up to this point, export sales had been based on local agents, the use of which had led to good results in countries such as South Africa, Norway, the Netherlands, and Germany. In other countries, opportunities had been wasted, and it had taken a very long time to build up strong market positions in those countries in which Storno had achieved successes. The conclusion was that in the future Storno itself would participate in the creation of the individual markets and contribute to building up a sales organization around suitable agents, which would require the immediate investment of 1.2 million kroner and probably the investment of more money during the coming years.

A factor that contributed to creating the new, focused strategy was the ongoing replacement of radio tubes by transistors everywhere in the electronics industry, which represented a technological breakthrough. In connection with the manufacture of mobile radio telephone systems, there were advantages to switching to transistors: The systems could be made significantly smaller, and electricity use could be reduced considerably. Because of the implications with regard to the company's market position, it was of decisive importance that Storno carry out this transition "as quickly as possible," and in this connection it was significant that the development budget would no longer be depleted by other business areas.

Storno already had a completely new mobile system, Viking I, that was 70 percent transistorized and used modular construction and printed circuits and was "technically and commercially in a high class in the context of the European market." In the course of a few years, it would become technically and economically practicable to produce a fully transistorized system, and the company already had a Viking II program under development.

The message conveyed by the report was that both commercially and technologically 1961 could be "a turning point in Storno's history." The question was whether Great Northern's board of directors would be willing to accept a transition period lasting an unspecified number of years during which significant investments would be required and despite the expectation of strong growth the company would only be able to produce "relatively poor results."[4]

When Bent Suenson presented the report at the meeting of Great Northern's board of directors on November 1, 1961, he declared that it could be assumed that the alternative to proceeding on the basis of this proposal was that "the business would slowly die." He noted that sales in the civilian sector had increased by approximately 30 percent since 1958, and Niels Erik Holmblad added a statement to the effect that it could be assumed that transistorization and the reduction in the size of the systems would result in their being more widely used.[5]

Bent Suenson reported that Storno's leadership, organization, and economy had been improved, and on this basis the board of directors approved Storno's pursuit of the new strategy and initial investments in the creation of a sales organization.

The turning point

The expected turning point came. After a predictable dip in revenues in 1961 as a result of the shutting down of the other business areas, sales of radio telephone systems really took off, and a decade of constant and significant growth followed. A contributing factor was that there was a general economic upswing of hitherto unseen strength that started in the late 1950s and was borne by a series of technological innovations including transistor technology and an opening of the international capital markets that made it possible for Danish companies to borrow money abroad.

In Europe, the development of new markets was stimulated by the 1957 establishment of the European Economic Community by means of the conclusion of the Treaty of Rome by West Germany, France, Italy, and the Benelux countries and the creation of the European Free Trade Association (EFTA), which included the United Kingdom, Denmark, Portugal, Norway, Sweden, Austria, and Switzerland, in 1960.

Storno adapted to the formation of these new markets by creating the sales organization Storno Funkgeräte G. m. b. H. in West Germany in 1960. This company took over the previous agent's sales and service organization. Also in 1960, Storno concluded a licensing contract with the British company Southern Instruments Ltd., which manufactured precision instruments. According to the contract, the British company was to manufacture Storno products under license, while sales and service would be handled by a commonly owned company, Storno-Southern Ltd., three-eighths of the share capital of which would be owned by Great Northern.[6]

Storno's exclusive commitment to mobile radio telephony produced quick results. Despite the company's abandonment of all other business areas, its revenues increased by almost 64 percent, to just under 20 million kroner, in 1962, and in 1963, revenues reached approximately 33 million kroner. This trend continued until revenues reached approximately 78 million kroner in 1967. This was more than six times the company's revenues at the historic turning point in 1961, and it looked as though the growth would continue unabated.

This trend was being driven by new models that used transistors. In 1960 the first Stornophone systems were introduced, and these systems won the company the Dutch Post, Telegraphy, and Telephone Authority as a customer. The Dutch national police force, too, acquired equipment from Storno when it began building a national radio telephony network that in 1963 included more than one thousand mobile radio telephones, including a few hundred for motorcycles. Storno's position in the Netherlands was particularly remarkable, as the Dutch electronics company Philips also manufactured radio telephony systems.[7]

In West Germany, there was competition from large national electronics manufacturers such as Siemens and Bosch, but Storno nevertheless won orders for systems for taxi companies in fifteen large and thirty small cities. In Hamburg, approximately 80 percent of all taxis used Storno equipment. The company received an order from Greenland for just under two hundred mobile and fixed stations.[8] In 1962, Storno introduced the Stornophone V car radio telephone, which had printed circuits and was 80 percent transistorized. This telephone quickly became common; it was used by companies including the taxi company Aarhus Taxa, which replaced its existing VHF systems with eighty mobile units.[9]

Parallel to the company's launching of new models, Storno developed expertise in large and integrated VHF systems that were adapted to the needs of the company's clients. This sector was handled by a special systems department offering "technical systems consultations," and according to Erik Petersen, this made the company "absolutely cutting-edge" in the international context in this area.[10]

A remarkable breakthrough came in the summer of 1962, when Storno, which had competed with twenty other companies, won an order from Stockholms Spårvägar (the Stockholm streetcar authority) for an integrated system including one thousand mobile VHF units to be installed in all of the buses, streetcars, and service vehicles in the Swedish capital and be connected to a traffic center and six remotely controlled main stations. The system was delivered in the summer of 1963 and was the largest civilian VHF network in Europe to date and according to the industry magazine *Ingeniøren* "the most modern collective traffic network in Europe." The agreement in question had been reached via negotiations by Storno in Denmark, and on January 1, 1963, a Swedish subsidiary, Svenska Storno AB, was created in reaction to Storno's previous nearly constant dissatisfaction with the company's changing Swedish agents.[11]

In the fall of 1963, Storno succeeded in winning a new order of a similar size. Gothenburg's fire department, harbor authority, and hospitals ordered a common VHF radio telephony network together with other organizations including the city's municipal libraries and housing authority and the city engineering office. A newly developed electronic selection system ensured optimal signal conditions, and in general the newest technology was used—for example, semiconductor components on printed circuits were used instead of traditional relays.[12]

A particularly important source of Storno's increasing revenues was the result of an agreement concluded with the German electronics manufacturer Siemens in the fall of 1962 with regard to the sales of Storno products on the German market. Siemens itself had been manufacturing mobile radio telephones but had been experiencing difficulties keeping up with technological developments. According to the agreement, Siemens was obliged to place orders for a total of 45 to 50 million kroner over the next five years, and as a result Storno decided to shut down its German sales company. All the equipment was to be manufactured by Storno, and this was to be indicated by the telephones despite the fact that they were sold under the Siemens brand. The first order, which had a value of just under 3 million kroner, was placed immediately, and in total, Siemens orders contributed 8.3 million kroner to Storno's revenues in 1963 and 10 to 11 million kroner each of the following two years. In 1966, a new agreement was concluded.[13]

Fully transistorized radio telephones

In the wake of the Stornophone V, Storno introduced the world's first fully transistorized so-called pocket radio telephone, which won a gold medal and a diploma at the Leipzig trade exhibition in 1963 because of its scientific and technical excellence. The task given to Storno's engineers and technicians had been to construct a portable telephone using duplex technology that satisfied the most exacting international standards, fit in a shirt or jacket pocket, and weighed a maximum of 750 grams. Storno's team succeeded in this after two and a half years of development work.[14]

The pocket telephone was a technological breakthrough and quickly achieved a high volume of sales. The first big order, which was for four hundred telephones and corresponding base stations, was placed by the Danish national police force, which after its first Storno order had bought all of its radio telephone systems from the British company Pye Telecom Ltd., which was Europe's biggest producer of radio telephones and Storno's biggest competitor.

In 1965, on the other hand, Storno supplied five hundred pocket radio telephones to London's police force, Scotland Yard, to be used by emergency response teams and task forces. These telephones were manufactured at a new factory that belonged to the newly established Storno Ltd., a company Great Northern had set up that same year in con-

nection with terminating Storno's cooperation with Southern Instruments Ltd. With its new subsidiary, Storno would now be responsible for its own production, sales, and service in the United Kingdom, and the company supplied products to the entire Commonwealth.[15]

The portable Stornophone 500 played a central role when Storno secured the largest European order yet for radio telephones for nonmilitary use, an order from the Dutch police for pocket radio telephones at a total price of approximately 8 million kroner.

The spring of 1967 saw another record set: Storno delivered goods for more than 10 million kroner when Scotland Yard acquired a system comprising three thousand of Storno's latest-model pocket radio telephones so that all of London's police officers could be equipped with them. The system was designed to cover five thousand square kilometers and connect each officer with his or her police station via a network of seventy-five base stations and seventy forward receiving stations. Scotland Yard was able to access the network directly and transmit messages to all street officers.[16]

Previously, Storno had supplied car and pocket radio telephones in various combinations to the police forces in Norway, Finland, Austria, West Germany, Portugal, Spain, and Sweden, and in the summer of 1967 the company received an express order from the police in Hong Kong, who had previously purchased a shipment of pocket radio telephones but in the wake of recent demonstrations and unrest wished to receive an express shipment containing fifty of the new remote-controlled devices.[17]

A further technological breakthrough was represented by the launch of the world's first fully transistorized car radio telephone, the Stornophone 600, which was awarded a gold medal in the fall of the same year at the international electronics exposition in Plovdiv, Bulgaria, and received a further gold medal at the Leipzig exhibition in the spring of 1967.

Among the first major customers for the Stornophone 600 was Stockholms Spårvägar, which, in November 1966, ordered 250 of the telephones for installation in the completely new ultramod-

It required great accuracy and a sure hand to perform the soldering necessary to manufacture Storno's radio telephones.

ern buses that were to be used the following year, when Sweden would switch from left-side driving to right-side driving. In the spring of 1967, Storno received an order for devices costing 1.6 million Swedish kronor for the subways in the Greater Stockholm area.[18]

In the socialist countries in Eastern Europe and in the Soviet Union, too, Storno made progress, partly as a result of participation in international trade fairs—the company first participated in the trade fair in Moscow in the fall of 1966—and of the company's touring with three vehicles including a six-ton Volvo exhibition bus and two accompanying vehicles to demonstrate the company's product assortment.[19]

However, the company's main market was Western Europe, where revenues for 1967 reached 35.1

million kroner, the United Kingdom, West Germany, the Netherlands, and France being the largest national submarkets within this market. Following the establishment of Storno Ltd. in 1965, the company created a German production company, Storno Electronic G. m. b. H., in Flensburg, and this company supplied its first four thousand systems to Siemens in 1967.[20]

Nordic sales revenues for 1967 amounted to 34.4 million kroner. In the Nordic region, the largest markets by far were Sweden and Denmark, after which came Norway, Finland, and Iceland. Total sales revenues for Europe's socialist bloc amounted to 5.7 million kroner; here, Romania and East Germany were the largest markets. Sales revenues for Asia amounted to a little under 1 million kroner, of which just under 200,000 kroner came from communist China, where Storno had participated in several Danish exhibitions. Sales revenues for Africa were under half a million kroner, as were sales revenues for South and Central America and the British Commonwealth.[21]

Of Storno's total 1967 sales revenues of a little over 77 million kroner, then, 83 percent came from the export markets, particularly from Western Europe and Scandinavia. There were no sales revenues from the United States, whose market Storno had not attempted to penetrate, partly because of the existing large American companies and partly because of the technical standards; frequencies and wavelengths used in the United States differed greatly from those used in Europe. European radio telephones could not easily be used in the United States, where they had to be approved by the relevant authorities, and for similar reasons American-produced systems could not simply be used in Europe.

A public Danish car telephone network

Though Storno developed into a predominantly export-oriented company, the Danish market was not without importance. In 1967, the company's Danish sales revenues reached 13.5 million kroner, which made Denmark Storno's second-largest single market, Sweden leading with 16.4 million kroner in sales revenues. However, it was not because of large orders for systems placed by public organizations that Denmark was a bigger market than countries such as the United Kingdom, West Germany, and the Netherlands, which had much larger populations and business communities than Denmark. Storno received few such orders from Danish public organizations, partly because Danish government authorities often preferred foreign-made products to those offered by Storno and other Danish electronics companies.

In contrast, Denmark had achieved relatively broad distribution of small private radio telephony systems at an early stage. By 1959, approximately five thousand radio telephones had been installed in cars in Denmark, which in the global context gave Denmark the second densest coverage per inhabitant, exceeded only by that of the United States. In 1962, according to P & T, the number had doubled, reaching approximately ten thousand, and thanks to the existence of the newest models, which were both simpler and more dependable, the trade magazine *Ingeniøren* expected sales to increase by four thousand new systems per year.

These expectations were also based on a relaxation of the previous rules, which had allowed only taxi companies, electric companies, and actual transport businesses as well as newspapers, physicians, and veterinarians to acquire their own car radio telephony systems. In July 1961, the rules were relaxed so that all private companies with a need for transportation could be issued permits—to begin with in Greater Copenhagen. A reason for the relaxation of the rules was that technological developments had made it possible to squeeze in more channels on a single frequency without having the various conversations disturb each other. The first company in Copenhagen to exploit the new possibility was J. C. Hempels Skibsfarvefabrik ("J. C. Hempel's Ship Paint Factory") A/S, which had Storno car radio telephones installed in its service vehicles.[22]

There was great interest among both small and large companies, and developments caused the daily newspaper *Politiken* to predict in the summer of 1962 that it would not be long before mobile radio telephony systems were available to ordinary consumers. "We talk to each other" was the headline over an article that foresaw that the Danes were approaching a time "when the possibility of contacting each other at any time will be something completely natural." This was a far-sighted observation, as was the following one. "This perspective might seem frightening, of course."[23]

In fact not much time passed before ordinary Danes had the opportunity to acquire the ability to reach each other constantly—if they could afford it, and there were more and more Danes who could. The economic upswing continued unabated throughout the 1960s and created the basis for increasing and increasingly widespread affluence. The Danish welfare state was born and engendered a large public sector including more and more modern libraries, hospitals, nursing homes, schools, gymnasia, and cultural centers. The number of public employees exploded, and large numbers of women entered the workforce.

Private affluence also increased and was reflected by the construction of large groups of detached houses with carports, multistory buildings containing large, well-lighted apartments, shopping centers with their own parking lots, and a network of highways. Automobile ownership became common—and so did telephone ownership, and when new residential buildings were built telephone jacks were preinstalled next to television and radio jacks, which now became standard features alongside the usual electrical outlets.

The time was ripe for car telephony, and in December 1963, P & T created what the organization itself characterized as "a modernized and simplified" new version of the public car telephony network for Greater Copenhagen from 1950, which had never become a success. The base station was supplied by Storno and placed in Telefonhuset ("the Telephone House") on Borups Allé with an antenna that reached a height of one hundred meters, so its signal would reach Køge, Roskilde, and Hillerød. According to *Politiken*, the opening of this base station had been coordinated with Storno's launch of its Stornophone V, which was much simpler and much easier

to use than earlier models. The installation of such a system in a car cost approximately 3,500 kroner, but a system could be rented from Storno for 135 kroner per month. In addition, the customer would pay an annual fee to P & T as well as a per-minute talk-time fee of 40 øre plus the other usual telephone charges.[24]

The creation of P & T's new system had an effect, though progress was slow. The number of subscribers in late March 1964 was 133, and at the end of the year, this number had increased to two hundred, and it was soon necessary to increase capacity. This was only the first step in the establishment of a national network served by Rigstelefonen, the Danish national telephone authority, and the next step consisted of the opening of a car radio telephony service in Aarhus in early April 1965, when the number of subscribers in Copenhagen had increased to three hundred. The base station in Aarhus was supplied by Storno; its antenna was placed on top of the two-hundred-meter-high television mast on P & T's Søsterhøj transmitter south of Aarhus. Because of the height, it was expected that this transmitter would have a significantly greater range than the one in Copenhagen and that it might even reach Skagen.[25]

When Funen was connected to the Danish car telephone network on March 1, 1967, the number of subscribers in Copenhagen was 450 and the number in Aarhus 60, and with the new Funen subscribers, the total number reached 600 by April 1. This put Denmark in second place after the United States with regard to coverage in relation to the number of inhabitants, while Sweden was number three and West Germany number four. On Funen, too, the base station had been provided by Storno, and of all the country's subscribers, approximately 90 percent had acquired a Stornophone.[26]

North Jutland was connected to the network late in 1967, and West and South Jutland followed in 1968 while capacity in Copenhagen was again increased as a result of a great increase in the number of subscribers. In 1969, Southern Zealand was finally connected to the network, and with this, Denmark had gotten a national car radio telephone service that covered approximately 95 percent of the entire country on the basis of Storno centers and with the Stornophone as the strongly dominant car radio telephone. The number of public subscribers passed two thousand, while the number of car telephones associated with twelve thousand private networks passed thirty thousand.[27]

Storno A/S

In 1967, with overall revenues—including the companies in Germany, the United Kingdom, and Sweden respectively—totaling 77 million kroner, Storno reached a size more than double that of Great Northern's telecommunications business, which had revenues of 33.6 million kroner that year. However, it was still the telecommunications area that, with 9 million kroner, delivered the lion's share of the mother company's earnings, while Storno contributed a surplus of 1.46 million kroner—the surplus was negatively affected by a deficit for the German company of 1.7 million kroner. After the deduction of a deficit for GNT Works, common administrative costs for Storno and the mother company's subsidiaries, interest on bank loans, and other expenses, Great Northern's overall surplus for 1967 amounted to 8.2 million kroner.[28]

Despite the unsatisfactory result, the prognoses for Storno were good: Continued growth and better results were expected. After several related discussions, Great Northern's board of directors therefore decided on January 1, 1968, that it was time to separate all the radio telephone activities and place them in an independent limited company that had Storno Danmark ("Storno Denmark") as a mother company and subsidiaries in Sweden, Germany, and the United Kingdom.[29]

The founding of Storno A/S took place on May 14, 1968, with Great Northern as well as the chairman of the company's board of directors, Hans-Henrik Stevenius-Nielsen and Vice Chairman Bent Suenson as founders. The share capital in the amount of 20 million kroner was distributed such that 19,998,000 kroner went to Great Northern and 1,000 kroner to each of the two cofounders, who were the chairman of the board of directors and vice chairman of Great North-

ern, respectively, and subsequently transferred their shares to Great Northern.[30]

When the new company was founded, assets from Great Northern amounting to a good 65.5 million kroner and liabilities from Great Northern amounting to a little over 33.4 million kroner were transferred to Storno A/S. The difference was converted into shares for 19,998,000 kroner at 103 points, corresponding to a little under 20.6 million kroner, while the remaining share capital, a little less than 14.5 million kroner, was provided by Great Northern as loan capital.[31]

The board of directors of the new company was comprised of five individuals, of whom Bent Suenson (chairman) and K. E. Bredahl Rasmussen of Great Northern's board of directors as well as the two directors from Great Northern, Niels Erik Holmblad and Werner Drenck, were voted onto the board of directors at the constituting general meeting. The last place on the board of directors remained unoccupied so the company would have the option of adding a board member from outside, and this occurred in May 1969, when Professor Niels Meyer of the Technical University of Denmark joined the board.[32]

As far as the new company's leadership was concerned, the top management team was expanded to four individuals in early August 1969, when Erik Petersen was appointed sales director, Leif Christensen technical chief, and O. Friis-Jensen, who was brought into the company from outside, chief financial officer. Officially, Børge Bentsen continued as the top director until he resigned at the end of the year, after which Storno was led by a three-person so-called collegial top management team with three equal directors—and Bent Suenson as the delegate of the board of directors at the company.[33]

"We want to be the world's leading [. . .]"

In its first year as an independent limited company, Storno A/S achieved revenues of 93 million kroner. The primary operating result ended up at 5.6 million kroner, but the annual result after tax and depreciations ended up at 1.6 million kroner. With outstanding orders for 80 million kroner at the end of the year, things looked promising in 1969, when revenues were budgeted at 120 million kroner and an operating surplus in the range of 10 to 12 million kroner was expected.[34]

In just ten years, Storno had increased its revenues tenfold, acquired 30 percent of the European market, and established subsidiaries in Sweden, Germany, and the United Kingdom. With more than 1,500 employees, Storno was the world's fourth largest producer of car telephones, ranking behind only the American companies General Electric and Motorola and the United Kingdom's Pye, which had been taken over by the Dutch company Philips at the beginning of 1967.

Because of the company's success, Storno appears to have attracted the attention of potential buyers among the big companies—at least Niels Erik Holmblad reported at the meeting of Great Northern's board of directors on December 5, 1967 that he and Poul Laursen had had a conversation with Admiral Ellery Stone, who was now vice president of ITT's European division and had expressed an interest in buying a bloc of shares in Storno or possibly taking over the company entirely. However, Storno was not for sale, and no action was taken with regard to the matter.[35]

Storno's development was remarkable, not least because the business lacked a large market in its home country that could have been used as a starting point for growth and because there were large local competitors in several of Storno's most important markets. If the growth continued at the current rate, revenues would pass half a billion kroner by 1975 at the latest, and indeed this was what Storno's leaders expected. Erik Petersen, one of the co-founders of the business, made no effort to conceal his ambitions when, looking back after Storno's first years as an independent limited company, he declared "We want to be world leaders."[36]

Storno's success no doubt had to do with the focus on mobile radio telephony systems in the early 1960s and the choice to eliminate all of the other products. According to Erik Petersen, it had also

been a contributing factor that while the global mobile radio telephony market had certainly been big to a company like Storno, it had been of a more modest size in the perspective of the really big companies who had not focused on research and development to the same extent as Storno. "A lucrative little corner of the electronics industry," Erik Petersen called the business area.[37]

It has been estimated that mobile radio telephony equipment accounted for only 1 percent of the global electronics market, and it is therefore the case that while the area constituted only a very small part of the big companies' total activities, it was for Storno "a matter of life and death to develop and manufacture products of high quality." The main cornerstone of the business was therefore research and development. It was necessary constantly to improve the company's products and introduce new ones, and it was important to adapt the products to new national and international standards that created new marketing possibilities when the company's customers were forced to acquire new models because of new standards. About 10 percent of the company's total expenses were accounted for by research and development costs, and there were about one hundred individuals working on research and development for Storno, mostly engineers and other technicians. [38]

In his retrospective, Erik Petersen noted that the business had already lived during three different electronic ages: that of radio tubes, that of transistors, in the middle of which the company currently found itself, and that of integrated circuits, in which Storno was already "making great strides." What would come next would be a continuation of the tendencies that had characterized the whole electronics industry, including mobile radio telephony, up to this point: The products would become cheaper, they would become more dependable and stable in their operations, and they would become smaller.[39]

However, not everything the company did had to do with research and development. The new products needed to be manufactured and marketed, and one goal that had been formulated for Storno was therefore that the company should strive to achieve sufficient sales that "[the company] can maintain a production capacity that will be able to assure the position of the business as a leading company on the international market."[40]

Up to this point, Storno had focused on the European market because the company had not had sufficient production and marketing capacity to go farther. If the company was to realize the predictions that it would have revenues of half a billion kroner in 1975, the company would need money—a great deal of money—to invest in production and marketing. The company was already having difficulty keeping up with demand, and this was af-fecting sales in the overseas markets. In addition, there was the constant need for research and devel-opment, a need that did not diminish. It was fore-seen that none of the products that would secure Storno's revenues in 1975 would be ones that exist-ed already in 1968—with the possible exception of products that were under development in the labo-ratories of the research division.[41]

Money was not a problem, however, if one was to believe the company's finance director, Ole Friis-Jensen. "Our expansion will be financed partly via our own earnings and partly via bank loans," he told *Berlingske Aftenavis* in early January 1969. The future looked bright.[42]

The Great Northern Electronics Group

CHAPTER 21

From telegraphy apparatus to GNT Automatic

Despite Storno's size, the attention paid to Storno by the public, and the pride Great Northern took in Storno, it was the telegraphy business that stole the spotlight at the celebration of Great Northern's hundredth anniversary on June 1, 1969. To be sure, the Far Eastern cable system had not yet been opened on that day, but preparations for its commissioning had gotten to the point where it was natural for this grand project to dominate the celebration of the anniversary. Both Great Northern itself and the press emphasized the direct lines that could be drawn all the way back to the laying of cables in the Far East in 1870 and 1871 and that the individual at the heart of the festivities, Bent Suenson, was the grandchild of Edouard Suenson, who had led the historic cable mission and subsequently become the company's first chief executive officer.

However, it was not as chief executive officer that Bent Suenson celebrated the hundredth anniversary. In accordance with his own wishes, he had resigned effective at the end of 1966 and been replaced by a collegial top management team con-

sisting of Technical Chief Niels Erik Holmblad; Poul Laursen, who was responsible for the telecommunications business; and Werner Drenck, who was responsible for the finances and organization of the mother company as well as for the manufacturing business. Poul Laursen had worked with the company's telegraphy business for many years, while Werner Drenck had previously been chief executive officer of Hellesens.

Despite the change, Bent Suenson was still the strong man among the company's leaders, as he remained vice chairman of the board of directors and had also been appointed the representative of the board of directors on the top management team and as such had his own office and secretary at Kongens Nytorv. He therefore retained decisive influence during the final phase of Great Northern's transformation from a classic telegraphy company into a modern industrial company, a transformation he himself had initiated during the first postwar years.

The creation of the collegial top management team reflected the fact that Great Northern had become a large and complicated company and that leading it had become correspondingly complicated, as it was involved in activities within two very different business areas, international telecommunications and industrial manufacturing, and in the latter area two subsidiaries had been added. One of these was Hellesens A/S, in which Great Northern had eventually acquired all of Landmandsbanken's shares so Great Northern owned 97 percent of the total shares and had established the battery factory as a subsidiary as of January 1, 1968. Given the fact that Great Northern had held a majority of the shares in Hellesens for years at this point, the establishment of the subsidiary could be viewed mostly as an organizational and accounting-related transaction, but it nevertheless signaled that the mother company planned to become more directly involved in managing Hellesens with Werner Drenck as the chairman of the board of directors.

In contrast, the other subsidiary, the telephone factory GNT Automatic, represented an entirely new activity, though GNT Automatic was deeply rooted in Great Northern's original division for the manufacture of telegraphy apparatus, GNT Works. During the Second World War, the division's leader, the head engineer K. L. Jensen, had lived in Great Britain, where he had worked on the development of a remote printer to be used with telex connections, which were a new type of telecommunications.

After the war, Great Northern's board of directors decided to continue the development work, in part because the volume of orders for telegraphy apparatuses had declined as a result of the growth of telex and international telephone connections. In March 1961, the board voted to discontinue the project as a result of ongoing technical prob-

lems, but just a year later, the board of directors voted to begin production after all.[1]

The reason for this was that after having received a prototype device as a test sample, Sweden's Telestyrelse ("Telecommunications Authority") had wished to receive a price offer with regard to the delivery of one thousand devices as soon as possible, which had caused Denmark's P & T to request a price offer for the delivery of this number of devices. This caused the project to appear in an entirely new light, as the two orders could be expected to lead to further orders from telecommunica-

At the celebration of Great Northern's one hundredth anniversary in 1969, Bent Suenson could note that the strategy he had pursued since the late 1930s consisting of switching the company from telegraphy to industry had succeeded, not least thanks to Storno, which was among the world's largest producers of car radio telephones. At the same time, he could look back on forty-four years of service at the company, thirty-seven of which he had spent as a director and twenty-two of which he had spent as vice chairman of the board of directors.

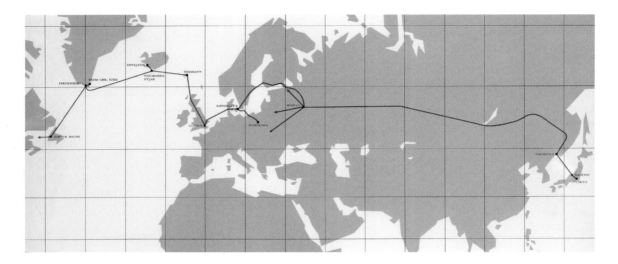

tions authorities and other organizations requiring telex connections such as the military, police and customs authorities, shipyards, and international companies. The decision to begin production was therefore made after a declaration from the chairman that "the company would now have to pull out all the stops in order to avoid delays in finishing work on the teleprinter and delivering it to the customers."[2]

It did not prove to be possible to avoid delays. Many of the parts in the teleprinters needed to be produced by GNT Works itself using special tools the company also had to produce itself. The consequence was that despite having promised to do so, the company was unable to deliver the first eight hundred teleprinters to the two telecommunications authorities by the end of 1964, and the quality of the few that were delivered was soon criticized both by the Swedish and by the Danish telecommunications authority. Great Northern had to admit that a large part of the parts that had been manufactured were not compliant with the relevant specifications and would have to be discarded and that "it [would] not be possible to deliver any teleprinters [that] year."[3]

A new promise to deliver 850 teleprinters in 1966 was not fulfilled either, and in fact, in early December, Niels Erik Holmblad was in doubt as to whether the company would even be able to deliver two hundred by the end of the year. The delay caused

Map of Great Northern's international telecommunications systems at the time of the company's hundredth anniversary in 1969. In the midst of the Cold War, it stretches across the two geopolitical blocs, from North America in the west through the Soviet Union to Japan in the east.

P & T to order five hundred teleprinters from Siemens, though P & T did assure Great Northern that P & T intended to retain Great Northern as its main supplier.[4]

In the meantime, global interest in teleprinters was increasing. In late August 1966, a total of twelve had been sold, and a further eighteen had been delivered for trial purposes. Orders had arrived from Spain and East Germany for fifty-five and forty-three machines respectively, and Great Northern had submitted bids for a further 1,200, 750 of which were for Venezuela.[5]

These orders were welcome confirmation that the teleprinter was competitive and that the company would need a plot of land in Ballerup that had been purchased for a new factory. The estimated costs for this construction project, which was to be begun in 1968, were 28 million kroner, but in the fall of 1967, when it had become clear that GNT Works would post a record deficit of 7 million kroner, Great Northern began looking for a different solution. In October 1967, Niels Erik Holmblad was able to inform the board of directors of "certain negotiations" that had been pursued in recent months

with regard to cooperation with L. M. Ericsson of Sweden that would involve Denmark's Telefon Fabrik Automatic A/S.[6]

In 1946, L. M. Ericsson had acquired 49 percent of this telephone factory to be able to supply telephones, switchboard centers, and other equipment to the Danish telephone companies, which were about to undertake a comprehensive modernization of the entire telephone network. In the summer of 1967, the company moved to a newly erected building in Søborg, outside Copenhagen, but around this time, there was a reduction in orders from the Danish telephone companies, as the modernization of the telephone network was nearing its completion, and the building in Søborg ended up being too big.

L. M. Ericsson had shown an interest in Great Northern's teleprinter earlier, and the two companies now agreed to merge GNT Works and Automatic and to use the facility in Søborg for all of the new company's manufacturing activities. In early December 1967, Great Northern took over the Danish shareholders' majority bloc of 51 percent of the shares in Automatic, while L. M. Ericson kept its 49 percent of the shares. The merger could be executed on January 1, 1968, and GNT Automatic A/S, as the new company was called, became a subsidiary of Great Northern. The board of directors of the new company consisted of five representatives of Great Northern and three representatives of L. M. Ericsson; Great Northern's Director Werner Drenck became the chairman of the board of directors.[7]

A hundred-year-old telegraph company with industrial subsidiaries

At the time of its hundredth anniversary, the Great Northern Telegraph Company, despite its name, was in particular an industrial company. While there were revenues from the telecommunications business amounting to 27.4 million kroner, the three subsidiaries had total revenues of 280 million kroner. The subsidiaries' contribution to the mother company in the form of dividend yields was modest, however; Storno contributed only 1.2 million kroner and Hellesens only 872,000 kroner, while because of a significant deficit, GNT Automatic paid out no dividend.[8]

In addition to the revenues from the telecommunications business and the subsidiaries, rev-

GNT Automatic's factory in Søborg. This factory had originally been built by the telephone manufacturer Automatic but was too large as the Danish telephone manufacturer significantly reduced their orders for new switching centers. After the telephone manufacturer and GNT Works had been merged, the factory became the site at which telephone equipment and GNT Works's teleprinter were manufactured, though production of the teleprinter was soon abandoned.

63 million kroner of which was in in stocks, while the remainder was distributed among bonds and properties. This distribution was the result of an increasingly conscious decision to invest in stocks.

The annual report did not specify the companies in which Great Northern had invested, but the biggest of these investments was in Denmark's second-largest electrotechnical company, A/S LK-NES, in which Great Northern purchased a bloc of shares with a nominal value of 13.25 kroner, which corresponded to one-fourth of the share capital. A bloc of shares in Nordisk Kabel og Tråd (NKT, "Nordic Cable and Wire") had a nominal value of 5.116 million and accounted for 5 percent of the share capital. Great Northern's involvement with these two companies was reflected by Bent Suenson's membership of both boards of directors—in the case of NKT, he had been chairman of the board of directors since 1963.

Among Denmark's largest electrotechnical companies, as measured in terms of revenues, Storno, GNT Automatic, and Hellesens were in third, fourth, and fifth place, respectively, while Great Northern, which was also viewed as an electrotechnical company, was in ninth place. Overall, the Great Northern group of companies had revenues of approximately 320 million kroner in 1969, which made Great Northern Denmark's second-largest electrotechnical group after Thrige-Titan, which had revenues of 333 million kroner.

Great Northern, then, was solidly anchored in Danish industry, and the company's leading position was reflected by Bent Suenson's position as the chairman of the board of directors of Privatbanken, a position he had held since 1963. His strategy from the postwar years of creating a new basis for Great Northern's existence consisting of manufacturing

enues from capital investments in the amount of 11.2 million kroner and net revenues from the real estate portfolio in the amount of 1 million kroner contributed to the company's total revenues of 40.5 million kroner. Without these revenues, the annual account would have shown a deficit of 3.6 million kroner—as it was, though, there was a surplus, so a dividend of 10 percent, corresponding to 7.2 million kroner, could be paid out.

The revenues from capital investments could be attributed to the fact that Great Northern remained well-consolidated, with a balance of just under 300 million kroner and equity of just under 150 million kroner. Of the company's assets, capital investments accounted for a little more than 107 million kroner,

activity had paid off, to the point where the company—despite its name—was much more an industrial electronics group than a telecommunications business.

In 1973, when Great Northern first presented an account for the entire group, the total revenues amounted to 599 million kroner. As for all of the postwar years, however, it was the capital investments that ensured a surplus large enough to make it possible to pay out a dividend. This is to say that Great Northern was having difficulty making money from its own operations, and this was true for both of the telecommunications business and—in particular—of the subsidiaries.

The telecommunications business: "A unique anachronism"

Despite the industrial transformation, Great Northern held on to its telecommunications business, though it was not unproblematic to ensure stable operations, particularly in the North Atlantic. The

In August 1969, Storno presented its fully automatic car telephone, the Stornophone Automatic, on which the dial found on earlier models had been replaced with pushbuttons so it would be easier to place calls while driving. Another special feature of this model was that the car telephone could be called directly from all other Danish telephones; correspondingly, it was possible to call all other numbers directly from the car.

reason for this was repeated, lengthy interruptions of service, in particular in the case of Icecan, where massive ice formations could hinder repairs for months at a time—in 1968, there was a single interruption lasting sixty-three days. The cable breaks typically occurred close to Greenland as a result of icebergs scraping against each other or on the big fishing banks off the coast of Newfoundland, where cables were broken by trawlers.

The breaks themselves led to an immediate reduction of traffic revenues, but they were probably also a contributing cause in connection with the United States government's notice of termination of the lease for two of four channels which caused

Hellesens batteries were sold in large parts of the world, including in Congo, where there was significant licensed production.

dum that was presented to the board of directors on September 11, 1972.[9]

This memorandum predicted that the decline in telecommunications revenues would continue while telecommunications costs would increase until, in 1975, Great Northern's telecommunications would no longer be able to produce a profit. The reasons for the decline were ongoing reductions in the volume of classic telegram traffic, the introduction of automatic telex technology, and in particular rapid growth in international telecommunications connections and an associated downward pressure on rates, which had been reduced by 95 percent since the commissioning of the Weybourne cable in 1950.

While the company's original telegraph cables between Denmark and Great Britain had had only a single telegraph circuit each, the Weybourne cable had been expanded over the years to eight telephone channels, which corresponded to 192 telegraph circuits. The direct government cable between Great Britain and Sweden that had been laid in 1960 had sixty telephone channels, and a government cable laid in 1964 between Great Britain and Denmark had 120 telephone channels, while a new Dano-British government cable would have 1,260 telephone circuits. The development was explosive and the same all over the world, and then there were also the satellites, the first of which had 240 telephone channels, and the latest of which had six thousand telephone channels each.

In Poul Laursen's words, the company's activity in Great Britain "had been superfluous for years," and no one would notice if the Weybourne cable were shut down. The British postal and telegraphy directorate had suggested a number of times that the epoch of Great Northern's telegraphy activity might be drawing to a close. A high-ranking official had called the company "an anachronism."

Indeed, Great Northern was the only company of its kind left in Europe and would hardly become involved in the establishment of new cable systems anywhere in the world. Poul Laursen therefore agreed with the British official that the company was an anachronism, even adding that it was "a

Great Northern to lose 2 million kroner in revenues annually. In contrast, the ICAO—the international aviation organization—displayed great patience and kept its channels, doubtlessly because there was no alternative.

A number of cable reinforcements and reroutings of cables near Greenland eventually helped to address some of the problems, but nevertheless, the telecommunications revenues from the North Atlantic steadily declined while revenues from the JASC contributed to an overall increase in revenues in 1973 to 31.3 million kroner. Revenues from telecommunications subsequently declined again, which caused the director of the telecommunications section, Poul Laursen, to prepare a memoran-

GNT Works's teleprinter, or telex, has been called the world's most advanced mechanical apparatus. It never worked dependably, however, and ultimately, production was discontinued.

unique anachronism." His conclusion was an "undramatic but melancholy one," namely that Great Northern would need to prepare to shut down its telecommunications activity around 1975 and to become a pure industrial business, which would turn out to be more problematic than he had suggested.[10]

The Hellesens-Tudor battery merger

During the 1960s, Hellesens had experienced significant increases in battery sales as a result of the rapid spread of transistor radios, but by the end of the decade, the European market was becoming saturated. At the same time, competition was increasing. American companies were seeking access to the European market, which depressed prices, while increasing salary costs and a shortage of labor at the company's factory in Copenhagen led to general cost increases. Some of the production was therefore moved to Thisted in 1972, and the following year, the remaining production was brought together at the company's factory in Køge.

The management of Hellesens had great expectations with regard to Denmark's entry into the Eu-

ropean Community on January 1, 1973, but steeply rising oil prices and an international economic downturn weakened the effect of European Community membership, while increasing competition and dramatic increases in the prices of raw materials continued to put pressure on the company. Sales stagnated, and surpluses were replaced by deficits. In the absence of prospects for an improvement in the situation, it was decided that Hellesens would seek to cooperate with one of the large international battery producers and that if necessary, Great Northern would be prepared to give up its majority position in Hellesens. The previous year, Great Northern had acquired the last 3 percent of the share capital, so it would not be necessary to take into account the wishes of minority shareholders.[11]

The solution ended up being a regional one instead. Great Northern and Hellesens had previously negotiated with the Swedish battery and accumulator manufacturer Tudor, but the Swedes had been reluctant to make a commitment to close cooperation. Now Tudor's owner, the industrial and gas concern AGA, contacted Great Northern with the proposal that the two companies negotiate regarding precisely such cooperation; AGA's reasons for presenting this proposal were similar to the reasons why Great Northern itself was seeking a cooperation partner for Hellesens.[12]

This time the parties were able to reach an agreement according to which Hellesens's and Tudor's dry-battery production would be placed in a new company, Hellesens-Tudor A/S, with share capital of 20 million kroner. Fifty-one percent of this company was to be owned by Hellesens and 49 percent by Tudor. Hellesens's top management team would continue its work as the top management team of the new, common company, and Hellesens's board

Mass production of batteries at Hellesens A/S, which became a subsidiary of Great Northern in 1968 after Great Northern had owned a decisive stake in Hellesens since 1939.

of directors would continue its work as the board of directors of the common company, though a Swede would be added to the board. The new company would have revenues of approximately 190 million kroner and a market share for the Nordic region of 75 percent.

The Danish shares in Hellesens-Tudor A/S were placed in A/S Hellesens, which simultaneously changed its name to Hellesens Invest A/S, as in reality it became a holding company—100 percent owned by Great Northern. Hellesens A/S retained its ownership of the buildings in Denmark, where Hellesens-Tudor rented space for 3 million kroner per year. With a further 2.4 million kroner in annual interest revenues from a loan to the merged company, Hellesens Invest could look forward to an annual surplus for 1975 of 7 million kroner, to which any

dividend from Hellesens-Tudor would be added. "It is therefore to be expected that future results for Hellesens will be quite nice," the top management team claimed in its recommendation to the board of directors, and the board of directors responded by approving the agreement unanimously.[13]

GNT Automatic

The process of getting GNT Automatic on the right track after that company had gotten off to a bad start proved to be more difficult and dramatic. The rationale behind the merger had been that the production of the teleprinter could compensate for declining deliveries of telephones and telecommunications equipment and produce increased revenues and profitable operations. Instead, the teleprinter became a problem child—in a major way, in fact.

From the beginning, the production of the teleprinter drained GNT Automatic of financial resources, and at the same time, only 60 percent of the planned number of teleprinters were being produced. To be sure, the company had been expected to post a deficit for the first year, but by October 1969, it could be foreseen that the deficit would be 3 million kroner more than what had been reflected in the budget. The company ended up requiring 5 million kroner in fresh capital, which Great Northern and L. M. Ericsson provided as a loan.[14]

Already in the spring of 1970, a new loan of 3 million kroner had to be provided, and a further 2 million kroner followed in the fall of that year, after which the first loan, of 5 million kroner, was converted into share capital. The difficulties with the teleprinter affected the annual account for 1970, which showed a deficit of 7.5 million kroner and did not suggest that 1971 would be any better, for which

reason there was a need for a further infusion of capital.[15]

The situation caused serious worry at Great Northern, and at a meeting of the board of directors on March 2, 1971, Werner Drenck was asked whether he had the impression that L. M. Ericsson believed in the teleprinter. Drenck said he did have that impression, and the chairman subsequently asked each individual member of the board of directors for his opinion. There was a unanimous agreement that production should continue. The board of directors subsequently voted to increase GNT Automatic's share capital by 10 million kroner.[16]

A new deficit in the annual account for 1971 necessitated a new infusion of capital in the amount of 8 million kroner, 5 million of which constituted an increase in the share capital. On the other hand, Great Northern could rejoice over the fact that production of the teleprinter had proceeded in accordance with plans to produce two thousand of the current printers and that an improved version was on the way.[17]

And then it was over, as there were difficulties in producing the improved teleprinter. The cus-

tomers lost confidence in the product, P & T and Sweden's Telestyrelse bought fewer than had been expected, and there was tough price competition from companies including Siemens of Germany. Given the prospect of further deficits, Great Northern proposed to L. M. Ericsson in September 1972 that the production of the teleprinter be discontinued. The loss would amount to about 20 million kroner, most of which, in accordance with existing agreements between the companies, would be borne by the Swedes.[18]

Nevertheless, L. M. Ericsson's top management were in agreement, and in late October 1972, it was decided that production of the teleprinter would be discontinued. Approximately 150 employees were dismissed immediately, while a further 250 workers would be dismissed as existing orders were filled, which would take two or three years. Given the budgeted loss of 20 million kroner, the share capital and reserves would be lost, but the negative equity was eliminated by L. M. Ericsson, which provided an operating supplement amounting to just under 2 million kroner, and early in 1973, the share capital was increased by 5 million kroner to 40 million kroner.[19]

The discontinuation of teleprinter production was a turning point for GNT Automatic. After a low point in 1972, there was an increase in revenues for 1973 of no less than 20 percent, to 119.4 million kroner. At the same time, the export share rose to 51 percent, which reflected the fact that the company moved away from a role as a supplier primarily of the Danish home market.

The improved situation was generated in particular by two new types of products, a new standard telephone with a keyboard called Dialog for the Danish telephone companies and a new generation of coin-operated telephones that could be used without calling a switchboard. In contrast, a product series comprising printers, perforators, and punched tape readers for computers, which were being used increasingly both by large companies and in the public sector, did not become the success it had been expected to become.

GNT Automatic had the sole right to supply the Dialog telephone to the Danish telephone companies, while the coin-operated telephones in particular became a popular product on the export markets with the bonus advantage that GNT Automatic was able to secure loans under favorable conditions from Eksportkreditrådet, the Export Credit Council. Already in November 1973, GNT Automatic's liquidity was 15 to 17 million kroner better than it had been expected to be, and for the first time in several years, the annual account showed a surplus, one that amounted to no less than 12.8 million kroner.[20]

The improvement continued in 1974, when revenues increased 19 percent, to 142 million kroner, and there was a surplus of 22 million kroner. No dividend was paid out in 1973 or 1974, however, as

rebuilding GNT Automatic's reserves was considered a priority.

Storno: Crown jewel and problem child

At the beginning of the 1970s, Denmark had a thriving electronics industry with considerable exports. Storno was considered that industry's crown jewel thanks to its leading position technologically, its product development, and its strong growth in competition with some of the world's largest electronics groups. In 1969, Storno's revenues increased by 25 percent, to 125 million kroner, and the value of orders received increased by 40 percent. The optimism of the leaders of both Storno and Great Northern was therefore great, and the budget for 1970 foresaw revenues of 180 million kroner. Already in May, however, this figure had to be adjusted downward to 161 million kroner, and the expectations of management took another shot across the bow when Siemens gave notice of termination of its cooperation agreement with Storno.[21]

West Germany was Storno's largest single national market, accounting for 24 percent of Storno's total sales, so this termination had a major effect. In addition to a decline in revenues, Storno had to expect considerable expenses in connection with the creation of a new sales organization in West Germany, though it would be possible to hire Siemens's employees there. Also, Storno would have to introduce its own name, as Siemens had sold telephones and systems in its own name, and Storno was therefore practically unknown in West Germany.

Furthermore, Storno was facing the need to build up a new sales organization in France after having given notice of termination of its previous agent, and Storno had just begun the construction of a new factory in Flensburg to be able to accommodate previously expected increasing sales in Germany. Increasing sales were no longer expected, but the construction project could not be stopped.[22]

Given the declining growth, the increasing costs, and the tendency for more and more money to become tied up in a growing inventory of finished goods, Storno's liquidity was getting tighter and tighter. Storno had had an outstanding debt to Eksportkreditrådet and Privatbanken amounting to a good 12.2 million kroner as well as a loan debt to Great Northern amounting to 14.5 million kroner, but Storno managed to get through 1970 without taking out new loans or receiving any other form of infusion of fresh capital. The revenues for the year ended up at 136 million kroner, which was 25 percent under the budgeted amount, and only an accounting reverse transfer of 5.2 million kroner from an account for tax depreciations secured a positive annual result of 1.5 million kroner, of which Great Northern received a dividend of 1.2 million kroner.

The first months of 1971 did not lead to a significant improvement of sales, and in late March, Great Northern's board of directors voted to provide Storno with a further loan in the amount of 10 million kroner. A major reorganization of the company involving streamlining measures including the dismissal of about four hundred employees was already under way, and there were also changes in Storno's leadership, as the company's cofounder Erik Petersen and Leif Christensen, who had been with the company since 1948, both left the top management team on July 1, 1971—the latter to become the technical chief of Great Northern when Niels Erik Holmblad retired.

That same day, Great Northern's board of directors received a report from the top management team on Storno's situation, and it was not inspiring. After the first five months of the year, revenues were 20 percent below the budgeted level, and if

Storno
ORIENTERING FOR MEDARBEJDERE

UDGIVET AF STORNO A/S
FABRIK FOR RADIOTELEFON-SYSTEMER
Ved Amagerbanen 21, 2300 København S
Telefon AS (0127) 6600, SU (0177) 6800
REDAKTION: K. ALKESKJOLD
BIRGITH RAUN
R. BILDSTED (ansv.)
TRYK: RONOTA
Eftertryk kun med redaktionens tilladelse
Tilsluttet Dansk Personalebladsforening.

CQM 700
— en ny radiotelefon

fortsættes side 3

In 1972, Storno presented its CQM car telephone with silicon transistors and integrated circuits, which allowed for a high degree of stability in operation and a long life span.

this trend continued, a deficit of 17 million would have to be expected. Production was limited, and a few hundred assembly-line workers went down to a three-day workweek. However, the liquidity situation became worse, and Great Northern had to go to Eksportkreditrådet and Privatbanken to secure additional credit for its subsidiary.[23]

Storno's revenues for 1971 ended up at 157 million kroner, which was 15 percent over the level for the previous year—but well under the budgeted 192 million kroner—and instead of showing a surplus

This photograph of a "bobby" from London's police force, Scotland Yard, with a mobile radio telephone that was very small for its time is an almost-iconic reflection of the extent to which Storno's equipment was distributed among police forces in Europe. In 1967, Storno delivered three thousand telephones to Scotland Yard together with an extensive network of stations with which to handle communication throughout London.

of 17 to 18 million kroner, the annual result ended up balanced. One reason for this was that the debts to Eksportkredtrådet and Privatbanken as well as the loans from Great Northern, which had gradually risen to a good 24.5 million kroner, were now really beginning to weigh on Storno's annual accounts in the form of significant interest payments. As long as no significant operating surplus could be presented, there was no prospect of the company's getting out of debt—if anything, the company was likely to

end up even deeper in debt than it was already. The crown jewel of the Danish electronics industry was turning into Great Northern's problem child.

Change of chief executive officer at Great Northern

To begin with, Storno appeared to regain its momentum in 1972, when the company presented a 31 percent increase in revenues, to a historic 205 million kroner. Liquidity was still tight, however, and in the fall, Great Northern had to provide a new loan in the amount of 2.5 million kroner, which was supposed to be paid back before the end of the year. In fact, it was not paid back before the end of the year, nor was it paid back in the following year.

This was because despite the increase in revenues and the record sales, Storno did not manage to produce a surplus, and in March 1973, Great Northern had to provide a new loan in the amount of 2.5 million kroner so that Storno would be able to pay its employees' wages for the month. At the same time, a liquidity budget showed that in the course of the year, Storno would need an infusion of 15 million kroner.[24]

A short time later, Storno received a further loan, in the amount of 4 million kroner, and in late May 1973, the need for liquidity in excess of the loans already received was estimated at 12 million kroner, half of which was to be received in June and half in July, but Storno's management believed that Storno would not require further cash infusions between then and the end of 1975. Great Northern's board of directors approved contributing the 12 million kroner, and the infusion was executed as a part of the increasing of Storno's share capital by 20 million kroner via the conversion of loans so that the mother companies' outstanding loans to Storno subsequently amounted to a little less than 25 million kroner.[25]

At this point, Great Northern's board of directors had long since lost patience with Storno. Already in the summer of 1972, several members of the board of directors had come to entertain doubts about Werner Drenck and his management of his respon-

sibility for the development of the subsidiary, and during the fall, the board of directors held a series of secret meetings in Bent Suenson's private residence without the knowledge of the top management team. Among the participants were the chief executive officer of Radiometer A/S, Erik B. Rasmussen, who had become a member of the board of directors in August 1971, and the chief executive officer of Finansieringsinstituttet for Industri og Håndværk ("the Financing Institute for Industry and Crafts"), Erik Mollerup, who had become a member of the board of directors a short time previously. Both of these men would play a central role in the events that followed.[26]

The topic of discussion at the confidential meetings of the board of directors was the subsidiaries and in particular Drenck's future at Great Northern, and the board of directors reached agreement

that a replacement for Drenck would have to be brought in from outside the company. Bent Suenson had previously put out a feeler to Erik B. Rasmussen, as had the chairman of the board of directors, Hans-Henrik Stevenius-Nielsen.

At the meeting of the board of directors on November 30, 1972, Erik Mollerup asked Erik B. Rasmussen directly whether he would take on the job of Great Northern's chief executive officer. After having taken a few weeks to think this over, he accepted taking over as Great Northern's chief executive officer on August 1, 1973, asking for this relatively late date because of his existing obligations at Radiometer. Werner Drenck left his position that day, while Poul Laursen stayed in the top management team with responsibility for the telecommunications sector. Leif Christensen left his post as technical chief on April 1, 1974. Alongside his post as chief executive officer, Erik B. Rasmussen retained a seat on Great Northern's board of directors, and he became the chairman of the boards of directors of the subsidiaries.[27]

There were changes to Great Northern's board of directors as well. After the general meeting in June

One of Storno's products was a so-called crane telephone that made it possible for a man on the ground to communicate with a crane operator who had difficulty seeing what was going on far beneath him.

1973, H. Stevenius-Nielsen resigned his position as chairman and was succeeded by Bent Suenson, while Erik Mollerup became the new vice chairman after just one year on the board of directors.

"[...] between hope and fear [...]"

Erik B. Rasmussen's first major task was to improve the situation at Storno, and he immediately began a thorough investigation of the subsidiary's economy. Already in November 1973, he warned the board of directors that by the middle of 1974, Storno would require a new capital infusion in the amount

of 20 to 22 million kroner to be able to finance the expected growth. On the other hand, he indicated that the prognoses for the coming year foresaw a surplus for Storno of 10 million kroner, though in the same breath he warned the board of directors "that it would not take much to reduce this result."[28]

This caused Erik Mollerup to declare that he "was tired of Storno's constant swinging back and forth between hope and fear." He had previously declared that he "found it incomprehensible that revenues like those of Storno could not generate a better result," and he asked how things were going with the evaluation of the subsidiary's economy.[29]

He and the rest of the board of directors had to wait until late January 1974, when the report on Storno had been finished. The situation was discussed at two meetings of the board of directors on February 1 and March 1, respectively, and Erik Mollerup characterized the report as "disturbing reading." Erik B. Rasmussen declared that he was in agreement but emphasized that the report "reflected his evaluation of Storno in the current situation."[30]

It did not come as a surprise to anyone that the company's liquidity was extremely strained or that the annual account for 1973 would end up showing a deficit of an estimated 5 million kroner. The final numbers were not yet ready, but it appeared clear that Storno would again require an infusion of fresh capital and that it would not be possible to secure further loans without having Great Northern become involved either as a direct lender or as a guarantor of repayment of a bank loan, and this should be avoided, as such involvement of Great Northern would have to be reflected in the annual account and would thus reveal the difficult situation in which Storno found itself.[31]

The report revealed that Storno's management, organization, and economic reporting system were "in a deplorable state and the possibilities with regard to normal administration of the company by the group management therefore restricted." Erik B. Rasmussen also noted that the numerous management changes had weakened Storno's management and led to a feeling of independence at the foreign subsidiaries, where the top management teams displayed "a lack of understanding of economic realities."

The message was that Storno had no management with an overview of the company's situation and that Storno's finances were out of control. This was confirmed by the fact that between the two meetings of the board of directors at which the matter was discussed, Storno's expected deficit increased from 5 to 12 million kroner despite an increase in revenues to 225 million kroner. It was therefore clear that Storno would need the capital infusion of up to 22 million kroner during the first five months of the year that had already been discussed, but Storno's leadership believed that Storno would subsequently be able to get through the rest of the year without further help.[32]

Great Northern's board of directors hardly felt confidence in this evaluation. Storno was like a bottomless pit, and the repeated infusions of capital were starting to have a noticeable effect on Great Northern's financial situation. In the words of Erik B. Rasmussen, a capital infusion of the desired size would "in itself put a major strain on Great Northern," and it would be necessary to ensure that there were no further liquidity demands.

The chairman of the board of directors, Bent Suenson, was also worried about the situation, and he proposed that an external audit be carried out, a proposal for which there was general support. On March 19, 1974, while the board of directors was waiting for this external audit to be completed, Storno again appeared on the board's agenda. A memorandum indicated that there was a need for an infusion of 28.6 million kroner in addition to 11 million kroner that had already been transferred to Storno to increase liquidity. Great Northern's own liquidity only made it possible for Great Northern to contribute 3 to 4 million kroner to Storno without having to start converting stocks or bonds into cash. Great Northern therefore got the company's line of credit at Privatbanken increased from 10 to 40 million kroner, and at the same time, Great Northern got the bank to abstain from terminating a temporary increase in Storno's credit in the amount of 7 million kroner in addition to the 30

Storno was the official supplier of the wireless telephony system for the Olympic Games in Munich in 1972, including base stations and mobile telephones.

million kroner the bank had already lent Storno.[33]

Erik Mollerup again warned that "the burdens with which Storno's problems [were] saddling Great Northern [were] of a significant size in relation to the company's resources," and he declared that "serious consideration should be given to the possibility of contacting companies that might be interested in Storno."[34]

Despite the care that had been taken to prevent Storno's economic difficulties from becoming known outside the Great Northern group, rumors had begun circulating in the industry—Erik B. Rasmussen could report that the American electronics companies Motorola, General Electric, and Thompson Ramo Woolridge Inc. had already been in contact with Great Northern, as had Europe's largest producer of car telephones, Pye-Philips, and Storno's partner of many years in Germany, Siemens. There was agreement that a cooperation partner should be sought, and Erik B. Rasmussen was authorized to undertake the preliminary discussions.

In the meantime, the external audit report was ready to be presented at the meeting of the board of directors on May 15, 1974, and it showed that Storno's situation "was much more serious than had previously been assumed." While Storno's own budget showed a surplus of 4.5 million kroner, the auditing company judged that there would be a deficit in the amount of 14 million kroner. The liquidity deficit was found to be just under 49 million kroner, and if the company were to continue its operations, Great Northern would have to anticipate providing considerable infusions of capital during the coming years.[35]

This being the case, Great Northern's board of directors agreed that the task of carrying out the necessary restructuring of Storno would be too heavy and economically risky for Great Northern to take on itself, and after discussion of several alternatives, the board unanimously voted to work toward selling Storno despite the fact that this "would be emotionally difficult and mean loss of face for Great Northern." A final decision in this regard was made at the meeting of the board of directors on May 21, 1974.[36]

Negotiations with Motorola

Immediately after the meeting of the board of directors, Erik B. Rasmussen visited Siemens in Germany and thereafter Motorola and General Electric in the United States. The best possibilities appeared to be offered by Motorola, which had attempted in vain to penetrate the European market and for which Storno's sales organization would constitute a good bridgehead at the same time as Storno's development and manufacturing activities would be continued. The Americans were willing to pay 16.6 million dollars—approximately 100 million kroner—for Storno, and this was the price Erik B. Rasmussen had named. The final price, however, would be dependent upon an economic and legal evaluation of Storno—so-called due diligence. Erik B. Rasmussen promised to recommend to his board of directors

that the offer be accepted, and indeed, the board of directors were in an excellent mood when they met on July 1, 1974. The board of directors congratulated Erik B. Rasmussen on the result he had achieved and unanimously approved proceeding on the basis of Erik B. Rasmussen's negotiations with Motorola.[37]

The result of the American due diligence process was that Motorola found the price too high. Around the same time, Storno was negatively affected by declining sales in Germany in particular as a result of the economic downturn, and an overview of the liquidity situation showed that Storno would require a new infusion of approximately 20 million kroner, which Great Northern "could just barely manage." Given the prospect of having to inject more capital into Storno, Great Northern's board of directors supported proceeding with the sale even if the price would be one that was "significantly lower than the price originally discussed."[38]

However, there were unexpected complications in the middle of October, when, during a visit to the United States, Erik B. Rasmussen was informed that Motorola had been warned by its attorneys that if Motorola acquired Storno, then Motorola might find itself in the spotlight of the American authorities because of a perceived violation of American antitrust laws. Storno had no sales in the United States, but the authorities might come to the conclusion that by acquiring Storno, Motorola would have put itself in a position to be able to prevent a competitor from entering the American market.

When Erik B. Rasmussen reported to Great Northern's board of directors following his return from the United States, he was therefore "somewhat pessimistic" with regard to whether Motorola would complete the transaction. His pessimism would prove to have been justified, as the Americans informed Great Northern in the middle of December 1974 that they had decided not to proceed with the matter.[39]

Storno is sold to General Electric

For the time being, then, Great Northern was stuck with Storno, which did increase its revenues once again in 1974, by 20 percent to 272 million kroner.

However, Storno had debts totaling 300 million kroner, 62 million kroner of which were owed to Great Northern, while Storno had equity of only 51 million kroner and had 130 million kroner tied up in inventory. There were some bright spots, however. The annual result before tax was a modest deficit of 1 million kroner, and the liquidity situation had improved, so there was hope that Storno might get through the first quarter of 1975 without needing an infusion of capital.

The decision to sell the business was unchanged, however, and the company now turned its attention to General Electric, with whom Erik B. Rasmussen had conducted ongoing discussions the entire time he had been engaged in negotiations with Motorola, just as he had maintained contact with Siemens. General Electric declared that it was quite interested—not in acquiring Storno, but in acquiring a majority position in a Danish-American joint venture—while Siemens were more hesitant and unclear in their way of expressing themselves.

In the summer of 1975, Great Northern's discussions with General Electric therefore moved into a decisive phase, and on December 9, Erik B. Rasmussen could finally present a complete draft contract to Great Northern's board of directors. According to this draft contract, General Electric acquired 50 percent of the shares in Storno effective on January 1, 1976, and a further 25 percent effective on January 1, 1978. Great Northern would retain the remaining 25 percent, which the company would be free to sell after 1982, though General Electric would have the right of first refusal. The price was set at approximately 94 million kroner, payment of 60 million of which would be due on January 1, 1976, and payment of the remainder of which would be due two years later. In addition, a bonus would be paid dependent upon Storno's results for the first four years.[40]

General Electric assumed full responsibility for the leadership of Storno and acquired a majority on the board of directors, while Great Northern would have the right to two seats on the board of directors and the right to appoint the chairman of the board of directors for the first two years. The Americans were supposed to exercise leadership "after consultation" with Great Northern, and the unanimous support of the board of directors would be required in connection with "major decisions that could have a significant effect on Great Northern's investment [. . .]."[41]

Great Northern's board of directors were satisfied with the fact that the company would remain involved with Storno, which had good prospects for growth, and the board therefore looked forward to "long-lasting cooperation" with General Electric. At the same time, the board of directors were relieved over no longer carrying all of the risk and all of the responsibility. During a meeting with the chairman of the board of directors of General Electric, Bent Suenson declared that it "had not been without some hesitation that Great Northern had relinquished its control over Storno, which had been so closely associated with Great Northern, and that nationalistic feelings had also played a role." General Electric's board chairman responded by saying that General Electric was glad to have Great Northern as a business partner.[42]

The agreement was approved by General Electric's board of directors on December 19, 1975, and by Great Northern's board of directors three days later. As agreed, Erik B. Rasmussen became the chairman of the board of directors of Storno; the top management team continued its work with Peter Vange as chief executive officer supplemented by two directors from General Electric. To the public, Storno appeared to be a Danish company despite the fact that from January 1, 1976, onward, it was a subsidiary of General Electric. It was emphasized in communications with employees and the public that Storno would continue as it had previously and that there would not be production changes or dismissals of employees.

As a result of the sale, Great Northern's annual revenues declined from 794 million kroner for 1975 to 563 million kroner for the following year, and the number of employees was reduced from 4,350 to 2,300. However, the group's other companies were growing, and new activities had been begun, and not much time passed before the hole left by Storno had been more than filled in.

From the Great Northern Telegraph Company to GN Store Nord

After the sale of Storno, Great Northern had four subsidiaries: on the one hand GNT Automatic and Hellesens Invest and on the other hand two very new subsidiaries, the wholesaler for electrical articles Havemanns Eftf. A/S, which in 1975 had revenues of 114 million kroner, and the data processing company Tiger Data A/S, which in 1975 had revenues of 16 million kroner. In the past, Havemanns had been the sole dealer for Hellesens batteries in Denmark, and in the second half of the 1950s, when the company had gotten into difficulties, it had been purchased by Hellesens. In 1973, Havemanns had been acquired by Great Northern as a fully owned subsidiary with share capital of 12 million kroner.

Tiger Data too had originated from Hellesens, whose electronic data processing division had carried out data processing for other companies using Hellesens's computers. In 1971, the department became a subsidiary of Hellesens, and the following year, Oliemøllen ("the Oil Mill") in Aarhus, Colon Emballage ("Colon Packaging"), and De forenede Papirfabrikker ("the United Paper Factories")—all customers of Tiger Data—became involved as part

owners. In the spring of 1975, Tiger Data merged with Store Nord Konsulent ("Great North Consultant") A/S, which had been founded three years previously and had become a subsidiary of Great Northern, which owned 51 percent of the shares, while the rest were owned by Colon Emballage, De forenede Papirfabrikker, and Oliemøllen.

The new subsidiaries did not add new activities or new revenues to the group; rather, the companies were created as the result of internal reorganization. However, new activities were on the way, as the main shareholder in and chief executive officer of the Danish hearing aid manufacturer Danavox, Gerd Rosenstand, had contacted Erik Mollerup early in 1975 to find out whether Great Northern would be interested in taking over the business.

Rosenstand offered to give Erik B. Rasmussen an opportunity to join Danavox's board of directors to follow the company's activities and get to know the leading staff members so that there would be a good basis for discussing a possible takeover of Danavox by Great Northern again in a year's time. Great Northern's board of directors were in agreement that Danavox could be of interest to Great Northern, and Rosenstand's offer was accepted.[1]

Danavox A/S and the Danish hearing aid industry

Danavox had a history that went back to before the company had begun to manufacture hearing aids as one of the first companies in Denmark to do so. In 1925, Nordisk Radio Industri A/S was founded. That company was located on Rådhuspladsen in Copenhagen and manufactured crystal radio receivers that were sold under the name Superphone and electrodynamic loudspeakers with the name Danavox—"the Danish voice." In 1930, the manufacture of loudspeakers was split off and placed in an independent division with the newly hired electrician Gerd Rosenstand as its head.

In 1943, the manufacture of loudspeakers was separated off in an independent limited company, Danavox, Fabrik for Elektroakustisk Materiale ("Danavox, the Factory for Electroacoustic Equipment") A/S with Gerd Rosenstand as its chief executive officer. The founders were Rosenstand, who provided half of the share capital, which amounted to a total of 100,000 kroner, and Nordisk Radio Industri and two leading staff members who together contributed the rest of the share capital. In addition to amplifiers, the company manufactured microphones and loudspeaker systems for stage performances as well as components and accessories such as various plugs, jacks, fittings, microphone stands, and cables—all under the brand name Danavox.

After the war, a new business area opened up when the development of new technology such as miniature radio tubes led to a revolution in the manufacture of hearing aids. Early in 1946, Danavox concluded a representation agreement with the British hearing aid producer Multitone, and in the summer of the same year, Danavox launched its first hearing aid via a sales office on Borgergade in central Copenhagen. The following year, at the same address, a hearing clinic, Nordisk Tunghøre Service ("Nordic Service for the Hard of Hearing"), opened. Here anyone who wished to could undergo an au-

ADITONE er den største Nyhed i mange Aar inden for Tunghøreapparater.
ADITONE er bygget efter de sidste akustiske Principper og giver en enestaaende kraftig Forstærkning, fri for „Sus" og Baggrundsstøj.

Det fine Præcisionsinstrument er indbygget i et elegant gyldent Metalkabinet, der næppe er saa stort som et Spil Kort, og det vejer ialt med Batterier 190 g.

Trods sine mange indlysende Fordele og Forbedringer er ADITONE takket være rationel Fabrikation endog væsentlig billige end de tidligere store Apparater med store, løse Batterier. ADITONE koster nemlig kun Kr. 525,00

ADITONE maa De se og prøve. De er velkommen i vore Servicelokaler uden Købelvang, og vi sender Dem gerne vor store Beskrivelse.

Eneforhandling for Danmark:

Nordisk Tunghøre Service
BORGERGADE 15 . KØBENHAVN . PALÆ 5946

Advertisement from October 1948 for Danavox's first device, which was marketed under the name Aditone and retailed through Nordisk Tunghøre Service, which was owned by Danavox and soon represented by branches in several Danish cities.

diological evaluation that would result in a printed audiogram showing any hearing loss for each ear.

The imposition of stricter import rules, however, meant that the components were to be manufactured in Denmark, and this established the course to be followed by Danavox, which produced the first hearing aid of its own, which was called Aditone, in the fall of 1948 and created its own sales organization. Danavox had an annual production of six thousand devices, 4,500 of which were for the export markets.

The Aditone hearing aid was a pocket model with a three-tube amplifier and a crystal microphone as well as a battery that was housed in the same metal case; the total weight of the device was 190 grams. An earplug with a little electroacoustic speaker was connected to the amplifier by a wire so that it could be placed in the ear. "One has the impression that everything smart from America has been combined with the fine execution of Danish craftsmanship, and the overall impression is therefore as good as could be imagined," the industry journal *Dansk Radio Industri* enthusiastically wrote.[2]

However, Danavox was not the only Danish manufacturer of hearing aids. In the 1930s, William Demant manufactured American Acousticon hearing aids under license, and in 1940, after the outbreak of the Second World War, he launched the first hearing aid that was entirely Danish-produced, the Acusticus, which was a copy of the American device.[3]

After the war, the production of the copied hearing aid led to a break with the American company, and in the spring of 1946, William Demant and the American hearing aid manufacturer Charles Lehman founded the American-Danish Oticon Company, which at the same time introduced the Oticon model TA hearing aid, which had a construction similar to that of the Multitone that was presented by Danavox in the summer of the same year—except that the Multitone had built-in batteries, while Oticon's model had external batteries, which led to a fair amount of problems with the wires.[4]

From the beginning, then, Danavox and Oticon were competitors on the Danish market, and from the beginning, both companies were export-oriented. Both companies sold products in Denmark by having representatives travel around and demonstrate the products at hotels and inns and in meeting houses. This changed in 1950, when a law was passed in Denmark establishing government economic support for hearing aids; all Danes with hearing problems thus acquired the right to receive free hearing aids. Public hearing aid centers were opened in Copenhagen, Odense, and Aarhus, and subsequently hearing clinics were opened at hospitals all over the country. During the first year after the law was adopted, a total of seven thousand applications for hearing aids were received, and this number was characteristic of the following years as well.[5]

This system fundamentally changed the Danish hearing aid market, as the customers became patients, and the government-run hearing centers became the only significant purchasers of hearing aids. One consequence of this development was that there was a marked increase in demand, but there was also increased competition between the two manufacturers—and in the long run, there was an enhancement of the quality of the devices.

For economic reasons, the government wished to offer a single high-quality device. The technology offered only limited possibilities with regard to variations among devices, and it was believed that approximately 80 percent of all individuals with hearing problems could be helped by a single standardized type of device. Statens Hørecentraler (the Danish government hearing centers) therefore purchased hearing aids in large quantities from licensed manufacturers that provided devices satisfying the government's specifications. In the beginning, the hearing aids were evaluated by Lydteknisk Laboratorium ("the Acoustic Laboratory"), a unit of the Danish Academy of Technical Sciences; later, the hearing aids were evaluated by a special council comprising representatives of the medical, hearing pedagogy, administrative, and technical sectors.[6]

The first round of licensing testing took place in May 1952, when only 25 percent of the thirty-six devices that were offered by Danish and foreign companies were approved. Oticon and Danavox both participated; the company chosen to be the largest supplier was Raaberg & Co., which imported British Fortiphone-brand hearing aids, while Danavox secured an order for 1,500 devices and Oticon failed to secure an order. In contrast to its competitor Oticon, Danavox was therefore able to brag about being a "supplier to the Danish hearing centers," but after the next licensing round, it was Oticon that was able to decorate itself with this title.[7]

The government's hearing centers constituted a de facto purchasing monopoly, and for the two Danish manufacturers, the licensing rounds became a recurring all-or-nothing contest. This sharpened their competition to use the latest technology and enhance quality, and the development processes for new devices were also driven by the fact that the companies received free access to all of the statistical material from the hearing centers, which they could use to develop their new devices.

In connection with the export markets, the two companies could also advertise the fact that their devices had been clinically tested—even in cases in which the devices in question had not been chosen to be ordered by the hearing centers—and this had a great deal of marketing value. The orders from the hearing centers were far from sufficiently large to ensure that production of the devices would be profitable, however, and both Danavox and Oticon were therefore very much export-oriented—and they experienced great successes on the export markets. During the first six years, Danavox increased its revenues for hearing aids tenfold, and exports accounted for 85 percent of the company's total sales.

In 1956, a further Danish hearing aid manufacturer came into existence when two leading employees broke with Oticon and founded Widex A/S. In 1963, after several years of hard competition, the three Danish hearing aid companies formed the cooperative company Otwidan—the name incorporated the respective first letters of the three original companies' names—through which they placed common bids for the Danish government's orders and distributed production and deliveries among themselves internally. This arrangement was approved by Denmark's newly created monopoly authority Monopoltilsyn and contributed to weakening large foreign competitors such as Siemens and Philips in Denmark while the Danish companies continued to compete on the export markets as they had in the past.

In 1964, the technical development process was further strengthened by the establishment of Laboratoriet for Teknisk-Audiologisk Forskning ("the Laboratory for Technical-Audiological Research"), which had the purpose of conducting research on hearing aids and other technical aids for individuals with hearing problems and functioning as a technical consultant for the Danish hearing-enhancement establishment to ensure that the newest technology was reflected in the specifications published in connection with rounds of bidding by potential suppliers of hearing aids.

Hearing aids, ear telephones, and stethosets

From the beginning, the hearing aid sector was characterized by constant technological development and probably the first civilian production in which the transistor technology of the postwar period was used. At the same time, improvements in battery technology involving the use of mercury elements in button-sized batteries contributed to reducing the size of hearing aids, so it became possible to wear them discreetly.

In 1953, Danavox, as one of the first hearing aid manufacturers in Europe to do so, could present an "all transistor" model, and in the summer of 1955, the first spectacle hearing-aid in Europe were introduced by Danavox. The spectacles had the earphone, the battery, and the sound control built into one stem and the rest of the apparatus built into the other. "The triumph of technology," the advertisement for the spectacles called them. Two years later, an improved version was presented that had a complete hearing aid built into each of the temples of the spectacles so that a stereo effect was achieved, and it thus became possible to determine the direction from which a sound was coming. A model for women with long hair was Baretten, "the Barrette," which consisted of a hearing aid built into a hair barrette and a wire to the earphone that could be concealed in the hair or in a tie pin with the wire leading back to the ear concealed behind the tie.[8]

In 1957, Danavox presented its first hearing aid for slightly hearing-impaired individuals to be placed in or rather on the ear—Aurette, it was called. Later the same year, Danavox presented a model called the ear-hanger that was placed behind the ear and had a short wire leading to the ear telephone. This type of device was included in the standard assortment of the Danish hearing centers

In contrast to eyeglasses, whose visibility was quickly accepted, and which were eventually seen as a means of forming the characteristics of the human face, the development of hearing aids was and is characterized by efforts to render them invisible. The picture shows two of Danavox's devices in 1957 that were designed with precisely this goal in mind; the hearing aids are concealed in a hair barrette and a pair of spectacles, respectively.

starting in the late 1960s and was supplied by Otwidan.[9]

In 1964, Danavox became the first European hearing aid manufacturer to use integrated circuits in an ear-hanger, and the following year, Danavox presented a so-called all-in-the-ear device, the model 661 IMC, which could be placed in the ear canal itself. All cords and wires could thus be avoid-

ed, and in *Ingeniøren*, the device was touted as "the most advanced device that has been built in Europe and one that sets the standards for the hearing aids of the future." Some years would pass, however, before the all-in-the-ear models became an element of the Danish hearing centers' assortment, which in the late 1960s included hearing-aid glasses, ear-hangers, and pocket models.[10]

Danavox had a business area in addition to hearing aids, as the company's self-developed components were sold to other manufacturers of hearing aids and also constituted the basis of a further product. This was earphones for Dictaphones and portable transistor radios, which were becoming increasingly popular in the United States. These earphones weighed between two and a half and nine grams, and in 1957, Danavox produced approximately five hundred thousand.

In 1951, the company could present a new earphone set, a so-called stethoset—later called a stethoclip—which had two hearing tubes for the ears and a lightweight earphone placed where the two hearing tubes met so that it was possible to carry on a conversation. This device—an early version of the headsets of the present day—was sold for use by telephone switchboard operators, among other uses.[11]

Later came over-the-head on-the-ear headphones, and in 1965, a mobile so-called boom-arm microphone that was attached to the headphones was presented and gave birth to a series of other new headsets. The same year, the Danasonic system was demonstrated—a wireless headphone with small radio receivers placed on the headband so instructions could be transmitted from a centrally placed microphone, tape recorder, or other devices.

Danavox marketed its hearing aids under the brand name Aditone until 1968, when the company began using the company name Danavox, which was also a part of the names of the nine subsidiaries in various countries the company had by that point. The occasion for which this change was made was the company's twenty-fifth anniversary on January 22, 1968, when the name got further exposure as a result of the fact that Gerd Rosenstand awarded 25,000 kroner to Laboratoriet for Teknisk-Audiologisk Forskning and at the same time announced the creation of Danavox Jubilæumsfond ("the Danavox Jubilee Foundation"), which was formally established on January 1, 1970.

Danavox—A subsidiary in the Great Northern group

Like Storno, Danavox contributed to building up an entirely new market for communications equipment. In the early 1950s, when Nordisk Radio Industri got into difficulties, Gerd Rosenstand bought the company's shares in Danavox, but in the late 1950s, the two other part owners had to provide fresh share capital to address a liquidity crisis. In early 1975, when Rosenstand contacted Great Northern, he therefore owned approximately 62 percent of the share capital. He now wished to sell the company because he planned to withdraw from his involvement with the company and retire in Switzerland.

The question of Great Northern's possible involvement with Danavox was back on the agenda when Great Northern's board of directors met on June 17, 1976, and Erik B. Rasmussen, having been a member of the board of directors for a year, declared that he considered Danavox to be "a good business," indicating that it could be of interest for Great Northern to become its sole owner. He had already had a preliminary discussion with Gerd Rosenstand and was now authorized to proceed with the matter and carry out a due diligence process with a view to taking over the business.[12]

Danavox had a complicated group structure with the holding company Danavox Invest A/S at the top and five subordinate companies with a further nine subsidiaries, two of which were production companies in Denmark and the United Kingdom and six of which were sales companies in the United Kingdom, France, the Netherlands, Germany, Switzerland, and the United States. Revenues for the last accounting year, 1975/1976, had amounted to a little under 67 million kroner with a surplus of 3 million kroner,

and for 1976/1977, revenues of 71 million kroner and a surplus of 1 million kroner were expected.[13]

Danavox's biggest product was hearing aids, which accounted for 42.5 percent of the company's revenues, while components for devices including hearing aids accounted for 13.5 percent and headsets for only 1.9 percent. The remaining revenues came largely from batteries and assorted accessories for the hearing-impaired as well as repairs and service.

Among the world's largest producers of hearing aids, Danavox was number eight, with 80,000 devices per year, while Denmark's Oticon was the largest, with 225,000; the American company Beltone number two, with 200,000; and Widex number three, with 120,000. Danavox had previously ranked higher, but in the last ten years, the company had slid down, which the due diligence process that had been completed suggested had been the result of a focus in recent years on short-term results and "the extraction of unreasonably large" dividends as well as "excessive salaries" paid to Gert Rosenstand in anticipation of his retirement.

As a consequence, there had not been enough money for development and investments, and there had not been a focus on long-term results. Assuming this trend would be corrected, Danavox was found to be "an exciting company with the potential for growth that fit with what Great Northern would be able to handle," and in terms of its earnings, Danavox was found to be basically healthy.[14]

Late in the year, Gerd Rosenstand received confirmation from the minority shareholders that they too would be willing to sell their shares to Great Northern, and what now remained was to agree on a price. In April 1977, after lengthy negotiations, agreement was reached that Great Northern would take over Danavox by the end of the year in a series of stages for a total price of 26.5 million kroner.[15]

Two new subsidiaries: Elmi A/S and LK-NES A/S

In the wake of the acquisition of Danavox, Great Northern acquired another company after a ne-

GNT Automatic developed and marketed apparatuses for the measurement of noise at various frequencies, which became the technological and commercial basis of the activity of the company Elmi, which became a subsidiary of Great Northern in 1971.

gotiation process that had gone both faster and more easily. This company was Elmi A/S, which had originated at GNT Automatic, which had begun developing electronic measuring equipment for telephone switchboard centers and telecommunications connections. In the summer of 1971, the division in question had been split off and turned into a limited company, Elmi. The name was an abbreviation of "Electrical Measuring Instruments." Forty-nine percent of the share capital was owned

by GNT Automatic and 51 percent by the head of the division, P. C. Beyer, who became the new company's chief executive officer.

Elmi started out with twenty-two employees and annual revenues of 2.8 million kroner, and by 1976, the company had forty employees and annual revenues had increased to just under 11 million kroner. From the beginning, the company's main customer was L. M. Ericsson, which had originally received about 50 percent of Elmi's production, but Elmi had a growing number of other customers, including government telecommunications authorities. At the same time, L. M. Ericsson was reducing its orders, and in 1976, they constituted only 20 percent of Elmi's total sales. About 19 percent of Elmi's revenues came from export markets in thirty countries.

In the summer of 1977, Elmi's two shareholders offered Great Northern an opportunity to acquire Elmi. Great Northern's leaders were quite familiar with Elmi, naturally, and in December 1977, the parties reached agreement on a price of 10 million kroner plus a possible bonus for P. C. Beyer, who continued in the role of chief executive officer. The purchase of Elmi was subsequently executed effective February 1, 1978.[16]

Shortly thereafter, another purchase—though not a complete one —followed, and in this case too, the process went smoothly. Since 1968, Great Northern, with 25 percent of the share capital, had been the biggest single shareholder in LK-NES, where Bent Suenson had been chairman of the board of directors since 1973. The company manufactured articles for electrical installations, low and high voltage equipment, electrical measurement devices, and fuses as well as various electronic control systems. The company's largest business area was electrical installation articles, an area in which, because of national technical specifications, LK-NES had a de facto monopoly in Denmark on electrical plugs and other products that produced annual revenues of approximately 500 million kroner.

The second-biggest shareholder was Ulf Ekmann, whose father had founded one of the two companies that became LK-NES and who was willing to sell his bloc of shares, which comprised 11.3

percent of the total shares. Other shareholders too were willing to sell, and effective April 1, 1978, Great Northern acquired shares accounting for a little more than 53 percent of the share capital in LK-NES. At the next general meeting thereafter, Bent Suenson resigned his position as chairman of the board of directors and was succeeded by Erik B. Rasmussen.[17]

Electronics conglomerate with continuing telecommunications operations

With its acquisition of Danavox, Elmi, and not least LK-NES, Great Northern had more than filled the hole in the group revenues left by the sale of Storno, and in 1978, the group received revenues in excess of 1 billion kroner for the first time. Revenues for that year exceeded those for the previous year by almost 450 million kroner, mostly thanks to the acquisition of LK-NES even though the company had contributed only for nine months.[18]

The following year, revenues increased to more than 1.4 billion kroner, partly as a result of organic growth and partly because LK-NES now contributed revenues for an entire year, in the amount of 600 million kroner. With the revenues from Aage Havemanns Eftf., which amounted to 187 million kroner, the production and sale of articles for electrical installations and related items accounted for almost 57 percent of Great Northern's total revenues. Hellesens Invest contributed 226 million kroner, GNT Automatic 216 million kroner, Danavox 100 million kroner, Tiger Data 25.5 million kroner, and Elmi just under 21 million kroner.[19]

While the purchases contributed to an almost explosive increase in the group's revenues, the earnings situation was less positive. In 1976, the subsidiaries contributed a total of 7 million kroner in dividends to the mother company, but such contributions dramatically declined, to 1.4 million kroner, in 1977. The main reason for this was that Sweden's AGA group sold its stake in Hellesens-Tudor to the American battery giant ESB Inc. effective February 1, 1977, and the lucrative agreement with regard to

Hellesens Invest was thus nullified. After this, the subsidiaries' dividends increased to 5.3 million kroner in 1978, when 2.2 million kroner came from LK-NES, and then to 8.9 million kroner in 1979.[20]

The small dividends from the subsidiaries were due to an economic downturn that had commenced after steep increases in the price of oil in 1973, and both LK-NES and Havemanns were also affected by economic trends in the construction sector. Hellesens faced the particular challenge that the market for traditional dry batteries was declining while the market for alkali battery types was growing and the use of lithium was increasing, which resulted in large development costs. Things were going better for Tiger Data, where Great Northern took over the leadership of the company completely at the beginning of 1976. Tiger Data was delivering both growth and nice surpluses, as were Elmi and GNT Automatic.[21]

On the other hand, Danavox did not contribute a dividend in 1977, 1978, or 1979, as the company was not able to produce a surplus despite the fact that the company had undergone a thorough streamlining process.

In contrast, the telecommunications business had become a stable source of income. The group's expectation that it would discontinue its activities in this sector notwithstanding, telecommunications revenues grew until they stabilized at approximately 40 to 42 million kroner annually. One of the reasons for this was that in 1976, Great Northern had exercised its right to increase its share in the Japan-Russia cable—the JASC—to 50 percent, which had doubled Great Northern's earnings from the cable, and at the same time, more and more circuits were being leased as a result of the economic growth in Japan and the country's increasing importance in the global economy. As had been expected, classic telegram traffic declined, but in 1979, it was still contributing revenues of 4 million kroner. The surplus for telecommunications in their entirety fluctuated approximately in the range of 10 to 12 million kroner annually, which was constantly more than the corresponding amount for all of the subsidiaries together.

Great Northern's last cable ship, the *Northern*, on a voyage in the North Atlantic in 1976. In addition to maintaining the Scotice-Icecan connection, the ship's crew maintained cables for other companies and telegraphy authorities.

Despite the continuing significance of the telecommunications activity, the acquisition of the new subsidiaries completed Great Northern's transformation into an electronics conglomerate that was engaged in the manufacturing of products for various—and varied—different markets as well as in wholesaling. The conglomerate was a form of organization that had become more and more popular in large companies because it made it possible to increase revenues by means of the spreading of the respective company's activities to more markets. At the same time, risks were spread so that the company was not dependent upon developments within a single market.

The many companies with their individual challenges created a growing workload for the company's management, however, and this caused Erik B. Rasmussen to present plans, in September 1975, for the establishment of a group secretariat to assist

the chief executive officer and strengthen the relationship with the subsidiaries, which he characterized as "weak." In addition to the secretariat, there was a need for overall strategic planning and control of the development of the entire group of which the existing organization was not capable, and there was a lack of resources for carrying out the analyses that were necessary when new companies were acquired.[22]

The new leadership organization was implemented in January 1977, when an actual group administration was created. At the same time, a new position was created for a vice director for financial control with responsibility for contact with the subsidiaries, and this position was filled on March 1, 1977, with René Tang Jespersen, who came to Great Northern from the American computer and electronics group Honeywell. At the same time, P. E. V. Jørgensen became the new head of the telecommunications division, while Erik B. Rasmussen, as chief executive officer, had the superordinate leadership responsibility for the whole group.[23]

Economic downturn and disappointments

After the sale of Storno and the acquisition of the share majorities in Elmi and LK-NES, Great Northern still had such a significant liquidity reserve that its size, as Erik B. Rasmussen put it at a meeting of the board of directors in late August 1979, "in itself was sufficient incentive to make new investments." Nevertheless, he felt that given the need for consolidation in the wake of the latest purchases, Great

Northern should not make new purchases in the near future.[24]

A few months later, Erik B. Rasmussen was nevertheless involved in negotiations regarding the acquisition of a company, as the American battery group ESB wished to sell the stake in Hellesens it had purchased less than three years previously. For Great Northern, this was not a dream scenario, as Hellesens had long been viewed as a problem child due to failure to produce earnings—Great Northern, then, would have preferred not to have received an unexpected opportunity to become sole owner of Hellesens.[25]

For Great Northern, the alternative to purchasing ESB's shares was that someone else would purchase the shares and that it would be impossible for Great Northern to be certain beforehand who the purchaser would be. In that case, the sale could result in an undesirable focus on Hellesens's difficult situation. "Everything taken into consideration, a purchase of ESB's share by Great Northern must be viewed as least disadvantageous," the chairman concluded, and indeed, Great Northern did acquire the stake effective January 1, 1980, for the price of 32 million kroner.[26]

Great Northern became sole owner of Hellesens at the worst possible time. In the wake of the 1973 oil crisis, there was a general trend toward economic recovery in the late 1970s, and as in the rest of the business world, there was optimism at Great Northern, where, in 1979, Board Chairman Erik Mollerup expressed "a reasonable amount of confidence" that 1980 would bring a slightly better annual result.[27]

Instead, Great Northern was hit hard by a new oil crisis and subsequent economic downturn in the wake of the Iranian revolution and the collapse of Iran's oil production in 1979. At a meeting of the board of directors in June 1980, Erik Mollerup had to conclude that "the picture of the group one can see is bleak" and that the situation at Hellesens in particular was "worrying."[28]

When the group's annual account for 1980 was ready, it in fact proved to be the case that Hellesens, which presented a deficit of 27 million kroner, had suffered most, while LK-NES followed with a deficit of 13.8 million kroner. Danavox, Tiger Data, and Havemanns too had deficits; only Elmi and GNT Automatic posted surpluses. In contrast to the subsidiaries' overall situation, revenues from the telecommunications sector significantly increased to 57.6 million kroner and delivered a surplus of just under 30 million kroner, while yields from stocks and bonds contributed 23 million kroner. However, this did not prevent the group's ordinary result from being a surplus of only 5 million kroner—61 million kroner less than for the previous year despite the fact that revenues had increased by 200 million kroner, to just under 1.6 billion kroner.[29]

This situation caused brows to be furrowed deeply on the board of directors, who were particularly disappointed in Danavox, which again had a deficit, this time in the amount of 4.4 million kroner. The chairman was especially critical. He had repeatedly expressed dissatisfaction with Danavox, and in June 1980, he had said that the board of directors "would hardly have any more patience if the company did not present a better result for the current year."[30]

Danavox, then, had in fact failed to produce a better result; nevertheless, the board's patience did last a while longer after a new chief executive officer and a new chief financial officer had been hired. In addition to these leadership changes, a new headset, a so-called Stetomike, was introduced and quickly generated strong demand, being chosen as the official model for the soccer world championships in Spain in 1982. Also, Danavox was ahead of its two Danish competitors with regard to the development of a new thick-film technology to be used in the production of electronic circuits, and in the United States, the Sears chain added Danavox rather than Oticon to its assortment, while the new Stetomike was approved by the American authorities.[31]

In 1981, it proved possible to increase Danavox's revenues by 30 percent, to 145 million kroner, and achieve a modest surplus of 700,000 kroner. Havemanns too had a small surplus, while Elmi and GNT Automatic again had good results and Hellesens again brought up the rear, with a deficit of 13 million kroner. An increase in revenues for the telecommunications sector to 65.5 million kroner combined with cost-cutting measures implemented across the whole group contributed to an improvement of the group's ordinary result, which increased from 5 million to 65 million kroner. Given that the group's revenues had increased by 200 million kroner, to 1.8 billion kroner, however, the ordinary result was not exactly splendid—particularly not in view of the fact that the group had sold its remaining stake in Storno to General Electric, which, together with Great Northern's share of Storno's surplus for 1980, had provided net revenue of 31 million kroner.

The negative economic trend continued during the following years, and Great Northern achieved only very weak real growth during this period. Along the way, the wholesaler Havemanns disappeared; it merged with the Swedish company Asea Skandia, which received an option to purchase Great Northern's 50 percent of the shares, which it subsequently did in several stages.

Despite the economic downturn, Elmi continued to post good results both on the top line and on the bottom line, but otherwise, there were disappointments across the board. With stagnating revenues, GNT Automatic presented a deficit of 5.7 million in 1983, while Danavox delivered a deficit both in 1982 and in 1983. LK-NES too posted large deficits, but a thorough restructuring of the company and a new upswing in the construction sector made it possible for the company to post positive results again in 1983 and 1984.

In contrast, it did not prove to be possible to reverse the trend at Hellesens. After the poor results in 1980 and 1981, the company did succeed in producing small surpluses for two years, but in 1984, the result dramatically plunged, to a deficit of 20 million kroner. This deficit was discussed at length by GN Store Nord's board of directors, in connection with which the chairman declared "that the board cannot accept deficits of that size."[32]

In the spring of 1985, it was clear that Hellesens was again heading for a significant deficit. Also, an overview showed that during the period 1975–1985, the company had increased its revenues from 200 million to 400 million kroner but only presented small annual surpluses four times, in 1975, 1976, 1982, and 1983. For all of the other years in that period, Hellesens had posted deficits, and Great Northern had infused Hellesens with 114 million kroner, either in the form of loans or as increases in the share capital. In the words of the chairman, the situation looked "extremely difficult," and the board decided to look for potential buyers.[33]

Microprocessors, digitalization, and fiber optic cables

Tiger Data was also affected by the economic downturn and posted large deficits in 1980 and 1981, after which there were again surpluses, though modest ones. In addition to the economic downturn, the little data company was challenged by a new technological revolution that in the long run would revolutionize not only the data and electronics industry but the whole global economy.

In the 1960s, large mainframe computers had gained a place in large companies and public institutions, but in the early 1970s, the first microprocessor, the Intel 4004, which housed the computer's central processing unit in an integrated circuit, was marketed. The following year, its successor, the Intel 8008, became available, and after this, things went only one way, with microprocessors that were ever smaller, faster, and more powerful, which led to the production of so-called minicomputers that won a place in small and medium-sized businesses.

Computers are built on digital technology that converts all information to zeroes and ones, which are represented by the absence and the presence of a signal respectively. In the late 1960s, data transmission began to become common. Special modems were used to transmit computers' digital data via the telephone network. By the beginning of 1970, 420 telephone modems had been connected to the Danish telephone network.

Another technological breakthrough arrived in 1970, when the American company Corning Glass

Works took out a patent on fiber optic cables—or light conductor cables—in which copper in cables was replaced by glass fibers and electrical impulses were replaced by flashes of light, which resulted in a much greater transmission capacity and much higher transmission speeds. This technology created the infrastructure foundation for the establishment of a telecommunications infrastructure that in addition to providing telephony and telex connections also made possible the rapid transmission of pictures, film, and all kinds of data in the same cable and network on the basis of digitalization.

For the time being, the new technology was still in its infancy, but already from the middle of the 1970s onward, the big telecommunications companies were fully committed to digital transmission, and the first digital switchboards were installed at Danish companies. In 1980, two Danish telephone companies and P & T requested bids for orders for no fewer than 125 digital telephone switchboards, and the same year, the laying of the first fiber optic cables in Denmark was begun—and there were similar trends elsewhere in the industrialized world.

Elmi was able to get through the economic downturn better than the other subsidiaries not least because the company quickly adapted to the new information and communication technologies. Already in 1978, Elmi introduced a new generation of programmable testing and measuring instruments based on the use of microprocessors, and Elmi was also developing new instruments for the measuring and control of digital telephone switchboard centers and transmission systems.

Tiger Data also sought to adapt, beginning to change its business model in the late 1970s. Until then, Tiger Data's business model had consisted of

While, by far, the largest part of Great Northern's revenues were coming from the industrial companies, the telecommunications area, including the maintenance and repair of cables in the North Atlantic, was still an important source of income for the company. The picture shows the placement of an undersea amplifier in September 1975.

batch processing of data including accounts and salary payments that had been generated by its mainframe computer to its owners and other clients. Elmi began instead to deliver "intelligent terminals" for companies that, with their own monitors and programs for word processing, economic administration, administration of orders, and invoicing were connected to Tiger Data's systems via telephone modems. Parallel to this activity, Tiger Data expanded its sales and servicing of minicomputers to include the supplying of a standard program for clients including auditors and payment card companies, who represented rapidly growing business areas.

The new products created a need for nationwide direct contacts with customers, and in 1980, Tiger Data purchased the company Dansk Data A/S, which had branches in Esbjerg, Kolding,

Aarhus, and Odense. In 1981, the two companies merged under the name Tidana A/S, and in June 1982, Tidana became a fully owned subsidiary.

Meanwhile, technological developments continued at accelerated speed. In 1981, the American computer group IBM introduced a so-called personal computer, a type of minicomputer that was soon known as a PC and was sold via chains of stores such as Sears and Computerland. The door to the private consumer market was opened, and other computer companies soon produced cheap copies of IBM's PC that had been created with a so-called open architecture that had not been created for IBM's use alone. The term *PC* soon became a general designation for the new microcomputers, whose rapid spread caused the basis for Tidan's data business to crumble but also created new possibilities.

Great Northern: A data company?

In the middle of this technological revolution, there was a leadership change at Great Northern when Erik B. Rasmussen, who had been chief executive officer for just under ten years, left effective March 1, 1983, to become chief executive officer of the cement and machine industry group F. L. Smidth. Great Northern's new chief executive officer was René Tang Jespersen, who was supported by Jan Frøshaug, who became group director and joined the top management team after having been the chief executive officer of Norsk Hydro. It was these two men who would be responsible for guiding Great Northern into the new digital age, and they started by trying to make the new information and communication technology the basis of a new business area at Great Northern.

In 1983, Tidana concluded an agreement regarding the retailing of L. M. Ericsson's PC, Step One, at the same time as the company increasingly concentrated on consultancy activity and the delivery both of standard programs and of sector-oriented programs for small and medium-sized companies. A large development project financed by the Computing Fund (Edb-fondet) was begun, and in Sep-

tember, Great Northern and five other Danish companies started the company Danish Information Systems, or DAISY, for export to five of the so-called ASEAN (Association of Southeast Asian Nations) countries: Thailand, Singapore, Indonesia, Malaysia, and the Philippines.[34]

Apparently, this development project never materialized, nor did exports to the ASEAN countries ever take off. In contrast, the PC sector grew very rapidly, and in October 1985, Tidana entered a new market by becoming half owner of the Danish division of the Computerland chain, which sold PCs to both the business community and private individuals.

Computerland was an international United States–based franchise chain that had been among those chosen to sell IBM's first PC. The chain had grown to include eight hundred stores and was now the world's largest retailer of PCs and sold 30 percent of IBM's PCs. The chain's three branches in Denmark had been started by "three young people without capital," as the minutes of one of the meetings of Great Northern's board of directors have it, and had 40 million kroner in revenues, while Tidana sold PCs for 18 million kroner. The cooperation was established by means of the creation of an equally owned general partnership, GN Data System, which took over both the Computerland stores and Tidana's existing PC activities and became a subsidiary of Tidana.[35]

Not all of the members of Great Northern's board of directors viewed this acquisition positively, though Jan Frøshaug presented the initiative as a "significant strengthening of this business area." Erik B. Rasmussen argued against the acquisition, noting that "Computerland's business area [deviated] from the business areas with which [Great Northern was] usually involved" and that it therefore meant taking on "a different type of risks." He was not alone in his criticism, but the chairman of the board of directors supported the purchase and characterized the acquisition as "a natural expansion of Tidana [. . .] which already sells microcomputers"—and the acquisition went ahead on that basis.[36]

In fact, the takeover of the Computerland stores dovetailed with another initiative undertaken around the same time. In late August 1984, the internationally recognized Danish computer company Chr. Rovsing A/S went bankrupt, and Great Northern was offered an opportunity to purchase the company's Information System Division, which manufactured the CR 16 microcomputer and an open local network, X-net, for internal communications among computers and terminals of various makes. An electronic archiving system, ODIN, was also included. Kommunedata, which supplied equipment to the Danish municipalities, had agreed to purchase two hundred CR 16s and expected to order a further four hundred over a period of two years, while P & T had ordered an unspecified number.[37]

Already on September 17, 1984, Great Northern's board of directors were to discuss an acquisition that according to the chairman would represent "a leap forward." Erik B. Rasmussen found it to be "advantageous to acquire advanced knowledge in packaged form, as had been proposed here," but it would be a slow process for the company to build up such knowledge itself. In 1981, the company had considered acquiring a stake in the Danish data company Regnecentralen, which was experiencing an economic crisis, but the poor annual result in 1980 had caused the board of directors to abstain. Now there was a new opportunity, and taking advantage of it, according to Erik B. Rasmussen, would mean a technological boost for several of Great Northern's subsidiaries and offer a good synergy effect relative to Tidana. The biggest concerns had to do with the management of the company, but there was otherwise general support for the takeover, and it was realized for 23 million kroner.[38]

The Rovsing activities were placed in a new company, GN Netcom A/S, which started out with 160 employees plus ten employees from a development project that was moved over to the new company from Tidana. With the two data companies and the stake in Computerland, Great Northern had built up a small cluster of data companies with development, production, sales, and consultancy in hardware, software, and networks. The goal was to ensure the group a place in the rapidly growing data sector.

GN Store Nord

When Great Northern held its general meeting on May 15, 1986, the group had approved a new name, GN Store Nord—"Great Nordic" in English. The new name was intended to give the subsidiaries a common profile with a common logo and contribute to shifting into the background the dusty image that the name "the Great Northern Telegraph Company" had associated with the whole group. All of the subsidiaries had "GN" added to their company names, and several got completely new names. GNT Automatic became GN Telematic, while Tidana became GN Data, and LK-NES became GN Laur. Knudsen. The telecommunications activity remained a part of the mother company's activities as a division with the name GN Store Nordiske Telegraf-Selskab with Vice President Frits Larsen as its leader.

The name change was implemented at a time when an economic upswing was in progress and things were again going well for the group. Revenues for 1985 exceeded those for the previous year by 18 percent or nearly 2.6 million kroner, and the group had an ordinary result of 107 million kroner. After extraordinary revenues and expenses and tax, the net result was 131 million kroner.

The mood at the general meeting was certainly good, and an injection of capital by means of the issuing of shares with a face value of a little more than 100 million kroner at four hundred points was unanimously approved, while employees could also purchase shares with a total nominal value of just under 5 million kroner at two hundred points. In all, the emission gave GN Store Nord just under 400 million kroner after deduction of costs.

The top earner among the subsidiaries was GN Laur. Knudsen, with a record surplus before tax of 65 million kroner, while GN Telematic came second with a surplus of 25.5 million kroner, and GN Elmi reached 14.1 million kroner. In contrast to what had been the case previously, GN Store Nord received

GN Telematics's entire surplus, as GN Store Nord had purchased L. M. Ericsson's bloc of shares effective January 1, 1985. GN Laur. Knudsen's positive development caused GN Store Nord to purchase all of the minority shares in this company as well, in the spring of 1986.

Once again, the company that performed worst was the company now known as GN Hellesens, which presented a deficit of 15.9 million kroner, which caused the group leadership to intensify its efforts to sell the company. Things again went wrong for the company now known as GN Danavox, which delivered a deficit of 6.1 million kroner despite an increase in revenues by 20 percent, to 330 million kroner.

Within the data cluster, GN Data, including GN Store Nord's stake in Computerland, delivered a surplus of 1.9 million kroner, having received revenues of 86 million kroner, and things went completely wrong for the newly established GN Netcom, which, with revenues of 99 million kroner, delivered a deficit of 8.4 million after the company had been expected at least to present a balanced account.

In contrast, there was a striking success for the telecommunications activity for which GN Store Nordiske Telegraf-Selskab was responsible; that company increased its revenues by 45 percent, to 98.1 million kroner, and increased its operating surplus by 9 million kroner. At the same time, operations had been secured for some years to come, as the contract with KDD regarding the operation of the JASC had been extended until the end of 1994, and the contract with the ICAO for the operation of those parts of the Scotice and Icecan cables that connected the Faroe Islands, Iceland, and Greenland had been extended, the remainder of the cables having been shut down. At the same time, GN Store Nord had gotten the right to use the government-owned cable between Great Britain and the Faroe Islands extended. Also, a telex and data transmission office that had been established earlier in London, GN Citytel, had grown considerably, and there were still good revenues from the repair work carried out on behalf of other telecommuni-

cations companies and telecommunications authorities by the cable ship *Northern*.

With GN Hellesens up for sale, the group's only money-losing companies were GN Danavox and GN Netcom. With regard to GN Danavox's result, the annual report declared that this was "a very unsatisfactory operating loss," and in internal discussions at GN Store Nord, the tone was even sharper. According to the minutes of a meeting of the board of directors, "the chairman found it incomprehensible that one could end up with a negative result when one had three hundred million kroner in revenues," and he emphasized "that Danavox cannot continue to perform poorly." Jan Frøshaug was therefore asked to prepare a report on the company.[39]

The board of directors moved quickly with regard to GN Netcom, parts of which the board had decided to sell off already before the general meeting, as there were significant technical problems both with the CR 16 computer and with X-net. The buyer was the Italian office machine and data group Olivetti, which took over most of the activities. "Unfortunately, this was a poor decision," GN Store Nord's chief executive officer René Tang Jespersen concluded with regard to the group's purchase of the activities of Chr. Rovsing. The vision of a large data business had taken a major hit, and GN Netcom ended up having the archiving system ODIN as its only business area.[40]

The splitting up of GN Danavox

In the middle of May 1986, GN Store Nord's top management team presented a preliminary report for the first quarter, according to which GN Danavox's operating result was 1 million kroner under budget and the result for the first half year, given the current trend, would be a deficit of 7 million kroner. It was the sales of hearing aids in the United States that failed to perform, as had been the case the previous year, while things were going better with the Stetomike headset, which benefited from strong growth in the number of so-called call centers.[41]

As far as its product line was concerned, Danavox did not have a competitive all-in-the-ear hearing aid despite the fact that this was the type of hearing aid that was most widely used in the United States and the type that was currently most in demand there. In addition, the company suffered from a lack of economic management and serious leadership problems both in Denmark and in the United States. The chairman of the board of directors, Erik Mollerup, characterized it as "very worrisome that GN Danavox still [had] quite unsatisfactory results despite the company's many declarations that improvements were expected." He felt that "something must be fundamentally wrong at the company," and he demanded that the report that had been requested be finished in time to be presented at the next meeting of the board of directors.[42]

When the board of directors met on September 22, most of GN Netcom's activities had been sold to Olivetti, and GN Store Nord had finally found a buyer—Duracell—for most of Hellesens's activities. GN Store Nord retained the production of especially long-lived batteries in the company GN Batteries, which was continued as a supplier to the big battery companies. At this point, then, GN Danavox was the only money-losing company in the GN Store Nord group, and Jan Frøshaug's report showed that the situation was worse than had previously been assumed, as the company was losing about 5 million kroner per month.[43]

While the Stetomike business was developing reasonably well, posting a positive operating result for the first half year, things were going poorly in the hearing aid business. According to Frøshaug, the company had created its problems itself, as the number of employees involved in production had increased by 100 percent since 1983, while revenues had increased by only 50 percent. Also, there were quality problems with the latest model because of insufficient cooperation between development and production, which had led to "dangerously low customer confidence in the company."

According to Frøshaug, one solution would be to split the company into two independent divisions that corresponded to the very different markets at which hearing aids and Stetomikes were directed—hearing-impaired individuals in the one case and customers in the office and call center sectors in the other. While the Stetomike division could quickly build up a healthy business, it would take the hearing aid division longer to do this. Frøshaug emphasized that in his view, "it would be constructive to make an effort on GN Danavox's behalf" and the company "could be made to produce a reasonable surplus."

When the proposal with regard to splitting up GN Danavox was presented to the board of directors in the middle of December 1986, it was clear that the company was heading for a deficit in excess of 40 million kroner. "A disaster" and "completely incomprehensible," the chairman of the board of directors declared. Jan Frøshaug presented a new rescue plan according to which the Stetomike activities would be transferred to GN Netcom, which would simultaneously take over the factory in Great Britain, while GN Danavox would become a pure hearing aid company with production in Præstø.[44]

The chairman declared that "things [had] gone completely wrong for GN Danavox," but he nevertheless expressed his support for the rescue plan, as he believed he could see signs of a changing trend. He also stated that while GN Danavox had certainly been poorly led, GN Store Nord's top management team bore some of the responsibility for GN Danavox's problems because the top management team had not reacted to the danger signals quickly enough. The rescue plan was subsequently approved, and at the same time, it was decided that 45 million kroner of the mother company's loans would be converted into share capital, as the company's equity would otherwise be lost, and to transfer 6 million kroner to GN Netcom as starting capital. The ODIN project was simultaneously transferred to GN Data.

Turnaround with Rebirth of the Telegraph Company

CHAPTER 23

"A very bleak picture"

The first year for the newly named GN Store Nord did not go well, and already when the account for the first quarter was presented in May 1986, the trend caused brows to be furrowed on the board of directors. Things looked worse for GN Danavox, but in the words of the chairman, the financial result was generally "very bad." In the course of the year, the situation got even worse, and after the third quarter, the group's revenues were 200 million kroner under the budgeted amount. Only GN Data and GN Elmi satisfied expectations, and all in all, in the words of the chairman, "a very bleak picture" had emerged.[1]

The situation was also embarrassing because the emission brochure published in connection with the capital expansion in the spring had expressed positive expectations with regard to the group account for 1986 and the future generally, and late in the year, the board of directors therefore decided to send a message to the Copenhagen Stock Exchange regarding the poor prospects for the annual account.

In fact, the financial result did end up being very poor; it showed group revenues that had declined by

almost 160 million kroner in relation to the previous year. However, extraordinary revenues from the sale of activities at Hellesens and Netcom brought the net result up to 80 million kroner—a drop of 27 million in relation to the previous year. Particularly GN Danavox hurt the group, as the company posted a deficit of just under 50 million kroner, while GN Netcom posted a deficit of 17 million kroner in the wake of the year's turbulence from the sale of the Rovsing activities and the transfer of the Stetomike business.

On the other hand, GN Data posted a surplus of a little more than 3 million kroner on the strength of the Computerland activities in particular, and as usual GN Elmi posted a good result, a surplus of more than 17 million kroner in this case. For GN Laur. Knudsen, the surplus declined to 48 million kroner, while GN Telematic saw its surplus sharply drop, by nearly 20 million kroner to 5.5 million kroner, despite the fact that its revenues had increased. GN Batteries posted a surplus of over 50 million kroner because of the revenues from the sale to Duracell.

The telegraph company experienced setbacks not only with regard to its revenues but also with regard to its geographical coverage. At the end of 1986, the Weybourne cable was decommissioned after having been operated for thirty-six years, as the company's Danish concession would expire just over half a year later. The remaining parts of the Scotice-Icecan connection would be decommissioned at the end of 1987, while the ICAO's connections would be provided via a satellite earth station in Greenland operated by the telegraph company in the future. The JASC—the cable between the Soviet Union and Japan—was still a source of steady income, but on the other hand, GN Citytel in London posted a very poor result.

GN Store Nord's subsidiaries and activities were like a bag of mixed sweet and sour bonbons, and on January 1, 1987, when Jan Frøshaug left his director's post to become the chief executive officer of Egmont A/S, it was left to new group leadership to create a more focused foundation for new successes with regard to both revenues and surpluses.

On May 1, 1987, Thomas Duer, whose most recent previous position had been that of chief executive officer of the shipyard Aarhus Flydedok, was hired as the new chief executive officer of GN Store Nord alongside René Tang Jespersen, but nevertheless in a leading position as chairman of the top management team. This was an unusual structure, and in fact, René Tang Jespersen resigned from his position on April 1 of the following year, after which Thomas Duer continued at GN Store Nord as sole director. On the same occasion, Erik B. Rasmussen became the representative of the board of directors on the top management team.

There was a change of board chairman as well, as Erik Mollerup reached the age limit of seventy years and left the board of directors at the general meeting in May 1987. The new chairman was Ebbe J. B. Christensen, who had just left the post of chief executive officer of Gutenberghus Gruppen ("the Gutenberghus Group"). He ended up leading GN Store Nord for a single year, as he resigned at the general meeting in May 1988, when he had to present an account that was even worse than the one for the previous year, and the group posted a negative result for the first time ever.

With a decline in revenues by 346 million kroner to just under 2.1 billion kroner and a net result of minus 153 million kroner, this annual result was, as the understated formulation chosen for the annual report has it, "highly unsatisfactory." Poor performance was seen across a broad range of the group's companies; only GN Elmi and GN Laur. Knudsen achieved surpluses—in the amount of 18.9 million kroner and 3.4 million kroner, respectively—and there were red numbers on the bottom line for all of the other companies.

In just two years, GN Store Nord had lost half a billion kroner in revenues, and it was only a transfer of 135 million kroner from the reserves that made it possible to pay an unchanged dividend of 12 percent of the share capital to the shareholders. The board of directors had discussed the possibility of not paying a dividend but had ultimately reached agreement that they should maintain the dividend "to emphasize that things are again going well for the company," as the minutes of a meeting of the board of directors have it.[2]

After the general meeting, the board of directors constituted itself with Erik B. Rasmussen as its new chairman. Thanks to his time as a member of the board of directors since 1971 and as chief executive officer during the years 1973–1983, he knew the group from the inside as few other people did, and in connection with the election, the board of directors reached agreement that he should continue as the board's representative on the top management team for a further year: "It will be valuable to Thomas Duer to have Erik B. Rasmussen to support him in connection with the many challenges that need to be confronted."[3]

Trimming and selling off of companies

There *were* many challenges that needed to be confronted. The setbacks, which had surprised both GN Store Nord's top management team and the group's board of directors, were rooted in a global market trend that had established itself while the digital revolution continued unabated. Starting in the early 1980s, a new neoliberal agenda became internationally dominant. This agenda was focused on deregulation and liberalization and on giving market forces free rein and creating increased competition both nationally and internationally, across national borders. The banner bearers for this trend were the British prime minister Margaret Thatcher and the American president Ronald Reagan. The European Community followed this agenda and in 1986 approved the so-called European Community package, which was to establish an open inner market featuring the free movement of people, goods, capital, and services by January 1, 1993, at the latest.

It was within the framework of continuing technological development, liberalization, and internationalization that Thomas Duer began the cleaning up of GN Store Nord. The first company to be affected by the cleanup was GN Data, which felt the effects of massive losses experienced by the Danish Computerland stores along with approximately eight hundred other Computerland stores around the world. Late in the year, facing a deficit of 25 million kroner, GN Store Nord unloaded its stake in the chain, and a short time later, the board of directors decided that the group "[should] get out of the data sector," and GN Data was sold.[4]

However, GN Store Nord did retain the electronic archiving system called ODIN, which had originally come from Chr. Rovsing. Late in 1989, a number of large orders arrived from German and Danish companies and from Denmark's Postgiro, and this business area was subsequently split off and given its own company, GN FileTech, with the German ball-bearing manufacturer INA as its main customer, distributor for the German market, and part owner—INA accounted for 49 percent of the share capital.

GN Telematic, which was directly affected by the deregulation and liberalization, was also trimmed. Beginning already in the early 1980s, there were increasing imports of cheap telephones from the East that put the Danish market under pressure. These pirate telephones, as they were called, had features such as redial buttons and memories that could store ten telephone numbers, but it was illegal to connect them to the telephone network. However, it was legal to import them and sell them to customers who used them as extra devices despite the prohibition. In 1984, one hundred thousand pirate telephones were sold via mail order, and the same year they found their way to the shelves of the supermarket chain Føtex.

In 1986, the market for switchboards was liberalized, and in 1988, it was the telephone modems' turn. In 1987, retailing of teleprinters and extra telephones was liberalized, and in 1988, the provision of text and data communication services was opened up. The same year, a directive from the European Community Commission established that free trade with regard to telephones was to be legalized by 1990 at the latest.

In the fall of 1988, GN Store Nord's board of directors therefore decided to shut down the entire telephone area in GN Teleautomatic and divide up the remaining activities into two companies: GN Communications, which produced pay telephones, for which there was still a demand, and GN Datacom, which developed programs for paper-tape automation equipment for production control as well as terminals for the Dankort, the Danish national payment card.[5]

GN Laur. Knudsen, which had revenues of nearly 1 billion kroner, was believed unsuited for surviving on its own in a liberalized European market without great difficulties. A number of the company's products, such as electric and other plugs, had been protected by special Danish standards up to this point, but that would soon no longer be the case. After having investigated a number of possibilities with regard to potential mergers, GN Store Nord sold the whole company to Nordisk Kabel og Tråd for 576 million kroner in cash in March 1990.[6]

In September 1988, GN Store Nord succeeded in selling the lithium division of GN Batteries to a Swedish battery manufacturer, and the following year, GN Store Nord signed a letter of intent to the American battery manufacturer Ray-O-Vac with regard to the sale of the alkali division. Ray-O-Vac pulled out after having completed a due diligence process, however, and the remainder of GN Batteries was therefore still for sale.[7]

Finally, the telegraph company's business disappeared on its own when the cables in the North

Great Northern's last cable ship, the Northern, was purchased and refitted for cable work in the North Atlantic in 1968. The ship was sold in 1987 when the last parts of the company's cables in the North Atlantic were decommissioned. The picture shows the ship on its way through the Øresund, with Kronborg Castle to starboard.

Atlantic were decommissioned at the end of 1987, and the group's share of the cable between Poland and Denmark was transferred to the two countries' telegraphy authorities the same year. In December 1987, the cable ship *Northern* was sold, and all that remained thereafter was the JASC, the cable between the Soviet Union and Japan, the operation of the satellite earth station on Greenland having been transferred to Greenland's telegraphy authority on January 1, 1990.

The telecommunications and data communications company in London, GN Citytel, disappeared as a subsidiary, as its activities, following major losses in 1987 and 1988 totaling more than 60 million kroner, were merged with those of its competitor One to One in a new company, Comtext International Ltd., 43 percent of the shares of which were owned by GN Store Nord. As a consequence, the telegraph company's revenues for 1989 were reduced

to half of those for the previous year, declining to a little less than 16 million kroner, and in 1990, when there was a surplus of 1.4 million kroner, revenues declined to 9.3 million kroner. The JASC was the only source of income—and was all that was left of the honored telegraph company.[8]

Strategy for a turnaround

During the years 1987–1990, GN Store Nord underwent what a stockbroking company later called "spring cleaning of its businesses" that reduced the group's revenues from just under 2.4 million kroner in 1986 to 1.4 million kroner in 1990—a drop of more than 40 percent. It was particularly some of the activities related to the group's home market that were eliminated, and such eliminations brought Denmark's share of the group's revenues down from 47.4 percent to 27.2 percent so that the group became very predominantly internationally oriented. Investments also declined, from 187 million kroner annually to a little more than 73 million kroner annually.[9]

The only companies spared from elimination were GN Elmi and GN Netcom, which both delivered constant growth in revenues, reaching 102 million kroner and 187 million kroner, respectively, and also posting good surpluses, and GN Danavox, whose revenues increased from 218 million kroner to 292 million kroner. GN Danavox continued to have difficulty earning money, however.

As results of the cleanup, GN Store Nord saw an increase in its ordinary operating result to just under 40 million kroner in 1988 and a little more than 87 million kroner in 1990. GN Store Nord also had extraordinary and financial revenues that in combination with other revenues produced a net result of 185 million kroner, following a modest deficit of 8 million kroner in 1988.

In addition to the selling off of activities and trimming of the group, the group's major decline in 1986 and 1987 led to strategic discussions—the first such discussions since Bent Suenson had shifted Great Northern's course toward becoming an industrial company during the postwar years—and to the adoption of the first strategy plan the company had ever had.

In September 1988, Chief Executive Officer Thomas Duer presented an initial draft strategy plan with the introductory remark that "GN Store Nord had not previously had a clearly defined goal and strategy." This was to be changed, and in the spring of 1989, GN Store Nord asked the consultancy company McKinsey to prepare a proposal with regard to a group strategy.[10]

McKinsey's report was completed late in 1989 and was thoroughly discussed at the meeting of GN Store Nord's board of directors on January 25, 1990. The report's message was that in the future, the group should concentrate on GN Elmi as well as GN Laur. Knudsen's electrical installation business, while the latter company's divisions for low voltage and measurements and electronics should be sold. GN Danavox and GN Netcom should also be sold, the report indicated, because they were too small to survive in the global marketplace, and GN Communications as well as all other small business areas should also be sold.[11]

As was soberly noted in Thomas Duer's introductory commentary, proceeding as McKinsey proposed would mean that GN Store Nord would be left with two subsidiaries and 38 percent of its current revenues. It could also be noted that GN Laur. Knudsen's installation business was very predominantly oriented toward the home market and threatened by the European Community's coming inner market. In fact, GN Store Nord went a different way, selling GN Laur. Knudsen in its entirety two months later.

In general, McKinsey's recommendations dovetailed poorly with the path on which GN Store Nord had already set forth. In his first strategy presentation, Thomas Duer had identified precisely GN Netcom as a company for which things were going well, a company that should be expanded, while GN Danavox, in Thomas Duer's view, should be supported and reinvigorated. GN Netcom had more than lived up to expectations with strong growth and the creation of sales companies in the United States, the United Kingdom, Canada, and Germany, while it was hard to get GN Danavox on the right track, as Jan Frøshaug had concluded earlier.

Structurally, the hearing aid sector was in a general consumer transition: customers were switching from behind-the-ear devices to in-the-ear devices, and GN Danavox had fallen behind its competitors in adapting to this trend. In 1986, however, the company had introduced the smallest model on the market, which was selling well, and the same year, the company entered into cooperation with Oticon and Widex with regard to a research project on digital signal development lasting several years. This project was specifically focused on the development of a new generation of hearing aids.

In 1987, as one of the first Western companies to do so, GN Danavox established production in Xiamen, which was one of four so-called new economic zones in China in which foreign companies were allowed to establish themselves. GN Danavox entered into a joint venture with a Chinese partner, the purpose of which was to establish a hearing aid factory that would manufacture devices for the Western markets but also a cheap pocket model for the Chinese market, which was extremely large and promising but thus far lacked great purchasing power.

Late in 1988, GN Store Nord's board of directors found that GN Danavox was on "the right path," though there were still great difficulties, particularly in the United States, which were the world's largest national hearing aid market. In 1989, GN Store Nord therefore purchased the American hearing aid manufacturer Hearing Technology, which doubled GN Danavox's market share in the United States—though this only brought it up to 4 percent—and right around the time McKinsey presented their report to GN Store Nord's board of directors, GN Danavox got out of 1989 with a surplus of 12 million kroner.[12]

Both GN Netcom and GN Danavox were experiencing a positive and promising development, and while several members of the board of directors supported McKinsey's view of GN Danavox, the board moderated McKinsey's recommendations in its final strategy plan. Both GN Danavox and GN Netcom—like GN Communications—were given two to three years to live up to expectations before the board of directors would discuss a possible sale of the respective company. During this period, the mother company would provide financial support for investments and possible acquisitions.[13]

GN Netcom repaid this confidence with an immediate increase in revenues—the figure for 1990, 187 million kroner, represented an increase of 40 percent in relation to revenues for the previous year—and a doubling of its surplus to 18 million kroner. The company became the world's second-largest manufacturer of headsets. In a sector in which design was becoming increasingly important as a competitive parameter, the company could also rejoice over winning two prestigious design prizes, in Sweden and at the Hannover Exposition respectively.

In contrast, 1990 was another disappointing year for GN Danavox, which saw its revenues increase by only 6 percent and its surplus drop markedly. This trend supported the view of the skeptics on GN Store Nord's board of directors that the company should be sold, but on the other hand, two strategic investments suggested there could be hope of improvements in the future.

One of these was the purchase of 90 percent of the shares in the Danish company Madsens Electronics, which manufactured audiological measuring equipment used at both public and private hearing clinics all over the world. Thanks to this acquisition, GN Danavox was able to become a one-stop supplier to its customers, which consisted of hearing clinics that recommended and sold devices to consumers after having tested their hearing. At the same time, the company wanted to adapt to the closer relationship between the measurement of hearing ability and individual adjustment of hearing aids that would accompany the introduction of a new generation of programmable hearing aids. GN intended to develop a total concept for a "total hearing clinic" of the future.[14]

With an eye on this new generation of hearing aids, GN Danavox purchased a fourth of the share capital in the French hearing aid manufacturer Intrason SA, which had made more progress than its competitors with the development of a programmable hearing aid. With this investment, GN Danavox gained access to new technology while continuing to carry out its own research on digital signal processing in cooperation with Widex and Oticon.

Despite McKinsey's recommendations, then, GN Netcom and GN Danavox were allowed to remain in the group, and indeed, analysts and investors viewed GN Store Nord's development positively. In February 1991, the stockbroking company Unibørs described the stock as "extremely attractive," as GN Store Nord was on the way out of "a turnaround situation," in which, following the sale of several subsidiaries and the restructuring of others, a "clearly defined growth strategy" had been implemented and the "basis for significant growth" established."[15]

In addition to describing the turnaround with regard to the subsidiaries, Unibørs noted that GN Store Nord was in the startup phase with regard to new major cable projects in the Soviet Union and Poland. The first investments were not to be made until 1992, and the first revenues would arrive even later, but according to the stockbroking company, these were activities with "high earnings potential." Things had been quiet for many years now as far as the cable activities were concerned, but here too there was a turnaround—and more.

Cable projects for the Soviet Union and in Poland

GN Store Nordiske Telegraf-Selskab was not affected by the strategy work, and given the prospect that the JASC contract would expire at the end of 1994, the apparently moribund company's days seemed to be numbered. During the second half of the 1980s, however, geopolitical developments took an unexpected turn that opened up new possibilities.

In March 1985, the fifty-four-year-old Mikhail Gorbachev was elected general secretary of the Communist Party of the Soviet Union and thus became the de facto leader of the Soviet Union. Not only was he significantly younger than his predecessors, he also introduced a new political age when, with slogans about glasnost and perestroika and extensive reform policies, he placed openness and democracy on the agenda. These reform policies embraced a new approach to and openness to the West and a desire for reduction of international tensions and for nuclear arms reductions as well as increased trade and enhanced economic relationships. This created great opportunities for the Great Northern Telegraph Company.

In the middle of December 1988, Thomas Duer could inform the board of directors that GN Store Nord had received a message from the government of the Soviet Union, which wished to know whether GN Store Nord was interested in cooperating with regard to the establishment of a fiber optic cable connection from Denmark to Japan via European Russia and Siberia. The original "lifeline" of the Great Northern Telegraph Company," as Edouard Suenson had called it in 1896, was awakened, and so was the telegraph company.[16]

Already in February 1988, Statens Teletjeneste (the Danish telecommunications authority) had presented the Soviet Union's Ministry of Communications with a proposal with regard to a fiber optic cable connection between Denmark and the Soviet Union, and the Russians had now expanded the project to include the whole trans-Siberian connection—and wished to have GN Store Nord involved in the project.[17]

Corresponding messages had been sent to GN Store Nord's cooperation partners of many years, KDD and Cable & Wireless, and a number of other international actors and telecommunications authorities. The project would cost 600 to 700 million dollars, and a preliminary meeting between the old cooperation partners—the Ministry of Communications of the Soviet Union, KDD, and GN Store Nord—was scheduled for early in the new year. At Kongens Nytorv, GN Store Nord's leaders rejoiced over having been invited at all, and of course the grand project was assigned to the telegraph company, which had the requisite technical, political/diplomatic, and linguistic competencies—and not least a thorough knowledge of conditions in Japan and Russia as well as good contacts with key individuals in both Japan and Russia.

At a meeting in Moscow in February 1989, the Ministry of Communications of the Soviet Union, KDD, and the telegraph company reached agreement to move forward with the project, which soon began to take shape. The American telecommunications company US West International was involved by the Russians because of its experience with fiber optic cables in areas with climatic conditions like those of Siberia and in particular for the sake of enhancing the likelihood of receiving permission for relevant technology to be exported to the Soviet Union. Such permission needed to be issued by the organization Cocom, which had been created under NATO in 1949 to prevent the export of strategically important goods to the Eastern bloc.

At a subsequent meeting in April 1989 with Statens Teletjeneste—which was the successor organization to P & T—the Russians insisted that GN Store Nordiske Telegraf-Selskab participate in the establishment of a Dano-Russian cable connection. The Russians lacked money, and in this connection, their Danish cooperation partner of nearly 125 years could help.[18]

After a feasibility study had been completed, all of the participants in the project participated in a common steering committee meeting in late November and early December 1989, when a memorandum of understanding was signed that was intended to result in the creation of a common company that would be responsible for the establishment and operation of the complete connection between Denmark and Japan. A week later, the parties published a joint press release regarding the initiative.[19]

The meeting took place in the wake of the dramatic events in Berlin on October 9 and 10, when the border crossings between East and West Berlin were opened and the tearing down of the wall that had divided the city since 1961 was begun. The fall of the Berlin Wall had no immediate impact on the trans-Siberian project, but the events in Berlin gave an extra impetus to the dissolution of the Eastern bloc, which in March 1990 spread to the Soviet Union when Lithuania, as the first Soviet republic to do so, declared itself independent and strong independence movements evolved in the two other Baltic countries and in a number of other Soviet republics.

This development caused the Soviet Union to wish the cable to follow a different route. Originally, the cable was to have been landed in the Russian enclave of Kaliningrad, between Poland and Lithuania, but the Russians now wished to have it moved to Leningrad, which made the cable project 25 million dollars more expensive.[20]

However, the major obstacle was the as-yet-outstanding approval of the project by Cocom, which it was expected would be dependent upon the outcome of an upcoming summit between the president of the Soviet Union, Mikhail Gorbachev, and the president of the United States, George Bush, which, to the joy of the project participants, further reduced international tensions.

In the meantime, there were disagreements among the participants in the trans-Siberian consortium, which had grown to include a large number of European telecommunications authorities with an interest in a trans-Siberian connection. The creation of a common company was therefore abandoned, and instead, the overall project was divided into three stages, of which GN Store Nordiske Telegraf-Selskab and Statens Teletjeneste, in cooperation with the Soviet Union's Ministry of Communications, would be responsible for stage one, which would consist of the establishment of a fiber optic cable connection between Denmark and the Soviet Union. The other two stages respectively consisted of the establishment of a fiber optic cable connection via Russia and Siberia and the laying of an undersea fiber optic cable between the Russian Far East and Japan. The Danes were interested in all of the stages, but to begin with, they focused on the cable between Denmark and the Soviet Union, and in cooperation with the Danish Ministry of Foreign Affairs and the Industrial Council, an application for approval of the project was sent to Cocom in late October 1990.

Around this time, another opportunity arose for the telegraph company because Statens Teletjeneste and the Polish telegraphy authority laid a fiber optic undersea cable between Denmark and Poland in July 1990. The Polish government wished to lay an adjacent fiber optic land cable from north to south through the entire country as the spine of a modernization of the Polish telecommunications system but could not afford to finance such a cable.[21]

On the initiative of the Danish company Nordisk Kabel og Tråd, which was to supply the cable to the Poles, the telegraph company successfully moved to become involved in this project, investing 160 million kroner to pay for the cable and associated equipment, while the remaining 85 million kroner, which would cover labor and other expenses, were paid by the Polish national telegraphy authority. The company was not to be a traffic operator but was solely to be responsible for the agreed-upon financing and repayment of the principal and interest and a surplus margin to be achieved via traffic invoices.[22]

On December 13, 1990, GN Store Nord's board of directors gave the telegraph company approval for proceeding with the project but required the company to seek to minimize the risk, which was judged to be of a political nature in particular. To do so, the company entered into a 75-25 percent joint venture with Telecom Danmark A/S—the successor to P & T and Statens Teletjeneste—to finance and execute the project. The partners succeeded in getting the Danish Ministry of Foreign Affairs to provide guarantee coverage of 90 percent of the investment for the eventuality that political developments in Poland should change conditions that were of relevance for the project, and on February 21, 1991, the project received final approval from GN Store Nord's board of directors.[23]

As had been feared, political disagreements arose in Poland with regard to the project, which required both a permit for the import of the equipment and a permit allowing the Danish consortium to export the surplus. On April 17, 1991, however, the final contract could be signed, and the telegraph company's first cable contract since the JASC agreement was a reality.

In the meantime, the telegraph company, Telecom Danmark, and the Ministry of Communications of the Soviet Union signed an agreement in Moscow with regard to the financing of an undersea cable connection between Denmark and the Soviet Union—an investment of a total of 80 million dollars, or approximately 500 million kroner, that was to be shared by the two Danish companies. The details were to be agreed upon when the project became a reality, but for the time being, the parties were awaiting a decision from Cocom, which the Danish consortium strongly hoped to be positive—also because it had already ordered the cable.[24]

Dansk MobilTelefon I/S

With its involvement in the trans-Siberian and Polish cable projects, GN Store Nordiske Telegraf-Selskab was back in its accustomed role as an actor in the global telecommunications infrastructure. The context was a world undergoing dramatic change as a result of the systemic changes in the Soviet Union and Eastern Europe and the simultaneous spread of digital technology and internationalization and liberalization of the Western economies, which changed the ground rules for a

number of business sectors. This had put several of GN Store Nord's subsidiaries under pressure but also opened up new possibilities that the telegraph company did not hesitate to exploit.

In January 1982, a common Nordic mobile telephony system had been commissioned as a replacement for the national car telephone systems, and in Denmark, this new system had acquired approximately fifteen thousand subscribers. This new Nordisk Mobiltelefon System (Nordic Mobile Telephone System [NMT]) was the first system in the world to be fully automated and international in the sense that one could direct-dial all numbers and use one's telephone across all Nordic national borders. And the system was open to mobile telephones, which was permitted in Denmark starting in 1987. Among the leading suppliers of telephones were Storno, now owned by Motorola, and the newly established Danish mobile telephone company Dancall in North Jutland.

The system, which used the frequency range around 450 MHz, had an initial capacity of thirty thousand subscribers that was quickly reached and, therefore, increased by means of some technical modifications. An upper limit of 56,000 subscribers was reached in 1986, however, and a parallel system was introduced in the frequency range around 900 MHz.

In 1990, NMT-450 and NMT-900 together had 140,000 subscribers, and the telephones were steadily becoming smaller and more portable. The system was owned and operated by the national postal and telecommunications authorities of the Nordic countries, and the same technology was used in the Benelux countries, for example, while large countries such as the United Kingdom, France, and Germany had their own national systems.

In the late 1980s, both the technology and the model of ownership and operation were undermined by technological developments and the liberalization of the European Community. The NMT system was analog, but in June 1987, after the European association of postal and telecommunications authorities had agreed on specifications for a digital mobile telephone system, the European Community's Council of Ministers adopted a directive regarding the establishment of a common European digital mobile telephone system called GSM (Global System for Mobile communication). The implementation of the system was to begin by 1991 at the latest and create an opportunity for private actors to create competition.

In Denmark, the directive was executed via a decision by the Folketing on November 8, 1990, that gave the newly established TeleDanmark A/S, which had been created by means of a merger of the old regional telephone companies, permission to operate a public GSM mobile telephone network starting on March 1, 1992, and authorized the minister to permit the existence of a competing private network starting on the same date. This was a historic decision as it represented the first break with the public telephone monopoly since the passage of the Telephone Law of 1897.

At an early stage, GN Store Nordiske Telegraf-Selskab considered participating in the construction of a Danish GSM mobile telephone system that at the same time would compete with the existing NMT system and TeleDanmark's coming GSM system. Doing so would mean taking on a major risk, and because the company lacked experience with mobile telephony, it negotiated with a number of companies in Denmark and elsewhere with regard to the creation of a consortium that would apply for a concession for the private GSM system. In late November 1990, GN Store Nordiske Telegraf-Selskab concluded an agreement with the American telephone company BellSouth with regard to investigating the possibilities of an actual application.[25]

BellSouth was the largest of seven regional telephone companies in the United States that had been created in connection with the splitting up of the telephone corporate group AT&T by the American authorities in 1982. The company had revenues of thirty million dollars and operated landline telephony in an area in which fifty million people lived and mobile telephony systems in thirty-six US states as well as in Buenos Aires and Mexico City. As recently as in June 1990, the company had received a license to operate a mobile telephony system in New Zealand.

BellSouth's motive for seeking cooperation did not involve the Danish market alone; rather, the company wished to use Denmark as a springboard to the rest of the European Community. GN Store Nord was motivated to seek an alliance by its need for a strong partner who possessed both technological and commercial knowledge relevant to the establishment and operation of mobile telephony. Sweden's Nordic Tel, which had been established in 1990 by companies such as SAS and Volvo to acquire a Swedish GSM license, showed interest in participating.[26]

Any application for a concession would need to be delivered to the Danish Ministry of Communications by March 1, 1991, at the latest, and among the four applicants were the general partnership Dansk MobilTelefon I/S, which consisted of GN Store Nord, which represented a 51 percent share; BellSouth, which represented a 29 percent share; and Nordic Tel, which represented a 20 percent share. The reason for this distribution was that for political reasons, the existence or absence of a Danish majority would be taken into consideration in connection with the awarding of a concession. GN Store Nord planned to reduce its stake and thus the economic risk if the concession were awarded to the consortium by transferring 30 percent to other Danish investors or to BellSouth and Nordic Tel within the context of a company structure that ensured a continuing Danish majority of 51 percent.[27]

The other applicants were Interfon, a consortium consisting of partners including the Danish shipbuilding and petroleum group A. P. Møller and the British mobile telephony company Racal (now Vodafone); Mobicon, which consisted of the toy company Lego and the insurance company Baltica and had the IT specialist Christian Rovsing as its front figure; and finally a purely foreign consortium that called itself Danmobil, probably to distract attention from its actual lack of a Danish component.

Formally, the decision regarding the awarding of the license was to be made by Conservative

Minister of Communications Torben Rechendorff, though he was required to have the support of the Danish government's so-called coordinating committee, which included two ministers from each of the parties represented in the Danish government, the Conservatives and Venstre; the Danish Liberal Party; and Prime Minister Poul Schlüter. The political game in which the applicants attempted to influence the ministers, other politicians, and centrally placed officials had begun already before the deadline for the submission of applications, and there was also a great deal of agitation via the press—the GN Store Nord consortium chose to maintain a low profile in this connection, however.

Late in the afternoon on May 31, 1991, Thomas Duer received a telephone call from Torben Rechendorff, who informed Thomas Duer that the license for the GSM network had been awarded to Dansk MobilTelefon. On the recommendation of Telestyrelsen, Torben Rechendorff himself had endorsed the GN Store Nord consortium, but the government's coordinating committee had been divided with regard to the matter as the two Venstre ministers had supported the A. P. Møller consortium. The Conservative prime minister, Poul Schlüter, had ended the dispute by choosing Dansk MobilTelefon.[28]

There was great surprise at this decision among both the applicants and the public as A. P. Møller had been considered the clear favorite. Opinions with regard to which proposal was actually best varied greatly, as did assumptions about why the license had been awarded to the GN Store Nord consortium. A later account of A. P. Møller's actions in connection with the fight for the license concluded that "there was certainly no doubt about who was best at playing the political game."[29]

After three months of negotiations with Telestyrelsen, the final license was presented to Dansk MobilTelefon by Torben Rechendorff at a ceremony on September 9, 1991, on Kongens Nytorv. The board of directors of the mobile telephony company would consist of Thomas Duer (chairman) and the head of the telegraphy company, Vice Presi-

dent Frits Larsen, and two representatives of Bell-South and one of Nordic Tel.

Subsequently, Kryolitselskabet Øresund A/S purchased 15 percent of the shares from GN Store Nord, which was left with 36 percent. This was 15 percent more than the 21 percent originally foreseen, but Thomas Duer and the telegraphy company convinced the board of directors that the mobile telephony project was attractive enough to justify refraining from reducing GN Store Nord's stake more.[30]

The construction of the GSM system began immediately. It was carried out by BellSouth with Nokia of Finland as the supplier of infrastructure, including antenna masts and transmission stations. The first part of the network was opened on March 1, 1992, under the name Sonofon. Meanwhile, TeleDanmark built the other GSM network via the newly established subsidiary Tele Danmark Mobil with the Swedish company L. M. Ericsson as a supplier.

Despite the fact that both systems were commissioned by the agreed-upon date, they did not immediately acquire any subscribers as there were no approved GSM telephones. However, Sonofon did succeed in acquiring a permit to purchase and distribute one thousand mobile telephones so it would be possible to test the system and eliminate flaws. It was not until early September 1992 that the two networks acquired ordinary subscribers.

Coup in Moscow

A few days after Thomas Duer received notification that the GN Store Nord consortium had been awarded the GSM license, Cocom granted its permission for the establishment of an undersea fiber optic connection between Albertslund, near Copenhagen, and Kingisepp, near Leningrad, as well as for the creation of two digital radio chains from Kingisepp to Leningrad and Moscow, respectively. Permission was granted on condition that the landing station for the cable in Kingisepp would be manned by Danish personnel and that the radio chain would be used only for international traffic.

On this basis, the Danish consortium concluded a final contract with the Soviet Ministry of Communications that same month.[31]

GN Store Nordiske Telegraf-Selskab and Telecom Danmark were to establish the cable connection in cooperation, and while Telecom Danmark was to finance and own the western part of the cable, GN Store Nord was to finance and own the eastern part, which was to be taken over by the Soviet ministry when the company's construction costs had been fully covered. All revenues from the Russian half then were to belong to the telegraph company until the financing amount of approximately 250 million kroner had been paid back with interest, after which the traffic revenues were to be divided between the company and the Soviet ministry in accordance with an agreement between those two parties. There was also the possibility of taking on the construction and financing of the radio chain connection between Kingisepp and Moscow, which would involve total expenditures of 80 to 100 million kroner, if an agreement between the Soviet ministry and US West did not become a reality.[32]

In early July 1991, when GN Store Nord's board of directors was to make a final decision on participation in the Denmark-Russia cable project, it was underscored in a preparatory presentation by the telegraph company that the value of the project could not be calculated in money alone. Rather, the telegraph company argued, the project should be seen as "GN Store Nord's springboard to participation in future telecommunications projects not only in the USSR but also in Europe and the Far East."[33]

According to the presentation, the agreement was an indication that the Soviet ministry saw its cooperation with GN Store Nordiske Telegraf-Selskab as valuable and attractive and as "a continuation of a cooperation that has lasted more than a hundred years" that could open the door to similar projects in the future. In addition, there was the value of the cooperation with Telecom Danmark, which all the evidence suggested could be expanded in the years to come. The project could give GN Store Nord an international future in telecommunications and, therefore, had great potential strate-

gic significance, while rejecting the project would "have a negative effect not only nationally and internationally but also in relation to Telecom."[34]

According to the minutes of the meeting of the board of directors, no critical views were heard from the members of the board, who declared that they were in agreement that the project had "great strategic significance for the Telegraph Company," and the company received the desired authorization to move forward and begin negotiations with possible cable suppliers.[35]

However, only a short time passed before everything appeared to be lying in ruins. On August 19, 1991, an attempt to remove the president of the Soviet Union, Mikhail Gorbachev, by means of a coup began. The leaders of the coup attempt were several members of the government, including the vice president, the prime minister, the minister of defense, the minister of the interior, and the head of the secret police, the KGB. These individuals felt that Gorbachev's reforms went too far and that a planned new Union treaty that would make the republics largely autonomous would lead to the dissolution of the Soviet Union.

While tanks and other military vehicles rolled into Moscow and headed toward the Kremlin and a state of emergency was declared for parts of the country, Gorbachev was placed under house arrest in Crimea. However, despite the positions of power held by the organizers of the coup attempt, it soon became clear that their actual power base was weak and lacked significant support in the general population and in the army. When the president of the Russian Federation, Boris Yeltsin, went out onto the streets of Moscow and denounced the coup, it crumbled quickly, and while the plotters of the coup sought to flee, Gorbachev returned to Moscow on August 22, just three days after the coup attempt had begun.

The whole world followed developments in Moscow excitedly. On Kongens Nytorv, there was particular interest in those developments, and indeed, the coup attempt had consequences for the Dano-Russian cable project. While Gorbachev was restored to his position as the president of the Soviet Union, he lacked real political authority and power, while Yeltsin began systematically transferring the power of the Soviet government to Russia's ministries in anticipation of the dissolution of the Soviet Union.

As a consequence, GN Store Nord received a message in early September to the effect that responsibility for the cable project had been transferred from the Soviet government to the Russian government, which could be bad enough in itself. What was worse was that GN Store Nord learned that for a lengthy period of time, the Russian government had been negotiating with parties such as Cable & Wireless with regard to a potential competing project involving a cable laid from Aberdeen to Kingisepp via Sweden.[36]

In a somewhat understated formulation, the top management team's report to GN Store Nord's board of directors remarked that the situation was "rather complicated." The reality covered by this formulation was that the telegraph company and Telecom Danmark had an agreement with a Soviet ministry that lacked authority, while Cable & Wireless was sitting at the table with those who were now in power.

Therefore, a Danish delegation from GN Store Nord and Statens Teletjeneste, including the respective chief executive officers, Thomas Duer and Jens Kiil, traveled to Moscow, where, on September 19, 1991, they met with the Russian minister. By the time they returned to Denmark, they had secured confirmation that the Russian government would be a party to the original agreement, which was expanded late in the year to include the radio chain from Kingisepp to Moscow on a corresponding financing basis.[37]

The participation of the telegraph company in the trans-Siberian project, at least as far as the Denmark-Russia cable was concerned, had been ensured. The telegraph company's role was expanded in November 1991 when GN Store Nord, Telecom Danmark, Russia's Rostelecom A/O, Japan's KDD, and Korea Telecom signed an agreement to complete a feasibility study for an undersea fiber optic cable connection linking the three countries and giving them access to the modernized trans-Sibe-rian connection. In the Far East, the telegraph company was also on its way to reestablishing its position on the basis of the technology of a new age and a new political world order.[38]

Rebirth of the Great Northern Telegraph Company

After decades during which GN Store Nord had focused on building an industrial sector and there had been one prediction after another of the imminent death of telecommunications activities, GN Store Nordiske Telegraf-Selskab found itself at the center of the group leadership's actions with projects that required investments that were similar in size to those required for the building up of the GSM network and had not been seen since Tietgen's establishment of the Great Northern Telegraph Company. The driving force behind the rebirth of the company was a small group of employees of many years around the leader of the telegraph company, Frits Larsen.

The agreements regarding the Polish cable project, the GSM project, and the Dano-Russian cable created a need for total investments by the end of 1993 of 500 to 600 million kroner, which caused GN Store Nord's board of directors to add capital via a stock emission. According to the top management team, there was "no obstacle" to the financing of the three projects by the group itself, but in this case, further investments in the telegraph company itself and in the subsidiaries could be blocked because of a shortage of capital, which "would be an unfortunate signal to send."[39]

The stock emission was executed in late November and early December 1991 and gave the group approximately 490 million kroner in capital that appeared likely to be needed. The dissolution of the Soviet Union and the collapse of the Eastern bloc created extensive opportunities as the telecommunications infrastructure in the former Soviet republics and in the Eastern European countries was inadequate and old-fashioned.

However, the countries in question had the problem that they lacked both capital and technologi-

The official opening of the fiber optic cable took place on April 10, 1993, when Denmark's prime minister Poul Nyrup Rasmussen and Russia's president Boris Yeltsin exchanged a thumbs-up via a television link between Taastrup and Moscow.

cal know-how. To be sure, organizations such as the World Bank and the European Investment Bank were already providing large sums of money for the expansion and modernization of the telecommunications infrastructure in Eastern Europe and the former Soviet Union, but the application and approval processes were lengthy and involved subsequent rounds of bidding for licenses. Many countries did not wish to take the time to go through such a process, and this created opportunities for GN Store Nordiske Telegraf-Selskab, which could supply both financing and know-how.

In the fall of 1991, there were possibilities with regard to several cable projects in Estonia, Latvia, and Lithuania, and the telegraph company secured an agreement regarding the completion of a fea-

sibility study for a possible cable connection from Warsaw to Kaunas and Vilnius in Lithuania with a possible later extension through Latvia and Estonia and finally to Kingisepp, where the Dano-Russian cable was to be landed. However, only a cable system in Lithuania between Vilnius and Kaunas and with an extension to the Polish border was ultimately actually realized. On the other hand, the telegraph company concluded an agreement regarding a feasibility study for an extension of the Polish north-south cable into and through Czechoslovakia. In Ukraine and Belarus, the telegraph company established connections in anticipation of possible projects branching off from the Poland project.[40]

The telegraph company's strategy was to sign contracts for as many feasibility studies as possible with no guarantee that these studies would result in new projects. Other Western telecommunications companies, including British, Turkish, Italian, and American ones, were also active in this connection, but, as is noted in a blueprint presented

GN Store Nord's chief executive officer Thomas Duer with Captain Jens Pedersen aboard P & T's cable ship Peter Faber, which laid the fiber optic cable between Denmark and the Soviet Union. This picture was taken in connection with an earlier visit by a Russian delegation that was to inspect the cable ship and watch while it plowed a submarine cable into the sea floor. In the background is Head Engineer Erik Boye Jensen of GN Store Nord.

in March 1992, the telegraph company—in addition to knowledge of the world of international communications resulting from many years of experience as well as a tradition of cooperation with several Eastern countries stretching back over many years—had an advantage not shared by any of its competitors.

"At the same time, the telegraph company has its origins in a small country, which means that the telegraph company does not dominate its partners in the East. The telegraph company has the potential to be a builder of bridges between the East and the West."[41]

Reading this was like hearing C. F. Tietgen's original vision of the establishment of the Great Northern Telegraph Company in 1869 and the subsequent expansion in East Asia. The company's weaknesses, however, were also the ones that had characterized the company back then: a lack of international size in relation to the company's competitors and ultimately a lack of organizational and economic capabilities for which the company's cooperation with Telecom Danmark now compensated.

In the blueprint, the money required for investments in the currently active projects, including the construction of the Danish GSM network, as well as for future projects expected to be established by the end of 1995, was calculated to be a good 1,125 million kroner. Subsequently, smaller investments in the amount of 80 million kroner would be required for the period through 2000. In addition, the telegraph company would require further investments for any new projects for which the company was able to conclude contracts.[42]

This did not frighten off GN Store Nord's leadership, however. The group's total liquidity reserve at the beginning of 1992 was 1.1 billion kroner, excluding the 490 million kroner from the stock emission in December 1991. The blueprint for GN Store Nordiske Telegraf-Selskab was, therefore, approved by the board of directors on March 27, 1992, in connection with which the board of directors declared that "[t]he Telegraph Company [would] continue to constitute a central and significant part of GN Store Nord."[43]

The Denmark-Russia cable and the radio chain connection between Kingisepp on one hand and Moscow and Saint Petersburg, respectively, on the other was commissioned as planned in 1993, as was the Lithuanian cable system establishing a line leading from Vilnius to Kaunus and on to the border with Poland. Also, in 1993, the telegraph company, in partnership with Telecom Danmark, concluded an agreement with Rostelecom regarding the financing of leases for international fiber optic cables that would extend Rostelecom's international connections through Denmark to other European countries and to the United States.

On the other hand, the Polish north-south cable, contrary to expectations, was not commissioned until February 1994 as a result of internal disagreements among the Polish partners and a large number of errors in the laying of the cable that had no practical significance in themselves but that the Poles insisted be corrected. In 1994, revenues for all the connections amounted to a good 182 million kroner, which generated an account surplus of just over 108 million kroner.[44]

There was more on the way from the revitalized 125-year-old telegraph company, which in June 1993, in partnership with Telecom Danmark, signed a contract with Rostelecom for the financing of the Russian portion of a fiber optic cable connecting the Russian Far East, Japan, and Korea; an agreement was also concluded with regard to the financing of Rostelecom's leases for telecommunications connections between Japan and Korea on one hand and other Asian countries, Australia, and the United States on the other. The required cables were laid late in 1994, and the entire system was opened to traffic on February 15, 1995.

Around the same time, the JASC, the cable between Russia and Japan, was shut down. For many years, this cable had been not only a stable source of revenues but also the link between the telegraph company's past and GN Store Nord's modern international telecommunications activities.

The telegraph company did not succeed in becoming involved in the construction of a radio chain connection extending 9,500 kilometers from Moscow to Khabarovsk that was to connect the fiber optic cable systems in the Baltic region and in the Far East, respectively, as salaries demanded by the Danish engineers were too high for the telegraph company to compete successfully for the project as regards the price. However, the telegraph

company and Telecom Danmark were engaged by Rostelecom as technical consultants in connection with the preparation and execution of the project. The connection in question was expected to open in 1995.

In December 1994, on the other hand, the telegraph company concluded an agreement with the Swedish government-owned telecommunications company Telia and the Estonian telephone company Eesti Telefon with regard to the establishment of a fiber optic cable connection between Sweden and Estonia with a link to Kingisepp so that the cable could serve as a reserve connection in relation to the Denmark–Russia cable.

One of the more spectacular of the telegraph company's actions was the acquisition of 25.5 percent of the shares in two small Russian companies. One of these, AO Neda Paging, opened a personal paging system in Saint Petersburg in the spring of 1994, while during the same year, the other, AO St. Petersburg Taxophones, began setting up 5,500 payment card telephones that were supplied by GN Communications.

The scale of these activities was modest, and they did not lie within the usual business areas of the telegraph company or of GN Store Nord. Strategically, however, they were of interest to the telegraph company as they could provide important knowledge conditions with regard to local telecommunications and open up new opportunities as not only the local telephone company in Saint Petersburg but also corresponding companies in other Russian cities wished to modernize their systems and equipment. The telegraph company itself had the ambition of exploiting its experiences with Sonofon to become involved in the establishment of GSM systems in Russia and Eastern Europe.[45]

It was also for strategic reasons that in June 1994, the telegraph company decided to spend 10 million kroner to acquire a small stake—half a percent—in Rostelecom, which was to be privatized. Rostelecom itself had indicated that "it would be seen positively" if GN Store Nord acquired a small stake.[46]

Telephony and Industry

CHAPTER 24

Mobile growth and stagnating cable business

Among the applicants for the Danish GSM license, Dansk MobilTelefon had the lowest investment costs for the first five years, 1.1 billion kroner, which had to do with the fact that Dansk MobilTelefon had used the most conservative estimate of the number of future subscribers—72,000 in 1996, increasing to 180,000 by 2001. These expectations were based on the assumption that the NMT system would still be in operation and that TeleDanmark would construct a GSM network parallel to that of Dansk MobilTelefon. TeleDanmark's network was expected to have approximately one hundred thousand subscribers by 2001. Dansk MobilTelefon had also assumed that mobile telephony would be attractive primarily to businesspeople and to the well-to-do part of the population. Cellular telephones were, in fact, quite expensive—they cost 15,000 to 20,000 kroner—and using them cost 2.80 kroner per minute.

However, cellular telephone use expanded much more quickly than had been expected, generating a much greater need for investments. By the end of 1993, Sonofon had thirty thousand subscribers, having expected only sixteen thousand, and the vast majority of telephones were not car telephones with eight-watt radio transmitters but two-watt handheld mobile telephones with a shorter range. Also, the buyers expected to be able to use their telephones indoors, where the signal was weaker; therefore, it became necessary to reconfigure the entire system and set up a large number of new masts to ensure denser coverage and sufficient capacity.

The growth in the number of subscribers accelerated in 1994 so that by the end of the year, Sonofon had approximately one hundred thousand customers. This growth was driven by sharp price competition with Tele Danmark Mobil, which had the advantage of having an established network of retailers because it had been operating the NMT system since 1982, for which Sonofon compensated by hiring its own salespeople who focused on the business community as well as concluding contracts with nationwide retailers of radios and televisions such as FONA and Fredgaard and the everyday goods retailer Bilka to facilitate sales to ordinary customers.

Both Sonofon and Tele Danmark Mobil advertised aggressively and paid large bonuses to retailers of SIM cards and subscriptions. Also, telephones were sold at considerably reduced prices if customers signed contracts for multiyear subscription periods, so in the summer of 1993, a cellular telephone could be purchased for under 1,000 kroner. Both companies were quite imaginative in connection with their sales methods, and there were mutual accusations of rule violations and complaints about the respective other party to Telestyrelsen and the ministry.

In its fight to attract subscribers, Sonofon sought to maintain a profile as the mobile telephony company of the business community, and the company was quick to introduce new technical facilities such as an advanced telephone answering system called sonoMEMO. In the spring of 1994, the company became the first to offer two-way data transmission via the GSM network, and in the fall of the same year, two-way fax transmission became a reality, after which the company introduced the Mobil Office concept for the business community. On the other hand, the subscribers of both Sonofon and Tele Danmark had the advantage of being able to use their Danish telephones outside Denmark, thanks to the so-called roaming agreements with GSM operators in countries other than Denmark. At the end of 1994, Sonofon had agreements with operators in twenty-five countries.

The increased investments and marketing costs had a significant effect on Sonofon's economic situation, and in turn, this had a significant effect on GN Store Nord's account of July 1, 1994, when Sonofon's establishment phase was viewed as completed and the establishment costs had been activated. Given an ownership share of 36 percent, GN Store Nord's share of Sonofon's annual result for 1994 ended up being revenues of a good 73 million kroner—and an accounting deficit of 55 million kroner and the prospect of further large deficits in the years to come. The first surplus was expected to arrive only in 1997. However, the deficit was more than compensated for by the annual results

from the telegraph company's cable projects in the Soviet Union, Lithuania, and Poland.[1]

From ugly duckling to beautiful swan

While the telegraph company and Sonofon were experiencing strong growth, the thorough cleaning up of GN Store Nord's industrial sector was completed. In the summer of 1992, GN Store Nord finally succeeded in selling the last remnants of GN Batteries; the buyer was the Hong Kong–based battery manufacturer Gold Peak Batteries International's branch in Singapore. Around the same time, GN Store Nord closed GN DataCom's division for paper tape–based automation equipment, which did not survive a quick technological shift to computer-controlled automation. The remainder of the company's activities, including the manufacturing of terminals for payments with the Dankort and other payment cards, were taken over by GN Communications.

However, GN Communications had come under pressure because of the liberalization of telecommunications. The national telecommunications authorities, which were facing privatization, had until now been the main customers for the company's advanced and, therefore, expensive coin- and card-operated telephones, but now these authorities began to focus more on prices. In the spring of 1992, to supplement the GN Communications product portfolio, GN Store Nord purchased the British company Rathdown Industries Ltd., which manufactured simple, cheap card telephones, which were aimed mostly at private-sector customers and were intended to be installed indoors.

However, this did not help GN Communications, which was sold in April 1994, while GN Store Nord kept GN Rathdown. In the same month, GN File-Tech, with its ODIN archiving system, was sold after having experienced several years of declining performance; the German part owner had sold its stake in GN FileTech in 1992.

On the other hand, a new subsidiary was added to the group in 1992 when GN Store Nord acquired all the share capital in the London-based company Comtext International Ltd. This company, the name of which was changed to GN Comtext, offered telex and telefax via its global telecommunications network, had built up considerable business generating revenues of nearly 150 million kroner, and was represented in thirty-five countries on five continents.

Also, the cleaning up of the group was beginning to be reflected in GN Store Nord's results. After a low point in 1991, revenues for 1992 rose to 1,335 million kroner, but the annual result, nevertheless, sank from 93 million kroner for 1991 to just 31 million kroner for 1992. The reason for this was extraordinary expenses totaling nearly 73 million kroner, 23 million kroner of which had come from the restructuring of GN Datacom, nearly 37 million kroner from depreciation of stocks and a stake in the troubled Danish insurance company Hafnia Holding A/S, and just over 13 million kroner from a decline in the share price for GN Store Nord's own stock and for shares in GN Store Nord Holding.

The declining share price for GN Store Nord's own stock reflected the fact that investors were not displaying much interest in the stock despite Unibørs's recommendation, but this soon changed. After having been at just over four hundred points in the summer of 1991, the stock fell to 260 by the fall of 1992, after which it again began to climb. Investors' confidence that GN Store Nord was finally on the right track was supported in the summer of 1993 by a thorough stock analysis by the stock-broking company Alfred Berg Børsmæglerselskab, which compared the group to the ugly duckling transformed into a beautiful swan in Hans Christian Andersen's fairy tale. "Wearing the yellow leader shirt in two of the most profitable growth areas of this decade, GN Store Nord can look forward to a very bright future," Alfred Berg wrote with reference to the international cable projects and the Danish GSM system.

However, Alfred Berg also had words of praise for the developments at GN Danavox and GN Netcom, as well as GN Elmi, which had just purchased the Canadian manufacturer of data measurement equipment Navtel Communications, and it was underscored that the industrial companies would continue to be of central significance as a component of the basis for the group's earnings. That GN Store Nord continued to have a focus on the industrial companies was indicated on March 1, 1993, when the group hired Jørn Kildegaard as a corporate director and member of the top management team with particular responsibility for the industrial companies so Thomas Duer would be able to concentrate on the telegraph company and Sonofon.[2]

By the end of 1993, GN Store Nord's stock reached six hundred points, where it was stabilized, and GN Store Nord had no difficulty attracting buyers in May 1994 when the group executed a combined share emission with a right of first refusal for existing shareholders and issuance of a convertible bond loan that brought the group a total of 660 million kroner to be used for new investments and purchases in both the telecommunications sector and the industrial sector.

The emission took place just before GN Store Nord celebrated its 125th anniversary and showed that despite its advanced age, the group was vigorous indeed. In the anniversary year, the group had revenues of 1.7 billion kroner—and most importantly, an operating result of 177 million kroner, the largest ever. The telecommunications activities resulted in revenues of just under 500 million kroner, while the industrial activities brought in more than twice as much—just under 1.2 billion kroner. However, given the prospects for the future of the telegraph company and Sonofon, it was to be expected that revenues for the group's two types of business activities would soon be equalized.

Of the telecommunications companies, GN Comtext, with revenues of 243.3 million kroner and a surplus of 105.7 million kroner, was the largest. The second-largest was GN Store Nordiske Telegraf-Selskab, with revenues of 182.1 million kroner and a surplus of 105.7 million kroner. Last came Sonofon, with revenues of 73.1 million kroner and a deficit of 45 million kroner.[3]

The leader among the industrial companies was GN Danavox, which, after several years of stag-

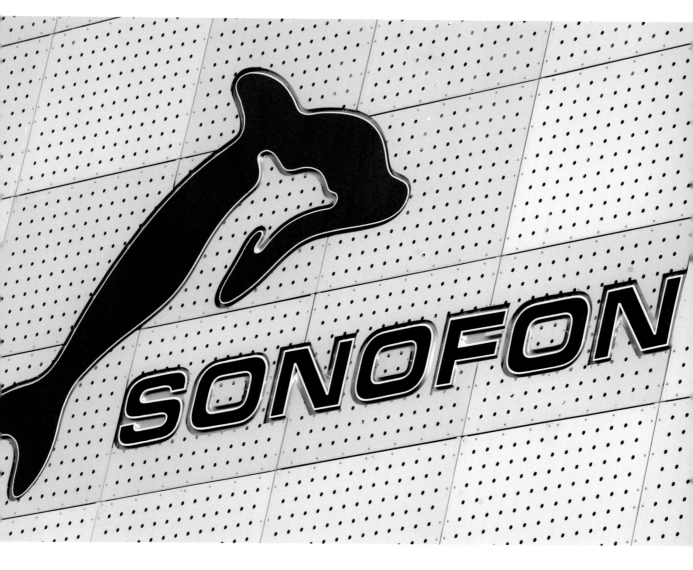

Sonofon's logo, a jumping dolphin, was created by the Danish designer Johan Adam Linneballe.

nation, had revenues of 410 million kroner; an increase in revenues by 35 million kroner could be attributed to the purchase of a Norwegian manufacturer of audiological accessories. The company itself had, in fact, presented several innovations, including two programmable hearing aids presented in 1991. The following year came the world's first partially digital behind-the-ear hearing aid, the DFS Genius, which reduced the squealing created by acoustic feedback, and in 1991, GN Danavox

presented new and updated models of both programmable and partially digital devices. GN Danavox also focused on retailers, presenting a "Hear for life" concept involving a broadly conceived support package, though this did not result in a marked increase in sales and the surplus increased only a little (to 19.3 million kroner in 1994) in relation to the previous year.

The second-largest industrial company was GN Elmi/Navtel, with revenues for 1994 of 321.1 million kroner, which represented a decline in revenues by nearly 80 million kroner. This was the first time the company had ever posted revenues that failed to exceed those for the previous year, and the company posted its first deficit ever in the amount of 9.4 million kroner. The reason for this was the liberalization of the telecommunications sector, which in many cases caused the government telecommunications authorities to refrain from making investments; the German market, in particular, was disappointing. Late in the year, however, the company strengthened its market position by acquiring the Laser Precision Corporation of the United States, which manufactured testing equipment for fiber optic networks.

GN Netcom was much more dynamic. The company was successful in all markets in 1994 and increased its revenues over those for the previous year by nearly 20 percent, to 312.6 million kroner, while the company's surplus increased by 80 percent over that for the previous year, 70.1 million kroner, which corresponded to a degree of surplus of 22.4 percent. Factors contributing to this success were several improvements to both the Stetomike series and the Profile series, as well as a new generation of amplifiers with a newly developed integrated circuit called ASIC. While there were no radical innovations, the company was far along with its development of the first wireless headsets, which the company expected to launch in 1996.

Finally, there was GN Rathdown, which, with revenues of 115 million kroner, was the smallest of the industrial companies by a good margin. However, GN Rathdown had a surplus of 19 million kroner, which was larger than that of GN Danavox and represented a surplus percentage that was close to that of GN Netcom. The company contrasted with the others because of its low-tech product line, but while this product area did not offer great prospects for the future, the respectable and dependable surpluses benefited the group's bottom line.

Industrial growth through purchases

The stock emission shortly before the anniversary was intended to provide funds partly for an ongoing investment in Sonofon and partly for the financing of a targeted growth strategy for the industrial sector involving, on one hand, investments that could lead to organic growth and, on the other hand, the purchasing of companies that could increase the subsidiaries' revenues and market share. The strategic goal was that each of the subsidiaries would be a leader in its business area.[4]

This was an ambition to which GN Netcom had already lived up as the company, with an increase in revenues to 351 million kroner in 1995 and to 428 million kroner in 1996 and with a surplus that continued to grow, reaching 71.5 million kroner and then 83 million kroner, had reinforced its position as the world's second-largest manufacturer of headsets. With its strong organic growth and conviction that there were hardly any possibilities with regard to significant purchases, GN Netcom did not have a purchasing strategy, but that did not keep the company from making purchases when the opportunity did present itself. In October 1996, GN Netcom bought its American competitor UNEX Corporation, which was the fourth-largest manufacturer both in the world and in the United States. The purpose of this acquisition was to complement GN Netcom's product range and strengthen the company's position on the American market in particular; GN Netcom kept UNEX's name and independent marketing.

In terms of GN Netcom's product range, the company's purchase of UNEX revealed its importance late in 1996 when GN Netcom presented its first wireless headsets in no fewer than three models. Two models were based on radio technology and used various frequencies for the North American and European market, respectively, and one model was based on technology using infrared light so it could be marketed worldwide.

With its acquisition of UNEX, GN Netcom reached a global market share of an estimated 24 percent, so it was still a long way up to the world's leading company, Plantronics of the United States, which had an estimated 54 percent. Plantronics had by far the largest share of the North American market—65 percent to GN Netcom's 25. With a 50 percent market share in Europe to Plantronics's

48 percent, GN Netcom led the European field by a slim margin.

For GN Netcom, it was a decisive goal to narrow the gap between GN Netcom and Plantronics on the North American market. Back in the fall of 1992, GN Netcom had attempted to take over the American company ACS Wireless, which was the third-largest on the American market with a share of 12 percent, but an unresolved patent lawsuit involving ACS Wireless and Plantronics had gotten in the way. In the spring of 1996, ACS contacted GN Netcom to find out whether GN Netcom was still interested in taking over ACS. While this new contact did not lead to practical negotiations, GN Netcom was, in fact, still interested in taking over its competitor.[5]

GN Danavox was working in a more targeted fashion on growing via purchases. Worldwide, there were ten to fifteen international manufacturers, the largest of which had a market share of approximately 15 percent, while GN Danavox, with a global market share of approximately 6 percent, was estimated to be the world's sixth-largest manufacturer; among the companies with larger market shares than GN Danavox's were Widex and Oticon. For Scandinavia, GN Danavox's market share was 20 percent, for the rest of Europe 5 percent, and for the United States 3 percent.

While GN Danavox's revenues grew steadily, reaching 450 million kroner in 1995 and 484 million kroner in 1996, this was far from enough to push the company up among the sector's leaders. Also, the sector was undergoing a market shift toward expensive high-tech devices at the expense of low-end devices like those marketed by GN Danavox. The company was therefore subjected to strong technological pressure while it was still behind in the in-the-ear market. In seeking to acquire companies then, GN Danavox was seeking to acquire technological know-how, new products, and increased revenues.

However, the group of realistic candidates was relatively small. Early in 1994, GN Danavox had contacted Phonak of Switzerland and Beltone of the United States and put out feelers with regard to possible takeovers, but neither company had shown any

interest. Negotiations late in the year with the Swiss company Ascom Audiosys, which had been put up for sale, ended when Oticon bought the company.

On the other hand, Beltone contacted GN Danavox in the spring of 1995 and informed GN Danavox that the family-owned company was for sale because of a generational shift. With a market share of 12 percent, Beltone was among the five largest companies on the American market, selling its products via one thousand hearing clinics, and a takeover would, therefore, give GN Danavox a significant boost in the American market. GN Store Nord's board of directors gave GN Danavox authorization to begin negotiations, though the chairman noted that "there [were] two paths that could be chosen for GN Danavox, one being to purchase more companies that can ensure growth and the other being to sell the company." The board of directors was still in doubt as to whether GN Danavox had an independent future or should be sold to a competitor. Therefore, the chairman asked the top management team to evaluate the possibilities with regard to selling GN Danavox if the negotiations with Beltone went nowhere.[6]

In the fall of 1985, when the negotiations with Beltone were ongoing, GN Danavox entered into a strategic alliance with the American technology company Audiologic involving the simultaneous purchase of up to 20 percent of the share capital. This alliance gave GN exclusive access to digital technology and algorithms that in GN Danavox's view were extremely attractive. In connection with approving this arrangement, GN Store Nord's board of directors expressed the wish that by 1997 at the latest, the cooperation would result in a fully digitalized hearing aid, an innovation the world's leading manufacturers of hearing aids were racing to be the first to present.[7]

The conclusion of this alliance stopped the discussion by GN Store Nord's board of directors of the possible sale of GN Danavox, which was still attempting to take over Beltone. However, the negotiations were dragged out because of disagreements about the price, and despite the fact that agreement was reached in March 1996, it all ended with the

American owner family notifying GN Danavox that the company was not for sale.[8]

In the spring of 1996, to compensate for the breakdown of GN Danavox's negotiations with Beltone, GN Danavox and Audiologic expanded their strategic alliance to include the American hearing aid manufacturer ReSound in cooperation to develop a digital hearing aid. ReSound occupied a position at the top end of the sector's technology scale and could contribute additional know-how as well as financing to the development project, which was expected to produce its first products by the end of 1997.[9]

Before then, in the fall of 1996, GN Danavox presented its first high-tech device, Danasound, which, to be sure, was analog, but used technology that was adapted to individual users, measuring hearing loss and adjusting the device in a single process. This device was presented in behind-the-ear and in-the-ear versions and in a form that took into account the anatomy of the human ear. The design of this device earned GN Danavox several industrial design prizes.

Also, in 1996, Oticon launched its first fully digitalized hearing aid, followed by Widex only two days later, and once again, GN Danavox was behind. Danasound filled up part of the hole while GN Danavox cooperated with Audiologic and ReSound with regard to the development of a fully digitalized hearing aid that was referred to as second-generation and superior in relation to the existing digital devices.

Technologically then, GN Danavox was on its way to catching up with its competitors, and what remained to be done was to execute a major purchase that could boost revenues significantly, and such a purchase did not seem to be just around the corner after the negotiations with Beltone had been terminated. Late in the year, GN Danavox negotiated with regard to a possible takeover of the Dutch company Philips's hearing aid division, which had revenues of 300 million kroner, most of which were generated in Europe, but these negotiations produced no positive result. GN Danavox did succeed in acquiring the Italian manufacturer and distributor of hearing aids Italiana Audioprotesi Primo and thus gaining greater access to the Italian market, where GN Danavox's position was weak, and increasing overall revenues by 4 percent.

GN Elmi/Navtel, which changed its name to GN Nettest following the acquisition of Laser Precision, was still negatively affected by the reluctance of the telecommunications authorities to make purchases and the technological shift, which created major problems for the Elmi division in particular, while the other two divisions presented respectable surpluses. In 1995, revenues increased to 381 million kroner, but the company, nevertheless, presented an increased deficit of nearly 13 million kroner. A further increase in revenues to 432 million kroner in 1996 resulted in a new deficit in the amount of 12 million kroner.

The growth in 1996 was due in part to the acquisition of the American company Azure Technologies, and in general, GN Nettest actively worked to create growth via purchases and to reach critical mass. However, the particular structure of the business sector, which was characterized by either small companies or divisions within large global corporate groups, made it difficult to execute purchases that would contribute significantly to GN Nettest's revenues.

Despite the company's difficulties, GN Store Nord's board of directors still had confidence in this subsidiary, which was maintaining its strong position in a market that was growing rapidly, borne along by the new global communication platform known as the Internet and related groundbreaking services such as those provided by the Web browser Netscape, which was launched in 1994; the search engine Yahoo, which was launched the following year; and various e-mail programs. The constant expansion of the global digital communications system of fiber optic cables, radio chains, and local, regional, and national networks as well as new GSM systems created a need for an ever-increasing system monitoring and more measurements and testing of the infrastructure and thus created optimal growth conditions for GN Nettest.

GN Rathdown's days as a part of GN Store Nord were numbered, however. The company had no realistic way of living up to the goals of the growth strategy, and in 1996, when British Telecom chose a different supplier of pay telephones, the company was sold off.

Great Northern as a Danish telephone company?

Despite the successes of the industrial companies, the biggest engine of growth at GN Store Nord was Sonofon, which had been activated by the telegraph company and had quickly grown to become a serious competitor of Tele Danmark. However, the telegraph company also had an eye on further opportunities that came with the liberalization of telecommunications in the European Union, opportunities that were further enhanced in November 1994 when the EU's Council of Ministers decided to liberalize the telecommunications market in all the member countries by January 1, 1998, at the latest. The liberalization was to cover traditional landline telephony, and in this connection, the existing cable network was to be either divided among special companies or—as ended up being the case in Denmark—remain the property of liberalized former national monopoly organizations that would allow competitors to lease their infrastructure.

Immediately after this decision was made, the telegraph company began working to bring it about that a consortium led by GN Store Nord would become the so-called second operator for the Danish landline telephony network already before January 1, 1998, possibly with the exclusion of voice telephony to ensure a gradual transition to free competition and secure jobs and know-how in Denmark. A corresponding arrangement had been adopted in the Netherlands. A discussion with Denmark's Minister of Research early in 1995 made it clear that GN Store Nord's proposal would not, in fact, be approved, but this did not change GN Store Nord's strategic goal "that GN shall establish itself as a telecommunications operator for the land line network in Denmark."[10]

The telegraph company had already contacted several Danish infrastructure companies with existing cable systems: the electric companies NESA and SEAS as well as Københavns Belysningsvæsen (the Copenhagen Lighting Authority), De Danske Statsbaner (DSB, the Danish National Railways), and A/S Storebæltsforbindelsen (Great Belt Connection). The telegraph company also contacted several international telecommunications concerns—BellSouth, Telia, and France Telecom—with a view to acquiring a strong business partner as this would be necessary if the telegraph company were to be able to match TeleDanmark as well as the international corporate groups that were likely to try to penetrate a liberalized Danish telecommunications market with or without an alliance with GN Store Nord.[11]

The Danish infrastructure companies responded positively, and a working group was appointed to investigate the amount of free telecommunications capacity as well as possible forms of cooperation. Among the international telecommunications concerns, Telia, in particular, was interested, and at a summit between the respective chief executive officers of the two corporate groups in late February 1995, agreement was reached to continue the dialogue. A short time later, Telia presented a draft proposal for the establishment of a holding company that in addition to landline network activities would include Sonofon, Comtext, and the cable television company Stofa, which Telia was currently in the process of taking over and whose cable network with its connections with the end users now became of interest in the context at hand.[12] At a new summit in early May 1995, the two chief executive officers reached a principal decision regarding the two companies' approaching each other via an equally owned holding company to which GN Store Nord would contribute Sonofon and Comtext, while Telia would contribute Stofa. Late in the month, an agreement was signed with regard to investigating the market possibilities for an operator of landline telephony in Denmark. Working groups were established to prepare common reports on legal, financial, organizational, and other aspects of cooperation so the two boards of directors could be presented with a basis on which to make a decision in August. At the same time, the other part owners of Sonofon were informed that GN Store Nord wished to purchase their stakes, which was a prerequisite for the implementation of the proposed construction.[13]

When GN Store Nord's board of directors assembled for an extraordinary meeting on August 18 to discuss and take a position on whether to continue cooperating with Telia, the top management team reported that the negotiations had been frozen by Telia early in July. The reason for this was that the other part owners of Sonofon had not yet clarified their positions with regard to the possible sale of their stakes and that it was expected to take up to nine months for this to happen.

A short time later, the entire liberalization process was forced forward when the EU's Council of Ministers moved up the liberalization of the landline network to the summer of 1996. This caused GN Store Nord to contact the Danish investment company Incentive A/S informally and offer to purchase that company's stake in Sonofon, which Incentive had acquired in connection with its earlier acquisition of Kryolitselskabet. Acquiring Incentive's stake in Sonofon would provide GN Store Nord with an ownership percentage of 51 percent, which would make it possible to proceed with the negotiations with Telia.[14]

Shortly before Christmas 1995, GN Store Nord reached agreement with Incentive regarding a price and signed a declaration of intent, but a few days later, Telia informed GN Store Nord that for the time being, Telia was not interested in cooperating with GN Store Nord. The first company to challenge Tele Danmark's monopoly on landline telephony was, therefore, the Swedish telecommunications company Tele 2, which opened its network in October 1996, and was soon followed by Telia. Both companies leased access to Tele Danmark's network, while GN Store Nord abandoned its efforts to become an operator of landline telephony and focused on the cellular telephony network alone.

Declining cable business despite great efforts

In 1996, GN Store Nord's telecommunications sector achieved revenues at the level of those of the industrial sector. "A milestone in the adaptation process initiated in the late 1980s," the annual report declared. However, it was very predominantly Sonofon that had driven the growth in the telecommunications sector, with an increase in its revenues of nearly 500 million kroner to 771 million kroner, while in the same year, GN Comtext contributed with an increase in revenues of 90 million kroner to 356 million kroner. In contrast, GN Store Nordiske Telegraf-Selskab had to record a decline in revenues of 75 million kroner to 173 million kroner.[15]

Sonofon's gains could be attributed partly to significant growth in the number of subscribers, which reached five hundred thousand, but also partly to the fact that in August 1996, GN Store Nord and BellSouth bought out the other two owners, so they owned 53.5 percent and 46.5 percent, respectively. The negotiations with Incentive had been dragged out, but GN Store Nord was still attempting to become the sole owner of Sonofon, now with a view to a possible stock exchange listing. BellSouth did not wish to give up its stake, however, and while GN Store Nord did acquire a majority, the two parties made an agreement to the effect that they would have equal influence over the cellular telephony company.[16]

GN Comtext's gains could be attributed to the acquisition of two British companies that developed communications software for the shipping industry in particular; the shipping industry was the company's largest customer category, followed by the banking and travel sectors. Despite the revenue gains, the result was modest, a surplus of only 4 million kroner, but this was to be viewed positively given that the company had posted a deficit of 16 million kroner the previous year.[17]

In contrast, the telegraph company delivered a surplus of 54 million kroner despite the decline in revenues. However, this was less than half of the surplus for the previous year, which, in addition to the drop in revenues, could be attributed to the fact that Rostelecom had insisted on early repayment of the Danish financing of the Denmark–Russia cable and the radio chains to Saint Petersburg and Moscow, respectively, so the debt had now been paid back. This meant a loss of revenues for GN Store Nord as the Russian repayment was with interest and interest on the interest, which now disappeared, so the group received only an agreed-upon portion of the traffic revenues.[18]

The telegraph company was a partner in the cable between Sweden and Estonia that opened in October 1995, and in Moldova, a north–south fiber optic land connection through the whole country was opened late in the year, while the second part, as well as a digital international switching center in the capital city of Chișinău, opened in December 1996. However, the revenues from these two projects were far from sufficient to replace the loss of revenues from the Russian system.

At this time, it was also becoming more difficult to get involved in Russian projects. The company was invited to join an international consortium to complete a feasibility study for a trans-Siberian fiber optic cable connection with an option to become a shareholder in the company that was to lay the cable. Ultimately, however, Rostelecom decided to finance the entire project itself, and the telegraph company did not succeed in becoming a part of a Sino-Russian project to lay a cable between Harbin and Khabarovsk despite the fact that a delegation from GN Store Nord visited China, nor did GN Store Nord succeed in participating in the establishment of a fiber optic cable connection between Saint Petersburg and Moscow.[19]

It also became more difficult to become involved in projects in the Eastern and Central European countries, which obtained access to more advantageous financing options as their economic situations improved, and competition became stiffer as a number of international telecommunications concerns and, in particular, suppliers of cables and other telecommunications equipment copied GN Store Nord's financing model. The telegraph company, therefore, turned to more distant and backward parts of the former Soviet Union in Transcaucasia and Central Asia.

In the spring of 1995, the company was invited to participate in a cable project in the Black Sea involving Bulgaria, Ukraine, Russia, Georgia, Greece, and Cyprus with a view to GN Store Nord's possible participation in the financing. The result of negotiations with the national telecommunications authorities of Ukraine, Bulgaria, and Georgia was that in May 1996, the telegraph company submitted bids to all three countries, the total value of which was 31.3 million dollars.[20]

Around the same time, the company succeeded in concluding an agreement with Georgia and neighboring Azerbaijan with regard to a feasibility study for a possible fiber optic cable connection through the two countries from the Black Sea to Baku. Assuming that the project became a reality, a cable would be laid under the Caspian Sea to Türkmenbaşy in Turkmenistan so the Black Sea project could be connected to a planned fiber optic connection from China to Europe via Central Asia. In Armenia, the telegraph company also entered into an agreement regarding a feasibility study; this one was for a connection to the cable through Georgia. In Moldova, a feasibility study was completed for the cable connection from Chișinău to Odessa, where the Black Sea cable was to be landed. Negotiations in Turkmenistan with regard to this project led to the undertaking of preliminary studies related to a cable connection from Türkmenbaşy and the capital city of Ashgabat.[21]

In September 1995, Thomas Duer, Frits Larsen, and Erik Boye Jensen of the telegraph company visited communist North Korea, where they negotiated with the postal and communications ministry, which wished to undertake the modernization of the telecommunications system, including the establishment of a fiber optic network in a new free trade zone. In March 1996, a delegation was in Mongolia, where they entered into an agreement regarding a feasibility study for a radio chain connection from the capital city of Ulaanbaatar to the Russian border.[22]

Neither of these two projects ended up being realized, however, and the same is true of the Black Sea project. The cable projects in Georgia and Armenia were not realized either, while the project in Azerbaijan, including the cable under the Caspian Sea to Turkmenistan, was sent out for a round of bidding in the spring of 1997 when the telegraph company participated in the financial tender. This project was not realized either despite the fact that a delegation visited Turkmenistan and despite direct negotiations with the president of Azerbaijan, Heydar Aliyev, and GN Store Nord's leaders on Kongens Nytorv had to recognize that the age of participation in big cable projects was drawing to a close.[23]

Closer to home, however, the telegraph company did participate in a Nordic cable project called Baltica, which established a new undersea cable system connecting the Nordic countries and Poland. However, Great Northern's role was limited to a small investment—300,000 kroner—and a small stake in a cable between Poland and Bornholm.[24]

And then in the spring of 1998, there was an investment of just under 45 million kroner in a fiber optic cable connection in the Black Sea between Poti in Georgia and Sochi in Russia. The basis for this business was the poor relationship between the two countries, which were not on speaking terms, which create a space in which the telegraph company could act as a buffer—a familiar role. This would be the last time the company was involved with undersea cables, and while the existing cable and radio chain systems would continue to generate steady revenues for some years to come, it was clear that the time of the once-so-honored Great Northern Telegraph Company was drawing to a close.[25]

Stock emission, cross-ownership, and restriction of voting rights

The subsidiaries' interest in purchases and other investments was great, but it was an entirely new investment opportunity that would set the agenda for GN Store Nord's development during the years leading up to the turn of the millennium. During the fall of 1996, the Danish government announced that it would be accepting applications for four licenses for the operation of a new DCS 1800 system at a higher frequency that could accommodate several simultaneous conversations and would permit the provision of a number of service functions that were otherwise available only to landline users. Sonofon submitted its application on December 2, 1996, as did Tele Danmark, France Telecom, and the Swedish companies Telia and Netcom Systems, the latter being the second operator in Sweden, while Tele Danmark Mobil was guaranteed to receive one of the four licenses.

The recipients of the licenses were to be notified on March 19, 1997, and both GN Store Nord and Sonofon were reasonably certain that they would be among the chosen. Already in February, GN Store Nord's board of directors discussed the addition of up to 900 million kroner in capital for the expected investments in the construction of the new DCS system as well as the continuation of the purchasing strategy to continue to strengthen the subsidiaries.[26]

However, a stock emission would require that GN Store Nord Holding be dissolved and that its cross-ownership relationship with GN Store Nord be eliminated. This structure, which had originally been put in place to secure the control of the board of directors over the company and protect it against an otherwise possible foreign takeover, had for some years already been provoking institutional investors such as Lønmodtagernes Dyrtidsfond (LD), Arbejdsmarkedets Tillægspension (ATP), and other pension funds, the administrators of which were dissatisfied with the fact that in reality, they were without influence despite the size of their investments.

However, this had not prevented the two pension funds from acquiring significant stakes in both the company and the holding company. ATP had a 12.89 percent stake in GN Store Nord and LD a stake of 8.42 percent. The largest shareholder was GN Store Nord Holding, which owned 27.26 percent.[27]

The largest stakeholder in GN Store Nord Holding was LD, with a stake of 12.10 percent, while ATP owned 12.09 percent and GN Store Nord 9.99 percent. Other large stakeholders in the holding company were two insurance companies, with 9.91 percent and 8.8 percent, respectively, and Danske Bank, which owned 5.57 percent. GN Store Nord then could end up well short of a majority in the holding company and thus in GN Store Nord, but the rules governing the composition of the board of directors meant that GN Store Nord would, nevertheless, have the deciding vote.[28]

In connection with the stock emission in 1994, GN Store Nord's board of directors had suggested that the cross-ownership would be eliminated when the big cable projects had been completed—and it was to be expected that this would be within five years. In the stock market, the declaration had been interpreted as a promise—and it was to be expected that in connection with a new stock emission, there would be a demand that the structure be eliminated—not least because the East Asiatic Company had just eliminated a corresponding structure. It was also of significance that the holding structure doubtless weakened the stock on the Copenhagen Stock Exchange.[29]

According to the minutes of a meeting of the board of directors, it was after "much thinking" that the chairman had reached the conclusion that the time had come for the elimination of the cross-ownership—if some other kind of protection against a hostile takeover could be put in place. A number of possibilities were discussed, and after consultation with LD, ATP, and other institutional investors, it was decided that a voting rights limitation to 7.5 percent would be introduced regardless of the size of the respective shareholder's stake.[30]

As expected, GN Store Nord received one of the licenses for the DCS 1800 network, while the two others went to France Telecom, which established a Danish cellular telephony company, Mobilix, and Telia. Subsequently, at an extraordinary general meeting on August 27, 1997, GN Store Nord Holding decided to eliminate the holding structure and instead introduce a voting rights limitation. GN Store Nord's general meeting also voted to carry out a stock emission for a nominal 112 million kroner, with expected actual revenues of 700,000 to 1 billion kroner. Approximately half of the new share capital was to be used for investments in Sonofon, including the establishment of the DCS 1800 network, while the rest was to be used for purchases to be made by GN Comtext, GN Nettest, and GN Danavox. According to the emission brochure, GN Netcom and GN Store Nordiske Telegraf-Selskab were expected to finance both organic growth and any purchases themselves; in the case of the latter company, this was no doubt on the basis of the assumption that there would hardly be any more major investments or purchases.

The day before the general meeting, GN Store Nord's headquarters received a telefax addressed to Thomas Duer. It was from Aros Securities, which led the consortium that was administering the emission, and contained a "Business Briefing" from the news agency Reuters. "GN Store Nord will have an unusually difficult time getting the expected revenues," a number of stock analysts Reuters had spoken with agreed. "There is no interest in buying . . . the company does not have anything interesting to sell . . . it is a company that is treading water," were some of the comments. Several commentators recommended that GN Store Nord sell the industrial companies and concentrate solely on the telecommunications activities, focusing on Sonofon and Comtext. "It is as if the companies have to fail completely on their own before they will sell them," wrote one analyst, who felt that the company had spread itself out too much.[31]

The emission was executed during the period of September 11–22, 1997, and it went better than the analysts had predicted, though at 775 million kroner, the actual revenues generated were at the low end of GN Store Nord's own expressed expectations. Danish investors purchased 49 percent of the shares offered. For the first time, the company had had investor presentations in Sweden, Norway, Finland, the Netherlands, France, and the United States.

Acquisitions, Selling Off of Companies, and Stock Exchange Listing of GN Nettest

CHAPTER 25

New growth strategy: Acquisition after acquisition after acquisition

Around the time of the stock emission, GN Store Nord got a new chief executive officer as Thomas Duer had reached the sixty-five-year age limit and stepped down after more than ten years in the position. His replacement was Jørgen Lindegaard, who had been the chief executive officer of Kjøbenhavns Telefon Aktieselskab, a company in the Tele Danmark group, until he became a group director at GN Store Nord in March 1996, with telecommunications as his primary area of responsibility. He assumed the position of corporate group leader and chief executive officer on October 1, 1997, when it became his task to administer the new capital from the stock emission together with Group Director Jørn Kildegaard—and the money was soon needed.

Jørgen Lindegaard took over the leadership of a concern that was much more trimmed and focused than the one Thomas Duer had once taken over, though the concern was still characterized by a conglomerate structure with GN Store Nord,

which in reality was a holding company. This opened up the possibility of a new and focused strategy of purchases and growth that GN Store Nord presented in connection with the stock emission. As a whole, the group was to double its 1996 revenues by 2000, reaching 5.4 billion kroner. During the same period, the operating result was to increase by at least 30 percent per year and the ordinary result by at least 15 percent, and the earnings margins of the subsidiaries were to be among the best in their business sectors.

These were goals that could not be achieved by means of organic growth alone, and during the preparations for the stock emission in the spring of 1997, the group's leaders already exploited several purchase opportunities. In two cases, the purchases in question had been executed by the end of the year; in one, the outcome was different from what had been expected. At the meeting of the board of directors on June 2, Jørgen Lindegaard informed the board that Cable & Wireless had offered GN Store Nord an opportunity to take over two of the British telecommunications group's telefax companies, Fax Italy and Fax Switzerland, as well as the telefax company Bimcom, which was among GN Comtext's biggest competitors.[1]

These three companies fit into GN Comtext's business area, and while the use of telex was declining and the use of fax and in particular e-mail messages was on the rise, telex was still dominant in the shipping industry, which was GN Comtext's biggest market. At its next meeting, GN Store Nord's board of directors, therefore, voted to spend 11 million pounds sterling to acquire the three companies.[2]

With regard to GN Store Nord's industrial sector, Jørn Kildegaard reported that the German electronics concern Siemens wished to sell its division for testing equipment for protocol analysis for the telecommunications area, which had a global market share of 18 percent in this area, while GN Nettest had a global market share of 11 percent. Purchasing this division would make GN Nettest the biggest company in this market, ahead of Hewlett-Packard of the United States, and GN Nettest, therefore, submitted a bid in competition with four other bidders.[3]

On August 14, 1997, Siemens informed GN Nettest that for "reasons of group strategy," Siemens had chosen to proceed with one of the other companies, but Siemens did offer to sell GN Nettest a small company based in the United States, Siemens Optical Test Equipment. GN Nettest found this company "very attractive" partly because of its distribution channels, which, in addition to Siemens itself, included an American joint venture between Siemens and Corning Inc., a company that was very strong in the area of private cable and television networks in the United States.[4]

Jørn Kildegaard made another announcement at the meeting of the board of directors on June 2, one with potentially greater consequences: GN Netcom's American competitor ACS Wireless had been put up for sale, and GN Netcom was working on putting together a nonbinding bid. Also, the American hearing aid manufacturer ReSound had proposed a merger of GN Danavox and ReSound, and ReSound should be the company that would continue to exist following the merger. The board of directors authorized the top management team to proceed with processing this proposal but required that GN Danavox simultaneously investigate the possibilities with regard to other cooperative arrangements or acquisitions as it could otherwise be difficult to lift GN Danavox "up to a satisfactory level."[5]

For GN Netcom and GN Danavox, taking over ACS Wireless and ReSound, respectively, was a dream scenario, and it was GN Netcom that reached its goal first. Late in January 1998, a nonbinding letter of intent could be signed, and on March 16, 1998, GN Store Nord's board of directors approved spending 11 million kroner on the acquisition of ACS Wireless. Because of some irregularities revealed during the due diligence process, however, a purchase agreement could be signed only on July 8, 1998. With this acquisition, GN Netcom secured the position of second-largest company in the sector, and the company significantly increased its market share in the United States to 27 percent, though Plantronics, with a good 60 percent of the market, remained the leader by a large margin.[6]

Parallel negotiations with ReSound were dragged out following a change of leadership at the American company, but in May 1998, the parties reached principal agreement regarding a merger with GN Store Nord as the main shareholder in the new company with a stake of 40 percent. Given that agreement had been reached regarding aspects including the composition of the board of directors and the structure of the organization, all the prerequisites for the conclusion of an agreement were in place, but early in June, ReSound froze the process until further notice. The reason for this was probably concern on ReSound's board of directors about excessive Danish influence on the company that would result from a merger; ReSound was owned mostly by small and medium-sized shareholders.[7]

In the middle of July 1998, while GN Store Nord was waiting for the Americans, GN Comtext acquired just under a fourth of the shares in the American provider of fax services FaxNet Corporation as a component of a strategic alliance. For GN Comtext, the purpose was to penetrate the American fax market and expand the company's own product portfolio with a FaxNet platform for FaxNet services.

GN Nettest was also strengthened by means of the acquisition of 50 percent of the shares in a Czech software company with a view to gaining access to more engineering resources, and in October 1998, GN Nettest acquired the French company Fastware, which had expertise within monitoring systems for so-called Wide Area Networks, networks covering large geographic areas.

In all, GN Store Nord spent 302 million kroner on acquisitions in 1998, having spent 194 million kroner the previous year, but the expenditures for 1998 were nothing compared to what would come when GN Store Nord was again in contact with ReSound. The Americans had abandoned the notion of a merger, and early in February 1999, ReSound's board of directors instead asked GN Danavox to present an offer with regard to the acquisition of the entire company. GN Danavox offered eight dollars per share, which corresponded to a total of approximately 1.244 billion kroner, and an exclusivity agreement was made in the middle of April, signed, and followed by a due diligence process lasting until early May when the negotiations took a surprising turn.[8]

At a meeting of the board of directors of ReSound late in April 1999, neither the company's chief executive officer nor the mergers and acquisitions bank whose services had been retained was given the opportunity to present the preliminary results of the negotiations. Instead, a committee led by the chairman was appointed to evaluate ReSound's strategy in its entirety, and a subsequent meeting at Kongens Nytorv with the American board chairman did not lead to agreement regarding how things should proceed.[9]

What Jørn Kildegaard called the Americans' "highly surprising and unprofessional" behavior caused GN Store Nord—very unusually—to send a letter to each individual member of the board of directors of ReSound. This letter described both the acquisition offer and the "duties and responsibilities" of the members of the board of directors in relation to a possible decision not to accept the offer, which consisted of a cash payment that exceeded the current stock price by approximately 50 percent.[10]

This letter produced quick results. Early in May, ReSound's board of directors appointed a negotiating committee, which did not include the board chairman, who was opposed to the sale. A purchase agreement was soon in place, and on May 10, 1999, GN Store Nord officially presented a purchase offer to the American shareholders of eight dollars per share. By the June 11 deadline, 92 percent of the shareholders had accepted the offer, and the remaining 8 percent could, therefore, be forced to cash in their shares. Three days later, the acquisition was executed, and the integration of the two companies was immediately begun. In terms of development and production, the process benefited from the two companies' strategic alliance with the company Audiologic, because of which their newest hearing aids were largely based on the same technology.

The name of the post-acquisition company would be GN ReSound, which, with annual revenues of approximately 1.5 billion kroner, became the world's fourth-largest in the sector, with a global market share of 14 percent, the sector's leaders being Siemens of Germany, Starkey of the United States, and Oticon of Denmark. The headquarters of GN ReSound were located in Redwood City, California, while the company had production facilities in three locations in the United States as well as in China, Denmark, Ireland, and Austria. Production in Austria was associated with an American owned division, Viennatone, which manufactured inexpensive digital and analog hearing aids that were still responsible for a considerable part of GN ReSound's total revenues.

The headquarters were subsequently moved to Denmark and the production of hearing aids in Denmark and Austria to Ireland and China, where GN ReSound purchased the originally Chinese share of the ownership of the factory in Xiamen, which had been taken over by the Investment Fund for the Developing Countries. In August, GN ReSound purchased the Danish manufacturer of audiological equipment Danplex A/S and merged it with the Madsen division, which, after having supplemented its own Aurical system for the adjustment of hearing aids with the Millennium system from Danplex, became the clear global leader within most areas of audiological measurement technology.

Early in July 1999, GN Nettest benefited from the acquisition of the American company PK Technology Inc., which was a leader in the area of testing and measuring equipment for fiber optic cables and networks. The price was fairly large—45 million dollars or approximately 324 million kroner—but the acquisition made GN Nettest the world's leading retailer of systems for the monitoring and control of fiber optic cables and networks. Following this acquisition, the sector made up 40 percent of GN Nettest's total revenues, and it was estimated that more than 95 percent of all the world's fiber optic cables had been tested by one or more of GN Nettest's instruments.[11]

Subsidiaries in growth and decline

The acquisition of ReSound was by far GN Store Nord's largest acquisition ever, and including the acquisition of PK Technology, the group spent a total of 1.777 billion kroner on acquisitions in 1999. This was considerably more than double the amount of real capital yielded by the share emission in 1997, and then there had been the acquisitions of the previous years, which had accounted for a total of nearly 500 million kroner. In addition, there had been investments in fixed assets over the past three years, totaling 1.842 billion kroner; most of this money was spent on the construction and expansion of Sonofon's system following the acquisition of the DCS 1800 license.

The goals of the growth strategy of 1997 were, therefore, more than achieved as revenues for the group reached 5.415 billion kroner, while the primary operating result increased to 440 billion kroner and the ordinary operating result to 660 billion kroner. The account for 1999 cannot be compared to accounts for previous years, however, as starting in 1999, GN Store Nord used the International Accounting Standard as the basis for its accounts, so the results could be compared with those of other international concerns, which was seen as desirable in view of the increasing foreign interest in the company's stock.[12]

However, the company achieved its goals within four years as indicated by a calculation based on the old accounting principles and in terms of the new ones. A decisive increase in revenues of just under 1.4 billion kroner in 1999 can be attributed mostly to the acquisition of ReSound and PK Technology. The growth seen since 1996 cannot be explained by acquisitions alone, however; in part, it was because of organic growth in several of the companies.

Particularly in GN Netcom, the organic growth was remarkable; in that company, it was driven by the development of new products at the same time as the company maintained all three brands after the acquisition of UNEX and ACS, thus maintaining a very broad product range. In the wireless headset sector, the company acquired a decisive lead over its competitors, who were forced to withdraw their products from the market early in 1997 because of quality control problems.[13]

In the meantime, GN Netcom consolidated its position as the leader in wireless technology, so early in 1998, the company was able to launch its next generation of wireless headsets, the Ellipse headsets. New products such as GN Express and Activa were developed for PC and telephone use; the latter product was the world's first headset with a built-in amplifier that made it possible for the headset to be connected with almost all telephones without an amplifier box.

GN Danavox's organic growth was more modest partly because the company's first fully digitalized hearing aid, the Danalogic, was not introduced to the market until October 1998. However, it was the first second-generation device on the market and had the most powerful chip yet presented and an open software platform that made it possible to run several programs at the same time, which in turn made possible more precise adjustment to the needs of the individual user. It was soon clear that the device lived up to expectations and that it would be GN Danavox's best-selling device ever.

Parallel to the preparations for the introduction of the Danalogic device, GN Danavox began a transition from cheap analog devices to high-priced products, focusing in particular on the rapidly growing market for digitalized devices, where prices were higher and there was greater potential for generating earnings. However, it was not until GN Danavox had acquired ReSound that the company got a broad high-tech profile that included ReSound's fully digitalized Digital 5000, and the acquisition of ReSound also brought with it the company's first so-called CIC (Completely-in-the-Canal) device, which was placed entirely inside the ear canal and was, therefore, nearly invisible. On the other hand, Viennatone contributed to maintaining the company's position in the market for less advanced analog devices, which would continue to be large.

Finally, there was GN Nettest, which, after some difficult years in the middle of the 1990s, performed a turnaround in 1997, achieving an increase in revenues of 20 percent, to 509 million kroner, and a positive annual result. Borne by the rapid spread of the Internet and information technology, the company's success continued during the following years with growth rates of 43 and 46 percent and revenues for 1999 of 1.059 billion kroner.

In contrast, the London-based telex, fax, and e-mail company GN Comtext fell behind. Despite the acquisition of the three Cable & Wireless companies in the fall of 1997, GN Comtext achieved only a modest increase in revenues of 5 percent, to 519 million kroner, in 1998, while a primary operating result of 18 million kroner became a deficit of 41 million kroner. The company found itself in a crumbling market; use of telex technology was declining steadily, and the fax service too was beginning to feel the competition from the Internet. Attempts to sell the company failed, and after a sharp drop in revenues to 456 million kroner and a new deficit in 1999, the dissolution of the company was begun.

For the telegraph company, which maintained annual revenues of approximately 150 million kroner from its land and undersea cable projects, time was also inevitably running out, despite the fact that the company was making determined attempts to discover new business opportunities. The company's stakes in the paging and card telephone companies in Saint Petersburg had not led to new opportunities as the telegraph company had hoped they would. The telegraph company was also disappointed when it acquired 50 percent of an Internet provider in Moscow and got nothing out of it when, in February 1998, the company and two Russian partners created a company in Moscow, RTC Page, with a license for the establishment of a country-wide Russian paging system.

Together with France Telecom, the telegraph company presented an ambitious bid to acquire Moldova's national telecommunications authority, which was to be privatized, but the telegraph company abstained from making a formal offer. A last attempt to remain in the international telecommunications sector via so-called brokering—reselling of traffic and transmission capacity in international telecommunications connections—via a switching center at GN Comtext in London came to naught.

In 1999, the telegraph company achieved revenues of 169 million kroner and a solid primary result of 90 million kroner. The reason for this was payments from Lithuania and Russia in the amount of 50 million kroner that had been moved up, and facing the prospect of a significant drop in revenues the following year, GN Store Nord's board of directors decided in the spring of 2000 to move the company into the remaining maritime division in GN Comtext. At the telegraph company, however, people continue to struggle, developing a strategy plan that in the middle of August 2000 was presented to a kind of miniature board of directors of the company that had been created in 1998 and consisted of Jørgen Lindegaard, Jørn Kildegaard, and GN Store Nord's chief financial officer, Poul Erik Tofte. This plan was not discussed; it was shelved, and the telegraph company was informed that its activities were to be discontinued.[14]

After the remnants of GN Comtext had been sold in July 2001, however, the telegraph company remained intact for several more years because of agreements that had not expired or been nullified, including the agreement regarding the optic fiber cable through Poland, in connection with which disagreements concerning the invoices had arisen. The matter was brought before the international court of arbitration in Vienna by GN Store Nord and Tele Danmark, and until it had been resolved, the telegraph company formally continued to exist.

Sonofon caught between Telia and BellSouth

In contrast, Sonofon was still experiencing considerable success, and a central component of GN Store Nord's growth strategy was to develop the cellular telephony company into a so-called full-service telephone company that offered the same services that were offered to landline users and new services as well. The company was to be based solely on wireless technology using a nationwide network of microwave radio chains that would make it possible to be liberated from Tele Danmark's landline network, which Sonofon had been forced to use for transmissions between radio masts up to this point. The goal was to make the landline network superfluous in cases in which cellular telephony subscribers did not need landline telephones in their homes. A first step in this direction was taken in 1997 when Sonofon introduced a UnoFon subscription that let users pay a low per-minute rate, at the level of the landline rate, in zones around their homes and otherwise pay the usual rate for cellular telephony. The goal was to get users of landline telephony to switch to cellular, and the expectation was that within five years, Sonofon would capture what was described as "a significant part" of the landline market, which had been liberalized on January 1 and with which a number of foreign companies were becoming involved.[15]

However, developments took an unexpected turn late in May 1998 when Erik B. Rasmussen informed GN Store Nord's board of directors that he had been contacted by the vice chairman of Telia's board of directors, Björn Wolrath, who had asked to have a meeting "to discuss [GN] Store Nord." The chairman had found out from another party that Telia had also contacted some of GN Store Nord's

Among the phones that subscribers could buy from Sonofon, this was from the Danish producer named Dancall. The company started to make mobile phones for the Nordic NMT network and was among the first to manufacture and market GSM phones. However, the company was soon outperformed by global competitors such as Nokia and Ericsson.

shareholders and asked them what their attitudes would be toward Telia's becoming the controlling shareholders in GN Store Nord. Also, Telia had been in contact with the president of BellSouth, Buddy Miller, who had informed Jørgen Lindegaard that Telia had wished to acquire BellSouth's stake in Sonofon in return for transferring a license for cellular telephony in São Paulo, Brazil's industrial and financial center, to BellSouth. Buddy Miller had not said anything about BellSouth's view of this proposal.[16]

The chairman indicated that the reason for the Swedish feelers was that Telia had not succeeded in establishing itself on the Danish cellular telephony market and that with two well-established companies, Tele Danmark Mobil and Sonofon, as well as the capital-rich company Mobilix, which was backed by France Telecom, Telia had no prospect of attaining the central position it wanted to have. Acquisition of GN Store Nord or of BellSouth's stake in Sonofon would be significant progress for the Swedes and at the same time would eliminate a competitor. GN Store Nord's voting rights limitation did not provide absolute protection against a hostile takeover, though executing such a takeover would be difficult.

As expected, Erik B. Rasmussen and Jørgen Lindegaard were asked about the possibility of cooperating with regard to the Danish cellular telephony market at the meeting with Björn Wolrath that took place the day after the meeting of GN Store Nord's board of directors. No one would want the series of price wars that would necessarily result if Telia tried to fight its way into the Danish market. The Danes indicated that their attitude toward such possible cooperation was positive, and it was agreed that Jørgen Lindegaard—after having informed BellSouth—would meet with Telia's chief executive officer, Lars Berg, to investigate the possible forms of cooperation.[17]

The chief executive officers met in Stockholm on June 3, 1998, and agreed to proceed on the basis of the Swedish proposal regarding Telia's acquisition of BellSouth's stake in Sonofon. This part of the complex of agreements was to be negotiated directly between Telia's concern leadership and BellSouth's president, while GN Store Nord and Telia continued working on clarifying the details of the cooperation with regard to Sonofon. GN Store Nord had previously assured BellSouth that no one wanted to push the Americans out but that cooperation with Telia would eliminate a competitor in the Danish market.[18]

The Swedes had great ambitions: They wanted to establish a new commonly owned company that would become number 1 in Denmark in cellular telephony, number 1 or 2 in Internet provision, and number 2 in landline telephony. Also, Telia believed that in the long run, GN Store Nord "could participate in the creation of a cellular telephony company that would be a European—perhaps a global—leader."[19]

GN Store Nord could join with the Swedes in their ambitions, but the Danes had a reserved attitude toward Telia's wish for the common company to be equally owned. GN Store Nord could accept an equal partnership like the one with BellSouth—but with a Danish majority of 50 percent so the company was perceived as Danish. And Jørgen Lindegaard found it necessary to emphasize that GN Store Nord "[desired] long-term cooperation with Telia on the basis of mutual respect and not on the basis of hostile share purchases." This could be ensured by an agreement that Telia would neither directly nor indirectly acquire shares in GN Store Nord without the approval of GN Store Nord's board of directors.

There is further evidence that GN Store Nord was not entirely comfortable with regard to the Swedes' intentions, in that around this time, GN Store Nord's board of directors began work on a defense manual containing guidelines for how to respond to hostile purchases of shares in the concern. To be sure, it had also been indicated to Jørgen Lindegaard at a meeting at Skandinaviska Enskilda Banken, as he reported at the meeting of GN Store Nord's board of directors in May, that Oticon had considered trying to take over GN Store Nord.[20]

Immediately after the meeting in Stockholm, working groups including representatives of both companies were created, and during the summer, there were a large number of meetings, including two attorney meetings, to discuss the composition of a memorandum of understanding. There was also a telephone meeting between Jørgen Lindegaard and Lars Berg, but after discussion of four draft memoranda, the negotiations broke down on September 16, 1998, and the parties went their separate ways without having agreed on a time for a new meeting.

The obstacles were GN Store Nord's demands that, on one hand, ownership should be divided 51 percent to 49 percent in favor of the Danes and, on the other hand, Telia would be forbidden to purchase shares in GN Store Nord representing more than 5 percent of the share capital. Along the way, Telia had demanded a 10 percent stake in GN Store Nord and a seat on the board of directors in return for accepting a Danish ownership share of 51 percent in the common company, which GN Store Nord had rejected outright. Also, GN Store Nord wished to have a permanent right to appoint the chairman of the board of directors of the common company, while Telia wished to have GN Store Nord and Telia take turns appointing the chairman.[21]

Subsequently, Telia's vice chairman, Björn Wolrath, indicated in a letter to Erik B. Rasmussen that the company would have difficulty accepting being a minority shareholder in Denmark, which was viewed as a key market. At the same time, GN Store Nord was put under a certain amount of pressure when the president of BellSouth Enterprises, which owned the American telecommunications company, came to Denmark and, at a meeting of Sonofon's board of directors, declared that his concern would like to see a solution that involved Telia.[22]

When GN Store Nord's board of directors discussed the situation in the beginning of December 1998, one question that was raised was whether it would be possible in the long run for Sonofon to stand on its own in a future consolidated telecommunications market in Europe and whether it might be time to find a strategic—and bigger—partner. Telia was obviously the most logical partner, but if Telia achieved success in Denmark on its own, the Swedes could become difficult to negotiate with, and if things ended with a fiasco, there was a risk that in desperation, Telia would attempt to take over GN Store Nord. Therefore, it was agreed that GN Store Nord should continue to seek to cooperate with Telia, and the board decided that GN Store Nord should present what was characterized as a compromise proposal to the effect that GN Store Nord would insist on everything it had previously insisted on, and the compromise would be that the chairman of the board of directors of the common cellular telephony company would not have a deciding vote.[23]

This proposal was discussed at a meeting on Kongens Nytorv on December 14, 1998, that was attended by Jørgen Lindegaard, Erik B. Rasmussen, and Vice Chairman Elvar Vinum from GN Store Nord and Björn Wolrath and Assistant Executive Officer Stig-Arne Larsson of Telia. Subsequently, on January 13, 1999, a nonbinding memorandum of understanding could be signed, and GN Store Nord's leaders hoped to have a contract before the company's general meeting on January 13, 1999, so the cooperation could be presented then.

The prospects of concluding a real agreement were in fact not good, however. On one hand, the negotiations between BellSouth and Telia were being dragged out because the Americans were reevaluating their future role in Europe in light of the fact that BellSouth had an opportunity to purchase a cellular telephony company in Germany. On the other hand, Telia was very busy with negotiations regarding a possible merger with the Norwegian government-owned telecommunications company Telenor that involved both governments and were the focus of a great deal of public attention, which made it difficult for the Swedes to make a final decision regarding Denmark.[24]

Also, Telenor had indicated during conversations with Jørgen Lindegaard that they were interested in strategic cooperation with Sonofon, and the French company Mobilix too had indicated that they were interested in cooperation on the basis of a model similar to that GN Store Nord was discussing with Telia. For the time being, however, GN Store Nord was focused on Telia as a potential cooperation partner, and Jørgen Lindegaard, therefore, adopted a reserved attitude in answering a letter from Mobilix's chief executive officer that proposed cooperation.[25]

Almost all of 1999 went by without a resolution of the matter, and then in early December, the plan for a fusion of Telia and Telenor fell apart in the wake of a major political scandal in both Norway and Sweden. This left Telia more or less paralyzed, and when BellSouth notified GN Store Nord that clarity with regard to the company's European role could not be expected before the spring of

Originally, Sonofon was located in Aalborg, but in 1999, the company built a brand-new headquarters at Frederikskaj in the south harbor of Copenhagen, designed by the architect firm DISSING + WEITLING. The following year, Sonofon was sold to the Norwegian company Telenor.

2000 at the earliest, this finally wrecked the whole project.

An alliance with Telia would have completely changed the conditions for Sonofon's and thus GN Store Nord's further development, but at the end of 1999, the situation was the status quo to the extent that Sonofon was alone in the Danish market and lacked a partner for a strategic alliance.

GN Store Nord had succeeded in keeping its negotiations with Telia a secret, but the Danish press was taking a strong interest in consolidation in the telecommunications sector and in the future of Sonofon—including in whether GN Store Nord

would be willing to sell part or all of Sonofon if the right offer were put on the table. This created uncertainty with regard to the cellular telephony company's future, not least among the company's employees, and when the possibility of an entirely different solution to the problem of Sonofon presented itself, GN Store Nord took advantage of it.

Sale of Sonofon

It was with a new chairman of the board of directors that GN Store Nord would discuss Sonofon's future, Erik B. Rasmussen having stepped down at the general meeting in April 1999. Elvar Vinum became the new chairman after having spent less than a year on the board as vice chairman. He was also a vice chairman of the boards of directors of Kapital Holding A/S, Investeringsforeningen BG Invest, BG Bank, and dk-invest management a/s, and he, therefore, very much represented an investor view of GN Store Nord's development.

Elvar Vinum was a proponent of the American-inspired shareholder value concept, according to which a company's primary task is to create value for the shareholders in the form of high yields and a rising share price. This was a concept that had become increasingly influential in the Danish stock market during the 1990s, and indeed, GN Store Nord's new growth strategy after Jørgen Lindegaard had become board chairman in 1997 had been a reflection of this.

However, it was only after the election of Elvar Vinum to the chairmanship that it was clearly formulated that GN Store Nord's vision was "to create high yields for the shareholders," the vision for the previous year primarily having been to create "value for the customers." In general, shareholder value became the foundation of the future development of the concern—not least because the whole stock market was permeated by the notion.[26]

The first order of business was to determine what was to be done with Sonofon. In 1999, Mobilix had executed several very aggressive campaigns involving large dealer grants aimed at acquiring new subscribers, and early in 2000, Tele Danmark followed suit. This put pressure on Sonofon, which had a hard time keeping up, and at the same time, Telia announced that it was planning to concentrate more on the Danish market.

Around this time, Telestyrelsen was planning to issue new GSM 900 and 1800 licenses, and bids would also be accepted for licenses for the establishment and operation of so-called 3G—third generation—cellular systems with much greater capacity that offered much higher speeds and would accommodate data transmission at a completely different level in relation to what had been seen thus far. Therefore, it was to be expected that Sonofon would again have to make huge investments—an auction of 3G licenses in the United Kingdom had resulted in astronomical prices—and new foreign competitors could be expected to seek to penetrate the Danish market, which would lead to increased competition and lower rates.

GN Store Nord's top management team believed that with the increasing competition, it would become increasingly difficult to earn money in the cellular telephony industry in Denmark—at least at a level that would satisfy the earnings goals of GN Store Nord's companies. Also, a very significant amount of money would be tied up if Sonofon were to bid on a 3G license, which would restrict options with regard to investments and purchases by GN Store Nord's other companies.[27]

Therefore, at the meeting of the board of directors on May 18, the top management team proposed that preparations be initiated to sell Sonofon on the basis of a preliminary estimate of a value of approximately 10 billion kroner for GN Store Nord's share of the company, an estimate produced by the Swiss investment bank UBS Warburg. There had already been informal discussions with BellSouth, which would not stand in the way. The board of directors authorized the top management team to proceed and have UBS Warburg investigate the market for potential buyers, though the board did not wish to initiate a formal sale process on the basis of the current foundation. If there were an attractive offer, however, the board of directors would consider a possible sale.[28]

Among the potential buyers that were contacted was Telenor, which had previously proposed cooperation with Sonofon and which immediately indicated strong interest in acquiring GN Store Nord's stake in the Danish cellular telephony company. On June 6, 2000, Telenor already offered 14 billion kroner for the stake, and two days later, GN Store Nord and Telenor signed an exclusivity agreement valid until June 20, after which the composition of a contract was begun. Telenor was expected to make a decision on June 15, and after consulting with the chairman, Jørgen Lindegaard requested an extraordinary meeting of the board of directors on June 19.[29]

Already the following day, Jørgen Lindegaard, having consulted with the chairman, moved the meeting up to June 12 at 5:00 p.m. as Telenor wished to have the process hurried along as much as possible so a contract could be signed the same evening and the acquisition publicized the following morning. For this reason, a delegation from Telenor, led by the chief executive officer, arrived in Copenhagen that day and checked in to the Hotel d'Angleterre, right next to GN Store Nord's headquarters on Kongens Nytorv.[30]

Everything had been gotten ready for the signing of an agreement then, but shortly after noon, the entire scenario was changed when Jørgen Lindegaard received an e-mail from the German cellular telephony company T-Mobile, which was a part of the Deutsche Telecom group. T-Mobile offered 16 billion kroner for GN Store Nord's stake in Sonofon, but on one hand, this bid was indicative and not binding, and on the other hand, T-Mobile had mistakenly assumed that GN Store Nord controlled Sonofon via its majority.[31]

Nevertheless, T-Mobile's bid was so high that despite Telenor's exclusivity, it could not be ignored. After he had spoken with Board Chairman Elvar Vinum by telephone, Jørgen Lindegaard visited Telenor's delegation at the Hotel d'Angleterre and told them about the German offer, demanding that Telenor raise its offer by 5 percent, to 14.7 billion kroner, and indicating that if Telenor did not do so, GN Store Nord would have to consider an open bidding process. The Norwegians did not take long to decide. After Telenor's chief executive officer had conferred with his chief executive officer, who was in Norway, Telenor took only five minutes to increase their bid by 700 million kroner.[32]

When GN Store Nord's board of directors met at 5:00 p.m., Jørgen Lindegaard and Jørn Kildegaard recommended accepting the Norwegian offer of 14.7 billion kroner because of the uncertainty surrounding the German offer. Two representatives of UBS Warburg took part in the meeting of GN Store Nord's board of directors, and they concluded that the Norwegian offer constituted "a very attractive price and one that [was] significantly higher than the most optimistic valuation" that the investment bank had been able to calculate.[33]

In response to a question with regard to whether an open bidding process could result in the payment of a higher price, the two representatives responded that it was impossible to give a precise answer to this question but that such a process would be negatively impacted by the relatively limited amount of information about Sonofon that was available and that Telenor would not be able to participate as the Norwegian company was facing an initial public offering. Finally, they pointed out that the timing was good as the opening up of a round of bidding for the new 3G licenses later in the year would make a sale more difficult and push the price downward.

The board of directors subsequently unanimously approved the transaction, and the next morning, the contract having been signed, the stock exchange notice was sent out. However, a prerequisite for the finalization of the transaction was that it be approved by Denmark's Telestyrelse and by the EU Commission, so it was only on August 10, 2000, that the transaction in fact became final.

The Norwegians had paid for a debt-free company, so after having covered Sonofon's debts, GN Store Nord received revenues from the transaction amounting to 12.9 billion kroner, which, according to the stock exchange notice, would be used partly to pay off bank debts of 3 to 4 billion kroner and partly to strengthen the development of GN ReSound, GN Netcom, and particularly GN Nettest—"in order to realize that company's potential for achieving significant gains in revenues in the course of a few years"—via acquisitions. The paying of an extraordinary shareholder dividend or repurchasing of some of the company's own shares might also "be considered," but investments in the subsidiaries, particularly in GN Nettest, would be the focus.[34]

The year 2000: The year of big purchases

As was indicated in the stock exchange notice, the revenues from the sale of Sonofon were a welcome addition of capital to GN Store Nord in a year that was historic when it came to the acquisition of companies. In the middle of February 2000, Chief Financial Officer Poul Erik Tofte informed the chairman and vice chairman of the board of directors that Jørgen Lindegaard had asked Unibank to evaluate whether the bank could provide up to 6 billion kroner in financing for possible purchases within the next three months. The reason for this was that three purchase opportunities had presented themselves: the American manufacturer of hands-free headsets for cellular telephones Jabra, a possibility for GN Netcom; the American hearing aid company Beltone, a possibility for GN ReSound; and finally, the American network company Hekimian, a possibility for GN Nettest. Hekimian was bought by a competitor following an auction, while Beltone and Jabra were both bought by GN Store Nord in the course of 2000.[35]

The agreement with Beltone Electronics Corporation was signed on April 26, 2000, and the company was acquired on June 7—in the middle of the hectic final phase of the sale of GN Store Nord's stake in Sonofon—after the American authorities had approved the transaction. This acquisition was GN Store Nord's biggest acquisition ever; the purchase price was 3.2 billion kroner, 1.8 billion kroner of which was paid in cash, while the remainder was paid in newly issued shares in GN Store Nord.

Beltone had taken over Philips's audiological division the previous year and was the world's seventh-largest hearing aid company. With this acquisition, GN ReSound became the world's second-largest, with estimated annual revenues of 378 million dollars, only a little behind Germany's Siemens, which had revenues of 388 million dollars—and well ahead of Denmark's Oticon, which was third-largest and had revenues of 300 million dollars. Next came Starkey of the United States with a little less than 300 million dollars in revenues and Widex with 171 million dollars.[36]

The acquisition brought with it a significant strengthening of GN ReSound's position in North America and Japan, where GN ReSound became second-largest and largest, respectively. Beltone was known in particular for very small in-the-ear devices and was the best-known hearing aid brand in the United States, where the company's organization was retained, while in the rest of the world, it was integrated into GN ReSound.

In the second half of May 2000, GN Store Nord undertook another large purchase, spending 331 million kroner, which were paid in the form of shares in GN Store Nord. Jabra was the strongest brand and the largest provider in the United States of advanced headsets for cellular telephones and was second-largest worldwide. With the acquisition of Jabra, GN Netcom significantly strengthened its position in the area of headsets for cellular telephones, where GN Netcom had had a weak presence, and in reality, GN Netcom acquired a whole new business area. At the same time, the company strengthened its sales channels in the United States, while Jabra, via GN Netcom's sales organization, got access to the European and Asian markets.[37]

The acquisition of Jabra was executed in late August as GN Netcom had had to wait for the American competition authorities to approve the transaction, and a short time later, GN Netcom was further strengthened by the acquisition of the American company Hello Direct, which had a leading position in the area of sales of headsets and telephony solutions to the American office market. This was a market in which GN Netcom had been weak in relation to Plantronics but now gained access to Hello Direct's sales channels and marketing, which consisted in part of the sending out of around twenty-nine million catalogs per year, and a well-functioning and quickly growing Internet business. The price was 810 million kroner.[38]

It took a little longer for GN Nettest to acquire new companies, and when GN Nettest did so, this took place in the wake of the sale of Sonofon, so the capital foundation was more than adequate. GN Nettest started out big, buying the French company Photonetics A. S. for no less than 9.1 billion kroner, 6.4 billion kroner of which was paid in cash and the remainder in shares in GN Store Nord. Photonetics had modest revenues of 510 million kroner per year but had several groundbreaking technologies that complemented GN Nettest's.

This acquisition made GN Nettest the world leader by a good margin as a provider of systems and equipment for monitoring optical communications systems—and more. In the words of the chief executive officer of GN Nettest, GN Nettest wanted to reach "an absolutely leading position in testing and control of next-generation networks." A few days later, a more modest acquisition followed: For 90 million kroner, GN Nettest acquired the little French company GM Iris, which had developed the Compass software, which identified problems in GSM networks.[39]

Only a week later, GN Store Nord's board of directors decided to purchase the French company Optran, which specialized in testing high-speed data transmission and strengthened GN Nettest's position in optical broadband communications. The price was approximately 159 million kroner, and in all, GN Store Nord had spent 9.149 billion kroner in just two weeks to strengthen GN Nettest by means of acquisitions. In addition, GN Store Nord had spent a total of 34 million kroner on two key technologies for Internet testing earlier in the year.[40]

Headed for the stock market listing of GN Nettest

With a few more relatively small purchases, including the acquisition of two measuring instrument companies for GN ReSound, GN Store Nord spent a total of approximately 14.258 billion kroner on acquisitions in 2000. This was a historically large amount and was eight times larger than the amount for the previous year and a clear expression of the will of the group's leaders to pursue their strategy of strengthening the subsidiaries by means of acquisitions; the revenues from the sale of Sonofon were fully exploited.

However, there was also an underlying agenda that was reflected by the acquisition of Photonetics. At a meeting of GN Store Nord's board of directors on August 29, 2000, by way of preparation for the imminent acquisition, GN Nettest's chief executive officer, Jens Maaløe, gave a presentation on the subsidiary's strategic possibilities and attractive candidates for acquisition. Among these candidates was Photonetics, which had been put up for sale via a bidding process in an auction in which GN Store Nord had just gone on to the second round.[41]

The top management team then took over and presented a justification of an application to begin preparations for a stock exchange listing of GN Nettest. The basis of the application was that the two investment banks Merrill Lynch and UBS Warburg judged that GN Nettest's stock exchange value as an independent company probably would amount to 5 to 5 billion dollars, which was by no means reflected in GN Store Nord's stock price. There was then considerable hidden inner value in GN Store Nord that could be freed via a stock exchange listing of GN Nettest and could thus benefit the shareholders. This argument was supported by a comparison with the competing Canadian company Exfo, which had been listed on the American technology exchange, Nasdaq, in June.

The advantages of a stock exchange listing consisted of a likely increase in the value of GN Store Nord's shares and the fact that both GN Nettest's and GN Store Nord's shares would take on greater weight as a so-called acquisition currency to be used in connection with the acquisition of companies, a practice that was becoming increasingly common and had been used in connection with several of GN Store Nord's most recent acquisitions.

In the long run, however, a stock market listing and separation of GN Nettest could have serious consequences for the entire corporate group. If GN Nettest used large blocs of shares to pay for acquisitions, GN Store Nord's proportion of the total shares could be reduced so much that GN Store Nord lost control over its subsidiary. It could also increase pressure for stock market listing of the two other subsidiaries and thus for the splitting up of GN Store Nord, a possibility that had been discussed for some time by stock market analysts and in the business press.

There were then arguments both for and against, but in the view of the top management team, a stock exchange listing would be most advantageous in terms of shareholder value, and it would strengthen GN Nettest's potential to develop into one of the three largest companies in its sector. Specifically, Jørgen Lindegaard and Jørn Kildegaard, therefore, recommended to the board of directors that preparations be begun for simultaneous listing of 15 to 25 percent of GN Nettest's shares on the Copenhagen Stock Exchange and on the Nasdaq. The board of directors approved this course of action but wanted to have an opportunity at future meetings of the board of directors to discuss the possible consequences of a stock exchange listing of GN Nettest for the group's other two companies.

The decision was announced to the stock market the following day in GN Store Nord's half-year report, which attracted appropriate attention. "GN Store Nord is well on its way to being scattered to the four winds," wrote *Jyllands-Posten*, which quoted Jørgen Lindegaard as having declared that "the board of directors has asked us to evaluate the possibilities and the consequences for GN Store Nord in its entirety if we list GN Nettest on the stock exchange independently." If the consequences would be the total splitting up of the group, then he was prepared for that if it should be in the interests of the shareholders. "Nothing is holy for us," he had said, noting that the subsidiaries were valued low in relation to their competitors.[42]

Internally, however, there was a different tone as the top management team noted in their recommendation to the board of directors regarding the stock exchange listing of GN Nettest that in their view GN Netcom and GN ReSound "were only partially or not at all ready to be listed by a stock exchange." This being the case, the desire of the board of directors to discuss the consequences before making a final decision does not seem unnatural—particularly because if the top management team's proposal were adopted, it would be the first time ever that the group carried out a stock market listing and splitting off of a subsidiary.[43]

The turning point came in late September with the acquisition of Photonetics, which in the view of the board of directors was of such a significance and size that a stock exchange listing would be "the natural next major step for GN Nettest." However, the board of directors still wished to discuss the consequences for the GN Store Nord concern and the other subsidiaries, and when Jørgen Lindegaard and Jørn Kildegaard subsequently began a series of meetings with six of the world's largest investment banks—Morgan Stanley, Goldman Sachs, CSFB, Merrill Lynch, Deutsche Bank, and UBS Warburg—to discuss the stock exchange listing, these investment banks were asked to judge the consequences for the GN concern and present recommendations with regard to a future structure.

The Danish business press was in no doubt as to the consequences, however. "Without a doubt, this means the end of GN Store Nord as we know the concern today," wrote *Jyllands-Posten*'s business section and predicted that the stock market listing of GN Nettest was "the first step on the way in the final splitting up of GN Store Nord." Jørn Kildegaard told *Berlingske Tidende* that the stock exchange listing was planned for the first half of 2001 and that it was more likely to be in the first than in the second quarter.[44]

Two months later, Jørgen Lindegaard announced that he wished to leave GN Store Nord on June 1, 2001, to become the new chief executive officer of the Scandinavian airline SAS. He would stay in the company long enough to execute the stock market listing, after which Jørn Kildegaard would become the new chief executive officer.[45]

Flying high ...

The preparations for the stock market listing began immediately. A thorough internal due diligence process for GN Nettest revealed no reasons for concern, and on December 4, 2000, an almost-complete stock exchange brochure could be presented to GN Store Nord's board of directors at a meeting with advisors from the investment bank Morgan Stanley, the auditing firm KPMG, and two law offices, Denmark's Gorrissen Federspiel Kierkegaard and Davis Polk & Wardwell of the United States. Just under three weeks later, an updated brochure was sent to the United States' Security and Exchange Commission and the Copenhagen Stock Exchange for approval.[46]

During the second half of January 2001, GN Store Nord's board of directors approved the articles of association for the separated company, which got the name NetTest, and the entire detailed plan for the stock market listing was gone over and also approved. It was agreed that a final decision would be made on February 23, and in the meantime, the recruitment of international board members for NetTest was begun, and the first interviews with potential candidates were carried out.[47]

When GN Store Nord's board of directors and top management team met on February 23, 2001, as agreed to make a decision, advisors from KPMG, Gorrissen Federspiel Kierkegaard, and, by telephone from New York, Morgan Stanley and the investment bank Gleacher & Co., Elvar Vinum asked the advisor from Gleacher & Co. to present an update on the market situation, and the news that reached the meeting room on Kongens Nytorv in this connection was not inspiring.[48]

According to the advisor, the Nasdaq was in "a very volatile period," and the market for new stock market listings was weak. Therefore, it could not be guaranteed that all shares offered would be purchased unless the price was set so low that it could negatively affect GN Store Nord's stock price. The advisor recommended postponing the stock market listing and following the market situation closely, week for week, with a view to listing NetTest when there was a market turnaround. Morgan Stanley fully supported this analysis, and GN Store Nord's board of directors subsequently expressed their confidence in it, and the listing was indefinitely postponed.[49]

The two advisors had referred to dramatic drops in share prices on the Nasdaq, which, since reaching a peak index of 5,049 on March 10, had been in constant decline, having fallen to just under 2,500 by the beginning of 2001. This decline had a strong negative effect on the information, communications, and technology sector, spreading to stock exchanges all over the world and continuing into 2001 with no prospect of a reversal.

GN Store Nord was among the companies affected, seeing its stock fall from 250 points in August 1999 to under 150 at the end of the year. Nevertheless, the company—applauded by advisors and stock market analysts—set course for a stock market listing of NetTest, and this course was not changed despite the fact that monthly sales of GN Store Nord's shares—after having constantly reached more than 8 billion kroner during the period from June to November 1999—dropped by half by the end of the year.

The drop in prices for technology stocks came after years of constant positive developments for such stocks and nearly constant price increases in 1999 and during the spring of 2000 before the so-called IT or dot-com bubble broke with dramatic consequences in the wake of the previous years' explosive growth in the number of Internet-based companies. Not only did the fall of technology stocks lead to a global wave of bankruptcies of Internet and information and technology companies, but the massive expansion of the infrastructure of the Internet also stopped, which in the spring of 2001 first negatively affected Photonetics and then the rest of GN Nettest.

In the midst of this decline, the change of chief executive officers at GN Store Nord was moved forward to April 1, 2001, so it was Jørn Kildegaard who had to notify the board of directors in late April that there would be no appropriate basis for a stock market listing in the immediate future. Late in August 2001, the plug was pulled completely after Morgan Stanley, Deutsche Bank, JP Morgan, and Goldman Sachs had all advised against a stock exchange listing, and for the first time, it was mentioned that a sale to a competitor could be better for GN Store Nord's shareholders. To begin with, however, the board of directors decided to postpone the stock exchange listing until the spring of 2002 at the earliest, but the process was moved forward by dramatic events in the United States.[50]

On September 11, 2001, the World Trade Center in New York and the Pentagon—the headquarters of the United States Department of Defense—were subjected to a terror attack; Islamist terrorists flew two passenger planes into the World Trade Center and one into the Pentagon. The world was in shock, and once again, the global economy experienced a downturn that affected GN Store Nord and not least NetTest, as the former GN Nettest was now called in preparation for a stock market listing.

In January 2002, GN Store Nord's board of directors decided to force the splitting off of NetTest, either via a stock market listing or via a sale, as uncertainty with regard to NetTest was affecting the whole group and not least GN Store Nord's stock price negatively. A short time later, GN Store Nord's board of directors again got a new chairman as Elvar Vinum resigned at the general meeting in April 2002. His replacement was Vice Chairman Mogens Hugo, who had been a member of the board of directors since 1994 and had thus been a part of the board during the entire period since the acquisition strategy had been launched.

Mogens Hugo faced a major task. The market situation was difficult for NetTest, whose revenues were in free fall, and it was difficult to find potential buyers for the company. Furthermore, pressure from investors, including the major shareholders Arbejdsmarkedets Tillægspension and Lønmodtagernes Dyrtidsfond, for a solution was increasing. In August 2002, the stock exchange listing was finally abandoned, and a course was set directly toward the sale of the company via a bidding process.[51]

Potential buyers were not exactly growing on trees, and at the same time, it was constantly becoming more difficult to keep NetTest together; late in the year, the company's revenues were around 830 million kroner—a third of what they had been the previous year—and the number of people employed by the company was halved. A widely held view in the market was that the large telecommunications companies would not begin to make major infrastructure investments again before 2004, and the prices proposed by potential buyers of NetTest, therefore, moved downward constantly.

When GN Store Nord's board of directors met on December 30, 2002, it was to consider an offer from the Danish capital fund Axcel to buy NetTest debt-free for one krone, which would mean that GN Store Nord would have to transfer 155 million kroner to NetTest. In addition, GN Store Nord would need to finance up to 100 million kroner in restructuring costs for NetTest 50 million kroner for a number of unexploited leases over the next ten years.[52]

The board of directors was divided on the question, as was the top management team. The decision was postponed until the following day, and the top management team was asked to finish negotiating with Axcel so there would be a final draft contract on which to take a position.

On December 31, 2002, when the board of directors held a telephone meeting to reach a decision, it was still equally split. While the chairman, Mogens Hugo, and two other members of the board of directors favored a sale, the vice chairman, Finn Junge Jensen, and two others opposed a sale. The decision of the top management team was also split as Chief Executive Officer Jørn Kildegaard was in favor of a sale, while Executive Vice President Jens Due Olsen opposed a sale. However, agreement was reached to follow the board chairman's recommendation and accept the offer from Axcel, and NetTest was subsequently sold on the last day of the year.[53]

The New GN

CHAPTER 26

"Danish record in deficits"

The cancellation of the stock market listing of NetTest and the subsequent major decline hit GN Store Nord like a hammer. While the annual account for 2000 was reason for festivities, showing an increase in revenues by 30 percent and a historic surplus of 12 million kroner after the sale of Sonofon, it was clear by the late summer of 2001 that the group was headed for a historic deficit.

In addition to NetTest's crisis, GN ReSound and the otherwise stable GN Netcom were both negatively affected by a general slump in the American economy, which caused a particularly strong decline in revenues at the newly purchased hearing aid manufacturer Beltone and the headset distributor Hello Direct and also caused a decline in revenues at Jabra. Also, GN ReSound was affected both by negative sales synergies and significant integration costs as a result of the merger of Danavox, ReSound, and Beltone.

The downturn on the Nasdaq and the American slump did not affect the United States alone; their effects spread to Europe and the rest of the world and led to a general economic slump. There was a particular decline in the information and commu-

nication sector, so a number of large technology companies were forced to adjust their expected annual results downward and carry out major goodwill depreciations.

In late August, GN Store Nord followed suit with depreciations of the values of goodwill and other immaterial assets totaling 6 billion kroner, 4.5 billion kroner of which was accounted for by Photonetics, 1.25 billion kroner by Beltone, and 250 million kroner by Hello Direct. "GN sets a Danish record in deficits" was *Børsen*'s headline, which referred to the fact that the group's expected deficit of 6.5 billion kroner would be the largest ever posted by a Danish industrial company. *Berlingske Tidende* noted that with its declining stock price, the group had lost over 40 billion kroner in market value in just a year. "GN Store Nord is hemorrhaging value" was the headline.[1]

The three companies had been acquired at the top of a stock market bubble, and now, things were going the other way, so late in the year, GN Store Nord had to record a new depreciation for Photonetics in the amount of 2.5 billion kroner. Despite a modest increase in revenues to 7.3 billion kroner, the annual account for 2001, therefore, reflected an even worse disaster than foreseen by *Børsen*, as the

420   FROM INDUSTRIAL CONGLOMERATE TO THE NEW GN

deficit amounted to no less than 9.176 billion kroner. Not surprisingly, there was no dividend for the shareholders.

The slump continued in 2002 with a decline in revenues by 1.8 billion kroner and another monumental deficit, this one in the amount of 5.114 billion kroner—and again, there was no dividend for the shareholders. In particular, the poor result reflected depreciations of NetTest and losses in connection with the sale of the company totaling 4.386 billion kroner. However, while the sale of NetTest cost GN Store Nord a great deal of money, it lifted a millstone from around the group's neck—and now, a new strategy for the group's future without NetTest began to emerge.

At the meeting of the board of directors on February 23, 2001, Jørn Kildegaard informed the board of a McKinsey project to determine whether GN Netcom's and GN ReSound's business areas could be better exploited through cooperation. This project resulted in a new group strategy that was first described in the annual report for 2001, which defined GN Store Nord as a global group with a focus on "intelligent, high-tech solutions for personal communication." While each of the two companies had its own products and its own markets, they were linked by their common roots in the original Danavox and in common values and competencies.[2]

The core of "the new GN" consisted of realizable synergies between the two companies on the basis of common technologies such as digital signal processing, audiology, and wireless technology; of common production based on microelectronics, microtechnology, and the exploitation of components; and of standardized forms of marketing based on brand building and marketing to end users.[3]

When Mogens Hugo became the chairman of the board of directors in the spring of 2002, the definition of the new GN was sharpened. The motto was "From conglomerate to a single company," and the group was defined as a global innovator in the area of personal communication based on acoustics and sound processing, as well as the designing of products that increased customers' comfort, mobility, and quality of life.[4]

The group would no longer consist of a mother company with two subsidiaries, though this structure would continue to exist formally and legally but would be a single company divided into four business areas: headsets for call centers and offices, headsets for cellular telephones, hearing aids, and audiological diagnostic equipment—in the case of the last area, the activities in question had been brought together in the company GN Otometrics in 2000.

A common economic and financial function and an HR function for the entire group had already been created, and the integration of a number of further functions was on the way. In May 2003, the managerial integration was completed when the group's top management team was expanded so that in addition to Chief Executive Officer Jørn Kildegaard and Chief Financial Officer Jens Due Olsen, it included the two chief executive officers of GN Netcom and GN ReSound, Niels B. Christiansen and Jesper Mailind, respectively, who at the group level became the directors of the divisions for headsets and for hearing aids and audiological diagnostic equipment, respectively.

In the near future, the new GN's administration and the expanded top management team were to move into a common headquarters, which was symbolically expressed when the building at Kongens Nytorv 26, which had been the company's domicile since 1879, was put up for sale. Until a new group headquarters could be acquired, the group leadership worked from two addresses: Jørn Kildegaard and Jens Due Olsen moved in with Jens Mailind in GN ReSound's building in Taastrup, while Niels B. Christiansen had his office in GN Netcom's building in Ballerup.

"GN's bloody turnaround"

The announced integration of GN Netcom and GN ReSound was a major task in itself, but both companies also faced their own challenges. In the fall of 2000, GN Netcom had presented the world's first headset based on the completely new Bluetooth wireless technology, as well as a new series of dig-

GN Netcom was the first in the world to use the all-new Bluetooth technology in wireless headsets, giving the company an important technological edge over its competitors. For customers, the new product meant that they became "cordless," which provided more comfortable working conditions.

ital headsets that represented a technological lead over competitors. Nevertheless, excluding revenues from the acquisition of Jabra and Hello Direct, revenues declined in 2001, and the slump was reflected in a dramatic decline in the surplus margin in relation to operations, the so-called EBITA, from 21.6 percent in 2000 to 6.7 percent in 2001.

GN Netcom did not lose market share but, like its competitors, was negatively affected by the economic downturn. In 2002, revenues fell by 9 percent, to 1.754 billion kroner, while there was a modest increase in the surplus margin to 8.5 percent, which was far from satisfactory.

It was the call center and office market in particular that was in decline, while GN Netcom saw growth in its sales in the cellular telephone market after the first Jabra Bluetooth headsets were introduced in April 2002. In 2003, growth in the cellular telephone market was equal to the decline in the call center and office sector, so GN Netcom's overall

revenues were stagnant. In contrast, extensive restructuring and streamlining as well as the transfer of all headset manufacturing to GN ReSound's factory in Xiamen contributed to lifting the surplus margin to 10.1 percent.

A reason for the strong growth of the cellular telephone division was that in 2001, GN entered into a so-called OEM agreement regarding the supplying of Bluetooth earphones to Motorola, which sold them together with its own cellular telephones under its own name. The following year, a similar agreement was concluded with the cellular telephone manufacturer Samsung, and in 2004, GN Mobile, as the cellular telephony division was now called, more than doubled its revenues, which reached nearly 1.2 billion kroner. Because of the low prices, the EBITA margin ended up at a modest 1.7 percent, but the goal was to reach 10 percent in 2010. On the other hand, GN Netcom, as the call center and office division were now called, achieved a surplus margin of 19.5 percent after an increase in revenues to over 1.3 billion kroner.

While it was new for there to be a decline in the headset business, low organic growth and low earnings were more or less normal for GN ReSound, which since the days of Danavox had had difficulties creating a stable operating surplus on the level of those of its competitors. In 2001, to be sure, GN ReSound, including GN Otometrics, saw a modest increase in its surplus margin from 6.4 to 7 percent, but this was far short of its competitors' surplus margins of approximately 20 percent.

Therefore, the most important strategic goal of the company was to improve the surplus margin and move up to the level of the company's most successful competitors via a so-called closing the margin gap project. The four acquired companies, each of which had its own company culture and procedures, were to be integrated into ReSound to create a balanced whole so the expected synergy effects could be exploited. This led to the closing of ten factories and the placement of the manufacturing of standard devices in fewer units. The product range was rendered smaller and more comprehensible by means of the phasing out of the Danavox, Vienna-

In 2004, the Danish business press paid tribute to the managing director of GN Store Nord, Jørn Kildegaard, for having completed what the business magazine *Berlingske Nyhedsmagasin* named "a bloody turnaround." The annual result also had a profit of more than half a billion, the best ever, except from year 2000 when the proceeds from the sale of Sonofon boosted the result. Here, a couple of months later, Jørn Kildegaard presents the expectations for 2005.

metrics, which presented a negative annual result, was viewed separately for accounting purposes, but in any event, ReSound had seen a marked increase in just three years.

When the results really became evident late in 2004, *Berlingske Nyhedsmagasin* published a lengthy interview with GN Store Nord's chief executive officer, Jørn Kildegaard, who had been strongly criticized since he had taken over in the position. Now, the newspaper adopted a different tone. "GN's bloody turnaround" was the headline of an article that described the process of closing factories and replacing two thousand employees as "a business measure without many parallels in recent Danish industrial history." When Tietgen had sent cable ships to East Asia in 1870, it had been risky, but he had dared to do so and won a great victory for his company in the process, and Jørn Kildegaard had now profited from being equally daring, in the view of the magazine.[5]

In February 2005, when GN Store Nord published its annual account for 2004, the numbers in fact showed dramatic improvement; the company posted revenues increased by 800 million kroner to 5.548 billion kroner, and a surplus of 504 million kroner. "GN has become a normal company," wrote *Jyllands-Posten*, reporting that "almost five years of wild expenditures for restructuring have come to an end."[6]

GN ReSound merger with Phonak?

Parallel to closing the margin gap and integrating GN Store Nord into a single company, a development took place that could ultimately have led to the splitting up of the group. This development had begun on January 3 2003, immediately after the sale of NetTest, when the chairman of the board of directors of William Demant Holding, Niels Boserup, had declared to *Berlingske Tidende* that "if the hearing aid division of GN Store Nord were put up for sale, [William Demant Holding] would be interested in buying it." William Demant Holding was the owner of GN ReSound's perennial competitor Oticon.[7]

tone, and Philips brands. The entire organization was to be generally streamlined via rationalization, effectivization, and the optimization of the supply chain from suppliers of raw materials and components to the distribution of the finished products.

The costs of closing the margin gap ended up amounting to 600 million kroner, but the effort soon paid off. In 2002, the degree of surplus for ReSound increased to 9.5 percent; the figure for 2003 was 14.8 percent; and in 2004, the goal was achieved with a surplus of 19.8 percent for the hearing aid division. To be sure, a contributing factor was that the division for audiological diagnostic equipment, GN Oto-

Niels Boserup had noted at the company's spring general meeting GN Store Nord's board of directors had recommended to the shareholders that the voting rights limitation to 7.5 percent be nullified, which not only Boserup but also a number of analysts had interpreted as an invitation to a takeover. William Demant was not interested in a possible hostile takeover, but if GN ReSound were put up for sale, that would be "a new situation."[8]

GN Store Nord's chief executive officer, Jørn Kildegaard, immediately rejected the possibility of a sale. "We are interested in acquiring companies, not in selling them," he said, declaring that GN Store Nord intended to strengthen its business areas via acquisitions. He saw the elimination of the voting rights limitation as "an expression of self-confidence," and he believed that the best defense against being taken over was a good stock price, which the group was in the process of achieving.[9]

In April 2003, however, the topic of a sale came up again, and GN ReSound's chief executive officer, Jesper Mailind, had to reject the possibility of a sale or merger with Oticon. "That would result in very negative sales synergies," he said to *Jyllands-Posten* in early April, declaring that GN ReSound intended to be among the world's top three with regard to degree of surplus.[10]

It was not only William Demant Holding that showed an interest in GN ReSound. In early May 2003, Jørn Kildegaard informed his board of directors that the Swiss hearing aid manufacturer Phonak had requested a meeting to discuss "the potential exploitation of certain synergies between the companies [Phonak and GN Resound]," which was an obvious invitation to a merger.[11]

Like GN ReSound, Phonak had a global market share of approximately 15 percent; the only companies with larger global market shares were Germany's Siemens, which had 23 percent, and Denmark's Oticon, which had 17 percent. Phonak and GN ReSound were followed by Starkey of the United States, which had a global market share of 13 percent, and Widex of Denmark, which had a share of 8 percent. Therefore, a merger of GN ReSound

and Phonak would create the world's largest hearing aid company.

Immediately after the meeting of the board of directors, Jørn Kildegaard, Jens Due Olsen, and Jesper Mailind met with Phonak's chief executive officer, Valentin Chapero, who explicitly indicated his interest in a merger. GN Store Nord did not reject this possibility, and in late August, the board of directors decided that its chairman, Mogens Hugo, should contact the head of the Swiss owner family and chairman of Phonak's board of directors, Andy Rihs, to arrange for a private conversation about his interests and the goal of his overture to GN Store Nord.[12]

Mogens Hugo met with Andy Rihs and—to his surprise—Valentin Chapero in Zurich on November 13, 2003. Rihs and Chapero were both eager to execute a merger but unclear when it came to the central question of the distribution of ownership shares. However, GN Store Nord's board of directors decided to continue the dialogue, partly to keep the discussions of a possible merger going and partly to keep Phonak from seeking alternative partners.[13]

It became clear that Phonak was serious when the chairmen of the boards of directors and the chief executive officers of the two companies met in Frankfurt in late February 2004. Andy Rihs and Valentin Chapero presented a plan for a merger according to which the company that existed following the merger would be GN ReSound, which would primarily be listed in Zurich. While the decisive question of ownership remained unresolved, the ball was now in GN Store Nord's court. At a meeting of GN Store Nord's board of directors in the first half of May, Mogens Hugo, therefore, reported that the top management team was working on a report that would be sent out and discussed after the summer vacation.[14]

On October 5, GN Store Nord's board of directors and top management team met for a day-long strategy meeting at Havreholm Castle in North Zealand. After going over the top management team's overall strategic perspective for the years through 2010 as well as the strategies for the individual business areas, the participants turned to an agenda item with

The chairman of GN Store Nord's board of directors, Mogens Hugo, presents his first report to the company's general meeting in Falkoner Centret on April 3, 2003. Mogens Hugo had been a member of the board of directors of GN Store Nord and had become chairman in the spring of 2002 in the wake of the failed stock exchange listing of GN Nettest and the major losses to which it had led. It proved to be possible to turn the group around, but Mogens Hugo was forced to put GN ReSound up for sale, as several major shareholders were dissatisfied with the company's growth. This resulted in the conclusion of an agreement regarding the sale of GN ReSound to Phonak, but the sale was not approved by the German competition authority, and GN Store Nord in its entirety therefore faced a new crisis. He resigned from his post as chairman of the board of directors in June 2008.

the heading "Project Rose," which stood for the possible merger with Phonak. The use of this code name reflected the fact that there was now a specific possibility on which to take a position.[15]

Already in August, the board of directors had received a twenty-page report from the top management team that noted that a merger would create value but established that the top management team could not recommend the merger "at the present time." While GN ReSound and Phonak had roughly the same revenues, Phonak's market value, given current stock prices, was roughly equivalent to that of GN Store Nord in its entirety. Therefore, a merger of GN ReSound and Phonak would hardly be on an equal basis, and there was no prospect of gaining significant influence over the merged company, which made the transaction uninteresting for GN Store Nord. Also, there were a number of unresolved critical "soft issues" such as the location of the headquarters and stock exchange listing and the selection of a chief executive officer.[16]

Before the report had been sent to the board of directors, Jørn Kildegaard had sent a draft to Mogens Hugo and expressed the view that a sale to William Demant or a sale of GN ReSound at an auction would be "more interesting" than a merger. The important thing to realize, Jørn Kildegaard felt, was that the time had now come for the board of directors to determine what it wanted to do with GN ReSound and which path it wanted to tread—and indeed, this was the message of the final report.[17]

At the strategy seminar on October 5, Jens Due Olsen presented the top management team's report, after which he, Jørn Kildegaard, and the secretary were sent out of the boardroom for the duration of the board's discussion. When they returned, they were informed that Mogens Hugo had been contacted by the chairman of the board of directors of William Demant Holding, which owned Oticon, who had wanted to know whether "there was any interest in discussing strategic possibilities," by which a merger had been implied. There had in fact not been any such interest, as a merger would make GN ReSound's Danish competitor the largest part of the new company. Subsequently, the chairman reported on the board's discussion of Project Rose, which had led to the board's following the top management team's recommendation and deciding "that it was not in the company's interests to advance the discussions of a possible merger on the basis of the conditions discussed thus far." However, it had been agreed that the chairman should continue the dialogue and schedule a new meeting with Phonak.[18]

At the end of the year, no new meetings had been held, and in the meantime, the integration of GN into a single company had continued. This integration process was made material by a decision to acquire a property at Lautrupbjerg 7–11 in Ballerup and carry out extensive remodeling and expansion, as well as modernization so the building could be used as the company headquarters and house the whole top management team and the whole administration and also create synergies across the business areas.

A short time previously, the chief executive officer of GN Netcom, Niels B. Christiansen, had resigned to become deputy chief executive officer of Danfoss A/S. He was replaced by Hans Henrik Lund, who did not become a member of the group's top management team, however; and GN Mobile was led by Morten Steen-Jørgensen. The group's top management team subsequently consisted of Jørn Kildegaard, Jens Due Olsen, and Jesper Mailind.

Inadequate growth at GN ReSound

Eventually the inquiries from Phonak appeared to die out, and when some of GN Store Nord's large foreign shareholders contacted the company's leaders early in 2005 and asked for a meeting to be arranged, it was not to discuss the hearing aid business. The topic was the company's capital structure, and the investors wanted a buyback program as well as the depreciation of the share capital, and they also wanted GN Mobile to be sold off and the money to be sent to the shareholders instead of risking a development like the one with GN Nettest, where the market suddenly disappeared and the company became worthless.[19]

The company's biggest shareholder, ATP, had wished to have a meeting to discuss the same topics, but this Danish major shareholder also brought up the possibility of a Danish consolidation in the hearing aid industry—a merger of GN ReSound and Oticon. ATP was in favor of such a merger, aktiekapitalen med XX mio. Den ak.irksomhed derfor være fifty-fifty, . ovember, uden der kom noget ud afdet. .

GN Store Nord accommodated the demand that the company buy back its own shares and depreciate the share capital in March 2005, when the general meeting extended an existing authorization for the repurchasing of shares at a stock exchange value of 400 million kroner and for a subsequent depreciation of the share capital. In contrast, the company did not have immediate plans to sell GN Mobile, as the company had concluded an OEM agreement with Samsung in 2004 and another such agreement as recently as in January 2005, this one an agreement with Nokia's gaming division with regard to the provision of earphones for portable game consoles and other devices.

Despite the wish expressed by ATP, GN Store Nord also did not intend to merge GN ReSound with Oticon or another company. However, in early June 2005—more than a year having passed with no meetings—Mogens Hugo again met with the chairman of Phonak's board of directors, Andy Rihs, at Rihs's request. The Swiss now indicated that the only possible merger that interested him was a merger of the two hearing aid businesses and that GN Netcom and GN Mobile would have to be split off if the merger were to become a reality. As a basis for a merger, Andy Rihs cited his view—the same view previously expressed by GN Store Nord's top management team—that Phonak and GN Store Nord in its entirety were of roughly similar value, which came as a surprise to GN Store Nord's board of directors when it met later in the month. GN ReSound and Phonak's global market shares were about the same size, and nevertheless, Phonak was supposed to be worth as much as all of GN, including GN Netcom and GN Mobile.[20]

The board of directors believed that a possible merger would take place on an unequal basis, but the top management team explained that Phonak's description was accurate, given the existing stock prices, and as a next step, the board of directors decided to get an investment bank to undertake a valuation of GN Store Nord. In the meantime, the chairman would indicate to Andy Rihs that "the yields relationship would be a challenge" but that the board of directors could see the argument for the creation of a "powerhouse" and would, therefore, work on the matter over the summer.[21]

It was J. P. Morgan that took on the valuation, which was presented at a two-day board of directors seminar with the leaders of GN ReSound in Xiamen on September 20 and 21 in 2005. After a discussion of strategy and visions for each of the four business areas, the floor was turned over to two representatives of the American investment bank, who soberly declared that GN was "fairly valued" by the stock market. The reason for Phonak's high stock price in relation to GN Store Nord's was primarily that the market expected higher organic growth from Phonak than from GN ReSound, which had historically always had low organic growth. J. P. Morgan also pointed out that in case of declining revenues or a shrinking surplus margin, GN Mobile could have a negative effect on GN Store Nord's stock price, which would further weaken the company in relation to Phonak.[22]

J. P. Morgan's presentation was followed by a lengthy discussion that ended with a decision by the board of directors that neither the mobile division nor the entire headset business was for sale and that a merger of GN ReSound and Phonak "was not to be pursued for the time being, as what would create the most value would be to enhance GN's own performance."[23]

The idea of a possible merger had not been irrevocably killed, but the focus was henceforth on creating organic growth at GN ReSound, which, given the surplus margin that had been achieved, would result in an increased surplus, while increased sales would result in the benefits of economies of scale and, therefore, an increased surplus margin. Another consequence would be that GN ReSound would be stronger in a merger situation.

Now, a new agenda had been set for GN ReSound; a consequence of the closing the margin gap project had been a decreased focus on growth. According to the annual report for 2001, GN ReSound, in addition to working to increase its surplus margin, wished "to retain and ideally increase its market share." This passive formulation was reflected by stagnating revenues in the hearing aid business of approximately 2.6 billion kroner during the years 2001–2004, a period during which the competitor companies achieved annual growth rates of approximately 10 percent. This meant that GN ReSound lost market share despite the successful launches of the groundbreaking ReSound Air and Canta 7 Open devices in 2003. The time had come for a closing the growth gap project, as a member of the board of directors put it.

The course toward increased growth for GN ReSound was set by the budget for 2006, which the top management team presented to the board of directors in early December 2005. The meeting took place in the shadow of persistent merger rumors, both Phonak and Oticon having publicly expressed interest in acquiring GN ReSound. The chairman of the board of directors had received several proposals related to the possibility of creating a "big Danish player." He had reacted "reservedly" to these proposals—but he had not rejected them outright.[24]

The top management team characterized its own budget as "aggressive." The budget foresaw growth in GN ReSound's revenues of no less than 9 percent, in contrast to organic growth of only 3 percent in 2005, excluding the German hearing aid company Interton, which GN ReSound had acquired in November 2005. For the sake of caution, the predicted growth rate announced to the public was reduced to 7 percent, which still represented a leap in relation to earlier years. The board of directors remarked on the top management team's great expectations with regard to growth and characterized the budget as "ambitious."[25]

The growth message was emphasized in the business press, as Jesper Mailind had announced already in late August 2005 that GN ReSound was now earning money as it should be and was "ready to expand." The message was sharpened after the end of the year. "GN gives its growth a kick" was a headline in *Jyllands-Posten*, which, in January 2006, presented an announcement by Jesper Mailind to the effect that with the introduction of a series of new products, GN ReSound would create strong organic growth and "knock out the competition."[26]

Major shareholders demand increased growth

Only a few months later, however, it was clear that the budgeted growth rate was too ambitious. At a meeting of the board of directors, a few hours before the general meeting on 21 March 2006, the top management team admitted that it would be "challenging to hit the growth targets that had been set." The previous year's success with ReSound Air was under pressure from competitors who had presented competitive similar products, and the launch of a new top-class product in the uppermost price class, the Metrix, had not been a success. Also, the organization was "taxed to the utmost" because of the pressure to launch more new hearing aids that could increase revenues.[27]

Newspapers had published articles criticizing GN ReSound's inability to keep up with its competitors, and at the board meeting, the chairman reported that he had been summoned to a meeting with Nordea and BankInvest, both of which banks had wished to discuss the lack of growth at GN ReSound. Therefore, he proposed that the top management team consider more radical measures to increase growth—and he remarked that it could be worth considering whether "a consolidation might not be a possibility after all."[28]

ATP, Nordea, and BankInvest had all announced that they would be presenting critical remarks at the general meeting that was held immediately after the meeting of the board of directors. A total of 1,200 shareholders had registered to attend, and the board's count indicated that, as the biggest shareholder, with an ownership share of 7.5 percent, ATP had 35 percent of the votes behind them, while the chairman of the board of directors had control over 40 percent of the votes, including some represented by powers of attorney.

Despite an annual account that showed an increase in the group's revenues by 20 percent, to more than 6.6 billion kroner, and the biggest surplus ever, 850 million kroner, the institutional investors were not satisfied. This was clearly expressed at the general meeting when ATP's portfolio manager Henning Skov Jensen addressed the 1,200 shareholders. "It is worrying that GN ReSound is no longer in the hearing aid sector's top league," he declared. "My question is what it will take to secure GN ReSound's place in the top league."[29]

There were similar questions from Nordea and BankInvest, in connection with which it was remarked that when Phonak and Oticon launched new high-end devices, they showed growth rates of up to around 20 percent, while in the fourth quarter—after the launch of the Metrix—GN ReSound had had organic growth of only 1 percent.[30]

In his response, Mogens Hugo avoided really engaging with the three major shareholders' declarations and questions, but these declarations and questions attracted attention from the press and on the stock market. The chairman of the board of directors began the board meeting of May 9 by remarking that there were quite a few rumors in circulation about GN Store Nord and that he had exchanged messages with Andy Rihs via telephone answering machines. Phonak's board chairman had expressed worry that GN Store Nord "would forget Phonak," and several times, he had proposed that he and Mogens Hugo should have lunch together, but Mogens Hugo had not accepted any of these invitations.[31]

Subsequently, Jørn Kildegaard had asked the head of GN ReSound's international sales division, Steen Bindslev, to give a presentation on the company's efforts to create growth. He began by remarking that the closing the margin gap project had taken a great deal of effort and that Oticon currently had at least one hundred more development engineers than GN ReSound. Furthermore, GN ReSound's team was relatively young and had only been gaining experience in the hearing aid sector for a relatively short time. The launch of the Metrix had not been a success because the development division had been under great pressure and had ended up with a device that was larger than the competitors' devices. This problem would be addressed by the launch of a new product in June, the mini Metrix, which featured the same technology in a smaller housing.

Asked what it would take to pass Oticon and Phonak, the companies that GN ReSound was always lagging behind, Steen Bindslev replied that it would take a long time to pass those companies in a traditional way. Technological leaps like that represented by the ReSound Air could make a great difference, but the company would have to be prepared "to remain a follower" in the area of traditional products.

During its presentation of the first-quarter report, the top management team noted that April had been a very poor month for GN ReSound and that there had been only 1.5 percent growth for the first four months of the year. It was, then, a long way up to the officially announced 7 percent, and in the words of the chairman, "everything [would] have to go optimally from now on for the predicted growth to materialize."[32]

The poor result in April was not reflected in the official quarterly notice that was sent out the same day and only gave the result for the year's first three months, when GN ReSound had had organic growth of 5 percent. As the predictions with regard to the year-end result were not modified, the notice provoked no reactions from the press or among the shareholders—no public ones, in any event.

However, the major shareholder ATP was not satisfied with developments, and at a meeting late in the spring of 2006, it was made clear to Mogens Hugo and Jørn Kildegaard that if GN ReSound could not achieve the same growth rates as its competitors, then the shareholders' interests would probably be best served by the sale of GN ReSound.

The pressure from the influential Danish major shareholder and the disappointing development in April caused both concern and considerable activity at GN Store Nord. This culminated with the scheduling of an extraordinary meeting of the board of directors on June 2, which began without the participation of the top management team. In connection with the main agenda item "Strategic Considerations," the chairman declared that during the past few months, and in particular during the past few weeks, he had had many conversations with Jørn Kildegaard and the other members of the top management team about the lack of growth at GN ReSound.[33]

All the evidence suggested that the month of May would be as bad as April, with almost no growth, and it, therefore, appeared clear that the coming quarterly result would be very poor and that expectations with regard to the annual result would have to be adjusted downward. At the same time, Oticon and Phonak had very high organic growth and were taking market share from GN ReSound, which was exactly what the major shareholders had warned against at the general meeting. At a recent meeting with the board chairman, the top management team had indicated that they were very worried about how difficult it would be to create organic growth at the level of the company's competitors' growth, and in the words of the chairman, the meeting had ended with the top management team, "throwing in the towel." Therefore, he found it necessary for the board of directors to take a position on what was to be done about the weak development of GN ReSound.

The top management team then came in, and Jørn Kildegaard could confirm the board chairman's description of the situation; Jørn Kildegaard added that all the evidence suggested that June, too, would see low organic growth. GN ReSound's chief executive officer, Jesper Mailind, added that despite the many launches of new devices, it would be difficult to address the situation effectively. The overall hearing aid business in the United States had not increased since 2003, and in France, the company was losing a large amount of market share, while Germany was still a problem child.

In contrast to Oticon and Phonak, which announced growth of 10 percent, GN ReSound could achieve only 3 to 4 percent, which was about half of the market growth rate and meant that GN ReSound was losing market share. He did not believe it would be possible to create much greater growth in the short run, but he believed that the major investments currently being made "would have to increase [the company's] organic growth later."

The board of directors concluded that GN ReSound's technology was among the best in the industry and that the company had an excellent supply chain as a result of the closing the margin gap project but that there were great difficulties in marketing. It was also mentioned that the mood in the organization was not as good as it could be and that the organization was "perhaps a little tired" in the wake of closing the market gap.

The prospect of having to adjust expectations with regard to the annual result downward did not appeal to the board of directors, as it could be assumed that reactions from the major shareholders would be "extremely negative." This was confirmed by two representatives from J. P. Morgan who participated in the rest of the meeting. They emphasized that the major active shareholders "viewed current developments very critically" and that a possible downward adjustment would be reacted to with strong criticism "and possibly also active interference in GN's leadership."

According to the two consultants, the major shareholders were quite aware of the very great synergy effects that would result from a consolidation and would "therefore insistently push for such a solution if GN ReSound did not develop as well as other companies." For GN Store Nord's board of directors, this was the writing on the wall, and according to the minutes, the meeting ended, with the chairman saying that "it was shocking that things had turned around this quickly and that he did not expect the board of directors to make a decision at this board meeting but would summon the board to a new meeting in the very near future at which the board could discuss what actions should be taken on the basis of what had been said at today's meeting."

GN ReSound for sale

Only a year had passed since Jørn Kildegaard had been praised in the business press for his bloody turnaround, and at the spring general meeting, GN Store Nord had presented an annual result so good it had to be called historic. Nevertheless, the big shareholders were not satisfied, and already on June 5 and 11, there were again extraordinary meetings of the board of directors excluding the top management team and under the main heading "Project Fahrenheit," which was the code name for the sale of GN ReSound. The possibility of selling GN Store Nord in its entirety was also discussed until the chairman concluded that there was a major-

ity on the board of directors in favor of selling only GN ReSound, including GN Otometrics; two board members asked for it to be recorded in the minutes that they were not in agreement.[34]

GN ReSound was to be sold at auction, a possibility to which Jørn Kildegaard had referred back in 2004. On June 22, the top management team again participated in an extraordinary board meeting; at this meeting, the schedule for the process and a deadline for bids in the middle of July were established. On June 28, the board of directors received a message from the chairman to the effect that the process had been begun and that he had spoken by telephone with the chairmen of Phonak and William Demant, respectively, that same day.[35]

On July 5, 2006, GN Store Nord's board of directors met in the new headquarters at Lautrupbjerg 7–11 in Ballerup, where GN had begun moving in a short time earlier. The chairman began by welcoming the attendees and remarking that because of the circumstances, a tour of the facility would have to wait until a later occasion.[36]

A representative of J. P. Morgan then informed the board of directors that six potential buyers had been contacted: the three major hearing aid companies William Demant, Phonak, and Siemens, as well as three global technology and medical conglomerates. Further interested parties—including capital funds—would probably be in contact when the decision to sell GN ReSound was announced later in the day. This occurred at 1:00 p.m, when a stock exchange notice was sent out and the entire organization was informed.

The process that followed was watched closely by the stock market and not least by the major shareholders; behind the scenes, ATP was working to bring about a Danish solution in the form of a sale to William Demant. In addition, the Danish pension fund and other Danish investors demanded that the revenues from the sale immediately be paid out to the shareholders—the sale of Sonofon six years earlier had not been forgotten.[37]

In late September 2006, there were two interested potential buyers left, Phonak and William Demant, who were offering 15.5 billion kroner and 12.5

billion kroner, respectively. However, Phonak's offer contained a number of conditions, and the payment was to be divided up so that 50 percent was payable immediately and 50 percent was to be acquired via a share emission, GN Store Nord's proceeds from which would be dependent on the share price, though a decline of up to 15 percent would be covered by Phonak. Therefore, four to five months would pass before the sale could be finally closed, while William Demant's offer was of immediate full payment—literally "money in the bank," as one of the advisors from J. P. Morgan put it.[38]

Apart from the share emission aspect, Phonak's offer was very attractive. The acquisitions of Beltone nad others in 1999 and 2000 had cost about 4.5 billion kroner, while the integration process and the closing the margin gap project had cost 600 million kroner. Now, the business could be sold for three times the total of these costs.

Indeed, GN Store Nord's board of directors chose Phonak and approved the sales agreement, which was announced to the Copenhagen Stock Exchange and the public on Monday, October 2, at 7:00 a.m. At the same time, it was announced that GN would send approximately 13 billion kroner to the company's shareholders when the transaction was final. As a member of the board of directors noted, the sale of GN ReSound was "a major event in GN's history." The board member in question emphasized that "it was important that the name GN [could] live on." It would be "necessary to 'reinvent' GN if the company were to survive in the long run."[39]

New leadership facing great challenges

It would be up to new top management to reinvent GN, as Jørn Kildegaard resigned his position as previously planned after the signing of the agreement with Phonak. At the same time, Jesper Mailind left GN Store Nord's top management team, while he was to remain the chief executive officer of GN ReSound until Phonak took over the company. Chief Financial Officer Jens Due Olsen was to leave when the transaction was finally executed.

GN Netcom too was to have new leadership, as the head of the mobile division, Morten Steen-Jørgensen, had given notice already around the end of 2005 that for private reasons he wished to leave GN, and a few months later, the chief executive officer of GN Netcom, Hans Henrik Lund, had given notice that, also for private reasons, he wished to leave GN by the end of the year at the latest.[40]

The timing of the announced departures was critical, as GN Store Nord was in the process of preparing for the merging of GN Netcom's two divisions in the middle of May 2006. The technologies in the two divisions were converging as wireless technology in general and Bluetooth in particular gained ground in the call center and office area, in part because of the increasing use of IP telephony via the Internet, and there was also increasing pressure from customers, particularly in the United States, for a merger that would mean they would need to deal with only one supplier.

The top management team immediately began a search for a replacement for Hans Henrik Lund, who led the merging of the two divisions of GN Netcom in the meantime. At the same time, the decision to sell GN ReSound meant that the leadership question was now lifted up to a higher level, as the object of the search was now a chief executive officer for GN Store Nord in its entirety.

The individual chosen was the Dutchman Toon Bouten, who was seeking new challenges after having spent two and a half years as the director of the Dutch electronics group Philips's division for consumer electronics in Europe, the Middle East, and Africa. He was able to begin working at GN immediately, and on October 2, 2006—the day the sale of GN ReSound was announced—Toon Bouten was presented as the new chief executive officer of GN Store Nord. At Philips, Bouten had been responsible for annual revenues of approximately 75 billion kroner; he now became the leader of a more modest Danish company that, following the sale of its hearing aid business, would have revenues of approximately 3.5 billion kroner. On the other hand, there were plenty of challenges.[41]

With the merger, GN Netcom had become the world's largest manufacturer of headsets. This was a position owed not least to the OEM business involving delivering earphones to the major manufacturers of cellular telephones, which increased by 70 percent and passed 1 billion kroner in revenues in 2005, while the Jabra brand, with growth of 36 percent and revenues of 924 million kroner, was also doing well. In total, the mobile business had revenues of 1.95 billion kroner, while the call center and office business, with growth of 17 percent, to revenues of just under 1.54 million kroner, had become the little brother of the company.

In general, the mobile business was the engine of GN Store Nord's overall revenue growth, but when Toon Bouten joined the company, it had gotten into the situation J. P. Morgan had warned against at the strategy seminar organized by the board of directors in Xiamen the previous year: the revenues, and therefore the surplus for the mobile business, were in decline as a result of a significant drop in deliveries to Motorola as well as to the American telecommunications company Verizon, both of which companies were experiencing a major decline in revenues. The previously expected annual revenues of 2.7 billion kroner were, therefore, now expected to be reduced to 1.8 billion kroner—or even less.[42]

In the call center and office business too, there were problems. Early in the year, the American company Hello Direct had launched a try-and-buy campaign, allowing customers to order headsets to try them and subsequently return them—or pay for them. It soon proved to be the case that a large part of the customers neither returned the headsets nor paid for them, and already in June, GN Store Nord's top management team foresaw a significant downward adjustment of the annual result because of the depreciation of headsets considered lost. Furthermore, the business area was negatively affected by a general economic downturn in the United States, and when Toon Bouten joined the company, it was estimated that the call center business would generate annual revenues of 1.6 billion to 1.7 billion kroner, not the predicted 1.8 billion kroner, and it appeared likely that the headset area would at best stagnate and post a negative operating result of approximately 50 million kroner.[43]

Overall, the situation at GN Netcom, in the words of the chairman of the board of directors, was "not tenable," but he was confident that Bouten was "the right man to confront the challenges that [awaited]." One member of the board of directors wanted to know "whether Toon Bouten [was] familiar with the latest estimates regarding Netcom's results for 2006," that is, whether Bouten knew what he was getting himself into, and the board chairman said that this was the case.[44]

German prohibition of the sale of GN ReSound

Toon Bouten was going to have a great deal of work to do. In addition to GN Netcom's difficulties, there was the whole process of splitting off GN ReSound after the two companies and the group leadership had worked hard for the past five years to become a single company. GN Netcom could no longer straightforwardly get its headsets manufactured at GN ReSound's factory in Xiamen, and Phonak wished to rent parts of GN Store Nord's headquarters in Ballerup, which would, therefore, need to be remodeled.

A more complicated process was the separation of the integrated financial and economic functions, IT systems, and HR functions, as well as all cooperative relationships and lateral group formations with regard to technology, design, and development. The creation of the annual account for 2006 would be a challenge in itself, as it would involve the separation of the two business areas and a division of activities into terminated and continuing ones. Employees felt uncertainty about the future—particularly in GN ReSound—and particularly in the integrated functions, many left GN Store Nord.[45]

The process into which GN Store Nord was thrown was both extensive and intensive, and while this process was going on, both GN Netcom and GN ReSound were to continue to be operated until the sale could be finally completed after having approved by the competition authorities, which was expected to occur early in the new year and after Phonak had carried out a share emission expected to occur during the first half of the new year.

The major shareholders and the stock market could not wait that long. They wanted clear information about the future of GN Store Nord and its remaining subsidiary GN Netcom, and they were concerned about possible hostile takeover attempts. The Swedish capital fund EQT Partners had already—without having been asked—offered an estimate of GN Netcom's value of 4 billion to 4.4 billion kroner. The fund's interest had been rejected, but the fund would probably not let itself be stopped.[46]

Toon Bouten's main task was to get GN Netcom on its feet and create a new strategy for the future, and shortly before Christmas, there was a strategy plan and an action plan that were to be implemented early in the new year. At the same time, the company's name was in play, as the chairman of the board of directors and Bouten proposed that the new company should be called GN JABRA. At the end, though, everybody agreed on GN as the new name of the company.

A monkey wrench was thrown into the works before then, however. The evening before the board of directors was to meet on December 6, the board received word that the Bundeskartellamt, the German antitrust authority, had proposed that Phonak send in a revised application. Phonak had applied for approval of the acquisition of GN ReSound under § 35 of the German antitrust law, which had to do with the merged company's possible acquisition of a dominant market position. There was no prospect of that, as Siemens had a market share of approximately 35 percent in Germany, while the merged Phonak/ReSound would have a market share of approximately 25 to 30 percent and Oticon had 20 to 25 percent.[47]

However, the Bundeskartellamt had also decided to process the application in view of § 40 of the antitrust law, which had to do with the consequences for the market structure and competitive situation in Germany, which, assuming it were in fact done, would occur in a so-called phase two that could take up to a year. Phonak—and GN Store Nord—could save time and get a decision in the course of the spring of 2007 if the application was changed to a § 40 application so the Bundeskartellamt could proceed immediately to processing the application in accordance with § 40.[48]

GN Store Nord's board of directors had no choice but to recommend that Phonak change the application and send it in again, which occurred the following week. Approval would not be given before the last days of February 2007 at the earliest, which would complicate the situation, as Phonak wanted to send out its share emission brochure in the middle of February, and GN Store Nord's annual account was to be published on February 22—before the Bundeskartellamt made its decision.[49]

However, GN Store Nord's board of directors still felt fully confident that the decision would be an approval, and the board, therefore, decided to summon shareholders to an extraordinary general meeting on January 5, 2007, at which the board proposed and got approved the reduction of GN Store Nord's share capital to a fourth of its previous value and the distribution of 13 billion kroner to the shareholders when the transaction had been completed. The reason for scheduling the general meeting before the decision of the Bundeskartellamt was that such a transaction required a three-month statutory notice period, and this period could thus subsequently elapse so the money could be paid out to the shareholders as soon as possible after the decision in Germany and Phonak's share emission.

As had been expected, the German antitrust authority had not made a decision when GN Store Nord's annual account was published—nor had a decision been made when GN's general meeting was held on March 21, 2007. At that point, however, GN Store Nord's top management and board of directors did not lack knowledge of which way things were going, as Jens Due Olsen, Jesper Mailind, and GN Store Nord's legal experts, as well as a similar delegation from Phonak had been to a meeting at the Bundeskartellamt two days earlier at which they had been presented with a draft decision that would forbid the merger between GN ReSound and Phonak.[50]

GN Store Nord's board of directors was informed at a meeting immediately before the general meeting, and Jens Due Olsen was able to inform the board that the German rejection of the merger was because of the fact that a consequence of it would be the strengthening of an existing oligopoly, consisting of Siemens, Oticon, and Phonak, which had a combined market share of 81.1 percent. The Bundeskartellamt wished to keep GN ReSound in the market as a challenger to the three big companies despite the fact that including Interton, the company had a market share of only 8 percent. With the support of Phonak, Jens Due Olsen had offered various possible solutions such as splitting off Interton and GN ReSound's own activities in Germany so there would still be an independent competitor to the big three, and the Bundeskartellamt would consider these offers in connection with its ongoing deliberations, with which it expected to finish in the course of the week.[51]

Not only the Danish but also Phonak's delegation was shocked, but for the time being there was nothing to do but wait. Mogens Hugo emphasized that his message was strictly confidential, and as GN Store Nord had not received an official decision, the company had no obligation to inform the market.

Immediately after the meeting of the board of directors, Mogens Hugo took the podium at Falkonersalen in Frederiksberg to present the board's report on the past year's events—fully aware that the basis for the sale of GN ReSound and of the decision made at the general meeting in January to depreciate the share capital was crumbling. He presented the annual report that had been prepared, and without knowledge of what was going on behind the scenes—and with the prospect of the imminent distribution of 13 billion kroner—none of the approximately seven hundred shareholders who had come to the meeting had critical comments on the annual account. In fact, that account showed a decline in revenues for the remaining headset business of 120 million kroner and a negative annual result of 55 million kroner.

Those present also accepted that no dividend would be paid out, but a number of small investors were provoked by the fact that the chairman announced that the board of directors would propose at the following year's general meeting that the chairman be paid triple the ordinary compensation and the rest of the board members double the ordinary compensation in order to compensate the board for the significant amount of work it had done, in connection with the sale of GN ReSound. "But now we just have to finish up with the sale of GN ReSound," he declared. He finished by saying, "Now, I've provided notice in good time."[52]

The day after the general meeting, GN Store Nord received the official indication from the Bundeskartellamt of the expected rejection of the merger. On the morning of 23 March, the company sent out a stock exchange notice regarding the German antitrust authority's reservations about the sale of GN ReSound, noting that the result could be the prohibition of the sale. At a new meeting in Bonn on March 30, the Bundeskartellamt presented its arguments in detail—and representatives of Phonak and GN Store Nord likewise presented their arguments but without making any headway.[53]

The Bundeskartellamt's 110-page, densely printed decision to prohibit the merger was published on April 12, 2007, and in early May, GN Store Nord and Phonak both appealed the decision to the highest court of the local German federal state, the Oberlandesgericht in Düsseldorf, as they found the decision illegal. The alliance held only until the middle of August, when Sonova—as Phonak was now called—nullified the acquisition deal and pulled out of the appeal case, as the Oberlandesgericht had rejected an application to have the prohibition suspended until the court's decision had been handed down. GN Store Nord decided to maintain its appeal despite the fact that the matter risked taking until 2010 to resolve.

It ended up taking even longer. In April 2010, the German Supreme Court determined that the prohibition of the sale on GN ReSound was illegal. As a consequence, GN Store Nord sued the Bundeskartellamt late in the year, demanding 8.2 billion kroner in damages. GN Store Nord lost this case, as the court recognized that the prohibition was illegal but found that there was no valid basis for the demand for compensation for damages. GN Store Nord appealed the decision, but the appeals court in Düsseldorf declined to hear the case, and the court's decision was supported by the German Supreme Court as recently as in October 2015. At this point all legal options had been exhausted; all instances had recognized the illegality of the Bundeskartellamt's prohibition, but none of them had found that the authority could be held responsible and made to pay compensation for the losses GN Store Nord had suffered because of the illegal prohibition.

Sell or keep GN ReSound?

Thanks to Phonak's pullout, GN Store Nord found itself in a completely new and entirely unexpected situation. GN Store Nord's leaders had feared a strong negative reaction from the shareholders, who had lost 13 billion kroner overnight, but—in addition to natural disappointment—the decision of the Bundeskartellamt elicited sympathy for GN Store Nord, and ATP even offered to help if it were possible. The board of directors now needed to decide what was to happen with GN ReSound, which had lost both market share and employees since the sale to Phonak had been announced. Jesper Mailind had warned earlier that the situation had constantly been getting worse since the Bundeskartellamt had presented its indication.[54]

When GN Store Nord's board of directors met on 15 August 2007, Mogens Hugo and Jens Due Olsen had met a few days previously with ATP, which had expressed concern about GN ReSound's future and recommended selling the company off even if the price were as low as 10 billion kroner. Jens Due Olsen added that he had been in contact with a number of major shareholders who together represented more than 20 percent of the shares in GN Store Nord and that there was a consensus that GN ReSound should be sold. This provoked an immediate reaction from the board's vice chairman, the newly elected board member Bill Hoover, an American who knew GN Store Nord from his nearly thirty years at McKinsey. "Why would one do that?" he asked rhetorically. Jens Due Olsen answered that investors seemed to take the view that "a line in the sand [had] been crossed" but that ultimately, the key issue was of course the price.[55]

Bill Hoover was not alone in his skepticism about a sale. In a memorandum to the board of directors, the chairman and Jens Due Olsen recommended that GN ReSound be sold off, in reaction to which one of the board members asked how that would add value and whether GN ReSound could not grow in GN Store Nord's ownership. Another board member doubted that the timing was good and argued that at a later time, GN ReSound would be much more well-functioning and, therefore, worth more—after which Bill Hoover declared that

The American William "Bill" Hoover joined GN Store Nord's board of directors in 1997 and became the board's vice chairman the following year. He had previously spent thirty years working for the consulting firm McKinsey, in connection with which he had advised companies including GN Store Nord, and he therefore knew the company better than most when he was elected to the board. He was the first member of GN Store Nord's board of directors to argue against selling GN ReSound to another buyer following the failed sale of that company to Phonak, and he has since played a central role at the GN group as the vice chairman of the board of directors of GN and the boards of directors of the two subsidiaries.

he was in agreement with the two previous speakers. The chairman subsequently concluded that GN Store Nord would not sell off GN ReSound in the fall but rather wait for the annual account for 2007.[56]

Nevertheless, a sale was discussed again in early October, when the board held its regular strategy meeting at Højstrupgaard in North Zealand. The question had not originally been on the agenda but was added to it—probably because of a memorandum from J. P. Morgan presented by Gary Weiss, who had been involved in the entire sales process.[57]

In J. P. Morgan's view, the board of directors should remember the mandate from the shareholders, which was to sell GN ReSound, which was also what the market expected. In a more or less didactic tone, Gary Weiss had said that in his view, the board of directors did not have a mandate to keep GN ReSound and go on as in the past, and if the board did so it could cause the more active shareholders to take action. He judged a realistic price level to be 10 to 12 billion kroner, or possibly as little as approximately 7.5 billion kroner—to which several members of the board of directors responded that they would oppose a sale at a price under 10 billion kroner.

The board of directors was under time pressure, as the shareholders and the market expected to see a plan soon that detailed what was to happen with GN ReSound and with GN Store Nord generally—the deadline for publication of such a plan was November 6, when the third-quarter report would be sent out. The conclusion was, therefore, that J. P. Morgan should be asked to arrange an auction with a deadline of October 15 for bids, after which the board of directors would make a final decision.[58]

When the bids were reviewed on October 16, there were not any from the leading hearing aid manufacturers—for good reason, as they could have looked forward to the rejection of the transaction by the Bundeskartellamt if they had bid and been selected. However, there were twelve bids from capital funds ranging from 7.5 billion kroner to 10.5 billion kroner, the highest of which had come from two relatively small capital funds. The bids had been presented on the basis of the half-year ac-

count, but new numbers showed a worsened situation for GN ReSound, and it was, therefore, to be expected that the bids would be lowered. This caused Bill Hoover to declare that he would resign from the board of directors before he would agree to sell for 8 billion kroner.[59]

It was decided that the board of directors would await the publication of the quarterly account on November 6 and then set a new deadline for bids of November 15, but eight days later, the process was stopped after GN ReSound's quarterly result had turned out to be so poor that it would hardly be possible to get an acceptable price for the company. The board discussed the possibility of splitting the company off instead, but in the words of the chairman, the result would be "two weak companies," as GN Netcom too had posted poor results. "Right now, they will both be stronger together," he believed, and the other board members agreed.[60]

However, the decision to keep GN ReSound did not mean a return to the concept of the new GN as a single company. On the contrary—the two subsidiaries, GN ReSound and GN Netcom, were to be separated to the greatest possible extent and have their own boards of directors with leading specialists as well as representatives of GN Store Nord among their members. Each subsidiary was to have its own chief executive officer, and the chief executive officers of the subsidiaries were to be equal chief executive officers of GN Store Nord, which was to have only a small secretariat covering areas such as investor relations, tax, and law. It would not be completely possible to separate the two chief executive officers' duties and responsibilities, but it was believed that their job descriptions could reflect a very considerable degree of separation.

This structure created the problem that Toon Bouten would no longer be the chief executive officer of GN Store Nord in its entirety but only of GN Netcom and thus would have to share the leadership of GN Store Nord with the chief executive officer of GN ReSound. He recognized that he was not the right individual to lead GN ReSound but viewed the new structure as a violation of his contract. However, he was willing to continue after having renegotiated his contract and established that he would deal only with GN Store Nord's board of directors, not with the board of directors of GN Netcom.

It was also decided that GN ReSound would have a new chief executive officer. After Jesper Mailind's very aggressive public statements regarding the expected strong growth in 2016 that had failed to materialize, the market's confidence in him was weak, and the board of directors had developed doubts of its own as to whether he was the right individual to create growth. A change of chief executive officer could demonstrate that the board of directors was taking action to address the lack of growth at GN ReSound.

On the morning of Sunday, November 1, 2007, before the decision was made public, Mogens Hugo and Bill Hoover met with the fund director and head of the investment division of ATP, Bjarne Graven Larsen, at Graven's office in Hillerød. To their relief, Graven viewed the decision positively; he agreed that selling at a very low price did not make sense. He was uncertain with regard to the leadership structure with two equal chief executive officers but recognized that it made sense in this specific situation. He made it clear that he regarded this structure as temporary by remarking that it would doubtless become evident in a year or two which of the two chief executive officers was best suited to lead all of GN Store Nord.[61]

ATP's support also manifested itself in a spontaneous offer from Bjarne Graven to publish a message of support the day GN Store Nord published its quarterly report, and it was agreed that he would receive the report's storyline before composing his message of support so the two texts would be harmonious. However, he proposed that the quarterly report should clearly state that when the time was appropriate, the two companies in GN Store Nord would be independently listed on a stock exchange.[62]

When Mogens Hugo told the board about the meeting in Hillerød during a telephone meeting that afternoon, the relief was evident. At a further two meetings of the board of directors, respectively, held on Saturday, November 3, in the afternoon and on Monday, November 5, in the evening, the quarterly notice was polished ahead of its publication on November 6.[63]

With regard to GN ReSound, it announced that the board of directors had decided to cancel the sale and that the company would be operated as an independent unit alongside GN Netcom. GN Store Nord's top management team would henceforth consist of the two equal chief executive officers; Toon Bouten would continue as the chief executive officer of GN Netcom, while Jesper Mailind would resign as soon as a new chief executive officer had been found for GN ReSound. Deputy Chief Executive Officer Jens Due Olsen would leave the top management team immediately and the company later, while the new chief financial officer would be the recently hired Anders Boyer.[64]

The notice included a detailed argument for the decision to keep GN ReSound that was supported by ATP's stock administrator, Claus Wiinblad, who declared to the press that "in view of recent developments [GN Store Nord had] made the right decision." However, this did not prevent GN Store Nord's stock price from tumbling—having been given a good downward push by reduced expectations regarding the results of both GN ReSound and GN Netcom.[65]

The following day, Mogens Hugo declared at an investor conference that GN Store Nord would come back and that after a year in which to get back on its feet, GN ReSound would again be able to deliver a surplus margin of 20 percent. Many analysts were somewhat doubtful about this, but that is not to say that they found it unrealistic. "It all depends on their new CEO," said an analyst from Danske Market. "If they find the right person, it may prove to have been a good idea to have turned down the capital funds [who had bid on GN ReSound]," the analyst continued. ABM Ambro was in agreement, and there were corresponding statements from Capital Markets and Jyske Bank. "The person they get to lead ReSound will be of decisive importance for the development of GN's stock price. This will determine whether shareholders can again come to feel trust in the company," Jyske Bank believed.[66]

The Road to GN Group

CHAPTER 27

Change of chairman and other changes to the board of directors

GN Store Nord's board of directors was well aware of the importance of being able to present a new, strong chief executive officer of GN ReSound, and the board indicated that it expected to hire an individual from the hearing aid or medical technology industry. The board was also aware that it needed to hurry, both for the sake of the company itself and out of consideration for the stock market's attitude. In early December 2007, the board chairman, Mogens Hugo, stated to the press that the board had "a very fine list of candidates" and that the goal was to fill the position before Christmas.[1]

That is not how things ended up going. GN Store Nord had a candidate who was both well qualified and desired, but time went by, and in the business press and in the stock market, surprise was expressed over not hearing any news. The reason was that GN Store Nord's board of directors did not believe it could meet this individual's salary demands, and on February 1, 2008, the board decided to end the negotiations. The time pressure was great, and the board of directors, therefore, turned its atten-

tion to a kind of internal candidate: an external board member.[2]

At the previous year's general meeting, the Dutchman Mike van der Wallen had been elected to GN Store Nord's board of directors with the expectation that thanks to his long career in the electronics and cellular telephony groups Sony and Ericsson, he could help to strengthen GN Netcom's development in the cellular sector. Now, he instead became the chief executive officer of GN ReSound, which was announced in a message to the Copenhagen Stock Exchange on February 12, 2008. after a very quick negotiation process.[3]

Like Toon Bouten, Mike van der Wallen had a great deal of work to do. The sales process, which had lasted almost a year and a half, and the uncertainty in the wake of the prohibition of the sale to Phonak by the German antitrust authority left a clear mark on GN ReSound, which managed to achieve as much as 15 percent negative growth in the fourth quarter of 2007. The poor fourth quarter dramatically affected the whole annual account for 2007, which was published on February 21. For GN Store Nord in its entirety, there was a decline in revenues of 785 million kroner, to 5.981 kroner, though

GN ReSound was only responsible for a good two hundred million kroner of this amount.

In particular, it was GN Netcom's cellular telephony business that pulled GN Store Nord down; Netcom's cellular sector saw a decline in revenues of 530 million kroner, to 1.279 billion kroner, mostly because of a steep reduction of deliveries to Motorola, which had experienced a dramatic drop in sales of cellular telephones. For the same reason, the sector posted a negative surplus margin of 18.7 percent, while the other business sectors achieved positive margins—of 17.9 percent in the case of the call center and office area and of 10.2 percent in the case of GN ReSound despite the company's decline in revenues and the inclusion of GN Otometrics's modest margin of 3.6 percent. The overall group result was a deficit of 67 million kroner and no dividend for the shareholders.

The two companies' poor results were good arguments for the new leadership structure with two chief executive officers, each of which could focus fully on his own business area. However, ATP wished to go further and appoint two vice chairmen to GN Store Nord's board of directors—"crown princes," as Mogens Hugo put it—who would both have been selected to be board chairmen when GN was ready to be split up into two independent businesses.[4]

Mogens Hugo was informed of this at a meeting with ATP on February 14 at which he was also informed that the pension fund had been in contact with Marathon Asset Management in London and that the two major shareholders, who together held 16 percent of the shares, wished to see a professionalization of the board's work. A change of chairperson was also brought up, and a week later, Mogens Hugo informed his board of directors that he planned to leave the board completely at the next general meeting. Vice Chairwoman Lise Kingo had previously indicated that she would leave the board, and Mike van

der Wallen had indicated that he would leave the board as a result of his appointment to the post of chief executive officer of GN ReSound.[5]

Theoretically, then, GN needed to find three new board members, including a chairperson, by the time of the general meeting on March 11, which would not be possible. Also, a number of major shareholders, including the Danish pension funds ATP and PFA, as well as the British hedge funds Marathon Asset Management and Parvus Asset Management, wished to be involved in the selection of a new chairperson of the board of directors. ATP asked Mogens Hugo to continue in the position until this selection could take place.[6]

Per Wold-Olsen makes his first report as the chairman of the board of directors of GN Store Nord at the company's general meeting in the SAS Radisson Falconer Center in Frederiksberg on March 23, 2009. Per Wold-Olsen had spent a lifelong career in the pharmaceutical industry, first in the Norwegian company MSD (Norge) AS (1976–1991) and then in the American company Merck & Co. Inc. (1993–2006). When he was elected chairman of the board of directors of GN Store Nord in June 2008, he had become the chairman of the board of directors of the Danish pharmaceutical company Lundbeck A/S the previous year—a post he left in 2011.

On February 25, GN Store Nord sent out a stock exchange notice announcing that, in cooperation with its major shareholders, the group was seeking three new board members with competencies and experience who could be elected at an extraordinary general meeting later in the spring. Aside from Lise Kingo, the entire board of directors would continue until then, after which Mogens Hugo and Mike van der Wallen would resign to make room for the new members.[7]

It was a calm general meeting; the major shareholders had previously indicated that they would support the board of directors and its proposals, including the proposal regarding an extraordinary general meeting with elections to the board of directors on its agenda. The extraordinary general meeting was scheduled for June 16, 2008, with only that one point on its agenda. The new chairman of the board of directors was the Norwegian Per Wold-Olsen, who had spent more than thirty years working for the global American medical company Merck & Co. and been a professional board member since 2006. The two other members were the German physicist Wolfgang Reim, PhD, who had had a career at Siemens and was now an independent consultant with a particular focus on the medical industry, and the chief financial officer of DONG, Carsten Krogsgaard Thomsen. All three were unanimously elected and were now to work with the rest of the board of directors and the Dutch two-man top management team to get the crisis-impacted GN Store Nord back on its feet. The first initiatives had already been launched.[8]

"Close it, fix it, or sell it"

Early in 2007, Toon Bouten had presented his strategy plan for GN Netcom, which would involve the dismissal of up to eight hundred employees and the shutting down of independent production in Xiamen, so the company would subsequently have all its devices manufactured by sub-suppliers. Research and development remained in Xiamen, however. The steep decline in the cellular telephony sector radically changed the basic conditions on

which the plan had been based, however, and eventually, the board of directors came to discuss what was to be done with this area.

Consultants from McKinsey became involved, and eventually, three possible scenarios emerged that were characterized thus by a member of the board of directors: "Fix, sell, or terminate." In the final formulation of the board of directors, this had become "Close it, fix it, or sell it," and while all of these options were unattractive and involved great economic risks, "fix it" appeared to be the least of the evils.[9]

The goal was to make the cellular sector profitable by the end of 2009, which would require major reductions in costs, but without a simultaneous increase in revenues, this would not be possible. In the wake of the merging of the call center and cellular business areas in 2006 and in response to a proposal from Toon Bouten, the board of directors now decided to separate the two areas as much as possible and have an independent leader for the cellular sector and create two dedicated sales organizations.[10]

In the meantime, together with McKinsey, the top management team prepared an extensive cost reduction plan, which was presented to the board of directors on May 28, 2008, at the first meeting of the board of directors attended by Per Wold-Olsen, who had not yet been elected and, therefore, participated as a guest. Toon Bouten presented a program of drastic streamlining and cost reduction in the cellular telephony business called FAST, for Fast and Simplifying Turnaround. The execution of the plan, which had been prepared by Chief Financial Officer Anders Boyer, would cost 175 million kroner and involve the risk of a possible depreciation of goodwill for the cellular division amounting to 160 million kroner. If the "fix it" plan failed, however, the money would not have been completely wasted, as FAST would be part of the path to the "close it" scenario in that case.[11]

FAST consisted of a number of elements, including the reduction of operating costs by a third and of employees in the cellular sector from 380 to 250; a reduction of the number of customers by 80 percent, so only the largest customers remained; re-

In 1987, Great Northern returned to China and opened a hearing aid factory in Xiamen, where the company had opened a telegraph station 114 years earlier. The factory has since been expanded and is still manufacturing hearing aids—today for GN Hearing.

duction of the sales organization by half; reduction of the number of products by half; and a transition to a production strategy based on orders received rather than on expectations and prognoses.

However, FAST was not sufficient to save the cellular sector, which was under pressure because of a declining OEM market and lack of resources for branding of the Jabra brand as well as out-of-control logistics and IT and financial control that did not work optimally. These were all problems that needed to be addressed, and at the same time, the call center and office business area was plagued by high costs and a surplus margin that was far below its competitors.

Therefore, FAST was expanded to include all of GN Netcom and involve a restructuring and streamlining of the organization at the same time as the two business areas were separated to the greatest extent possible. It was expected that up to 250 of the total of 1,200 employees would be dismissed, and annual savings achieved were expected to amount to approximately 150 million kroner.

It was left to the chairman of the board of directors and his successor, Per Wold-Olsen, to discuss the organization of the entire program with the top management team, which resulted in a division of labor such that Toon Bouten became responsible for increasing revenues with a focus on strategy, sales, degree of surplus, and the creation of value, while Chief Financial Officer Anders Boyer became responsible for implementing the FAST program. Immediately after the general meeting on June 16, at which Per Wold-Olsen was elected chairman, the board of directors voted to implement FAST.[12]

Financial crisis and downward adjustments

While up to the time of Per Wold-Olsen's assumption of the chairmanship and the board of directors was very much occupied with the difficulties at

GN Netcom, there was greater calm around GN Re-Sound, which started the year well with the launch of the world's smallest behind-the-ear hearing aid, dot by ReSound, in three price classes. After the first quarter, the expected annual revenues were increased from 2.9 billion kroner to approximately 3 billion kroner—not much, but important as a signal of new success—and after the second quarter, there was a new upward adjustment to revenues over 3 billion kroner. The fact that GN ReSound did not see a greater increase in revenues despite the success of dot by ReSound was because of the loss of ground in the highest price category.

In contrast, GN Netcom experienced a slight decline in revenues during the second quarter, and expectations with regard to the year's revenues were, therefore, adjusted downward from over 2.7 billion to approximately 2.7 billion kroner—not much, but enough that it would be noticed by the stock market along with the other small adjustments. On the other hand, Toon Bouten expected increases in revenues of 10.5 and 8.3 percent in the third and fourth quarters, respectively, as a result of launches of new products and a positive outlook for the OEM business area. With regard to FAST, Anders Boyer could report that the program had already produced "significant progress," including the elimination of 125 jobs and savings of 90 million kroner and that there was the prospect of saving a further 140 million kroner.[13]

With its successful implementation of FAST and the prospect of two-digit growth numbers, GN Netcom seemed to be back on the right track, but a little over a month later, the situation had changed dramatically. Instead of a two-digit growth number, revenues had declined by as much as 13 percent, and the prospects for the rest of the year were not encouraging as a result of a sudden economic slump, in North America in particular, that had hit the call center and office area hard. On the other hand, FAST was proceeding faster and working better than had been expected, and at a meeting of the board of directors on September 24, as a result of the worsened market conditions, Anders Boyer announced the implementation of a more radical version of the program that would save 328 million kroner instead of the planned 250 million kroner—a measure the board of directors welcomed and wished to see carried out "as soon as possible."[14]

For the moment there was no reason to announce reduced expectations with regard to the year's operating surplus, but the chairman declared that Toon Bouten would now have to do "everything that [was] possible" to acquire new customers and push revenues upward, a position Bill Hoover supported. Bouten replied that the market was not there, after which the chairman ended the discussion by declaring that it was all well and good for FAST to follow the plan but that "the only path to prosperity is to improve the top line. Toon Bouten must use all available means to improve the top line."[15]

Only two weeks later, however, Bouten had to inform the board of directors that, owing to the financial crisis and the general macroeconomic situation, Netcom's own situation had become worse. What he was referring to was the American investment bank Lehman Brothers' declaration of bankruptcy in the middle of September, which had been the beginning of a global financial crisis, in the course of which a large number of big and small banks went bankrupt or had to be saved by government intervention. As a consequence, the world was thrown into an economic slump that turned into a serious recession in a number of places.

GN Netcom immediately felt the effects of the crisis in the form of an almost total freeze in sales to the financial sector, which represented 30 percent of the call center and office market, the whole of which was expected to shrink by 10 percent. Also, all deliveries to the second-largest cellular market, Russia, had been halted because of credit risks, and in the United States, one of the company's biggest customers, the telecommunications company Verizon, had cancelled all orders.[16]

The financial crisis and its effects and the late time of year made it difficult to increase revenues via new markets and sales channels. Nevertheless, the chairman of the board of directors repeated his demand that Toon Bouten do everything possible to boost sales during the last months of the year—and the chairman wanted to see FAST moving at maximum speed. Anders Boyer was already working on increasing the savings by a further 72 million kroner, to 400 million kroner, though this would have an effect only starting the following year. Asked what acute crisis measures could improve the numbers for 2008, Anders Boyer replied that GN Netcom had already been in a state of crisis for two years and that further cost-cutting measures in 2008 would be "very damaging to the business."[17]

In contrast to GN Netcom, GN ReSound was relatively unaffected by the financial crisis, though the customers did tend to switch to cheaper product classes. Nevertheless, there was a major unexpected negative cash flow of 84 million kroner in the second quarter, which caused Per Wold-Olsen to demand "serious and immediate measures" to get the company back on track.[18]

In September 2008, GN ReSound launched the new ReSound hearing aid, which was the world's first in-the-ear hearing aid with an external microphone and completely new so-called invisible open technology. To begin with, the device was a success, and while it did not sell as well as had been expected, it contributed to bringing customers to the retail stores and to increasing the sales of GN ReSound's other products. This in turn contributed to increasing revenues over those of the previous year by 9 percent, but nevertheless, the operating surplus amounted to only 4 million kroner—58 million kroner less than expected. A large part of the devices that had been sold were returned and contributed to an unexpectedly large negative cash flow of 52 million kroner. GN ReSound, in other words, was still spending more money than the company was earning.

The chairman of the board of directors once again emphasized that getting the cash flow under control was a top priority, and when Mike van der Wallen remarked that new systems were being implemented but that it took time to achieve momentum, the immediate and firm response was that "time [was] a luxury [the company] did not have."

The third-quarter results should be a wake-up call for all leaders, the chairman declared, insisting that "this [needed] to be managed brutally."[19]

GN ReSound's chief financial officer drew attention to the fact that ReSound would need to make some strategic and defensive investments with consequences for the cash flow situation, to which the chairman replied that "if that [was] the case, something else [would need] to be removed." Brutality in prioritizing would need to be shown, he declared, remarking that there must be some fat in the organization that could be cut. "Management needs to identify the low-hanging fruit that will give us immediate savings," he insisted. According to the minutes, he ended by saying, "Management needs to act now."[20]

Liquidity problems

The pressure put on the management of GN Netcom and GN ReSound to retain and ideally increase sales and meet expectations with regard to the year's revenues and surplus was massive. Given the developments during the third quarter of 2008, however, there was no alternative to adjusting expectations for both GN Netcom and GN ReSound downward, and at the same time, pressure on GN Store Nord's liquidity built up.

During the first half of August, the board of directors had been presented with a financial overview that had shown that the group's cash flow had been weak in 2007 and would be again in 2008—though somewhat improved. GN Store Nord still had unused credit facilities amounting to 850 million kroner, but there was a risk that Danske Bank's conditions in the form of demands with regard to the company's economy (key covenants) would be violated during the third quarter, which could mean that the credit facilities would be terminated. For this reason, it was of decisive importance that GN Store Nord keep an eye on the cash flow and the credit facilities, which was the reason for Per Wold-Olsen's sharp reaction to the negative cash flow at GN ReSound that was covered by the credit facilities.[21]

In early October, GN Store Nord had drawn a total of 1.5 billion from the credit facilities, so 500 million kroner remained unused. In the view of Chief Financial Officer Anders Boyer, the group was, therefore, not facing an immediate liquidity crisis, but the rapid worsening of the financial crisis and its possible consequences made a liquidity buffer of five hundred million kroner appear too small. Given a combination of events such as the total collapse of the financial headset market, the termination of Nordea's short-term credit facilities in the amount of 250 million kroner, product recalls, and the shutting down of the cellular sector, GN Store Nord could end up in serious economic difficulties and risk being unable to pay its creditors.[22]

While the risk that the four scenarios would materialize was low, the top management team felt that GN Store Nord should strive to increase its liquidity buffer to one billion kroner. They mentioned possibilities including a sale-and-lease-back-arrangement for the headquarters at Lautrupbjerg, the taking out of a mortgage loan secured by the headquarters, and an expansion of the engagement with Nordea. The board of directors was in agreement that the buffer should be expanded and felt that the specific proposals should be investigated; the board of directors itself made suggestions including selling GN Otometrics and renting out some of GN Store Nord's facilities.[23]

In early November, the liquidity situation had been further worsened, so only two hundred million kroner in credit facilities remained unused—a worsening by 350 million kroner in just a month. A meeting with Danske Bank a short time previously had not improved the situation, as the downward adjustment of GN Store Nord's expectations with regard to the annual result and the comments on it made by the bank's representatives gave no hope that the bank would expand the existing short-term credit facilities.[24]

At a minimum, GN Store Nord needed a cash reserve of 500 million kroner, and a buffer of a further 250 million was recommended. With the existing credit facilities of 200 million kroner and an expected negative cash flow for the rest of the year of 150 million kroner, the situation could quickly become serious. GN Store Nord needed to acquire capital reserves of 400 million to 500 million kroner as soon as possible, and the board of directors decided to take out a mortgage loan in the amount of 250 million secured by Lautrupbjerg and initiate negotiations with the bank regarding 250 million kroner in further credit facilities.[25]

Because of the cash flow situation and the shrinking liquidity, GN Store Nord had become heavily dependent on the banks, but because of the financial crisis, there was a great reluctance to take risks, and only Nordea was willing to help. Since the establishment of the Great Northern Telegraph Company in 1869, Privatbanken, as Nordea was called back then, when it was led by C. F. Tietgen, had been the company's main banking partner, and now the bank was willing to step in to secure the company's liquidity in a situation that had the potential to become life-threatening.

Before the bank took a position on the matter, however, it wanted to see a budget for 2009, which was not entirely easy to provide. Late in 2008, GN Netcom's sales declined drastically, so revenues for the call center and office business area dropped 14 percent in the fourth quarter, while cellular business dropped 32 percent. As Bill Hoover put it, the financial crisis and the market situation meant that "no budget [would] remain valid in 2009," and this was true both of GN Netcom and of GN ReSound. In contrast to GN Netcom, the latter company had had a good fourth quarter, experiencing a growth rate of 10 percent in a flat market and winning market share, but this could quickly change, so the budget for 2009 was planned to take into account "significantly worsened conditions."[26]

GN Store Nord managed to put together a budget—one that stressed significant cost reductions achieved via restructuring and streamlining of GN ReSound—that could be approved by Nordea, so Per Wold-Olsen succeeded in securing a further one-year credit facility of 200 million kroner that was dependent upon a satisfactory operating surplus in the first two quarters of the year. With this, the worst was over, and in the spring of 2009, GN Store Nord sailed into calmer waters, though the group had not yet overcome all of its difficulties.[27]

New leadership structure and new products

In his report at the general meeting on March 23, 2009, Per Wold-Olsen could look back on a year that had been both eventful and demanding. The financial crisis had hit the group hard, but the shareholders could rejoice over how the FAST program had gotten GN Netcom's expenditures under control. A corresponding program had been implemented to reduce costs at GN ReSound, which had contributed to creating a positive cash flow of 55 million kroner at the company during the last quarter of the year.

However, the many measures taken could not prevent GN Store Nord from posting a very discouraging annual account for 2008, one that showed declining revenues for the second year in a row—this year they fell to 5.264 billion kroner—and the annual result was a deficit of 56 million kroner. For the third year in a row, no dividend was paid to the shareholders, and there was no prospect of a dividend in the coming year, either, when the focus would be on increasing the cash flow and strengthening earnings via restructuring and cost reductions. On the other hand, Per Wold-Olsen declared that he was convinced that "already in 2010, GN Store Nord would once again be able to deliver a profit to its many loyal shareholders."[28]

On the board of directors and in the top management team too, changes had been made. Despite skepticism among the major shareholders with regard to the group's leadership structure with two chief executive officers, the board of directors voted in late December 2008 to continue with this system, though with the significant change that all operational decisions were moved down into GN Netcom's and GN ReSound's boards of directors, which were to have a new structure and be professionalized. Up to this point, all important decisions had been made by GN Store Nord's board of directors, while the meetings of the boards of directors of the subsidiaries had had the character of brief informational meetings. This was now to be changed such that in the future, the mother company's board of directors would discuss only general matters that were of consequence for the entire group.

The central individuals in the whole structure were GN Store Nord's chairman and vice chairman, Per Wold-Olsen and Bill Hoover, who were also the chairman and vice chairman on the boards of directors of the two subsidiaries. Therefore, these two men came to play the role of top group management with control of decisions and measures taken at all levels and close contact with the chief executive officers of GN Netcom and GN ReSound.

During the spring of 2009, GN Store Nord got completely out of its liquidity problems as the effect of FAST took full effect at GN Netcom and GN ReSound got its cash flow under control after restructuring that immediately led to two hundred dismissals. The sale of one of the three buildings at Lautrupbjerg to the Danish investment company C. W. Obel A/S gave GN Store Nord a net capital infusion of 150 million kroner, so there was no need for the expanded credit facility from Nordea.[29]

The financial crisis and its consequences continued negatively to affect GN Netcom's business; the revenues for the call center and office market declined by 22 percent, which reflected the trend for the market in general, so the company did not lose market share. In the cellular area, revenues declined by no less than 40 percent, but for the first time in four years, the company managed to post an operating result of zero—not a negative number—for the fourth quarter. The reason for this was FAST, which generally contributed to a positive cash flow at GN Netcom despite the steep decline and an operating deficit of 184 million kroner.

GN ReSound experienced a modest decline of 6 percent, which resulted in an operating surplus of 225 million kroner and an increase in the surplus margin (EBITA) to 7.5 percent. The market grew by 2 to 3 percent, and GN ReSound lost market share, though not much—GN ReSound remained the world's fourth-largest manufacturer of hearing aids, with a global market share of 14 percent.

Primarily as a result of GN Netcom's decline, GN Store Nord's revenues declined by a good 900 million kroner, to 4.279 billion kroner, which resulted in a deficit of 70 million kroner. As announced, no dividends were paid to the shareholders, but the optimization of the entire organization had laid the foundation for new growth and earnings in 2010.

At the same time, a number of new product launches showed that the group planned to remain a leader in technology and innovation. In October, the group launched the hearing aid families ReSound Live and dot² by ReSound, which used an entirely new Surround Sound by ReSound technology that used a special processor to mimic the sound streams in the natural human ear and thus created a significantly better experience of sound.

Beltone and the German company Interton also presented a series of new products, as did GN Netcom, which launched new technologies such as Noise Blackout, which filtered out background noise, and the innovative Jabra Stone, which featured an entirely new design and a portable wireless charger that functioned as a holder as well. Late in the year, GN Netcom presented two new wireless headsets that were the first to be designed for so-called unified communications, meaning they could be used with both traditional landline telephones and cellular telephones as well as with IP telephony.

The new technologies and products provided encouragement during the crisis and in the somewhat resigned mood in the wake of the prohibition of the sale of the hearing aid business by the German competition authority. While GN Store Nord got through the liquidity crisis as a result of FAST and the other restructuring and cost-saving measures, new success and growth would require new technologies and products as a prerequisite for increasing revenues and thus the bottom line.

"It is time to celebrate"

At the meeting of the board of directors back in May 2006, the head of GN ReSound's international sales division had declared that a technological leap would be required if the company was to pass its competitors and not remain a "follower." The ReSound Air had been such a product, but partly because of the closing the margin gap project, the company had not been able to follow up on this success.

At the same time, other devices with new technologies and properties had not become the successes they had been expected to become because of a lack of user-friendliness and an inappropriate design. This was true of the Metrix and the Pulse, both of which were too large. There were also technical problems with the Pulse, which was the first hearing aid on the market with rechargeable batteries but had an unstable charger.

For Per Wold-Olsen, the failure to achieve more than limited successes at best was a reflection of a lack of a market focus that would be centered on the customers and their needs and wishes rather than centered on technology. Technological development and innovation were still a necessity, but GN ReSound needed a change of mentality that would make the company more driven by the market and less driven by engineers. "We need to become better at transforming innovation into business success in a cost-effective manner," he wrote in his first annual report, the report for 2008.[30]

Nevertheless, the company would need a product with groundbreaking new technology if it was to regain its position in the market. The financial crisis had hit sales of the most expensive devices hard, and GN ReSound had suffered a greater decline than its competitors, but a development project had been launched early in 2008 that could become the game changer that would change the market and make GN ReSound an industry leader.

In contrast to its competitors, GN ReSound did not have a wireless device, as work on wireless technologies had been stopped following the decision to sell GN ReSound. Early in 2008, work on wireless technologies resumed, however, and the company's position as a "follower" was underscored in April, when its competitor Oticon presented what was called the world's first completely wireless binaural solution, where the two devices in the ears communicated with each other wirelessly—ear-to-ear—and functioned as one. The devices could also communicate with and stream from cellular telephones, portable music players, and other electronic devices, though this required a special extra router typically worn around the user's neck.

GN ReSound could have presented a similar product, but refrained from doing so, instead making a commitment to 2.4 GHz technology. GN ReSound was convinced that this technology was superior to all other technologies, partly because the hearing aids using it would be able to communicate directly and at a much greater distance with other electronic technology, including computers—up to seven meters as opposed to the competitors' fifty centimeters, which made the router worn around the neck superfluous.

There were great difficulties with working with the 2.4 GHz technology and making it usable for hearing aids; several competitors had tried in vain to do so. GN ReSound's developers were convinced that the problems could be solved, but they expected to be able to present a wireless device only in the spring of 2010—on the other hand, they believed that the device would have the potential to make 2.4 GHz technology the new industry standard.

GN ReSound knew that its competitor Starkey was also working on a wireless device without a dedicated router and with a long range. However, the American competitor was using the 900-MHz frequency band also used by pacemakers and other medical equipment. For this reason, the technology was not legal in all countries, but the 2.4 GHz technology was, and this meant all markets were open to it and users would be able to use their devices everywhere in the world.[31]

To the end, there was doubt as to whether GN ReSound's technicians would be able to solve the

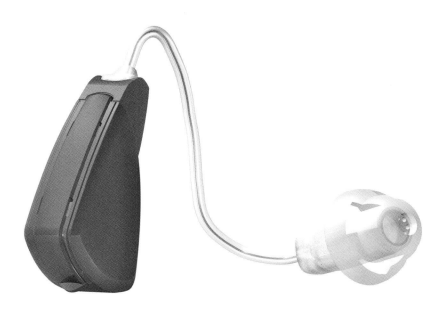

GN ReSound's first wireless hearing aid was based on 2.4 GHz technology, an achievement the company's competitors had believed impossible. The presentation of this device at the annual conference of the American Academy of Audiology, AudiologyNow, in April 2010 was therefore a triumph.

problems that had made competitors give up, but in early February 2010, the development work had reached the point at which GN ReSound was ready for the last critical test, which would indicate whether it would be possible to present the device at the American Academy of Audiology's annual conference in April, AudiologyNOW! The conference brought together audiologists from all over the world and was the largest conference of its kind; for this reason, the hearing aid producers used it to present their new products. For safety's sake, GN ReSound had a plan B involving the launching of two other devices.

But no plan B was needed. On February 16, GN ReSound's board of directors held a hastily scheduled telephone meeting, which Per Wold-Olsen began with a calming remark to the effect that this was not a crisis meeting. All the technological hindrances to presenting the world's first—and thus far only—2.4 GHz hearing aid had been eliminated, partly by using GN Netcom's Bluetooth software. Not everything had been worked out, but only "hard work remained," and the chairman could end the meeting with an almost exuberant remark. "We are back in business. It is time to celebrate."[32]

The presentation on April 15 of the GN ReSound Alera, as the wireless 2.4 GHz came to be called, was a triumph. Oticon had already presented its second-generation wireless device, which was based on the company's existing technology, and the company's chief executive officer claimed on the first day of the conference that creating a 2.4 GHz device was not possible.

The following day, GN ReSound demonstrated to an audience of five hundred that it was possible after all. For the time being, the technology worked only with external sound units, not with an ear-to-ear connection. However, this drawback was overshadowed by the general sense of a great breakthrough, and GN ReSound subsequently worked on solving the last technological problems. In June came the launch of both the GN ReSound and the corresponding Beltone True in the United States and other selected markets. Success had been achieved.

"Back on the growth track" with a new top management team

GN Netcom too put itself at the front of the pack in connection with new product categories such as headsets for unified communications, which represented a quickly growing area within the call center and office market, and this was also true of Bluetooth-based speakerphones for meetings with external participants. These were not technological innovations like GN ReSound's 2.4 GHz technology, but they sufficed to lift revenues to the point where GN Netcom adjusted expectations with regard to the annual operating result upward twice in the course of 2010. At the same time, the cellular business managed to deliver a modest positive operating result after several years of losses.

In May 2010, GN ReSound also adjusted expectations with regard to its operating result upward,

and it was a reflection of the fact that the company was back in its usual form that in the fall, it attempted—in vain, to be sure—to acquire the American company Otix Global Inc., which was the world's eighth-largest manufacturer of hearing aids and had a presence in the United States and Australia.

In general, 2010 was the necessary turning point for the whole group that GN Store Nord had worked to reach, and in the annual report for 2010, Per Wold-Olsen could report that GN Store Nord was "back on the growth track." GN Netcom had delivered organic growth of 9 percent (18 percent without Mobile's OEM activities), while GN ReSound had organic growth of 2 percent. Following a constant decline in revenues during the previous three years, GN Store Nord's total revenues increased by 5 percent. The increase in the fourth quarter, borne by the GN ReSound Alera and other new products, reached 10 percent.[33]

A further gain for GN ReSound was that the company had become a supplier to the United States Department of Veterans Affairs, a unit of the federal government whose responsibilities included providing health services to veterans and their families and survivors. The group of individuals for which the department was responsible represented approximately 20 percent of the American population, so becoming a supplier to the department was a breakthrough for GN ReSound both in terms of prestige and in terms of sales, and it contributed to a general enhancement of GN ReSound's position in the overall United States market.

The result for primary operations in 2010 was 469 million kroner, in contrast to only 8 million kroner the previous year, and for the first time in five years, GN Store Nord paid out a dividend, of 15 percent, to its shareholders. Furthermore, the company planned to send more money back to its shareholders—approximately 200 million kroner—via a buyback program in 2011.

The announcement that the company expected 6 percent organic growth for the whole group and an increase in the operating result to 675 million to 775 million kroner in 2011 was not the only indication that GN Store Nord was back on the growth track. The company declared that its strategic goal for the coming three years was that in 2013, it would exceed group revenues of 6.3 billion kroner, representing growth of more than 22 percent, and achieve nearly a doubling of the EBITA, or operating surplus margin, to approximately 19 percent, so the company would be at the level of its best competitors.[34]

The strategic goals were announced already in November 2010 in connection with the publication of the report for the third quarter and were received with some skepticism by the analysts. "Now, GN Store Nord is again setting up a financial goal that, seen objectively and neutrally, could only be considered extreme," wrote *Jyllands-Posten* in its business section. A drop in the company's stock price indicated that the stock market also saw the company's announcement as extreme, and *Jyllands-Posten* attributed this to the fact that a number of the analysts were the same ones who had been there six years previously and that "they wanted to see real improvements quarter after quarter before they dared believe in the visions."[35]

It would be up to a new top management team to realize the ambitious announcements of growth and growing surpluses that had been made by the board of directors. Toon Bouten had originally been brought to Denmark under the Special Tax Scheme for Researchers, which had made it possible for him to pay only 25 percent tax for a period of three years—and this period would end at the end of September, as would the period of validity of his contract. Also, as has been mentioned, the basis for his contract had been radically altered in relation to when he was hired as the chief executive officer of GN Store Nord in its entirety. At the meeting of the board of directors on February 25, 2009, after lengthy negotiations with Per Wold-Olsen regarding the conditions under which he might continue to work for GN Store Nord, Toon Bouten announced that for tax-related and personal reasons, he would leave GN Store Nord and return to the Netherlands when his contract expired.[36]

The individual who took on the position of new chief executive officer of GN Netcom was the Danish

Apple's iconic leader Steve Jobs presents the new iPhone at the Mac World Conference and Expo in San Francisco on January 9, 2007. The iPhone revolutionized the global cellular telephone market and, together with other so-called smartphones, had soon largely pushed aside the ordinary cellular telephones. This negatively affected GN Netcom, which provided earphones to some of the big manufacturers of cellular telephones, but in 2012, GN ReSound began cooperating with Apple in connection with the development of Made for iPhone hearing aids based on GN ReSound's 2.4 GHz technology. The first products were launched the following year.

engineer Mogens Elsberg, who had worked at IBM and Microsoft and been the chief executive officer of Aston Business Solutions. He started work at Lautrupbjerg on August 10, 2009, and just over half a year later, GN ReSound too got a new chief executive officer in the wake of increasing dissatisfaction on the board of directors with the lack of growth at the company. In late March 2010, it was announced that Mike van der Wallen was resigning and that his replacement was the Norwegian physician Lars Viksmoen, who had held leading positions at the American medical company Merck & Co. for eighteen years and been the chief executive officer of a Norwegian biotech company for four years.[37]

2.4 GHz technology and unified communications

The goals of the strategy plan were fully achieved by an annual account for 2013 that showed revenues of 6.791 billion kroner, which corresponded to total growth for the period 2011–2013 of a good 32 percent, while the operating surplus was 1,284 million kroner, which corresponded to an EBITA margin of 18.9. GN ReSound and GN Netcom contributed equally to the growth, achieving revenues for 2013 of 4.179,000 kroner and 2.612 million kroner, respectively, which corresponded to respective growth rates for the two companies of a good 32 percent over the three years.

Quite extraordinarily, GN ReSound had succeeded in winning market share fourteen quarters in a row, with the 2.4 GHz technology as the decisive engine of growth, one whose full effect was seen in 2011 thanks to the ReSound Alera hearing aid and its American parallel Beltone True. A special model was intended for hearing aid users who were suffering from tinnitus. This attracted great interest from the United States Department of Veterans Affairs which had many clients who had worked in environments in which they had been subjected to high levels of noise. The delivery of the Alera series was supported by a growing assortment of various accessories, including wireless streamers for television, radio and music systems, and cellular telephones.

GN ReSound followed up on this success in 2012, when the company could present what was called the second generation of devices with 2.4 GHz technology with the respective launches of the hearing aid ReSound Verso and its parallel device, the Beltone First. Once again, GN ReSound achieved "the impossible," this time by creating an ear-to-ear connection using 2.4 GHz technology, so the two hearing aids functioned as one. Also, the ReSound Ver-

so was simultaneously launched in all price classes with devices in no fewer than fifteen different forms designed respectively for behind-the-ear devices, in-the-ear devices, etc.

GN ReSound was still alone in using the 2.4 GHz technology, but the conviction of the company and GN Store Nord in its entirety that it was superior to other technologies and represented the future of the industry was supported by the conclusion of two cooperative agreements. One of these was a development and licensing contract concluded in the spring of 2011 with the Australian company Cochlear Ltd., which was—and is—the leading supplier of advanced implants and bone-mounted hearing solutions for severely hearing-impaired or deaf individuals and wished to use GN ReSound's 2.4 GHz technology.

The other agreement was concluded in 2012 with the American IT company Apple, which over the years had launched groundbreaking products such as the Macintosh computer, the iPod music player, and, in 2007, the iPhone, which had revolutionized the cellular telephony sector. Apple had developed a menu system for the iPhone that made it possible for blind and sight-impaired individuals to have individual menu items read aloud—now the company wanted to develop a product that would help the hearing-impaired.

Apple contacted the leading manufacturers of hearing aids regarding the possibility of cooperating to create a direct connection between Apple's products and hearing aids. Apple ended up working closely with GN ReSound, which, with its 2.4 GHz technology, already had a suitable technology in its hearing aids, and on June 11, 2012 Apple announced that their new operating system, iOS 6, would support the use of Made for iPhone hearing aids based on the 2.4 GHz technology.

Early in 2013, GN ReSound presented the first Made for iPhone products, the ReSound Unite Phone Clip and the ReSound Control app, and in the fall of that year the first Made for iPhone hearing aids, which bore the name ReSound LiNX, were presented. A limited number of devices were presented as an element of a market test that received

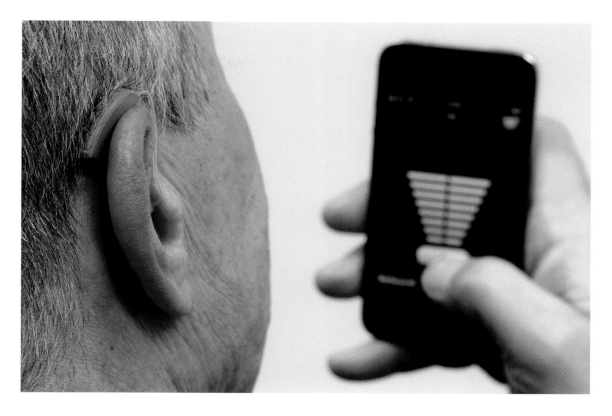

The hearing aid ReSound LiNX was the world's first Made for iPhone hearing aid. It was launched in the fall of 2013.

a positive response, and subsequently, the company exerted maximum efforts to realize a full-scale launch in the first quarter of 2014, when the corresponding Beltone First was also to be released.

GN Netcom too was driven by constant innovation, but this innovation was not characterized by technological breakthroughs like those at GN ReSound. The decisive engine of growth was unified communications, or UC, which was rapidly becoming more widespread globally, at the same time as GN Netcom marketed new products almost constantly. The development in question meant that the company was now really beginning to acquire very major customers as global companies chose the company as their preferred supplier of total solutions in unified communications. At the end of 2011, GN Netcom had ninety-nine of the world's largest one hundred companies as its customers;

ten of these companies accounted for 23 percent of total revenues, while the largest single customer accounted for approximately 6 percent. The company's position was further strengthened by respective partnerships concluded first with Cisco and then with Microsoft, and in 2013, GN Netcom was the preferred supplier to all of the leading providers of networks and complete UC solutions.

The largest business area was call centers and offices, which accounted for approximately 60 percent of revenues for 2013, while the cellular area accounted for approximately 40 percent. The Jabra brand alone accounted for all revenues, including in the cellular area, as the company had decided to abandon the volatile OEM business with its low surplus margins.

Dragged-out arbitration proceedings with cash yield

GN Store Nord's success benefited the shareholders in the form of annual increases in the dividend, from 15 percent in 2010 to 18 percent in 2013. In addition, the company repurchased shares for a total of 3.195 million kroner during the period 2010–2013—including a repurchase for no less than 1.614 million kroner in 2012—but there were other reasons for this than the company's success.

Since 2001, GN Store Nord had been involved in arbitration proceedings related to the company's involvement with the fiber optic land cable system in Poland the company had established in the first half of the 1990s in cooperation with Telecom Danmark. According to the agreement with the Poles, the two Danish companies were to receive 14.8 percent of the traffic revenues from the cable connection during the years 1994–2004, but after a few years, disagreements arose with regard to the calculation of the volume of traffic and the revenues. In 1999, the Poles unilaterally began reducing their payments to the Danish consortium, making reference to "errors in the calculations" but showing no willingness to provide details regarding the basis for this claim.[38]

In June 2001, the Danish consortium brought the matter before the Austrian court of arbitration, which, in September 2010, ordered the Poles to pay 2.9 billion kroner for the period up to 2005. GN Store Nord and Telecom Danmark subsequently presented a further demand, for the payment of 2.4 billion kroner for the remaining years through 2009, but the Polish party in the dispute, the telecommunications company TPSA, refused after the nine-year trial to recognize the decision made by the court of arbitration and refused to pay.

TPSA was a subsidiary of France Telecom, which was partly owned by the French government, and at the same time as the Danish consortium began so-called enforcement proceedings against TPSA in Poland, the Netherlands, the United Kingdom, and Germany, the Danes attempted to get the matter raised via diplomatic channels and in the political systems of Poland, Austria, France, and the EU. The Danes also launched a campaign in the international press, which greatly irritated the Poles and the French, who publicly complained of the Danes' "harmful lobbying activity," but in the end, the Poles and the French had had enough and sought a negotiated settlement.

On January 12, 2012, the parties concluded an agreement according to which TPSA would pay a total of 550 million euros, of which GN Store Nord received 75 percent, corresponding to approximately 3.1 billion kroner. After tax and costs, the net yield amounted to approximately 2.5 billion kroner, 1.2 billion kroner of which was used to pay off GN Store Nord's entire debt, while 1.3 billion kroner were sent to the shareholders via the repurchasing of shares. After the matter had been concluded, the telegraph company—the GN Store Nord group's original company—was shut down, the last share in the Black Sea cable between Russia and the Republic of Georgia having been shut down some years earlier.[39]

Innovation and growth

With the paying off of the group's debt, GN Store Nord acquired a new and strong financial basis for investments in continuing growth. In the middle of November 2013, the company announced a new strategy plan featuring new ambitious goals for both growth and surplus margins. The plan was called "Innovation and Growth," which indicated a continuation of the developments of the previous years, and indeed the basis of this plan was the idea that the company had found "a formula that [worked]" and that what was now the goal was to improve this formula to benefit the shareholders. In connection with this announcement, Per Wold-Olsen emphasized the importance of GN Store Nord's *pipeline*—a term from the medical industry that refers to coming products that are in various stages of development and on their way to being launched. The message was that the company could not rest on its laurels and that what was most important was not the existing products but the ones that were on the way, both in the short term and in the long term.[40]

The company needed to constantly be able to introduce new and innovative products, and in this connection, the 2.4 GHz and Made for iPhone technology became the crucial platform for GN ReSound, which delivered a constant stream of hearing aids with new functions and characteristics that were aimed at new groups of customers. There was an open playing field in this regard, as none of the company's competitors was using the new technology except for Starkey, which launched a Made for iPhone device in the spring of 2014.

With the launch of the Alera hearing aid and the 2.4 GHz technology in 2010, Per Wold-Olsen had in fact warned that no more than two years would pass before competitors would be on the heels of GN ReSound. It was indeed common in the hearing aid industry that technological innovations and gains were quickly adopted by competitors, usually in connection with supplementary qualities so the company in question could be the first to present something new. However, it is difficult to use 2.4 GHz technology in connection with hearing aids particularly in the smallest in-the-ear devices that are preferred by many users. For this reason, about six years passed before, in the fall of 2016, Oticon and Widex followed suit with their first generation of devices using 2.4 GHz technology, while Sivantos—previously Siemens Hearing—presented its first such device in the spring of 2017 and Sonova later the same year.

The hesitation of the company's competitors gave GN ReSound freedom to cement its leading position and indeed to increase its lead via the continued development and dissemination of 2.4 GHz technology. This began in 2014 with the respective launches of the ReSound LiNX and the corresponding Beltone First, which featured direct streaming from the iPhone, iPad, and iPod Touch, all of which devices the user could use to regulate his or her hearing aid via an app. In September, the company followed up with the devices ReSound Enzo and Beltone Boost, which used the same technology and were intended for individuals who had suffered great or very great loss of hearing as well as the ReSound Up Smart for children and the ReSound LiNX for individuals with tinnitus.

Early in 2015, apps for mobile phones using the Android operating system were added—to begin with the Samsung Galaxy S5 and later in the year three further Samsung Galaxy models. In March came the ReSound LiNX² devices, which were upgrades to the first Made for iPhone devices and became the company's fastest selling hearing aids to date, and the corresponding Beltone Legend devices. In August of the same year, the company launched the ReSound Enzo², which featured similar upgrades for individuals with great or very great hearing loss, and in September, the devices ReSound Enya and Beltone Ally followed in the lowest price class.

In 2016 a more modest set of innovations was presented. In March, sales of the ReSound Enzo² were expanded to include the whole world, and the same month the device, together with the ReSound LiNX, was presented in three camouflage designs intended for the United States Department of Veterans Affairs, where the company achieved a market share of 20 percent. On the same year, Oticon and Widex presented their first 2.4 GHz devices, while GN ReSound announced that in the new year, it would present what it called the fifth generation of devices using 2.4 GHz technology, which had now really become the technological platform for a transformation of the global hearing aid industry.

Two thousand sixteen was also the year in which the manufacturer of audiological diagnostic equipment GN Otometrics was sold off, effective at the end of the year, to Natus Medical, a company with which GN ReSound simultaneously entered into a strategic partnership. The cooperation in question included the development and marketing of the world's first 3D ear scanner, the Otoscan, on which GN Otometrics had been working for a number of years.

During the same period, GN Netcom launched a steady stream of Jabra products, some of which were aimed at a new growth area in mobile communications, so-called sport audio, a term that covered headsets for sports and training. GN Netcom entered this area in 2013 with the Jabra Sport Wireless headset, which was designed for use by runners, and the original device was soon followed by an updated version as well as the Jabra Sport Rox.

In 2014, the company launched the Jabra Sport Pulse Wireless, which, when used with the Jabra Sport Life app, made possible real-time coaching and measurement of the pulse via the ear, while a following updated device featured automatic measurement of the runner's oxygen consumption. The following year, the assortment was expanded to include the Jabra Sport Coach Wireless, which enabled coaching for cross training, and in 2016, the absolute top-of-the-line model Jabra Elite Sport was released.

Sport Audio was a business area experiencing strong growth, but it could not completely compensate for the decline in the traditional market for Bluetooth mono headset, so after some years of stagnation, the mobile area experienced negative growth in 2016. On the other hand, the call center and office area continued its strong growth on the basis of a number of new products and the cooperation with Cisco, Microsoft, and the other leading providers of unified communications solutions.

In 2016, GN Netcom achieved total revenues of just under 3.495 billion kroner, which represented growth of just under 34 percent since 2013, while the EBITA margin was 17.1 percent. GN ReSound, not including GN Otometrics, had revenues for 2016 of 5.156 million kroner, which represented total growth since 2013 of almost 42 percent, while the

GN's headquarters in Ballerup after the launch of a new branding strategy in the spring of 2016, when the group began calling itself GN.

FROM INDUSTRIAL CONGLOMERATE TO THE NEW GN

EBITA margin was 20.6 percent. For GN Store Nord as a whole, revenues for 2016 amounted to 8.651 kroner, and the EBITA margin was 18.3 percent.

GN Group, GN Hearing, and GN Audio

GN ReSound and GN Netcom as well as the entire GN Store Nord concern appeared to have been transformed since the crisis years just before 2010, and in a deeper historical perspective too, there was now a hitherto unseen development dynamic and an entirely new ability to create growth and surpluses. The basis of the company's business activity and the product groups, hearing aids and headsets, were the same as before the crisis, but GN Store Nord was nevertheless a transformed company.

This was emphasized by the introduction of a new basic branding platform in May 2016, one that presented insight into the human ear, work with the processing of sound, and wireless technologies as the group's common core competencies. At the same time, the conglomerate changed its name to GN Group, or just GN, while GN ReSound's name was changed to GN Hearing and GN Netcom's to GN Audio. The various product brands were also emphasized: the flagships ReSound and Jabra as well as Beltone and Interton in the hearing aid area and BlueParrott in the headset area—the latter brand having been a GN Store Nord brand since the group's acquisition of the American headset manufacturer VXi Corporation.

The group's logo and overall visual design were also altered in connection with the creation of the new branding platform, the overall goal of which was to create a better and more direct connection between the group's product brands and their relationship with GN and GN's technologies. This was intended to clarify the synergies across the two business areas and why it made sense to have them both under a single roof.

Actually, the new branding strategy dovetailed with the presentation of "the new GN" and the brand strategy presenting GN Store Nord as a sin-

In March 2015, René Svendsen-Tune was appointed managing director of GN Netcom after having been on GN's board of directors for eight years. René Svendsen-Tune came from an executive position in Nokia Networks where he had been responsible for the European and Latin American markets. He implemented a new strategy for the headset business by focusing on three product series for office use, leisure, and customer service centers, respectively, leading to a significant increase in growth.

gle company back in 2001, when the core idea had been precisely to present the common technologies as a basis for synergies among the four business areas. Back then, however, the point of departure had been a desire quickly to create a new group profile in the wake of the sale of NetTest, and the only result had been the merging of a number of internal group functions that were subsequently split up in connection with the failed sale of GN ReSound.

This time, the new branding strategy was based on an earlier process involving the exploitation and realization of synergies based in particular on 2.4 GHz technology, which, with GN ReSound's wireless hearing aids, had become a common technological platform for both business areas and could now to a much greater extent than previously exploit each other's development work in the area of sound processing as well as enjoying marketing advantages.

In September 2016, the introduction of the new branding platform was followed up by a new group strategy for the years up to 2019 under the slogan "Hear more, do more, be more." Once again, there were ambitious financial goals for organic growth and EBITA margins, but no changes to the overall strategy were announced—on the contrary, the company wanted to "strengthen GN's winning formula."[41]

It was clear that the formula had not lost its effect in April 2017, when the hearing aid ReSound LiNX 3D and the corresponding Beltone Trust were released. As the name of the ReSound device suggests, these devices offered improved spatial reproduction of sound and new possibilities with regard to adjusting individual devices. The devices contributed to organic growth in 2017; GN Hearing reached revenues of 5.615 million kroner and an EBITA margin of 20.5 percent. While GN Audio did not deliver a similar technological innovation, the company did produce a series of new products that contributed to organic growth of 10 percent, to revenues of 3.970 million kroner, and an EBITA margin of 18.2 percent. At the same time, GN increased revenues by nearly 1 billion kroner, to just over 9.5

billion kroner, in 2017, while the EBITA margin remained at the level of 18.2 percent.

Continued growth, new products— and a possible third pillar

This development continued unabated in 2018, when GN Audio opened the year with a completely new product series, the Jabra Elite series, which featured three new in-the-ear earphones. In August, the company launched a special Copper Black version of the Elite Active 65t called the Amazon Edition Color. This version could only be purchased through Amazon.com, and it made possible the use of Amazon's voice assistant, Alexa 2, and provided access to Amazon Music, Audible, and Prime Video.

The Elite series was an element of a completely new product strategy in which the previous frequent and unfocused launches of many new products were replaced by three well-defined series, or families, as they were called: Jabra Evolve for office use, Jabra Elite for recreational use, and Jabra Engage for call centers. The purpose of this strategy was to create a clearer product profile so customers could get a better overview of the product portfolio; the series were developed using common technological platforms, which made frequent product launches more cost-effective.

Also in August, GN Hearing launched a new top-class product with a completely new chipset, the ReSound LiNX Quattro and the corresponding Beltone Amaze, which, as the first hearing aid to do so, established a completely new top-class category called Premium-Plus for those who desired "the best of the best." The LiNX Quattro products were based on a new chip platform offering better sound quality and the option of having rechargeable batteries with wireless charging in a charging station included with the device. The same month, the company entered into a cooperative agreement with Google regarding the development of technology that would enable direct streaming to this new top-class product from all Android devices.[42]

Two thousand eighteen was also the year in which new products were introduced that were uncategorized in the sense that they belonged neither in GN Hearing's nor in GN Audio's product assortment but had their own product brand, FalCom, which was organizationally placed under GN Hearing. FalCom was an innovation in the sense that this was the first time a focused combination of technologies and competencies from both GN Hearing and GN Audio had resulted in the development of a completely new product group.

FalCom manufactured headsets and communications solutions for defense and security forces and others who needed to protect their hearing in situations involving extreme levels of noise and at the same time needed to be able to identify important sources of sound 360 degrees around the users. The target group was soldiers and security forces in particular, as well as firefighters and other emergency response personnel who operated in extreme situations involving high levels of noise and needed both to protect their hearing and have access to communication across 360 degrees.

The global market for the new products was valued at 300 billion kroner, but for GN, this was a completely new business area with established suppliers, and the company, therefore, did not have great immediate expectations with regard to it. The chief executive officer of GN Hearing nevertheless indicated that GN saw perspectives in the new business area when he said to Ritzau Finans, a unit of the news agency Ritzaus Bureau, that "this definitely has the potential to become a third pillar of our business activities, but that would require the products we have developed to be able to acquire the market share we both hope and believe they can."[43]

For the time being, however, it was the two established pillars that were driving business, with GN Audio in the driver's seat in the wake of the implementation of the new product strategy. During the first quarter of 2018, the headset business achieved organic growth of 16 percent, and the tempo was increased in the second quarter with organic growth of 19 percent, a level not previously seen. This led to no fewer than three upward adjustments of the expected organic growth for the whole year, from the originally predicted 7 percent to 16 to 19 percent, an expectation that was maintained after the third quarter, in which GN Audio had achieved organic growth of 20 percent. Expectations with regard to the EBITA margin were adjusted upward in June, from over 18 percent to over 19 percent.

While GN Audio delivered results that far exceeded expectations, GN Hearing's development was more stable; the company had organic growth of 5 to 6 percent for the first three quarters, while the expectation for the whole year was that there would be organic growth of more than 6 percent. Similarly, the EBITA margin was stable at around 19.3 percent for the first three quarters, while the expectation for the whole year was that there would be an EBITA margin of more than 20 percent. As several analysts noted, GN Hearing would, therefore, have to "get moving" in the last quarter of the year if the expectations regarding 2018 were to be met.[44]

The acting chief executive officer of GN Hearing, Marcus Desimoni, was confident. The new Premium-Plus device, the ReSound LiNX Quattro, had only made a moderate contribution to growth in the third quarter because of its late launch, but it had been very positively received both by audiologists and by users. At the same time, there was still strong demand for the other top-class product, the ReSound LiNX 3D, so GN Hearing felt "very comfortable" about being able to increase growth further. According to Marcus Desimoni, the company was, therefore, "well on its way to achieving its goals for 2018."[45]

GN 150 Years: From diplomacy to steady innovation and growth

GN Store Nord's annual report for 2018 was historic, as it was the 150th annual report since the founding of the Great Northern Telegraph Company in 1869. Another reason for this annual report to be considered historic is that it was the tenth annual report after the major changes to the board of directors that had followed the failed sale of the hearing aid business, after which GN had set course for a turnaround.

Since then, things had gone only one way, with constant and accelerating growth, until revenues for 2018 represented more than a doubling of those for the previous year, reaching 10.6 billion kroner, and GN achieved an EBITA margin of 19 percent. Once again, both business areas contributed to the success. With a strong performance in the last quarter of the year, GN Hearing lived up to its expectations of annual organic growth of 7 percent, revenues of 5.8 billion kroner, and an EBITA margin of 20.5 percent, and things went even better for GN Audio, which posted organic growth of no less than 21 percent, revenues of 4.8 billion kroner, and an EBITA margin of 18.4 percent. By itself, then, each of the two business areas was bigger than the entire group had been in 2009, and at the same time, the size difference was being equalized so that with its current level of growth, GN Audio would soon reach GN Hearing's level of revenues.

One hundred and fifty years after it was founded, GN found itself at the peak of a long period of strong growth—growth that appears likely to continue. In a deeper historic perspective, however, the group can also rejoice over having found itself following a long and sometimes turbulent transition from a classical telegraph company to an innovative and successful electronics company. This was a transition that was begun with the establishment of Storno seventy years previously but was not completed until the turnaround that was executed after the aborted sale of GN ReSound during the years 2006 and 2007.

Neither C. F. Tietgen nor the other founders of the Great Northern Telegraph Company would have been able to imagine that the company that was to realize Tietgen's visions of an international Danish telegraph company with connections with East Asia and North America would develop into today's GN. Nevertheless, this is how things have gone after 150 years of constant global and dramatic changes, not only in the areas of technology, economics, and politics but also in all aspects of social life.

Companies change over time—this is a prerequisite for their survival. It is unusual, however, for companies to reach the age of 150 years and still be in the best of health—and it is even more unusual for them to change as radically along the way as Tietgen's original telegraph company has changed. The world of today is very different from the world as it existed when Great Northern was founded, and the company has not only changed along with social changes; through the years, it has also made its mark on developments and participated in creating the world of today.

The foundation of the Great Northern Telegraph Company on June 1, 1869, was a grand and daring project—not least because the company was the first to challenge the many British actors in the telegraphy sector and their monopoly on undersea telegraph connections. The laying of the cable in East Asia that followed in 1870 and 1871 bordered on the foolhardy and was an extremely risky project with the potential for enormous economic losses.

The British attempted to sabotage the cable project but had to give up trying to bend the obstinate Danish company to their will. Great Northern based its position on the trans-Siberian connection and thus on the support of Russia, one of the great powers. On the other hand, the Danes had to recognize that there were limits to their freedom to act as they wished, as the British telegraphy interests were closely connected with the British imperium, which Great Northern would not be able to defy in the long run.

It was in the midst of these geopolitical tensions that Great Northern established itself as an important international telegraph company from a little neutral country; the regional political and sometimes military conflicts in East Asia were also significant in this connection. Denmark became a nexus of international telegraphy, and in a global perspective, the cables laid by Great Northern in East Asia contributed to connecting China and Japan telegraphically with Europe and the rest of the world.

In China, Great Northern made a special and significant contribution to the country's development when the company developed a Chinese telegraph code that made it possible to send telegrams in Chinese and subsequently participated in the construction of a national telegraph system.

With its two cable systems in Northern Europe and East Asia, which were connected by the strategically important trans-Siberian connection, Great Northern played an important role in the construction of the global communications network of undersea telegraph cables that constituted a decisive prerequisite for the first wave of globalization that picked up speed during the second half of the nineteenth century.

Great Northern did not succeed in realizing Tietgen's vision of a cable connection between Europe and the North America, though the cable laid to Iceland in 1906 did take the company part of the way. During the period 1902–1905, on the other hand, the company participated in creating the last significant link in the so-called Victorian Internet when it played a role in the laying of the United States' first—and only—cable connection across the Pacific Ocean. The company's system subsequently stretched all the way around the northern hemisphere with the exception of the Atlantic Ocean, though the company's involvement with the Pacific cable was kept secret for political reasons.

The first years of the twentieth century saw the culmination of Great Northern's time of greatness as an international telegraph company, and the company was subsequently put under increasing pressure that finally brought it to its knees. The turning point came with the First World War, which changed the geopolitical map and brought the Bolsheviks to power in Russia in 1917, while Japan strengthened its position as a major industrial and military power with expansionist ambitions.

The Russian Civil War interrupted the trans-Siberian connection, but in 1921, Great Northern made world history when, as the first foreign company to do so, it secured a concession from the Soviet government, which allowed it to operate the trans-Siberian connection. Things went differently in Japan, which, despite Denmark's smallness and neutral status, wished to free itself from the company that Japan believed was violating the country's sovereignty and honor. However, Great Northern managed to withstand the Japanese pressure thanks to the company's agreements and the tensions between China and Japan.

The biggest threat to the company, however, was the wireless telegraph, which made great gains after the First World War and could not be stopped by means of negotiations and diplomatic maneuvers. Not only Great Northern but all cable companies increasingly lost telegram revenues, and after mergers between large cable and wireless companies in the United Kingdom and the United States, Great Northern alone remained without an alliance partner.

The world economic crisis of the 1930s led to further major declines in telegram revenues, and ultimately, conventional telegraphy became unprofitable. For the first time ever, Great Northern's board of directors discussed the possibility of dissolving the company, which at the same time was being put under increasing pressure in the Soviet Union as the Stalinist terror increased.

In East Asia, the company's situation worsened in the wake of Japan's major military attack on China in 1937. Great Northern had its back to the wall but fought with determination to hold its positions. The company was forced to remove all Danish personnel from the Soviet Union, however, and in Japan, the company was unable to prevent its landing permit from being terminated.

With the German occupation of Denmark in April 1940, Great Northern's connection with London was interrupted, and after Germany invaded the Soviet Union in June 1941, the headquarters at Kongens Nytorv lost their connection with all of the company's stations. Telegraphy activity stopped, and the company sought to secure its continued existence by investing in Danish stocks and property.

When peace came in 1945, Great Northern's international telegraphy system lay in ruins. All of the company's cables had been cut, and in Japan, the company lacked a landing permit, while China was heading into a civil war. The prospects for the future were bleak, and a group of Danish shareholders demanded that the company be dissolved and its assets distributed among the shareholders.

The company's leadership did not give up, however, and despite the beginning of the Cold War, the company managed to reestablish its cable connections with the United Kingdom and the Soviet Union. The connection with Japan was also reestablished, and the trans-Siberian connection was reopened, but despite long and determined efforts to avoid this, the company had to give up its activities in China, where the foundation of the company's age of greatness had once been laid.

In Europe, undersea telegraphy became very predominantly the domain of national governments, and while Great Northern did succeed in laying a coaxial cable between Denmark and England in 1950, it was clear that telegraphy activity did not represent the future of the company. A repositioning was necessary—and more than that. Great Northern would need to reinvent itself and establish itself in an entirely different industry if the company was to survive in the long run.

Already before the war, Great Northern had taken its first small steps into manufacturing activity with its acquisition of a significant stake in the battery company Hellesens A/S in 1939. However, it was the establishment of the radio electronics company Storno in the spring of 1947 that put the company on course toward becoming the high-tech GN of today. This was a radical change of course, as Great Northern lacked experience with industrial activity, and the technology and products in question were of a new type and needed to be developed before they could be sold in a market that did not yet exist.

As Bent Suenson had once put it, Great Northern's position in international telegraphy had been based on the ability to carry out "diplomacy on a technological basis." Now, new and very different abilities would be demanded of the nearly eighty-year-old company.

From the beginning, Storno was a technological leader in the development of car radio telephone systems, which became the company's core business area. At a global level too, the company succeeded in competing, as it was the first in the world to present devices offering two-way speech and selective calls. The first customers were taxi companies, power plant administrators, and others who needed to have their own car radio networks. When the first public car telephone service opened in Copenhagen in 1950, it used technology from Storno.

In the course of the 1950s, Storno established itself in the export markets, primarily in Europe but eventually also on other continents. This occurred in sharp competition with foreign companies, but the company managed to remain at the front of the pack technologically.

During the economic upswing of the 1960s, Storno greatly increased its growth, and the company established subsidiaries in Germany, Sweden, and the United Kingdom. The company had developed into a great Danish industrial adventure, and in 1963, when Denmark's Postal and Telegraphy Directorate began the construction of a nationwide car radio network, it was with equipment from Storno, which also provided 90 percent of the car telephones. The same year, the company presented the world's first transistor-based portable telephone with duplex technology that would fit in a jacket pocket—in fact a very early mobile telephone or cellular telephone.

Despite its technological leadership and rapidly growing revenues, however, Storno never managed to achieve profitable operations, and Great Northern constantly had to infuse the company with capital. In 1968, however, this was to come to an end when the company was split off from Great Northern as an independent limited company. The point of departure for this decision was that with 30 percent of the European market, 1,500 employees, and annual revenues of 100 million kroner and as the world's fourth-largest manufacturer of car telephones, Storno should be able to stand on its own two feet.

Storno was no longer Great Northern's only industrial company, as the division for the production of telegraphy apparatuses had begun to manufacture a newly developed teleprinter. In 1968, the division merged with the telephone factory Automatic to become a new company, GNT Automatic, which became a subsidiary of Great Northern. The battery manufacturer Hellesens too became a subsidiary in 1968, Great Northern having acquired 97 percent of the company's share capital over the years.

On June 1, 1969, when Great Northern celebrated its hundredth anniversary, it was as Denmark's second-largest electronics group, with revenues of approximately 320 million kroner. Of this amount, the industrial companies contributed a total of 280 million kroner, while just under 28 million kroner came from the telecommunications activities and the rest from real estate and capital investments. The transformation of Great Northern from a classic telegraph company into a modern industrial group appeared to have been successfully realized.

However, the industrial companies made only a modest contribution to Great Northern's surpluses, and the group's ability to pay out dividends to its shareholders was largely because of the fact that the group had not forgotten the art of diplomacy but acquired contracts for the Scotice-Icecan cables that had been opened in the early 1960s. Subsequently, a diplomatic triangle drama involving the company, the Soviet Union, and Japan played out over several years and ultimately resulted in a modernization of the Far Eastern cable system, which opened in 1969. Measured in revenues, the continuing telegraphy activity was of modest importance, but in reality, it was from this activity and from the company's properties that the surpluses came. The industrial companies presented only modest surpluses—and GNT Automatic in fact presented a significant deficit.

This did not change during the following years, when the three industrial companies achieved only small surpluses or even posted deficits, while the telegraphy activity remained a stable source of income that, along with capital investments and property, secured the company's surpluses.

At GNT Automatic, the main problem was the teleprinter, the production of which was discontinued in 1973. In the case of Hellesens, the trend was turned around in 1975 by means of a lucrative merger agreement with the Swedish company Tudor. In contrast, there appeared to be no way out for Storno, which, despite constantly increasing revenues, was not able to create profitable operations. On the contrary—again and again, Great Northern had to provide loans and infusions of capital of a size that ultimately threatened the mother company's own liquidity. In May 1974, Great Northern's board of directors, therefore, made the difficult decision to sell Storno, and the company was sold to the American company General Electric the following year.

With the imminent shutdown of the teleprinter production, both of Great Northern's own industrial projects would have been discontinued, and all that would remain would be the acquired companies Hellesens and GNT Automatic. As a consequence, Great Northern's annual revenues for 1976 decreased to just over 560 million kroner, but new revenues would soon be secured by new acquisitions.

In 1973, Great Northern took over the wholesaler of electrical articles Havemanns Eftf., and in 1975, the electronic data processing company Tiger Data became a subsidiary. In 1977, Great Northern acquired the hearing aid manufacturer Danavox, and the following year, Great Northern acquired first ELMI, which manufactured measurement equipment for the telecommunications industry, and then the electrical installations company LK-NES. These acquisitions were not the result of a focused strategy, apart from a desire to increase revenues—and indeed revenues passed 1.4 billion kroner in 1979.

In contrast, there were problems with achieving profitable operations. Things went very wrong in 1980, when most of the group's companies—exceptions being ELMI and GNT Automatic—posted large deficits despite increased group revenues of 1.6 billion kroner. In contrast, the telecommunications business generated a large surplus and, together with yields from stocks and bonds and property, secured a modest overall surplus of 5 million kroner despite the weak results at the industrial companies.

During the following years, Great Northern achieved only weak growth, and in 1982, the wholesaler Havemanns Eftf. was sold. On the other hand, a different business area was strengthened when Tiger Data acquired half of the Computerland chain as the result of a merger. In 1984, parallel to this development, Great Northern took over part of the bankrupt data company Chr. Rovsing A/S and placed its activities in a newly founded company, Netcom A/S. The goal of this was to secure a place for Great Northern in the rapidly growing data sector.

In the spring of 1986, Great Northern changed its name to GN Store Nord to give the various activities a common brand, and at the same time, the trend had been reversed and most of the subsidiaries were producing surpluses. A striking exception was the battery manufacturer Hellesens, which was sold after several years of unprofitable operations. Things went completely wrong for the newly established Netcom, and efforts to become a part of the Danish data sector were abandoned.

The hearing aid manufacturer GN Danavox was also unable to create surpluses, and after several years of poor results, GN Store Nord's board of directors was losing its patience. The company was given another chance, however, as a product line comprising headsets was split off, and the activities in question were shifted to GN Netcom, which thus took on new life. The expectation was that the two separate business areas could develop into profitable businesses under respective focused leadership.

That is not how things went—at least not right away. In general, 1986 and 1987 were bad years for GN Store Nord, which lost half a billion kroner in revenues and in 1987 posted a record deficit of 153 million kroner. The decline was due in part to international deregulation and liberalization of markets, which, in combination with digital developments, undermined several of the subsidiaries' business areas.

When the company got a new leadership team in the spring of 1987, the team's main task was to adjust the group to the new times and develop a clearly defined growth strategy. During the period through the end of 1990, the leadership carried out "spring cleaning of [the company's] businesses," meaning that subsidiaries were sold off or trimmed. What remained was the measurement equipment company GN ELMI, which had always delivered growth and healthy surpluses, and GN Danavox and GN Netcom, as well as three smaller companies that disappeared in the course of the 1990s.

The consulting company McKinsey recommended selling GN Danavox and GN Netcom as an element of the work on GN Store Nord's strategy, as McKinsey considered GN Danavox and GN Netcom too small to survive in the global market. If the board of directors had followed this recommendation, GN would hardly have existed today. In fact, GN Danavox and GN Netcom, together with GN ELMI, became the core group of companies on which GN Store Nord staked its future.

In contrast, the days of the telecommunications business finally appeared to be numbered. The North Atlantic connections had been shut down, and only the JASC—the cable between Russia and Japan—remained, and it was due to be shut down in 1994. However, geopolitical developments opened up new and unexpected opportunities. The Soviet Union got a new general secretary who introduced a period of economic reforms, reduced tensions, and increased trade with other countries.

In 1991, GN Store Nord concluded an agreement with the Soviet Union regarding a fiber optic cable between Denmark and Russia, and two years later, the company concluded another agreement, this one regarding a connection linking Russia, Japan, and South Korea. Also in 1991, the company had concluded an agreement regarding a cable through Poland, and the ailing telecommunications company had now been resurrected.

As a completely new phenomenon, an opportunity arose for the telegraph company to become involved with telecommunications activities within Denmark's borders when the company formed a consortium that in the fall of 1991 was granted a license for a nationwide cellular telephony network that opened in the spring of 1992 with the name Sonofon. This was a major event in Danish histo-ry, as it was the first time the government monopoly on telecommunications activities established by the Telephone Law of 1897 had been broken. Efforts to become an operator on the Danish landline network in cooperation with the Swedish company Telia came to naught, however.

The resurrection of the telegraph company meant a significant increase in GN Store Nord's revenues and surpluses, but soon, the revenues from the cables began to decline, and the prospects of acquiring large new projects diminished. In 1998, it was, therefore, decided that the activities of the telegraph company would be discontinued, though the company continued to exist as a legal entity because of the ongoing arbitration case regarding the revenues from the cable through Poland.

At the same time, the industrial companies were growing, particularly GN Netcom and GN ELMI, which changed its name to GN Nettest. The industrial company that had the most difficulty overcoming its problems was GN Danavox, but following the acquisition of ReSound and Beltone, the company, under the new name GN ReSound, became the world's second-largest manufacturer of hearing aids—only Germany's Siemens was slightly larger.

A short time later, it was GN Netcom's turn to execute a major acquisition, the purchase of the American company Jabra, but the biggest event of the year was GN Store Nord's sale of the cellular telephony company Sonofon to Norway's Telenor for no less than 14.7 billion kroner. The revenues were used to strengthen GN ELMI, when the French company Photonetics had been acquired for no less than 9.1 billion kroner. The course was set for a stock exchange listing of GN Nettest with the new name NetTest and, as a consequence, an uncertain future for the rest of GN Store Nord—a future that might see the group split up.

Things did not get that far. On the very day in February 2001, on which the decision regarding a stock exchange listing was to be made, the entire foundation for such a listing crumbled as a result of a dramatic decline in the American Nasdaq index in the wake of the collapse of the dot-com bubble.

The stock exchange listing was postponed and then cancelled, and late in 2002, NetTest was sold for one krone, in connection with which GN Store Nord had to pay 300 million kroner to cover costs including the repayment of debts and restructuring costs.

GN ReSound and GN Netcom shared the fate of remaining in the GN Store Nord group, which in 2001 and 2002 amassed historic deficits totaling more than 14 billion kroner. The future did not look bright, but a new top management team and a new chairman of the board of directors took up the gauntlet to create "the new GN" by integrating the hearing aid and headset activities in one company.

In 2004, after what the business press called a "bloody turnaround," GN achieved an increase in revenues to 800 million kroner, corresponding to growth of 17 percent, and a historically large surplus of half a billion kroner. However, this was not enough for several of the big shareholders, who demanded more growth at GN ReSound and would have liked to see a merger with Denmark's Oticon. Instead GN Store Nord agreed in the fall of 2006 to sell GN ReSound to the Swiss company Phonak.

The sale left GN Store Nord and its remaining subsidiary GN Netcom in an uncertain situation that became extremely problematic in April 2007, when the German competition authority prohibited the sale of GN ReSound to Phonak. While the major shareholders wished to see the hearing aid business sold, opinions on the board of directors were divided.

The decision made was to keep operating both the hearing aid business and the headset business, and at an extraordinary general meeting in June 2008, three new members were elected to the board of directors, including a new chairman. The course was set for the creation of a new GN when, in the fall of the same year, the group was hit hard by the international financial crisis, which created serious liquidity problems for the group.

The group's critical situation was made clear when the group posted significant reductions in revenues three years in a row, through 2009, totaling over 36 percent, and posted deficits for all of the same three years. However, the implementation of the streamlining program FAST in the summer of 2008 eventually led to positive results, and at the beginning of 2009, a new leadership structure was put in place that moved the operational decisions down into the boards of directors of GN ReSound and GN Netcom respectively. At the same time, the competencies and structures of those boards of directors were strengthened.

The turnaround came in 2010, when GN ReSound presented the first generation of wireless hearing aids based on 2.4-GHz technology, which had previously been used at GN Netcom, and which now became the technological foundation of both business areas. "Back on the growth track" was the message, and since then, things have only been moving forward, with constant growth and dependable surpluses year after year on the basis of innovation and a constant stream of new products that have resulted in GN Store Nord's current position as a world leader in the production of hearing aids and headsets.

The distance between now and the time of the foundation of the Great Northern Telegraph Company is great—both in temporal terms and in terms of business activities. There is an unbroken connection, however, in the form of communication between people based on electronics and the most modern technology, which was the basis of the foundation of Great Northern in 1869, the creation of Storno in 1947, the development of the teleprinter in the 1950s and 1960s, the acquisition of Danavox in 1977, the attempt to enter the data industry in the 1980s, and the creation of Sonofon in 1992. ELMI— later GN Nettest—also rested on this foundation, as the company's business area was the production of equipment for the maintenance of communication networks.

The will to reinvent the company and tread new paths has provided constant momentum in the development of Great Northern and later GN Store Nord since the company began its transformation into an industrial group in 1947. By no means all of the projects and measures undertaken have been successful, and there have been failed investments and wrong decisions. The willingness to take risks, however, has been a constant factor since C. F. Tietgen founded the telegraph company back in 1869 and decided to lay cables to China and Japan.

Precisely the telegraph company played a decisive role in the shift to the status of an industrial group that followed during the years after the Second World War. In part, this was because of the significant wealth that had been created by the telegraph company's surpluses during the previous years and that became economic ballast for the shift in business areas. However, the telegraph company was also a constant source of revenues and surpluses all the way through the end of the twentieth century, and there were periods in which this, in combination with yields from the investment of accumulated wealth, played a decisive role in securing surpluses for Great Northern as a whole.

This is because, with a few individual exceptions, Great Northern, and later GN Store Nord, never succeeded in securing stable profitable operations in the group's industrial and other subsidiaries. This only occurred after the fresh start the group in a sense got after the sale of the hearing aid company collapsed and the group once again had to reinvent itself—and finally found itself and its raison d'être in a world far from that of the original telegraph company.

This does not mean that all of the intervening developments have been meaningless—on the contrary, for while there were problems with profitability, Storno did contribute to creating the technological, product, and marketing basis for the cellular telephony and smartphones of our age, while Sonofon contributed to breaking down the government monopoly on telephony and paving the way for a competition-driven globalized cellular telephony market that also embraces data communications and everything that comes with it.

In a historical perspective, today's GN has its real root in Danavox, which was founded in 1943 and became a part of Great Northern in 1977. With the splitting off of the headset business to create GN Netcom in 1987, the business foundation of today's GN was created with GN Hearing and GN Audio. The continuity with the original Danavox, then, is intact both as regards technology and as regards the products offered, but it is without a doubt their relationship with GN that has ensured the survival of both the hearing aid business and the headset business as autonomous companies and ultimately also their respective breakthroughs as leaders in their fields.

All of this, however, rests on the original Great Northern Telegraph Company and the historic, economic, and business legacy that the company left behind.

Sources and literature

This book is based predominantly on materials from the archives of the Great Northern Telegraph Company and GN Store Nord at the Danish National Archives and GN's headquarters in Ballerup. In cases in which the notes do not indicate the location of the sources used, they are from the above-mentioned archives.

In addition, other materials from the Danish National Archives and materials from archives in Russia, the United Kingdom, and China have been used. I consulted the archives of the British telegraph companies—Eastern, Eastern Extension, and Cable & Wireless—in the middle of the 1990s, when they were kept respectively at Warwick University and Electra House in London. Today, these archives are kept at the Telegraph Museum in Porthcurno, to which the overview of sources therefore refers. The bibliography refers only to books and other material that are cited in the text.

Archive materials

The Danish National Archives:

The archive of the Great Northern Telegraph Company

The archive of the Danish Ministry of Foreign Affairs (UM)

The archive of the Ministry of Greenland

C.F. Tietgen's private archive

The telegraphy depository

Other archives:

GN's archive, Ballerup

The Russian State Historical Archive (RGIA), Saint Petersburg

The Russian State Archive of the Economy (RGAE), Moscow

The Foreign Policy Archive of the Russian Federation (AVP), Moscow

The Archive for the NKVD Administration, Rostov Oblast, Delo No. 4060

The State Archive of the Russian Federation (GARF), Moscow

The Public Record Office (PRO), London: The Archive of the Foreign Office (FRO)

Cable & Wireless Ltd.'s Archives, Porthcurno

Shanghai Telecom Museum: The Great Northern Telegraph Company's Shanghai Archive

Literature

Ahvenainen, Jorma, The Far Eastern Telegraphs:The History of Telegraphic Communications between the Far East, Europe, and America before the First World War. Printed in Annales Academiæ Scientiarum Fennicæ, Ser, B, tom 216, 1981.

Alfred Berg Børsmæglerselskab A/S, *Aktieanalyse GN Store Nord, 13. August 1993.*

Baark, Erik, *Lightning Wires: The Telegraph and China's Technological Modernization, 1860–1890* (Greenwood Press 1997).

Barty-King, Hugh, *Girdle Around the Earth.* The Story of Cable and Wireless and Its Predecessors to Mark the Group's Jubilee 1929–1979 (William Heinemann Ltd 1980).

Bestaaende Overenskomster mellem Det Store Nordiske Telegraf-Selskab og forskjellige Regeringer, Autoriteter, Selskaber og Personer, Copenhagen 1873.

Buhl, Hans, *Buesenderen: Valdemar Poulsens radiosystem* (Aarhus Universitetsforlag 2005).

Codding, George Arthur Jr., *The International Telecommunication Union: An Experiment in In-*

ternational Cooperation (Université de Genève. Institut universitaire de hautes Études internationales. Thèse no. 88, Genève 1952).

Det Store Nordiske Telegraf-Selskab 1869–1894 (the Great Northern Telegraph Company 1894).

Hanaoka, Kaoru, One Hundred Years of Submarine Cables (1968). Translation from Japanese kept at the Danish National Archives.

Hansen, Jens Chr. and Domino, Søren, Søderberg – Mand af Mærsk (Gyldendal 2011).

Harmsen, Peter, Shanghai 1937: Stalingrad on the Yangtze (Casemate 2013).

Headrick, Daniel R.,The Invisible Weapon: Telecommunications and International Politics, 1851–1945 (Oxford University Press 1991).

Henningsen, Jacob, Under Punkahen: Skitser af Livet i Kina (Gyldendalske 1897).

Jacobsen, Kurt, editor, Dagbog holdt af Rasmus Petersen (GN Store Nord 1994).

Jacobsen, Kurt, Den Røde Tråd: Det Store Nordiske Telegraf-Selskabs storpolitiske spil efter den russiske revolution (Gyldendal 1997).

Kiil, Jesper, Midt i en teletid – Erindringer fra 40 år i teleteknik (Post & Tele Museum 1997).

Lange, Ole, Finansmænd, stråmænd og mandariner: C.F. Tietgen, Privatbanken og Store Nordiske. Etablering 1868–76 (Gyldendal 1978).

Lange, Ole, Partnere og rivaler. C.F. Tietgen, Eastern Extension og Store Nordiske. Ekspansion i Kina 1880–86 (Gyldendal 1980).

Marquard, Emil, Danske gesandter og gesandtskabspersonale indtil 1914 (the Danish National Archives 1952).

Mintz, Morton and Cohen, Jerry C., America, Inc. Who Owns and Operates the United States (Pitman 1972).

Mollerup, Erik, Hvad Formanden gør – (Gyldendal 1992).

Rasmussen, Erik B., Upublicerede erindringer om Store Nordiske as well as Radiometers historie fra 1956–1976.

Schønebeck, Alfred, Hovedtræk af den sibiriske Transitrutes Udvikling gennem et halvt Aarhundrede (the Great Northern Telegraph Company 1921). Unpublished manuscript kept at the Danish National Archives.

Standage, Tom, The Victorian Internet: The Remarkable Story of the Telegraph and the Nineteenth Century's Online Pioneers (Walker and Company 1998).

Statstelegrafens Virksomhed med tabellarisk Oversigt 1861–1863.

Suenson, Edouard, Det danske Telegrafanlæg i Østasien. Printed in Fra alle Lande, 1873, II.

Thestrup, Poul, 1850–1927: vogn og tog - prik og streg. P&T's historie volume 3 (Generaldirektoratet for Post- og Telegrafvæsenet 1992).

Yang, Daqing, echnology of Empire: Telecommunications and Japanese Expansion in Asia, 1883–1945 (Harvard University Press 2011).

Yang, Daqing, From Cooperation to Conflict: Ending Great Northern Telegraph Company in Japan.

Hubert Bonin et al, editors, Transnational Companies 19th–20th Centuries (Éditions P.L.A.G.E. 2002).

Zhang, Zhong, The Transfer of Networks Technology to China 1860–1898 (PhD thesis, University of Pennsylvania, 1989).

Journals etc.

Dansk Radio Industri.

Det danske post- og telegrafvæsen: Beretning om virksomheden.

Ingeniøren.

Tidsskrift for Tunghøre.

Various newspapers.

Materials from the website Stornotime.dk.

Notes

CHAPTER 1

1   Except where there is an explicit indication to the contrary, the entire description of the development of the telegraph in Denmark, including plans for and projects involving the establishment of cable connections with other countries, is based on Paul Thestrup, *Vogn og tog – prik og streg. P&T's historie 1850–1927*.

2   *Statstelegrafens Virksomhed med tabellarisk Oversigt 1861–1863*.

3   *Generalpostdirektøren til Udenrigsministeriet, undated*, RA, UM A2342/1863.

4   *Statstelegraphens Virksomhed med tabellarisk Oversigt, 1863* and *1866*.

5   *Kgl. Gesandtskab i Skt. Petersborg til Udenrigsministeriet, 1. April/21. Marts 1866*, RA, UM, A 3607/1866.

6   *Dagbladet*, 11. Januar 1868.

7   *Tietgen til Erichsen, 10. September 1867*, Kopibog 4. Juni 1864–17. Juli 1868. *Tietgen til Erichsen, 3.* and *4. Januar, 1868*, Kopibog 3. Januar 1868–28. Maj 1869. C. F. Tietgen's private archive.

8   *Forhandlingsprotokol for det Dansk-Norske-Engelske Telegraf-Selskab, 4. April* and *7. Maj 1868. Love for det Dansk-Norsk-Engelske Telegraf-Selskab*.

9   *C.F. Tietgen til Finansministeriet, 2. Marts 1868. Finansministeriet til C.F. Tietgen, 3. marts 1868*. Telegrafafleveringen, pk. 25.

10 *Memorandum om tildeling af økonomiske subventioner til Det Dansk-Norske Telegraf-Selskab, 4. Juni 1868*. RGIA, fond 1289, opis 1, delo 2827.

11 Ole Lange: *Finansmænd, stråmænd og mandariner*, p. 71. *C.F. Tietgen til Hans Pallisen, 13. August 1868. Hans Pallisen til C.F. Tietgen, 31. August 1868*. C. F. Tietgen's private archive.

12 *Hans Pallisen til C.F. Tietgen, 8. September 1868*. C. F. Tietgen's private archive.

13 *Tietgen til Erichsen, 30. januar 1868*. C. F. Tietgen's private archive.

14 *Det Store Nordiske Telegraf-Selskab 1869–1894*, p. 14–15.

15 Ibid.

16 Ibid., as well as *Tho. Joh. Heftye: Telegram til Tietgen, 28. September 1868*. C. F. Tietgen's private archive.

17 Ole Lange: *Finansmænd, stråmænd og mandariner*, p. 80.

18 Ibid., p. 77f.

19 Quoted from ibid., p. 88.

20 *C.L. Madsen til C.F. Tietgen, 5. November 1868*. C. F. Tietgen's private archive.

CHAPTER 2

1   Ole Lange, *Finansmænd, stråmænd og mandariner*, p. 70.

2   Zhong Zhang, *The Transfer of Networks Technology to China 1860–1898*, p. 4.

3   Erik Baark, *Lightning Wires. The Telegraph and China's Technological Modernization, 1860–1890*, p. 74–85.

4   Quoted from Ole Lange: *Finansmænd, stråmænd og mandariner*, p. 63.

5   *Burlingame to Secretary of State, Beijing May 22, 1867*.

United States Department of State: *Executive documents printed by order of the House of Representatives, during the second session of the fortieth Congress, 1867–68, Vol. I.* U.S. Government Printing Office, 1867–1868.

6   Ibid.

7   *Journal of the Telegraph*, New York, July 1, 1868.

8   Ole Lange, *Finansmænd, stråmænd og mandariner*, p. 83. Materials in RGIA, fond 1289, opis 1, delo 2827.

9   *C.L. Madsen til C.F. Tietgen, 2. November 1868*, C. F. Tietgen's private archive.

10 *C.L. Madsen til C.F. Tietgen, 5. and 8. November 1868*, C. F. Tietgen's private archive.

11 Ole Lange, *Finansmænd, stråmænd og mandariner*, p. 94–95.

12 There is a detailed description of John George Dunn's work on the project and his connection with Russian authorities and agencies in several files in RGIA, fond 1289, opis 1, delo 2835.

13 Files in RGIA, fond 1289, opis 1, delo 2835 as well as *Chadwicks, Adamson, Collier & Co. til Tietgen 22. October 1869*, which contains a transcript of Burlingame's letter.

14 Files in RGIA, fond 1289, opis 1, delo 2835. Ole Lange: *Finansmænd, stråmænd og mandariner*, p. 95.

15 Ole Lange, *Finansmænd, stråmænd og mandariner*, p. 102f.

16 Ibid., p. 110 as well as files in RGIA, fond 1289, opis 1, delo 2835.

17 Quoted from Ole Lange, *Finansmænd, stråmænd og mandariner*, p. 111.

18 Quoted from ibid., p. 113.

19 What follows is based on ibid., p. 115f.

20 David Chadwick's association with the British telegraph group is indicated by the company's application for a concession. RGIA fond 1289, opis 1, delo 2835.

21 Tietgen's application is in German and is kept in RGIA, fond 1289, opis 2, delo 2835.

22 Ole Lange, *Finansmænd, stråmænd og mandariner*, p. 123f., on which this description is based.

23 Quoted from ibid., p. 135.

24 Quoted from ibid., p. 139.

25 *Tietgen til Burlingame (udkast), 21. October 1869. Burlingame til Tietgen, 22. October 1869.*

26 *Chadwicks, Adamson, Collier & Co. til Tietgen 22. October 1869*, which contains a transcript of Burlingame's letter.

27 *Dagens Nyheder, 1. November 1869.*

28 Ole Lange, *Finansmænd, stråmænd og mandariner*, p. 149.

29 *Forhandlingsprotokol for Det Store Nordiske China & Japan Extension-Telegraf-Selskab, 9. Januar 1870.*

30 Ole Lange, *Finansmænd, stråmænd og mandariner*, p. 150.

31 C. F. Tietgen, *Erindringer og Optegnelser*, p. 89. GN's ar-

chives contain no papers that can illuminate the circumstances surrounding the public offering.

32 Ole Lange, *Finansmænd, stråmænd og mandariner*, p. 155f.

33 *Forhandlingsprotokol for Det Store Nordiske China & Japan Extension-Telegraf-Selskab, 3. Februar* and *28. Marts 1870.*

34 Ibid., *9. April 1870. Tietgen til McLeavy Brown, 20. April 1870.* Ole Lange, *Finansmænd, stråmænd og mandariner*, p. 175.

35 Ibid., p. 166.

36 The agreement is recorded in *Bestaaende Overenskomster mellem Det Store Nordiske Telegraf-Selskab og forskjellige Regeringer, Autoriteter, Selskaber og Personer*, Copenhagen 1873.

CHAPTER 3

1   The negotiations are described in detail in Erik Baark, *The Telegraph and China's Technological Modernization 1860–1890*, pp. 77–81.

2   *Edouard Suenson til C.F. Tietgen, 16. Juni 1870.*

3   Ibid., *26.* and *28. Juni 1870.*

4   Ibid.

5   Ibid.

6   *Convention passée entre le Gouvernment Japonais et l'Envoy Extraordinaire de Sa Majesté le Roi de Danemark, Yedo 20. September 1870.* The convention is recorded in *Bestaaende Overenskomster mellem Det Store Nordiske Telegraf-Selskab og forskjellige Regeringer, Autoriteter, Selskaber og Personer*, Copenhagen 1873.

7   *Det Store Nordiske Telegraf-Selskab 1869–1894*, p. 44.

8   *Edouard Suenson til C.F. Tietgen, 24. August 1870.*

9   Ibid., *28. September 1870.*

10 Ibid., *9. Oktober 1870.*

11 Ibid.

12 Ibid.

13 Ibid.

14 Ibid., *17. Oktober 1870.*

15 Ibid., *23. og 30. Oktober 1870*, and enclosed newspaper clippings.

16 Ibid.

17 *Store Nordiske Telegraf-Selskab 1869–1894*, p. 45.

18 *Edouard Suenson til C.F. Tietgen, 20. og 29. November 1870.*

19 Ibid., *3. December 1870.*

20 Ibid., *19. December 1870.* Kurt Jacobsen (editor), *Dagbog holdt af Rasmus Petersen.*

21 Ibid.

22 Ibid., as well as *Det Store Nordiske Telegraf-Selskab 1869–1894*, p. 48.

23 *Edouard Suenson til C.F. Tietgen, 4. Januar 1871. Edouard Suenson to G. B. Dixwell, January 5, 1871.* Great Northern's Shanghai archive.

24 Is indicated by Edouard Suenson's correspondence

with the company and with the Municipal Council of January and February 1871. Great Northern's Shanghai archive. The agreement with W. Keswick was is recorded in *Bestaaende Overenskomster mellem det Store Nordiske Telegraf-Selskab og forskjellige Regeringer, Autoriteter, Selskaber og Personer.* Desuden *Det Store Nordiske Telegraf-Selskab 1869–1894*, p. 48.

25   *Det Store Nordiske Telegraf-Selskab 1869–1894, pp. 51–52* as well as *Edouard Suenson til C.F. Tietgen, 11. og 23. Marts, 4. og 10. April 1871.*

26   A copy of the letter to the consuls is in Box A 694-1, Great Northern's Shanghai archive.

27   *Edouard Suenson til C.F. Tietgen, 1. Februar 1871.*

28   Is indicated by *C.F. Tietgen til McLeavy Brown, 20. April 1871.*

29   Edouard Suenson, *Det danske Telegrafanlæg i Østasien*, p. 26–27.

30   Ibid., *Hans Schjellerup til C.F. Tietgen, 19. April 1869* as well as *McLeavy Brown til C.F. Tietgen, 25. april 1871.*

31   Several systems are briefly described in *The Chinese Recorder and Mission Journal*, January-February 1874, pp. 53–54. *Edouard Suenson til C.F. Tietgen, 28. Juni 1870.* There is an example of Viguier's code in GN's archive.

32   *Ibid., 23. Oktober 1870.*

33   *Ibid., 3. December 1870.* The system is described in *Det Store Nordiske Telegraf-Selskab 1869–1894*, p. 50 and Edouard Suenson, *Det danske Telegrafanlæg i Østasien*, pp. 28–29.

34   *Ibid., 19. December 1870.*

35   *S. A. Viguier til E. Suenson, Shanghai 27. April 1870.* Great Northern's Shanghai archive. The demonstrations are described in *Det Store Nordiske Telegraf-Selskab 1869–1894*, p. 50 and Edouard Suenson, *Det danske Telegrafanlæg i Østasien*, pp. 28–29.

36   Is indicated by *S.A. Viguier til Løjtnant Dreyer, Shanghai 1., 16., og 19. Juni samt 11. December 1871.* Great Northern's Shanghai archive.

37   *Løjtnant Dreyer til Bestyrelsen, 22. September 1871.*

38   *The Chinese Recorder and Missionary Journal*, January and February 1874.

39   *Berlingske Tidende, 2. Januar 1872.*

40   *Fælles bestyrelsesmøde 9. Januar 1872. Det Store Nordiske Telegraf-Selskab1869–1894*, p. 60–61.

41   Ibid.

42   *Stemmeliste til Generalforsamlingen i Store Nordiske China & Japan Extension Telegraf-Selskab den 22. Februar 1872.*

43   *Generalforsamlingen i Det Store Nordiske Kina & Japan Extension Telegraf-Selskab, Torsdagen den 22de Februar 1872, kl. 6.*

44   *Bestyrelsesmøde, 20. Marts 1872.*

45   Minutes of the general meeting. *Fædrelandet, 1. Maj 1872* and *Dagens Nyheder, 1. Maj 1872.*

46   Ibid.

47   Ibid.

48   The agreement is recorded in *Bestaaende Overenskomster mellem det Store Nordiske Telegraf-Selskab og forskjellige Regeringer, Autoriteter, Selskaber og Personer.*

CHAPTER 4

1   Tom Standage, *The Victorian Internet.* Daniel Headrick, *The Invisible Weapon.*

2   *Berlingske Tidende, 26. April 1873.*

3   Tom Standage, *The Victorian Internet*, p. 146–47.

4   Quoted from ibid.

5   Ibid, p. 156.

6   The description of the creation and early development of the ITU is based on George Arthur Codding, *The International Telecommunication Union.*

7   Ibid., p. 25. *Det Store Nordiske Telegraf-Selskab 1869–1894*, p. 136.

8   *Bestyrelsesmøder, 20. Marts, 28. Maj, 12. Juni, 27. August* and *19. November 1873.*

9   Ibid. *9. Juli, 19. November* and *18. December 1873.*

10   Ibid., *12. Juni 1872, 25. Oktober 1873, 13. August 1875, 4. Maj, 14. Juni* and *28. Juli 1876.*

11   Alfred Schønebeck, *Hovedtræk af den sibiriske Transitrutes Udvikling gennem et halvt Aarhundrede*, p. 4–5.

12   Ibid., p. 8.

13   *Bestyrelsesmøde, 19. November 1872* and *14. Januar 1873.*

14   Ibid., and *23. januar 1874. Det Store Nordiske Telegrafselskabs generalforsamling, Leverdagen den 25de April 1874.*

15   The entire Svend Petersen affair is covered in Ole Lange, *Finansmænd, strømænd og mandariner*, pp. 219–258.

16   *Bestyrelsesmøder, 21. Marts, 5. april, 4. Maj, 14.* and *28. Juni, 25. august samt ekstraordinær generalforsamling 26. August 1876.*

17   *Bestyrelsesmøder, 28. Juni, 25. August* and *16. December 1876.*

18   *Bestyrelsesmøde, 25. Januar 1877.* Its progression can be followed in *Den administrerende Direktørs maanedlige Beretninger.* The current account is also based in part on *Det Store Nordiske Telegraf-Selskab 1869–1894*, p. 125ff.

19   Ibid.

20   *Det Store Nordiske Telegraf-Selskab 1869–1894*, p. 128.

CHAPTER 5

1   *Bestyrelsesmøde, 24. April 1873.*

2   Ibid., *25. Oktober 1873. Løjtnant Dreyer til bestyrelsen, 23. August 1873.* Also Ole Lange, *Finansmænd, Strømænd og Mandariner*, p. 265–68 og Erik Baark: *Lightning Wires*, p. 82–83.

3   Ibid.

4   Erik Baark: *Lightning Wires*, p. 83.

5   *Bestyrelsesmøde, 23. Januar 1874.*

6   Ibid. as well as *Det Store Nordiske Telegrafselskabs generalforsamling, Leverdagen den 25de April 1874.*

7   Ibid. as well as materials in RGIA, fond 1289, opis 1, delo 2835.

8   *C.F. Tietgen til Eugine de Bützow, 3. November 1873 (udkast).*

9   *Det Store Nordiske Telegrafselskabs generalforsamling, Leverdagen den 25de April 1874.*

10 Ibid.

11 Ibid.

12 The circumstances surrounding this event are not entirely clear. See Erik Baark, *Lightning Wires*, p. 89 and *Det Store Nordiske Telegraf-Selskab 1869–1894*, p. 140.

13 *Det Store Nordiske Telegraf-Selskab 1869–1894*, p. 140. *Løjtnant Dreyer til bestyrelsen, 24. Juli 1874.*

14 Erik Baark: *Lightning Wires*, p. 109–110.

15 Ibid., p. 111. *Bestyrelsesmøde, 3. Juli 1874.*

16 *Bestyrelsesmøde, 3. Juli 1874.*

17 Ibid., *18. Juli 1874.*

18 Ibid.

19 *Løjtnant Dreyer til bestyrelsen, 22. August* and *5. September 1874.* Erik Baark: *Lightning Wires*, p. 111–12.

20 *Bestyrelsesmøde, 11. august 1874.* Erik Baark: *Lightning Wires*, p. 112–13.

21 Ibid., p. 112–113.

22 Ibid. as well as *Bestyrelsesmøde, 3. Juli 1874*, from where the quote regarding Li Hongzhang was taken.

23 Ibid.

24 *Det Store Nordiske Telegraf-Selskab 1869–1894*, p. 143.

25 *Løjtnant Dreyer til bestyrelsen, 5. September 1874.*

26 Erik Baark: *Lightning Wires*, p. 113.

27 Ibid., p. 114.

28 Ibid.

29 Ibid., p. 115.

30 *Det Store Nordiske Telegraf-Selskab 1869–1894*, p. 144.

31 Erik Baark: *Lightning Wires*, p. 116.

32 Ibid., p. 118–19. *Bestyrelsesmøde, 23. Januar 1875.*

33 *Bestyrelsesmøde, 3. Juli 1874.*

34 What follows is based on Ole Lange, *Finansmænd, stråmænd og mandariner*, pp. 277–281.

35 Ibid., p. 286. Erik Baark, *Lightning Wires*, pp. 120–21. A lengthy excerpt from the note is recorded in *Det Store Nordiske Telegraf-Selskab 1869–1894*, pp. 96–97, which is the source of the current quote.

36 Quoted from Ole Lange, *Finansmænd, stråmænd og mandariner*, p. 286.

37 Erik Baark, *Lightning Wires*, p. 118–20.

38 Ibid. and Ole Lange, *Finansmænd, stråmænd og mandariner*, p. 294–95.

39 Ole Lange, *Finansmænd, stråmænd og mandariner*, p. 292–93, the source of this quote.

40 *Aarsberetning paa Store Nordiskes Generalforsamling, 28. April 1875.*

41 Ibid.

42 Ole Lange, *Finansmænd, stråmænd og mandariner*, p. 295. Erik Baark, *Lightning Wires*, p. 124–25.

43 Erik Baark, *Lightning Wires*, p. 126.

44 Jacob Henningsen, *Under Punkhaen: Skitser af Livet i Kina*, p. 51–52.

45 Ibid., p. 53–54.

46 *Bestyrelsesmøde, 8. September 1875.* What follows is based on this source.

47 Ibid.

48 Ibid., *25. Januar 1876.*

49 *Årsberetning på Store Nordiskes Generalforsamling, 29. April 1876.*

50 Ibid.

51 Erik Baark, *Lightning Wires*, p. 131.

CHAPTER 6

1   *Bestyrelsesmøde, 16. December 1876.*

2   Ibid.

3   *Bestyrelsesmøde, 14. December 1877.*

4   *Det Store Nordiske Telegraf-Selskabs Generalforsamling, Onsdagen den 16de April, kl. 7.*

5   Based on Ole Lange, *C.F. Tietgen, Store Nordiske og Eastern Extension. Ekspansion i Kina 1880–86*, p. 40–41.

6   Quoted from ibid.

7   *Den administrerende Directeurs maanedlige Beretninger, Maj 1880.*

8   Ibid., *Juli 1880.*

9   Erik Baark, *Lightning Wires*, p. 163–64. *Den administrerende Directeurs maanedlige Beretninger, November 1880.*

10 Ibid.

11 *Det Store Nordiske Telegraf-Selskabs Generalforsamling, Tirsdagen den 12te April 1881.*

12 This development is described in *Den administrerende Directeurs maanedlige Beretninger* for the years in question and is also described in *Det Store Nordiske Telegrafselskab 1869–1894*, pp. 155–56.

13 Quoted from *Den administrerende Directeurs maanedlige Beretninger, Maj 1881.*

14 Ibid.

15 A transcript of a translation into English is attached to ibid., *Juli 1881.*

16 Ibid.

17 Ibid., *Juni* and *Juli 1881.*

18 Ole Lange, *Partnere og rivaler*, p. 52.

19 Ibid., p. 54.

20 *Den administrerende Directeurs maanedlige Beretninger, Juli 1881.*

21 Ole Lange, *Partnere og rivaler*, p. 60.

22 Dunn's extensive information and evaluations are thoroughly described in ibid.

23 *Den administrerende Directeurs maanedlige Beretnin-ger, Januar* and *Februar 1882.*

24 Ole Lange did not have access to this part of Great Northern's archive when he wrote his book on Tietgen and the company, nor did Jorma Ahvenainen have such access.

25 *Edouard Suenson: Confidentiel Beretning om mine Forhandlinger med Eastern Extension Company i London, 8. Marts 1882.* Attached to *Den administrerende Directeurs maanedlige Beretninger, Marts 1882.*

26 Ibid. as well as Ole Lange, *Partnere og rivaler,* p. 86.

27 *Bestyrelsesmøde, 2. Januar 1883.*

28 The entire sequence of events related to the cable and the Guangzhou–Hong Kong connection is described in ibid. A Danish perspective on the events in question can be found in Great Northern's archive: *Den administrerende Directeurs maanedlige Beretninger Januar–Maj 1882.*

29 *Det Store Nordiske Telegraf-Selskabs ordinaire Generalforsamling, Lørdagen den 15. April 1882.*

30 Ibid.

31 *Den administrerende Directeurs maanedlige Beretninger, Maj 1882.* Ole Lange, *Partnere og rivaler,* p. 90.

32 Edouard Suenson's letter to Lüders is enclosed with *Den administrerende Direkteurs maanedlige Beretninger, Maj 1882.*

33 The negotiations are described in ibid., *Juli 1882.*

34 Ole Lange, *Partnere og rivaler,* p. 99ff.

35 *Den administrerende Directeurs maanedlige Beretninger, September 1882.*

36 Ibid.

37 Ibid., *November 1882.*

38 Ibid., *November* and *December 1882,* to which the contract is attached.

39 *Bestyrelsesmøde, 4. December 1882.* Ole Lange, *Partnere og rivaler,* p. 117–20.

40 *Bestyrelsesmøde, 2. Januar 1883. Den administrerende Directeurs maanedlige Beretninger, December 1882* and *Januar 1883.*

41 Ibid.

42 Ibid.

43 Ole Lange, *Partnere og rivaler,* p. 122. *Bestyrelsesmøde, 22. Januar 1883.*

44 *Bestyrelsesmøde, 22. Januar 1883.*

45 *Den administrerende Directeurs maanedlige Beretninger, Marts 1883.*

46 *Det Store Nordiske Telegraf-Selskabs ordinære Generalforsamling, Lørdagen den 28de April 1883, Kl. 7.* What follows is based on this source.

47 *Det Store Nordiske Telegraf-Selskabs ordinære Generalforsamling, Lørdagen den 26de April 1884, Kl. 7.*

48 Except where there is an explicit indication to the contrary, what follows is based on Jorma Ahvenainen, *The Far Eastern Telegraphs,* p. 102ff and Ole Lange, *Partnere og rivaler,* p. 163ff.

49 Quoted from Ole Lange, *Partnere og rivaler,* p. 163.

50 Ibid., p. 165, 179. Jorma Ahvenainen, *The Far Eastern Telegraphs,* p. 105.

51 *Den administrerende Directeurs maanedlige Beretninger, Juli 1884.*

52 *Kjær til Udenrigsministeriet, 1. Juni 1884,* UM, SNTS, journalnr. 8413.

53 *Bestyrelsesmøde, 31. Juli 1885.* The sequence of events is described in *Den administrerende Directeurs maanedlige Beretninger April–Juli 1885.*

54 *Confidentiel Beretning om den internationale Telegraf-conference i Berlin,* attached to *Den administrerende Directeurs maanedlige Beretning, August 1886. Bestyrelsesprotokol, 31. Juli 1885.*

55 Ibid.

56 *Bestyrelsesmøde, 7. Oktober 1885.*

57 *Den administrerende Directeurs maanedlige Beretning, Februar 1886.*

58 Ibid., *August 1886. Bestyrelsesmøde, 21. August 1886.* What follows is based on the second of these two sources.

59 *Heads of Agreement come to at Copenhagen between the Eastern Extension and Great Northern Telegraph Companies.* Attached to *Den administrerende Directeurs maanedlige Beretninger, August 1885.*

60 *Bestyrelsesmøde, 21. August 1886.*

61 *Det Store Nordiske Telegraf-Selskab 1869–1894,* p. 109. The book was written by Edouard Suenson and reviewed and approved by Tietgen.

CHAPTER 7

1 *Heads of Agreement between the Eastern Extension and Great Northern Telegraph Companies.* Attached to *Den administrerende Directeurs maanedlige Beretninger, August 1886* and *Marts 1887.*

2 Ibid.

3 *Joint Letter to Viceroy Li Chungtang, 30. November 1886* and *Memorandum relating to China Telegraphs, November 1886.* Attached to *Den administrerende Directeurs maanedlige Beretninger, November 1886.* What follows is based on this source.

4 Ibid.

5 *Den administrerende Directeurs maanedlige Beretninger,* April 1887.

6 Ibid., *Maj 1887.* What follows is based on this source.

7 Ibid.

8 Ibid.

9 Ibid., *Juli* and *August 1887.*

10 Ibid. as well as Jorma Ahvenainen, *The Far Eastern Telegraphs,* pp. 113–15.

11 Ibid., *Oktober 1887.*

12 Ibid., *December 1887* and *Juli 1889.*

13 Ibid., *September 1892.* What follows is based on this source.

14   Ibid.

15   *Det Store Nordiske Telegraf-Selskabs ordinaire Gene-ralforsamling, Lørdagen den 25de April 1891, kl. 3.*

16   *Det Store Nordiske Telegraf-Selskabs ordinaire Gene-ralforsamling, Lørdagen den 21de April, 1894, kl. 3.15.* Except where there is an explicit indication to the contrary, what follows is based on this source.

17   *Det Store Nordiske Telegraf-Selskab. Regnskab for Aaret 1893.*

18   Suenson's and Tietgen's role is indicated by the records of the company's board of directors.

19   *Bestyrelsesmøde, 8. Februar 1898.*

20   *Den administrerende Directeurs maanedlige Beretnin-ger, Januar-Maj 1895.* Jorma Ahvenainen, *The Far Eastern Telegraphs,* p. 133.

21   The sequence of events can be followed in Edouard Suenson's monthly reports to the board of directors and is described in Jorma Ahvenainen, *The Far Eastern Telegraphs,* p. 134ff.

22   *Det Store Nordiske Telegraf-Selskabs ordinaire Gene-ralforsamling, Lørdagen den 24de April 1897, Kl. 3.*

23   *Den administrerende Directeurs maanedlige Beretninger, Januar-Marts 1899.* Jorma Ahvenainen, *The Far Eastern Telegraphs,* p. 141ff.

24   Ibid., *Maj 1899.*

25   Ibid., *April–August 1895* and *Maj 1896.*

26   *Det Store Nordiske Telegraf-Selskabs ordinære Gene-ralforsamling, Lørdagen den 20de April 1895, Kl. 3.*

27   *Den administrerende Directeurs maanedlige Beretninger, Juni 1899* and *Bestyrelsesprotokol, 22. Marts 1899.*

28   Ibid., *September 1899.*

29   *Den adm. Directeurs maanedlige Beretninger, November 1899* and *januar 1900.*

30   Ibid., *27. Marts 1900.* A copy of the Japanese declara-tion is attached to ibid., *May 1900.*

31   Ibid., *Juli 1900.*

32   *Nationaltidende, 31. Juli 1900.*

CHAPTER 8

1   Edouard Suenson, *Forslag om Selskabets Deltagelse i Kabelanlæg i det stille Hav, 20. Januar 1896.* Attached to *Den administrerende Directeurs maanedlige Beretninger, Januar 1896.* What follows is based on this source.

2   Described in *Det Store Nordiske Telegraf-Selskabs bestyrelsesprotokol, 3. Februar 1896.*

3   Ibid.

4   Ibid.

5   *Den administrerende Directeurs maanedlige Beretninger, Februar 1896.*

6   Ibid.

7   Ibid., *Marts 1896.*

8   *Heads of Agreement, 18. Marts 1896.* Attached to ibid.

9   Ibid., *Maj 1896.*

10   Ibid. and *Bestyrelsesmøde, 8. August 1896.*

11   *Bestyrelsesmøde, 8. August* and *23. Oktober 1896.*

12   *Den administrerende Directeurs maanedlige Beretninger, Oktober, November* and *December 1896.*

13   Ibid., *Oktober 1896.*

14   *Edouard Suenson til F.C. Hesse, 16. December 1896.* Transcript attached to *Den administrerende Direct-eurs maanedlige Beretninger, December 1896.* What follows is based on this source.

15   Ibid.

16   Ibid., *December 1896.*

17   Ibid.

18   Ibid., *Januar 1897.*

19   Ibid.

20   Ibid.

21   *Edouard Suenson til James A. Scrymser, 19. Januar 1897.* Transcript attached to *Den administrerende Directeurs maanedlige Beretninger, Januar 1897.*

22   *James A. Scrymser til Edouard Suenson, 2. Februar 1897.* Transcript attached to ibid.

23   *Edouard Suenson til James A. Scrymser, 18. Februar 1897.*

24   Ibid.

25   *Den administrerende Directeurs maanedlige Beretninger, Maj 1897. Edouard Suenson til James A. Scrymser, 24. Maj 1897.* Attached to ibid.

26   *Den administrerende Directeurs maanedlige Beretninger, Juni 1897. Store Nordiskes bestyrelsesprotokol, 26. Juni 1897.*

27   *Memo om Forhandlingerne i London med Eastern Sel-skaberne og med Pacific Cable Company of New York,* on which what follows is based. Attached to *Den administrerende Directeurs maanedlige Beretninger, Juli 1897.*

28   Ibid., *December 1898. Bestyrelsesmøder, 16. Oktober* and *22. November 1897.*

29   *Den administrerende Directeurs maanedlige Beretninger, September-December 1898.*

30   Quoted from Daniel Headrick, *The Invisible Weapon,* p. 100.

31   Ibid.

32   *Den administrerende Directeurs maanedlige Beretninger, Juni-August 1901.*

33   Ibid., *September 1901.*

34   Ibid., *August 1901.*

35   Ibid.

36   Ibid. as well as *September 1901.*

37   Daniel Headrick, *The Invisible Weapon,* pp. 100–101 and Jorma Ahvenainen, *The Far Eastern Telegraphs,* p. 171.

38   *Den administrerende Directeurs maanedlige Beretninger, Oktober* and *November 1901* as well as Daniel Headrick, *The Invisible Weapon,* p. 100–101.

39   Ibid., *Juni 1902.*

40 *Bestyrelsesmøde, 24. September, 6. Oktober* and *1. November 1902.*

41 *Den administrerende Directeurs maanedlige Beretninger, December 1904.*

42 *Det Store Nordiske Telegraf-Selskabs ekstraordinaire Generalforsamling, Mandag den 23de Maj 1898, kl. 3.*

43 *Det Store Nordiske Telegraf-Selskabs ordinaire Generalforsamling, Torsdag den 30te April 1903, kl. 3.*

CHAPTER 9

1 *Den administrerende Directeurs maanedlige Beretninger, December 1897.*

2 Ibid., *Marts, April* and *December 1898.*

3 *Den administrerende Directeurs maanedlige Beretninger, Juni 1900. Det Store Nordiske Telegraf-Selskabs ordinære Generalforsamling, Tirsdag den 30te April 1901, kl. 3.* What follows is based on this source.

4 *Den administrerende Directeurs maanedlige Beretninger, Juni 1900.*

5 Ibid., *Juli-August 1900.*

6 Ibid., *Oktober 1900.*

7 Ibid., *Januar 1901.*

8 Ibid.

9 *Det Store Nordiske Telegraf-Selskabs ordinære Generalforsamling, Lørdag den 28de April 1900, kl. 3.*

10 *Tilbageblik på 1899.* Attached to *Den administrerende Directeurs maanedlige Beretninger, December 1899.*

11 *Det Store Nordiske Telegraf-Selskabs ordinære Generalforsamling, Tirsdag den 30th April 1901, kl. 3.*

12 Examples of the French ambassador's anti-British attitude: *Den administrerende Directeurs maanedlige Beretninger, November 1899* and *Juni 1900.*

13 Ibid., *Januar 1901.*

14 A detailed description of the sequence of events in question can be found in *Den administrerende Directeurs maanedlige Beretninger,* and it is briefly described in Jorma Ahvenainen, *The Far Eastern Telegraphs,* pp. 175–78, which was written without access to detailed documentation of the negotiations. The signing of the complex of agreements is referred to in *Bestyrelsesmøde, 10. August 1904.*

15 Ibid., *Marts 1901.*

16 *Forhandlinger i Skt. Petersborg angaaende Peking-Kiachta-Nystad Ledning.* Attached to *Den administrerende Directeurs maanedlige Beretninger, Juli 1901.* What follows is based on this source, which is also the source of the relevant quotes.

17 Ibid.

18 *Det Store Nordiske Telegraf-Selskabs ordinære Generalforsamling, Torsdag den 30te April 1903, kl. 3.*

19 Ibid. as well as *Den administrerende Directeurs maanedlige Beretninger, Marts* and *Maj 1904.*

20 *Den administrerende Directeurs maanedlige Beretninger, Februar 1904.*

21 Ibid.

22 Ibid., *Januar 1905.*

23 Ibid., *Juni* og *Juli 1905.*

24 Is described in ibid., *October–December 1905.*

25 Ibid., *Januar 1906.*

26 Ibid., *December 1905* and *Februar 1906.*

27 *Den administrerende Directeurs maanedlige Beretninger, Januar–Marts 1904.*

28 Ibid., *Marts–Juli 1904.*

29 Daqing Yang, *Technology of Empire,* p. 39.

30 *Bestyrelsemøde, 7. Marts 1907.*

31 *Bestyrelsesmøde, 8. April 1907.*

32 *Det Store Nordiske Telegraf-Selskabs ordinære Generalforsamling, Lørdag den 25de April 1908, kl. 3.*

33 *Bestyrelsesprotokol, 18. Juli* and *30. September 1908.*

34 The sequence of events is described in ibid., *October 1911–March 1912.*

35 *Den administrerende Directeurs maanedlige Beretninger, August-September 1910.*

36 Emil Marquard, *Danske gesandter og gesandtskabspersonale indtil 1914.*

37 Great Northern's initiatives in connection with Count Ahlefeldt-Laurvig's diplomatic career are indicated by *Den administrerende Directeurs maanedlige Beretninger, April 1908, April–Maj 1910, Juli 1911* as well as *Bestyrelsesmøde, 30. April* and *7. September 1910, 12. Juli* and *28. Oktober 1911.*

38 *Den administrerende Direktørs maanedlige Beretninger, Juli* og *August 1912.*

39 Ibid., on which the following description is based.

40 Ibid., *November* and *December 1912.*

41 Ibid.

42 The negotiations are described in *Den administrerende directeurs maanedlige Beretninger* up to August 1913. For the Japanese attitude: Kaouro Hanaoka, *100 Years of Submarine Cables.*

CHAPTER 10

1 Daqing Yang, *Technology of Empire,* pp. 57–58.

2 Ibid., pp. 56–57.

3 *Den administrerende Directeurs maanedlige Beretninger, April 1904. Det Store Nordiske Telegraf-Selskabs ordinære Generalforsamling, Lørdag den 29de April 1905, kl. 3.*

4 *Den administrerende Directeurs maanedlige Beretninger, August 1897.*

5 Ibid., *Oktober 1899.*

6 Ibid., *Marts 1902.*

7 Ibid., *December 1901.*

8 Ibid., *Januar 1902.*

9 *The Electrician (London), February 7, 1902, page 600.* Accessed via http://earlyradiohistory.us/ on November 8, 2017.

10 *Den administrerende Directeurs maanedlige Beretninger, December 1902.*

11 Ibid., *December 1896.*

12 Is indicated by *Den administrerende Directeurs maanedlige Beretninger 1880–1882* as well as *December 1896*
and *Januar 1897.*

13 Ibid., *Januar 1897.*

14 These efforts are described in *Den administrerende Directeurs maanedlige Beretninger.*

15 Ibid., *Marts 1898.*

16 Ibid., *Februar 1902.*

17 Ibid., *Marts 1902.*

18 Ibid., *Marts* and *Juli 1902.*

19 Ibid., as well as *November 1902* and *Juni 1903.*

20 Ibid., *Juni* and *December 1903* as well as *Juli 1904.*

21 Ibid., *November 1903.*

22 Ibid.

23 *Det Store Nordiske Telegraf-Selskab til Christian Hage,
16. November 1903.* Supplement to ibid.

24 Ibid.

25 Ibid.

26 *Den administrerende Directeurs maanedlige Beretninger, Januar, Februar* and *April 1905.*

27 Ibid.

28 *Det Store Nordiske Telegraf-Selskabs ordinære Generalforsamling, Lørdag den 29. April 1905, kl. 3.*

29 Hans Buhl, *Buesenderen. Valdemar Poulsens radiosystem.*

30 *Bestyrelsesmøde, 28. Januar 1904.*

31 Hans Buhl, *Buesenderen. Valdemar Poulsens radiosystem,* pp. 51–56.

32 Ibid., p. 78. *Den administrerende Directeurs maanedlige
Beretninger, Maj, Juni* and *Juli 1906.*

33 Ibid., *Januar 1907.*

34 Hans Buhl, *Buesenderen. Valdemar Poulsens radiosystem,* pp. 79–80.

35 Ibid., p. 80–82.

36 Ibid., p. 91–92 and 95.

37 Ibid., p. 99–101.

38 *Den administrerende Directeurs maanedlige Beretninger, Oktober–December 1907* and *Februar, Marts og Maj
1908.*

39 *Det Store Nordiske Telegraf-Selskabs ordinære Generalforsamling, Lørdag den 25de April 1908, kl. 3.*

40 *Den administrerende Directeurs maanedlige Beretninger, Maj 1908.*

41 Ibid., *Oktober* og *November 1908. Bestyrelsesmøde, 28.
November 1908.*

42 Ibid.

43 Ibid., *Marts 1909.*

44 Ibid., *Marts, Oktober* and *December 1909.*

45 Ibid., *April–Juni* and *August 1909.*

46 Ibid., *Oktober 1910* as well as *Marts* and *Maj 1912.*

47 Ibid.

48 Hans Buhl, *Buesenderen. Valdemar Poulsens radiosystem,* p. 111ff. What follows is based on the description in
this source.

49 Ibid., and pp. 124–126, the source of the quotes. *Den administrerende Direktørs maanedlige Beretninger, August 1912.*

50 *Den administrerende Direktørs maanedlige Beretninger, Oktober 1912.*

51 Hans Buhl, *Buesenderen. Valdemar Poulsens radiosystem,* p. 208–209.

CHAPTER 11

1 Alfred Schønebeck: *Hovedtræk af den sibiriske Transitrutes Udvikling gennem et halvt Aarhundrede,.* p. 115–
116.

2 Ibid.

3 *Fortroligt Memorandum fra Formanden, 3. September
1910.* Enclosed with *Den administrerende Direktørs
maanedlige Beretninger, Oktober 1910.* What follows is
based in this memorandum.

4 Ibid.

5 *Bestyrelsesmøde, 7. September 1910.*

6 *Den administrerende Direktørs maanedlige Beretninger, December 1910* and *Januar 1911.*

7 What follows is based on Alfred Schønebeck, *Hovedtræk af den sibiriske Transitrutes Udvikling gennem
et halvt Aarhundrede,* pp. 126–33, where the development in question is described in detail.

8 Ibid., p. 138–40.

9 *Den administrerende Direktørs maanedlige Beretninger, August 1914.*

10 Ibid., *August* and *September 1914.*

11 Ibid., *Januar, Februar* and *Marts 1915.*

12 Ibid., *Januar 1915.*

13 Ibid., *December 1914* and *Januar 1915.*

14 Ibid., *Juli* and *Oktober 1915.*

15 Ibid., *December 1915.*

16 Ibid., *Januar* and *Februar 1916.*

17 Ibid., *Juni 1916.*

18 Report in ibid., *July 1916.*

19 Ibid.

20 Ibid.

21 Ibid., *September* and *November 1916.*

22 Ibid., *Oktober 1916.*

23 Ibid.

24 Ibid.

25 Ibid., *November 1916.*

26 Ibid., *November* og *December 1916.*

27 Ibid., *Marts 1917.*

28 Ibid., *April* og *Maj 1917.*

29 Ibid., *April 1917.*

30 Ibid., *September 1917.*

31 Ibid.

32 *Den administrerende Direktørs maanedlige Beretninger, December 1917.* Alfred Schønebeck, *Hovedtræk af
den sibiriske Transitrutes Udvikling gennem et halvt
Aarhundrede,* p. 155f.

33 *Den administrerende Direktørs maanedlige Beretninger,*
    November 1917.

34 Ibid., *December 1917* and *January–July 1918.* Also materi-
    als in RGAE, fond 3527, opis 3, delo 42.

35 Ibid., *Georg van Wendt til Udenrigsministeriet, 3. decem-*
    ber 1917, UM 92. Dan 5/31. What follows is based on *Den*
    administrerende Direktørs maanedlige Beretninger, De-
    cember 1917 and *Januar 1918* as well as *Referat af Møde*
    mellem Dr. Adolf Törngren og Professor Georg von Wendt,
    udsendte af den finske Regering, og Direktionen for Det
    Store Nordiske Telegraf-Selskab, 14. december 1918, UM
    92. Dan 5/31.

36 *Den administrerende Direktørs maanedlige Beretninger,*
    Januar 1918.

37 What follows is based on Kay Suenson's report, which is
    attached to ibid., as well as Kurt Jacobsen, *Den Røde Tråd,*
    pp. 12–22, which describes in detail Kay Suenson's stay
    and negotiations in Helsinki.

CHAPTER 12

1   Quoted from Bent Jensen, *Danmark og det russiske*
    spørgsmål 1917–1924, p. 128–29.

2   *Den administrerende Direktørs maanedlige Beretninger,*
    August 1918.

3   Ibid., *September 1918* and Hans Schønebeck, p. 155.

4   Bent Jensen, *Købmænd og kommissærer,* p. 114–15.

5   *Repræsentanten i London til Direktionen, 30. Oktober*
    1918.

6   The description of Kay Suenson's negotiations is based
    on *Den administrerende Direktørs maanedlige Beretnin-*
    ger, December 1918 and *Memorandum til Post Office,* a
    copy of which is attached to *Repræsentanten i London til*
    Direktionen, 20. December 1918.

7   Ibid.

8   *Repræsentanten i London til Direktionen, 28. Januar 1919.*
    Den administrerende Direktørs maanedlige Beretninger,
    December 1919.

9   *Den administrerende. Direktørs maanedlige Beretninger,*
    Marts 1919.

10 Ibid.

11 Kurt Jacobsen, *Den Røde Tråd,* p. 60–61.

12 *Den administrerende Direktørs maanedlige Beretninger,*
    December 1919 and *Januar 1920.*

13 Ibid.

14 Ibid., *August 1919.*

15 Ibid. samt *Bestyrelsesmøde, 11. november 1919.*

16 Ibid., *September 1919.*

17 Ibid., *Marts 1920.*

18 *Notat ved Kaptajn Cramer om Møde med Per Michelsen*
    20. Marts 1920 and *Memorandum v/ Henrik Kauffmann*
    til Hjalmar Lange, 24. Marts 1920, UM 92.P.42.

19 What follows is based on *Den administrerende Direktørs*
    maanedlige Beretninger, Marts 1920 as well as *Store Nor-*
    diske til Litvinov, 29. marts 1920 and *Udkast til Aftale mel-*

lem *Store Nordiske og Sovjetregeringen,* both of which
are in UM 92.P.42.

20 Ibid.

21 *Direktionen til Repræsentanten i London, 28. Marts 1920,*
    UM 92.P.42. Kurt Jacobsen, *Den Røde Tråd,* on which
    what follows is based.

22 *Den administrerende Direktørs maanedlige Beretninger,*
    April 1920. Direktionen til repræsentanten i London, 20.
    April 1920, UM 92.P.42.

23 *Protokol vedrørende Rusland, økonomiske Spørgsmål,*
    23. April 1920, FO 371/4041.

24 *Tjitjerin til Litvinov, 22. April 1920,* AVP, opis 3, fond 85,
    delo 45. *Den adm. Direktørs maanedlige Beretninger, Maj*
    1920.

25 Ibid., *Maj 1920.*

26 Ibid., *Juni 1920.*

27 A transcript of the telegrams is in AVP, fond 85, opis 3.
    delo 47.

28 *Den administrerende Direktørs maanedlige Beretninger,*
    Juli–August 1920.

29 Ibid., *September 1920.* The report was written in late Oc-
    tober. *Litvinov til Tjitjerin, Kristiania 21. September 1920,*
    AVP, fond 85, opis 3, delo 45.

30 *Udenrigskommissariatet, økonomisk-juridisk afdeling,*
    til formanden for Sovnarkom, kammerat Lenin, 26. okto-
    ber 1920. GARF, fond 130, opis 5, delo 74.

31 Ibid.

32 *Udenrigskommissariatet, økonomisk-juridisk afdeling,*
    til sekretær for Sovnarkom, kammerat Fotijeva, 4. de-
    cember 1920 as well as *Protokoludskrift fra møde i Folke-*
    kommissærernes Råd, 11. december 1920 both in GARF,
    fond 130, opis 5, delo 74.

33 *Den administrerende Direktøres maanedlige Beretnin-*
    ger, Februar 1920.

34 Ibid. as well as *Udenrigskommissariatet, økonomisk-ju-*
    ridisk afdeling, til sekretær for Sovnarkom, kammerat
    Fotijeva, 3. februar 1920, GARF, fond 130, opis 5, delo 74.

35 *Repræsentanten i London til Direktionen, 18., 19.* and *23.*
    marts 1921. English materials related to this matter are
    in FO 372 372/145/38, N. 5464 (1921).

36 *Krasin til Tjitjerin, London 23. marts 1921* as well as
    Georgij Tjitjerin til Lenin, Moskva 23. marts 1921. Both in
    GARF, fond 130, opis 5, delo 74.

37 *Georgij Tjitjerin til Lenin, Moskva 24. marts 1921,* GARF,
    fond 130, opis 5, delo 74.

38 Lenin's intervention is indicated by *Justitskommissaria-*
    tet til Sovnarkom, 26. Marts 1921, GARF, fond 130, opis 5,
    delo 74 as well as Lenin's notes on Krasin's and Chicher-
    in's telegrams and letters.

39 *Protokol nr. 653, møde i den lille Sovnarkom, 30. marts*
    1921, GARF, fond 130, opis 5, delo 74.

40 *Den administrerende Direktørs maanedlige Beretninger,*
    Marts 1921. Store Nordiske til Litvinov, 1. April 1921, AVP,
    fond 85, opis 4, delo 7.

41 *Kjær til Store Nordiske, Moskva 10. maj, 1921,* AVP, fond 85,

opis 4, delo 8.

42 *Den administrerende Direktørs maanedlige Beretninger, Maj 1921.* The report was not written until June.

43 The insertion into the protocol is indicated by a written note on the copy that was sent to Great Northern.

44 *Frederik Kjær i Petrograd i Direktionen, 12. August 1921,* UM 92 Dan. 5/42.

45 Ibid.

46 *Den administrerende Direktørs maanedlige Beretninger, April 1923.*

47 *Store Nordiske Telegraf-Selskab til Udenrigsministeriet, 28. Maj 1923,* UM 64. DAN.65.

48 Ibid.

49 *Ministermødeprotokol, 29. Maj 1923.*

CHAPTER 13

1 *Store Nordiske til Ministeriet for Offentlige Arbejder, 16. Februar 1921,* UM 92 Dan. 5/3. What follows is based on this source.

2 Ibid.

3 *Den administrerende Direktørs maanedlige Beretninger, Marts* and *Maj 1921.*

4 Ibid.

5 *Repræsentanten i London til Direktionen, 26. oktober 1921.*

6 *Herluf Zahle til O.C. Scavenius, 2. December 1921,* UM 92 Dan.5/3.

7 *Den administrerende Direktørs maanedlige Beretninger, Marts* and *April 1922.*

8 Ibid., *November 1924.*

9 Ibid.

10 *Bestyrelsesmøde, 16. Februar 1925.*

11 Ibid., *15. April 1924.*

12 Hans Buhl, *Buesenderen - Valdemar Poulsens radiosystem,* p. 151.

13 Ibid. p. 148.

14 *Den administrerende Direktørs maanedlige Beretninger, December 1920.*

15 *Generalforsamling 30. Juni 1922.*

16 These developments are described in detail in Hugh Barty-King, *Girdle Around the Earth,* pp. 203–27.

17 *Nationaltidende, 26. Marts 1928. Den adm. Direktørs maanedlige Beretninger, Marts 1928.*

18 Is indicated by the annual accounts.

19 *Bestyrelsesmøde, 30. November 1927.*

20 Ibid.

21 Ibid., *13. April 1928.*

22 *Bestyrelsesmøde, 2. Januar 1929.*

23 *Bestyrelsesmøde, 27. November 1928.*

24 Ibid.

25 Ibid.

26 *Den administrerende Direktørs maanedlige Beretninger, Juli 1928* and *September 1928. Bestyrelsesmøde, 27. November 1928.*

27 Ibid., *November 1928* and *Januar 1929.*

28 *Bestyrelsesmøde, 22. April 1929 inklusive bilag.*

29 Ibid.

30 *Den administrerende Direktørs maanedlige Beretninger, November 1929.*

31 Ibid.

32 Ibid.

33 Ibid.

34 Daniel Headrick, *The Invisible Weapon,* p. 208.

35 *Den administrerende Direktørs maanedlige Beretninger, Februar 1918* and *Marts 1919.* Daqing Yang, *Technology of Empire,* p. 65. Daniel Headrick, *The Invisible Weapon,* p. 188.

36 Ibid., *September 1922.*

37 Ibid., *November 1922.*

38 Ibid., *Januar 1923.*

39 Ibid.

40 Daqing Yang, *Technology of Empire.*

41 *Den administrerende Direktørs maanedlige Beretninger, December 1930.*

42 Ibid.

43 Ibid., *Juli 1931.*

44 *Den administrerende Direktørs maanedlige Beretninger, Januar–Maj 1932* as well as the brochure *The Shanghai Incident and Great Northern,* which the company published in the fall of 1932.

45 Kaoru Hanaoka: *One Hundred Years of Submarine Cables and the Pacific.*

46 Ibid., p. 84.

47 The entire sequence of events with the repeated complaints is described in detail in Daqing Yang, *From Cooperation to Conflict: Ending Great Northern Telegraph Company in Japan.*

48 Ibid. as well as Kaoru Hanaoka, *One Hundred Years of Submarine Cables,* p. 84.

49 Daqing Yang: *From Cooperation to Conflict: Ending Great Northern Telegraph Company in Japan.*

50 Peter Harmsen: *Shanghai 1937. Stalingrad on the Yangtze.* Except where there is an explicit indication to the contrary, what follows is based on *Den administrerende Direktørs maanedlige Beretninger, Juli 1937–Januar 1938.*

51 *Den administrerende Direktørs maanedlige Beretninger, November–December 1937.*

52 *Store Nordiske (Shanghai) til Hovedkvarteret (telegram), 7. December 1937,* UM 92 Dan. 5/5N I. Daqing Yang, *From Cooperation to Conflict: Ending Great Northern Telegraph Company in Japan.*

53 *Store Nordiske til Udenrigsministeriet, 30. August 1938* and *12. November 1938. Den danske Ambassadør i London til Udenrigsministeriet, 12. November 1938.* UM 92.Dan. 5/5I.

CHAPTER 14

1 *Den administrerende Direktørs maanedlige Beretnin-*

ger, *Marts 1926*. The entire debt matter is described in Kurt Jacobsen, *Den Røde Tråd*, *74f*.

2 *Den administrerende Direktørs maanedlige Beretninger*, *September 1926*.

3 Quoted from *Notat om Litvinof v/ AU/EM*, *SNTS*, *15. januar 1935*, UM 92 Dan 5/53.

4 *Den adm. Direktørs maanedlige Beretninger, Januar* and *Maj 1928*.

5 Alfred Schønebeck: *Beretning til Store Nordiske, 28. November 1929*. UM 133 D 12. The reports were transferred to the Danish Ministry of Foreign Affairs by Great Northern.

6 Alfred Schønebeck, *Foredrag i Gosplan, 30. Januar 1930*.

7 *Den administrerende Direktørs maanedlige Beretninger, December 1933 og Februar 1935*. Also documents in RGAE, fond 3527, opis 13, delo 315.

8 *Internt Notat til Folkekommissær, Kammerat A.I. Rykov, 17. maj 1933*, RGAE, fond 3527, opis 13, delo 315.

9 *Den administrerende Direktørs maanedlige Beretninger, Maj 1934*.

10 Ibid., *November 1934*.

11 *Christiansen til Folkekommissariatet, 23. December 1934* and *Udateret udkast til brev fra Folkekommissariatet til Christiansen*, AVP fond 85, opis 18, delo 13.

12 *USSR's Folkekommissariat for Kommunikationsvæsenet til SNTS's Befuldmægtigede, Borger Christiansen, 8. Januar 1935*. RA, UM 92 Dan 5/53. The letter was transferred the following day.

13 *Kgl. Dansk Gesandtskab i Moskva til UM, 9. Januar 1935*, RA, UM 92 Dan 5/53.

14 Ibid. as well as *Den administrerende Direktørs Beretninger, Januar 1935*. NKVD is actually an abbreviation for the Russian for People's Commissariat of Domestic Affairs, and in the 1930s the secret police were officially referred to as one of "NKVD's organs." Usage here, however, reflects the established and more efficient usage where "NKVD" is understood as simply referring to the secret police.

15 *Bestyrelsesmøde, 14. Januar 1935*. What follows is based on this source.

16 Ibid., *28. December 1934* and *14. Januar 1935*.

17 The information provided by telephone is indicated by a written note on *Kgl. Dansk Gesandtskab i Moskva til UM, 14. Januar 1935*, RA, UM 92 Dan 5/53.

18 *Memo v/ AU/EM, SNTS, 15. Januar 1935*, RA, UM 92 Dan 5/53.

19 Ibid.

20 *Notat om Litvinov v/ AU/EM, SNTS, 15. Januar 1935, UM til P. Munch i Genève, 16. januar 1935*, RA UM 92 Dan 5/53.

21 *Kgl. Dansk Gesandtskab i Moskva til UM, 14. and 17. Januar 1935*, RA, UM 92 Dan 5/53.

22 *Notat, u.d. Januar 1935, UM til Kgl. Dansk Gesandtskab, 5. februar 1935*, RA, UM 92 Dan 5/53.

23 *Christiansen til direktionen, Moskva 23. Februar* and *5. Marts 1935*, RA, UM 92 Dan 5/53. *Den administrerende Direktørs maanedlige Beretning, Februar 1935*.

24 Ibid.

25 *Store Nordiske til Udenrigsministeriet, 11. Marts 1935. Udenrigsministeriet til Store Nordiske, 24. April 1935*, RA, UM 92 Dan 5/53.

26 *Den administrerende Direktørs maanedlige Beretninger, Juni 1935*.

27 Ibid., *Maj* and *Juli 1936*.

28 *Christiansen til Direktionen, Moskva 21. Juli 1937*, RA, UM Dan 5/53.

29 Ibid. as well as *Kgl. Danske Gesandtskab i Moskva til Udenrigsministeriet, 21. Juli 1937*, RA, UM 92 Dan 5/53.

30 *Christiansen til Direktionen, Moskva 21.–22. juli 1937*, RA, UM 92 Dan 5/53.

31 *Rådslagning om spørgsmålet vedrørende en uformel henvendelse til Store Nordiske i spørgsmålet om en likvidering af koncessionen, 19. juli 1937. Notat om likvideringen af Store Nordiske Telegraf-Selskab v/ Anikejev, 23. juli 1937*, AVP fond 085, opis 20, delo 233.

32 *Leningradskaja Pravda, 11. juni 1937*.

33 *Christiansen til Direktionen, Moskva 21.–22. Juli 1937*, RA, UM Dan 5/53.

34 *Bestyrelsesmøde, 17. August 1937*, RA, SNTS. The account that follows is based on these minutes.

35 Ibid.

36 The letter from Great Northern that was dated August 11, 1937, has not been found, but its existence, contents, and date are confirmed by other sources.

37 Reports in UM Journalsager 35.J.1.

38 *Berman og Potemkin til Stalin, 8. september 1937. Lapsjov til Mikojan, 9. september 1937. Lapsjov til Belenkij, 14. september 1937*. GARF, fond 5446, opis 22a, delo 207.

39 *Belenkij til Molotov, 23. november 1937*. GARF, fond 5446, opis 22a, delo 207.

40 There are a number of drafts of a government decision with this formulation, the latest dated 11 November 1937, in GARF, fond 5446, opis 22a, delo 307.

41 *Bestyrelsesmøde, 20. Oktober 1937*. The following description is based on this source.

42 *Kgl. Dansk Gesandtskab i Moskva til UM, 24. november 1937*, RA, UM Dan 5/53.

43 *Den administrerende Direktørs maanedlige Beretning, Oktober 1937*.

44 An internal Soviet government document of August 21, 1939, referring to the entire sequence of events, indicated that "in 1939 there was apparently an instruction regarding the liquidation of the Great Northern Telegraph Company's old agreement, but there is no record of any particular decision with regard to this matter in the archives of the People's Commissariat for Communications." Some documents did indicate that the concession was not to be formally nullified but that the Danish functionaries were to be replaced

with Russian workers. There was no particular agreement in this regard, however. *Memorandum vedrøren-de spørgsmålet om likvidering af Det Store Nordiske Telegraf-Selskabs koncessioner, Folkekommissariatet for Kommunikationsvæsen, 21. august 1939.* AVP, fond 085, opis 22, delo 259.

45 Materials in AVP, fond 085, opis 22, delo 259.

46 Ibid.

47 *Bestyrelsesmøde, 20. Oktober 1937,* RA, SNTS.

48 *Det Store Nordiske Telegraf-Selskab: Beretning for* året *1937,* RA, SNTS.

49 *Bolt-Jørgensen til Udenrigsministeriet, Moskva 19. april 1938.* UM, journalsag 17.m.539.

50 Ibid.

51 NKVD authority in Rostov Oblast, Delo No. 4060.

52 *Kgl. Dansk Gesandtskab til Udenrigsministeriet, Kode-telegram 20. Januar 1939* and *Kgl. Dansk Gesandtskab til Udenrigsministeriet, 9. Februar 1939.* UM, journalsag 17.m.539.

CHAPTER 15

1 *Den administrerende Direktørs maanedlige Be-retninger, Oktober 1929.*

2 Ibid., *Juli 1930.*

3 Ibid.

4 *Regnskab og Aarsberetning 1930.*

5 *Bestyrelsesprotokol, 9. April 1930.*

6 *Regnskab og* Aarsberetning, 1931.

7 Ibid., *1932.*

8 Ibid., *1933.*

9 *Bestyrelsesmøde, 6. April 1934.*

10 *Den administrerende Direktørs maanedlige Beretninger, September 1938.*

11 Ibid.

12 Ibid.

13 Ibid., *September 1939.*

14 Ibid., *November 1939.*

15 Ibid., *November* and *December 1939.*

16 Ibid., *December 1939, Januar–Marts 1940.*

17 Ibid., *Marts 1940.* What follows is based on this source.

18 Daqing Yang, *From Cooperation to Conflict,* p. 239.

19 Quoted from ibid.

20 *Den administrerende Direktørs maanedlige Beretninger, April/Maj* and *Juli/August 1940.*

21 Reproduced as a supplement to *Den administrerende Direktørs maanedlige Beretninger, Juni/Juli 1946.*

22 Is indicated by a supplement to ibid. as well as FO 371, F W 6044/5876/49 (1940).

23 Materials in FO 371, F 2984/2854/10 (1940); FO 371, W 7117/97/47 (1940). Also materials in Cable & Wireless's archive: Brown Shelf on GNTC, sector 2: cable stocks, Woosung depot, Shanghai; sector 3: Hong Kong ... GNC affairs.

24 *Statement by F.W. Phillips, Director of Telecommunica-tions, General Post Office, 1 June 1940.* Supplement to *Den administrerende Direktørs maanedlige Beretninger, Juni/Juli 1946.*

25 *Cable & Wireless to O.E. Nielsen, GNTC, 30 August 1940.* Brown Shelf on GNTC, Sector 4; Japan and consolidation agreement. *General position to Great Northern,* Cable & Wireless Archive.

26 *Den administrerende Direktørs maanedlige Beretninger, Juli–Oktober 1945* and *Juni–Juli 1946 inklusive bilag* as well as materials from Cable & Wireless's archive: *Note, 7 January 1941,* Brown Shelf on GNTC, Sector 4; *Japan and Consolidation Agreement. General Position to the Great Northern.*

27 *FO to the Treasury 21st March 1941.* In F.O. 371 N 1040/142/15 (/1941), where the exchange of memoranda and letters between the various British government organs can be found in its entirety.

28 *Internal letter to Room 17, FO, 3 August 1943,* FO 371, W 12145/987/801 (1943).

29 *Den administrerende Direktørs maanedlige Beretninger, April-Maj 1940.*

30 Ibid., *Juni 1940.*

31 Ibid.

32 Ibid., *Oktober 1940–Februar 1941.*

33 Ibid., *Marts–April 1941.*

34 Documents in RA, UM 17 E. Sovj. 10/1. Sovjetrusland og Danmark.

35 *Den administrerende Direktørs maanedlige Beretninger, Maj/Juni 1941.*

36 Ibid.

37 Ibid., *September–Oktober 1941.*

38 Ibid., *Maj–Juli 1942.*

39 Ibid., *November/December 1943, second halfyear of 1944* and *second halfyear of 1945.*

40 Ibid., *first halfyear of 1945.*

41 Ibid., *Januar–Februar 1942.*

42 Ibid., *Maj–Juli 1942.*

43 Ibid., *April–May 1943.*

44 *Bestyrelsesmøde, 28. Juli 1939* including supplements.

45 Ibid.

46 Ibid., *9. September* and *20. Oktober 1939.*

47 *Bestyrelsesmøde 8. September 1943* and *Den administrerende Direktørs maanedlige Beretninger, September–December 1943.*

48 The investments can be followed in the top management team's monthly reports to the board of directors.

49 *Bestyrelsesmøde 1. Februar 1940.*

50 Ibid., *6. November 1942* and *Den administrerende Direktørs maanedlige Beretninger, August–Oktober 1942.*

51 *Indbydelse til Tegning af indtil 12 mill. Kr. Aktier i Det Danske Luftfartsselskab A/S, Juni 1943.* Supplement to *Bestyrelsesmøde 25. Juni 1943.*

52 Ibid.

53 *Den administrerende Direktørs maanedlige Beretninger, Februar–April 1943.*

54 Bent Suenson: Memorandum af 27. februar 1943. Attached to Den administrerende Direktørs maanedlige Beretninger, Februar–April 1943.

55 Ibid.

56 Ministeriet for Handel, Industri og Søfart til Store Nordiske, 19. Juni 1943. Supplement to Bestyrelsesmøde, 25. Juli 1943.

57 Den administrerende Direktørs maanedlige Beretninger, September-December 1943. Bestyrelsesmøde, 30. November 1943.

CHAPTER 16

1 Bestyrelsesmøde 17. April 1945, with enclosure.

2 Ibid.

3 Den adm. Direktørs maanedlige Beretninger, 1. Halvaar 1945.

4 Ibid.

5 Bestyrelsesmøde 29. Maj 1945, including the enclosure.

6 Ibid., 12. Juni 1945 og Den adm. Direktørs maanedlige Beretninger, 1. Halvaar 1945.

7 Den adm. Direktørs maanedlige Beretninger, Juli/Oktober 1945 and Bestyrelsesprotokol 17. September and 20. Oktober 1945.

8 Den adm. Direktørs maanedlige Beretninger, November and December 1945. Bestyrelsesmøde 18. December 1945.

9 Ibid.

10 Den adm. Direktørs maanedlige Beretninger, Juli–Oktober 1945.

11 Ibid.

12 Den administrerende Direktørs maanedlige Beretninger, December 1945.

13 Ibid., Juli-Oktober 1945.

14 Ibid.

15 Ibid.

16 Ibid.

17 Ibid.

18 Ibid., December 1945.

19 Ibid.

20 Bestyrelsesmøde 20. November 1945.

21 Ekstraordinær Generalforsamling, Regnskab for 1944 and Beretning.

22 Ibid.

23 Ibid.

24 Generalkonsul Th. Olesen til Bestyrelsen for det Store Nordiske Telegraf-Selskab, 3. November 1945. Bilag til Bestyrelsesprotokol, 20. November 1945.

25 Ibid.

26 Bestyrelsesprotokol, 7. Februar 1946. Den adm. Direktørs maanedlige Beretninger, Januar–Februar 1946.

27 Ibid., Juni–Juli 1946.

28 Ibid., April 1946.

29 Ibid., April 1946, Marts–April and Oktober–November 1947.

30 Ibid., Januar–Februar 1946.

31 Ibid., Marts 1946.

32 Ibid., Juni–Juli 1946.

33 Ibid., August–Oktober 1946.

34 Ibid., November–December 1946.

35 Ibid., Januar–Februar 1947.

36 Ibid. as well as Marts–April 1947.

37 Ibid., Maj/Juli 1947.

38 Ibid., December 1947/Januar 1948.

39 Ibid., Juni–August 1948.

40 Ibid., November–December 1948.

41 Ibid., Januar–Februar 1949.

42 Information, 5.–6. marts 1977.

43 Bestyrelsesmøde, 25. Maj 1946. The account notice was sent out the same day.

44 Store Nordiske til Generalkonsul Th. Olesen. Supplement 174 to Bestyrelsesmøde, 21. Juni 1946.

45 Det Store Nordiske Telegraf-Selskab: Regnskab for 1945 and Beretning.

46 Det Store Nordiske Telegraf-Selskab: Regnskab for 1946 and Beretning. Generalkonsul Th. Olesen til Det Store Nordiske Telegraf-Selskab, 22. April 1947, bilag 182 til Bestyrelsesmøde, 14. Maj 1947.

47 Store Nordiske til Generalkonsul T. Olesen., 14. Maj 1947, supplement 183 to ibid.

48 Vekselerer S.A. Jensen til Det Store Nordiske Telegraf-Selskab, 26. April 1948 and Store Nordiske til Vekselerer S.A. Jensen. 4. Maj 1948. Bilag 184 og 185 til Ibid., 7. Maj 1948.

49 Det Store Nordiske Telegraf-Selskab. Regnskab for 1947 and Beretning.

50 Ekstra Bladet, 26. Marts 1948.

51 Quoted from Bestyrelsesmøde, 25. Maj 1946, at which the matter was discussed.

52 Berlingske Tidende, Politiken and Nationaltidende 20. April 1949.

53 Det Store Nordiske Telegraf-Selskab. Regnskab for 1948 and Beretning.

54 Ibid.

55 Formandens omslag, generalforsamlingen 1949.

56 Ibid.

57 Berlingske Tidende, 13. maj 1949.

58 Bestyrelsesmøde, 27. marts 1950.

CHAPTER 17

1 Bestyrelsesmøde, 16. Oktober 1947.

2 Ibid.

3 Bestyrelsesmøde, 7. maj og 29. juni 1948.

4 Den adm. direktørs månedlige beretninger, august-november 1950.

5 Pressemeddelelse, 8. november 1950. Bilag til Den adm. direktørs månedlige beretninger, oktober/november 1950.

6 Ibid., april-juni 1956.

7 *Bestyrelsesmøde, 29. Maj 1945.* At the same time, O. C. Scavenius offered to resign, as he would soon be seventy years old and "did not himself have any wish to remain." The other board members asked him to remain on the board, however.

8 Ibid., 13. Juni 1945.

9 Ibid., 29. Juni 1945,

10 *Bestyrelsesmøde, 3. Juni 1949,* including supplement no. 205.

11 *Den adm. direktørs månedlige beretninger, juli-august 1949.*

12 Ibid.

13 Ibid. as well as *september/november 1949* and *Bestyrelsesmøde, 26. august 1949.*

14 *Den adm. direktørs månedlige beretninger, september/ november* and *december 1949.*

15 Ibid.

16 Ibid., *juni–juli 1950.*

17 Ibid., *december 1950–juli 1951.*

18 Quoted from ibid., *marts–april 1952.*

19 Ibid.

20 Ibid., *maj–juli, oktober–december 1952* og *januar–juni 1953.*

21 The report is contained in ibid., *april–juni 1953.*

22 *Bestyrelsesmøde, 1. oktober 1953.*

23 Ibid., *Januar–Februar 1946* and *Maj/Juli 1947.*

24 Ibid., *februar–marts* and *september–oktober 1948.*

25 Ibid., *august–september* and *oktober–november 1950.*

26 Ibid., *februar–april 1951.*

27 Ibid., *marts–april 1949.*

28 Ibid., *juli–august 1949.*

29 *Den adm. direktørs månedlige beretninger, november– december 1951.*

30 *Bestyrelsesmøde, 20. marts 1952.*

31 *Den adm. direktørs månedlige beretninger, marts– april 1952.*

32 Ibid.

33 *Bestyrelsesmøde, 28. august 1952. Den adm. direktørs månedlige beretninger, december 1952/januar 1953.*

34 Ibid., oktober–december 1953.

35 *Bestyrelsesmøde, 17. december 1953.*

36 Supplement no. 238 to *Bestyrelsesmøde, 8. april 1954.*

37 *Den adm. direktørs månedlige beretninger, april–juni* og *juli–september 1955.*

38 Ibid.

39 Translated and quoted from Hanaoka Kaoru, *Hundred Years of Submarine Cables,* p. 123-24.

40 *Den adm. direktørs* månedlige beretninger, august-september 1954.

41 Ibid., januar–juni 1955.

42 Ibid., november 1955

43 *Bestyrelsesmøde, 7. marts 1955.*

44 *Den adm. direktørs månedlige beretninger, januar– februar 1957.*

45 Ibid., *marts–maj* and *juli–august 1958.*

46 Ibid., *januar–februar 1959.*

47 Ibid., *juni 1959.*

48 Ibid., *juli–august 1958.*

49 Ibid., *juni–august 1961.*

50 Ibid., *september–december 1961.*

51 Ibid

CHAPTER 18

1 *Bestyrelsesmøde 21. August 1946,* including supplement 175.

2 Ibid.

3 Ibid.

4 *Overenskomst mellem A/S Det Store Nordiske Tele- graf-Selskab og Einar Arp (indehaver af firmaet Viggo Arp), 17. December 1942.*

5 Ibid. as well as *Den adm. Direktørs maanedlige Be- retninger, Juni-Juli 1946.* The factory and the lot on which it stood were taken over on August 1, 1946.

6 Ibid., *August–September 1946.*

7 Proposal in *Formandens Omslag til Generalforsamling 1947.*

8 Referat i ibid.

9 Erik Petersen og Svend Falck Larsen, *Memorandum Ang. Firma for FM Tovejsradio, Maj 1947.* www.storno- time.dk. What follows is based on this source.

10 Ibid.

11 *Bestyrelsesprotokol, 7. August 1947.* The date of the es- tablishment of the company is indicated by *K.L. Jensen til Stornos direktion, 2. Marts 1981.* www.stornotime.dk. At that time, K. L. Jensen was the head of the division that manufactured telegraphy instruments and control clocks.

12 *Den adm. direktørs månedlige beretninger, Maj-Juli 1947.*

13 *Det Store Nordiske Telegraf-Selskab til Generaldirek- toratet for Post- og Telegrafvæsenet, 15. September 1947* (two letters).

14 *Bestyrelsesprotokol, 16. Oktober 1947.*

15 *K.L. Jensen til Stornos direktion, 2. marts 1981.* www. stornotime.dk. *Dansk Radioindustri, nr. 5, 1948.*

16 *Den adm. direktørs månedlige beretninger, marts/april 1949.*

17 *Social-Demokraten, 24. april 1949.*

18 *B.T., 3. august 1949.*

19 *Berlingske Aftenavis, 21. november 1949.*

20 *Teknikens Värld, nr. 1 1950.*

21 *Brandskydd.* Supplement to *Den adm. direktørs måned- lige beretninger, marts/april 1949. Berlingske Aftenavis, 21. november 1949.*

22 *B.T., 3. august 1949.*

23 *Politiken, 4. november 1949. Det danske post- og tele- grafvæsen: Beretning om virksomheden 1949-50.*

24 Ibid.

25 *Politiken, 2. marts 1949.*

26 *Ekstra Bladet, 10. oktober 1949. B.T., 23. november 1949. Politiken, 24. november 1949.*

27 Ibid.

28 *Ingeniøren, 5. januar 1952. Den adm. direktørs månedlige beretninger, august/oktober 1951.*

29 *Ingeniøren, 3.* and *10. januar 1953.*

30 Ibid.

31 *Ingeniøren 10. januar 1953. Den adm. direktørs månedlige beretninger, august/oktober 1951.*

32 *Den adm. direktørs månedlige beretninger, juli/september 1953. Ingeniøren, nr. 2, 1954.*

33 *Dansk Radio Industri, nr. 9, 1950.*

34 *Populär Radio, nr. 5, 1951. Det danske post- og telegrafvæsen: Beretning om virksomheden 1950-51.*

35 Ibid.

36 *Den adm. direktørs månedlige beretninger, august/oktober 1951* as well as www.storno.se.

37 *Den adm. direktørs månedlige beretninger, august/oktober 1951.*

38 Ibid. as well as *juli/september 1953.*

39 Ibid.

40 Ibid., *december 1952/januar 1953.*

41 Ibid., *juli/september 1953* as well as *oktober/december 1954.*

42 *Bestyrelsesmøde, 20. marts 1951.*

43 Is indicated by continually updated accounts in *Den adm. direktørs månedlige beretninger,* where one can follow the orders received and invoices issued.

44 *Bestyrelsesmøde, 28. august* and *4. december 1952.*

45 Ibid.

46 Ibid., *6. marts 1953. Dansk Ingeniørstat 1955.*

47 *Bestyrelsesmøde, 17. december 1953* and *8. april 1954. Den adm. direktørs månedlige beretninger, december 1953.*

48 *Den adm. direktørs månedlige beretninger, oktober/december 1954* and *oktober/december 1955.*

49 Ibid., *oktober/december 1955* and *Ingeniøren, nr. 1, 1956.*

50 Ibid.

51 Ibid., december 1956. *Ingeniøren nr. 1, 1957.*

52 *Danmarks Handels- og Søfarts-Tidende, 14. september 1956.*

53 *Bestyrelsesmøde, 29. november 1955* and *8. juni 1956.*

54 Ibid., *26. september 1956 og 16. marts 1957.* The streamlining report is not extant.

55 Ibid.

56 Ibid.

57 Ibid., *11. oktober 1957.*

58 Ibid., *29. november 1957* and *4. februar 1958.*

59 *Bestyrelsesmøde, 14. april 1959.*

CHAPTER 19

1 *Bestyrelsesmøde, 18. februar 1954.*

2 *Den adm. direktørs månedlige beretninger,* m*aj–juli 1954.*

3 Ibid.

4 Ibid., *maj–juni 1958* as well as *Bestyrelsesmøde, 6. juni 1956.* Morton Mintz og Jerry S. Cohen, *America, Inc. Who Owns and Operates the United States,* p. 330-37 describes the background of the project and its development based on documents from a lawsuit that was later brought against the United States government by ITT's subsidiary Commercial Cable Company and in connection with which it was alleged that the United States government had not supported the project energetically enough.

5 *American Embassy in Copenhagen to the Danish Ministry for Foreign Affairs, Confidential August 19, 1954.* Statsministeriet, Grønlandsministeriet: Departementschefarkiv (confidential), journalsager (1950-1978) 14: XXIV Icecan.

6 *Referat af møde i Udenrigsministeriet, lørdag 28. august 1954. Udenrigsministeriet: Note Verbale to the Embassy of the United States of America, Copenhagen, September 1st, 1954.* Statsministeriet, Grønlandsministeriet: Departementschefarkiv (confidential), journalsager (1950–1978) 14: XXIV Icecan.

7 The *Embassy of the United States to the Danish Ministry for Foreign Affairs, Confidential, September 8, 1954.* Statsministeriet, Grønlandsministeriet: Departementschefarkiv (confidential), journalsager (1950-1978) 14: XXIV Icecan.

8 *Referat af møde i Generaldirektoratet for Post- og Telegrafvæsenet, 15. oktober 1954.* Statsministeriet, Grønlandsministeriet: Departementschefarkiv (fortroligt), journalsager (1950–1978) 14: XXIV Icecan.

9 *Minutes of a meeting held in the Ministry for Foreign Affairs on November 9, 1954, Secret. Notater fra møde i Generaldirektoratet for Post- og Telegrafvæsenet, 10. november 1954.* Statsministeriet, Grønlandsministeriet: Departementschefarkiv (confidental), journalsager (1950-1978) 14: XXIV Icecan.

10 Ibid., as well as *Den adm. direktørs månedlige beretninger, september–december 1954.*

11 Is indicated by ibid. as well as materials in Statsministeriet, Grønlandsministeriet: Departementschefarkiv (confidential), journalsager (1950-1978) 14: XXIV Icecan.

12 Ibid. as well as Morton Mintz og Jerry S. Cohen, *America, Inc. Who Owns and Operates the United States,* p. 330-37

13 *Ingeniøren, 15. maj 1964.* What follows is based on this article, which was written by Niels Erik Holmblad.

14 *Bestyrelsesmøde, 10.* and *24. juni 1954.*

15 *Bestyrelsesmøde, 24. juni 1954.*

16 Ibid., *Den adm. direktørs månedlige beretninger, oktober–december 1954.*

17 Ibid.

18 Ibid.

19 Ibid.

20 Ibid. as well as *july–september*, from which the letter from the British postal minister is quoted. *Bestyrelsesmøde, 29. november 1955.*

21 Ibid.

22 *Den adm. direktørs månedlige beretninger, september–oktober 1959. Bestyrelsesmøde, 20. september 1960.*

23 Ibid., as well as *Den adm. direktørs månedlige beretninger, juli–oktober 1956 og Bestyrelsesmøde, 26. september 1956.*

24 *Den adm. direktørs månedlige beretninger, juli–oktober 1956.*

25 *Bestyrelsesmøde, 5. december 1956.*

26 *Den adm. direktørs månedlige beretninger*, november–december 1956.

27 Ibid., *januar-februar 1957. Ingeniøren, 15. maj 1964,*

28 Ibid., *marts–maj 1957* and *Bestyrelsesmøde, 28. maj 1957.*

29 *Bestyrelsesmøde, 29. november 1957. Den adm. direktørs månedlige beretninger, oktober–november* and *december 1957.*

30 The negotiations are described in detail in *Den adm. direktørs månedlige beretninger, december 1959.*

31 Ibid., *maj–juni 1958.*

32 Ibid.

33 Ibid., as well as *Bestyrelsesmøde, 6. juni 1958.*

34 Ibid.

35 Ibid., *juli–august 1958.*

36 A copy of this note is attached as a supplement to ibid. *Danish Embassy. P.M. Washington D.C., 31. July, 1958.* Statsministeriet, Grønlandsministeriet: Departementschefarkiv (confidential), journalsager (1950-1978) 14: XXIV Icecan.

37 The note dated August 4 is attached as a supplement to ibid. *Embassy of the United States of America to Danish Ministry of Foreign Affairs, August 4, 1958.*

38 *Den adm. direktørs månedlige beretninger, juli–august 1958.* Materialer i Statsministeriet, Grønlandsministeriet: Departementschefarkiv (confidential), journalsager (1950-1978) 14: XXIV Icecan.

39 Ibid. *Notes of a meeting held in London on 28th August, 1958 at Post Office Headquarters.* Statsministeriet, Grønlandsministeriet: Departementschefarkiv (confidential), journalsager (1950-1978) 14: XXIV Icecan.

40 Ibid. *Den danske ambassade i Reykjavik til Udenrigsministeriet 4. september 1958. Foreign Office to the American Ambassor, September 9, 1958. The Danish Ministry of Foreign Affairs to The Embassy of United States of America, the 10th of September 1958.* Statsministeriet, Grønlandsministeriet: Departementschefarkiv (confidential), journalsager (1950-1978) 14: XXIV Icecan.

41 Ibid.

42 The negotiations are detailed in ibid., September–October 1958. *Minutes of a meeting held at P.O. Head-*

quarters on 9. October to discuss the "Quick Freeze" Project and ICAO Requirements. Notat v/ Kgl. Dansk Ambassade i London, 15. oktober 1958. Notat til sagen vedrørende ICAO, November 14, 1958. Statsministeriet, Grønlandsministeriet: Departementschefarkiv (fortroligt), journalsager (1950–1978) 14: XXIV Icecan.

43 Ibid.

44 Ibid.

45 Ibid., *juli–august 1958.*

46 *Hemmeligt notat ved Bent Suenson, 21. November 1956. Hemmeligt notat v/ Eske Brun, 10. september med tilføjelse 22. september 1956.* In the file "DEW og andre warning systemer".

47 Ibid.

48 *Fortroligt referat af møde i Grønlandsministeriet, 8. juli 1957, vedrørende DEW-line.* In the file "Dew og andre warning systemer".

49 Ibid.

50 *Notat v/ Bent Suenson om Ingeniør Rasmussens udlån til Ministeriet for Grønland, 8. august 1957.* In the file "Dew og andre warning systemer".

51 *PL: Samtale med afdelingschef Finn Nielsen, Grønlandsministeriet, den 21. Oktober 1957.* In the file "Dew og andre warning systemer".

52 *Bestyrelsesmøde, 29. november 1957.* The following messages from the Ministry of Greenland and Great Northern's responses are indicated by materials in the file "Dew og andre warning systemer."

53 A description of the course of events is contained in *Notat af 15. maj 1964 ved Poul Laursen om nye amerikanske planer om et telekommunikationskabel mellem Kulusuk, Grønland og Keflavik, Island.* The file "Greenice 1958-".

54 *Fortroligt referat af møde 15. december 1958 om Dew-Line-systemet i Grønland: Kabel fra Kulusuk til Island.* The file "Greenice 1958-".

55 Ibid.

56 Ibid.

57 *Den adm. direktørs månedlige beretninger, januar-februar 1959. Bestyrelsesprotokol, 27. januar 1959.* As the only delegation to do so, the French delegation refrained from voting at the meeting on January 12.

58 Ibid., *november–december 1959.*

59 Ibid.

60 Ibid.

61 Ibid.

62 Ibid., *marts–april 1960* and *november–december 1960.*

63 Ibid., *marts–maj 1961.*

64 Ibid., *juni 1962.*

65 Ibid., *august–oktober 1963.*

66 Ibid.

67 Ibid., *marts–april 1964.* What follows is based on this source.

68 Ibid.

69 Ibid., *august–oktober 1964.*

70 Ibid.

71 Ibid., *april 1965.*

72 Ibid.

73 *Bestyrelsesmøde, 27. september 1965,* including supplement no. 308. What follows is based on this source.

74 Ibid.

75 *Den adm. direktørs månedlige beretninger, september–december 1965.* What follows is based on this source.

76 Ibid.

77 *KDD til Store Nordiske, Tokyo 19. september 1965. Store Nordiske til KDD, Kbh. 6. december* 1965 and *Bilag til den adm. direktørs månedlige beretninger, september–december 1965.*

78 *KDD til Store Nordiske, Tokyo 13. december 1965.* Supplement to ibid.

79 *Den adm. direktørs månedlige beretninger, marts–april 1966.*

80 Ibid., *maj–november 1966.*

81 Ibid.

82 Ibid.

83 *Bestyrelsesmøde, 16. januar 1967.*

84 Ibid.

CHAPTER 20

1 The contact with Motorola is detailed in minutes of the meetings of the board of directors, the fall of 1959.

2 Ibid.

3 *Bestyrelsesmøde, 1. november 1961 med bilag.*

4 Ibid., as well as *Bestyrelsesmøde, 28. september 1961.*

5 *Bestyrelsesmøde, 1. november 1961.*

6 *Bestyrelsesprotokol, 5. februar 1960. Ingeniøren, 1. januar 1961.* Formally, the German company was a subsidiary of Great Northern, and the mother company concluded a licensing agreement with Southern Instruments in the United Kingdom.

7 *Ingeniøren, 1. januar 1961.*

8 Ibid.

9 Ibid., *1. januar 1962, 1. januar 1963* and *1. januar 1965. Tidsskrift for Bygnings- og Ingeniørvæsen, 10. juni og 25. juli 1962.*

10 *Tidsskrift for Industri, januar 1964.*

11 Ibid. as well as *Ingeniøren, 1. januar* and *5. oktober 1963.*

12 Ibid., *14. september 1963.*

13 *Storno. Årsberetning og regnskab for 1963. Bilag 288 til bestyrelsesmøde 9. april 1964. Storno Årsberetning og regnskab for 1966. Bilag 324 til bestyrelsesmøde 2. maj 1967.*

14 *Ingeniøren, 1. januar* and *2. maj 1964.*

15 Ibid., *25. februar* and *16. september 1966. Jyllands-Posten, 20. august 1966. Politiken, 18. september 1965.*

16 Ibid., *11. marts 1966. Tidsskrift for Industri, januar 1964.*

17 Ibid., as well as *30. juni 1967.*

18 Ibid., *11. november 1966* and *19. maj 1967.*

19 *Tidsskrift for Bygnings- og Ingeniørvæsen, 3. september 1965.*

20 *Politiken, 3. november 1966.*

21 *Storno. Årsberetning og regnskab for året 1967. Bilag 332 til bestyrelsesprotokol, 30. april 1968.*

22 Ibid., *1. januar 1962.* Various newspapers, November 1–3, 1961.

23 *Politiken, 11. august 1962.*

24 *Det danske post og telegrafvæsen: Beretning om virksomheden 1963-64. Politiken, 5. december 1963.*

25 *Ingeniøren, 1. januar 1965* and *Politiken, 24. marts 1965. Det danske post- og telegrafvæsen: Beretning om virksomheden 1965-66.*

26 *Det danske post- og telegrafvæsen: Beretning om virksomheden 1966-67.*

27 *Jyllandsposten, 2. marts 1967. Ingeniøren, 8. september 1967. Det danske post- og telegrafvæsen: Beretning om virksomheden 1967-68, 1968-69* and *1969-70.*

28 *Storno. Årsberetning og regnskab for året 1967. Bilag nr. 332 til bestyrelsesmøde 30. april 1968. Det Store Nordiske Telegraf-Selskab. Regnskab for 1967 og Beretning.*

29 *Bestyrelsesmøde. 5. december 1967* and *30. april 1968.*

30 *Stiftelsesoverenskomst, udateret. Bilag 336 til bestyrelsesmøde 30. april 1968.*

31 Ibid.

32 *Bestyrelsesmøde, 30. april 1968. Politiken, 7. maj 1969.*

33 Ibid., *15. januar 1968. Politiken, 3. august 1963.*

34 *Storno A/S. Driftsregnskab og status for året 1968.* The revenues of the subsidiaries are not indicated by the operating account, and the 93 million kroner referred to in the text are based on *Bilag nr. 343 til bestyrelsesmøde, 9. april 1969. Tidsskrift for Industri, januar 1964.*

35 *Bestyrelsesmøde, 5. december 1967.*

36 *Berlingske Aftenavis, 4. januar 1964.*

37 *Tidsskrift for Industri, januar 1964.*

38 *Berlingske Aftenavis, 4. januar 1969.*

39 *Tidsskrift for Industri, januar 1969.*

40 Quoted from *Berlingske Aftenavis, 4. januar 1969.*

41 Ibid.

42 Ibid.

CHAPTER 21

1 Based on *Bestyrelsesmøde, 18. september 1958* samt *Bilag nr. 269 til bestyrelsesmøde, 2. marts 1961,* which contains a historic account.

2 Ibid., *14. marts 1961.*

3 Ibid., *26. februar* and *17. juni 1965.*

4 Ibid., *31. august 1966* and *16. december 1966.*

5 Ibid.

6 Ibid., *9. oktober* and *5. december 1967.*

7 *Bilag nr. 328 og 329 til bestyrelsesmøde, 5. december*

1967. Den adm. direktørs månedlige beretninger, november/december 1967.

8 *Det Store Nordiske Telegraf-Selskab. Beretning og regnskab 1968.*

9 *Bilag 368 til bestyrelsesmøde, 11. september 1972.* What follows is based on this source.

10 *Bestyrelsesmøde, 11. september* and *7. november 1972.*

11 *Bestyrelsesprotokol, 1. februar* and *1. marts 1974.*

12 Ibid., *8. april* and *20. august 1974 inklusive bilag.* What follows is based on this source.

13 Ibid. and *26. september 1974.*

14 Ibid., *9. oktober 1969.*

15 Ibid., *20. maj* and *3. oktober 1970* as well as *2. marts 1971. Det Store Nordiske Telegraf-Selskab. Beretning og regnskab 1970.*

16 Ibid. as well as *Det Store Nordiske Telegraf-Selskab. Beretning og regnskab 1971.*

17 Ibid., *22. december 1971* and *8. marts 1972. Det Store Nordiske Telegraf-Selskab. Beretning og regnskab 1972.*

18 Ibid., *11. september 1972.*

19 Ibid., *7. november 1972* and *Det Store Nordiske Telegraf-Selskab. Beretning og regnskab 1972.*

20 Ibid., *13. november 1973* and *1. marts 1974.*

21 *Bestyrelsesmøde, 20. maj 1970.*

22 *Det Store nordiske Telegraf-Selskab. Beretning og regnskab 1970.*

23 *Bestyrelsesmøde, 1. juli 1971.*

24 Ibid.

25 Ibid., *23. maj, 13. juni 1973* and *11. september 1973* as well as *Bilag til bestyrelsesmøde, 13. november 1973.*

26 Except where there is an explicit indication to the contrary, what follows is based on Erik B. Rasmussen, *Upublicerede erindringer om Store Nordiske* as well as *Radiometers historie fra 1956–1976.* Erik Mollerup, *Hvad formanden gør . . .*, p. 96f. These meetings are not described in the minutes of the board of directors.

27 Ibid.

28 Ibid., *20. september* and *13. november 1973.*

29 Ibid.

30 Ibid., *1. februar* and *1. marts 1974.*

31 *Bilag til bestyrelsesmøde, 1. februar 1974.* What follows is based on this source.

32 *Bestyrelsesmøde, 1. marts 1974.* What follows is based on this source.

33 Ibid., *19. marts 1974.* What follows is based on this source.

34 Ibid.

35 *Bestyrelsesmøde, 15. maj 1974, inklusive bilag.* What follows is based on this source.

36 Ibid. as well as *21. maj 1974.*

37 Ibid., *1. juli 1974.*

38 Ibid., *26. september 1974.*

39 Ibid., *23. oktober 1974.*

40 Ibid., *9. december 1975 inklusive bilag.*

41 Ibid.

42 Quoted from ibid.

CHAPTER 22

1 *Bestyrelsesmøde, 26. februar 1975.*

2 *Dansk Radio Industri nr. 3, marts 1949. Ingeniøren 16. november 1957.*

3 *Bygget på omsorg – Oticon gennem 100 år* as well as www.oticon.dk.

4 *Ingeniøren, 21. december 1946.*

5 O. Bentzen, H.W. Ewertsen og G. Salomon (eds.), *Dansk Audiologi 1951-1976,* p. 1–5

6 *Ingeniøren, 17. april 1970.*

7 Claus Nielsen og Cecilie Wallengren, *William Demant – manden bag Oticon,* p. 110.

8 *Tidsskrift for tunghøre,* various volumes.

9 Ibid. as well as *Ingeniøren 17. april 1970.*

10 Ibid., *5. september 1965* and *1. januar 1966. Hørelsen, nr. 9, 1965.*

11 Ibid., as well as *9. juni 1951.*

12 Ibid., *17. juni 1976.*

13 *Bestyrelsesmøde, 26. april 1977,* including supplement 473.

14 Ibid.

15 Ibid.

16 Ibid.

17 Ibid., *12. april* and *13. september 1978.*

18 *Det Store Nordiske Telegraf-Selskab. Beretning og regnskab 1978.*

19 Ibid., *1979.*

20 Reports and accounts for the years 1973–1979. *Bestyrelsesmøde, 20. februar 1979.*

21 Ibid.

22 *Bestyrelsesmøde, 19. september 1975,* including supplement 433.

23 Ibid., *20. oktober 1976, 1. marts 1977* and *20. december 1978.*

24 *Bestyrelsesmøde, 28. august 1979.*

25 *Bestyrelsesmøde, 23. oktober* and *18. december 1979.*

26 Ibid.

27 *Bestyrelsesmøde, 18. december 1979.*

28 Ibid., *18. december 1979* and *3. juni 1980.*

29 *Det Store Nordiske Telegraf-Selskab. Beretning og regnskab 1980. Bestyrelsesmøde, 20. februar 1981.*

30 *Bestyrelsesmøde, 3. juni 1980.*

31 Ibid., *16. december 1978* as well as *18. maj* and *9. september 1981.*

32 *Bestyrelsesmøde, 21. februar 1985.*

33 Ibid., *22. maj 1985.*

34 *Det Store Nordiske Telegrafselskab. Beretning og Regnskab 1983.* The website of the Danish Business Authority, the VIRK registry.

35 *Bestyrelsesmøde, 16. december 1985.*

36 Ibid.

37 Ibid., *17. september 1984*.

38 Ibid. The discussions regarding Regnecentralen: ibid., *18. maj 1981*.

39 Ibid., *24. februar 1986*.

40 Ibid., as well as *22. september 1986*.

41 Ibid., *15. maj 1986*.

42 Ibid.

43 Ibid., *22. september 1986*, on which what follows is based.

44 Ibid., *18. december 1986*, on which what follows is based.

CHAPTER 23

1 *Bestyrelsesmøde, 15. maj 1986* and *16. december 1986*.

2 Ibid., *11. april 1988*.

3 Ibid., *25. maj 1988*.

4 Ibid., *28. september 1988*.

5 Ibid.

6 Ibid., *19. april 1990*.

7 Ibid., *22. december 1988, 24. februar* and *28. september 1989*.

8 The shares were owned via GN Citytel Ltd., which was one hundred percent owned by GN Store Nord and from this point onward was operated as a holding company.

9 Alfred Berg, *Aktieanalyse. GN Store Nord outperform, 13. august 1993 (bilag 853 til Bestyrelsesmøde, 31. august 1993)*.

10 *Bestyrelsesmøde, 28. september* and *14. december 1988* as well as *25. januar 1990*.

11 McKinsey's report has not been preserved, so the current account is based on *Direktionens strategiske oplæg til bestyrelsesmødet, 25. januar 1990* samt *Bestyrelsesmøde, 25. januar 1990*. What follows is based on this source.

12 Ibid., *14. december 1988*.

13 Ibid., *20. september 1989*.

14 *Bestyrelsesmøde, 22. februar 1990* including supplements.

15 *Bilag 786 til Bestyrelsesmøde, 11. april 1991*.

16 *Bestyrelsesmøde, 14. december 1988*.

17 Jesper Kiil, *Midt i en teletid*, p. 134.

18 *Bestyrelsesmøde, 14. april 1989*, including supplements.

19 Ibid., *14. december 1989*.

20 Ibid., *23. februar 1990*.

21 Ibid., *28. maj 1990*.

22 Ibid., *13. december 1990*.

23 Ibid., *21. februar 1991*.

24 Ibid., *10. april 1991*.

25 Ibid., *13. december 1990*, including supplements.

26 Ibid.

27 Ibid., *21. februar 1991*.

28 The whole sequence of events related to the granting of the license is described in detail in Jens Chr. Hansen & Søren Domino, *Søderberg – Mand af Mærsk*, the source on which this passage is based.

29 Ibid.

30 *Bestyrelsesmøde, 26. september 1991*, including supplements.

31 Ibid., *5. juli 1991*.

32 Ibid.

33 Ibid.

34 Ibid.

35 Ibid.

36 Ibid., *26. september 1991*. Jens Kiil, *Midt i en teletid*, p. 140.

37 Ibid.

38 Ibid., *12. december 1991*.

39 Ibid., *26. september* and *4. november 1991*.

40 Ibid., as well as *26. september 1991*, including supplements.

41 *Perspektivplan for GN Store Nordiske Telegraf-Selskab*. Supplement 818 to *Bestyrelsesmøde, 27. marts 1992*.

42 Ibid.

43 Ibid.

44 Ibid.

45 *Bestyrelsesmøde, 31. august 1993* and *2. juni 1994*.

46 Ibid., *5. april 1994*.

CHAPTER 24

1 *GN Store Nord. Beretning og regnskab 1994. Bestyrelsesmøde, 29. marts* and *31. august 1993*.

2 Alfred Berg Børsmæglerselskab A/S: *Aktieanalyse GN Store Nord, 13. august 1993*.

3 *GN Store Nord: Beretning og regnskab 1994*. Except where otherwise stated, what follows is based on this source.

4 *Strategiplan 1995-1997*. Supplement to *Bestyrelsesmøde, 25. oktober 1994*.

5 *Bestyrelsesmøde, 25. august* and *17. december 1992* as well as *20. marts* and *29. august 1996*.

6 Ibid., *5. april 1995*.

7 Ibid., *29. august 1995*.

8 Ibid., *20. marts, 7. maj* and *29. august 1996*.

9 Ibid., *20. marts* and *9. maj 1996*.

10 Ibid., *1. marts 1995*.

11 Ibid., *1. marts* and *5. april 1995*.

12 Ibid. At this time, GN Store Nord owned a sixth of the shares in Stofa, but together with the other owners, GN Store Nord was bought out by Telia.

13 Ibid., *16. maj* and *29. august 1995*.

14 Ibid. *12. december 1995*.

15 *GN Store Nord. Beretning og regnskab 1996*.

16 *Bestyrelsesmøde, 12. december 1995* and minutes of subsequent meetings of the board of directors.

17 *GN Store Nord. Beretning og regnskab 1996*.

18 Ibid.

19   Ibid., *1995. Bestyrelsesmøde, 29. august 1995.*

20   Ibid., *29. august 1996.*

21   *Bestyrelsesmøde, 29. august 1995 og 22. februar 1996.*

22   Ibid., *7. maj 1996.*

23   Ibid., *6. maj 1997.*

24   *GN Store Nord. Beretning og regnskab 1996.*

25   Ibid., *1998.*

26   *Bestyrelsesmøde, 25. februar 1997.*

27   *GN Store Nord. Børsprospekt 1997.*

28   Ibid.

29   *Bestyrelsesmøde, 25. februar 1997.*

30   Ibid.

31   The fax message in GN Store Nord's file containing supplements to the minutes of the meetings of the board of directors in August 1997.

CHAPTER 25

1   *Bestyrelsesmøde, 2. juni 1997.*

2   Ibid., *5. august 1997.*

3   Ibid., *2. juni 1997.*

4   Ibid., *28. august* and *3. november 1997.*

5   Ibid., *2. juni 1997.*

6   Ibid., *18. marts* and *25. juni 1998.*

7   Ibid., *25. maj* and *9. juni 1998.*

8   Ibid., *10. december 1998* and *10. marts 1999.*

9   Ibid., *27. april 1999.*

10   Ibid., *10. maj 1999.*

11   *GN Store Nord: Årsrapport 1999.*

12   Ibid.

13   *Bestyrelsesmøde, 25. februar 1997.*

14   *GN Store Nordiske Telegraf-Selskab, Strategi 2001–2003.*

15   *GN Store Nord. Beretning og regnskab 1997.*

16   *Bestyrelsesmøde, 25. maj 1998.* What follows is based on this source.

17   *Erik B. Rasmussen til GN Store Nords bestyrelse, 27. maj 1998.* Enclosed with the minutes of the meeting of the board.

18   *Lars Berg til Jørgen Lindegaard, 4. juni 1998* and *Jørgen Lindegaard til Lars Berg, 8. juni 1998.* Enclosed with the minutes of the meeting of the board.

19   Ibid.

20   Ibid. as well as *Bestyrelsesmøde, 15. maj* and *23. juni 1998.*

21   The negotiations are detailed in the minutes of the meetings of GN Stores Nord's board, *23. juni, 27. august* and *10. december 1998.*

22   Ibid., *10. december 1998.*

23   Ibid.

24   *Møde mellem Telia og GN Store Nord den 14. december 1998.* Enclosed with the minutes of the meeting of the board. *Bestyrelsesprotokol, 10. marts 1999.*

25   Ibid., *10. marts* and *27. april 1999.*

26   *GN Store Nord. Årsrapport 1998* and *1999.*

27   *Bestyrelsesmøde, 18. maj 2000.* There is, then, no evidence to support the claim in Martin Jes Iversen, *Turnaround*, pp. 44–52, that the sale of Sonofon was the first step in a "master plan" Jørgen Lindegaard had had since 1998 to split up GN Store Nord and list the subsidiaries on a stock exchange. The sale of Sonofon was a forced sale in the sense that the cooperation with Telia–which Martin Jes Iversen does not mention–never materialized and GN Store Nord faced the prospect of further huge investments, and it would have been difficult for Sonofon and GN Store Nord to continue as an independent player in the Danish cellular market. This is the case regardless of the fact that the proceeds from the sale of Sonofon were used to invest in and ultimately prepare for the stock market listing of one of GN Store Nord's subsidiaries.

28   Ibid.

29   *Jørgen Lindegaard til bestyrelsens medlemmer, 8. juni 2000.*

30   *Jørgen Lindegaard til bestyrelsens medlemmer, 9. juni 2000.*

31   *Bestyrelsesmøde, 12. juni 2000.*

32   Ibid. as well as Martin Jes Iversen, *Turnaround. Kampen om GN Store Nord,* p. 46–50.

33   *Bestyrelsesmøde, 12. juni 2000.*

34   *Fondsbørsmeddelelse, 10. august 2000.*

35   *Telefax til Elvar Vinum og Mogens Hugo Sørensen, 16. februar 2000. Bestyrelsesmøde, 1. marts 2000.*

36   *Bestyrelsesmøde 11. april* and *Fondsbørsmeddelelser, 26. april* and *8. juni 2000.*

37   Ibid., *18. maj 2000* as well as *Fondsbørsmeddelelse, 22. maj 2000.*

38   *Bestyrelsesmøde, 4. oktober 2000. Fondsbørsmeddelelse, 5. oktober* and *8. november 2000.*

39   *Fondsbørsmeddelelse, 25.* and *29. september 2000. Bestyrelsesmøder, 25. september* and *4. oktober 2000.*

40   *Bestyrelsesmøde, 4. oktober 2000. Fondsbørsmeddelelse, 27. oktober 2000.*

41   *Bestyrelsesmøde, 29. august 2000.* What follows is based on this source.

42   *Jyllands-Posten, 30. august 2000.*

43   *Bestyrelsesmøde, 29. august 2000.* The statement made by the top management team indicates that there was no master plan involving the listing of all of the subsidiaries on a stock exchange and the splitting up of the group, but also indicates that the possibility thereof had been discussed–and dismissed at the time.

44   *Jyllands-Posten, 26. september 2000.*

45   *Bestyrelsesmøde, 23. november 2000.*

46   Ibid., *4. december 2000.*

47   Ibid., *23. januar* and *23. februar 2000.*

48   Ibid., *23. februar 2000.*

49   Ibid.

50   Ibid., *29. august 2001.*

51   Ibid., *24. januar, 25. juni* and *16. august 2002.*

52   Ibid., *30. december 2002.*

53   Ibid., *31. december 2002.*

CHAPTER 26

1   *Børsen* and *Berlingske Tidende, 30. august 2001. Besty-relsesmøde, 23. februar og 22. juni 2001.*

2   *GN Store Nord. Årsrapport 2001.*

3   Ibid.

4   Ibid., 2002.

5   *Berlinske Nyhedsmagasin, 26. november-2. december 2004.*

6   *Jyllands-Posten, 22. februar 2005.*

7   *Berlingske Tidende, 3. januar 2003.*

8   Ibid.

9   Ibid., samt *7. januar 2003.*

10   *Jyllands-Posten, 2. april 2003.*

11   *Bestyrelsesmøde, 7. Maj 2003.*

12   Ibid., *21. august 2003.*

13   Ibid., *11. december 2003.*

14   Ibid., *26. februar* og *10. maj 2004.*

15   Ibid., *5. oktober 2004.*

16   *Project Rose. Board Information Pack til bestyrelsesmø-det, 19. august 2004.*

17   *Jørn Kildegaard til Mogens Hugo, 30. april 2004.*

18   Ibid. One of the main claims of Martin Jes Iversen, *Turn-around: Kampen om GN Store Nord* that Mogens Hugo and Jørn Kildegaard were deeply conflicted with regard to a possible merger of GN ReSound and Phonak. On the contrary, the whole course of events and the available source material show that they were basically in agreement. There is also no support in the sources for Martin Jes Iversen's claim that Mogens Hugo played a "double game" in relation to Jørn Kildegaard or to the rest of the board of directors. The sources also indicate that the driving force in the negotiations was Phonak, who were very eager, while GN Store Nord were more hesitant.

19   Ibid., *9. februar 2005* as well as *Jyllands-Posten, 4. april 2005.*

20   Ibid., *20. juni 2005.*

21   Ibid.

22   Ibid., *20.-21. september.*

23   Ibid.

24   Ibid., *8. december 2005.*

25   Ibid.

26   *Jyllands-Posten 29. august 2005* and *26. januar 2006.*

27   Ibid., *21. marts 2006.*

28   Ibid.

29   *Berlingske Tidende, 27. marts 2006.*

30   *Børsen, 22. marts 2006.*

31   *Bestyrelsesmøde, 9. maj 2006.* What follows is based on this source.

32   Ibid.

33   Ibid., *2. juni 2006.* What follows is based on this source.

34   Ibid., *5.* and *11. juni 2006.*

35   Ibid., *22. juni 2006. E-mail til bestyrelsens medlemmer, 28. juni 2006.* Attached to the minutes of the meeting of the board.

36   Ibid., *5. juli 2006.* Det følgende bygger på denne kilde.

37   Ibid., *11. august 2006.*

38   Ibid., *27. september 2006.*

39   Ibid., *29. september* and *1. oktober 2006.*

40   Ibid., *9. december 2005* and *22. februar 2006.*

41   There are indications in the international business press that Antonius Bouten—his actual name—had left his position with Philips shortly before he was hired by GN Store Nord, and in *Mandag Morgen, 3. December 2007,* he himself states that he was looking for a new job outside Philips when he was contacted by a head-hunting company on behalf of GN Store Nord.

42   Ibid., *19. september 2006.*

43   Ibid., *2. juni 2006. GN Store Nord. Announcement 2. Oc-tober 2006.*

44   Ibid., *19. september 2006.*

45   Ibid., *6. november 2006.*

46   *Ibid., 6. november* and *6.* december *2006.*

47   Ibid., *6. december 2006* as well as *Bundeskartellamt, 3. Beschlussabteilung: Beschluss in dem verwaltungsver-fahren der Phonak Holding AG, der GN ReSound A/G u.z.w 11. april 2007,* which contains a description of the course of events and a justification of the decision reached by the authority.

48   Ibid.

49   Ibid.

50   *Bestyrelsesmøde, 21. marts 2007.*

51   Ibid.

52   *Generalforsamling, 21. marts 2007.*

53   *GN Store Nord. Announcement 23. March 2007. Besty-relsesmøde, 1. april 2007.*

54   Ibid., *3. maj 2007* and *1. april 2007.*

55   Ibid., *15. august 2007.*

56   Ibid.

57   *Biannual strategy session, 3.-4. oktober 2007.*

58   Ibid.

59   Ibid. *16., oktober 2007.*

60   Ibid., *24. oktober 2007.* What follows is based on this source.

61   *Bestyrelsesmøde, 1. november 2007.*

62   Ibid.

63   Ibid., *1., 3.* and *5. november 2007.*

64   *GN Store Nord. Announcement no. 2, 6. november 2007. Q3 Interim Report 2007.*

65   Quoted in several media.

66   *Business.dk, 7. november 2007.*

CHAPTER 27

1   *Business.dk, 4. december 2007* and *Jyllands-Posten, 11. december 2007.*

2   *Bestyrelsesmøde, 13. december 2007* and *1.* and *12. feb-ruar 2008.*

3   *Berlingske Business, 12. februar 2008.*

4   *Bestyrelsesmøde, 17.* and *21. februar 2008.*

5   Ibid.

6   Ibid., as well as *11. marts 2008.*

7   *GN Store Nord. Announcement no. 4, February 25, 2008.*

8   *Generalforsamling, 16. juni 2008.*

9   *Bestyrelsesmøde, 11. marts* and *7. april 2008.*

10 Ibid., *21. april 2008.*

11 Ibid., *28. maj 2008.*

12 Ibid., as well as *16. juni. GN Store Nord. Announcement no. 14, June 17, 2008.*

13 *Bestyrelsesmøde, 11. august 2008.*

14 Ibid., *24. september 2008.*

15 Ibid.

16 Ibid., *9. oktober 2008.*

17 Ibid.

18 Ibid., *11. august 2008.*

19 Ibid., *3. november 2008.*

20 Ibid. Capital letters are used in the official minutes of the meeting of the board in question.

21 Ibid., *11. august 2008.*

22 Ibid., *9. oktober 2008.*

23 Ibid.

24 Ibid., *5. november 2008.*

25 Ibid.

26 Ibid., *10. december 2008.*

27 Ibid., *25. februar 2009.*

28 *Berlingske Tidende, 28. februar 2009.*

29 Ibid., *10. november 2009.*

30 *GN Store Nord. Årsrapport 2008.*

31 Ibid., *1. februar* and *3. november 2010.*

32 Ibid., *16. februar 2010.*

33 *GN Store Nord. Årsrapport 2010.*

34 Ibid., samt *GN Store Nord. Q3 Interim Report 2010.*

35 *Jyllands-Posten, 11. november 2010.*

36 *Bestyrelsesmøde, 25. februar 2009.*

37 *GN Store Nord. Announcement no. 13, June 26, 2009* and *Announcement no. 13, March 25, 2010.*

38 The description of the content and progression of the court case is based on supplements to *Besty-relsesmøde, 7. April 2008.*

39 The progression of the matter and the initiatives of the Danish consortium are described in the minutes of GN Store Nord's board.

40 *GN Store Nord. Årsrapport 2013.*

41 *GN Store Nord A/S. Company Announcement, Sep. 25, 2016.*

42 *GN News, August 13, 2018.*

43 *GN News, January 30* and *May 17* as well as *Euroinves-tor.dk* and *Ritzau Finans, 30. januar 2018.*

44 Quoted from *Medwatch, 15. november 2018.* The expression was repeated in a number of other analyses and evaluations of the quarterly account.

45 Marcus Desimoni had been appointed acting chief executive officer after Anders Hedegaard had announced in late October that he would leave the company to take a position as the chief executive officer of a foreign company. The quotes are from *Ritzau Finans, 15. november 2018,* and *Medwatch, 15. november 2018.*

Index of names

Illustrations

Except for the ones mentioned below, the illustrations in this book are from Great Northern's photo archive at the Royal Danish Library or from GN's headquarter.

Royal Danish Library: 14; 27; 28; 35; 38; 75 (Illustrated London News); 117; 122; 127; 177; 183, 191; 192; 198; 201; 211; 260; 318

Kbhbilleder.dk: 17

Getty Images: 29 (Bettmann)

Alamy Stock Photo: 36; 44 (Gibon Art); 112; 152; 187; 242 (Sputnik)

Atlantic-Cable.com: 139 (2)

Telegraph Museum, Porthcurno: 18

Ritzau Scanpix: 142 (Harlinge-Viollet); 154; 163 (Topfoto); 181; 210 (Topfoto); 223; 247; 248 (The Granger Collection); 251 (Ullstein); 254; 257 (Ullstein); 265 (Michael Barrett Boesen); 284; 287 (Charles Gorry); 304 (Lars Hansen); 314; 320; 341 (Bjarne Lüthcke); 389 (Linda Kastrup); 393 (Finn Heidelberg); 412 (Søren Steffen); 423 (Jens Nørgaard Larsen); 425 (Carl Redhead); 435 (Keld Navntoft); 449 (Paul Sakima); 451 (Heinz-Peter); 454 (Torben Klint)

WikiCommons: 232; 409

Hans Buhl, Buesenderen: 171; 212; 214

Hørelsen (magazine): 361; 364